The Selected Works of Antonia Darder

Also Available from Bloomsbury

The Student Guide to Freire's "Pedagogy of the Oppressed," Antonia Darder
Education for Critical Consciousness, Paulo Freire
Paulo Freire, Daniel Schugurensky
Paulo Freire's Intellectual Roots, edited by Robert Lake and Tricia Kress
Paulo Freire's Philosophy of Education, Jones Irwin
Pedagogy of Hope, Paulo Freire
Pedagogy of the Heart, Paulo Freire
Pedagogy of the Oppressed, 50th Anniversary Edition, Paulo Freire

The Selected Works of Antonia Darder

On Theory, Politics, and Struggle

Edited by
Kevin D. Lam and Kortney Hernandez

BLOOMSBURY ACADEMIC
LONDON • NEW YORK • OXFORD • NEW DELHI • SYDNEY

BLOOMSBURY ACADEMIC

Bloomsbury Publishing Plc, 50 Bedford Square, London, WC1B 3DP, UK
Bloomsbury Publishing Inc, 1359 Broadway, New York, NY 10018, USA
Bloomsbury Publishing Ireland, 29 Earlsfort Terrace, Dublin 2, D02 AY28, Ireland

BLOOMSBURY, BLOOMSBURY ACADEMIC and the Diana logo are
trademarks of Bloomsbury Publishing Plc

First published in Great Britain 2026

Copyright © Kevin D. Lam, Kortney Hernandez, and Contributors 2026

Kevin D. Lam and Kortney Hernandez have asserted their right under the Copyright,
Designs and Patents Act, 1988, to be identified as Editors of this work.

Cover design by Paul Smith
Cover artwork: The Offering by Antonia Darder

All rights reserved. No part of this publication may be: i) reproduced or transmitted in
any form, electronic or mechanical, including photocopying, recording or by means of
any information storage or retrieval system without prior permission in writing from
the publishers; or ii) used or reproduced in any way for the training, development or
operation of artificial intelligence (AI) technologies, including generative AI technologies.
The rights holders expressly reserve this publication from the text and data mining
exception as per Article 4(3) of the Digital Single Market Directive (EU) 2019/790.

Bloomsbury Publishing Plc does not have any control over, or responsibility for,
any third-party websites referred to or in this book. All internet addresses given
in this book were correct at the time of going to press. The author and publisher
regret any inconvenience caused if addresses have changed or sites have ceased
to exist, but can accept no responsibility for any such changes.

A catalogue record for this book is available from the British Library.

A catalog record for this book is available from the Library of Congress.

ISBN: HB: 978-1-3503-4901-8
       PB: 978-1-3503-4900-1
       ePDF: 978-1-3503-4902-5
       eBook: 978-1-3503-4903-2

Typeset by Integra Software Services Pvt. Ltd.
Printed and bound in Great Britain

For product safety related questions contact productsafety@bloomsbury.com.

To find out more about our authors and books visit www.bloomsbury.com
and sign up for our newsletters.

Contents

List of Figures and Table ... vii–viii
Teaching, Learning, and Loving for Transformation: A Foreword to
The Selected Works of Antonia Darder Gilda L. Ochoa ... ix
Words from a Mentor Carol Brunson Day ... xiii
Editors' Preface: In Relationship with Antonia Darder ... xvi

The Indispensable Praxis of Antonia Darder: An Introduction ... 1

Part 1 Reinventing Paulo Freire

1 Liberation: Our Historical Task ... 19
2 Teaching as an Act of Love: In Memory of Paulo Freire ... 45
3 Introduction: Pedagogy of the Heart ... 51

Part 2 The Politics of Biculturalism

4 A Critical Theory of Cultural Democracy ... 73
5 The Politics of Biculturalism: Culture and Difference in the Formation of *Warriors for Gringostroika and the New Mestizas* ... 97
6 Neoliberalism in the Academic Borderlands: An On-going Struggle for Equality and Human Rights ... 117

Part 3 Decolonizing Interpretive Methodology

7 Problematizing the Notion of Puerto Ricans as "Underclass": A Step Toward a Decolonizing Study of Poverty ... 133
8 Decolonizing the Flesh: The Body, Pedagogy, and Inequality ... 145
9 Decolonizing Interpretive Research: Subaltern Sensibilities and the Politics of Voice ... 159

Part 4 Toward a Critical Theory of Racism

10 Shattering the "Race" Lens: Toward a Critical Theory of Racism ... 177
11 What's So Critical about Critical Race Theory? A Conceptual Interrogation with Rodolfo Torres ... 191

12 Racism in a Medically Segregated World	211
13 A Marxist Challenge to the Concept of "Race" *Antonia Darder and Rodolfo D. Torres*	225

Part 5 Interrogating Latino Studies

14 Mapping Latino Studies: Critical Reflections on Class and Social Theory *Antonia Darder and Rodolfo D. Torres*	243
15 Radicalizing the Immigrant Debate in the United States: A Call for Open Borders and Global Human Rights	263
16 Latinos, Education, and the Church: Toward a Culturally Democratic Future	281

Part 6 Critical Pedagogy, Social Justice, and the Politics of Difference

17 Political Grace and Revolutionary Critical Pedagogy	315
18 Radio and the Art of Resistance: A Public Pedagogy of the Airwaves	323
19 Critical Leadership for Social Justice: Unveiling the Dirty Little Secret of Power and Privilege	337

Afterword: The Darder Question: "To End the World as We Know It" *João M. Paraskeva*	361
Epilogue: Teaching for the End of the World (As We Know It): Decolonizing the Curricular Limits of Modernity	371
Index	397

Figures

4.1 The Biculturation Process Represented along a Dialectical Continuum 79
4.2 Axis Relationship between Culture and Power 79
4.3 Sphere of Biculturalism 80

Table

4.1 Relationship of Cultural Response Pattern, Modes of Engagement,
and Cultural Identity 81

Teaching, Learning, and Loving for Transformation

A Foreword to *The Selected Works of Antonia Darder*

Gilda L. Ochoa

As a new professor in the mid-1990s, I began assigning Antonia Darder's scholarship. Her nuanced analysis was unlike anything I had read in sociology, education, or Chicana/o Latina/o Studies, and her co-edited book *Latinos and Education* with her longtime collaborator Rodolfo D. Torres became a staple in a class I was teaching by the same name. Then, in the early 2000s I had the opportunity to hear Doctora Darder at a conference on Aspiring Teachers of Color where she was the keynote speaker. She spoke with so much passion and conviction—in a way my family spoke but something I rarely observed in academic spaces. I was in awe. She linked the personal with the structural and accessibly broke down the political economy. I could feel the ballroom filled with hope and inspiration.

This volume—*The Selected Works of Antonia Darder*—is similar and will continue inspiring multiple generations. It is a gift to teachers and learners—those who are new to Darder's work and those who have had the privilege of reading, engaging with, and teaching her scholarship before. Among Darder's contributions are the many edited volumes she has produced. In addition to helping shape several fields, these edited volumes have nurtured a space for graduate students to more established professors often writing from the margins to share their insights. Thus, it is apropos that two of Darder's former doctoral students and now current professors have reciprocated by organizing this collection.

On the surface, much has changed in US educational institutions since Antonia Darder's first publications over three decades ago. The numbers of educators and administrators of color, K-6 dual immersion language programs, university Hispanic Serving Institutions, and Centers for Diversity, Equity, and Inclusivity have increased exponentially. And, after nearly sixty years of struggle for ethnic studies, California high schools are preparing to make ethnic studies a graduation requirement beginning in 2030. Meanwhile, concepts such as social justice, transformation, and intersectionality have become mainstream. Yet, as Darder presciently warned, we cannot be subdued into passively assuming that representation, discourses, and neoliberal multiculturalism mean that material conditions have improved for poor and working-class communities. What remains in our current period are vast inequities in schooling, housing, health, and other arenas. These will not be eradicated without radical socio-political *and* economic transformation.

Organized into six parts, this volume offers a critical lens, inspiration, and a vision of what is possible. It brings together some of the breadth of Antonia Darder's work, and each section complicates larger debates. Woven together are nuanced analyses of power and paradigms for change that do not ignore the social relations of production. Darder not only critiques conservative, liberal, and seemingly progressive political and academic approaches. She draws on her experiences and work in the classroom and community to offer "emancipatory" approaches to our teaching, research, activism, and being.

Given the transformational impact of Paulo Freire to generations of educators, communities, and activists, including Antonia Darder, the volume begins with Darder's detailed discussions of Freire's writings and his ways of being. Together, these chapters unpack the many lessons Freire offers. Starting with these chapters aid in understanding the sections that follow, and they help illustrate how thinking and learning are best done in collectivity as Darder's own approach has been influenced by Freire's teachings.

Part Two includes classic and newer pieces on Darder's foundational work on biculturalism. Early on, Darder was among a small group of scholars writing on the politics of culture and difference, and the chapters in this section map out her critical theory of biculturalism and bicultural pedagogy of education in conversation with the scholarship of others. She calls for culturally democratic environments where working-class bicultural students can participate freely and build on the knowledge they and their families bring to schools. Given US legacies of cultural genocide and language domination, this call is urgent. It must be heeded by conservatives and assimilationists who have historically endorsed biological and cultural deficiency frameworks, Americanization Programs, and English-Only policies. But Darder's call is also needed by liberals and progressives who often approach K-6 dual immersion language programs with a neoliberal frame that positions the Spanish language as a commodity to improve students' marketability in the capitalist structure rather than a potentially humanizing process. Missing in many language programs are attention to culture and power, English language learners, classroom pedagogies, relationships, communities, and histories—all aspects Darder shows are fundamental to culturally democratic environments.

At the crux of Darder's scholarship is a radical rethinking of Western constructions of knowledge production that privilege positivism and quantitative measurements of lives and realities. Positivism posits that there is one truth capturable via scientific research which is presumed to be neutral and value free. Yet, all knowledge is positioned, and there is a historical pattern of scientific research being used to create and then justify exclusionary policies and practices that maintain the status quo. As Darder argues, relying only on evidence-based research to understand social phenomena reduces our abilities to better comprehend the multi-faceted conditions (mis)shaping society and fueling oppression. The hyperfocus on high-stakes standardized test results and evidence-based practices without an understanding of power, inequities, and students' material realities is one devastating example in our schools. Part Three of this volume offers detailed discussions of the problematics of positivism, the overemphasis on empiricism, and the possibilities of decolonizing interpretive methodology.

Highlighting how the stakes are too high to only produce scholarship that simply describes or interprets phenomena for academic audiences in ivory towers, Darder affirms the need to combine our pedagogy, research, and activism as part of a larger "revolutionary praxis" that is anti-colonial, anti-capitalist, and anti-racist.

Parts 4 and 5 illustrate the possibilities of such a revolutionary praxis by focusing specifically on the limits of critical race theory (CRT) and the potentials of Latina/o Studies. Over the past several years, as conservative politicians have targeted critical race theory further denying K-12 students access to crucial histories, some scholars have reacted uncritically by championing CRT. And, in select fields CRT has become *the* paradigm for understanding schooling and human life. Together, this reaction and singular approach have minimized radical critiques on the limits of CRT and stunted the development of other paradigms. Part Four of this volume offers readers a much-needed nuanced reflection on CRT and the problematics of centering race, identity, and storytelling devoid of context. Along with critiquing liberal conceptions of race which can essentialize, homogenize, and reinforce binaries of us versus them, Darder and Rodolfo Torres posit that scholars of critical race theory who rely only on people's individual stories and stop their analysis at the micro level of identity and microaggressions inadvertently further a conservative agenda by camouflaging the salience of macro-structures and racist ideologies in maintaining the status quo. As such, as Darder does throughout her work, she offers a framework that names the significance of capitalism and does not invisibilize structures of power and inequality.

Part Five of this volume continues Darder's rigorous analysis by centering on Latina/o Studies. Like their critiques of CRT, Darder and Torres problematize scholarship on Latinidad, race, culture, identity, representation, and immigration that is divorced from macro-structural processes, including the capitalist state and the international division of labor. Recalling the more radical roots of Chicana/o Latina/o Studies, Darder and Torres (2004) map out an agenda for Latina/o Studies that is transnational, comparative, attends to the heterogeneity within panethnic categories, and "returns to the basics" of history, political economy, and public policy (p. 120). By spotlighting structural processes, Darder's framework enables more radical possibilities for change. This is made transparent in the chapter on "Radicalizing the Immigrant Debate in the United States" where she argues for open borders and "globalizing human rights" as fundamental aspects of the freedom of movement.

Darder's work is imbued from beginning to end with visions of possibilities. This is the case throughout the volume, and Part Six hones in on radical possibilities and multiple forms of resistance. The chapters in this section illustrate the significance of public radio as public pedagogy where community voices build solidarity and counter dominant narratives that maintain systems of power and inequality. Darder also unpacks the state of neoliberal universities where corporate interests prevail and careerist faculty are rewarded for garnering national-level grants that advance individual careers and institutional status over community-engaged work. As more working-class and students of color earn doctorates, they encounter a much smaller percentage of tenure track positions and universities that superficially celebrate diversity and multiculturalism while stifling dissent. Within this context, Darder leaves readers with clear ideas for creating "a critical praxis of leadership to support self-determination and culturally democratic life."

As I witnessed decades ago and was reminded while reading side-by-side the chapters in this essential volume, Darder's work and approach are not simply academic exercises. They are powerful calls to action embodying her ethos of love and possibilities in solidarity with all those committed to radical transformation.

Reference

Darder, A., and Torres, R. D. (2004), *After Race: Racism after Multiculturalism*. New York, NY, and London: New York University Press.

Words from a Mentor

Carol Brunson Day

I write this note as a story about a chapter in the life of Antonia Darder—when our paths first crossed early in the evolution of her professional journey. Although this chapter began while she was a graduate student in human development at Pacific Oaks College in the late 1970s, we have continued to stay in touch through the years. So much of what I want to say stems not just from old memories but grows from her earliest writings as a student, and our subsequent fifty years of correspondence and interactions. As I reflect on where this journey began, I remember a woman who on the surface was struggling to "know" who she really was, what she really wanted to do, and how to accomplish something meaningful in her life. Yet underneath the surface, but particularly transparent was her struggle with the burden of competing personal qualities—one that was in one moment fragile, in another fierce: on one occasion compassionate, and on another unsympathetic and hard.

I also remember knowing early on that she had an incredibly good mind—a brilliantly good mind. But she had no idea of the brain power she possessed due to the impact of the flagrant and repeated underestimation and neglect by school systems that purport to nurture good minds. Her boldness of character was tempered by an insecurity that prevented her from believing fully in her right to be her genuine, beautiful, and authentic self. Because she sought self-emergence so deeply in her heart and mind, her struggles were cogent and unceasing. During her time as a student, we watched her boldness grow as she searched for and uncovered scholarship and philosophies and built relationships that matched and supported her deepest convictions about her own life that would influence the direction of her professional life and her contribution to the world.

Throughout her journey through her master's degree studies, I had many opportunities to get glimpses of her thinking, questioning, grappling with emotions, in the process of framing what she wanted to give to the world through her professional work and through her "being."

In the years since, I have since witnessed a journey that I had hoped for early on, but the enormity of which I never could have predicted, evidenced by her academic career and the stunning consequence captured here in these writings. So skillfully and brilliantly gathered and grouped, the compilers have portrayed the incredible depth and complexity of the contribution that Antonia has made to the academy.

Solidly grounded in the works of Paulo Freire, a philosopher whom she has read, embraced, worked with, critiqued, and analyzed, she draws us into his thinking and its reinvention in her thinking. And while the topics are vast—from the political analyses of biculturalism, to decolonizing our minds, to Critical Race Theory, to Latino studies, to social justice—a central theme regarding a Freirean mission in life is clear as liberatory for ourselves, our people, our society, and our world. But know that the scope and range of the words on the pages that follow here pale in comparison to the person. The beauty and power of her passion and creativity, expressed in her poetry, song, and painting, are equally an expression of who she is being and becoming and what she wants for us and the world.

Excerpted from "rican woman madness is just another word for love"

Rican-woman-madness
is just another word for love,
she is born of the chains of slavery
and the genocidal history of the Taíno
brushing furiously against the backdrop of Spanish barbarism.
She is a fighter, warrior blood
oozes through her veins, …

Rican woman's rage runs deep,
but her love runs deeper,
she is the sensibilities of the
moon, sky, and earth combined,
they penetrate into the very core
of all lives natural existence …

The Rican woman is a wild woman,
it is true that she has been colonized
by the rabid thieves who stole her land,
and twisted her history to unrecognizable
proportions, but still and yet,
she refuses to be colonized in the spirit
and will fight to the death to protect
the integrity of the people's song …

Rican-woman-madness
is just another word for love,
a love that needs open, flowing life in
all its shapes and far reaching dimensions,
a love that will accept nothing but today
and refuses to be appeased with
translucent promises of tomorrow,
a love that will no longer tolerate the forces

of human cruelty and injustice,
a redemptive love that is completely
stripped naked and fully present
just for the asking,
(if you dare).

—Antonia Darder (1993)

As I look back on my own teaching and learning with faculty colleagues and students, few have touched me as deeply as Antonia—in terms of how she impacted and unleashed her own growth potential in teaching/learning within a human development environment. As you read, it is my hope that you too will be moved to get into the teaching/learning conversation with Antonia, and have moments when you will experience something so profound that you will want to stop and scratch your head and respond, "Wow, say that again?" And then you will go back and think about it again and again and in reflection be transformed.

For as you reflect on your own thoughts, it is my hope that you will be inspired as I have been, to deepen your thinking about how to truly represent yourself as liberator and activist in your work and in your life. Let me close by giving gratitude to the compilers Kevin Lam and Kortney Hernandez for bringing us their insightful choices of scholarship to provide a glimpse of the ways that Antonia Darder has chosen to share herself with the world across the full scope of her intellectual, emotional, and spiritual beings. Together, they beautifully offer to us her full self as a scholar, as an activist, and as a woman who loves.

Editors' Preface
In Relationship with Antonia Darder

As editors of this volume, we have sought to compile a reader that centers Antonia Darder's theoretical contributions to education and beyond. We have been deeply influenced by her scholarly work. But more importantly, our selections have been shaped by our personal relationships with Darder. We both had the privilege of being mentored by Darder as graduate students. We have seen the ongoing and necessary connection between theoretical, personal, and political in her life, and it has made us aware of these connections in our own lives. We begin with our stories, first, to share how this unfolded in our own development and second, to offer a way of reading these selected works of Antonia Darder that is connected to the reader's own life.

Kortney's Story

I (Kortney) still remember the first time I heard Dr. Antonia Darder speak. I had been finishing up the last year of my master's program and simultaneously working as a graduate assistant in the office where she spent much of her time and countless hours meeting with students and teaching. One day she walked by in between her back-to-back meetings and slid me a copy of one of her books. At the time, I honestly really did not like to read; so, I thanked her for the book and put it away in my bag (this book would sit unread for months). As fate would have it, one day Dr. Darder was giving a lecture to faculty, staff, and students on campus and asked if I would help her out by attending and supporting the technology of her talk. I agreed, having no idea that from that moment on my life would change.

Once a passive recipient of education, this lecture offered an awakening that nourished my soul to the core (this is the case every time I hear her speak publicly). The talk at the time was entitled, "A Critical Theory of Biculturalism," and it was my first introduction to the power of the words and critical ideas of Antonia Darder and radical scholars whom she engaged with in her talks. This lecture was so powerful for the loving force and presence that she brought to the space as she weaved lessons, possibilities, and the raw truths about education in a *"keep it real kinda way."* I was moved despite much of the language and concepts being new to me. She broke it down in ways that were linked to our lived histories and contexts. When I looked around the room, people were moved as well—some were holding back tears, and many were clapping and nodding along when she would mention particular struggles for bicultural communities. This was my first experience and entrance into the lively and loving force of Antonia Darder—an experience I will never forget and one which I credit with leaving an indelible mark on my life.

Needless to say, I was changed in such a way during her lecture that I was left grappling with what it meant for my own life and work. I was searching for more knowledge that could be delivered in this "keep it real kinda way" that I had only seen Darder deliver up until this point. So, I went home after her powerful lecture and searched for the book she had gifted me months before; and when I finally found it, I read it over and over again (because I didn't understand some of the words and concepts the first time around). That text was *Culture and Power in the Classroom*—her seminal book that opened an important portal and gateway into both a political and liberatory vision and an ethos for living in what felt like a dying world. In all of my years of schooling before this moment, I had never read anything that spoke with such authenticity about the conditions of the world—or if I had, I didn't have the capacity to hold on to it before then. What I remember from that time is that I craved more of this critical framing, and it was as if my being had been starved intentionally from learning a critical analysis of the world. And, as such, I had been rendered passive by the educational system that was supposed to educate me. When I think back on that time, I cannot thank Dr. Antonia Darder enough for her soulful essence and presence and for providing for me the conditions for a critical awakening, at such a fragile and important time in my life. I am grateful to her for so much, including that she opened my world to other readings by critical scholars, including Paulo Freire, her most cherished teacher.

I feel very fortunate to have completed my doctoral studies under the devoted tutelage of Darder, given that she is one of those rare intellectuals who engages the process of mentorship in a profoundly revolutionary way. She bestowed me with so many gifts of insight, whose impact on my life I am still working to uncover. As a cultural worker at heart who has utilized her artistry as an educator, activist, poet, and writer to labor persistently for a more just world, she has continuously shown us all through her mentorship that a more loving way is possible. As students, we were fortunate to be touched by the hands, words, and wisdom of "Dr. D.," to whom we owe tremendous gratitude. She walked with us, clearing the path, and removing the obstacles, so that we as free human beings could work to develop political clarity, embrace solidarity, and fight for liberation amidst debilitating structures of oppression. Her legacy will live on in the hearts and souls of the many lives she has touched.

Kevin's Story

I (Kevin) was first introduced to critical pedagogy and the Freirean tradition as a master's student at Cal State, Los Angeles and that changed everything for me. It dramatically shifted my intellectual and academic trajectory in ways I would never have imagined or anticipated. I was never a "good" student; having started in the community college ranks before matriculating at a large public university. My only objective at the time was to obtain a Multiple Subject credential for elementary education. I had no other intentions. I wanted to teach and work with young people as a way to give back to my community—continuing the work I was doing at a community-based organization, but in a school setting. However, after the first two classes in the credential program,

I decided to pursue a master's degree in Educational Foundations. I became more interested in the social, historical, and philosophical analysis and articulation of US schooling and wanted to further explore these critical principles in education.

As an undergraduate, I had read Marx, Durkheim, Weber, Rousseau, among others, but was not able to connect with these texts. Part of it had to do with the fact that, as a working-class student, I was not prepared academically or ready to engage theory (Lam, 2024). I was also taking Asian American Studies classes and wanted to know more about my history. However, even in the context of ethnic studies, I felt detached and removed from the very history that I am a part of—partly because it was not politicized in ways that I could understand. It seems like praxis (the alliance between theory and practice) was a discourse missing in action. In contrast, the theoretical language of critical pedagogy and Freirean-inspired pedagogy spoke to my core and the essence of who I am as a person and thinker. To be sure, the field of critical pedagogy (and my advisor at the time, Carlos Tejeda) made me want to dig deeper into my own subjectivity as a way to read the word and the world (Freire, 1993)—and to position myself not as an object, but a subject of history.

After working as a youth worker at a community-based organization and teaching 6th grade for a few years, I pursued a doctorate in my desire to work and think in the critical pedagogical and Freirean tradition. I went to work with Antonia Darder the first year she migrated out to the US Midwest to teach at the University of Illinois, Urbana-Champaign. I was particular about who I wanted to study with. Darder is the kind of scholar and intellectual I strive to be. Perhaps, just as significant here is that we share a working-class history, which is hard to replicate in academia, yet has served as the basis for work together the last twenty years. The question of class and class struggle, not surprisingly, has been central to our intellectual and political project. It is the lens in which we see through—in our desire to create a more democratically and economically just world. I understood at an intimate level the things that were being conveyed in her writings and teachings. They are not just words on papers, but ideas and concepts lived and embodied in the flesh. For this reason and more, she has been *the* most significant political mentor to me and the embodiment of what an *activist* scholar is and can be. This is not to suggest that it is always easy. In fact, most of the time, it can be very difficult. Additionally, we all have our shortcomings, carrying with us historical traumas and self-doubts that we also bring to the work. Most of us did not enter academic spaces that were set up for us to succeed, let alone thrive. More often than not, our survival mechanisms kick in. Darder would be the first to tell you that it is no different for her. That said, she also makes it very clear where she is coming from and where she wants to go. It is because of her clarity that her teachings and pedagogy have stayed with us long after we were done with graduate work.

An Invitation to the Story

The opportunity to immerse readers into the soul and power of Antonia Darder's writings has been nothing short of an honor, as well as a life-changing experience. We believe this book will be a gift for all who read it; but it is also a gift for Antonia, crafted with immense love and gratitude for all that she has been and done for us and for so many others around the world. In *The Selected Works of Antonia Darder: On Theory, Politics, and Struggle,* we hope readers will uncover the gifts and treasures Darder has borne from the depths of her soul; and, in so doing, begin to create your own story with this revolutionary human being. As you bear witness to the writings of Darder and the realities of injustice and oppression amongst us, which she so eloquently articulates, we also invite you to embrace within yourselves the courage it requires to see and honor your unfinishedness; and from here to make the commitment, as Freire and Darder illustrate through their lives, to always begin anew and to never stop challenging— with every fiber of your body—the injustices that perpetuate human suffering. What unfolds in this text is our story and an example of how to read Antonia Darder. Beyond this, we invite readers to add your own insights to our communal Darderian story, by studying, unveiling, resisting, transforming, reinventing, and daring to *teach for the end of the world, as we know it.*

The Indispensable Praxis of Antonia Darder: An Introduction

Antonia Darder's first book *Culture and Power in the Classroom* was published in 1991. It went on to garner much attention over the years for its prescient analysis of the schooling of subaltern/racialized students in the United States over the last half century. It was republished as a 20th anniversary edition in 2012. This first book, like many of the works that followed, has enjoyed a long and sustained shelf life for its scholarly significance and contributions to educational studies and beyond. It is with this in mind that we offer this collection of readings as an attempt to present the four decades-long intellectual and political formation and contributions of Darder as an internationally renowned critical education scholar, professor, and activist. *The Selected Works of Antonia Darder: On Theory, Politics, and Struggle* traces the literary evolution of one of the foremost radical thinkers of our time. It introduces readers to Darder's earliest scholarship beginning in the late 1980s to publications from recent years. Her scholarship has ventured into critical pedagogy, cultural studies, sociolinguistics, issues of the body, racism, political economy, liberation theology, critical interpretive research, and decolonial thought, among many others. Darder's work cogently examines questions of culture and power for democratic life. While her analysis is located within a particular time and place, the issues and concerns evoke much larger philosophical, political, economic, and pedagogical questions about culture, difference, identity, and the nature of American education under capital. Praxis, for Darder, is informed by a deep personal history of struggle, as well as scholarly rigor; her expressed focus on social justice and economic democracy is grounded in her material and ideological readings of the world. In alignment with Marxist sensibilities, Darder is not only interested in interpreting the world but in changing it.

Darder did not begin her working life as an academic. She labored as a pediatric nurse, psychotherapist, community organizer, and activist within Latino communities in Southern California. From her community work prior to becoming a faculty member, she brings a grounded understanding of the many issues that she has engaged as a scholar. Darder read Paulo Freire's *Pedagogy of the Oppressed* in the late 1970s and met the great Brazilian educational philosopher, who would become her *father in the struggle,* at a critical education conference in Irvine, CA in 1987. Many years later and across numerous scholarly endeavors, Darder always comes back to Freire, as she does to her grounded understanding of historical materialism. While the specific focus of

Darder's work as a scholar, thinker, and educator is constantly evolving and changing, there has always remained a deep coherence with the theoretical and political questions she has taken up throughout the years. In significant ways, her intellectual labor has always been informed by love for her students, communities, and the world.

Like Freire before her, "the world" is not just a poetic metaphor. It is much more. The world is the place where love abides, life intersects, and struggles for justice are forged. Freire (1993) wrote of his love for the world with respect to the "trees and animals" and "mountains and rivers," but was simultaneously intent on understanding the "social structures, politics, [and] history" that informed his pedagogy of the oppressed. Similarly, Darder makes a systematic attempt to read "the world" as she sees, lives, and experiences it around her. She is attentive to the superstructure when contending with questions of identity, culture, and difference—insisting that we must grapple with the ideological dimensions that are part and parcel of the schooling apparatus in the United States. For Darder, it is imperative that we recognize that the "task at hand is not to reproduce the traditional arrangements that support and perpetuate inequality and injustice, but rather to work toward the transformation of those conditions within the context of our vocation as human beings and our daily efforts as educators and community activists clearly committed to social change" (Darder, *United Opt Out*, 2017).

Darder has not sought research agendas in the traditional sense. Rather, her research questions and projects (by way of problem-posing education) have developed out of on-going struggles at work in whatever contexts she has found herself. This points to the vigilance and presence necessary when engaging with the larger goals of liberatory pedagogy, consciousness-raising, and what it means to be fully present in the world. Darder contends that we teach and learn in our bodies, each with our own histories and shaped by the material conditions and the social relations of power in which we exist.

> In our efforts to understand the dynamics of the classroom, teaching and learning have to be acknowledged as human labor that takes place within our bodies, as we strive to make sense of the material conditions and social relations of power that shape our particular histories. Only through such an approach can educators begin to build an emancipatory practice of education where youth are not expected to confront themselves, and one another, as strangers, but rather as fully embodied human beings, from the moment they enter the classroom.
> (Darder in Hernandez, et al., 2023, p. 191)

Those who "make revolution," in Grace Lee Boggs's (1974) words, must change themselves. This process of personal and societal transformation is forged by the kind of scholarship, teaching, and activism that embrace both the heart and mind as centers of intelligence. For Darder, neither community nor academic work can ever be done alone or in a vacuum. There must always be an acknowledged context to our research, teaching, and learning. Moreover, we must work alongside those with whom we share an emancipatory vision for a more loving world. In the sections below, we discuss Darder's contribution to the politics of biculturalism, Latino studies and education, the field of critical pedagogy, a critical theory of racism, an engagement with love as poetics and methodology, and her pedagogy of courage as an indispensable tool for living with what Paulo Freire termed our unfinishedness.

The Link between Culture and Power

In her early work, Darder engaged the relationship between culture and power in the context of schooling of bicultural students—students who were forced to navigate between the culture of their homes and the culture of the school. She argued that understanding this phenomenon dialectically is an important first step to developing a foundation for a critical bicultural pedagogy. She critiqued traditional ideas of culture tied to Western anthropological discourses and epistemologies as limiting and oppressive, given their "value-free," and thereby neutral assumptions. Darder was concerned for the ways in which earlier studies on culture failed to engage with the question of power (and power relations), when theorizing about historically marginalized and oppressed communities and student populations. Hence, for Darder, the relationship between power and truth is also not only important, but necessary in discussion of the social sciences and critical pedagogical work.

Drawing from Foucault (1980), Darder insists that any educational theory of cultural democracy must allow individuals from dispossessed groups to express and challenge "regimes of truth," imposed and perpetuated within the social relations of capitalist schooling. This signals the importance of interrogating questions of ideology, cultural politics, and the hidden curriculum within educational studies. Moreover, Darder's thesis also addresses the desire to know oneself—in relation to dominant discourses, paradigms, and ways of being. She consistently discusses the asymmetrical relations of power at work in the dominant and subordinate dynamics of oppression and the need to understand key terms like hegemony, cultural invasion, language domination, racism, and the politics of resistance. When structures of hegemony are enacted in schools and society, Darder contends, these structures can be unveiled, challenged, and transformed. Celebration of Cinco de Mayo and Martin Luther King's birthday are used as prime examples of initially radical concepts, once intended to push back, and resist cultural invasion, that were appropriated into the dominant culture, stripping them of their revolutionary and transformative vision.

For Darder, biculturalism speaks to the process by which bicultural individuals and students must traverse two distinct sociocultural environments: (1) the primary culture of their community and (2) the dominant culture of the school. In order to survive and thrive in societies like the United States, all bicultural individuals must ultimately learn to navigate and negotiate their lives along the borders where these intersect. Darder is particularly concerned with supporting the "awakening" and development of critical consciousness for students of color—a process through which they can reclaim their voices. In her work, Darder makes a clear distinction between being bilingual and bicultural—in that someone who is bilingual may not necessarily also be bicultural. Biculturalism refers to a lived and experienced knowledge of subalternity, rather than information that can be gathered from a book. Questions of power and privilege thus come into play, as learning a second language from a privileged or affluent social position is a very different story from that of bicultural students from working-class and racialized communities. In response, Darder proposes a philosophy of cultural democracy that provides key critical principles significant to teaching bicultural students in the United States and other subaltern contexts.

The Latino Question

In providing some specificity to the link between culture and power and a philosophy of cultural democracy, Darder takes on the "Latino" question within the United States in the context of schooling and society. For example, in their introduction to *The Latino Studies Reader*, Darder (and Rodolfo Torres) began by citing Chicano historian Juan Gómez-Quiñones (1977) on the centrality of political economy for theorizing Mexican American communities. Furthermore, Gómez-Quiñones's work supports Darder and Torres's claim regarding the inseparability of culture and class in understanding Latino life and society. Their introductory chapter offers an explicitly Marxist analysis to the field of Latino/Chicano Studies and Education. Darder and Torres expand the discussion of Latinos as a racialized group by utilizing an analytical lens that "forthrightly engages material conditions, class structure, and cultural change" as fundamental to understanding, reading, and analyzing this extremely diverse group—demographically, culturally, ideologically, and politically.

Darder and Torres made it clear (and it still holds now) that Latino Studies scholars, for the most part, have systematically ignored critiques of capitalism, engagement with class struggle, and the significance of the labor question. Darder and Torres situate Latino Studies and Education in context to the internationalization of capital and labor, its link to the "postmodern" project, identity politics, the language of "race," and the limits of cultural nationalism when forging a field of study that had its origins with Mexican American/Chicano struggles. As a way to address the heterogeneity of Latino populations and open up the discourse, Darder and Torres remind us of the scholarly formation of the field, whose beginnings were inextricably tied to the question of social justice *and* economic democracy.

Not surprising within the context of academic institutions, Darder and Torres argue that Latino Studies (and the institutionalization of ethnic studies and other anti-racist programming and curriculum) has been directed, explicitly and implicitly, to produce forms of research and pedagogy that are "commensurate with the needs of capital"; that is, consistent with the economic imperatives of the university. In alignment with the neoliberal multicultural logic of the academic industrial complex, Darder and Torres posit that many Latino Studies scholars reproduce and perpetuate forms of knowledge production that are positivistic, reductionist, and ahistorical. Accordingly, they engage in issues of cultural representation and racialized differences devoid of political and economic interrogations. For nearly four decades, Darder and Torres have called for scholarship grounded in a historical materialist analysis of society—an analysis they believe should be centrally important to Latino Studies. Moreover, Darder and Torres

(2004) consider questions of social class (and class struggle) as "intrinsic to all social relations, and thus, view all social arrangements as configured, dialectically, within the context of contemporary capitalist social formation." This is a perspective that aligns with long-time labor organizer and public intellectual Adoph Reed, Jr. (2018), who wrote:

> Anti-racist politics is a class politics; it is rooted in the social position and worldview, and material interests of the stratum of race relations engineers and administrators who operate in Democratic party politics and as government functionaries, the punditry and commentariat, education administration and the professoriate, corporate, social service and nonprofit sectors, and the multibillion-dollar diversity industry. That stratum comes together around a common-sense commitment to the centrality of race—and other categories of ascriptive identity— as the appropriate discursive framework through which to articulate norms of justice and injustice and through which to formulate remedial responses.
>
> (p. 111)

A Contribution to Critical Theory of Education

Antonia Darder has left an indelible mark on countless scholars in the fields who have come across her writings, but more broadly, she has made a significant contribution to educators and community activists on the left. But one has to be ready for her work—to be ready to engage in struggle and be willing to struggle internally with the contradictions of one's own life. In many ways, it is as much a matter of her work finding the reader, as it is the reader finding her work. This dialectic is profoundly embedded in scholars writing from the Freirean tradition and certainly can be traced back to Marx. As Shirley Steinberg writes in the foreword of Darder's compilation, *A Dissident Voice* (2011), one does not encounter Antonia, but in fact one is "invited in … to her paintings, her poetry, her speeches, her books, and her advocacy." Since the 1990s, Darder had been considered one of the most significant women in the field of critical pedagogy (Darder, 2011). Today, she still stands as one of the most significant scholars in the field, particularly for scholars from working-class and racialized communities. It is important here to note that the theoretical language of Western educational discourses has historically been structured by predominantly white, male, and academic elites (Darder, 1997; Lam, 2008). Even within the progressive scholarly context of critical pedagogy, this has not been an exception. Nevertheless, despite these barriers, the writings of Antonia Darder, as a working-class woman of color, ruptured this orthodoxy within critical pedagogy, inserting questions of cultural life, linguistic democracy, and historical specificities.

Darder is also recognized for her capacity to ground her praxis in creative, productive, and instructive ways. In working with historically marginalized populations, it is easy for educators to fall into the trap of rearticulating experiences of discrimination and racism as the only means for empowering students. Although these experiences may serve as a point of entry into our social analysis, it is also imperative that in the intellectual formation of students for subaltern populations, critical educators are able to facilitate their ability to move from the language of practice to the language of theory (Darder, 1997; Lam, 2008). In efforts to resist conservative forms of domination, educators may respond by disengaging from all forms of theoretical language. Darder warns of the dangers of such disengagement. Sharing her concerns, we recognize this dilemma and support the idea that minoritized populations must be able to theorize our own histories and lived experiences. It is fundamental that we have the knowledge and theoretical language to unveil, challenge, and work to transform the rampant forms of inequality that persist within a racializing capitalist society.

Given the genealogy of critical pedagogy, some scholars of color, consciously or unconsciously, have distanced themselves from the field. While some have used critical pedagogy as "jumping-off points" to other critical scholarship, most have not fully acknowledged or given proper due to this field of study and its genesis for much of the progressive work in education. In fact, critical pedagogical principles form the basis for much of the radical educational scholarship and literature on teaching written during the last fifty years. One can argue that the publication of Freire's *Pedagogy of the Oppressed* in English in 1970 profoundly impacted the intellectual direction of critical pedagogy in the North American context. In addition, the work of Henry Giroux (1983) in the early 1980s helped shape the field by connecting critical theory to critical pedagogy. The incorporation of some of the Frankfurt School's tenets into the pedagogical conversation paved the way for how we make sense of ideology and critique, culture industry, praxis, class struggle, etc. and its relationship to curriculum studies, educational theory and practice, and capitalist schooling more broadly. Here, we would be remiss to not mention that both Paulo Freire and Henry Giroux were two of Darder's most influential mentors.

In an era where new fads are recycled as "improved" theories reign supreme, critical pedagogy has often been thrown to the wayside. In what can appear to some like a theory without saliency today, Darder and other critical education scholars have contributed to critical pedagogy by their consistent willingness to acknowledge the power of its principles and the wherewithal to keep it alive. In Darder, we find a scholar who is able to share the power of critical pedagogy in expanding consciousness, without reliance or allegiance to recipes or formulaic strategies. Through her pedagogical praxis, Darder has honed critical pedagogy's potential to stretch students and linked this to a deeper cultural analysis of subaltern life. In this way, she has significantly opened critical pedagogy to reinvention and a fuller sense of commitment to the academic well-being of all students. For instance, the first edition of *The Critical Pedagogy Reader*, originally published in 2002, has seen four editions spanning two decades with over 100 articles included in these collections that offer powerful ways in which critical pedagogy represents a possibility for social change (Darder, et al., 2002; 2008; 2017; 2024). We, as editors, joined Darder on the fourth edition of the *Reader*, and witnessed her commitment to continuously opening the field of engagement with respect to the ways critical pedagogy can continue to support an alternative emancipatory vision for political change.

Despite efforts to cultivate critical dialogue, often competition and individualism in the academy undermine emancipatory discourses meant to expand and stretch us. This competition is exacerbated by animosity and skepticism even among scholars and activists who might be considered allies or on the "same side" of history, including those on the educational left from all populations. Instead of thinking about our work collectively, individuality and competition among us are often reinforced. There is a brutal dynamic of one-upmanship constantly at work to see who is the "smartest" or "most articulate" person in the room. This can be driven by the quantities of articles and books we publish. It is the desire to build on what is "yours/ours" without fully considering that we stand on the shoulders of people who have labored before us, with their blood, sweat, and tears (and at times, their lives) to make a way for us. It arises from the incessant expectation to develop "new" areas of study or coin "new" terms; and to be seen as "stars" or "innovative" thinkers in the field. In concert with Darder's frequently expressed concerns about the repressive culture of the academy, we are concerned about the ways in which our knowledge production and ways of being and knowing in the world get commodified—to be sold to the highest bidder without hesitation. Here, Darder's writings remind us that self-vigilance, humility, and solidarity are not just words to be written or spoken, they must be central to our lived intellectual and political project. Moreover, it is imperative that we rethink existing issues, questions, and concerns, but perhaps with more depth and clarity—as a way to begin anew.

Darder's concern with the "politics of forgetting" supports our commitment not to forget where we come from nor where we want to go. This is also in sync with the anticolonial intellectual and political leader, Amilcar Cabral, who beckoned us to always go "back to the source" (Cabral, 1972; Cabral, 1979; Darder & Torres, 2004; Valley & Motala, 2023), in order to understand ourselves. There is no question that a critical study of history, political economy, class, praxis, hegemony, and ideology belong at the forefront of our intellectual, political, and pedagogical work. For Darder, this work must also be grounded in the material conditions of the people. It is the pain and suffering of real people on the ground, in the streets, and our communities that give us voice, strength, and inspiration to move forward and to go out again the next day. What Darder consistently reminds us of is that intellectual work cannot solely exist in the abstract or in our heads, but rather it must also be familiar or recognizable to those with worn-out faces and tattered bodies. And simultaneously it must be an invitation to "look backward to look forward" (Kelley, 1997).

Toward a Critical Theory of Racism

Darder, with her comrade and long-time collaborator the aforementioned Rodolfo Torres, posited a critical theory of racism in their study of historically marginalized and racialized populations in the United States. By focusing their attention on the material conditions of racialized groups, their work is undeniably historical and comparative—both within and beyond its national and geographical borders. Their particularly provocative and challenging articulation of critical race theory (CRT) borrows from the British, French, and Marxist traditions, locating political economy/class as a primary unit of analysis in their work. Darder and Torres, in the late 1980s and early 1990s, were striving to speak about what they both experienced within their contexts as young scholars and professors. To be sure, their analysis stemmed from both growing up working-class in the barrios of Los Angeles and as colonized subjects of the United States of America. Similar to Darder's engagement with critical pedagogy, Darder and Torres sought to develop not just a language of critique, but also a language of possibility—in thinking and rethinking the notion of "race" and racism and its inextricable relationship to class formation.

Darder and Torres's writings were strongly aligned with Harry Winston, National Chairperson for the Communist Party USA for twenty years, who stated that "the fight against racism is the Achilles Heel of US Imperialism." Their concerns echoed that of William L. Patterson, the Civil Rights Congress, and those on the black left decades before whose goal was to internationalize the struggle against US imperialism (Patterson, 1951/1970/2017, p. x). In a similar vein, Darder and Torres continued in this line of thinking by taking up those writing and thinking within the Marxist tradition, in an effort to place questions of class at the center of analysis. Darder and Torres drew on trans-Atlantic literature on racism and migration from scholars from the UK beginning in the early 1980s. Engaging ideas advanced by radical sociologist Robert Miles (1982; 1989; 1993; 2003), Darder and Torres vehemently fought to break the false conceptual link between the notion of "race" and the phenomenon of racism, as a way to distinguish the significant analytical use of racism and re-center questions of social class and class struggle. In the process, they brought much-needed depth, rigor, and specificity to their analysis of racialized populations, given the major demographic shifts taking place amid a changing US/California political economy and international division of labor.

A central critique posited by Darder and Torres is the overwhelming use of "race" as a central unit of analysis in the post-1960s civil rights era. Their work expressed concern for the limits of CRT with its formation from critical legal studies in the late 1980s. Moreover, they viewed the US legal system as part and parcel of the ideological state apparatus, which more often than not is both shaped by and protects the imperatives of capitalism. Moreover, most CRT scholarship is grounded in intersectionality arguments of "race, class, and gender," presuming that each category should receive equal attention and status in the field. In their discussion, Darder and Torres provide a succinct critique of the intersectionality argument; often centered on storytelling modes of inquiry. Darder and Torres express concerns about its anti-dialectical stance, which often perpetuates a false binary between objectivity and subjectivity. Hence, storytelling methods are at issue here, given their tendency to essentialize social relations in the following ways: (1) romanticizing the experience of historically marginalized and dispossessed groups, (2) homogenizing of "white" and "people of color" tied to the question of voice and representation, and (3) inevitable "exaggerations, excesses, and ideological trends for which the only possible name is chauvinism."

In concert with the work of Paul Gilroy (2000), Darder and Torres are not interested in "short-cut" solidarity. Rather, they forthrightly call for a substantive critique of capitalism (and to that extent, a nuanced understanding of imperialism). While they recognize the important work done within CRT and intersectionality studies, they seek to forge a different political and analytical path. Their call for a historical materialist analysis of racism is an attempt to think more substantively about multi-ethnic organizing and building solidarity among working people in the United States and around the world. Given the adhesive nature of "race" and the commonsensical utility of the "race relations" paradigm, their call for a critical theory of racism has not been well-received, particularly within the CRT circle. Nevertheless, Darder and Torres have been willing to go where most scholars are unwilling to go politically and ideologically. They are clear that their efforts to push the envelope have been informed by their own material conditions and how they make sense of the world. Moreover, their work agreed with political theorist Ellen Meiksins Wood's (1995) contention that, "at a time when a critique of capitalism is more urgent than ever, the dominant theoretical trends on the left are busy conceptualizing away the very idea of capitalism" (p. 238).

As Darder reinvents critical pedagogical thought and Freire's writings (2002; 2015; 2018) in her analysis of American schooling under capitalism, she has also drawn several central tenets from the aforementioned Wood, including a radical rethinking of democracy without capitalism, the limitations of identity politics, a rereading of Gramscian "civil society," and the reimaging of class differences without exploitation and domination, when interrogating the plurality of racism (Wood, 1995; Darder & Torres, 2004). Darder and Torres (2004) build upon Wood's (1995) notion of "civil society" when contending with the intersectionality argument. Here, Wood argues that intersectionality arguments reflect a distorted appropriation of Gramsci's "civil society," which was "explicitly intended to function as a weapon against capitalism by identifying potential spaces of freedom outside the state for autonomous, voluntary organization and plurality" (Darder & Torres, 2004, p. 105). About this, Wood contends:

> The danger lies in the fact that the totalizing logic and coercive power of capitalism is reduced to one set of institutions and relations among many others, on a conceptual par with households or voluntary associations. Such a reduction is, in fact, the principal distinctive feature of "civil society" in its new incarnation. Its effect is to conceptualize away the problem of capitalism, by disaggregating society into fragments, with no overarching power structure, no totalizing unity, no systemic coercion—in other words, no capitalist system, with its expansionary drive and its capacity to penetrate every aspect of social life.
> (Wood in Darder & Torres, 2004, p. 106)

Similar to how Darder extends Freire's work when contending with capitalist schooling and its relationship to love, humanization, and pedagogy, she reinvents an analysis of racism and its manifestations by way of Wood's contribution to our understanding of contemporary capitalism. Darder evokes the very best of what good teaching and scholarship do—by making us think and ask questions. Over the years, she has consistently attempted to make intellectual and political interventions within multiple fields of study, including the study of race and racism. Darder's engagement with a critique of capitalism as antithetical to democratic ideals and values brings to the forefront tensions and contradictions inherent in our desire to create a culturally democratic classroom and society. Within the context of institutions like schools, Darder's writings signal the cracks and fissures in the system that can allow us to do critical work with others, even in spaces deemed as oppressive and colonizing, especially for working-class racialized populations.

Despite the wholesale disregard of *After Race: Racism after Multiculturalism* (2004) in the field, the volume has had a lasting impact over the last twenty years on many of us whose labor has questioned mainstream views of race. Darder and Torres's work on racism and class relations has been instructive to our thinking about "race" and racism with regards to economic restructuring in the metropole (specifically as a way to understand racialized populations comparatively) and placing class struggle in the center of the conversation when analyzing racialized class inequality in the twenty-first century. Studying *After Race* has allowed us to think about the relationship between democracy and capitalism, racism and capitalism, power and difference, the macro and micro, and the institutional and individual. Darder's location as a working-class Boricua woman, in conjunction with a particular history of violence, colonization, and subsequent migration to the metropole, undoubtedly shaped her commitment to the socialist and internationalist project.

Darder is not interested in producing scholarly work simply for the sake of publishing. Repeatedly, she has written with the clear purpose of expanding an understanding of the field and bringing together or presenting in new ways discourses that yet required consolidation to make the scholarship more accessible. This is well-illustrated by her publications, including *Culture and Power in the Classroom, Latinos and Education, The Latinos Studies Reader, After Race: Racism After Multiculturalism, The Critical Pedagogy Reader, The International Critical Pedagogy Reader, Decolonizing Interpretive Research*, and *The Student Guide to Pedagogy of the Oppressed*—award-winning and groundbreaking in their respective fields. More importantly, Darder's work has consistently been grounded in and committed to examining questions of social and material oppression—in ways that reclaim our histories, dignity, and humanity.

A Poetics and Methodology of Love: A World in Which It Will Be Easier to Love

If there is a concept that has been most profoundly reinvented (in the Freirean sense) by Darder, it is the pedagogical and political meaning of love. She has cultivated and drawn from the works and understandings of Paulo Freire's pedagogy of love, grasping intimately the soul behind his words and his life. Darder has accomplished this in a way that extends how we understand love beyond the realms of pedagogy, spirituality, education, and as a conscious embodied practice. Darder is able to do this because she labors with love, from the deepest parts of her soul, and in so doing, ruptures the mind/body split and commits to a life of coherence, unity, and integrity. Freire, as Darder has noted, is a profound example of an educator and philosopher who consciously embraced love as a necessary force in the struggle against the lovelessness of oppression and injustice. Similarly, it is valuable to "read" the world through the musings, writings, and ways of being of Antonia Darder, not just as written words but also as material labor that seeks to contribute to the world. In this way, the indelible markings she leaves behind on our consciousness and the world impact the bodies, hearts, and minds of those who read her. Her soulfulness is a quality of being, as it is a pedagogical life lesson that offers us a lived epistemology of love and makes tangible Freire's vision of a world in which it is easier to love. Birthed, forged, and honed over the years from struggle, Darder's way of being is informed by a historical presence, a comradely solidarity, and a love that she extends openly to all those with whom she comes into relationship.

Beyond debilitating judgments, an intimacy informs the relationships built on a Darderian poetics of love, in that this reflects a vision grounded upon an ethics and clarity, which understands that love is not "about absolute consensus, or unconditional acceptance, or unceasing words of sweetness, or endless streams of hugs and kisses" (Darder, 2011). The foundation and groundwork for Darder's vision and methodology can be first found in her seminal poesis, *Culture and Power in the Classroom*—a cultural love letter to educators who dare to take up the call to struggle for freedom (1991; 2012). She weaves love into the fabric of her passionate political treatise on culture and power. She does not romanticize love when she makes a case for the need to understand and problematize traditional American pedagogy—a form of pedagogy that has been used to pacify rather than create the conditions for a critical pedagogy and decolonizing analysis of society. It is her courage to name the material conditions of education; through an understanding of how spheres of culture and power collide, which ultimately constitutes an act of love. Similarly, offering us the possibility to embrace cultural democracy in the classroom also reflects the importance of love and freedom to a genuinely emancipatory pedagogy. As a teacher, writer, and activist, Darder always remains a cultural worker at heart, working with others to piece puzzles of possibility and liberation together, while all the time nurturing love as a political force.

Whether it is because she is a mother, a lover, or touched by both acts of love and lovelessness, Darder keenly came to see that what often was missing from pedagogical and political discourses alike was a practice of love—something that she learned so clearly as central to a Freirean vision of the world. Over the years, she has committed much of her life to living a praxis of love through her pedagogy, mentorship, activism, friendships, and everyday life. There is no question that love, for most, is a complex and elusive concept. In a critical pedagogical sense, the meaning of love is revealed only through the lived practice of the concept; there is no recipe, formula, or prescription for its enactment. Above all, then, love requires communal presence and engagement, which Darder terms as a political force. This signals the embodiment of a deeper understanding, an energetic relationship, a passion, a force, enveloped by an ethics of liberation—where the needs of the most oppressed are made central to our labor. Drawing from Freire's "revolutionary vision of consciousness and transformation," Darder (2016) also writes about love as political grace or spiritual force that is unleashed by our collective revolutionary efforts. Moreover, love as praxis is a regenerating process that grows and matures within our communal labor and within ourselves as evolving human beings. To say that love matures speaks to the ways that we gain deeper understanding, through "our social and material practices, as we work to live, learn, labor, and transform the world together" (Darder, 2016).

This discussion may help explain the reason why Darder's seminal piece, "Teaching as an Act of Love," is one of her most cited articles in the literature. In epistemologies of the West, any notion of love is generally decentered, leaving lovelessness to unfold undeterred. In contrast, Darder's critical analysis calls for a praxis of love to be integral to our daily lives and practices, whether within the classroom or beyond. She has formulated a poet(h)ics and methodology of love, grounded in critical philosophical principles, which she steadily embodies in her labor with individuals and communities around the world. Notably, for more than four decades, her revolutionary ethics, passion, intimacy, and love have served as a political force for building relationships that are never one-sided or top-down, but rather liberatory for those involved. Those who have been mentored by Darder would agree. For Darder, we are certain, this level of commitment has come at a cost, given the level of honesty, struggle, and presence required. Additionally, for Darder, as for many critical scholars who seek to live their politics, this way of being can make the often-lonely halls of academia intolerable. Collegial resistance and intellectual posturing can only be made bearable through our commitment and clarity about why we do the work. Ultimately, Darder's labor has never been in service of educational institutions that historically have been incapable of permitting genuine forms of love and justice to unfold in their ivory towers. Rather, Darder's political and intellectual project has steadfastly encompassed, as it did for Che Guevara, a commitment to revolutionary love—a love which requires our openness and willingness to love and "fight the good fight." By example, Darder has shown that love can build harmonious connections, but requires a consciousness of human inseparability and interconnectedness, given the alienating forces that divide and separate us from ourselves and one another.

In "The Establishment of Liberatory Alliances with People of Color: What Must Be Understood," Darder speaks of an embodied solidarity, as key to the struggle for liberation. In opposition to the unacknowledged racism and elitism of progressive movements—that have often replicated power dynamics and structures that repress the participation of people of color and working-class populations—Darder calls for "a new politics of liberation that truly encompasses the participation of all people." What Darder proposes here is the need for a profound commitment and sense of ownership in the fight for our liberation. That is, the authentic opportunities for full participation in movements, through genuine partnerships with working-class communities of color. As such, the establishment of liberatory alliances with oppressed communities brings to light the willingness to engage in intimate and authentic forms of solidarity across our differences, along with a commitment to labor together toward our common well-being. Consistently, solidarity has been one of the key political concerns in Darder's work, reflecting her efforts to embody it in her labor and everyday life. Still, what she and so many of us continue to experience are disingenuous forms of solidarity, marked by individualism and competition within institutions that negate authentic possibilities of solidarity. Yet, despite the many difficulties and tensions confronted over her forty years within the academy, Darder has never wavered in her courage to love.

A Pedagogy of Courage

As a teacher of praxis, Darder's research and pedagogy have consistently connected her objective and subjective world. Perhaps equally important, Darder recognizes that there are material implications and consequences that profoundly impact the lives of the dispossessed around the world. Moreover, one of her most significant contributions to our own formation as scholars and thinkers has been the humility, grace, and radical love she extends. What she asks from us, as Freire did before her, is to find the courage to reinvent ourselves—as we seek to understand and engage with issues of human sufferings and differences. She also speaks of the courage to push back against things and ideas that are deemed "common-sense" and the willingness to step into the unknown and to let go of certainties (Fromm, 2001).

As alluded earlier, the academy can be a difficult, lonely, and isolating environment. It is even more difficult when one's scholarship and activism are politically and ideologically dismissed by those in positions of power. We have witnessed Darder's scholarship marginalized even among marginalized scholarly circles. The commitment to activist scholarship, and if necessary, to stand alone on principled positions can result in having to contend with much consternation and tension. Darder's refusal to "play the game" has caused her much pain and anguish every step of the way. Often, it has left her open to criticisms that sought to delegitimize her contributions as an educational philosopher. Nevertheless, through her labor with institutions and organizations, her intellectual courage, and sense of moral ethics, has also given her much joy and redemption.

Darder, in every sense of the word, is a Gramscian organic intellectual. To be sure, her struggles with institutions have not occurred in a vacuum. Universities and colleges, for the most part, were fundamentally set up to either reproduce class relations and privileges of the elite or to be of service to the ruling class. Undoubtedly, institutions can change folks, in ways often unbeknownst to them. The tensions of such contentious environments can certainly mess with your head, as is often the case with radical scholars of color, or students who come from working-class and historically oppressed populations. In the midst of a capitalist ideology for intellectual consumption, competition, and neoliberal down-sizing (including cutbacks in funding or limiting resources for social justice or ethnic studies programs and classes), the values and practices of educational institutions can eat at your core. It can erode one's values and begin to numb principled sensibilities. When we reflect on Darder's experiences in the academy, it seems amazing that she is still alive and ready to fight another day. Moreover, we attribute her fortitude partly to survival mechanisms learned and developed, while growing up in deeply colonizing conditions of social, political, and economic dispossession.

In her formation as a dissident woman of our time, engaged public intellectual, and renowned scholar, Darder refused to be objectified and commodified as an exception. She writes, "I managed to remain more firmly anchored to an organic aesthetic and collective sensibility as a Puerto Rican working-class woman, who recognizes that it is by an inexplicable accident of history that I sit here now and write these words" (Darder, 2012, p. 7). Given the trajectory of her origins, she was in the words of Audre

Lorde and critical anthropologist João Costa Vargas (2008), "never meant to survive." Darder's analysis on this question is endowed with a revolutionary commitment:

> Mine has been a long and arduous journey. Yet, what has allowed me to survive and thrive has always been a deep sense of justice that has prevailed in my life and continues to inspire my research, scholarship, teaching, and my everyday relationships. Moreover, through every experience and expression of my life, a deep spiritual process has connected my being and my knowing with the suffering and struggle of others, as I have attempted in community to make sense of a world that was not constructed for our survival, in that it was not meant for the survival of subaltern populations.
>
> (Darder in Hernandez, et al., 2023, p. 50)

Darder's life and scholarship are the living, breathing, and walking embodiment of courage. Yet, if one were to ask her, she would be the first to say that it is not about having courage or being courageous, but rather out of political necessity. Nevertheless, her pedagogy of courage is unshakable, because it is grounded in personal history, community relationships, and decades of regenerative praxis, which has included reading, reflection, analysis, political dialogues, more reading, more reflection, more analysis, and so on. It is a pedagogy that is lived, articulated, and translated into the everyday. Darder has encompassed a commitment to stay grounded, to stand her ground, to live humbly, to say "I don't know," to do it with humor, and to do it with abiding love and integrity. And through it all, she has remained critically astute, present, and faithful to the unfinishedness of the journey.

Hence, Freire's notion of unfinishedness remains central to Darder's view of her personal life and her relationship with the larger political project. Darder (2015) recognizes our unfinishedness as a necessary pedagogical and philosophical tool in "diminishing fatalism and inspiring hope in new possibilities for collective change among the oppressed" (p. 40). Darder affirms in her writings, as did Freire, that without our unfinishedness, we would be unable to generate the force necessary to not only fight for liberation, but to also imagine a new world for generations to come. Darder (2015) reminds us that "at the heart of this concept of our humanity is the recognition that oppression is never a permanent condition; and it is, indeed, because no human condition is ever absolute or finished that the struggle remains viable and hope fertile, even within political and material conditions that appear desolate and barren" (40). With this, we sincerely hope that this volume of Antonia Darder's selected works will contribute to the rethinking and reinventing of your labor and your life.

Bibliography

Boggs, J., and G. L. (1974), *Revolution and Evolution in the Twentieth Century*. New York, NY: Monthly Review Press.

Cabral, A. (1972/2023), *Return to the Source: Selected Texts of Amilcar Cabral*. New York, NY: Monthly Review Press.

Cabral, A. (1979), *Unity and Struggle: Writings and Speeches of Amilcar Cabral*. New York, NY: Monthly Review Press.
Darder, A. (1991/2012), *Culture and Power in the Classroom: Educational Foundations for the Schooling for Bicultural Students*. New York, NY: Routledge.
Darder, A. (2002/2017), *Reinventing Paulo Freire: A Pedagogy of Love*. New York, NY: Routledge.
Darder, A. (2011), *A Dissident Voice: Essays on Culture, Pedagogy, and Power*. New York, NY: Peter Lang.
Darder, A. (2015), *Freire and Education*. New York, NY: Routledge.
Darder, A. (2016), "Political Grace and Revolutionary Critical Pedagogy," *Rizoma Freireano*. Retrieved from https://www.rizoma-freireano.org/articles-2121/political-grace-21.
Darder, A. (2017), "Paulo Freire and Our Continuing Struggle in Neoliberal Times" [video file]. United Opt Out Conference. Retrieved from https://www.youtube.com/watch?v=qx-qb1BC0kQ&t=752s.
Darder, A. (2018/2024), *The Student Guide to Freire's Pedagogy of the Oppressed*. London: Bloomsbury Academic.
Darder, A., and Torres, R. D. (1997/2013), *Latinos and Education: A Critical Reader*. New York, NY: Routledge.
Darder, A., and Torres, R. D. (2004), *After Race: Racism after Multiculturalism*. New York, NY: New York University Press.
Darder, A., Hernandez, K., Lam, K. D., and Baltodano, M. (2003/2008/2017/2024), *The Critical Pedagogy Reader*. New York, NY: Routledge.
Foucault, M. (1980), *Power/Knowledge: Selected Interviews and Other Writings* (edited by Colin Gordon). New York, NY: Pantheon Books.
Freire, P. (1993), *Pedagogy of the Oppressed*. New York, NY: Continuum.
Fromm, E. (2001), *The Fear of Freedom*, 2nd ed. New York, NY: Routledge.
Gilroy, P. (2000), *Against Race: Imagining Political Culture Beyond the Color Line*. Cambridge, MA: Harvard University Press.
Giroux, H. (1983), *Theory and Resistance in Education: Toward a Pedagogy for the Opposition*. Westport, CT: Bergin & Garvey.
Gómez-Quiñones, J. (1977), "On Culture." *UCLA-Chicano Studies Center Publications*, Popular Series, Issue 1.
Hernandez, K., Cronin, S., and Lopez, E. (2023), *The Antonia Darder Reader: Education, Art, and Decolonizing Praxis*. Gorham, ME: Myers Education Press.
Kelley, R. (1997), *Yo' Mama's disFUNKtional!: Fighting the Culture Wars in Urban America*. Boston, MA: Beacon Press.
Kohan, W. (2021), *Paulo Freire: A Philosophical Biography*. London: Bloomsbury.
Lam, K. D. (2008), "Relocating Critical Pedagogy." *Radical History Review*, Special Issue, History and Critical Pedagogies: Transforming Consciousness, Classrooms, and Communities (102): 12–14.
Lam, K. D. (2024), "Beyond 'Bread and Circus': Reading and Teaching *Pedagogy of the Oppressed*," in A. Darder (ed.), *The Student Guide to Freire's Pedagogy of the Oppressed*. London: Bloomsbury Academic, 212-6.
Miles, R. (1982), *Racism & Migrant Labour*. London: Routledge.
Miles, R. (1989), *Racism*. London: Routledge.
Miles, R. (1993), *Racism after "Race Relations"*. New York, NY: Routledge.
Miles, R., and Brown, M. (2003), *Racism*. London: Routledge.

Patterson, W. (1951/1971/2017), *We Charge Genocide: The Crime of Government against the Negro People*. New York, NY: International Publishers.

Reed., Jr., A. (2018), "Antiracism: A Neoliberal Alternative to a Left." *Dialect Anthropol* (42): 105–15.

Steinberg, S. (2012), "Foreword: Artist, Scholar, Poet, Teacher, Activist … Sister to the World," in A. Darder (ed.), *A Dissident Voice: Essays on Culture, Pedagogy, and Power*. New York, NY: Peter Lang, xv–xvi.

Vally, S., and Motala, E. (2023), *Against Racial Capitalism: Selected Writings of Neville Alexander*. London: Pluto Press.

Vargas, J. C. (2008), *Never Meant to Survive: Genocide and Utopias in Black Diaspora Communities*. Lanham, MD: Rowman and Littlefield.

Wood, E. M. (1995), *Democracy against Capitalism: Renewing Historical Materialism*. Cambridge: Cambridge University Press.

Part 1

Reinventing Paulo Freire

Introduction

Paulo Freire has had a profound impact on the work of many subaltern scholars working toward the transformation of society, including Antonia Darder. Considered as *her father in the struggle,* Darder has written about her deep love for Freire and in turn his influence on the awakening of her political bicultural voice. Intellectually rooted in Freire's pedagogical strength and wisdom, Darder has continuously and cogently taken up the invitation to reinvent his work. Through serious engagement and ongoing dialogue with Paulo's writings, Antonia rewrites, reinvents, and recreates through the Darderian corpus that will follow in this opening section and throughout this compendium. Without a doubt, she pays homage to Paulo Freire through her work which is an offering of solidarity and an unfolding letter of love to not only readers but in honor of Freire and his tremendous loving commitment to the oppressed.

Summary of Articles

This section begins with "Liberation: Our Historical Task," a chapter in the book *Freire and Education* in which Darder offers insight into some of the powerful theoretical contributions that impacted her personal reflections, scholarships, and loving reinventions of Freire's ideas. This guiding force of liberation as a historical task ushers us into a view of liberation as a necessary unapologetic struggle. This struggle Antonia acknowledges is key to a larger international struggle taking place globally and intimately tied to our collective liberation and solidarity as human beings. To honor Freire's writings, Darder offers a naming and reinvention of salient themes and elements of his central tenets and messages to the world. Through Antonia's tribute to Paulo's work on liberation as a central task, she reveals that it is inextricably linked to what Freire described as our "quest for human completion." Antonia has and continues to do her work through the act of teaching where she without a doubt embodies Paulo's liberatory spirit.

One of the most profound gifts bestowed upon Antonia Darder by Paulo Freire was the power of love in teaching. Undoubtedly, it has had an immense impact on her pedagogy and her life in that all she does and embodies in the world is done through intentional acts of love. As such, one of her most often cited and read texts is "Teaching as an Act of Love: In Memory of Paulo Freire," where she offers an extension and reinvention of Paulo's insistence that education is an act of love carried out through a deep commitment to the oppressed. A vulnerably tender and intimate text, "Teaching as an Act of Love," invites us into the relationship that Antonia had with Paulo. It is at the same time an insightful unveiling of the possibility and necessity of love, and a tribute to Freire that invites educators to reckon with the politics of love and the need for a critical understanding of love in the making of educationally democratic spaces. This text offers an understanding of the evolution of Paulo's thinking as well as his incisive critique of capitalism as a totalizing force that must be embraced through solidarity and across difference.

The final piece within this section is an introduction to one of Paulo's later texts, *Pedagogy of the Heart* or *Under the Shade of the Mango Tree* (its Portuguese title). Antonia writes from the heart as she offers this introduction grounded in a loving analysis of his work. She begins by offering readers a powerful understanding about the political act of translation where in that act something powerful is often lost. However, Freire's intellectual capacity and loving spirit shine through even in the translated forms of his writings. Intertwined with the current state of neoliberal politics, Covid-19, and global capitalism, Darder links Freire's work to his critique of capitalism and technology. In all of Darder's writings that appear in this section and throughout the book, she continues to pay homage to Paulo Freire—a beautiful soul that lives on through her and so many others—in struggle, politics, faith, hope, liberation, and love.

1

Liberation: Our Historical Task

The greatest humanistic and historical task of the oppressed: to liberate themselves...
—Paulo Freire (1970)

More than forty years after *Pedagogy of the Oppressed* was first released, the inequalities and injustices that Paulo Freire was addressing then continue to persist in the United States and around the world today. In many instances, these conditions have only worsened in the last two decades, with the steady infusion of neoliberal imperatives into education, focused on privatization, deregulation, and free-market enterprise. With this in mind, it is important to begin any discussion on the legacy of Freire here; in that, often, it has been precisely Freire's revolutionary critique of capitalism and the relationship of schooling to class formation that have been systematically stripped away, resulting in diluted versions of his ideas. As a scholar of color who was born in Puerto Rico, a colonized subject, and reared in the urban poverty of the United States, it is impossible to convince me, given my lived history, that oppression's center of gravity for those of us deemed as "other" is simply the psychological aberration (or microaggressions) perpetrated by white people toward our so-called race. Rather, I argue that the processes that reproduce racism at all levels of the society, including education, are intimately connected to the material domination and exploitation of our communities by the powerful elite—and enacted, for the most part, by those who are not themselves affluent, but answer daily its siren call.

Although seldom spoken or acknowledged in traditional discourses about Freire's work, there are particular ways in which radical black, Latino, Native American, and Asian-American working-class communities of the 1960s and 1970s embraced his revolutionary ideas and pedagogical assertions. Freire's observation, in contrast, acknowledged this phenomenon, when responding to those who deemed his work metaphysical, abstract, or dense: "Workers also understand my work, as well as those who have some experience of oppression. But I acknowledge there might be a problem of cross cultural translation with [more privileged and mainstream] U.S. readers."[1]

For many of us, Freire (2002) was one of the few philosophical educational theorists of the time that inspired us to struggle: "[We] were on fire with the love of freedom, and had found a point of reference in *Pedagogy of the Oppressed* " (p. 184). The distinctiveness of his radical discourse spoke to a grounded understanding of our racialized oppression and powerfully linked us to a larger international anti-imperialist struggle taking place around the world. In other words, if we were to counter the impact of the historical and contemporary impact of genocide, slavery, and colonialism, we had to begin by engaging the manner in which racism is inextricably tied to imperatives of social class formation and material exclusion. Freire (2005) contended that although "one cannot reduce the analysis of racism to social class, one cannot understand racism fully without a class analysis, for to do one at the expense of the other is to fall prey into a sectarianist position, which is as despicable as the racism that we need to reject" (p. 15).

Freire's work then was central to understanding movement strategies related to community struggles, educational politics, and theoretical formations, in that he specifically grounded his analysis in an understanding of poverty as oppression and capitalism as the root of domination. The struggle for radical activists of color was not foremost about "celebrating diversity," identity politics, or cultural legitimacy, but rather, it was a larger struggle for our humanity and our survival, given that we had suffered, in the flesh, the violence of oppression at every level of our existence. Hence, the more radical arms of the civil rights era recognized that local political struggles for self-determination had to also be connected to a larger international political project of class struggle and an incisive critique of capitalism, racism, and patriarchy. During that short-lived era, movement organizations of color came to understand their struggle within the context of a long history shaped by the violence of colonialism. Important links were made between the economic imperatives that led to the colonization of the land, exploitation of workers, and the enslavement of African Americans. As such, we recognized that the purpose of our engagement with Freire's work was as much about unveiling the structures of domination as it was about decolonizing our minds of hegemonic ideologies that made us complicit with our oppression.

Freire's philosophical insights about the oppressor/oppressed contradiction and its internalization among oppressed populations were echoed by writers of color of the twentieth century, who spoke to this phenomenon in their political articulations of the plights of impoverished racialized communities. Many authors of color also made references to a dual process of socialization, not found in ethnocentric theories of the dominant culture. In concert with Freire's (1985) understanding, "without a sense of identity, there can be no real struggle" (p. 186), theorists of color sought to better comprehend and posit theories of identity. These perspectives challenged Eurocentric epistemologies, notions of identity, and Western concepts of human development. Theorists of color, instead, spoke to the phenomenon of double consciousness, double vision, bicultural identity, diunital consciousness, multidimensional consciousness, duality, of our twin beings, and so on (Darder, 2012), referring to the collision of not only two cultures but of deep asymmetrical relations of powers, which led to the subordination and erasure of our histories and material oppression of our communities. Restoring the integrity of our voices and centering our cultural and historical knowledge of survival, in sync with Freire's pedagogy, became an important political quest, in an era where our voices and participation remained relatively silent and absent from the spheres of power.

As a young woman, meeting Paulo Freire, hearing him speak, and reading his work truly changed the course of my life, as an educator and political activist. This was for many reasons, of course. However, what cannot be denied is that this was partly so because he looked and felt more like people from my own community—people exiled by colonialism from or within our own lands. At the time, he was exiled from Brazil for his emancipatory literacy efforts with poor populations from the Brazilian countryside—those whom he credited for much of his ideas for *Pedagogy of the Oppressed*. Freire often spoke of his work as a manifestation of what he had learned through his relationship with those who were the most dispossessed in his country. His writings generated in activists and educators of color, in the United States and other parts of the world, greater political clarity and commitment.

Freire's writings also challenged educators to truly embody our commitment to political consciousness and social transformation, within the everyday relationships we forged with those within and outside our cultural communities. What we understood was that *pedagogy of the oppressed* was not pedagogy solely for the classroom, but rather a living pedagogy that has to be infused into all aspects of our lives, including our personal politics. This is to say that teaching to transgress had to constitute a moral stance, often belittled and diminished within mainstream political discourses, even on the left. So much so that it caused bell hooks (1994) to write, "It always astounds me when progressive people act as though it is somehow a naive moral position to believe that our lives must be a living example of our politics" (p. 48).

For communities betrayed by our schooling, Freire's message promised the possibility of an educational project for our children tied to a larger political democratic vision—one that resonated with our anticolonial struggles for self-determination and political aspirations to become full subjects of our histories, as well as control our own destinies. Pedagogy of the oppressed also signaled a pedagogy of transgression—transgression of oppressive ideologies, attitudes, structures, conditions, and practices within education and society that debilitate our humanity. It is not surprising that Freire's humanistic inclinations and political vision of education resonated deeply with movement demands of educators and activists of color who sought fundamental change to the process of schooling in this country and those societal structures that worked against the emancipatory interests of our children and our communities.

Through Freire's (1970) ideas, we came to acknowledge that education can serve as an important vehicle for the political formation of citizens within a democratic society. This pointed to a humanizing educational process that could prepare students from oppressed communities for voice, participation in civil society, and ethical decision making in all aspects of their life. A central political aim of such a humanizing process of education is to support the evolution of critical consciousness with an explicit aim toward the establishment of a more harmonious and peaceful world. Starting from the fundamental realization that we live in an unequal world, an emancipatory pedagogy had to encompass a collective "struggle for our humanization, for the emancipation of labor, and for the overcoming of our alienation" (p. 28), so that we might affirm ourselves as full political subjects of our lives.

Freire (1970) articulated a vision that he considered "an indispensable condition for the quest for human completion" (p. 31)—a completion that although would remain ever unfinished, nevertheless could enliven our imagination, creativity, hope, and commitment to resist the forces of domination and exploitation within education and the larger society. For Freire, freedom encompassed our human capacity "to be" and to exist authentically. Moreover, our capacity to live free required a fundamental shift in how we define ourselves and the conditions in which we exist. This entailed a humanizing process that could support and facilitate the ongoing development of critical consciousness, so that we might find the cognitive, emotional, psychological, and spiritual strength necessary to critique and denounce conditions of oppression, embrace a life of solidarity, and announce new possibilities for a more just world.

Toward this end, Freire (1970) understood that our task as teachers and students is to embrace a historical understanding of our relationship with the world and transform our teaching and learning into revolutionary praxis—a sound political pedagogy of "reflection and action upon the world to transform it" (p. 36). He argued that it is imperative that we, as educators, work in our communities to unveil and challenge the contradictions of educational policies and practices that objectify and dehumanize us, preventing our expression as full subjects of history. Indeed such a vision of education entails an ongoing political process. One that can only be sustained through collective labor—a labor born of love, but deeply anchored in an unceasing commitment to know, through both theory and practice, the nature of the beast that preys on our humanity.

Education as a Political Act

Education is part and parcel of the very nature of education… It does not matter where or when it has taken place, whether it is more or less complex, education has always been a political act.

—Paulo Freire (1993)

Freire (1993) was clear and forthright about his belief in the political nature of education. Furthermore, he believed that our political definition of our pedagogical orientation in the classroom and communities had to be understood explicitly with respect to our political responsibility as social agents for change. This view rips apart assumptions of neutrality in education, in that it demands from educators that we clearly take on our labor as a political act, defining ourselves "either in favor of freedom, living it authentically, or against it" (p. 64). Freire's personal enactment of this important principle in his work was made obvious when he wrote,

> In the name of the respect I should have for my students, I do not see why I should omit or hide my political stance by proclaiming a neutral position that does not exist. On the contrary, my role as teacher is to assent the student's right to compare, to choose, to rupture, to decide.
>
> (p. 68)

Thus, within the context of education, whether we are conscious of it or not, Freire recognized that all educators perpetuate political values, beliefs, myths, and meanings about the world. As such, education has to be understood as a politicizing (or depoliticizing) institutional process that conditions students to ascribe to the dominant ideological norms and epistemological assumptions of the prevailing social order. In addition, Freire helped us to understand how the hegemonic culture of schooling socializes students to accept their particular role or place within the material order—a role or place that historically has been determined by the colonizing forces of the dominant society, based on the political economy and its sorted structures of oppression. What Freire's writings made clear to educators and activists was that schools are enmeshed in the political economy of the society and at its service. As such, schools are political sites involved in the construction, control, and containment of oppressed cultural populations, through their legitimating function, with respect to discourse, meaning, and subjectivity. And, furthermore, "the more [we] deny the political dimension of education, the more [we] assume the moral potential to blame the victims" (Freire & Macedo, 1987, p. 123).

Freire's pedagogy of the oppressed courageously discarded an uncritical acceptance of the prevailing social order and its structures of capitalist exploitation, embracing the empowerment of dispossessed populations as the primary purpose of liberatory education. In essence, his revolutionary praxis turned the traditional purpose of public education on its proverbial head, to unveil its contradictions. Instead of educating students to become simply reliable workers, complacent citizens, and avid consumers, Freire called upon educators to engage students in a critical understanding of *the world* in order to consider emancipatory possibilities, born from the lived histories and material conditions that shaped their daily lives. Freire's (1993) common use of "the world" here is important to grasp, in that its meaning was both material and ideological, not merely poetic metaphor. Rather he explained:

> When I speak of the world, I am not speaking exclusively about the trees and the animals that I love very much, and the mountains and rivers. I am not speaking exclusively of nature which I am a part, but I am speaking also of the social structures, politics, culture, history, of which I am also a part.
>
> (p. 103)

This perspective of classroom and community life helped us to understand how historically, as a consequence of cultural and linguistic colonization and economic subjugation, populations of color in this country and abroad have been systematically oppressed. For more than forty years, this knowledge has helped to support radical educators in unveiling those hidden ideological values and beliefs that inform standardized curricula, materials, textbooks, testing and assessment, promotion criteria, and institutional relationships, in an effort to support and better infuse our teaching with an emancipatory political vision of schools and community life. In so doing, we came to recognize that the task at hand is not to reproduce the traditional social arrangements that support and perpetuate inequality and injustice, but rather to work toward the transformation of these conditions, within the context of our vocation as human beings and our daily efforts as educators and community activists committed to social change.

For Freire (1970), schools are inextricably linked to the hegemonic process of cultural, political, and economic life. He theorized that it is precisely these processes of domination that reinforce and give legitimacy to the reproduction of a "banking" system of education. The reflection of the dominant class and culture is inscribed in the educational policies and practices that shape hegemonic schooling. One of the most pervasive aspects of this approach has been the instrumentalizing practice of teaching-to-the-test. This sterile and enfeebling pedagogical approach functions to "minimize or annul students' creative power and stimulate their credulity" (p. 60) so as to reinforce intellectual submissiveness and conformity to the state's prescribed ideological definition of legitimate knowledge and academic measures of achievement.

Freire (1970) denounced instrumentalizing forms of pedagogy, given that these perpetuate cultural values of domination by teaching students they exist "abstract, isolated, independent and unattached to the world, that the world exists as a reality apart" (p. 69) from their control or influence. This deceptively and effectively works to structure the silences of students of color by relegating them to objects of their learning. Furthermore, this bankrupt logic of standardization adheres to a political message of conformity, which renders suspect social critique, particularly from those deemed deficient and unworthy to speak.

In powerful ways, Freire's pedagogical project assisted us to expose how most teachers are simply not prepared to critique the destructive impacts of disabling practices in schools nor able to support students in their political formation. Hence, alienated and powerless to challenge the oppressive apparatus of schooling that mythologizes the authoritarianism of standardized knowledge and curricula, teachers become complicit in concealing the class formation and colonizing role of schools. Over the years, "scientific" myths attached to the need for high-stakes testing, standardized knowledge, and meritocracy have only solidified in the popular imagination. Seasonal publication of test scores in local newspapers has been used to rank the achievement status of teachers and schools. This public exposition has placed increasing federal and state pressure on school districts; pressure that school district officials displace upon principals; which principals, in turn, displace on teachers; and teachers on their students and parents.

Freire's politics of education, in sync with our lived histories, highlighted for educators and activists of color how classroom practices often replicate similar fears, frustrations, and insecurities that mirror those of their students, when they hit unfamiliar territory and receive little substantive support in the process of their everyday practice. Consequently, educators experience enormous constraints due to the system of reward and punishment commonly employed by administrators to control teacher labor. This is reflected in the authoritarian manner in which school administrators can limit the decision-making role of teachers, through prescribing rules for dress, conduct, curricula, textbooks, lesson plans, classroom activities, student assessment, and the nature of parent participation. Freire (1998b) spoke to the political impact of prescribed behavior on teaching practice:

> Teachers become fearful; they begin to internalize the dominator's shadow and authoritarian ideology of the administration. These teachers are no longer with

their students because the force of the punishment and threatening dominant ideology comes between them... In other words, they are forbidden to be.

(p. 9)

Freire (1998b) also linked the destructive impact of the traditional punishment and rewards system to the politics of teacher evaluation. He highlighted the unfortunate manner in which traditional teacher evaluation methods tend to focus less on the teacher's practice and far more on evaluating the teacher's "personality"— namely the teacher's willingness to conform and comply with traditional roles and expectations. As a consequence, "we evaluate to punish and almost never to improve teacher's practice. In other words, we evaluate to punish and not educate" (p. 7). Freire, however, was not opposed to the practice of teacher evaluation. On the contrary, he firmly argued that "the evaluation of practice represents an important and indispensable factor" (p. 7) in the development of teaching practice, but it had to be grounded in a participatory approach if it was to be a useful tool in supporting the ongoing critical formation of educators. Anything short of this grounded approach results in a domesticating process that thwarts teacher responsibility, while rendering them ambiguous and indecisive. Freire asserted that this ambiguity and indecisiveness often lead us to grasp at "a false sense of security ... informed by the paternalistic nurturing" (p. 6) with which teachers are rewarded for their conformity.

In order to break out of the contradiction of false security, Freire urged us to establish collective relationships of struggle, in order to interrogate openly the consequences of educational practices and to consider more effective strategies for disrupting the political domestication that inanimate the intellectual and political formation of students from oppressed communities. Freire (1998b) considered that such collective empowerment reinforced the need for teachers to struggle together in identifying,

... the tactical paths that competent and politically clear teachers must follow... to critically reject their domesticating role; in so doing they affirm themselves as teachers by demythologizing the authoritarianism of teaching packages and their administration in the intimacy of their world, which is also the world of their students. In their classroom, with the doors closed, it is difficult to have their world unveiled.

(p. 9)

Freire's political understanding of teaching was deeply rooted in a democratic view of education as a permanent terrain of struggle, resistance, and transformation. The common perception of public schooling as a neutral or benevolent enterprise therefore is categorically dismissed. However, given the long history of conflicts and contradictions at work in the ideological formation of educational institutions in an ostensibly democratic nation like the United States, Freire's politics of education also guided us in recognizing that seldom has domination been absolutely deterministic in its reproduction. Wherever oppression exists, there also exist side-by-side the seeds for resistance, at different stages of expression and evolution. Freire's pedagogy of the oppressed nourished and cultivated the seeds of our political resistance—a resistance that we could link historically to a multitude of collective struggles waged around the world in efforts to genuinely democratize education and societies. Our pedagogical process of political empowerment, then and now, entails a long historical process—where our struggle in schools constitutes a significant political front.

Knowledge as Historical Process

> *Through their continuing praxis, men and women simultaneously create history and become historical-social beings... their history, in function of their own creations, develops as a constant process of transformation... Were this [not] the case, a fundamental condition of history—its continuity—would disappear.* —Paulo Freire
> (1970)

Freire asserted that a critical understanding of history and ourselves as historical subjects is fundamental to a revolutionary praxis. Yet, most educators have traditionally been socialized to think of history as frozen and fixed. For most teachers, history is a subject taught from a book about things that happened in the past—this points to a passive and reified notion of history that disembodies the oppressed, excluding our active participants in the making of history. To counter this debilitating view, Freire repeatedly noted that knowledge is the product of a historical process. Who we are and how we come to know the world is profoundly influenced by the particular historical events that shape our understanding of the world, at any given moment in time. By the same token, our collective responses to events also alter the course of history, as well. In this light, Freire (1998a) wrote,

> Even before I read Marx, I had made his words my own. I had taken my own radical stance on the defense of the legitimate interest of the human person. There is no theory of socio-political transformation that moves me if it is not grounded in an understanding of the human person as a maker of history and as one made by history.
>
> (p. 115)

From this empowering view of history, we also came to comprehend knowledge as a widely plural and partial phenomenon, constructed under a variety of material conditions, subject positions, geographical locations, and epochal formations. Yet, neither is this plurality or partiality of history acknowledged in the teaching of history nor are the hegemonic structures of power, which determine whose historical account will be preserved as official public record. In contrast, Freire posited that historical accounts of the dominant culture are deeply mired in the political and economic interests of the ruling class. Official historical accounts of the dominant society then do not miraculously appear within a vacuum, neutral, and untarnished by ideology and material aims. Instead, all readings of history are constructed within a set of values and beliefs that shape the ontological and epistemological interpretations given to particular societal relationships and events. Freire (1970) called for a critical perspective to unveil the dialectical tensions that are hidden underneath, in that "historical themes are never isolated, independent, disconnected or static; they are always interacting dialectically with their opposites" (pp. 91–2).

Understanding history from this vantage point sheds light on the whitewashed partiality and limitations of officially recorded accounts of history and, furthermore, reveals the historical absences of the oppressed who remained exiled and suppressed by *epistemicides* of power (Paraskeva, 2011). Through naming outright this historical injustice, Freire's vision reinforced the need for oppressed communities to recover and uncover our documented and undocumented histories, which have remained hidden from mainstream life. Nevertheless, Freire believed that one important place to begin the labor of uncovering the lived histories of oppressed populations is within the classroom.

To discover ourselves as historical beings constituted for Freire a significant emancipatory moment in the lived histories of the oppressed. He firmly believed that when we come to see ourselves as capable of affecting the course of history through our collective voices and actions, this emancipatory process also assists us to fend off the hopelessness of oppression. Educators, students, and communities working together gain greater insight into the historical process, by way of their collective efforts to name and change the world. In naming the world and constructing meaning, we begin to experience what it means to be subjects of our own lives; and through acting upon the world in meaningful ways, students from oppressed communities develop voice and social agency. Discovering this sense of being a subject of history and becoming comfortable in exercising our social agency constituted for Freire (1970) a significant liberatory process to the political formation of self-determination and community empowerment—both indispensable to our struggle for liberation.

Freire associated the historicity of knowledge with epochal shifts in the world that require our praxis to evolve, in sync with the new conditions that we must confront. Each epoch or era is defined by new historical circumstances and accompanying events that may require very different political strategies, tactics, or pacts than those of the past. This is to say that our work must draw from the events and lessons of the past, but also consistently work to *reinvent* unjust conditions, in order to remain grounded in the present needs of students and their communities. This critical approach is extended and deepened through our pedagogy, when we embrace a dialectical view of knowledge, history, and the world. It is, moreover, through our capacity to observe and interpret what Freire (1970) called *limit-situations* and to engage these objectively, alongside the historical conditions that inform them, that provides us new knowledge from which to make liberating decisions, within our classroom and communities. Of this, Freire (1970) wrote,

> ... as they locate the seat of their decisions in themselves and in their relations with the world and others, people overcome the situations which limit them: the "limit-situations." Once perceived by individuals as fetters, as obstacles to their liberation, these situations stand out in relief from the background, revealing their true nature as concrete historical dimensions of a given reality.
>
> (p. 99)

For Freire, the world exists as it does because of the multitude of relationships and structures, historical and contemporary, constructed by human beings, of which we are all a part. And, as such, our vision for transforming schools and society is not only plausible, but absolutely possible. We learned from Freire that to instill such radical hope in our students and communities required that we too be absolutely convinced of our right to struggle and to be sincerely committed to our revolutionary dreams.

Similarly, knowledge as a historical phenomenon implies that it emerges out of communal processes, produced dynamically, through our relationships with one another and the world. As noted earlier, Freire viewed emancipatory knowledge as a living process—a living historical process that grows and transforms within an environment of teaching and learning that is informed by a critical epistemological commitment to dialogue and the evolution of social consciousness. Here, Freire's (Freire & Macedo, 1995) notion of the dialogical must be understood as a relational way of knowing and being in communion with others, not manipulation or coercion.

> Dialogue is a way of knowing and should never be viewed as a mere tactic to involve students in a particular task. We have to make this point very clear. I engage in dialogue not necessarily because I like the other person. I engage in dialogue because I recognize the social and not merely the individualistic character of the process of knowing. In this sense, dialogue presents itself as an indispensable component of the process of both learning and knowing.
>
> (p. 379)

This relational understanding of dialogue is, again, in direct opposition to banking education, which predominantly anchors ideas of teaching and learning to values of individualism, independence, and competition. For this reason, Freire placed great emphasis on dialogue as an epistemological practice. He believed that only through love and trust, which generate and are generated by dialogue, could teachers and students come to know the world critically, recovering the power to transform our lives as historical subjects.

The Dialectical Relationship

Humans, however, because they are aware of themselves and thus of the world—because they are conscious beings—exist in a dialectical relationship between the determination of limits and their own freedom.
—Paulo Freire (1970)

Freire upheld in his work the importance of the dialectical relationship—that relational tension between seemingly opposites—as necessary to the critical process of consciousness and the construction of emancipatory knowledge. This radical perspective compels us to engage critically with those social and material conditions that emerge from the ideological differences in cultural values and beliefs, as well as asymmetrical relations of power that repress them. Again, also important here are the ways that limit-situations, which stem from such tensions, can also serve as unexpected creative venues in our pedagogical and political efforts. That is, through our openness to exploring limit-situations, critiquing the existing tensions and consequences, we can also create the means by which critical knowledge is constructed within particular historical moments. In other words, new knowledge forms result from our dialectical engagement with the historical and contemporary tensions that call forth new possibilities.

When dialectical tensions expressed as resistance to structures of domination are suppressed within traditional classrooms or communities, the critical reflection, dialogue, and action necessary for emancipatory knowledge are thwarted. Accordingly, students of color, who experience tremendous tensions due to conflicting values and beliefs between the classroom curriculum and their daily lives, are often silenced by mainstream values and expectations of schooling that curtail their participation. A revolutionary practice, on the other hand, strives to stretch the limited boundaries of what is considered permissible discourse, in order to create the pedagogical conditions for students to engage freely across their lived histories in the process of knowledge construction. By stretching the boundaries of what is deemed acceptable discourse and legitimate knowledge, educators construct counter-hegemonic or transgressive spaces that shatter the *culture of silence* (Freire, 2002). In so doing, the democratic potential of students who have been historically excluded from participation is nurtured.

Freire also linked this dialectical understanding of knowledge construction to the notion of ideology, for how we construct knowledge is directly connected to the set of values and beliefs we employ to make sense of the world. Yet, our ideological belief systems generally exist most steadfastly within the realm of unexamined assumptions, which are preserved by way of a historical commonsense (Gramsci, 1971). These antidialectical assumptions about the world generally impact our attitudes and practices about why we believe people are poor; what we think it means to be a person of color; the attitudes we hold about children and their rights; how we articulate the differences between men and woman; our views about God or spirituality; and what we perceive to be legitimate power relations within schools. Then, based on these underlying assumptions, we formulate pedagogical decisions about student expectations, classroom materials, interaction with students and parents, and expressions of authority in the classroom.

The issue of authority in the classroom is worth greater discussion. Within the context of schooling, most well-meaning teachers—particularly those working with working-class students of color—consider "strictness" a legitimate expression of teacher authority. However, often their discourse is mired by an authoritarian rhetoric of student control and containment "for their own good." In the process, the dialectical relationship between authority and freedom is negated. In contrast, Freire (2002) summons up the contradiction by which true freedom evolves, by arguing "there is no freedom without authority, there is no authority without freedom" (p. 21). His perspective retains the dialectical tension between authority and freedom, which reinforces the communal value and need for limits, if we are to exist in a genuinely democratic world. In *Pedagogy of the City*, Freire (1993) wrote,

> To create a practice of a democratic nature—a practice in which we learn how to deal with the tension between authority and freedom, a tension that cannot be avoided unless through the sacrifice of democracy… the more authentically I live the tension, the less I fear freedom and the less I reject the necessary authority.
>
> (p. 130)

Freire's view, moreover, refers to a process in which *both* teachers and students must enter into dialogue as subjects, with responsibility for the context created. As such, teachers have the responsibility to use their authority to create conditions where students are free to read their world, according to the authority of their lived histories and from there construct new knowledge. Given the uncanny manner that unexamined assumptions and beliefs about the world unexpectedly creep into our pedagogy, it is imperative that critical educators reflect often on their practice of authority and their educational decisions. To do so helps teachers to uncover contradictions that may inadvertently obstruct our efforts to construct a liberatory practice and thus make different choices. Freire (1998b) saw this process as an ongoing and necessary one for revolutionary educators striving toward greater coherence in our practice. In the struggle for coherence between what we say and do, Freire urged us to diminish the distance. However, he also acknowledged that it is not possible to be absolutely consistent, but rather, through moments of inconsistency, we are challenged to reflect anew upon our ambiguities.

> In the moment that I discover the inconsistency between what I say and what I do—progressive discourse, authoritarian practice—if, reflecting, at times painfully, I learn the ambiguity in which I find myself, I feel I am not able to continue like this and I look for a way out. In this way, a new choice is imposed on me. Either I change the progressive discourse for a discourse consistent with my reactionary practice, or I change my practice for a democratic one.
>
> (p. 67)

Given the covert manner that the political economy impacts the control of knowledge within the classroom, educators must align their practice with a democratic intent. Through the courage to pose difficult questions, expose the tensions, and refuse to fall into the complacency of privilege, teachers are in a key position to support new readings of the world and participate in unveiling the hidden faces of oppression. Moreover, to enliven democracy in the classroom, Freire (1997) argued that we had to nurture relationships of dialogue and solidarity within schools and communities—relationships grounded in our unwavering fidelity to break out of the domesticating conditions and institutional structures that dehumanize our lives and entrap us within a political economy that is primarily fueled by avarice, greed, and indifference.

Schooling and Capitalism

Brutalizing the workforce by subjecting them to routine procedures are part of the nature of the capitalist mode of production. And what is taking place in the production of knowledge in the schools is in large part a reproduction of that mechanism.

—Paulo Freire (in Freire & Faundez, 1989)

Freire, in no uncertain terms, saw capitalism as the root of oppression. He often made direct references to the logic of capitalism, with its debilitating impact on workers and the need to override the consumerism of the marketplace. Freire offered us a critical analysis of schooling situated firmly against the dynamics of capitalist accumulation and the reproduction of a deeply racialized and gendered labor force. He contended that the politics of schooling, informed by the economic interests of the ruling class, supports the reproduction of inequality, by replicating "the authoritarianism of the capitalist mode of production" (Freire & Macedo, 1998, p. 229). The impact of the political economy on the educational conditions of students from racialized communities is made visible in a variety of ways, including the types of academic expectations, financial resources, and other opportunities available to them, which contrast dramatically to those of affluent student populations.

Unfortunately for the majority of people, this distinction is seldom engaged beyond the belief that if a family can afford to pay for an excellent education for their children, then they deserve the privilege. In contrast, the majority of students from economically oppressed communities are positioned within schools, according to their class location within the racialized economic order. Meanwhile, blatant structural inequalities are successfully camouflaged by the myths that place exaggerated weight on "exceptional" success stories, despite the fact that only a small percentage of individuals from poor communities manage ever to achieve social mobility, despite educational attainment. Commonly repeated myths such as "education leads to social mobility" conceal, according to Freire (1997), "the class war raging throughout the country … a class war that hides and makes confusing a frustrated class struggle" (p. 50).

As a consequence, the class structure has remained unchanged during the last seventy years. Teachers, bridled by the myth that the United States is a classless society, blindly perpetuate contradictory teaching practices that deepen the structures of class inequality. In an effort to challenge glaring economic contradictions and the myths that sustain them, Freire proposed a pedagogy that would help to make visible and explicit issues of social class and its impact on schooling. For example, the class-bound arrangement of public schools has existed since their inception. Public schools designed to function as factories of learning for the future workers of the nation have sought to ensure their consensual participation in the process of capitalist accumulation. The majority of public school students were expected to move into a file-and-rank structure of labor. However, things have gone amuck due to the changing nature of work and the neoliberal emphasis on a globalized workforce. Rather than keeping jobs within the United States where union workers tirelessly struggled to obtain improved conditions of labor, capitalists have relocated or outsourced production to "undeveloped" countries, where massive worker exploitation is carried out with greater ease and few environmental regulations or restrictions.

Meanwhile, the United States, keeping with its privileged status as economic leader of the world, has become the knowledge society. The consequence of this shift in the nature of work is the virtual disappearance of thousands of well-paying jobs, through rampant technological development and computerization—factors that although they might increase efficiency of capitalist interests also exacerbate the level of alienation and joblessness. Workers are increasingly functioning within virtual contexts that are now so commonsensical, that few even notice the ever-growing disconnection from the products of their labor. Moreover, the alienation provoked by this intense separation of workers and the natural world has reached such proportions that few seem to have the wherewithal to halt its movement or to challenge the colonizing impact on our lives. Teachers too are implicated in this process as they are stripped of freedom to make decisions regarding curricula, while their pedagogical social agency is pacified with prepackaged materials, distance learning, and other technological devices linked to the control of teaching labor. For many, it just feels like an unstoppable "train of progress" on which one must board or be forever left in the obscurity of the past.

Even more disconcerting is the destructive impact that alienation and unbridled consumerism have had on working-class students and their education. People, places, and things are all potential commodities, whose value is determined by the whims of the marketplace. Of this, Freire (1970) argued, "Money is the measure of all things and profit the primary goal" (p. 44). Accordingly, the marketplace, through the process of fetishization, successfully "transforms everything surrounding it into an object of its domination. The earth, property, production, the creations of ... [human beings]—everything is reduced to the status of objects" (p. 44). The process of fetishization is equally at work within schools, as it is in the society at large. Schools are constantly courted by large publishing companies hawking the latest educational textbooks and curricular materials that are deceptively "divorced from the leading ideas that shape and maintain them" (Macedo, 1994, p. 182). Companies, seeking to establish name recognition with young consumers, are eager to generously provide teachers with logo-ridden materials. Meanwhile, teachers, forced by necessity to spend hundreds of dollars on materials for their classroom without compensation, are only too happy to receive classroom resources, without regard for the corporate manipulation of young minds.

Freire argued that educational policies and practices have real economic consequences, particularly for working-class students from racialized communities. In our work, we need to recognize that these consequences "are not just symbolic ... they shape people's lives and their places in the material world" (Carnoy, 1987, p. 16), and nowhere is this more evident than in the arena of education. Through an unjust system of meritocracy, schools sort, select, and exclude students. Testing, assessment, and promotion policies determine which students are deemed worthy of opportunities and which are not. And just as there is nothing neutral about how the political economy is reproduced, there is nothing neutral about the manner in which these education practices promote racialized class formation.

A dual process of domestication and massification is also implicated in the narrow definition of success offered to working-class students. Success is narrowly defined today as college entrance. Never mind that in the current neoliberal labor market, college graduates are greeted with shrinking job options. Never in the history of the United States have so many college graduates faced the prospects of underemployment or unemployment, after accumulating huge debt to attend university. Yet, despite these very real and concrete material conditions, schools continue to tout the college readiness mantra, without serious engagement with what is happening out in the world. Students, who defy, covertly or overtly, the limited choices handed them, find themselves generally ignored or eventually suspended or expelled, when teachers and school officials give up trying to "fix" their resistance and unwillingness to acquiesce to the hegemony of the college readiness code.

Freire (1983) viewed this limiting of student choices as entrenched within the capitalist mode of mass production—a culprit in the domestication and alienation of workers, their children, and their communities. Accordingly, he wrote:

> Mass production as an organization of human labor is possibly one of the most potent instruments of [human] massification. By requiring a man [or woman] to behave mechanically, mass production domesticates him [or her]. By separating activity from the total project, requiring no total critical attitude toward production, it dehumanizes him [or her]. By excessively narrowing a man [or woman's] specialization, it constricts horizons, making him [or her] a passive fearful being... reducing critical capacity.
>
> (p. 34)

Furthermore, Freire connected this process of massification with the domestication of students' critical faculties, which fools them into believing they have choices. But the limited choices offered work well in the service of social containment, in that the majority of the population is actually excluded from the sphere where decisions are made by fewer and fewer people. Simultaneously, students and their parents are maneuvered to accept mythical explanations of reality that whittle their life choices. In turn, the process of education too is whittled down, as greater emphasis is placed on "training" programs founded on neoliberal pragmatism. On this point, Freire (1998a) was exceedingly clear: "Purely pragmatic training, with its implicit or openly expressed elitist authoritarianism, is incompatible with the learning and practice of becoming a 'subject'" (p. 46).

This phenomenon is particularly alarming at a time when the safety net of the welfare system has been effectively eroded by neoliberal policies of the last thirty years. In the process, the poorest people in the wealthiest country in the world are stripped of limited state resources available for their meager material existence. These conditions have intensified during the last decade, given that the great mortgage debacle of 2006 that heavily affected working-class communities of color, leaving economists to predict that it will take another twenty-five years for our communities to recover from the collapse. Yet, in the midst of an increasing economic polarization, the meaning of democracy in this country remains synonymous with the freedom to consume. Seldom are students encouraged to critically interrogate what it means to be a free-market consumer or to consider the ecological downsides of overconsumption. Instead, capitalism has become the transcendent culture—a phenomenon that is achieved through the market's grip on the culture industry and its racialized manifestations. Through the hegemonic process, the marketplace homogenizes the dreams and desires of consumers, rendering cultural knowledges and indigenous wisdom inconsequential to the dictates of neoliberal rule.

Freire (1997) also expressed concern for the hidden curriculum of technology, which has become "a main bastion of capitalism" (p. 56). The global booming industry developed swiftly due to the enormously profitable connection it enjoyed with the burgeoning "information society," initiated in the late twentieth century and the increasing move toward virtual education. Yet, seldom are important critical questions raised, given the zeal that schools express as they mount the technology bandwagon. In whose interest and to what purpose is technology functioning? When teachers increasingly insert technology into the process of classroom learning, what is the impact of technology on student relationships to one another and the natural world? By failing to critically engage these questions, Freire (1997) argued that much of the rhetoric on technology obscures that "technological advances enhance with greater efficiency the ideological support for material power" (p. 36). Freire, nevertheless, retained the dialectical tension in his argument, in that he did not consider the answer to be the rejection of technology, but rather the process of our humanization. "I am a being who does not bow before the indisputable power accumulated by technology because, in knowing that it is a human production, I do not accept that it is, in and of itself, bad" (p. 35).

Deeply concerned with the contradictions inherent in the politics of the marketplace, Freire urged teachers to "detach ourselves from the idea that we are agents of capital" (McLaren, 2000, p. 191). Furthermore, he argued that teachers must struggle "to retain a concept of the political beyond a reified consumer identity constructed from the panoply of market logic" (p. 152). Moreover, Freire (1998b) believed that educators could support students from oppressed communities "to create a social, civic and political discipline which is absolutely essential to the democracy that goes beyond bourgeois and liberal democracy and that finally seeks to conquer the injustice and the irresponsibility of capitalism" (p. 89).

Freire (1997) asserted that the oppressive system of capitalist production could not be altered without simultaneous collective efforts to democratize schools and the larger society—which, incidentally, is exactly what most reform strategies stifle, given the logic of the marketplace and the quest for economic supremacy that inform the politics of reformism. Not surprisingly, he urged instead "fighting against reformism" and using "the contradictions of reformist practice to defeat it" (p. 74). To help counter these contradictions, Freire urged us to construct within schools and communities what he called "advanced forms of social organizations … capable of surpassing this articulated chaos of corporate interests" (p. 36). This again points to corporate policies of economic Darwinism that promote deregulation, the free market, nationalism, and militarism, through an ethnocentric ethos of "survival of the fittest." The focus, in this instance, is confrontation with the political economy of capitalism, which shamelessly justifies its perilous impact upon millions of people and the destruction of the Earth's ecosystem, by way of military supremacy and international speculation.

We need only consult history to confirm that the politics of colonization has been rooted in a violent project of economic exploitation and racialization, which has provided the hegemonic apparatus to justify imperial expansionism and unmerciful genocide and conquest of those deemed less human. Returning to Freire's notion of capitalism as the root of domination, it is useful in this analysis to also link past and current colonizing forces to the subordinating role of a population's perceived capacity for productivity within capitalist society. This is to say that the basic worth of an individual or a people has been literally tied to their capacity to contribute to the process of capitalist accumulation. Hence, rather than pedagogical concern for our humanity, sovereignty, or the evolution of critical consciousness in the interest of culturally democratic life, banking educational objectives emphasize to what extent students have the potential to participate as consuming citizens of the empire.

Moreover, schools, as economic engines, function effectively in the process of class formation and the production of a national workforce that is in sync with the requirements of the labor market and the military demands of a culture of perpetual war. It is here, where the politics of meritocracy in the United States, in conjunction with high-stakes testing, is effectively normalized and utilized to sort, sift, reward, or exclude students, accordingly. As would be expected, the children of the affluent rise to the top, while the majority of poor and working-class students of color continue to populate the rosters of the academically underachieving—where they, their families, their culture, and their language are held suspect and responsible for their failure. All the while, the larger economic inequalities and hegemonic educational forces that negatively impact the lives of working-class students remain veiled in a victim-blaming ideology of accountability and personal choice, along with the myth that equality and fair treatment are available to all deserving students who genuinely work hard. The unemployment crisis that has hit all sectors of the population in the last five years has begun to unveil this hypocrisy.

Coming to terms with the role of political economy in the process of schooling is essential to an emancipatory vision of schooling. Educators must not only come to accept responsibility for the power we hold within schools and communities, but also make wise decisions about how we use our power in the interest of constructing a practice that supports cultural and economic democracy. Freire contended that teachers who are unaware of the political nature of their power and authority will find themselves constantly falling into contradictions and unable to develop well-conceived alternative pedagogical approaches. This occurs most when educators lack coherent emancipatory principles from which to enact our teaching practice—outside the limiting culture of hegemony.

Betrayal of Multiculturalism

To underestimate the wisdom that necessarily results from sociocultural experience is at one and the same a scientific error, and the unequivocal expression of the presence of an elitist ideology.

—Paulo Freire (2002)

In the early history of the civil rights movement, educators and activists of color viewed multicultural education as a counter-hegemonic alternative for decolonizing the curriculum and transforming classroom life. In the 1970s, notions of biculturalism—also tied to the struggle for bilingualism—began to evolve and efforts were forged toward developing culturally relevant pedagogies. Many of these pedagogical efforts were founded on the principles that Freire first outlined in *Pedagogy of the Oppressed*. Those principles challenged cultural invasion and the banking model of education and called for a problem posing pedagogy that would support the evolution of critical consciousness in the education of children from oppressed communities. Freire's notion of cultural invasion was overwhelmingly salient to those of us from communities with histories of genocide, slavery, and colonization.

However, as critical multicultural education efforts began to take hold in the late 1970s and early 1980s, reactionary conservative backlash and liberal rewriting of multiculturalism began to steadily erode the transformative intent and counterhegemonic purpose. Many of the multicultural education efforts that took hold in schools during the 1980s and 1990s, born of the burgeoning Neoliberal age, conserved not only a racializing hierarchical structure of power but also deficit notions, which served to readily sustain the meritocratic process of class formation within working-class communities of color.

As communities of color employed the organizing potential of a politics of identity, in order to call for fundamental change to gross social and economic inequalities across the nation, the Reagan administration's *A Nation at Risk* report, issued in 1983, served as the perfect counter-revolutionary strategy to thwart our escalating movement for equality. With the veiled contention that schools should serve as economic engines to ensure the global superiority of the nation, the accountability movement began to gain steam. Neoliberal priorities of the state countered emancipatory agendas in every arena of social and economic policy, including education. The process of deregulation, privatization, and the erosion of the safety net resulted in an economic corporate boom in the decade that followed, while the burgeoning neoliberal agenda began to dismantle gains made by the civil rights movement. One disastrous impact to communities of color was the unprecedented increase in the number of US incarcerations from 1984 to 2008, increasing from less than 500,000 inmates to over 2 million—with an overwhelming number of poor, working-class inmates of color, 70 percent who were considered to be functionally illiterate.[2]

Rooted in a conservative ideology of deficit notions—whether of nature or nurture—"whitewashed" expectations of multicultural education became the norm, while discussions about the "race" problem or "race" as the determining factor in the academic underachievement of students of color prevailed in educational debates. In true colonizing and hegemonic style, many radical educators, particularly those of color, who remained aligned with Freire's pedagogical and political concerns, were pushed out and marginalized, as new "White" (liberal) multicultural education gurus descended on the stage to dominate and distort more revolutionary discourses born out of decolonizing struggles that had been waged by black, Latino, Asian, and American Indian educators. In their place, well-meaning discourses of urgency, justified by liberal "cycle of poverty" interpretations—which blamed our children, families, and culture for our personal and community dysfunctions—were used as rationales for obstructing newly gained opportunities to evolve and advance our participation in decision making, even in the education of our children.

As a consequence, many of us found our innovative efforts warped into unrecognizable proportions, rationalizing once again the superiority of mainstream multicultural educators. Token educators of color who followed their lead were effectively integrated into schools and teacher preparation programs to marginalize more overt decolonizing discourses and practices of radical educators of color—a phenomenon whose consequence is being dramatically felt across the entire educational landscape today, as scholarship tied to cultural and language subordination in schools has gone out of vogue and now considered passé in the "flat world"[3] of neoliberal multiculturalism. In the process, the transformative potential of multicultural curriculum, text, and pedagogy has been all but stripped away, while a fragmented curriculum of cultural songs, stories, holidays, and heroes prevails, if at all.

With the eclipse of the so-called multicultural age in education, persisting problems and concerns raised by educators of color and their allies for almost a century now fall on deaf ears, as the instrumentalizing ideology of neoliberal education has devised limiting matrices of accountability that deliberately discount historical and contemporary community concerns related to culture, language, class, pedagogy, power, and knowledge production. Instead, the numbers game of high-stakes testing, the standardization of knowledge, and teaching to the test are the order of the day. Consequently, we find ourselves today more deeply mired in Western ethnocentric notions of humanity, where individualism, object-based, future-focused, scientism, and materialism counteract the legitimacy of subordinate cultural community values and epistemological traditions of difference. Additionally, this leads to the negation of the worldviews of those deemed "other"—including the marginalization of communal strategies, ancestral knowledge, and spiritual traditions that might enhance the teaching and learning of our children. More often than not, well-meaning educators seeking to address the needs of working-class communities of color continue to be entrapped in a deficit paradigm of difference.

Even more disconcerting is when critical educators of color, at all levels of education, attempt to challenge these deficit notions in our teaching and research. Mainstream educators, many who pride themselves in being social justice advocates or antiracist, greet us with resistance and unparalleled requests for legitimacy of claims, when we seek to express or enact our particular cultural paradigms and philosophical assumptions of humanity and community self-determination. These paradigms and assumptions that often reside outside many well-intended, but still colonizing, social values and epistemological priorities or directives, inadvertently objectify and render students from poor and working-class communities of color passive agents of their own learning—in direct opposition to Freire's notion that students should reside at the center of their learning and that educators must begin with this as our starting point.

This, of course, echoes modernity's historical project of political and historical colonization, drafted from a conceptual narrative and societal design that legitimates and normalizes the economic and military domination, disempowerment, and dispossession of the majority of the world's population—in the name of democracy, progress, and profit. There is no question that the dehumanizing currents of the contemporary neoliberal agenda, which show trends of increasing inequalities in so-called developing countries, require us to grapple seriously with the struggle for our humanity, as Freire argued, in the face of hegemonic forces that seek to colonize every aspect of our lives, from birth to death. That is precisely why this issue is one that must remain central to any decolonizing epistemology, pedagogy, or methodology of classroom or community leadership.

The Cultural Context

Respect for the knowledge of living experience is inserted into the larger horizon against which it is generated—the horizon of cultural context, which cannot be understood apart from class particularities… Respect for popular culture, then, implies respect for cultural context.

—Paulo Freire (2002)

Central to Freire's (1983) pedagogical thesis of critical consciousness is an understanding of the significance of the cultural context in the process of knowledge production. Furthermore, he recognized culture as a collective human creation and "a systematic acquisition of human experiences" (p. 49). This is as true to the larger context of class formation as it is to the question of bicultural formation where students must daily navigate the tensions and power dynamics of the subordinate/dominant divide. Hence, Freire's work has been and continues to be fundamental to critical educators, educational leaders, and activists of color, in that it reinforces the political necessity of contextual knowledge. Culture is a systematic acquisition of human experience (p. 48). This concept of culture links decolonizing education to communal and ancestral knowledge, which transcends neither the individual subject nor the material conditions that shape the histories and everyday relationships of formerly colonized and enslaved populations.

From this standpoint, if we are to contend, in theory and practice, with the educational difficulties of students from working-class and racialized communities, we must look beyond simply the personal or individual. We must seek answers, as Freire argued, within the long histories of economic, social, and political oppression, so that we might better understand the forces and structures that give rise to inequalities and social exclusion, as they currently exist within our own lives and that of our students. Moreover, Freire's writings also make an important case for the embodiment of knowledge, which can potentially move us away from colonizing abstractions and separations of the body, a phenomenon that has always worked to the colonizing interest of the powerful and wealthy (Darder, 2011).

This is to say that the underlying purpose of hegemonic power is to legitimate and conceal the imperial and colonial relations that today still undergird capitalism. As such, the political work of the oppressed has always required the unveiling, naming, and challenging of asymmetrical relations of power and their consequences within schools, communities, and the larger society. There is no question that Freire's pedagogy of the oppressed was articulated precisely with the intent to *speak truth to power* and, in so doing, create classroom conditions whereby student self-determination and critical consciousness could more readily flourish, in concert with educators committed to their critical formation.

It is from this political imperative that philosophical critiques related to objectivity, absolute knowledge, reductionism, ethnocentrism, and elitism, as well as structural critiques of class inequalities, cultural invasion, racism, sexism, hetero-sexism, and so on, have been waged. For some, this may echo the mantra of intersectionality, so often heard in oppositional discourses. However, as Rodolfo Torres and I (2004) have argued in *After Race: Racism After Multiculturalism*, intersectionality arguments still fail to confront the totalizing impact of capitalism. That is, racism, sexism, heterosexism, disablism, and all forms of oppression are deeply implicated in an interlocking set of relations that preserve and sustain the interests of capital and, therefore, do not function independently of an unjust distribution of wealth and power.

Beyond the obvious material dispossession of the impoverished working class, Freire spoke repeatedly about the manner in which conditions of economic exploitation and domination dehumanize our relationships, distorting our capacity to love one another, the world, and ourselves. In concert with Antonio Gramsci (1971) before him, Freire was well aware of how even well-meaning educators, through lack of politics or critical moral leadership, participate in disabling the hearts, minds, and bodies of students—an act that interferes with the development of the social agency and political comprehension required to engage and transform the debilitating social and material circumstances that betray our humanity.

Our Unfinishedness

> [Our] own unity and identity, in regards to others and the world, constitutes [our] essential and irrepeatable way of experiencing [our selves] as cultural, historical, and unfinished beings in the world, simultaneously conscious of [our] unfinishedness... This unfinishedness is essential to our human condition. Wherever there is life, there is unfinishedness.
>
> —Paulo Freire (1998a)

Starting from the realization that we live in an unfree and unequal world, Freire affirmed that "our struggle for our humanization" had to evolve from our struggle for the emancipation of labor and the overcoming of our alienation,[4] so that we might affirm ourselves as full subjects of history. However, the pursuit of our full humanity, Freire (1970) argued, could not "be carried out in isolation or as individuals, but only in the fellowship and solidarity" (p. 85) of community and social movement. Thus, relationships of solidarity, built through collective labor, must remain central to our politics and our pedagogy, given that it is "in the process of revolution ... that human beings in communion liberate each other" (p. 133). This understanding of social struggle as a collective undertaking has resonated deeply and powerfully with those who possess little power or influence over their lives, given the contradictions and constrictions at work in capitalist societies.

Freire often called to mind the significance of *unfinishedness* as a necessary radical variable in diminishing fatalism and inspiring hope in new possibilities for collective change among the oppressed. This recognition of human unfinishedness can also help unveil the hidden or silenced contradictions at work behind what Freire termed *limit situations*—contradictions that we must challenge and overcome in our efforts to reinvent schools and communities. At the heart of this concept of our humanity is also the recognition that oppression is never a permanent condition; and it is, indeed, because no human condition is ever absolute or finished that the struggle remains viable and hope fertile, even within political and material conditions that appear desolate and barren. Freire (1983) explained,

> If this world were a created finished world, it would no longer be susceptible to transformation. The human beings exists as such, and the world is a historical-cultural one, because the two come together as unfinished products in a permanent relationship, in which human beings transform the world and undergo the effects of their transformation. In this dynamic, historical-cultural process one generation encounters the objective reality marked out by another generation and receives through it the imprints of reality.
>
> (p. 147)

For Freire, our capacity to live free requires then a fundamental shift in the "imprints" by which leaders, educators, and students define our lives and the conditions of our labor. This requires moving beyond the internalization of our oppression, the ejection of colonizing ideologies of domination, toward the establishment of solidarity with others, the recognition of ourselves as subjects of history, the courage to speak out when necessary, and a well-developed sense of empowerment, in order that we might name, critique, decolonize, and reinvent our world anew, in the interest of a truly just and democratic future. In waging struggles for social change, Freire considered it an imperative that those who are oppressed come to believe and understand that domination does not exist within a closed world from which there is no exit. Instead, Freire (1970) reminded us, "This struggle is possible only because dehumanization, although a concrete historical fact, is not a given destiny but the result of an unjust order that engenders violence ... which in turn dehumanizes the oppressed" (p. 44).

Freire's writings acknowledged the psychological, physical, and spiritual violence that oppressed populations have endured for centuries at the hands of the powerful—a meaningful insight, given the ruthless physical and psychological violence so often experienced by communities of color. In today's neoliberal world, psychological violence in the guise of accountability is made palatable through veiled deficiency discourses of "high-risk" students, which Freire (1970) likened to being "sweetened by false generosity, because it interferes with the [student's] ontological and historical vocation to be more fully human" (p. 55). He reasoned that situations of violence generally emerge out of subjugation and the negation of our humanity. About this, Freire wrote,

Violence is initiated by those who oppress, who exploit, who fail to recognize others as persons—not by those who are oppressed, exploited, and unrecognized. It is not the unloved who initiate dis affection, but those who cannot love because they love only themselves. It is not the helpless, subject to terror, who initiate terror, but the violent, who with their power create the concrete situation which begets the "rejects of life." It is not the tyrannized who initiate despotism, but the tyrants. It is not the despised who initiate hatred, but those who despise. It is not those whose humanity is denied them who negate humankind, but those who denied that humanity (thus negating their own as well).

(p. 55)

Freire, as Frantz Fanon before him, demonstrated political fortitude and intellectual courage when he linked the question of violence to intentionality. His view on violence has been particularly important to the struggle of the oppressed. That is to say that although Freire never condoned violence in any of his speeches or writings, he clearly recognized that there was a very different phenomenon at work in the violence engendered by those who seek to dominate and exploit and the violence generated by the fight of those who seek to counter their dehumanization. "And this fight, because of the purpose given it by the oppressed, will actually constitute an act of love, opposing the lovelessness which lies at the heart of the oppressors' violence, lovelessness even when clothed in false generosity" (1970, p. 45).

Through his solid ontological fidelity to our unfinishedness, Freire championed the possibilities of the oppressed to remake history, through our commitment to struggle. For, it is precisely because oppression exists as an impermanent, incomplete, and changing historical phenomenon—constructed by human beings—that we as decolonized and empowered subjects of history possess the possibility of transforming its configuration. Our task then as critical educators committed to a just world is to embrace fully this dialectical understanding of our relationship with the world, so that together we might transform our teaching and learning into a revolutionary praxis—a critical praxis that encompasses reflection, dialogue, and action, where theory and practice are regenerating and in alliance (Darder, 2002).

Freire (1997) knew that this way of life requires a critical commitment to move beyond piety, sentimentalism, and individualistic gestures, so that we might "risk an act of love" and enter into sustaining and nurturing political relationships of dialogue and solidarity—communal relationships grounded upon our unwavering fidelity to break out of the domesticating and colonizing conditions that trick us into complicity with "an economy that is incapable of developing programs according to human needs and that coexists indifferently to the hunger of millions to whom everything is denied" (p. 36).

In *Teachers as Cultural Workers*, Freire (1998b) acknowledged that radical struggles, by those who dare to exercise their political will and capacity within schools, could be severely curtailed by the tendency to become "hardened" by the dominant bureaucracy's oppressive expectations and dehumanizing posture toward those who critique the system and work toward social change. He recognized that, more often than not, this phenomenon is prevalent because critical educators—particularly educators of color—committed to a Freirian-inspired pedagogy of freedom are perceived by institutional gatekeepers as disruptive and destructive, while our efforts to achieve greater freedom and autonomy are discouraged or punished, even by those who would call themselves our allies. In efforts to control and "inanimate" teachers and students of color, conservative educational bureaucracies and policies of schooling often "deter the drive to search, that restlessness and creativity that characterizes life" (Freire, 1970, p. 46). In response, Freire argued that genuine forms of learning must aim critically to unveil the contradictions and courageously challenge practices that objectify, dispirit, and dehumanize, preventing our political expression as full cultural citizens. Educational oppression, in the flesh, consists of policies and practices of social control, by which teachers, students, and parents from historically oppressed communities are permitted, for the most part, only enough opportunity to fulfill roles prescribed by their social class.

Freire recognized and often spoke of the enormity and difficulty of the pedagogical vision that he proposed. Nevertheless, he could see no alternative for the restoration of our humanity than to eradicate the debilitating fatalism and imposed myths, which seek to alienate and render us passive, while underhandedly seeking our consensus and participation in our own oppression. Often, this is accomplished through bourgeois notions of morality that function to reinforce our disempowerment, bringing to mind the words by former Black Panther, Assata Shakur, who argued, "Nobody in the world, nobody in history, has ever gotten their freedom by appealing to the moral sense of the people who were oppressing them."[5] Hence, Freire (1970) repeatedly asserted that no one can empower the oppressed, but rather it is the oppressed who must empower themselves, if true emancipation is to prevail. That said, the role of the privileged ally is to use their privilege to create the conditions by which the disenfranchised can truly "become beings for themselves" (p. 74).

This political project of emancipation, however, requires our sustained collective labor—a labor born of love, but deeply anchored in an unceasing political commitment to know, through both theory and practice, the nature of the beast that preys upon our humanity; and with this knowledge, fight with unwavering hope and solidarity. For many of us from poor and working-class communities of color, the option of struggle was never a choice, but rather a political necessity, if we were to empower ourselves and ensure our right to exist in sync with the cultural wisdom forged from our own lived histories of survival as tribes, nations, and peoples. Indeed, Freire's revolutionary vision points to the need for an ongoing political process of personal and community struggle that demands ongoing critical vigilance. This demands a willingness to courageously and consistently persist in a process of personal and collective reflection, regarding the consequences of our theory and action. For Freire (1983), this is an essential component of our pedagogy and politics, for as educators are placed "face to face before themselves they investigate and question themselves" (p. 150), enlivening their practice. This intimate engagement of self underscores the revolutionary accountability that educators and leaders must enact in efforts to transform conditions of inequality. Through a sustained process of personal and political accountability, we can labor in schools and communities with greater coherence, humility, and love.

Notes

1. Cited in Facundo, B. How Is Freire Seen in the United States? Facundo's article here sets down a rather scathing critique of Freire that simply does not coincide with my experience of Freire's work in communities of color. Nevertheless, I respect her efforts here. See www.bmartin.cc/dissent/documents/Facundo/section2.html
2. See, The Punishing Decade: Prison and Jail Estimates at the Millennium. [1] May 2000. Justice Policy Institute; Historical Corrections Statistics in the United States, 1850–1984. NCJ 102529. Published in 1986; Correctional Population Trends Chart. U.S. Bureau of Justice Statistics. Number of prison and jail inmates from 1980 onwards; and Sourcebook of Criminal Justice Statistics (uses BJS data).
3. The reference here is to Thomas L. Friedman's *The World Is Flat*, a book that glorifies the accomplishments of a globalized neoliberalism but fails to engage the realities of an increasingly unequal world. What Friedman means by "flat" is "connected": the lowering of trade and political barriers and the exponential technical advances of the digital revolution, which have made it possible to do business, or almost anything else, instantaneously with billions of other people across the planet. Again, the question is who exactly can do business or anything else?
4. Freire (1970, p. 28).
5. Shakur, Assata. The People Record. See: http://thepeoplesrecord.com/post/31671382262/nobody-in-the-world-nobody-in-history-has-ever.

References

Carnoy, M. (1987). Foreword to *Pedagogy of the Heart* by P. Freire (pp. 7–19). New York: Continuum.

Darder, A. (2002). *Reinventing Paulo Freire: A Pedagogy of Love*. Boulder, CO: Westview Press.

Darder, A. (2011). *A Dissident Voice: Essays on Culture, Pedagogy, & Power*. New York: Palgrave.

Darder, A. (2012). *Culture and Power in the Classroom* (20th Anniversary Edition). Boulder, CO: Paradigm.

Darder, A., & Torres, R. D. (2004). *After Race: Racism After Multiculturalism*. New York: New York University Press.

Freire, A. M. A., & Macedo, D. (1998). "Introduction," in A. M. A. Freire & D. Macedo (Eds.), *The Paulo Freire Reader* (pp. 1–44). New York: Continuum.

Freire, P. (1970). *Pedagogy of the Oppressed*. New York: Continuum.

Freire, P. (1983). *Education for Critical Consciousness*. New York: Seabury Press.

Freire, P. (1985). *The Politics of Education: Culture, Power, and Liberation*. South Hadley, MA: Bergin & Garvey.

Freire, P. (1993). *Pedagogy of the City*. New York: Continuum.

Freire, P. (1997). *Pedagogy of the Heart*. New York: Continuum.

Freire, P. (1998a). *Pedagogy of Freedom: Ethics, Democracy and Civic Courage*. Lanham, MD: Rowman & Littlefield Publishers.

Freire, P. (1998b). *Teachers and Cultural Workers: Letters to Those Who Dare to Teach*. Boulder, CO: Westview Press.

Freire, P. (2002). *Pedagogy of Hope: Reliving Pedagogy of the Oppressed.* New York: Continuum.

Freire, P. (2005). *Pedagogy of the Oppressed* (30th Anniversary Edition). New York: Continuum.

Freire, P., & Faundez, A. (1989). *Learning to Question: A Pedagogy of Liberation.* Trans. Tony Coates, New York: Continuum.

Freire, P., & Macedo, D. (1987). *Literacy: Reading the Word & the World.* South Hadley, MA: Bergin & Garvey Publishers.

Freire, P., & Macedo, D. (1995, fall). "A Dialogue: Culture, Language, and Race." *Harvard Educational Review,* 65 (3), 377–402.

Gramsci, A. (1971). *Selections of the Prison Notebooks.* New York: International Publishers.

hooks, b. (1994). *Teaching to Transgress.* New York: Routledge.

Macedo, D. (1994). *Literacies of Power.* Boulder, CO: Westview Press.

McLaren, P. (2000). *Che Guevara, Paulo Freire, and the Pedagogy of Revolution.* Lanham, MA: Rowman and Littlefield.

Paraskeva, J. (2011). *Conflicts in Curriculum Theory.* New York: Palgrave MacMillan.

2

Teaching as an Act of Love: In Memory of Paulo Freire

For days, I have reflected on Paulo Freire's life. And with every turn of ideas, I'm brought back to the notion of love. But, let me quickly say that I am neither speaking of a romanticized or liberal notion of love nor the long-suffering and self-effacing variety. For nothing could be further from the truth. If there was anything that Paulo consistently sought to defend, it was the freshness, spontaneity, and presence embodied in what he called an "armed loved–the fighting love of those convinced of the right and the duty to fight, to denounce, and to announce."[1] A love that could be lively, forceful, and inspiring, while at the same time, critical, challenging, and insistent. As such, Paulo's brand of love stood in direct opposition to the insipid "generosity" of teachers or administrators who would blindly adhere to a system of schooling that fundamentally transgresses every principle of cultural and economic democracy.

Instead, I want to speak of the love I came to know through my work and friendship with Paulo—a political and radicalized form of love that was never tied to absolute consensus, or unconditional acceptance. Instead, it was a love that I experienced as unconstricted, rooted in a committed willingness to struggle persistently with an emancipatory purpose and to intimately connect that purpose with what he called our "true vocation"—to be human.

Hence for Paulo a democratic education could never be conceived without a profound commitment to our humanity—a humanity that was not merely some psychologized notion of "positive self-esteem," but rather a deeply reflective interpretation of the dialectical relationship between our cultural existence as individuals and our political and economic existence as social beings. From Paulo's perspective, if we were to solve the educational difficulties of students from oppressed communities, then educators had to look beyond the personal. We had to look for answers within the historical realm of economic, social, and political forms, so that we might better understand those forces that give rise to our humanity as it currently exists. In so many ways, Paulo bore witness to the dehumanizing consequences of injustice. In the tradition of Antonio Gramsci, Paulo exposed how even well-meaning teachers, through their lack of critical moral leadership, actually participate in disabling the heart, minds, and bodies of their students—an act that disconnects these students from the personal and social motivation required to transform their world and themselves.

There is no question that Paulo's greatest gift to the world was his capacity to be a loving human being. His regard for children, his concern for teachers, his work among the poor, his willingness to share openly his moments of grief, disappointment, frustration, and new love, all stand out in my mind as examples of his courage and unrelenting pursuit of a coherent and honest life. I recall our meeting in 1987, six months after the death of his first wife, Elza. Paulo was in deep grief. During one of his presentations, he literally had to stop so that he could weep the tears that he had been holding back all morning. For a moment, we were enveloped by his grief. I don't believe anyone left the conference hall that day, as they had arrived. Through the courageous vulnerability of his humanity—with all its complexities and contradictions—Paulo illuminated our understanding of not only what it means to be a critical educator, but what it means to live a critical life.

The next year, I was to experience another aspect of Paulo's living praxis. To everyone's surprise, Paulo remarried. Many were stunned by the news of his marriage, while his public gestures of affection and celebration of his new wife Nita were met with a mix of suspicion and fear. Despite these reverberations, Paulo spoke freely of his new love and the sensations that now stirred in him. He shared his struggle with loneliness and grief, challenging us to *live and love* in the present—as much personally as politically.

In *Pedagogy of the Oppressed*,[2] Paulo wrote about the *fear of freedom* that afflicts us, a fear predicated on prescriptive relationships. As critical educators, he urged us to question carefully our ideological beliefs and pedagogical intentions; and to take note of our own adherence to prescription. He wanted us to recognize that every *prescribed behavior* represents the imposition of one human being upon another—an imposition that moves our consciousness away from what we experience in the flesh to false abstractions of ourselves and our world. If we were to embrace a pedagogy of liberation, we had to prepare ourselves to replace the conditioned fear of freedom with sufficient autonomy and responsibility to struggle for a way of life that could support revolutionary dreams.

In Paulo's eyes, fear and revolutionary dreams were unquestionably linked. The more that we were willing to struggle for these dreams, the more apt we were to know intimately the experience of fear; but also how to control and educate our fear, and finally, how to transform that fear into courage. Moreover, we could come to recognize our fear as a signal that we are engaged in critical opposition and transformative work to bring to life our revolutionary dreams.

In many ways, Paulo's life showed us that facing our fears and contending with our suffering are inevitable and necessary in our quest to make and remake a new world. Often, he likened our movement toward greater humanity to *childbirth, and a painful one*. For Paulo this *labor of love* constituted a critical process in our struggle to break the *oppressor-oppressed* duality and the conflicting beliefs that incarcerate our humanity.

Paulo firmly believed that to embrace a pedagogy of freedom, we had to step out of this duality. We had to come to see how the domesticating power of the dominant ideology causes teachers to become ambiguous and indecisive, even in the face of blatant injustice. Critical educators had to struggle together against a variety of punitive and threatening methods used within schools to instill a fear of freedom. For if this domestication was not rejected, even progressive teachers could fall prey to *fatalism*—making them each day more politically vulnerable and less able to face the challenges before them.

Throughout his life, Paulo adamantly denounced fatalism. At every turn, he emphatically rejected the idea that nothing could be done to halt the consequences of social injustice. If the economic and political power of the ruling class denied subordinate populations the space to survive, it was not because "it should be that way."[3] Instead, the asymmetrical relations of power that fuel fatalism had to be challenged. This required teachers to problematize the conditions of schooling with their colleagues, students, and parents, and through a critical praxis of reflection, dialogue, and action, become capable of *announcing justice*.

In defining issues of justice, questions of culture and power were tied to class—a dimension of Paulo's work that is often negated or simply ignored by many who embrace his ideas. Nevertheless, when Paulo spoke of the *ruling class* or the *oppressors*, he was referring to historical class distinctions and class conflict within the structure of capitalist society—capitalism was (and is) the root of domination. As such, his theoretical analysis was fundamentally rooted in notions of class formation, particularly with respect to how the national political economy relegated the greater majority of its workers to an exploited and marginalized class. However, for Paulo, the struggle against economic domination could not be waged effectively without a humanizing praxis that could both engage the complex phenomenon of class struggle and effectively foster the conditions for critical social agency.

Although heavily criticized on the left for his failure to provide a more systematic theoretical argument against capitalism, Paulo's work never retreated from a critique of capitalism and a recognition of capitalist logic as the primary totalizing force in the world. This is to say that he firmly believed that the phenomenon of cultural invasion worldwide was fundamentally driven by economic imperatives. During my early years as a critical educator, I, like so many, failed to adequately comprehend and incorporate this essential dimension of Paulo's work. For critical educators of color in the United States, we saw racism as the major culprit of our oppression and insisted that Paulo engage this issue more substantively. Although he openly acknowledged the existence of racism, he was reticent to abandon the notion of class struggle and often warned us against losing sight of the manner in "which the class factor is hidden within both sexual and racial discrimination."[4] Our dialogues were often lively and intense, for in many ways, Paulo questioned the limits of cultural nationalism and our blind faith in a politics of identity. When educators of color called for separate dialogues with him, Paulo told us that he could not understand why we insisted on dividing ourselves. With true angst, he explained: "I cannot perceive in my mind how Blacks in America can be liberated without Chicanos being liberated, or how Chicanos can be liberated without Native Americans being liberated, or Native Americans liberated without Whites being liberated." Paulo insisted that the struggle against oppression was a human struggle in which we had to build solidarity across our differences, if we were to change a world engulfed by capitalism.

Paulo deeply believed that the rebuilding of multiethnic solidarity among educators was a vital and necessary radical objective, for such solidarity moved against the grain of "capitalism's intrinsic perversity, its anti-solidarity nature."[5] Throughout his writings, Paulo warned us repeatedly against sectarianism. "Sectarianism in any quarter is an obstacle to the emancipation of [human]kind."[6] "While fighting for my dream, I must not become passionately closed within myself"[7] (Freire, 1998, p. 88). In many instances, he linked our ability to create solidarity with our capacity for *tolerance*.

At a critical scholars' conference in Boston during the summer of 1991, I came face to face with Paulo's profound belief in the political necessity for tolerance. The meetings had been quite intense, particularly with respect to the concerns of feminist scholars within the field. In my frustration, I stood up and fired away at one of the participants. This same frustration also fueled my critique of academic notions of multiculturalism the following day. In response, Paulo besieged me to be more tolerant in the future. With great political fervor, I rejected his position, making the case for greater *intolerance* to oppression and social injustice! For years, I licked my wounds over being *scolded* in public by Paulo. But in retrospect, I must confess that I recognize the wisdom in his advice. Despite my undeniable political commitment, I was lacking the virtue of revolutionary tolerance—the wisdom of being able to struggle with [reconcilable political differences], "so as to be able to fight the common enemy."[8]

It is significant to note, that just as we all face political differences among ourselves, Paulo, too, had to deal with his share of conflicts. In 1964, after launching the most successful national literacy campaign Brazil had ever known, he was imprisoned and exiled for almost sixteen years. But despite the pain and hardships he and his family experienced, Paulo's work as an educator and cultural worker continued unabated. And although Paulo would speak openly of the pain and suffering he endured in exile, he refused to reduce his life to grieving alone. "I do not live only in the past. Rather, I exist in the present, where I prepare myself for the possible."[9]

As Paulo's work became more prominent within the United States, he also grappled with a variety of issues that both challenged and concerned him. For almost three decades, feminists across the country fiercely critiqued the sexism of his language. In some arenas, Marxist scholars criticized him brutally. To the dismay of many scholars, educators, and organizers of color, Paulo seldom engaged with much depth and specificity, the perverse nature of racism and its particular historical formations within the United States. Nor did he readily accept the identity politics of the Chicano movement and its emphasis on a mythological homeland, Atzlan. Paulo also questioned the uncompromising resistance (or refusal) of many radical educators of color to assume the national identity of "American,"—an act that he believed fundamentally weakened our political position and limited our material struggle for social and economic justice. Beyond these issues, he also harbored serious concerns over what he perceived as the splintered nature of the critical pedagogy movement in the United States. Yet, most of these issues were seldom discussed substantively in public, but rather were the subject of private dialogues and solitary reflections.

Nevertheless, it is a real tribute to Paulo, that in *Pedagogy of the Heart* written shortly before his death, he showed signs of change and deepening in his views on these issues. For example, the language in the book finally reflected an inclusiveness of women when making general references, which had been missing in his earlier writings.

He spoke to the issue of capitalism more boldly than ever before and considered the nature of globalization and its meaning for radical educators. Paulo also addressed issues of diversity and racism, acknowledging that although we cannot overlook class in formulating our understanding of different kinds of discrimination, neither can we "reduce all prejudice to a [class] explanation."[10] And more forcefully than ever, he spoke to the necessity of moving beyond our reconcilable differences so that we might forge an effective attack against the wiles of advanced capitalism in the world.

I share these examples with you, not to diminish the memory of Paulo's work, but rather to remember his totality as a human being. Beyond the conflicts and contradictions he faced, Paulo had an expansive ability for sustained reflection, inquiry, and dialogue and an enviable capacity to reconstruct and *begin always anew*. I'm convinced that this quality served as the foundation for his unrelenting search for freedom and his unwavering hope. In the tradition of Marx, he believed that we both make and are made by history and thus, knowledge could not be divorced from historical continuity. Like us, he would explain, "history is a process of being limited and conditioned by the knowledge that we produce. Nothing that we engender, live, think, and make explicit takes place outside of time and history."[11] And as such, educators had to recognize that "it was when the majorities are denied their right to participate in history as Subjects that they become dominated and alienated."[12]

Moreover, Paulo was convinced that this historical process needed to take place within schools and communities, anchored in sustaining relationships of solidarity. Paulo urged critical educators to build communities of solidarity—networks to help us problematize the debilitating conditions of globalized economic inequality and confront the devastating impact of neoliberal social policies on the world's population. He saw these critical networks directly linked to the practice of democracy and an expanded notion of citizenship. Paulo urged us to strive *for intimacy with democracy*, living actively with democratic principles and deepening them, so they would come to have real meaning in our everyday life. Inherent to this politic is a form of citizenship that could not be obtained by chance. Such citizenship required that we fight to obtain it—a fight that required *commitment, political clarity, coherence, and decision*.

Paulo possessed an unwavering *faith in the oppressed*. As he saw the gap widening between the rich and the poor everywhere, he would argue that "Never has there been a deeper need for progressive men and women ... to give testimony of their respect for the people."[13] Paulo consistently identified this respect for and commitment to the oppressed as an essential ingredient to the cultivation of democratic schooling. This implied a critical posture, as well as a preoccupation with the meanings that students used to mediate their world. He believed it was impossible to teach without educators knowing what took place in their students' world. Teachers "need to know the universe of their [student's] dreams, the language with which they skillfully defend themselves from the aggressiveness of their world, what they know independently of the school, and how they know it."[14]

In *Teacher as Cultural Workers: Letters to Those Who Dare to Teach*, Paulo argued passionately that teaching was a task that required a love for the very act of teaching; for only through such love could the political project of schooling become transformative and liberating. Hence, it could never be enough to teach only for critical reasons.

Instead, Paulo fervently argued that we must dare to do all things with feeling, dreams, wishes, fear, doubts, and passion.

Paulo Freire was an exquisite human being. He placed great faith in our ability to live joyfully, despite the multitude of external forces that constantly challenge our humanity. *Living with joy* personifies for me the ultimate purpose of both Paulo's work and life. In retrospect, I am filled with wonderful memories—the beauty of his language, the twinkle in his eyes, his thoughtful and respectful manner, the movement of his hands when he spoke, his lively enthusiasm when contemplating new ideas, and his candid expressions of love and gratitude. In his words and his deeds, Paulo persistently invited us to fully embrace the dignity, beauty, and power of a revolutionary life.

Notes

1. Freire (1998, p. 42).
2. Freire (1970).
3. Freire (1997, p. 41).
4. Ibid. (p. 86).
5. Freire (1998, p. 88).
6. Freire (1970, p. 22).
7. Freire (1998) ibid.
8. Freire and Faudez (1989, p. 18).
9. Freire (1998, p. 67).
10. Freire (1997, p. 86).
11. Freire (1998, p. 32).
12. Freire (1970, p. 125).
13. Freire (1997, p. 84).
14. Freire (1998, p. 73).

References

Freire, P. (1970), *Pedagogy of the Oppressed*. New York, NY: Seabury Press.
Freire, P. (1997), *Pedagogy of the Heart*. New York, NY: Continuum, 41.
Freire, P. (1998), *Teachers as Cultural Workers: Letters to Those Who Dare to Teach*. Colorado: Westview Press, 42.
Freire, P., and Faudez, A. (1989), *Learning to Question: A Pedagogy of Liberation*. New York, NY: Continuum, 18.

3

Introduction: Pedagogy of the Heart

I am ... a being in the world, with the world, and with others; I am a being who makes things, knows and ignores, speaks, fears and takes risks, dreams and loves, becomes angry and is enchanted. I am a being who rejects the condition of being a mere object.

—Paulo Freire

In *Pedagogy of the Heart*, we encounter a translation of Freire in a very contemplative and reflective state of mind, as he revisits philosophical ideas that for decades were central to his work. I choose to raise the question of translation, first, in that it is an essential political question about how we make meaning seldom acknowledged or considered by readers when reading Freire. Yet, this cultural and epistemological issue is palpable in even the translation of this book's Portuguese title, *Under the Shade of the Mango Tree*. Lost is the living manifestation of the mango tree as both organic and cultural metaphor, under which Freire ponders and unveils his reflections on a variety of themes. For those of us whose cultural and epistemological sensibilities are more deeply anchored in the South, something powerful can get lost or erased in translation: a diverse cultural essence, a bodily sensibility, a way of knowing the world, a cadence that echoes the suffering of colonized generations.

Yet, despite the inelegance so often encountered in translated texts, Freire's formidable intellectual capacity to engage lovingly, yet soberly, with his world remains evident here. In this instance, we find him in a hopeful state of mind, as he contemplates a *maturing of democracy* in his beloved Brazil, despite the pressures of encroaching neoliberal forces in the country and around the world. No doubt he would experience deep sadness and frustration should he have lived to see Brazil today, where conservative forces and neoliberalism have aligned against the genuine needs of the people. Under the right-wing leadership of Jair Messias Bolsonaro, the nation's poverty has intensified, while his gross mishandling of the coronavirus pandemic besieged the nation, which is now only second to the United States in total cases and deaths from Covid-19.[1]

Internationally renowned as one of the most cited progressive scholars of his time, Freire ought to be remembered as Brazil's most respected educational philosopher. However, in the current neoliberal climate, Bolsonaro's authoritarian government has proclaimed Freire an enemy of the people. More disheartening, Freire's pedagogy of the oppressed has been maligned on the streets by the reactionary Chega Freire[2] (Enough with Freire) movement, bolstered by right-wing proponents who seek to eliminate his legacy from schools and curriculum, advance a staunchly instrumental and prescribed form of education across the country, and move to outlaw teachers and educators who teach his works.[3] In response, Freirean opponents challenge the repression of Brazil's banking educational approach, which censors open dialogue and critical reflection within education, by way of a pedagogy that disembodied students from their own learning. Yet, we can surmise from Freire's reflections here that, despite whatever disappointment he would have felt if still alive today, he would be reflecting, writing, and speaking to *what is to be done*—actively engaging with the global conditions of poverty, participating in the struggle of the landless movement in Brazil, reflecting on the issues raised by the Black Lives Matters movement around the world, and speaking out against the environmental violence of global capitalism.

Freire gave serious attention to the relationship of human beings to history, making this concept central to his philosophy of education and to his critical reading of the world. In this volume, he wisely draws from his historical experiences as an educator, his fifteen years in exile, his tenure as Sao Paulo's secretary of education, and his participation in democratizing campaigns to expand the breadth of educational opportunities for students. It is, therefore, not surprising that shortly before the end of his life, he critically engages here with the contentiousness of political campaigns in his country, from the standpoint of popular movements and electoral politics. Freire advocates for a *language of historic possibility*, a concept that remains vastly salient to the larger struggles we face today against the destructive forces of advanced capitalism threatening the well-being of the planet. Freire also points to a critical notion of utopia, which does not relate so much to a concrete place of eventual arrival, but rather to an ethical vision against perversity to guide our politics. Armed with a socialist vision, Freire urges us to do all in our power to organize and mobilize in the name of a democratic citizenship that prepares to critique, challenge, and resist, as we struggle to denounce oppression and announce justice. And all this, he argues, must be enacted politically with a deep spirit of humility, generosity, acceptance, and an ease with the uncertainty that defines our existence as human beings.

In writing about his period of exile, Freire astutely notes, "In one's fight for justice, one neglects seeking a more rigorous knowledge of human beings" and, as such, we can underestimate the impact of domination upon our lives. He speaks of this through *suffering exile*—enduring the suffering of exile by embracing the pain of his experience and what it represented in his life. Despite this anguish, he was forced to accept the tragedy of his rupture, the loss of his homeland, existence in a borrowed context, and reconciliation with contradictions between his past life and his present, as he simultaneously longed for his return to Brazil. Freire recalls suffering exile with his *conscious body,* that is to say with both reason and feeling, where his body was deeply affected by the grief, bitterness, lament, and yearning for return. In the midst of this, he was forced to deal with the tensions of his new conditions, while remaining loyal to his political dreams. He openly confesses that, in the experience of his exile, his virtues and flaws became highlighted, as his ability to love, contend with anger, and find tolerance were frequently tested. Through such heartfelt reflections, we gain a glimpse into the inner personal struggles of this very thoughtful, loving, and soulful man to live coherently with both his pedagogy and politics.

Freire also expresses thoughtful concern for his own grappling with the question of human nature, within the realities that shape our historical experiences. This he considers an indispensable political question often overlooked by those who struggle on the left. He reminds us that we are unable to truly know ourselves independent of history or outside our relationship to the world. And as such, if we do not possess a clear understanding of the historical forces and systemic conditions that enhance or thwart our participation as democratic citizens, we are left impotent to transform the oppressive conditions of society. Here again, Freire underscores human nature as never absolute, a priori, or ahistorical, in that our lives are always constructed within history, as are our struggles for liberation. Similarly, he returns to the idea that fighting against all forms of oppression constitutes an ethical imperative, in that our liberatory struggles must fundamentally work against the negation of our humanity.

The Fate of Humanity Hangs in Balance

We are … at a moment of confluence of crises of extraordinary severity, with the fate of the human experiment quite literally at stake.

—Noam Chomsky[4]

At this precise moment, the question of history hangs heavy on the minds and hearts of many radical educators and activists. Around the world, we have endured ruthless neoliberal assaults on democracy, as the leaders of the United States, Great Britain, Brazil, Turkey, and other nations have taken a sharp turn to the right, betraying liberal ideals that formerly beckoned global social change. Instead, populist conservative discourses prevail unabated across these nations, as is well illustrated by the rancorous presidential rhetoric of Donald Trump in the United States. Neoliberal excesses, beginning with the overthrow of Chilean president Salvador Allende in 1973,[5] set forth the political stage for the current historical milieu, by systematically eroding social, educational, and labor gains of the twentieth century—hard-won gains achieved by people's movements and trade union struggles. Furthermore, the destructive seeds of the neoliberal era were sown when the industrialized West "decided its mission was to conquer and subdue the natural world, when it embraced an ideology that fetishized money and turned people into objects to be exploited."[6]

The outcome is, as Chomsky argues, that the fate of humanity now hangs in balance. The crises we are facing today are inextricably tied to neoliberal policies of globalization that have produced staggering poverty and deplorable environmental abuses around the world. In fact, Harvard scientists suggest that many of the root causes of climate change have also increased the risk of global pandemics.[7] Capital-led deforestation associated with climate warming, linked to a loss of habitat, is forcing wild animals to migrate and potentially spread pathogens to other animals and humans. High carbon-producing livestock farms are also sources for spillover of life-threatening infections. The lethal nature of the coronavirus (or Covid-19), for example, has left over 35 million cases worldwide, with over a million deaths in less than a year.[8] This viral outbreak has been rightly linked to the destabilization of our complex global ecosystem, and gross deficits in public health and environmental sanitation are the result of neoliberal disregard for life.[9]

The pandemic has, therefore, not only set off a global health crisis, along with distressing impacts on both education and worker conditions, but has also highlighted enormous cleavages in political, economic, and racialized inequalities across societies, which are expected to increase in the post-pandemic world. Black, Latino, Indigenous, and other racialized populations, in particular, are experiencing the distressing impact of the virus, where statistics show significant disparities in death rates among people of color from Covid-19 compared to white counterparts.[10] In education, where over a billion children have been affected worldwide by the move to virtual learning, racialized inequalities in digital access have widened the divide.[11] Similarly, subaltern workers typified as low-skilled and with few benefits have also shouldered disproportionately the burdens of neoliberal disregard.[12]

In the current political climate, emancipatory struggles against such uninhibited social Darwinism are belittled, while the accumulation of wealth and power among the few is openly normalized and defended as a sign of business acumen or personal fortitude. In the midst of fifty years of neoliberal economic plunder, all notions of shared social responsibility have been tossed out the window, leaving the majority of the world's population defenseless in the face of its wide-scale consequences. Nowhere has this dehumanizing spectacle been more apparent than in the confusing and inept handling of the coronavirus pandemic, which led to elderly, impoverished, and racialized populations suffering disproportionately, while politicians pondered theories of herd immunity and argued about personal protection equipment to safeguard against the spread of the virus. There is no question the proponents of global capitalism have sought to undermine political efforts to build a more humanizing and just social order, generating the conditions for the fiercest global-class struggle in the history of humankind.

Amid harsh political economic measures that have betrayed the heart of liberal democracy, people around the world are contending with what critical theorist Henry Giroux[13] terms *neoliberal fascism*, where the ironclad rule of the marketplace has replaced any formerly held social consensus of government responsibility for the people. In its place, the welfare state has been systematically dismantled, as the unbridled privatization of public institutions prevails, with education, health care, and even prisons converted into money-making enterprises. Concurrently, a neoliberal ideology of unimpeded authoritarianism wages war on democratic values, bolstered by an economic logic of political hyper-individualism, competition, and financial gluttony. The consequence is we are living in a world where not only has the gap between the rich and the poor continued to deepen, but the racial wealth gap is higher today than in the 1960s.[14] Moreover, if current economic disparities remain unchecked, economists predict that by the year 2030, the top 1 percent will own 64 percent of the world's wealth.[15]

It is worth repeating that these massive economic injustices are the direct result of five decades of neoliberal excesses made possible by the political consensus and social neglect of powerful governments around the world. In an effort to extract labor and exploit the financial opportunities of the globalized economy, national leaders followed the speculative initiatives of the International Monetary Fund and the World Bank, while looking the other way as workers' real wages diminished, educational resources dwindled, and key public welfare services were slashed by austerity measures that relentlessly persevered the interests of the global capitalism.

Critique of Global Capitalism

We truly face a crisis of humanity. Our very survival depends on us at the very least curbing the excesses of the out-of-control system of global capitalism, if not its outright overthrow.

—William I. Robinson[16]

It was precisely Freire's persistent concern for the dehumanizing impact of global capitalism on the lives of the majority of the world's population that fortified his enduring vision of education as a humanizing political project in the interest of freedom and equality. Freire wrote *Pedagogy of the Heart* during the mid-1990s, after witnessing the neoliberal project of global capital beginning to take hold like a vengeance. During the era of Margaret Thatcher in the UK and Ronald Reagan in the United States, right-wing agendas included repeated assaults on the welfare state, by way of draconian social policies and cuts in public spending, along with taxation laws and deregulation of the financial industry, prioritizing economic interests. As the two major world leaders in support of rising neoliberalism, Thatcher professed, "There's no such thing as society,"[17] promoting the supreme value of the individual, while Reagan defended the omnipotence of free-market competition, peddling the logic of his trickle-down economics. More to the point, both leaders used their executive powers to propagate the notion that schools should function as economic engines for the nation, while also utilizing national resources to drastically weaken the power of trade unions.

It is not surprising then to find that at the core of Freire's argument against neoliberalism is a direct and unapologetic critique of global capitalism. Freire openly chastises neoliberal disregard for the most vulnerable and argues against the corrupt nature of global financial initiatives. He condemns the politics of privatization that, openly or by stealth, have seized public resources worldwide to expand capital accumulation among the wealthy and powerful. Freire speaks adamantly to how neoliberalism undermines public access and limits the democratic participation of the masses in crucial decisions that impact their labor and daily existence. He argues that not just political economic vision can be actualized without the active participation of men and women, advocating for systems genuinely in sync with human needs. Similarly, his reflections point to a global capitalism that operates across terrains of class, race, and gender, invisibly and pervasively embedded in all of society's institutions. Freire's view echoes what Anibal Quijano[18] calls the *coloniality of power*—hegemonic societal structures of power inherent to the global reach of imperial capitalism that endure to the present.

Speaking out resolutely against the oppressive power of the ruling class, Freire reminds us about the power of ideology in the consolidation of material power and control. He calls upon us to demystify determinist discourses of neoliberalism that engender fatalism and obstruct open participation. Freire insists that such dystopian discourses impoverish democratic efforts, in both the north and the south, given how global neoliberalism functions to expand and consolidate power and wealth among the few. Here, he stalwartly contends, *capitalism is not the radiant future,* to make the point that it is impossible for us to overcome the abuses of capital without entering in a forthright negation of its oppressive ideology of extraction and accumulation. This points to a colonizing ideology anchored to a Western epistemology of conquest that reproduces what Boaventura de Sousa Santos[19] calls an *abyssal divide*—where all knowledge or meaning that does not serve the interests of capital is systematically invisibilized, rendering it nonexistent or irrelevant to our reading of the world.

Freire also unwaveringly asserts that the curricular injustices of capitalist educational systems function to obscure global class struggle. Class antagonisms within the classroom, veiled by instrumentalized curricula, intensify the labor of critical educators who struggle to enact practices of democratic learning. This lack of clarity about social class can also generate confusion and contradictions among many working-class teachers, students, and communities, disrupting their capacity for coherent participation in class struggle. As such, if we are to unveil the concrete conditions of oppression and fight to dismantle the structures of global capitalism, we must resist and challenge the oppressive ideologies of domination that betray our humanity. Freire further notes that a clear conceptual understanding of the complexities of global capitalism engenders social movements and civic organizations to enact and endorse more coherent political interventions and to reimagine a lucid, hopeful, and critically ethical leadership.[20] Indisputably, Freire points to ethical *coherence between what we do and say* as key to building social movement organizations that can inspire the confidence and solidarity necessary for global political mobilization in these times. At the core of Freire's message is the need for educators and activists to confront the deadly impact of global capitalism on our lives and to enter into political struggles *within* the actual circumstances we face within schools and communities. This mandate, however, is often very challenging for teachers, particularly within the rising global inequalities of today's virtual learning culture.

Virtual Learning and Technology

Human beings make their own history, but not under circumstances of their own choosing.

—Karl Marx[21]

The difficult circumstances of the coronavirus pandemic are certainly not of our own choosing. Given Freire's commitment to the humanizing purpose of education, he would undoubtedly experience much unease with the current proliferation of online teaching and widespread marketization of piecemeal curricula to accommodate the intensification of virtual learning. At the heart of his disquiet would be the lasting threat of continuing and expanding digital education, once the conditions of the pandemic recede. For Freire, classroom conditions of democratic education provide opportunities for students to critically grapple together across differences and likenesses, in an effort to learn, communicate, and transform their world within the complexity of our diverse humanity. Vital to the critical intellectual formation of students is the creative tension that unfolds in the context of lively human encounters and relationships, best enacted through their embodied presence within the everyday. Within the disembodiment of virtual education, students are expected to function in ways that, more than ever, alienate them from the processes of their learning and from their dynamic participation in their lived history.

Instead of rigorous classroom dialogues, key to Freirean-inspired question-posing pedagogies, students are expected to learn within lonely, detached, online spaces with minimal teacher attention. Nevertheless, they must readily respond to prescribed, standardized forms of curricula developed and designed for them by experts, often without teacher or student participation or input. Such virtual spaces reinforce neoliberal learning values that privilege individualization, memorization, and quantification, in ways that promote a stilted one-dimensionality in the production of knowledge. Instead of students being immersed in active learning processes that stimulate critical engagement, the development of voice, and the construction of participatory knowledge, they are now conditioned to learn sequestered and unaided, away from embodied human contact and the communal dialogical environments that best foster and cultivate empathy, openness, and acceptance across differences.

In contrast, virtual education, more single-mindedly than ever, reinscribes banking educational methods by way of standardized curricula and teaching-to-the-test, often resulting in undemocratic practices that inhibit students' understanding of themselves as empowered subjects of their own learning. In this sense, digital mainstream approaches transfigure students into objects to be manipulated and silenced, narrowing the scope and expectations of their contribution. Without student opportunities for critical reflection and dialogue with others, they are prevented from developing the social skills required for democratic interaction and collective participation. The outcomes are educational circumstances where students fail to garner a rich sense of their own social agency as loving, thinking, feeling, and conscious human beings, a vital quality in the political formation of democratic citizens. Moreover, when students' embodied experiences with others are severely curtailed or altogether absent in the e-learning experience of many students worldwide today, the impact of its alienating conditions cannot go unheeded. In the prevailing virtual educational context, Freire would likely argue that the epistemological curiosity of students is severely curtailed by a pedagogy and curriculum fixated on keeping the national economic engine revving, rather than creating conditions where students learn to critically challenge the injustices of their world.

Similarly, Freire would have expressed serious concern for the manner in which teaching in these new circumstances disfigures the labor of teachers. In the virtual classroom, the difficult labor of teachers has become even more routinized and tediously disembodied than previously, as they are expected to function as technological mediators, dispensers, and automatons of a growing virtualized pedagogical culture. Similarly, many young student teachers who should be receiving adequate pedagogical support and room to develop their practice are instead being overwhelmed by exploitative teaching loads. The consequence is a situation where students are often taught by teachers inadequately prepared and who must now also labor longer hours to demonstrate their students are fulfilling neoliberal standards of accountability put in place for digital learning.

No doubt, Freire would have objected to the dangers of this deeply technocratic educational culture, which further initiates and conditions teachers, student teachers, and students into a commonsensical acceptance of technological institutional practices, which provide "the grounds for a degree of surveillance never before experienced within the classroom."[22] Social media platforms for e-learning are not employed solely for teacher-student communication, but are widely used for monitoring student assessment, test results, attendance, class participation, chat-box, and many other virtual instructional activities. The extensive data collection and processing capabilities make these platforms privacy-invasive and insecure. Consequently, educational platforms can readily become "fodder for the government and private players to build a society of control and exploitation."[23] With this in mind, critical educators and activists cannot overlook how the more extensive use of social media platforms across society can function as a vehicle for state repression, threatening violation of human rights and civil liberties.[24]

Freire rightly asserts *technology is a bastion of capitalism*, given its instrumentalizing demands, its dizzying acceleration and movement of uncritical communication, and its shift to promoting a largely disembodied existence. He reasons that, despite the wonders attributed to technology, the domination and exploitation of the majority of the world's population by the few persists—globalized oppression more formidably intensified by *algorithmic capitalism*,[25] where algorithms, changing and opaque, are embedded within a mode of production that bolsters and fortifies structures of surveillance, social control, and domination. According to *The Social Dilemma*,[26] nowhere is this phenomenon more apparent than the arena of social media, whose pervasive proliferation remains in the hands of a small group of designers, eagerly attending to the profit motives of transnational corporations. As the wealthiest and most unregulated global industry under neoliberal rule, massive online corporations such as Apple, Google, Amazon, Facebook, Twitter, YouTube, and Pinterest ruthlessly extract data and sell users to the highest bidder. Accordingly, social media platforms have profoundly normalized the exchange of embodied public space for a virtual social existence, where messiness, contradictions, and complexities of human life give way to a cacophony of distorted and unsubstantiated truths, pontificated by disreputable "experts" whose aims are, at best, questionable and, at worst, politically authoritarian, violent, xenophobic, and misogynist.

It can be argued that social media represents not only the most sophisticated and effective operant and conditioning tool in the history of humankind, but also, in the Gramscian sense, the most complex hegemonic devise for securing a variety of streams of cultural consensus among the masses. Accordingly, "our minds are being aggressively rewired to hold their attention and then make them pliable for corporations to sell things."²⁷ Similarly, identities are being constructed by way of virtual images and disembodied artifacts that deceptively condition users to desire the uncomplicated perfection of a limited range of identities, which for all intents and purposes can only exist in the virtual zone. Within this dehumanizing or what some now call posthuman zone,²⁸ the commodification and exploitation of prefabricated archetypes that dictate personal behaviors (i.e., how we talk, walk, dress, live) and emotions (i.e., fears, insecurities, desires, and yearnings) become addictive drivers of personhood, replacing in-the-flesh relationships of human contact, community values, and shared experiences. In the process, the competitive financial and political agendas of capitalist zealots not only enjoy free reign over the marketplace, but also gain access to our hearts and minds. Through overwhelming sensory bombardment of virtual images, behind-the-scenes algorithmic wizards narrowly manipulate human consciousness in ways that can potentially disrupt democratic dialogue across political and cultural differences.

It goes without saying, there is a dire need for civil rights and social movement organizations to forge new tactics and strategies to contend with this technological assault on our humanity. However, these must go beyond simply urging users to get off these platforms or urging parents to restrict their children's screen usage. Needed are tougher global campaigns to defend public space, redistribute the wealth, and dismantle the overwhelming control of transnational corporations over life on the planet. In education, rather than surrender to neoliberal discourses that fatally portend the inevitable virtualization of education, we must work collectively to move schools, universities, and the public toward an unwavering democratic commitment to education for the well-being of humanity. Freire would also urge us to establish global networks and social movement campaigns that unveil, challenge, and fight against the oppressive structures of global capital responsible for the preponderance of profiteering technology and its increasing reification of human consciousness.

A foremost concern for Freire is that students evolve democratically into critically conscious adults, prepared to face the challenges and contradictions of a complex world. True to his philosophy, he also insisted on a critical reading of technology that retains a dialectical perspective. In this volume, he espouses a view of technology as a powerful tool utilized for oppressive as well as liberatory undertakings. This signals Freire's refusal to fall victim to an essentialist analysis of technology, one that fails to engage critically with its deeply contradictory nature. Here, we must consider how the oppressed have utilized technology for democratizing knowledge, the dissemination of unfairly censored information, and support of democratic dissent around the world. No doubt, if writing today, he might remind us about the significant emancipatory political role of technology to the anti-austerity campaigns in Europe, the global Occupy movement, pro-democracy movements of the Arab Spring, and worldwide protests of Black Lives Matter following the police killing of George Floyd. He might also note the risks taken by Chelsea Manning in exposing military war crimes or Edward Snowden in exposing government technological surveillance or Julian Assange in setting up WikiLeaks to expose the excesses and impunity of world leaders.

In the spirit of Freire, there are progressive educators who seek to bring criticality to the center of e-learning.²⁹ Toward this aim, Freirean educators engage with questions of power and decision-making by assessing with students their goals, prior to deciding how a virtual classroom or course is structured.[30] They work to keep the transformative aim of education at the forefront by creating e-learning opportunities that enhance dialogical interactions and activities by situating student learning in their lived experiences. These educators also focus on the development of voice; support students' strengths, abilities, and interests as they strive to engage new material; and emphasize horizontal relationships with students to create space for (re) negotiating together course strategies and materials. Most fundamentally, a Freirean approach to online teaching begins with building a community where dialogue can ensue and students can engage ideas openly, as well as experience opportunities for meaningful collaboration.[31] As noted earlier, practicing these strategies within the instrumentalized and fractured environment of virtual education is highly challenging. Larger structural changes are also needed to facilitate critical pedagogical efforts, including smaller class sizes; reduced virtual screen time, with adequate breaks; help for parents to assist their children; and a decrease in standardized material covered to ensure ample time for interactive virtual activities with and among students.

Freire would certainly have supported progressive educators who, in the midst of the pandemic, are laboring to bring criticality to virtual instruction. Amid this great challenge, he would have urged critical optimism, to not be left silenced, disempowered, or to become uncritical opponents of technology. He would have encouraged educators and activists to remain present and be involved in a critical relationship with the world of technology and virtual learning, *as it exists*, in the hopes of discovering the cracks by which a genuine liberatory position of struggle could be forged. And, more importantly, he would have considered this dedication to criticality, in the face of dehumanizing circumstances, to be the ethical and political responsibility of educators and activists committed to our fight against the common enemy.

Fighting the Common Enemy

> *Therefore, we tend to divide forces fighting among and against ourselves, instead of fighting the common enemy.*
>
> —Paulo Freire[32]

In Freire's reflections on his "first world" as a child, he argues that before we can become citizens of the world, we must be citizens of our place of origin. This is to say that we must embody an awareness of our existence, the place of our doing, the space of our dreaming, the geography of our identity. The profound political relevance of knowing ourselves fully across the many identities that shape our consciousness and our world is essential to our pedagogical and political work. In Freire's discussion of difference, there is an appreciation for the construction of political identity as a dynamic human factor that links each of us to our cultural, racial, linguistic, religious, political, and economic histories. Yet, simultaneously, he notes the limits of a politics founded solely on identity markers, which can obscure the commonalities in the suffering of oppressed peoples.

Freire argues, for example, that the perversity of racism is not inborn to human nature but arises from *the color of ideology*. This to say, racism arises from a dehumanizing ideology of race, historically linked to systems of exploitation or the colonial matrix of power responsible for the persistent brutality of colonization, slavery, and genocide. Freire's critical insights on this matter remain salient today, as we continue to grapple with an overwhelming tendency to divide our forces, fighting identity battles among and against ourselves. Troubled by struggles of disunity on the left that ultimately serve the hegemony of the ruling class, Freire urges us to embrace *unity within diversity*, a collective political vision for liberation, which aims for unity across diverse progressive political groups.

Cognizant of the growing need for political action on the left against the atrocities of neoliberal exploitation, Freire also voices his abhorrence of sectarianism and dogmatism, which impoverish democratic participation by way of vanguard solutions derived by the few *for* the many, rather than solutions generated *with and by* the people. Instead, he upholds the democratic capacity of workers, women, racialized communities, and other oppressed populations to name their own realities, to collectively labor for change and to assert their self-determination in the interest of a destiny where justice prevails. For Freire, it is an open, unfinished, and historically undetermined vision of the future that counters the historical stasis and fixity of modernity, by embracing movement, change, and the unpredictability inherent to liberatory struggles. Antonio Machado's words, which Freire often quoted to accentuate this point, come to mind: *se hace camino al andar*,[33] or "we make the road by walking."

Freire also expresses concern for leftists who enter into questionable alliances with conservative forces, which ultimately render them politically incoherent. He laments those on the left who take centrist or pragmatic positions, often justifying their decision by asserting that the significance of class has disappeared. Similarly, he warns against political infighting and debilitating ruptures among the left, as if those with whom we disagree are our enemies rather than simply comrades in struggle with whom we differ. Again, he makes a case here for *unity within diversity* as an irreplaceable value in the larger struggle for liberation, calling for political and pedagogical organizations to collectively address common struggles of our time, by way of democratic participation and interventions rooted in the needs of the oppressed. To enter political struggles across our differences requires great tolerance and patience, which Freire advocates in our speech, relationships, and actions, if we are to enter into the intimacy of democracy. This infers an active political process by which we cultivate relationships of struggle within social movements that transcend closed organizational borders. This entails a willingness to labor openly across diverse political fields of being, as we keep questions of culture, politics, economics, gender, skin color, sexuality, religion, and physical abilities at the center of our struggles for a better world.

Freire, of course, acknowledges the many challenges at work for leftist organizations and progressive political parties who aspire to gain political power for the emancipatory purpose of transforming society. Pedagogical qualities important to this crucial political task include curiosity, coherence, patience, faith, a sense of hope, dialogue that begins where people are at, communal goodwill, critical optimism, and ethical rigor. Freire affirms that through these qualities we can better remain open to the evolution of social consciousness, as we learn new language, strategies, and skills for critiquing capitalism and challenging conditions of suffering across communities. Freire underscores the importance of collective organizing that democratically supports oppressed communities to define strategies of resistance against forces that trample upon our humanity. A glimpse of this type of organizing in the United States was visible in the powerful efforts of CORE (Caucus of Rank-and-File Educators)[34] of the CTU (Chicago Teachers Union), who fought on behalf of the city's entire working class, uniting issues of education to racism, immigration, and the school-to-prison pipeline. More importantly, by embracing organizing strategies that brought teachers, students, parents, and community members together, their successful campaigns for educational justice helped to shift schools toward a more democratic balance of power.[35]

In instances, however, where organizing for change is not as successful, Freire reminds us of the grueling political conditions faced by those who endure daily conditions of oppression, where despair and hopelessness can ensue even for those committed to a socialist future. At such moments, educators and activists fighting across differences may be tempted to focus solely on issues associated with what they perceive as their own oppression, forgetting that all forms of human oppressions are inextricably linked. And although Freire empathizes with the temptation to struggle separately in the name of urgency, he also rightly compels us to reach across our own suffering and join in the suffering of others, so that we might struggle together against the common enemy. Rather than to wax cynical or surrender to despair, Freire maintains that it is precisely through the power of our solidarity, unity, and labor with those perceived as different that we generate the power of hope and commitment to persist in the arduous fight for liberation.

Nevertheless, Freire adamantly objects to *imposed transformation* in the name of the oppressed, which he argues reinforces blind obedience, immobilization, passivity, fear, and erosion of people's participation in making decisions vital to their lives. He also warns of the pressures, tensions, and confusion generated by the advance of political conservatism, where a sterile and necrophilic sectarianism can arise among the left, when what is most needed are open, creative, and life-affirming political stances that support critical democratic dialogue among people. This reflects his concern with growing authoritarianism and overbearing arrogance that is too often justified, in the name of political urgency. And, while Freire might be the first to assert the power of resistance and people on the streets, he also decries a politics predicated primarily on rally cries, slogans, prescriptions, indoctrination, and undemocratic forms of vanguard leadership. So, despite the everyday tensions generated by our differences, Freire provokes us to persevere in building political open-mindedness and solidarity across our differences by integrating values indispensable to democracy and to the making of a more loving world.

Values Indispensable to Democracy

I hope at least the following will endure—my trust in the people and my faith in human beings and in the creation of a world in which it is easier to love.

—Paulo Freire[36]

Freire's great concern for the fate of our humanity under the domination and exploitation of capitalism seems evermore relevant and salient today, given the unrelenting neoliberal war against democracy. In this volume, Freire asserts the liberatory intent of critical pedagogical and political projects as the fulfillment of our vocation: *to be human*. In *Pedagogy of the Oppressed*,[37] he distinctly connects this vocation to our capacity to love the people and the world. This humanizing intent, however, does not end with the classroom, but rather is meant to extend to the pedagogy and politics of social movements, trade unions, and other political organizations. Similarly, Freire advances love as an essential political force in our fight for liberation.[38] His meaning is well-articulated by bell hooks[39] when she writes, "The moment we choose to love we begin to move against domination, against oppression. The moment we choose to love we begin to move towards freedom, to act in ways that liberate ourselves and others." And although few references to love are included in *Pedagogy of the Heart* (whose title implies the significance of love in his philosophy), Freire offers pedagogical and political reflections on curiosity, faith, and hope—all akin to love—as values indispensable to democracy.

Epistemological Curiosity

For Freire, living a reflective life as that of teachers entails a willingness to ask questions by entering with an open sense of curiosity into the reality of students' lives and the conditions of the world around us. Epistemological curiosity, as he conceives of it, pertains to an openness to knowing and exploring our nature as human beings, as well as a willingness to discover the differences that exist across our lives. Such a pedagogical process supports a liberatory acceptance of the differences ever-present between schools, students, and communities. Curiosity also generates a greater realization of the many human possibilities that exist for knowing the world. As students evolve in their capacity to be open to differences, they can also better seek democratic ways to enter into conscious and humble communion with others across our diverse humanity. Freire demonstrates this even with his readers, by way of a cultural style of passionate engagement and use of language that brings body, mind, and emotions into conversation, enlivening his many personal and political reminiscences born of his own curiosity to know his world more fully.

Correspondingly, Freire opposes a closed pedagogical system or a *pedagogy of answers*, where abstracted, neutral, and decontextualized answers float in the air, devoid of the critical inquiry that opens doors to transformative knowledge—knowledge with the power to disrupt the authoritarian values deceptively embedded in the elite, patriarchal, and racializing culture of hegemonic schooling. Severely blunting students' curiosity, a pedagogy of answers (or banking education) erodes students' creativity, imagination, and social agency, reinforcing a frozen, ahistorical, and timeless view of knowledge. Freire posits that decontextualized knowledge of standardized or marketized curricula, wittingly or unwittingly, denies the democratic investigation and dialogical participation of students in their critical formation. In turn, authoritarian values and vertical approaches to teaching and learning are persevered, where students are perceived as objects to be filled.

Freire does not view epistemological curiosity as solely a cognitive exercise, but rather a dynamic process of knowing that relies on the entire body. The body is crucial to our knowing in that "once we start talking in the classroom about the body and about how we live in our bodies, we're automatically challenging the way power has orchestrated itself"[40] in our lives. It is no wonder that Freire poetically argues, both pedagogically and politically, for our *increasing solidarity between the mind and the hands*, in that social and material change are realized to the degree that our bodies are actively implicated in the remaking of our world. It is also through our physical participation that we renounce an existence as mere objects of an oppressive system that appropriates our human agency for the extraction of our labor. Similarly, a disembodied pedagogy of answers inhibits the development of voice, robbing students of opportunities to embody their thoughts and actions in the interest of their freedom to be.

In discussing epistemological curiosity, Freire also speaks to the pedagogical and political significance of wrestling with uncertainty (as opposed to settling for absolute ways of knowing). Uncertainty, he contends, is essential to the development of critical thought, in that historical conditions and therefore our lives are ever changing. This continuity of history shapes our production of knowledge, in that we are continuously developing knowledge, while simultaneously immersed in the historical movement of our lives. It is this view of history and knowledge that guides Freire's problem-posing philosophy of education, where epistemological curiosity drives the evolution of critical consciousness and, therefore, our political process as subjects of history. Moreover, it is curiosity, according to Freire, that stimulates teachers and students toward a critical process of making meaning, grounded in our embodied relationships with others. In this way, transformative forms of democratic knowledge can assist us to engender those material conditions and relations of power that support our liberation.

Politics of Faith

As is the hallmark of Freire's liberatory philosophy, he decisively reiterates faith as central to the transformative capacity of human beings. Freire reflects on the manner in which faith has served as an impetus for his ongoing participation in the fight for liberation—a fight that reaffirms a just vision of society, commits to stand for freedom, respects the self-determination of others, and strives to enact humility, coherence, and tolerance in our pedagogy and politics. In particular, faith in the people is underscored as a significant ethical and political commitment of those who fight for a more just world. Faith in the people respects the ability of others to evaluate, investigate, name, and transform their conditions. Faith in others allows us to support critical pedagogical and political practices that make feasible concrete opportunities for oppressed communities to critically engage collectively with their lived circumstances.

Freire also argues that it is this faith in people that cultivates and nurtures democratic relationships of solidarity where, through our collective labor with others, critical social consciousness evolves and transformative relationships develop. A formidable example is the miners' strike of 1984–5,[41] where 187,000 miners took to the streets in the largest class war in the history of Britain—with workers on one side and every conceivable ruling class weapon on the other. The size and year-long duration of the strike would have been impossible, if not for the participation of allies across communities. Many miners' wives participated, bravely venturing outside their immediate communities to speak publicly for the first time in their lives. Crucial to the campaign were Miners support groups formed in every town and city across the country, where Black students, lesbian and gay activists, and religious organizations supported the strike. Despite valiant efforts, the miners' strike was ruthlessly smashed by the Thatcher government's neoliberal onslaught against the power of organized class struggle.[42] Nevertheless, the labor and evolving political consciousness of the miners, their families, and supporters, who fought with faith in people's self-determination, transformed their lives forever.[43]

As the miners' strike above and Freire's own reflections attest, genuine political transformation is a process rooted in the decisions, relationships, and actions we undertake collectively and those we enact daily. For revolutionaries, revolution must be comprehended as an active, present, and living pedagogy of love and an ethical way of life. Our future is, therefore, undeniably tied to the allegiances and commitments that shape our consciousness, which in turn shape our political decisions and interventions in the world. Additionally, faith in others and political consciousness evolve in the community, through the radical collective actions we take to change the inequalities and social exclusions at work in our everyday lives. The political transformation of society and its democratic commitment to people is an ongoing matter that relies on our consistent reflection, dialogue, and democratic participation as critical citizens of our world. Hence, as Freire argues, education is an indispensable institution for the liberatory reinvention of society, in that emancipatory schooling, founded on our faith in students, critically prepares them for democratic life.

Hope as Ontological Requirement

In his personal reflections on exile, Freire affirms the importance of educators and activists being reflective about our human nature, in that many oppressed people exist in the half-free condition of *internal exile*, forced to exist in a borrowed context not of our own making. This echoes the experience of many working-class and racialized educators and activists who live as second-class citizens. In these difficult times, Freire's grief, bitterness, lament, and yearning for a more just world resonate deeply with the powerful longing of oppressed communities around the globe, where their conditions of exploitation, marginalization, and violence fuel bitterness, rage, and despair, that in turn engenders hopelessness. Here, Freire posits hope as the antidote to fatalism, inviting us to embrace an empowering understanding of our human nature.

As with curiosity and faith, our struggle to sustain hope must be permanent. It requires our ongoing critical engagement with the circumstances of schools and society, in that we find the strength to keep hope alive, only through our constant communion with others. Through hope forged collectively, Freire contends, we discover the courage, strength, and emancipatory possibilities to challenge social injustices taken for granted in the past. In this way, hope also inspires our collective vision and participation in changing the direction of our future, by opening us to new definitions of what it means to be human. With this in mind, Freire affirms, *hope is the ontological requirement of human beings*. A powerful example of abiding hope is the fight waged against anti-Black racism and police brutality by the Black Lives Matter movement, one of the largest movements in US history. The refusal of Black Lives Matter activists to be deterred in their struggle has led to dramatic shifts in how people today understand historical and contemporary expressions of anti-Black racism, across the nation and around the world.[44]

Freire rightly stresses that an education of answers functions in the service of domination, stripping hope away with pragmatic educational policies and practices that limit students' critical engagement. In the process, students are steered toward jobs that may fulfill the vocational needs of the neoliberal workplace, but leave workers empty and despairing. In opposition, a pedagogy of question, grounded in the lived histories and experiences of those populations most afflicted, aims to name, challenge, and resist root causes of oppression, in an effort to develop collective solutions for the future. An emancipatory vision of hope mobilizes students, educators, and activists past oppressive conditions of inequality and exclusion. Freire embraces the significance and necessity of rebelliousness, if another world is to be truly possible. Here, critical questions of power remain ever on the table, in that social and material conditions of domination cannot be altered outside of our critical interrogation and collective participation in the daily life of schools and communities. Furthermore, no genuine or lasting political change is possible outside a larger ethical struggle to end global poverty, the appalling abuses of the labor market, the unnecessary world health crisis, the unprecedented incarceration of subaltern populations, and the dreadful inequalities that persist in education.

Finally, Freire insightfully warns us that without hope, we would be fatally trapped in a predetermined world, where the oppressed would have little choice but to accept our fate within an oppressive order. Instead, Freire argues convincingly that it is free and empowered human beings in collective struggle who transform history. Without hope, our human suffering would remain unabated and the inhumanities of the wealthy and powerful unchecked. Hope illuminates our persistent and coherent opposition of oppressive ideologies, policies, and practices and fuels our revolutionary dreams. And, it is through the power of collective hope that we garner the strength and wherewithal to unite across our differences, *in the creation of a world in which it is easier to love.*

Notes

1   Malta, et al. (2020).
2   Darder (2015a).
3   Accioly (2020).
4   Chomsky (2020).
5   Lagos-Rojas and Gomez-Baeza (2019).
6   Cook (2020).

7   C-Change (2020).
8   European Centre for Disease Prevention and Control (2020).
9   Wallace, et al. (2020).
10 Yaya, et al. (2020).
11 International Task Force on Teachers for Education (2020).
12 Furceri, et al. (2020).
13 Giroux (2019).
14 Pathe (2015).
15 Sheen (2018).
16 Robinson (2019).
17 Moncrieff (2013).
18 Quijano (2000).
19 Santos (2007).
20 Darder (2018).
21 Marx (1852).
22 Luck (2012).
23 Bajpai (2020).
24 Timotijevic (2020).
25 Bilić (2018).
26 Orloeski (2020).
27 Cook (2020).
28 Rutsky (2018).
29 Kahn and Kellner (2007).
30 Carr-Chellman (2016).
31 Informedia Services (2020).
32 Freire, P. (2021), Pedagogy of the Heart. London, UK: Bloomsbury Academic.
33 See: https://www.espoesia.com/poesia/antonio-machado/caminante-no-hay-camino-antonio-machado/.
34 Uetricht (2019).
35 Jaffe (2019).
36 Freire (1970).
37 Ibid.
38 Darder (2015b).
39 hooks (2006, p. 298).
40 hooks (1994, p. 137).
41 Mitchinson (2005).
42 Green (1990).
43 Bannock (2015).
44 Buchanan, Bui and Patel (2020).

References

Accioly, I. (2020), "The Attacks on the Legacy of Paulo Freire in Brazil: Why He Still Disturbs so Many?" in S. L. Macrine (ed.), *Critical Pedagogy in Uncertain Times*. Cham: Palgrave Macmillan, 117–38. https://link.springer.com/chapter/10.1007%2F978-3-030-39808-8_8.

Bajpai, H. (2020), "Surveillance on Students Raises Privacy Concerns on Online Education Platforms." *The Leaflet* (August 14). https://www.theleaflet.in/surveillance-on-students-raise-privacy-concerns-on-online-education-platforms/#.

Bannock, C. (2015), "Miner's Strike 30 Years On: 'I Fought Not Just for 'My Pit' but for the Community.'" *The Guardian*. https://www.theguardian.com/politics/guardianwitness-blog/2015/mar/05/miners-strike-30-years-on-i-fought-not-just-for-my-pit-but-for-thecommunity.

Bernstein, A. (2020), *Coronavirus, Climate Change, and the Environment*. C-Change. Boston, MA: Harvard T. H. Chan School of Public Health. https://www.hsph.harvard.edu/c-change/subtopics/coronavirus-and-climate-change/.

Bilić, P. (2018), "A Critique of the Political Economy of Algorithms." *Triple C* 16(1): 315–31.

Buchanan, L., Bui, Q., and Patel, J. K. (2020), "Black Lives Matter May be the Largest Movement in U.S. History." *New York Times* (July 3). https://www.nytimes.com/interactive/2020/07/03/us/george-floyd-protests-crowd-size.htm.

C-Change (2020), "Coronavirus and Climate Change. Harvard T. H. Chan School of Public Health." https://www.hsph.harvard.edu/cchange/subtopics/coronavirus-and-climate-change/.

Carr-Chellman, D. (2016), "Freirean Principles for E-Learning." *ELearn* (December). https://elearnmag.acm.org/featured.cfm?aid=3026475.

Chomsky, N. (2020), "The Fate of Humanity Hangs in the Balance." *ROAR* (September 18). https://roarmag.org/essays/noam-chomsky-the-fateof-humanity-hangs-in-the-balance/.

Cook, J. (2020), "Why Is the World Going to Hell? Netflix's Social Dilemma Tells Only Half the Story." Jonathan Cook Blog (September 25). See https://www.jonathan-cook.net/blog/2020-09-25/netflix-social-dilemma/.

Darder, A. (2015a), "Countering the 'Chega Freire' Campaign in Brazil: Our Emancipatory Struggle Continues." *Truthout* (April 22). https://truthout.org/articles/countering-the-chega-freire-campaign-in-brazil-our-emancipatory-struggle-continues/.

Darder, A. (2015b), *Freire and Education*. New York, NY: Routledge.

Darder, A. (2018), "Critical Leadership for Social Justice," in S. Soohoo, P. McLaren, and L. Monzo (eds.), *Radical Imagine-Nation*. New York, NY: Palgrave, 139–64.

European Centre for Disease Prevention and Control (2020), COVID-19 Situation Update Worldwide as of 23 of October 2020. https://www.ecdc.europa.eu/en/geographical-distribution-2019-ncov-cases.

Freire, P. (1970), *Pedagogy of the Oppressed*. New York, NY: Seabury Press.

Freire, P. (2021), *Pedagogy of the Heart*. London: Bloomsbury, 44.

Furceri, D., Loungani, P., Ostry, J. D., and Pizzulo, P. (2020), COVID-19 Will Raise Inequality if Past Pandemics Are a Guide. VOX/CEPR (May 8). https://voxeu.org/article/covid-19-will-raise-inequality-if-past-pandemics-are-guide.

Giroux, H. (2019), *The Terror of the Unforeseen*. Los Angeles, CA: Los Angeles Review of Books.

Green, P. (1990), *The Enemy Without: Policing and Class Consciousness in the Miners' Strike*. New York, NY: McGraw-Hill Education.

hooks, b. (1994), *Teaching to Transgress*. New York, NY: Routledge.

hooks, b. (2006), *Outlaw Culture: Resisting Representations*. New York, NY: Routledge.

Informedia Services (2020), "Critical Pedagogy in an Age of On-line Learning. StCloud State University." https://blog.stcloudstate.edu/ims/2020/05/06/critical-pedagogy-in-an-age-of-online-learning/.

International Task Force on Teachers for Education (2020), COVID-19 Highlights the Digital Divide in Distance Learning. https://teachertaskforce.org/news/covid-19-highlights-digital-divide-distance-learning.

Jaffe, S. (2019), "The Chicago Teachers Strike Was a Lesson in 21st Century Organizing." *The Nation* (November 16). https://www.thenation.com/article/archive/chicago-ctu-strike-win/.

Kahn, R., and Kellner, D. (2007), "Paulo Freire and Ivan Illich: Technology, Politics and the Reconstruction of Education." *Policy Futures in Education* 5(4): 431–48. https://www.researchgate.net/publication/242103754_Paulo_Freire_and_Ivan_Illich_Technology_Politics_and_the_Reconstruction_of_Education.

Lagos-Rojas, F., and Gomez-Baeza, F. (2019), "Chileans Have Launched a General Strike against Austerity." *Jacobin* (October 19). https://www.jacobinmag.com/2019/10/chile-protests-fare-hike-general-strike.

Luck, M. (2012), Surveillance in the Virtual Classroom. *The Virtual Learning Environment*. doi: 10.4018/978-1-4666-0011-9.ch808.

Malta, M., Murray, L., Passos da Silva, C. M. F., and Strathdee, S. A. (2020), "Coronavirus in Brazil: The Heavy Weight of Inequality and Unsound Leadership." *EClinicalMedicine* 25(1–2): 1–2. https://doi.org/10.1016/j.eclinm.2020.100472.

Marx, K. (1852), "The Eighteenth Brumaire of Louis Bonaparte." *Die Revolution*. New York. https://www.marxists.org/archive/marx/works/1852/18th-brumaire/ch01.htm.

Mitchinson, P. (2005), "Faith: A Dramatic Tribute to the Miners' Strike of 1984–85." *Defense of Marxism* (June 15). https://www.marxist.com/britain-faith-miners-strike090305.htm.

Moncrieff, C. (2013), "Margaret Thatcher: In Her Own Words in Independent (April 13)." Retrieved from: https://www.independent.co.uk/news/uk/politics/margaret-thatcher-her-own-words-8564762.html.

Orloeski, J. (2020), *The Social Dilemma*. Exposure Labs Production: Netflix Original Documentary. https://www.thesocialdilemma.com/thefilm/credits/.

Pathe, S. (2015), "Today's Racial Wealth Gap is Wider than in the 1960s." *PBS News Hour*. https://www.pbs.org/newshour/nation/todays-racialwealth-gap-is-wider-than-in-the-1960s.

Quijano, A. (2000), "Coloniality of Power, Eurocentrism and Latin America." *Nepantla: Views from the South* 1(3): 533–80. *Project MUSE* muse.jhu.edu/article/23906.

Robinson, W. I. (2019), *Into the Tempest: Essays on the New Global Capitalism*. Chicago, IL: Haymarket Books.

Rutsky, R. L. (2018), "Technological and Posthuman Zones." *Genealogy of the Posthuman* (November 19). https://criticalposthumanism.net/technological-and-posthuman-zones/.

Santos, B. de Sousa (2007), "Beyond Abyssal Thinking." *Eurozine*. http://www.euro-zine.com/pdf/2007-06-29-santos-en.pdf.

Sheen, M. (2018), "Richest 1% on Target to Own Two-Thirds of All Wealth by 2030." *The Guardian* (April 7). https://www.theguardian.com/business/2018/apr/07/global-inequality-tipping-point-2030.

Timotijevic, J. (2020), "Society's 'New Normal'? The Role of Discourse in Surveillance and Silencing of Dissent during and Post Covid-19." *First Look: Social Science and Humanities Open*. https://ssrn.com/abstract=3608576 or http://dx.doi.org/10.2139/ssrn.3608576.

Uetricht, M. (2019), "Chicago Teacher Militancy Is Up for Reelection." *Jacobin* (May15). https://www.jacobinmag.com/2019/05/chicagoteachers-union-caucus-of-rank-file-educators.

Wallace, R., Liebman, A., Chaves, L. F., and Wallace, R. (2020), "COVID-19 and Circuits of Capital." *Monthly Review* 72(1) May. https://monthlyreview.org/2020/05/01/covid-19-and-circuits-of-capital/#en38backlink.

Yaya, S., Yeboah, H., Charles, C. H., Otu, A., and Labonte, R. (2020), "Ethnic and Racial Disparities in COVID-19 Deaths: Counting the Trees, Hiding the Forest." *BMJ Global Health* (6). http://dx.doi.org/10.1136/bmjgh-2020–002913.

Part 2

The Politics of Biculturalism

Introduction

Darder's *Culture and Power in the Classroom: Educational Foundations for the Schooling of Bicultural Students* begins an arduous journey in that this seminal book is the gateway for many readers into Darder's theoretical contributions to the world, especially with respect to understanding the experiences of bicultural students in the United States. Built upon a foundation of love for teachers, students, and communities, *Culture and Power in the Classroom* crystallized a language of critique and hope through a political project committed to coherence, theoretical principles, and cultural democracy. Darder seeks to understand the theoretical and practical concerns with US education under capitalism for students and those who are most marginalized and dispossessed. Darder is interested in understanding the material and ideological conditions for bicultural students and how students must negotiate and traverse the neoliberal logic and structure of schooling. Hence, Darder is concerned with creating conditions needed for cultural democracy—in the push for economic democracy.

Summary of Articles

In this seminal article, "A Critical Theory of Cultural Democracy," Darder thinks about the link between culture and power. She sees the need to develop, in theory and practice, an emancipatory political construct upon which to build a critical bicultural pedagogy. When thinking of human emancipation and social justice, Darder connects to Dewey's (1916) writings on democratic schooling and Giroux's (1988) theorizing of critical democracy—and offers a critical theory of cultural democracy. For her, this educational and pedagogical construct is essential for transforming classroom life, ourselves, and society. Building on earlier works done by Valentine (1971), deAnda (1984), Ramirez and Castaneda (1974), and others, Darder insists on engaging substantively with the politics of biculturalism—and to foreground a clear and succinct understanding of power, truth, and social, political and economic relations under capitalism.

Darder's "The Politics of Biculturalism: Culture and Difference in the Formation of *Warriors for Gringostroika* and the *New Metizas*" is a yearning to remember who we are as people, individually and collectively. It is, as she states, rarely discussed in traditional academic discourse. That is, their histories of interactions and engagements with the dominant cultures have "required consistent forms of adaptational behaviors which have, in many instances, eroded, restructured, and reconstructed the language system, cultural beliefs, and social traditions of these groups." As a way to rethink identity formation, Darder engages with Stuart Hall's notion of ethnicity—with respect to a critical biculturalism. She does so by asking us to do a dialectical reading of the category that "retrieves" from (1) the political opportunism and academic domain of neo-conservatives, and (2) to challenge critical scholars to reconceptualize the liberatory potential of the category by thinking about it in more class-specific ways.

Darder is invested in creating space for scholars of color to insert their voice, and following hooks (1994), to speak not from the "authority of experience," but rather from the passion of experience, the passion of remembrance (p. 90). Darder asks us to consider and critically engage with consciousness and decolonization, to think about identity not decontextualized from material conditions, media/ideological distortions of "difference," oppositional consciousness, border-crossing as transgressive politics, and revolutionary love. Darder closes the chapter by re-engaging with the critical politics of re-presentations. By enlivening the border culture writings of Guillermo Gomez-Pena's *Warriors for Gringostroika* and Gloria Anzaldua's *New Metizas*, Darder calls for theorizing from the "passion of experience, the power of reflection, and the courage to act."

In "Neoliberalism in the Academic Borderlands: An On-going Struggle for Equality and Human Rights," Darder thinks about the politics of biculturalism, cultural democracy, and the negative impact of neoliberal policies and practices on the labor of "border" or "subaltern" intellectuals within the university. Despite a long history and tradition of progressive struggle with the academy, a liberal multiculturalism has taken shape for quite a long time. Darder speaks to how careerist orientation alienates us from ourselves, to each other, and to the world we imagine differently. However, working within the logics and structures of the institution, it fundamentally takes scholars from the critical principles and foundations of progressive and radical scholarship. The desire to be competitive in the neoliberal marketplace takes precedence as academics develop a research agenda that will "procure them greater access to private and public funds" (p. 415). Hence, border intellectuals are asked to transverse through the changing "minefields" of the academy.

In the process, Darder is troubled that border intellectuals find themselves even more marginalized the very moment they come into scholarly and political maturity and are able to forge more democratic ways of thinking about research, teaching, and learning. The institution and its loyal gatekeepers are sure to find ways to call into question their collegiality, legitimacy, and place within the academy. Darder notes that radical scholars find themselves exiled from meaningful participation in the evolution of university programs and departments "by an antidemocratic wave that silences and banishes their contributions to the wasteland of irrelevancy" (p. 422). Citing Mike Neary's "violence of abstraction" and Raya Dunayeskaya's articulation of critical thought, Darder reiterates the need of "unquestionable Marxist ethos of equality and human rights"—both within and without the university.

4

A Critical Theory of Cultural Democracy

> *Education has to be linked to forms of self and social empowerment if the school is to become ... a force in the ongoing struggle for democracy as a way of life.*
> —Henry Giroux, *Schooling and the Struggle for Public Life*, 1988

In examining the link between culture and power, it becomes quite evident that in order to move toward a genuinely liberatory form of education, there must exist in theory and practice an emancipatory political construct upon which to build a critical bicultural pedagogy. This is particularly true given the asymmetrical power relations in American society and the disproportionate number of injustices suffered by students of color in the public schools. Significant to this discussion is the notion of student voice and empowerment and the conditions required for bicultural students to develop their bicultural voice and to actually experience a process of empowerment in the classroom. In more specific terms, there must exist a democratic environment where the lived cultures of working-class bicultural students are critically integrated into the pedagogical process. Keeping these principles in mind, a critical theory of cultural democracy emerges as part of a language of possibility and hope.

In the same spirit of human equality and social justice that is so clearly found in John Dewey's (1916) writings on democratic schooling and in the work of Henry Giroux (1988b) on critical democracy, a critical theory of cultural democracy seeks to function as an educational construct that can transform the nature of classroom life. Above all, it represents a concerted effort to awaken the bicultural voice of students of color and cultivate their critical participation as active social agents in the world. This is particularly essential in light of the many social forces of domination at work in the lives of bicultural students.

A philosophy of *cultural democracy* was first defined by Mexican American educators Manuel Ramirez and Alfredo Castañeda (1974). Their notion is based primarily on the principle that every individual has the right to maintain a *bicultural identity*. Because the critical theory of cultural democracy to be developed in this chapter is an effort to expand on some of the ideas formulated in the original theory, the meaning of biculturalism and its implications for establishing a culturally democratic environment must first be considered as a necessary part of a culturally emancipatory discourse.

Biculturalism

Biculturalism speaks to the process wherein individuals learn to function in two distinct sociocultural environments: their primary culture, and that of the dominant mainstream culture of the society in which they live. It represents the process by which bicultural human beings mediate between the dominant discourse of educational institutions and the realities that they must face as members of subordinate cultures. More specifically, the *process of biculturation* incorporates the different ways in which bicultural human beings respond to cultural conflicts and the daily struggle with racism and other forms of cultural invasion.

It is essential that educators recognize that just as racism constitutes a concrete form of domination directly experienced by people of color, biculturalism specifically addresses the different strategies of survival adopted by people of color in response to the dynamics of living in constant tension between conflicting cultural values and conditions of cultural subordination. Although the responses may bear a similarity to those that result from conditions of class oppression, an analysis of biculturalism cannot be reduced simply to class conflict. The "attack on culture is more than a matter of economic factors …. It differs from the class situation of capitalism precisely in the importance of culture as an instrument of domination" (Blauner, 1972, p. 67). Thus, to consider the lived experiences of bicultural populations as only dictated by forces related to the economy is to fall into a reductionistic theoretical trap that trivializes and distorts the struggles for equality of people of color in the United States.

It is worth noting here that studies grounded in traditional psychological or anthropological paradigms tend to theorize biculturalism in ways that render individualistic and relativist readings of this phenomenon. Whereas bicultural scholars who contend more directly with the political and economic ramifications of subordinate-dominant relations tend to be far more clear about the manner in which questions of culture and power impact the process of response patterns, particularly in individuals who are forced to negotiate two cultures from a very young age, from necessity rather than choice. This is an important distinction in that there are some who would claim that if you are bilingual, you are also bicultural. This, in fact, is not the case. To learn a second language from a privileged mainstream or affluent position in society results in a very different experience from that of being a working-class child from a racialized community, who must contend not only with learning a second language but also with the negative messages about the primary culture and language that abound in assimilative classroom environments. Needless to say, the work here seeks to arrive at not only an individual understanding of biculturalism but also a communal concept of biculturalism that will help to inform a critical theory of cultural democracy.

In examining the notion of biculturalism, it is significant that, since the early 1900s, writers, educators, and social theorists of color have made references in their work to the presence of some form of dual or separate socialization process among their own people. These references have included a variety of terms used to describe the personality development, identity, or traits of nonwhites socialized in a racist society: double consciousness (Du Bois, 1903), double vision (Wright, 1953), bicultural

(Valentine, 1971; Ramirez & Castañeda, 1974; Solis, 1980; Rashid, 1981; Red Horse, et al., 1981; deAnda, 1984), diunital (Dixon & Foster, 1971), multidimensional (Cross, 1978), and other references that closely resemble notions of duality and "twoness" (Memmi, 1965; Fanon, 1952; Kitano, 1969; Hsu, 1971; Sue & Sue, 1978).

In the last twenty years, another generation of bicultural scholars in education, sociology, and psychology has continued to engage this phenomenon (Chau, 1991; Tatum, 1992; LaFramboise, Coleman, & Gerton, 1993; Suárez-Orozco, 1998; Gutiérrez, Baquedano-López & Tejeda, 1999; Rodriguez, 1999; Sheets & Hollins, 1999; Chapman, 2002; Trueba, 2002; Cronin & Massó, 2003; Kanno, 2003; Sheets, 2005; Trumbull & Pacheco, 2005; Vargas-Reighley, 2005; Lomawaima & McCarty, 2006; Olivos, 2006; Cronin, 2008; Dennis, 2008; Hepi, 2008; Diaz-Soto & Haroon, 2010; Doerr, 2009; Smokowski & Bacallao, 2011). Many of the very same issues raised by earlier scholars (and in this book twenty years ago) are also found in newer works on biculturalism, including questions of identity development, anxieties, and consequences of negotiating across dominant–subordinate cultural milieus; contending with conflicting values across cultures; language differences and community struggles for bilingualism; as well as common institutional issues of subordination and marginalization associated with racialization and class formations within bicultural communities.

That said, studies of Black, Latino, Asian, and Native American populations clearly indicate that a bicultural phenomenon is present in the development of members from subordinate cultures. They also support the notion of biculturalism as both a social process and psychological mechanism of survival that constitutes forms of individual and collective adaptive alternatives in the face of hegemonic control and institutional oppression. Furthermore, these alternatives must be also understood as forms of resistance, as discussed earlier, that may—or may not—function in the emancipatory interest of the individuals who utilize them in their lives. In order to better understand the role of biculturalism in relation to a critical theory of cultural democracy, it is helpful to examine some of the early studies more closely.

Charles Valentine (1971) was one of the first social theorists to consider the concept of a *bicultural model of human development*, based on his work with Black children. His work represents an early attempt to expand on the *cultural difference model* and to challenge and displace the *cultural deprivation model*, which has failed to portray with accuracy the socialization process of children of color in the United States. Valentine suggests that bicultural groups undergo a dual socialization process that consists primarily of enculturation experiences within one's culture of origin (subordinate culture), in addition to less comprehensive but significant exposure to the socialization forces within the dominant culture. In reference to this notion of development, he writes,

> The idea of biculturation helps explain how people learn and practice both mainstream culture and ethnic culture at the same time. Much intra-group socialization is conditioned by ethnically distinct experience, ranging from linguistic and other expressive patterns through exclusive associations like social clubs and recreational establishments to the relatively few commercial products and mass media productions designed for ethnic markets. Yet at the same time,

members of all [subordinate cultures] are thoroughly enculturated in dominant culture patterns by mainstream institutions, including most of the contents of the mass media, most products and advertising for mass marketing, the entire experience of public schooling, constant exposure to national fashion, holidays, and heroes.

(p. 143)

Diane deAnda's (1984) efforts to examine the bicultural process and to explain the differences found among bicultural individuals led her to suggest six factors that she argues have an influence on the level of biculturalism in the individual. These factors include the following:

1. The degree of overlap or commonality between the two cultures with regard to norms, values, beliefs, perceptions, and the like;
2. The availability of cultural translators, mediators, and models;
3. The amount and type (positive and negative) of corrective feedback provided by each culture regarding attempts to produce normative behaviors;
4. The conceptual style and problem-solving approach of the bicultural individual and their mesh with the prevalent or valued styles of the majority culture;
5. The individual's degree of bilingualism; and
6. The degree of dissimilarity in physical appearance from the majority culture, such as skin color, facial features, and so forth.

The major conceptual difference between Valentine's and deAnda's models of biculturalism lies in the manner in which the individual is considered to interrelate with the two distinct cultures. Whereas Valentine's model of biculturalism perceives the process as resulting from the bicultural individual stepping in and out of two separate and distinct cultures, deAnda's argues that the bicultural experience is possible only because an overlap exists between the two cultures. The more overlap there is between the two cultures, the more effective the bicultural process of dual socialization. This difference that de Anda posits may help to explain why immigrants with more affluent backgrounds and whose worldview is more in sync with the dominant worldview—heavily influenced by a mix of Anglo-Saxon roots, modernism, and capitalism—might more readily integrate into mainstream American life.

The bicultural world of Mexican American children is described by Ramirez and Castañeda (1974) as encompassing the realities that Mexican American children must learn in order to function effectively in the mainstream of the American cultural community, and to continue to function effectively in and contribute to the Mexican American cultural community. They characterize this phenomenon as follows:

If a Mexican-American child has been raised during his [or her] preschool years in the sociocultural system characteristic of the traditional Mexican American community, the socialization practices pertaining to (1) language and heritage, (2) cultural values, and (3) teaching [and cognitive] styles will be unique to that system, and the child will have developed a communication, learning, and motivational style which is appropriate to it. At the same time the child begins his experience in the public schools he is required to relate to a sociocultural system whose socialization practices pertaining to language and heritage, cultural values, and teaching [and cognitive] styles are different from those experienced during his preschool years. In effect, it is a new cultural world which he must come to explore and understand. At the same time, he must continue to explore, understand, and learn to function in the heretofore familiar sociocultural system ... represented in his home and community. These demands placed on many Mexican-American children in one sense constitute the reality of a bicultural world.

(p. 29)

In addition, Ramirez and Castañeda posit a summary of characteristics for what they term *traditional, dualistic, and atraditional communities*. The schematic presentation for their framework incorporates the categories of general community characteristics; the degree of identification with the family, community, and ethnic group; the definitions of status and roles; the religious ideology espoused; and the preferred cognitive mode. Individuals from *traditional* communities hold a strong Mexican worldview, speak Spanish as their primary language, have a field-sensitive cognitive style, espouse a strongly Catholic ideology, and tend to live in relative isolation from the mainstream culture. Those individuals who are said to be *dualistic* incorporate cultural values from both the Mexican and Anglo-American cultures, are bilingual, Catholic, utilize mixed cognitive styles, and live in more ethnically heterogeneous communities. *Atraditional* individuals maintain an Anglo-American orientation, speak English exclusively, are field independent, Protestant, and live in communities that are predominantly Anglo-American. In addition, Ramirez and Castañeda attribute the diversity observed in Mexican American communities to these seven variables:

1. distance from the Mexican border;
2. length of residence in the United States;
3. identification with Mexican, Mexican American, or Spanish American history;
4. degree of American urbanization;
5. degree of economic and political strength of Mexican Americans in the community;
6. degree of prejudice; and
7. degree of contact with non-Mexican Americans.

Ramirez and Castañeda also view the notion of bicognitive functioning as a most important goal in the development of bicultural human beings. This relates not only to the issue of cognitive flexibility but also to the fact that functioning effectively in two cognitive styles allows bicultural students to participate more fully in both their culture and the mainstream American culture; this can then help them to achieve a strong bicultural identity. Consequently, the concept of *bicognitive development* is a vital component of the Ramirez and Castañeda methodology, which evaluates both teachers and students in terms of field-sensitive and field-dependent cognitive styles. This assessment is primarily conducted with instruments that measure preferential modes in terms of cultural values, relational styles, incentive motivation, and other behavioral and attitudinal criteria.

Based on his work with Black children, Hakim Rashid (1981) defines biculturalism as "the ability to function effectively and productively within the context of America's core institutions while simultaneously retaining [an] ethnic identity" (p. 55). He strongly argues that biculturalism is an essential developmental process if children of subordinate cultures are to develop the ability to cope with the racism and classism that permeate American society. Related to this view, Rashid posits the notion that biculturalism should also be considered an important component of the cognitive and behavioral repertoire of all American children,

> for it is only through recognition of the need for biculturalism that a foundation for true multiculturalism [in society] can be built. When children have developed the ability to survive and thrive within the context of their own culture as well as that of the broader society, a genuine appreciation for the variety of cultures that comprise America is the next step.
>
> (Rashid, 1981, p. 61)

A *theory of biculturality* is described by indigenous psychologist Arnoldo Solis (1980), based on his work with Chicano populations. He defines "biculturality" (biculturalism) in an individual as the result of existing in and adapting to two cultures having substantial dissimilarity. Solis argues that the more similar the cultures, the lesser the degree of biculturality; and on the other hand, the more the dissimilarity between the two cultures, the greater the degree of biculturality. For Solis, the dynamics of biculturation are considered to begin when the dominant culture exerts increasing influence on the subordinate culture to accommodate and assimilate to the dominant culture's values, language, and cognitive style. At this point, a dynamic of resistance is said to develop, which causes the individual to experience a cultural crisis. Within this construct, the process of biculturation is viewed as an attempt to reestablish the intrapsychic harmony of the primary culture that is threatened by the tensions arising as a result of pressure by the dominant culture to renounce subordinate cultural values. The resolution of the bicultural crisis is brought about through a series of developmental stages whereby the individual becomes increasingly able to recognize the value of and is able to utilize adaptive functions from both cultures in a harmonious manner (Solis, 1981).

Although there are some differences in the manner in which these bicultural theorists have conceptualized the notion of biculturalism, it is nonetheless evident from this discussion that an understanding of what constitutes the dynamics of biculturalism is essential to any foundations of education that are designed to meet the needs of racialized students. This is particularly true because what has often been missing (although often mentioned) from many of the earlier and more recent theories of biculturalism is a serious confrontation of the power relations that shape the nature of how working-class bicultural students respond to the tension of cultural conflicts and the pressure to assimilate so highly prevalent in traditional American schools. This phenomenon has once again gained steam, given current neoconservative efforts to eliminate multiculturalism in the curriculum and the prevalence of neoliberal educational initiatives anchored to government and corporate efforts to ensure the standardization (or homogenization) of knowledge. Hence, a contemporary reading of biculturalism cannot be reduced to an absolute fixed moment or a linear developmental stage. On the contrary, its critical dimensions must be retained through its formulation of bicultural existence as a deeply complex process encompassing a variety of both conscious and unconscious contradictory, oppressive, and emancipatory responses that are at work along a continuum that moves, conceptually, between the primary culture and the dominant culture (see Figure 4.1).

Educators who possess this dialectical understanding of biculturalism will be better equipped to assist their working-class racialized students in critically examining their lived experiences in an effort to genuinely reveal the impact that cultural domination has on their lives. Furthermore, given the nature of cultural domination and resistance, the process of biculturation can also be understood as patterns of responses that are shaped by the manner in which bicultural students react, adjust, and accommodate to the emotional anxiety and physical stress that result from the persistence of cultural dissonance. These response patterns can be perceived in a more critical manner when understood in terms of an axis relationship between culture and power that on one hand moves between the dominant and subordinate cultures, and on the other hand moves between the forces of dominance and resistance (see Figure 4.2).

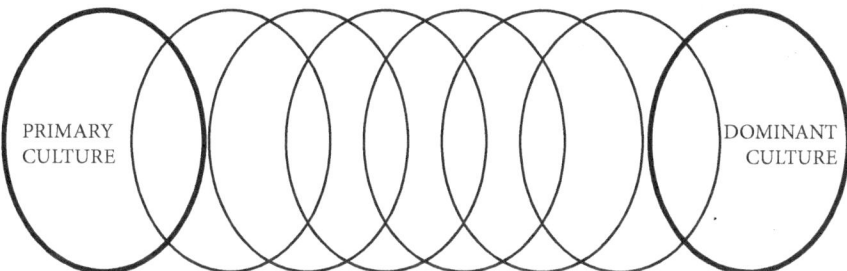

Figure 4.1 The Biculturation Process Represented along a Dialectical Continuum.

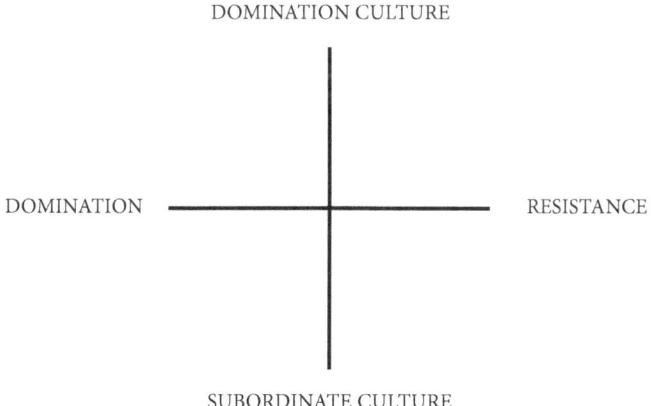

Figure 4.2 Axis Relationship between Culture and Power.

With this in mind, four major response patterns related directly to the biculturation process can be identified: alienation, dualism, separatism, and negotiation. Responses categorized under *cultural alienation* reflect those that suggest an internalized identification with the dominant culture and a rejection of the primary culture. Some examples of alienation include a bicultural student's exclusive preference for identifying herself/himself as "American" or seen as "acting white," refusal to speak their primary language, belief in the inferiority of their primary culture, and denial of the existence of racism. A *cultural dualist* (or non-negotiation) response pattern is informed by a perception of having two separate identities: one that is identified with the primary cultural community, and one tied to acceptance of mainstream institutional values. An example of a dualist response is found among members of an all–Black social club who embrace the practices and values of the dominant culture's elitist ideology. The *cultural separatist* response pattern identifies those responses associated with remaining strictly within the boundaries of the primary culture while adamantly rejecting the dominant culture. A cultural nationalist group's responses geared toward complete self-sufficiency for its members, outside of the dominant culture, represent an example of this mode. The cultural negotiation response pattern reflects attempts to mediate, reconcile, and integrate the reality of lived experiences in an effort to retain the primary cultural identity and orientation while also functioning within the dominant culture for social transformation of the society at large. Examples of cultural negotiation are present in community struggles for bilingual education or immigration rights within the United States. It must be stressed that these patterns are conceptualized within a social domain that can be conceptualized as a *sphere of biculturalism* (see Figure 4.3).

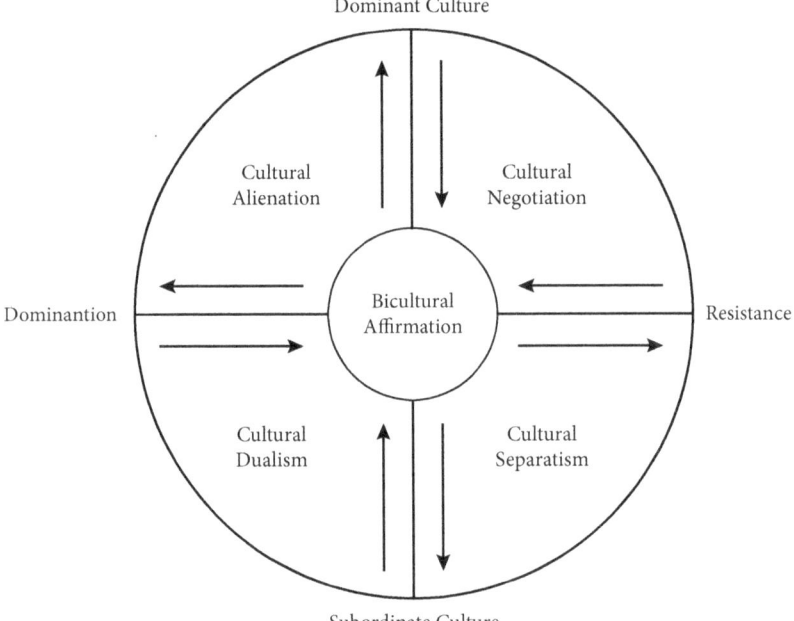

Figure 4.3 Sphere of Biculturalism.

As such, these four patterns reflect major modes of engagement that are directly influenced by power relations that result from the axis relationship between culture and power. Within such a sphere of biculturalism, student responses can also be considered with respect to the degree that they can function within a context of *bicultural affirmation*. For example, cultural alienation and cultural separatist responses move the individual away from bicultural affirmation responses, in that they require a conscious or unconscious denial of the primary culture or the dominant culture in which the individuals must survive. In this sense, alienation responses tend to move the bicultural student more exclusively toward the context of the dominant culture, while cultural separatist responses tend to move the student more exclusively toward the primary (subordinate) cultural context.

On the other hand, cultural dualism and cultural negotiation responses, which result from some effort to contend with the reality of both the dominant and subordinate cultural realities, are more likely to result in moving student consciousness toward bicultural affirmation. It might be helpful to point out here that there are some scholars who prefer to use such terms as *hybridity* or *hybrid identity* (Suárez Orozco, 1998; Gutiérrez, Baquedano-López & Tejeda, 1999; Tate, 2005) or *panethnic identity* (Espiritu, 1993; Ricourt & Danta, 2002) or *biracial identity* (O'Hearn, 1998; Shankar, 1998; Root, 1999; Rockquemore & Brunsma, 2002; Womack & Dingle, 2010) when referring to many aspects similar to those that are integrated into a critical theory of biculturalism.

Nevertheless, what is key here is that educators remain mindful of the forces of hegemony that are constantly at work in shaping material conditions and the shifting social relations that shape the bicultural experience within the United States. Hence, just as other cultural response modes cannot be essentialized, responses which might seem to serve bicultural affirmation may not necessarily result in supporting the emancipatory interests of bicultural students. Examples of this were evident in the uneven manner in which multicultural programs were practised. Nevertheless, it is safe to say that bicultural affirmation response patterns may hold the greatest emancipatory promise for both individuals and communities, with respect to the struggle for cultural democracy in schools.

Also vital to an understanding of biculturalism is recognition of the relationship that exists between cultural response patterns, modes of engagement (thinking), and cultural identity (see Table 4.1). Here again, it is helpful to utilize the four previously

Table 4.1 Relationship of Cultural Response Pattern, Modes of Engagement, and Cultural Identity.

Cultural Response Pattern	Mode of Engagement	Cultural Idenlity	
		Individual	Social
Alienation	Absolute	Dominant	Dominant
Dualism	Dichotomized	Primary	Dominant
Separatism	Absolute	Primary	Primary
Negotiation	Critical	Primary	Bicultural

discussed response patterns to illustrate the dynamics inherent in the relationship between these three variables. In addition, the variable of cultural identity is presented with respect to both an individual and a social subcategory.

Cultural alienation and separatist responses, commonly reflective of a mode of engagement associated with absolute thinking, generally seek to negate, eliminate, or move away from the tension, conflict, and contradictions that result from cultural differences. This mode of engagement reinforces a form of cultural identity that is also absolute or totalizing in nature. Hence, an alienation response pattern is commonly associated with individuals who espouse an exclusive identification with the dominant culture, whereas cultural separatism response patterns are associated with individuals who tend to embrace an exclusively primary cultural identity. A dichotomized mode of engagement generally results in dualism response patterns, which are likely to result from a cultural identity that is also dichotomized between the primary culture and the dominant culture. It is important to note that although the dualist context acknowledges the existence of both cultures, its dichotomized mode of engagement also results in undialectical responses due to its efforts to avoid or deny the tension and contradictions that result from cultural conflicts. Cultural negotiation response patterns most commonly result from a critical mode of engagement that seeks to contend with the tension and contradictions inherent in cultural differences and conflicts. This mechanism functions to affirm a bicultural social identity while sustaining an unambiguous individual identification with the primary culture.

Although these categories can assist educators to understand better the dynamics of the biculturation process, it is critical to remember that these patterns are not fixed. Given the contradictory nature of human consciousness and the complexity of the survival mechanisms that motivate these response patterns, bicultural students will exhibit many different variations of tactical responses, depending on the extent of their primary cultural socialization; the degree of their bilingualism; their personal and collective tensions related to class, gender, sexuality, and ability; their consistent association with other bicultural students with schools; the teacher's cultural and political orientations; the degree of peer pressure; institutional constraints; and a myriad of other social and economic variables.

In many ways, this concept of bicultural consciousness echoes certain aspects of Sandoval's (2000) notion of "differential consciousness" found in her writings on US Third World feminism. What Sandoval's work harkens is "a new subjectivity, a political revision that denie[s] any one [fixed identity] as the final answer, while instead positing a *tactical subjectivity* with the capacity to de- and re-center, given the forms of power" (p. 59) that must be engaged or confronted by students.

> Differential consciousness requires grace, flexibility, and strength: enough strength to confidently commit to a well-defined structure of identity for one hour, day, week, month, year; enough flexibility to self-consciously transform that identity according to the requisites of another oppositional ideological tactic if readings of power formation require it; enough grace to recognize alliance with others committed to egalitarian social relations of race, gender, and class justice, when readings of power call for alternative oppositional stands.
>
> (p. 60)

From this discussion, it should be readily apparent that some of the response patterns described previously incorporate principles set forth in the various bicultural theories discussed previously. But the critical bicultural perspective proposed here attempts to challenge reductionist and deterministic influences that shape many of the earlier and current theories of biculturalism. If educators are to meet the pedagogical needs of bicultural students, they must recognize the ideological foundations that shape bicultural responses and the contradictions and tensions that result from students' efforts to survive in the midst of serious forms of educational oppression.

In contrast to notions of biculturalism that define it as a more deliberate and volitional phenomenon, here it is argued that, whether or not a student from a subordinate culture perceives him- or herself as a *bicultural being*, the fact that the working-class student from a subordinate culture is raised within the sociocultural and class constraints dictated by the dominant culture locates that student, from a sociopolitical standpoint, in a culturally subordinate position within the school and society. It is the pervasive quality of hegemonic control that so often obscures the truth of this reality, particularly for those bicultural individuals who perceive themselves as adjusting successfully to the social constraints through their identification with the culture of the oppressor (Freire, 1970) or what Fordham (1991, 1988) at one point in her work termed "racelessness" or "acting white." This, again, emphasizes the importance of educators to examine critically bicultural responses in terms of resistance, particularly when these responses fail to result in behaviors, attitudes, or relationships that empower bicultural students by preparing them to engage as full subjects in their world.

As a consequence of traditional pedagogical theories and practices, working-class bicultural students often face isolation, alienation, and despair in public schools because few opportunities exist for these students to reflect together on their collective histories and lived experiences, and to explore critically how these experiences relate to their participation in the larger society and to their process of emancipation. Instead, student voices are often silenced, as "the discourse of the other" is systematically ignored in the process of schooling (Giroux, 1988b). If the bicultural voice is to be awakened and students of color are to become active social agents in the world, educators must create the conditions for a genuine form of cultural democracy to take root in the classroom—one that not only creates the space for all aspects of their humanity to be expressed but also allows their cultural particularities to be in critical conversation with the universal human dimensions that are also vital to their identities and relationships with others.

A Philosophy of Cultural Democracy

In an effort to develop a critical theory of cultural democracy, it is useful to first examine Ramirez and Castañeda's (1974) philosophy of cultural democracy for the bilingual classroom. One of the primary objectives of their work is to challenge the negative effects of what they term the "Anglo conformity/assimilation ideology" of the melting-pot theory, which—by implication—reduces all other cultural forms to one of inferior value, status, and importance. Hence, their notion of cultural democracy argues that an individual can be bicultural and still be loyal to American [democratic] ideals. Cultural democracy is a philosophical precept which recognizes that the way a person communicates, relates to others, seeks support and recognition from his [and her] environment... and thinks and learns. [Cognition] is a product of the value system of the home and community. Furthermore, educational environments or policies that do not recognize the individual's right, as guaranteed by the Civil Rights Act of 1964, to remain identified with the culture and language of his cultural group, are culturally undemocratic.

(p. 23)

More specifically, a philosophy of cultural democracy argues for the right of each individual to be educated in her or his own language and learning style, which, according to Ramirez and Castañeda, has been found to be integrated with one's language community. This also implies that all children have the right to maintain a bicultural identity—that is, the right to retain their identification with their culture of origin while simultaneously adopting American values and an American lifestyle. This philosophy encourages institutions to develop learning milieus, curriculum materials, and teaching strategies that are sensitive to the child's cultural orientation, and thus language and cognitive styles (Hernandez, Haug, & Wagner, 1976).

Furthermore, the education of bicultural students within the context of a culturally democratic environment is considered by Valverde (1978) to support five specific purposes for students and the school:

1. reducing language and educational disabilities through the opportunity to learn in one's native language;
2. reinforcing the relations of the school and the home through a common bond;
3. projecting the individual into an atmosphere of personal identification;
4. giving the student a base for success in the field of work; and
5. preserving and enriching the cultural and human resources of a people.

In contrast to the "exclusionist Anglo conformity" view, Ramirez and Castañeda characterize the culturally democratic environment as one that

1. considers the student's language, heritage, cultural values, and learning styles as educationally important;
2. views the home culture as determining unique communication, relational, incentive motivational, and cognitive styles and utilizes these styles as a basis for teacher training;
3. recognizes the child's personality as acceptable and as a means whereby the child can explore new cultural forms related to communication, human relations, incentive motivation, and cognition;
4. works to change the educational style of the school through greater parent participation, new teaching strategies, curriculum development, and assessment of techniques; and
5. holds as one of its major goals the child's formation of a bicultural identity.

Despite the many contributions of Ramirez and Castañeda's philosophy of cultural democracy to the field of bicultural education and its promise as a politicizing educational construct, it nonetheless lacks many of the critical qualities essential to the education of bicultural students as members of a subordinate culture. The deficits of the model are most apparent in the fact that it can too easily deteriorate into a positivist instrumentalist modality that perceives culture as predictable, deterministic, neutral, oversimplified, and at moments even relativistic in nature. And although it argues for changing the cultural realities of classrooms, it fails to address critically the necessary shift in power relationships required in schools and society, in order to involve bicultural students in an active process of empowerment, one that can assist them to effectively find their voice, enhance their intellectual formation, and support their development of both individual and collective identity and political solidarity.

Critical Democracy and the Process of Schooling

In an effort to expand on the emancipatory intent of Ramirez and Castañeda's philosophy of cultural democracy, it is helpful to examine the concept of *critical democracy*, particularly as it relates to the process of schooling. This would provide the critical dimension that is missing in the work of Ramirez and Castañeda and can be useful in specifically addressing the relationship of democracy to notions of student participation and solidarity, as well as the development of voice in the process of schooling.

The term "democracy" is derived from the Greek words *demos* and *kratos*, meaning rule by the people or the many; in addition, because there were so many poor in Greece, it was taken to mean rule by the poor. Hence, despite the fact that democracy seldom has been equated with overt social conflict, historically it has never been realized without dissent and struggle, and that struggle has always been associated with social and economic equalities (Arblaster, 1987). Even today, the American struggle for democracy and equality, particularly in the classroom, continues to be reflected along the lines of social class and racialized inequalities.

The recognition of democracy as a site of struggle is one of the most important principles of a theory of cultural democracy, where the struggle is focused directly on the issue of culture and power and who controls cultural truths. Unfortunately, democracy in the United States often has been reduced simplistically to an unqualified principle of majority rule, enacted primarily through the electoral process—while simultaneously the voices of minority groups are systematically silenced within the larger society. Paul Carr (2010), in *Does Your Vote Count: Critical Pedagogy and Democracy*, expresses concern for the manner in which the electoral process too often is utilized both to silence the voices of marginalized populations and to justify the existence of inequalities, as if all members of US society were equally situated, with power and privilege, to influence policies and practices that impact the education of their children. Instead, Carr asserts:

> It would be an affront to all people, including aboriginal/indigenous peoples, marginalized groups, and those traditionally kept out of decision making circles,

if the act of voting could stifle debate about what democracy is simply because elections have provided people with a supposed "free choice." Democracy must be constantly worked and reworked, with less dependence on the formal process and cycle of elections, and it must consider how a more humane, decent, meaningful society can be constructed, outside of the trappings of power elites and constitutional maneuvers that trivialize the aspirations of all people.

(p. 5)

When the power of "majority rule" prevails in the classroom or the larger society, minority interests, views, and convictions are generally disregarded in the process of decision making, and certain groups are permanently relegated to a marginal position. Unfortunately, such an understanding of democracy is likely to become unstable and lose legitimacy in the eyes of its citizens. This becomes so because democracy cannot function where there does not exist room to organically develop a common will or common interest, and this cannot develop where a foundation of both social and economic equality is missing. Arblaster (1987) addresses this need more specifically in his writings on democracy:

[Democracy] needs a foundation not only of shared values but also of shared experience, so that people identify with the political system to which they belong, and can trust its procedures and outcomes. This means not only that those procedures are seen and felt to be fair. It is also necessary that no significant minorities feel themselves to be permanently excluded from power and influence; that groups and individuals sense that they are roughly equal in their ability to influence the outcome of communal policymaking; and that those outcomes embody what people recognize to be the general interests of society rather than merely the combination or balance of the interests of various particular and organized groups or specific interest.

(p. 78)

From this perspective, it can be better understood why gross and excessive forms of inequality existing in the process of American schooling threaten the coherence of society and hence negate the principles of equality, of which democracy is an expression. It also clearly supports the notion that the contradiction between an espoused theory of democracy and a lived experience of inequality (and the obvious diffusion of power that results) is greatly responsible for the growing social tensions existing in the relationship between subordinate cultural groups and public schooling, whose pedagogical aim centers around the perpetuation of cultural domination and technocratic control. And as a further consequence, it is precisely this form of social disequilibrium that also functions effectively to prevent the concrete development of a genuine common interest and a spirit of solidarity among different groups in society. John Dewey (1916), in writing about democratic schooling, addresses the impact that this form of inequality has on students:

In order to have a large number of values in common, all members of the group must have an equitable opportunity to receive and to take from others. There must be a large variety of shared undertakings and experiences. Otherwise, the influences which educate some into masters educate others into slaves. And the experience of each party loses in meaning when the free interchange of varying modes of life experience is arrested .... [This] lack of free equitable intercourse which springs from a variety of shared interests makes intellectual stimulation unbalanced .... The more activity is restricted to a few definite lines—as it is when there are rigid class [cultural] lines preventing adequate interplay of experiences—the more action tends to become routine on the part of the class at a disadvantage, and capricious, aimless, and explosive on the part of the class having the materially fortunate position.

(pp. 84–5)

Dewey also argues formidably that schooling in the United States should function to develop in students an ethical foundation for their participation in the democratic process and a critical understanding of democracy as a moral ideal. Such knowledge establishes a sense of community and struggle for principles like freedom, liberty, and common good. But for schools to meet this challenge, Dewey proposes that educators create environments where mutual interests are clearly recognized as the basic factor in social control, and where a commitment exists to continuously readjust as necessary when new situations produced by a variety of social discourses arise. He believes an essential step in deconstructing the "fear of intercourse with others" is to permit conflict between students to occur, thereby enabling them to learn from each other and expand their understanding of the world. In this context, Dewey (1916) defines democracy as:

primarily a mode of associated living, of conjoint communicated experience. The extension in space of the numbers of individuals who participate in an interest so that each has to refer [her or] his own action to that of others and to consider the action of others to give point and direction to his [or her] own is equivalent to the breaking down of those barriers of class, race, and national territory which kept men [and women] from perceiving the full import of their activity. These more numerous and more varied points of contact denote a greater diversity of stimuli to which an individual has to respond; they consequently put a premium on variation in [her or] his action. They secure a liberation of powers which remain suppressed as long as the invitations to action are partial, as they must be in a group which in its exclusiveness shuts out many interests.

(p. 87)

This notion of schools as apprenticeships in democracy is also shared by Freire. In *Education for Critical Consciousness,* Freire (1973) points to the "habit of submission" that curtails subordinate classes from seeking to integrate themselves with reality, which, he argues, results from a phenomenon of socially conditioned dependency and a lack of experience with participation in the democratic process. He argues that it is only through participation in an educational climate in which open dialogue is fostered that students can develop the skills for critical engagement with their world and a genuine sense of participation in a common democratic life.

Thus, Freire posits this axiom: Without dialogue, self-government cannot exist. Here, he speaks to the notion of the free and creative consciousness that results from dialogue, indispensable to authentically democratic environments. He elaborates on the relationship of democracy and this idea of "transitive consciousness":

> Democracy requires dialogue, participation, political and social responsibility, as well as a degree of social and political solidarity .... Before it becomes a political form, democracy is a form of life, characterized above all by a strong component of transitive consciousness. Such transitivity can neither appear nor develop except as men [and women] are launched into debate, participating in the examination of common problems.
>
> (pp. 28–9)

From this standpoint, it also becomes evident that a student's ability to participate and enter into dialogue within the classroom and, as a result, participate in a democratic social process in the world is also critically connected to the development of voice—that is, voice as it relates to the variety of ways by which students actively participate in dialogue and attempt to make themselves heard and understood, as well as the manner in which they define themselves as social beings. Giroux (1988b) describes this concept of student voice in the following way:

> Voice refers to the principles of dialogue as they are enunciated and enacted within particular social settings. The concept of voice represents the unique instances of self-expression through which students affirm their own class, culture, racial, and gender identities. A student's voice is necessarily shaped by personal history and distinctive lived engagement with the surrounding culture. The category of voice, then, refers to the means at our disposal—the discourses available to use—to make ourselves understood and listened to, and to define ourselves as active participants in the world .... The concept of voice ... provides an important basis for constructing and demonstrating the fundamental imperatives of a critical democracy.
>
> (p. 199)

The notion of student voice is fundamental to the struggle for democracy and equality in the classroom, particularly as it relates to the development of voice in students of color. It is connected to the control of power and the legitimation of specific student discourses as acceptable truths or rejected fallacies, and consequently determines who speaks and who is silenced. When working-class bicultural students are consistently silenced in the process of their schooling, they often are trapped in classrooms with teachers who not only prevent them from finding their voice but also thwart their organic and contextual understanding of how what they are learning in the classroom can be used to transform their lives. As a result, they are conditioned into a state of dependency on a system that they do not understand (nor which respects them) and are unable to influence because they lack the critical skills and the social- and self-empowerment necessary to make their needs, interests, and concerns heard. This, then, leads to a form of social isolation that prevents the development of a sense of community and solidarity and negates any possibility for a genuine process of democracy to take place in society.

Giroux (1988b), in his articulation of voice and active citizenship, speaks to the kind of environment teachers must cultivate in the classroom to prevent the silencing of students:

> Organize classroom relationships so that students can draw on and confirm those dimensions of their own histories and experiences that are deeply rooted in the surrounding community .... assume pedagogical responsibility for attempting to understand the relationships and forces that influence students outside the immediate context of the classroom .... develop curricula and pedagogical practices around those community traditions, histories, and forms of knowledge that are often ignored within the dominant school culture .... create the conditions where students come together to speak, to engage in dialogue, to share their stories, and to struggle together within social relations that strengthen rather than weaken possibilities for active citizenship [and democracy].
>
> (pp. 199–201)

What emerges from this discussion on democracy and the process of schooling are the fundamental principles on which to develop further a critical theory of cultural democracy. Central to any theory that seeks to speak to the notion of democracy in the classroom is the requirement that it address seriously the themes of student participation, solidarity, common interest, and the development of voice (hooks, 1994, 1989). It is not enough to focus on specific cultural and/or cognitive determinants or questions related to curricular content. This is not to say that certain aspects of these educational concerns are not vital to a bicultural pedagogy, but rather to emphasize that these alone will not necessarily ensure a democratic environment.

If bicultural students are to become competent in the democratic process, they must be given the opportunity to experience it and live it actively, as it gradually becomes a part of their personal history. But this can only be accomplished if a culturally democratic educational environment exists, one in which students may participate actively and freely. It must also be one where they will receive the consistent support and encouragement required for them to develop their bicultural voice, so they may learn to use it toward their collective empowerment and emancipation. This is to say that the process of awakening the bicultural voice requires a culturally democratic process and loving community, in which students not only feel heard but also feel free to talk—and to talk back (hooks, 1989).

Awakening the Bicultural Voice

The concept of voice constitutes one of the most important democratic principles of student empowerment and the evolving ability to participate in and influence the manner in which power is relegated in society—so much so that any theory of cultural democracy must specifically consider the development of voice as it relates to the pedagogical needs of bicultural students. This is particularly significant given the forces of hegemony and cultural invasion at work in the manner that bicultural students perceive themselves, their communities, and their ability to participate in the world.

As suggested in the previous section, students can only develop their voice through opportunities to enter into dialogue and engage in a critical process of reflection from which they can share their thoughts, ideas, and lived experiences with others in an open and free manner. Herein lies a necessary ingredient so often missing in the classroom experience of bicultural students. Again, this generally occurs because the dominant pedagogy of American schools predominantly reflects the values, worldview, and belief system of the dominant culture and class, while neglecting or ignoring the lived experiences of subordinate cultures (Diaz Greenberg, 2003; Rubin & Silva, 2003; Rabow, 2006; Vuckovi, 2008). Hence, students of color are silenced and their bicultural experiences negated and ignored, while they are systematically educated into the discourse of the dominant culture—an ethnocentric ideology that perceives the discourse of the other as inferior, invaluable, and deficient in regard to the aims of American society. This manifests itself in various forms of cultural invasion that, consciously or unconsciously, teach bicultural students to deny their lived cultures and their bicultural voice, and to take on uncritically the ideology of the dominant culture.

In light of the hegemonic forces active in the hidden curriculum and in classroom relations, the bicultural voice can seldom develop within the school context unless students of color receive the opportunity to enter into dialogue with one another. It is primarily through the dynamics of the *bicultural dialogue* that students can come together to reflect on the common lived experiences of their bicultural process and their common responses to issues of cultural resistance, alienation, negotiation, affirmation, and oppression. In this way, bicultural students begin to break through the rigidly held perspectives that can result when those who hold power inauthentically name their experience for them. Also important to this process is the role of the bicultural educator who functions as guide, model, and support, and who facilitates the critical (and often fearful) journey into the previously prohibited terrain of the bicultural discourse—a discourse that is so often only felt or sensed, but seldom articulated, within the classroom.

Despite this pedagogical need, most teachers of color, unfortunately, repeat the educational patterns they experienced as children and later learned in teacher education programs. Hence, what generally occurs in many classrooms is the inadvertent silencing of the bicultural experience by teachers who have been trained to concentrate their efforts on creating an inauthentic climate of cohesion, conformity, and harmony. By doing so, they fail to involve bicultural students in their own learning and to provide opportunities for them to enter into dialogue regarding the cultural conflicts and social contradictions they experience in the classroom and in their communities.

It is precisely in meeting the students' need to participate in bicultural dialogue with others that the bicultural teacher can most provide assistance in facilitating the process across this terrain of struggle, and thus cultivate through a critical process with students a spirit of possibility and empowerment (Nieto, 1999/2009, 2002/2010, 2005;

Darder, 2002). Bicultural educators who have found their own voice can provide an effective *bicultural mirror*, through which they can validate, support, and encourage students going through this process during moments of cognitive disequilibrium. These teachers can also help bicultural students discover a language that accurately describes the feelings, ideas, and observations that previously have not fit into any of the definitions of experience provided by the dominant educational discourse. Above all, this represents a critical effort to assist students in integrating themselves as complete human beings in the world by recognizing the truths embedded in their personal reflections and the substance of their everyday lives—in essence, to awaken the bicultural voice. The development of voice and social empowerment go hand in hand as bicultural students peel away the layers of oppression and denial, undergo a deconstruction of the conditioned definitions of who they are, and emerge with a sense of their existence as historically situated social agents who can utilize their understanding of their world and themselves to enter into dialogue with those who are culturally different.

At this point, it is imperative to note that this does not mean that the bicultural voice is the only voice bicultural students need. But it does suggest that it represents a major step toward their self-empowerment because it is the voice most intimately linked to their personal identity and their "authority of experience" (hooks, 1994, p. 81). Furthermore, it is by way of the bicultural voice that students can develop the self-empowerment required to participate in the collective public voice—a voice that must be built around a collaborative effort and commitment of the many to examine critically their collective lived experiences so that together they might discover the common good. In this manner, bicultural students can also develop the ability, confidence, and desire to acknowledge the similarities, honor the differences, examine the possibilities, and struggle openly with a genuine spirit of solidarity in the context of a complex and ever-changing multicultural society.

The role of the Euroamerican educator in the development of the bicultural voice is also significant to this discussion. Often the white teacher is one of the few people from the dominant culture with whom working-class bicultural students have any contact on a regular basis. Consequently, the white teacher can become for the bicultural student the primary reflection of not only public institutions but also the society at large. How conscious teachers are of this phenomenon, as well as of the histories and stories of the bicultural communities in which bicultural students reside, is fundamental to their ability to assist students in developing their voice. White educators who are working with bicultural students must first come to acknowledge their own limitations, prejudices, and biases, and must be willing to enter into dialogue with their students in a spirit of humility and with respect for the knowledge that students bring to the classroom (Pearce, 2005; Howard, 2006; Bartolomé, 2007; Landsman & Lewis, 2007).

Despite how well-meaning many teachers may be, often it is at this juncture of power (and control) that they fail bicultural students. This commonly occurs because any genuine acknowledgment of one's limitations is closely related to letting go of the control (power) associated with knowing (or authority), and in the process permitting the student to teach the teacher (Freire, 1970). This process truly requires the teacher to engage more horizontally and, in so doing, create conditions that empower students.

This is achieved by critically engaging, challenging, and affirming students, and by incorporating into the classroom the knowledge that bicultural students bring about self and community. The emphasis here is placed on the recognition that the white critical educator has much to learn from as well as to teach bicultural students in the context of a culturally democratic classroom. Teachers can discover from bicultural students how they feel, think, dream, and live. In turn, they can provide for their students the opportunity to develop critical academic skills, examine their histories, reflect on the world, and engage in dominant educational discourses as free social agents with the potential to influence and transform their individual and collective conditions.

Most important to any educational theory of cultural democracy is recognition by the educator—regardless of her or his class, culture, or ethnic identity—of the emancipatory needs of working-class students of color. In order for bicultural students to develop critical skills in the classroom, there must first exist a culturally democratic environment where students find opportunities to participate freely with others as they enact pre-existing and developing "funds of knowledge" (Moll, et al., 1992; González, et al., 2005) within the classroom. This critical pedagogical process constitutes the integration of cultural knowledge that is tied to important values and social practices necessary to understanding how society works, where students are located within society, and what opportunities or inequalities are at play in their lives. Educators must also remain conscious of the fact that bicultural students shape and are shaped by their cultural values, as well as by their constant struggles to survive within the myriad of cultural contradictions they face each day.

References

Arblaster, A. (1987), *Democracy*. Minneapolis, MN: University of Minnesota Press.
Bartolome, L. (2007), *Ideologies in Education: Unmasking the Trap of Teacher Neutrality*. Bel Air, MD: Peter Lang.
Blauner, R. (1972), *Racial Oppression in America*. New York, NY: Harper & Row.
Carr, P. (2010), *Does Your Vote Count? Critical Pedagogy and Democracy*. New York, NY: Peter Lang.
Chapman, F. (2002), *Race, Identity and Myth in the Spanish Speaking Caribbean: Essays on Biculturalism as a Contested Terrain of Difference*. Santo Domingo, Domingo Republic: Chapman and Associates.
Chau, K. L. (1991), *Ethnicity and Biculturalism: Emerging Perspectives in Social Group Work*. New York, NY: Haworth.
Cronin, S., ed. (2008), *Soy Bilingue: Adult Dual Language Model for Early Childhood and Elementary Teacher Education*. Seattle, WA: Center for Linguistic and Cultural Democracy.
Cronin, S., and Masso, C. (2003), *Soy Bilingue Seminar Workbook*. Seattle, WA: Center for Linguistic and Cultural Democracy.
Cross, W. E. (1978), "The Thomas and Cross Models on Psychological Nigrescence: A Literature Review." *Journal of Black Psychology* 5(1): 13–31.
Darder, A. (2002), *Reinventing Paulo Freire: A Pedagogy of Love*. Boulder, CO: Westview Books.

DeAnda, D. (1984), "Bicultural Socialization: Factors Affecting the Minority Experience". *Social Work* 29(2): 101–7.
Dennis, R. (2008), *Biculturalism*. Stamford, CT: JAI Press.
Dewey, J. (1916), *Democracy and Education*. New York, NY: The Macmillan Group.
Diaz-Greenberg, R. (2003), *The Emergence of Voice in Latino/a High School Students*. New York, NY: Peter Lang.
Diaz-Soto, L., and Haroon, K. (2010), *Teaching Bilingual/Bicultural Children*. New York, NY: Peter Lang.
Dixon, V., and Foster, B. (1971), *Beyond Black or White*. Boston, MA: Little Brown.
Doerr, N. M. (2009), *Meaningful Inconsistencies: Bicultural Nationhood, the Free Market, and Schooling in Aotearoa/New Zealand*. Oxford: Berghahn Books.
Du Bois, W. E. B. (1903), *The Souls of Black Folk*. Chicago, IL: A. C. McClurg.
Espiritu, Y. L. (1993), *Asian American Panethnicity: Bridging Institutions and Identities*. Philadelphia, PA: Temple University Press.
Fanon, F. (1952), *Black Skin, White Masks*. New York, NY: Grove Press.
Fordham, S. (1988), "Racelessness as a Factor in Black Student Success: Pragmatic Strategy or Pyrrhic Victory." *Harvard Educational Review* 58(1): 176–296.
Fordham, S. (1991), "Racelessness in Private Schools: Should We Deconstruct the Racial and Cultural Identity of African-American Adolescents." *Teachers College Record* 92(3): 470–84.
Freire, P. (1970), *Pedagogy of the Oppressed*. New York, NY: Seabury Press.
Freire, P. (1973), *Education for Critical Consciousness*. New York, NY: Seabury Press.
Giroux, H. (1988), *Schooling and the Struggle for Public Life*. Minneapolis, MN: University of Minnesota Press.
Gonzalez, N., Moll, L. C., and Amanti, C. (2005), *Funds of Knowledge: Theorizing Practices in Households, Communities, and Classrooms*. Mahwah, NJ: Lawrence Erlbaum Associates.
Gutierrez, K., Baquedano-Lopez, P., and Tejeda, C. (1999), "Rethinking Diversity: Hybridity and Hybrid Language Practices in the Third Space." *Mind, Culture, and Activity* 6(4): 286–303.
Hepi (2008), *Pakeha Identity and Māori Language and Culture: Bicultural Identity and Language in New Zealand*. Saarbrucken: VDM Verlag.
Hernandez, C., Haug, M., and Wagner, N., eds. (1976), *Chicanos: Social and Psychological Perspectives*. St. Louis: Mosby.
hooks, b. (1989), *Talking Back*. Boston, MA: South End Press.
hooks, b. (1994), *Teaching to Transgress: Education as the Practice of Freedom*. New York, NY: Routledge.
Howard, G. R. (2006), *You Can't Teach What You Don't Know: White Teachers, Multicultural Schools*. New York, NY: Teachers College Press.
Hsu, F. (1971), *The Challenge of the American Dream: The Chinese in the United States*. Belmont, CA: Wadsworth.
Kanno, Y. (2003), *Negotiating Bilingual Bicultural Identities: Japanese Returnees Betwixt Two Worlds*. New York, NY: Routledge.
Kitano, H. (1969), *Japanese-Americans: The Evolution of a Subculture*. Englewood Cliffs, NJ: Prentice-Hall.
LaFramboise, T., Coleman, H., and Gerton, J. (1993), "Psychological Impact of Biculturalism: Evidence and Theory." *Psychological Bulletin* 114(3): 395–412.

Landsman, J., and Lewis, C. (2007), *White Teachers/Diverse Classrooms: A Guide to Building Inclusive Schools, Promoting High Expectations, and Eliminating Racism*. Sterling, VA: Stylus Publishing.

Lomawaima, K., and McCarty, T. (2006), *To Remain an Indian: Lessons in Democracy from a Century of Native American Education*. New York, NY: Teachers College Press.

Memmi, A. (1965), *The Colonizer and the Colonized*. Boston, MA: Beacon Press.

Moll, L. C., Amanti, C., Neff, D., and Gonzalez, N. (1992), "Funds of Knowledge for Teaching: Using a Qualitative Approach to Connect Homes and Classrooms." *Theory into Practice* 31(2): 132–41.

Nieto, S. (1999/2010), *The Light in Their Eyes: Creating Multicultural Learning Communities*. New York, NY: Routledge.

Nieto, S. (2002/2010), *Language, Culture, and Teaching: Critical Perspectives*, vol. 2. New York, NY: Routledge.

Nieto, S. (2005), *Why We Teach*. New York, NY: Teachers College Press.

O'Hearn, C. C., ed. (1998), *Half and Half: Writers on Growing Up Biracial and Bicultural*. New York, NY: Pantheon.

Olivos, E. (2006), *The Power of Parents: A Critical Perspective of Bicultural Parent Involvement in the Public Schools*. New York, NY: Peter Lang Publishers.

Pearce, S. (2005), *You Wouldn't Understand: White Teachers in Multi-Ethnic Classrooms*. Sterling, VA: Trentham Books.

Rabow, J. (2006), *Voices of Pain and Voices of Hope: Students Speak about Racism*. Dubuque, IA: Kendall Hunt.

Ramirez, M., and Castañeda, A. (1974), *Cultural Democracy: Bicognitive Development and Education*. New York, NY: Academic Press

Rashid, H. (1981), "Early Childhood Education as a Cultural Transition for African-American Children." *Educational Research Quarterly* 6(3): 55–63.

Redhorse, J. G., Lewis, M., Feit, M., and Decker, J. (1981), "Family Behavior of Urban American Indians," in R. Dana (ed.), *Human Services for Cultural Minorities*. Baltimore, MD: University Park Press, 67–72.

Ricourt, M., and Danta, R. (2002), *Hispanics de Queens: Latino Panethnicity in a New York City Neighborhood*. Ithaca, NY: Cornell University Press.

Rockquemore, K., and Brunsma, D. (2002), *Beyond Black: Biracial Identity in America*. Thousand Oaks, CA: Sage Publishers.

Rodriguez, G. (1999), *Raising Nuestros Ninos: Bringing Up Latino Children in a Bicultural World*. Los Angeles, CA: Fireside.

Root, M. P. P. (1999), "The Biracial Baby Boom: Understanding Ecological Constructions of Racial Identity in the 21st Century," in R. H. Sheets and E. R. Hollins (eds.), *Racial and Ethnic Identity in School Practices: Aspects of Human Development*. Mahwah, NJ: Lawrence Erlbaum Associates, 67–89.

Rubin, E., and Silva, B., eds. (2003), *Student Voices in School Reform: Students Living Through Change*. New York, NY: RoutledgeFalmer.

Sandoval, C. (2000), *Methodology of the Oppressed*. Minneapolis: University of Minnesota Press.

Shankar, L. (1998), *A Part/Yet Apart: South Asians in Asian America*. Philadelphia, PA: Temple University Press.

Sheets, R. H. (2005), *Diversity Pedagogy: Examining the Role of Culture in the Teaching-Learning Process*. Boston, MA: Allyn & Bacon.

Sheets R. H., and Hollins, E. R., eds. (1999), *Racial and Ethnic Identities in School Practices: Aspects of Human Development*. Mahwah, NJ: Lawrence Erlbaum Associates.

Smokowski, P., and Bacallao, M. (2011), *Becoming Bicultural: Risk, Resilience, and Latino Youth*. New York, NY: New York University Press.

Solis, A. (1980), "Theory of Biculturality." *Calmecac deAztlan en Los* 1(1): 7–12.

Suarez-Orozco, M., ed. (1998), *Crossings: Mexican Immigration in Interdisciplinary Perspectives*. Cambridge, MA: David Rockefeller Center for Latin American Studies and Harvard University Press.

Sue, S., and Sue, D. W. (1978), "Chinese-American Personality and Mental Health." *Amerasia Journal* 1: 36–49.

Tate, S. A. (2005), *Black Skins, Black Masks: Hybridity, Dialogism, Performativity*. Surrey: Ashgate Publishing.

Tatum, B. D. (1992), "Talking about Race, Learning about Racism: An Application of Racial Identity Development Theory in the Classroom." *Harvard Educational Review* 62(1): 1–24.

Trueba, H. T. (2002), "Multiple Ethnic, Racial, and Cultural Identities in Action: From Marginality to a New Cultural Capital in Modern Capital." *Journal of Latinos and Education* 1(1): 7–28.

Trumbull, E., and Pacheco, M. (2005), *Human Development, Culture and Cognition*. Providence, RI: Brown University Press.

Valentine, C. (1971), "Deficit, Difference, and Bicultural Models of Afro-American Behavior." *Harvard Educational Review* 41(2): 137–57.

Valverde, L. (1978), *Bilingual Education for Latinos*. Washington, DC: Association for Supervision and Curriculum Development.

Vargas-Reighley, R. V. (2005), *Bi-Cultural Competence and Academic Resilience among Immigrants*. El Paso, TX: LBF Scholarly Publishing.

Vuckovi, M. (2008), *Voices from Haskell: Indian Students between Two Worlds, 1884–1928*. Lawrence, KS: University Press of Kansas.

Womack, L., and Dingle, D. T. (2010), *Post Black: How a New Generation Is Redefining African American Identity*. New York, NY: Lawrence Hill Books.

Wright, R. N. (1953), *The Outsider*. New York, NY: Harper & Row.

5

The Politics of Biculturalism: Culture and Difference in the Formation of *Warriors for Gringostroika and the New Mestizas*

There is a whisper within you that reminds me of who I am ...
—Guillermo Gomez-Pena (1993)

The dormant areas of consciousness are being activated, awakened.
—Gloria Anzaldúa (1987)

The yearning to remember who we are is a subject that is rarely discussed in the realms of traditional academic discourse. It is not easily measured or observed by the standard quantification of scientific inquiry, nor is it easily detected in the qualitative dimension of focus groups and ethnographic research methods. It is a deeply rooted quality, obscured by layers upon layers of human efforts to survive the impact of historical amnesia induced by the dominant policies and practices of advanced capitalism and postmodern culture.

For these reasons, efforts to articulate a conclusive politics of biculturalism is a highly complex and messy endeavor. Yet it is significant to note that even the naming of such a phenomenon clearly is linked to an experience of listening to "the whisper within" and giving voice to an unspoken, yet ever-present memory of difference—"dormant areas of consciousness" that must be awakened. This view is readily supported by the fact that despite countless studies and writings about people of color by white researchers, none names or engages the experience of two-worldness or double consciousness. It was not until scholars of color, such as Du Bois (1903), Fanon (1967), Valentine (1971), Ramirez and Castaneda (1974), Solis (1980), Rashid (1981), Red Horse (1981), deAnda (1984), Buriel (1984), and others began to posit specific theoretical frameworks grounded in their own community histories and cultural knowledge that notions of biculturalism began to appear in the discourse of the social sciences and historical studies. These scholars of color during the last thirty years have made significant contributions to an understanding of biculturalism. As a consequence, there has been a slowly, but consistently, emerging body of work that has attempted to give voice to a variety of explanations of bicultural processes and identities. These efforts, to a greater or lesser degree, have discussed the societal and psychological impact of living between two world views. In more recent years, a new wave of critical scholars of color (Darder, 1991; Akinyela, 1992; Millan, 1993; Romay, 1993) in different disciplines has also begun to address the notion of biculturalism in their work.

Toward a Critical Theory of Biculturalism

> *The story never stops beginning or ending. It appears headless and bottomless for it is built on differences* (p. 2).
> —TRINH MINH-HA (1989)

Within a critical theoretical tradition, biculturalism must be understood as a contested terrain of difference. It is upon this highly complex and ambiguous ground that subordinate groups create both a private and public space in which to forge battle with the faces of oppression, while flying high their banners of cultural self-determination. Biculturalism as a critical perspective acknowledges openly and engages forthrightly the significance of power relations in structuring and prescribing societal definitions of truth, rules of normalcy, and notions of legitimacy which often defy and denigrate the cultural existence and lived experiences of subordinate groups.

The story of where, when, and how biculturation processes and identities begin, move, and end is generally a difficult one to recount, given the historical and contextual dimensions which shape the particular survival requirements of different groups at any given moment in their histories. This is to say that each subordinate group grapples with the effects of cultural imperialism according to the manner in which geographical, political, social, and economic forces shape and influence the efforts of members of a group to resist, oppose, negotiate, or even accept passive or voluntary assimilation into the dominant group.

Furthermore, given the wide-reaching effects of advanced capitalism and a deeply rooted tradition of cultural oppression and domination in the United States, African Americans, Chicanos, Puerto Ricans, Native Americans, Asians, and other subordinate cultural groups for the most part exist in a hybridized state. This is to say that their histories of forced interaction with the dominant culture have required consistent forms of adaptational behaviors which have, in many instances, eroded, restructured, and reconstructed the language system, cultural beliefs, and social traditions of these groups.

Michael Omi and Howard Winant (1983a) argue that throughout most of the history of the United States, the discourses of subordinate cultures received very little political legitimacy. "However democratic the United States may have been in other respects, with respect to racial [and cultural] minorities it may be characterized as having been to varying degrees despotic for much of its history" (p. 55). Given a collective history of social marginalization, exploitation, cultural invasion, powerlessness, and systematic violence,[1] all subordinate cultures in this country currently experience an advanced state of hybridization. Understanding this phenomenon requires that we acknowledge the deep historical consequences of being driven out of the dominant political space and relegated to a subordinate position. Black, Indigenous, and mestizo communities across the United States evolved over the last 400 years through their efforts to survive conditions of oppression, develop alternative structures, and resist annihilation of cultural knowledge and traditions.[2]

It cannot be denied that patterns of cultural, economic, and political oppression have been repeated in the international arena wherever European colonizers and their descendants have appropriated the land and resources of indigenous populations. Usurping the people's natural resources, destroying their economic and agricultural self-sufficiency, placing the children in foreign educational environments, devaluing the language community, and interfering with the generational transmission of spiritual knowledge are all common strategies of cultural imperialism. As such, every subordinate cultural group in the United States, to one extent or another, has been required to contend with the destructive impact of all or some of these strategies. Most insidious are the established relationships of domination and dependency which, despite ongoing and persistent group efforts to resist cultural oppression, further complicate the struggle to affirm the cultural integrity and self-determination of subordinate cultural groups.

Rethinking Ethnicity and the Formation of Identity

We will not remain the same. Either we re-make ourselves or we will be remade by others (p. 24).

—Gonzalo Santos (1992)

In many respects, biculturalism entails an ongoing process of identity recovery, construction, and reconstruction driven by collective efforts of subordinate cultural groups to build community solidarity, engage tensions surrounding nationality differences, revitalize the boundaries of subordinate cultures, and redefine the meaning of cultural identity within the current social context (Nagel, 1994). Furthermore, this phenomenon is influenced by the persistent efforts of those who have been historically marginalized to establish a sense of place from which to struggle against relations of domination. Along the same lines, Stuart Hall (1990a) argues that a notion of ethnicity is required in order to truly engage the relationship between identity and difference.

> There is no way, it seems to me, in which people of the world can act, can speak, can create, can come in from the margins and talk, can begin to reflect on their own experience unless they come from some place, they come from some history, they inherit certain cultural traditions. What we've learned about the theory of enunciation is that there's no enunciation without positionality. You have to position yourself somewhere in order to say anything at all ... the relation that peoples of the world now have to their own past is, of course, part of the discovery of their own ethnicity. They need to honor the hidden histories from which they

come. They need to understand the languages which they've been taught not to speak. They need to understand and revalue the traditions and inheritances of cultural expression and creativity. And in that sense, the past is not only a position from which to speak, but it is also an absolutely necessary resource in what one has to say.

(p. 19)

Hall's use of the term *ethnicity* provides us with a framework upon which to rethink the analytical value of ethnicity with respect to biculturalism, particularly as it relates to identity formation. This requires a dialectical reading of ethnicity[3] that, first of all, retrieves the category from the political opportunism and academic domain of neo-conservatives, and secondly, challenges the failure of critical scholars to conceptualize the liberatory dimensions of this category in more fully class-specific terms. Thus, a critical definition of ethnicity is one that engages, in both concept and articulation, a politics of difference and class specificity within the context of a changing economy and postmodern world.

On Essentialism

I voice my ideas without hesitation or fear because I am speaking, finally, about myself (p. 189).

—June Jordan (1992)

In conventional critical debates about culture, there is generally a tremendous uneasiness when there is any effort made to seriously explore notions of cultural consciousness and the merits of knowledge that is rooted in the lived cultural experience of marginalized communities.[4] Often this uneasiness seems to stem most directly from an overarching commitment to protect Western assumptions of individualism, objectivity, and universal truth which deceptively conceal institutionalized structures of entitlement and privilege embedded in critiques of identity politics that, intentionally or unintentionally, function as "the new chic way to silence … marginal groups" (hooks, 1994, p. 83). And though it is true that cultural groups are not entities that exist apart from individuals, neither are they just arbitrary classifications of individuals by attributes which are external to or accidental to their cultural identities.

Group meanings partially constitute people's identities in terms of the cultural forms, social situations, and history that group members know as theirs, because their meanings have been either forced upon them or forged by them or both. Groups are real not as substances, but as forms of social relations A person's sense of history, affinity, and separateness, even the person's mode of reasoning, evaluation, and expressing feelings, are constituted partly by her or his group affinities.

(Young, 1990, pp. 44–5)

Along with the traditional academic anxiety over obliterating the individual as subject are the overzealous denouncements of essentialism whenever scholars of color attempt to grapple with those actual experiences of cultural identity rooted in social and material conditions of racialized relations—experiences that, more often than not, reinforce a strong sense of cultural consciousness and solidarity among members of subordinate cultural communities. There is an expectation that they abdicate the power of their experience, without concern for the fact that "only the powerful can insist on a neat separation between the thought and reality separation that serves them well" (Sampson, 1993, p. 1227). It is not surprising then to note that often critiques of essentialism embody the mistaken dichotomous notion that inquiry focused on subordinate life experiences automatically precludes recognition of in-group differences and cultural change, and amounts to nothing more than the act of reducing culture to a theory of reifying collectivity. As a consequence, scholars of color whose research engages cultural questions in their own communities are often marginalized by the "enlightened" mainstream of their disciplines, while those who are deemed more "open-minded" by Eurocentric standards are permitted to play freely in the arena of intellectual thought.

At this point, it is imperative to stress that I am not suggesting that subjective interpretations of lived experience alone can suffice in the struggle to overcome and transform structural conditions of domination, whether in theory or practice. And further, it cannot be denied that claims to exclusive "authority" derived solely from lived experience can be misused to silence and undermine the possibility of dialogue. Yet, despite these possible dangers, we must find the manner to incorporate in our intellectual work those ways of knowing that are rooted in experience. hooks (1994) addresses this idea eloquently in the following passage from her essay "Essentialism and Experience."

> Though opposed to any essentialist practice that constructs identity in a monolithic, exclusionary way, I do not want to relinquish the power of experience as a standpoint on which to base analysis or formulate theory. For example, I am disturbed when all the courses in black history or literature at some colleges and universities are solely taught by white people, not because I think that they cannot know these realities but that they know them differently. Truthfully, if I had been given the opportunity to study African American critical thought from a progressive black professor instead of the progressive white woman with whom I studied ... I would have chosen the black person. Although I learned a great deal from this white woman professor, I sincerely believe that I would have learned even more from a progressive black professor, because this individual would have brought to the class that unique mixture of experiential and analytical ways of knowing this is a privileged standpoint. It cannot be acquired through books or even distanced observation and study of a particular reality. To me this privileged standpoint does not emerge from "the authority of experience" but rather from the passion of experience, the passion of remembrance.
>
> (p. 90)

Cultural Consciousness and Decolonization

Whereas the colonized usually has only a choice between retraction of his being and a frenzied attempt at identification with the colonizer, the [decolonized] has brought into existence a new, positive, efficient personality, whose richness is provided ... by his certainty that he embodies a decisive moment of [cultural] consciousness (p. 103).
—Frantz Fanon (1964)

It is impossible to arrive at an emancipatory politics of biculturalism without questions of cultural consciousness and knowledge derived from lived experience receiving a rightful place within critical discourses on culture and difference. Likewise, the reality of subordinate groups cannot be sufficiently grasped without a foundational understanding of culture as an epistemological process that is shaped by a complex dialectical relationship of social systems of beliefs and practices which constantly moves members between the dynamic tension of cultural preservation and cultural change. This is to say that no culture (particularly within the Western postmodern context of advanced capitalism) exists as a fixed, static, or absolute entity, since culture, and hence cultural identity, is a relationally constituted phenomenon, activated and produced through constant social negotiation between others and one's own integration in the daily life and history of the community (Epstein, 1987). "It is something that happens over time, that is never absolutely stable, that is subject to the play of history and the play of difference" (Hall, 1990a, p. 15).

Nevertheless, forms of cultural consciousness, grounded in collective memories of historical events, language, social traditions, and community life, exist. This collective experience of affinity that emerges from such forms of cultural knowledge is often echoed in historical discursive accounts of African Americans, Latinos, Native Americans, and Asian Americans in this country. For example, it is not unusual for a person who identifies ethnically with the Latin American cultural experience to readily discuss the differences in affinity experienced when immersed within a Spanish-speaking versus an English-speaking context. This experience of affinity is a powerful connecting and perpetuating force in the lives of members of subordinate cultural groups—a force so strong that it continues to play a significant role in supporting a politics of identity, resistance, self-determination, and cultural nationalism among members of historically disenfranchised cultural communities worldwide.

In light of this, it is no wonder that all strategies of colonial oppression, to one extent or another, function to interfere with cultural community beliefs and practices that foster cultural integrity and cohesion among colonized subjects (Fanon, 1964). This process of cultural subjugation continues within the current so-called post-colonial era. This is readily evident in a multitude of economic, political, legal, educational, and religious institutional policies and practices in the United States aimed at furthering the assimilation process of subordinate groups. More specifically, we see it at work today in the forging of trade agreements that solidify the labor market's exploitation of workers of color, English-only initiatives to interfere with the advancement of bilingualism, covert and overt educational strategies that support cultural domination, laws to prevent particular religious activities of groups who exist outside Judeo-Christian traditions, the current inflammatory politics of immigration control as evidenced in California's passage of Proposition 187, and the worldwide commodification of subordinate cultural forms as multinational profit ventures.

There can be no question that biculturalism in the United States has evolved from a set of conscious and unconscious adaptational strategies to preserve significant dimensions of cultural knowledge and collective identity, adapt to changing material conditions, and resist institutional forms of psychological and physical violence (Young, 1991). In many respects, the bicultural process reflects what Frantz Fanon (1963) describes as a process of decolonization where "the meeting of two forces, opposed to each other by their very nature, which in fact owe their originality to the sort of substantiation which results from and is nourished by [the political and economic context of domination]." Biculturalism can then best be understood as incorporating the complex multilayered realities that shape a people's cultural and material struggle for survival. It is a phenomenon that "is born of violent struggle, consciousness raising and the reconstruction of identities" (West, 1993, p. 15), and one that is most intensely felt within those subordinate cultural contexts that most greatly differ from the established social beliefs, expectations, and norms of the dominant group. As such, subordinate communities continue to be stigmatized by both external and internalized perceptions of inferiority and deficit, whereby their members are, for the most part, viewed as inadequately prepared or socially unfit to enter mainstream American life.

Growing Poverty and the Evasion of Class

[P]olitical [economic] questions are disguised as cultural ones, and as such become insoluble (p. 149).
—Antonio Gramsci (1971)

At this juncture, it must be stressed that the dominant culture and its fabrication of the American middle-class mainstream are clearly driven by the political economy of advanced capitalism, with its overwhelming emphasis on the interests of the marketplace and its "tendency to homogenize rather than diversify human experience" (Wood, 1994, p. 28). Even more important is the recognition that postmodern mechanisms of cultural domination in the United States and abroad are most directly linked to the domination of multinational firms and new international divisions of labor. The impact of these rapidly changing and deepening economic and class relations serves to perpetuate the embroilment of subordinate cultural communities in a fierce struggle for economic survival with fewer and fewer possibilities of self-sufficiency. And despite the growing number of professionals of color and the glossy image portrayal of their success, the majority of American institutions, with their accompanying resources, continue to be overwhelmingly controlled by a cadre of elite white males who are, slowly but steadily, being joined by their female counterparts.

The consequences have resulted in an actual decrease in the proportional wealth and resources of communities of color over the last thirty years (Children's Defense Fund, 1994).[5] This widening economic gap is directly linked to what Xavier Gorostiaga (1993) characterizes as the "dominant fact of our age—growing poverty" (p. 4). In his analysis of a 1992 United Nations report, he explains:

> [T]hroughout the world the last decade has been characterized by the rise of inequality between the rich and the poor ... In 1989 the richest fifth controlled 82.7 percent of the revenue; 81.2 percent of world trade; 94.6 percent of commercial loans; 80.6 percent of internal savings and 80.5 percent of investment. If in terms of distribution the panorama is untenable, it is equally so regarding resources: The rich countries possess approximately one-fifth of the world population but consume seventy percent of world energy, seventy-five percent of the metals, eighty-five percent of the timber, and sixty percent of the food. Such a pattern of development ... is only viable in the degree to which the extreme inequality is maintained, as otherwise the world resources would be exhausted. Therefore, *inequality is not a distortion of the system. It is a systematic prerequisite for growth and permanence of the present system.*
>
> (p. 4, author's emphasis)

It is the tendency to ignore or overlook this "systematic prerequisite" of capitalism in discussions of culture, difference, and identity politics in the United States that motivates Ellen Meiksins Wood (1994) to question why "having recognized the complexities, diversities, and multiple oppressions in the so-called postmodern world, we can't also recognize that capitalism is not only dominant but massively present in every aspect of our lives and in all our 'identities'" (p. 28). Wood's critique rightly challenges class-blind notions of cultural identity and argues that identity politics decontextualized from material conditions only limits and narrows the impact of such discourse upon the deep structures of economic inequality. Furthermore, the absence of class discourse in the politics of marginalized communities in no way lessens the exigencies of class struggle. In fact, "since the discourse of justice is intimately tied to class, ethnicity, race, and gender, the absence of one of its most salient components—class"—(Aronowitz, 1992, p. 59) foredooms the transcultural solidarity required to effectively address the plight of economically dispossessed people, not only in this country but around the world. Stanley Aronowitz (1992), in his writings on working-class identity,[6] sheds light on this issue. The American evasion of class is not universal. We have no trouble speaking of ourselves as a "middle class" society or, indeed, endowing the economically and politically powerful with the rights and privileges of rule. American ideology identifies the middle class with power and, in its global reach, has attempted to incorporate manual workers into this family. The anomaly of the large and growing working poor, some of whom are hungry, others homeless and, indeed, the increasing insecurity suffered not only by industrial workers but also professional and clerical employees in the service sector, makes some uneasy but have, until recently, failed to faze the ongoing celebration. Or, to be more accurate, class issues are given other names: crime, especially drugs; teenage pregnancy and suicide; homelessness

The Media and Ideological Distortions of Difference

Mass media in the United States exploit ... representations of race and racialized contact in various ways daily: angry black folks doing violence, somebody—usually a young black man—dying (p. 173).

—bell hooks (1990)

It is impossible to fully grasp the social formation of ideological distortions about class, "race," and gender in the postmodern world if we ignore the overwhelming impact of today's accelerated media and communications technology. Through its captivating influence on "mental production" and its false presentation of democratic cultural differentiation, the media increasingly give shape to new forms of postmodern repression while sustaining common-sense approval for their capital-ist representations. Within the structured relationships between the media and the ideas they extend forth to the public, the ideological function is deceptively concealed. Hall and his colleagues (1978) explain this relationship in terms of Marx's basic proposal that "the ruling ideas of any age are the ideas of its ruling class."

> [The] dominance of the "ruling idea" operates primarily because, in addition to its ownership and control of the means of production, this class also owns and controls the means of "mental production." In producing their definition of social reality and the place of "ordinary people" within it, they construct a particular image of society which represents particular class interests of all members of society; this class's definition of the social world provides the basic rationale for those institutions which protect and reproduce their "way of life." This control of mental resources ensures that theirs are the most powerful and "universal" of the available definitions of the social world. Their universality ensures that they are shared to some degree by the subordinate classes [and cultures] of the society.
> (p. 59)

The media, with a highly centralized and almost monolithic structure, provide an essential link between the ruling ideology of the dominant culture and the society at large (Winston, 1982). In a society such as the United States where most people do not have any direct access to nor power over the bulk of decisions that affect their lives, the media play a powerful legitimating role in the social production of mass consensus. And although it may be argued that the power of the media is not absolute, in that there frequently exist counter-ideologies and definitions which challenge its legitimacy by way of dissident voices,

> many emergent counter-definers however have no access to the defining process at all ... [for] if they do not play within the rules of the game, counter-spokesmen

[sic] run the risk of being defined out of the debate (because they have broken the rules of reasonable opposition) ... Groups which have not secured even this limited measure of access are regularly and systematically stigmatized, in their absence, as "extreme," their actions systematically deauthenticated by being labeled as "irrational."

(Hall, et al., 1978, p. 64)

Oppositional Consciousness

This means locating the structural causes of unnecessary forms of social misery, depicting the plight and predicaments of demoralized and depoliticized citizens caught in market-driven cycles of therapeutic release and projecting alternative visions, anal-yses, and actions that proceed from particularities and arrive at moral and political connectedness (p. 35).

—Cornel West (1992)

It is against such a backdrop of societal contradictions and mainstream cultural complexities that subordinate cultural groups must endeavor to rethink past strategies for cultural survival that now prove ineffective and to discover new ground upon which to carry out political projects of resistance and negotiation. This also includes the need to forge a new consciousness of opposition, in light of assimilationist postmodern rhetoric and right-wing conservative backlash.[7]

In the face of wide social and economic inequalities, biculturalism as a political construct must move beyond simple notions of individual psychological theories of identity, liberal paradigms of pluralism, and unproblematic notions of two distinct cultural worldviews interacting. Instead, the genealogy of biculturalism must be theoretically grounded in the historical intricacies of social formations that emerge from the collision between dominant/subordinate cultural, political, and economic relations of power which function to determine the limits and boundaries of institutional life in this country. Given the hegemonic nature of American institutions, marginalized communities must develop the ability to negotiate and navigate through the current social complexities and co-opting nature of postmodern conditions of cultural domination. This requires a mode of oppositional consciousness that depends on the ability to read actual situations of power and to choose and adopt tactics of resistance that are best suited to push against the different forms of power configurations that shape actual experiences of injustice and inequality. Chela Sandoval (1991), in her work on US Third World feminism and oppositional consciousness, describes this as a "differential mode of oppositional consciousness" which provides members of subordinate groups with

> enough strength to confidently commit to a well-defined structure of identity ... enough flexibility to self-consciously transform that identity according to the

requisites of another oppositional ideological tactic, if readings of power's formation require it; enough grace to recognize alliances with others committed to egalitarian social relations and race, gender, and class justice, when their readings of power call for alternative oppositional stands.

(p. 15)

In historical struggles against cultural oppression, bicultural communities have oftentimes joined together, albeit not always smoothly or easily, to oppose practices of social injustice directed against those groups in the United States who have been perceived consistently as unentitled to a rightful place within the mainstream. These coalitions and movement organizations have generally been primarily founded upon bicultural affinities of struggle rooted in the shared historical opposition of African Americans, Latinos, Asians, and Native Americans to cultural, class, and gender subordination. As the "nature" of postmodern social oppression presents itself in a more highly sophisticated, differentiated, and confusing manner, there is a greater necessity for members of subordinate groups to incorporate a differential mode of oppositional consciousness in order to build expanding alliances of struggle. Such alliances can serve as vehicles by which to more effectively identify and challenge actual relations of power at work and to select more effective modes of intervention that are directed toward actualizing an alternative vision of both institutional and community life.

Racialization and Notions of Difference

[W]here cultural difference is represented as natural and immutable, then it has all the qualities signified by the notion of biological difference, with the result that the distinction between racism and nationalism seems to have been dissolved (p. 100).
—Robert Miles (1993)

As discussed earlier, expressions of bicultural affinity among members of subordinate cultural groups are generally linked to experiences of difference and the role that difference plays in the social construction of both dominant and subordinate attitudes, beliefs, and practices in the United States. This is particularly at play when both dominant and subordinate groups struggle to challenge racism and the problematic inherent in notions of "race relations"; for the manner in which these notions are commonly used, more often than not, implies "an acceptance of the existence of biological differences between human beings, differences which express the existence of distinct, self-producing groups" (Miles, 1993, p. 2). Robert Miles (1993), in his book, *Racism After Race Relations,* challenges this racialization of groups by arguing that all forms of racism "are always mediated by and through other structures and social relations, the most important of which are class relations and the political reality of the nation state" (pp. 12–13). Therefore as relations of economic domination intensify worldwide, subordinate cultural groups must not fall into the trap of defining cultural differences as a "race problem" or a "race struggle." Instead what must be confronted is

> the problem of racism, a problem which requires us to map and explain a particular instance of exclusion, simultaneously in its specificity and in its articulation with a multiplicity of other forms of exclusion. Hence, we can now confront the fundamental issues concerning the character and consequences of inequality reproduced by and in contemporary capitalist social formations, freed from a paradigm which finds an explanation for that inequality within the alleged "nature" of supposedly discrete populations rather than within historical and so humanly constituted social relations.
>
> (Miles, 1993, p. 23)

From this vantage point, we must also understand notions of "race identity and difference" as politically formed rather than embedded in the color of the skin or a given nature (Hall, 1990a, 1990b). In other words, to identify as Black or Chicano is not so much a question of color as it is a question of cultural, historical, and political differences. Hence, to conceptualize accurately the social construction of bicultural identity formation requires an understanding of the process of racialization. In other words, the theoretical foundation of a politics of biculturalism challenges the "common sense" discourse of "race" and problematizes its utility as an analytical category. This summons a bold analytical transition from the politics of "race" to recognizing the centrality of racism and racialization in the interpretation of exclusionary practices.

Life on the Border

> *The prohibited and forbidden are its inhabitants. Los atravesados live here: The squint-eyed, the perverse, the queer, the trouble- some, the mongrel, the mulatto, the half-breed; in short, those who crossover, pass over, or go through the confines of the "nor-mal" (p. 3).*
>
> —Gloria Anzaldua (1987)

The transcultural dimensions of biculturalism must then be situated within a continually changing process of cultural identity formation, as much as within complex human negotiations for social and material survival. The place where these processes and negotiations evolve and shift, construct and reconstruct is what Homi Bhabha (1990) terms "the third space." It is also in his discussions of the third space that Bhabha engages the "process of hybridity." Hybridity here does not represent a relativist notion of culture, but instead challenges the global structures of domination which shape the lives of subordinate groups and creates a space for new formations of cultural identity to take hold. "This process of hybridity gives rise to something different, something new and unrecognizable, a new area of negotiation of meaning and representation" (p. 211).

It is then this "process of hybridity" that constitutes one of the central characteristics of border existence where the border itself becomes a political terrain of struggle and self-determination. Lawrence Grossberg (1993) expounds on the nature of this "in-between" place by engaging the work of Gloria Anzaldua, *Borderlands/La Frontera: The New Mestizo.*

> Here the subaltern is different from the identities on either side of the border, but they are not simply the fragments of both. The subaltern exists as different from either alternative in the place between colonizer and the (imagined) precolonial subject or, in Gloria Anzaldua's borderland, between the Mexican and the American: "A border land is a vague and undetermined place created by the emotional residue of an unnatural boundary .... People who inhabit both realities ... are forced to live in the interface between the two." ... Anzaldua describes the third space as "a shock culture, a border culture, a third culture, a closed country."
>
> (p. 97)

In the safety of the "third space," notions of bicultural identity are constructed, deconstructed, and reconstructed anew, all while negotiating the tension of ongoing interactions with social and material conditions of subordination. This suggests "a form of border crossing which signals forms of transgression in which existing borders forged in domination can be challenged and redefined" (Giroux, 1992, p. 28). In short it is a "transborder" experience of identity that "is involved in constantly struggling to emerge from the bottom-up" (Santos, 1992, p. 16).

In many respects at its very core, this "bottom-up" act of challenging and redefining reflects an effective strategy of cultural survival that Trinh Minh-ha (1992) terms "displacing."

> Displacing is a way of surviving. It is an impossible truthful story of living in-between regimens of truth. The responsibility involved in this motley in-between living is a highly creative one; the displacer proceeds by increasingly introducing difference into repetition. By questioning over and over again what is taken for granted as self-evident, by reminding oneself and the others of the unchangeability of change itself. Disturbing thereby one's own thinking habits, dissipating what has become familiar and cliched, and participating in the changing of received values—the transformation (without master) of the selves through one's self ... Strategies of displacement defy the world of compartmentalization and the system of dependence it engenders, while filling the shifting space of creation with a passion named wonder.
>
> (pp. 332-3)

The meaning and complexity of this culture of hybridity, transgressing nature, and bottom-up displacement that shapes and enlivens a critical politics of biculturalism are fiercely echoed in the border culture manifesto of Guillermo Gomez-Pena's *Warrior for Gringostroika.*

Border culture means boycott, complot, ilegalidad, clandestinidad, contrabando, transgresion, desobediencia, binacional; en otras palabras, to smuggle dangerous poetry and Utopian visions from one culture to another, desde alia, hasta aca. But it also means to maintain one's dignity outside the law. But it also means hybrid art forms for new content-in-gestation ... to be fluid in English, Spanish, Spanlish, and Ingefiol, 'cause Spanglish is the language of border diplomacy ... But is [sic] also means transcultural friendships and collaborations among races, sexes, and generations. But it also means to practice creative appropriation, expropriation, and subversion of dominant cultural forms a multiplicity of voices away from the center ... to return and depart once again ... a new terminology for new hybrid identities.

(p. 43)

Bicultural Re-presentations and a Solidarity of Difference

The insidious colonial tendencies we have internalized—and that express themselves in sadistic competition for money and attention, political cannibalism, and moral distrust—must be overcome. We must realize that we are not each other's enemies and that the true enemy is currently enjoying our divisiveness (p. 62).
—Guillermo Gomez-Pena (1993)

The bicultural re-presentations of Gomez-Pena and Anzaldua, as the *warrior for gringostroika* and the *new mestiza,* unmistakably emerge from the passion of experience, the power of reflection, and the courage to act. From these examples, we can glimpse at the face of revolutionary commitment—a grounded commitment to struggle against any and all forms of theory or practice that imprison our minds and incarcerate our hearts. Collectively these bicultural re-presentations not only call forth themes of opposition to dominant structures and cultural forms that impede the humanity and liberation of subordinate subjects, but also signal new ways of perceiving our dialectical capacities to transform the social and material conditions of our communities. It is through their vibrant discourses of simultaneous deconstruction and reconstruction, undoing and redoing, embracing and releasing, that we find the hidden seeds of self-determination and catch glimpses of the possibilities awaiting us, possibilities that are given birth through our courage to transgress the antiquated "sacred cows" of profit and privilege, and that join us together in a solidarity of difference—a solidarity that is ever mindful of the manner in which

> [i]nstitutionalized rejection of difference is an absolute necessity in a profit economy which needs outsiders as surplus people. As members of such an economy, we have all been programmed to respond to the human differences between us with fear and loathing and to handle that difference in one of three ways: ignore it, and if that is not possible, copy it if we think it is dominant, or destroy it if we think it is subordinate. But we have no patterns for relating across

human difference as equals. As a result, those differences have been misnamed and misused in the service of separation and confusion.

(Lorde, 1992, pp. 281–2)

Audre Lorde's words strongly reflect one of the most important questions we must openly acknowledge and consistently address in our efforts to establish a solidarity of difference. How do we move across a multiplicity of subjectivities rooted in both material conditions and diverse orientations that historically shape our worldviews? For example, so often we hear people, even within bicultural communities, bemoan the "loss of community." Yet, if the truth be told, a return to the good old days of such an imagined community actually would require returning to a simpler, unproblematic vision of community—a vision that, in fact, was often theorized in monolithic and solely essentialist terms and enacted through exclusionary practices that precluded the full participation of women, poor and working-class people, gays, lesbians, and those perceived as "racially" inferior.

As critical beings, we must consistently recognize the dangers of falling into the hidden traps of both absolutely exclusionary (assimilationist) and relativistically inclusive (liberal pluralist) theories and practices. A solidarity of difference instead challenges us to actively struggle across human differences within the ever-present dialectical tension of inclusionary/exclusionary personal and institutional realities and needs. For the purpose is not to obscure or obliterate differences or diminish and destroy cultural self-determination in the search for "common values"; rather, our greatest challenge is to negotiate the ongoing construction and reconstruction of relations of power and material conditions that both affirm and challenge our partialities in the interest of cultural and economic democracy, social justice, human rights, and revolutionary love.

Conclusion

The theoretical foundation for a politics of biculturalism posited upon these pages represents, above all, one effort to articulate a dialectical reading of issues that are central to extending our political understanding of culture and difference and the impact of these forces upon the identity formation of members from subordinate communities. In so doing, this has entailed (1) a reexamination of notions of identity and ethnicity; (2) the reclamation of the power of experience in the construction of cultural knowledge; (3) the reconsideration of colonization, decolonization, and the development of cultural consciousness; (4) the reinstitution of class relations and material conditions as central to identity formation; (5) the distorting impact of the media on social perceptions of difference; (6) a move away from race-based specificity to a clear focus on racism and racialization; (7) an engagement with transcultural notions of border existence; and (8) the necessity for a solidarity of difference as a significant strategy of struggle against the forces of domination that shape our world.

Most importantly, this work embodies a recognition that critical bicultural scholars must engage actively and persistently with the political challenges faced by our communities—not through simplistic platitudes of hope, but rather the committed intellectual discipline and critical practice required to boldly imagine and bring into existence a world that up to now has existed only in our dreams.

Notes

1   See Iris Marion Young's (1991) text *Justice and the Politics of Difference* for an excellent critical analysis of the sociopolitical contexts that shape the histories of subordinate cultural groups in the United States.
2   Although there no longer exist cultural groups in the United States untouched by the dominant artifacts, structures, and economic relations of power, the beginning stages of this hybridization process can be observed in Indigenous cultures that exist in remote regions of the world. One such example is the culture of the Q'.eros in Peru. The Q'.eros are the remaining community of people in the Peruvian highlands who are the direct descendants of the Inca. To flee the violent rampage of the conquistadors in the 1500s and to protect their way of life, the Q'.eros fled into the Andes, living virtually in isolation for 500 years. It is only recently that the Q'.eros have begun to have some contact with the West. Government projects to assimilate the Q'.eros into the mainstream of Peruvian life have taken the form of setting up farm collectives and Spanish-language educational programs for the children. As the Q'.eros begin to have greater contact with the West, it is expected that away of life conserved for hundreds of years will undergo dramatic reconstruction, if not be lost altogether. This is already evident in those members of the Q'.eros who have moved into the cities, only to face harsh conditions of poverty and very few opportunities for a better life amid the Peruvian mainstream (Cohen, 1993).
3   For a more extensive and thought-provoking discussion of ethnicity, see "Ethnicity: Identity and Difference" and "Cultural Identity and Diaspora," by Stuart Hall (1990a, 1990b); and Stanley Aronowitzs (1992) *The Politics of Identity*.
4   See chapter 6, "Essentialism and Experience," in Teaching to Transgress, by bell hooks (1994) for an incisive discussion and critique of Diana Fuss's *Essentially Speaking: Feminism, Nature, and Difference*, particularly with respect to the manner in which Fuss problematizes student voices that she characterizes as speaking from the "authority of experience."
5   According to the Children's Defense Fund yearbook, The State of America's Children: In 1992, more children lived in poverty than in any year since 1965; the share of family income received by the poorest one-fifth of families shrank to 4.4 percent in 1992, while the share going to the richest one-fifth reached 44.6 percent. In *Who We Are: A Portrait of America*, among other income inequities, Roberts (1993) shows that despite an increase in total Black families who earn more than $50,000 (from 7 percent to 15 percent), the total number of Black families earning under $5,000 has risen from 8 percent in 1967 to 12 percent in 1990. Edward Luttwak (1993) bemoans the "Third-Worldization" of America in his book *The Endangered American Dream*. He writes: "America s slide toward Third World conditions is

even now being prepared by the sheer force of demography: the proportion of poor Americans is increasing, the concentration of wealth in the hands of the richest one percent is also increasing, and the proportion of Americans in between who have enough wealth and income to claim genuine middle-class status is therefore in decline" (153). Luttwak also provides the following figures: between 1979 and 1990, the number of workers below the poverty line nearly doubled, from 7.8 million to 14.4 million; the combined net worth of the richest 1 percent was greater than the total net worth of the bottom 89.9 percent of all American families, at $5.2 trillion.

6 For an eloquent discussion of the history of working-class identity, see *The Politics of Identity: Class, Culture, Social Movements*, a text by Stanley Aronowitz (1992).
7 Michael Omi and Howard Winant (1983b) in their essay "By the Rivers of Babylon: Race in the United States (Part II)" provide an informative and useful discussion of the New Right's "programmatic attempts to limit the political gains of the minority movement (and its successors) by reinterpreting their meanings." In their work, the authors outline several of the major currents in the rearticulation process that have fueled the right-wing conservative backlash in the United States.

References

Akinyela, M. (1991), "Critical Afrocentricity and the Politics of Culture," in *Wazo Weusi (Think Black)* (Fall). Fresno, CA: California State University.
Akinyela, M. (1992), "Critical Afrocentricity and the Politics of Culture," in *Wazo Weusi* (A Journal of Black Thought) (Fall). Fresno, CA: California State University.
Anzaldua, G. (1987), *Borderlands/La Frontera: The New Mestizo*. San Francisco, CA: Aunt Lute.
Aronowitz, S. (1992), *The Politics of Identity: Class, Culture, Social Movements*. New York, NY: Routledge.
Bhabha, H. (1990), "The Third Space," in J. Rutherford (ed.), *Identity, Community, Culture Difference*. London: Lawrence and Wishart, 207–21.
Buriel, R. (1984), "Integration with Traditional Mexican-American Culture and Sociocultural Adjustment," in J. Martinez (ed.), *Chicano Psychology*, 1st ed. New York, NY: Academic Press.
Children's Defense Fund (1994), *The State of America's Children Yearbook*. Washington, DC: US Department of Justice/Office of Justice Programs.
Cohen, J. (1993), *Q'eros: The Shape of Survival*. New York, NY: Mystic Fire Video.
Darder, A. (1991), *Culture and Power in the Classroom: A Theory for a Critical Bicultural Pedagogy*. Westport, CT: Bergin and Garvey.
deAnda, D. (1984), "Bicultural Socialization: Factors Affecting the Minority Experience." *Social Work* 29(2): 101–07.
Du Bois, W. E. B. (1903), *The Souls of Black Folk*. Chicago, IL: A.C. McClurg.
Epstein, S. (1987), "Gay Politics, Ethnic Identity: The Limits of Social Constructionism." *Socialist Review* 17 (May–August): 9–54.
Fanon, F. (1963), *Wretched of the Earth*. New York, NY: Grove Press.
Fanon, F. (1964), *Toward the African Revolution*. New York, NY: Grove Press.
Fanon, F. (1967), *Black Skin, White Masks*. New York, NY: Grove Press.
Giroux, H. (1992), *Border Crossings*. New York, NY: Routledge.
Gomez-Pena, G. (1993), *Warrior for Gringostroika*. St. Paul, MN: Graywolf Press.

Gorostiaga, X. (1993), "Is the Answer in the South?" Paper presented at the international seminar "First World Ethics and Third World Economics: Christian Responsibility in a World of Plenty and Poverty," Sigtunn, Sweden.

Gramsci, A. (1971), *Selections from the Prison Notebooks*. New York, NY: International Publishers.

Grossberg, L. (1993), "Cultural Studies and/in New Worlds," in C. McCarthy and W. Crichlow (eds.), *Race, Identity, and Representation* in *Education*. New York, NY: Routledge, 89–105.

Hall, S., Critcher, C., Jefferson, T., Clarke, J., and Roberts, B. (1978), *Policing the Crisis*. London: Macmillan.

Hall, S. (1990a), "Ethnicity: Identity and Difference." *Radical America* 13(4): 9–20.

Hall, S. (1990b), "Cultural Identity and Diaspora," in J. Rutherford (ed.), *Identity, Community, Culture, Difference*. London: Lawrence and Wishart, 222–37.

hooks, b. (1990), *Yearnings*. Boston, MA: South End Press.

hooks, b. (1994), *Teaching to Transgress*. New York, NY: Routledge.

Jordan, J. (1992), *Technical Difficulties*. New York, NY: Vintage Books.

Lorde, A. (1992), "Age, Race, Class, and Sex: Women Redefining Difference," in R. Ferguson et al. (eds.), *Out There: Marginalization and Contemporary Culture*. New York, NY: New Museum of Contemporary Art.

Luttwak, E. (1993), *The Endangered American Dream*. New York, NY: Simon and Schuster.

Miles, R. (1993), *Racism after Race Relations*. London: Routledge.

Millan, D. (1993), "The Chicano Collective Bicultural Consciousness: Identity and the Politics of Race," in A. Darder (ed.), *Bicultural Studies in Education: The Struggle for Educational Justice*. Claremont, CA: Institute for Education in Transformation/Claremont Graduate School.

Minh-ha, T. (1989), *Woman Native Other*. Indianapolis: Indiana University Press.

Minh-ha, T. (1992), "Cotton and Iron," in R. Ferguson et al. (eds.), *Out There: Marginalization and Contemporary Culture*. New York, NY: New Museum of Contemporary Art.

Nagel, J. (1994), "Constructing Ethnicity: Creating and Recreating Ethnic Identity and Culture." *Social Problems* 41(1) (February): 152–76.

Omi, M., and Winant, H. (1983a), "By the Rivers of Babylon: Race in the United States (Part 1)." *Socialist Review* 13(5): 31–65.

Omi, M., and Winant, H. (1983b), "By the Rivers of Babylon: Race in the United States (Part 2)." *Socialist Review* 13(6): 35–68.

Ramirez, M., and Castañeda, A. (1974), *Cultural Democracy: Bicognitive Development and Education*. New York, NY: Longman.

Rashid, H. (1981), "Early Childhood Education as a Cultural Transition for African-American Children." *Educational Research Quarterly* 6(3): 55–63.

Redhorse, J., Lewis, R., Feit, M., and Decker, J. (1981), "Family Behavior of Urban American Indians," in R. Dana (ed.), *Human Services for Cultural Minorities*. Baltimore, MD: University Park Press, 67–72.

Roberts, S. (1993), *Who We Are: A Portrait of America*. New York, NY: Random House.

Romay, E. (1993), "Policy Implications for the United States through Mexican Immigration Bilingual Teachers' Experiences of Bilingual-Bicultural Education: A Participatory Research Process." Ph.D. dissertation, University of San Francisco.

Sampson, E. (1993), "Identity Politics: Challenges to Psychology's Understanding." *American Psychologist* 48(1):1. (December): 1:1. 19–30.

Sandoval, C. (1991), "U.S. Third World Feminism: The Theory and Method of Oppositional Consciousness in the Postmodern World." *Genders* 10 (Spring): 1-24.

Santos, G. (1992), "Somos RUNAFRIBES? The Future of Latino Ethnicity in the Americas," *National Association of Chicano Studies Annual Conference Proceedings*.

Solis, A. (1980), "Theory of Biculturality." *Calmeccac de Atzlan en Los* 2(1): 36-41.

Valentine, C. (1971), "Deficit, Difference, and Bicultural Models of Afro-American Behavior." *Harvard Educational Review* 41(2): 137-57.

West, C. (1992), "The New Politics of Difference," in R. Ferguson et al. (eds.), *Out There: Marginalization and Contemporary Culture*. New York, NY: New Museum of Contemporary Art, 19-38.

West, C. (1993), *Race Matters*. Boston, MA: Beacon Press.

Winston, M. (1982), "Racial Consciousness and the Evolution of Mass Communications in the United States." *Daedalus* 8: 171-82.

Wood, E. M. (1994), "Identity Crisis." *In These Times* (June 13): 28-9.

Young, I. M. (1990), *Justice and the Politics of Difference*. Princeton, NJ: Princeton University Press.

Young, I. M. (1991/2022), *Justice and the Politics of Difference*. Princeton, NJ: Princeton University Press.

6

Neoliberalism in the Academic Borderlands: An On-going Struggle for Equality and Human Rights

This chapter examines the negative impact of neoliberal policies upon the work of border intellectuals within the university, whose scholarship seeks to explicitly challenge longlongstanding structural inequalities and social exclusions. More specifically, the notion of neoliberal multiculturalism is defined and discussed with respect to the phenomenon of economic Darwinism and the whitewashing of contemporary academic labor, despite a tradition of progressive struggle within the academy. In response to the current counter-egalitarian climate of neoliberalism, a call is issued for a critical pedagogy that supports a revolutionary vision of human rights and democratic life.

At the heart of neoliberal policies of education is a veiled pursuit to destroy any tacit notion that we in the United States may have once had about the importance of the common good and public education as a human right. Instead, schooling and other public goods have been thrown underhandedly into the up-for-grabs conservative arena of privatization and deregulation. An unrelenting neoliberal culture of rampant greed, wholesale surveillance, and the regulation and monitoring of our humanity has subsumed notions of equality and public responsibility. Similarly, critical notions of multiculturalism and diversity in higher education have been pushed back by an economic ethos that has rendered difference a whore to its own utilitarian pursuits or an enemy of the state.

In the process, scholarship and activism for structural equality, political inclusion, economic access, and human rights have given way to an emphasis on multiculturalized market niches, the management of an international workforce, a frenetic focus on the globalization of education through technology, and the occasional portrayals of colored faces and celebratory rhetoric for public relations pamphlets and Web sites. In the efficient, cost-effective, and competitive neoliberal world, questions of difference have been neatly conflated and diffused by a hypocrisy fueled by racism, elitism, and a tenacious disbelief in the equality of those who exist outside the narrow rationality of its profit logic. As a consequence, "deficient" subjects of difference, unable to march to the homogenizing and bootstrap neoliberal refrain, are conveniently tossed aside or criminalized and held behind iron bars, without concern for their numbers or their fate. This disregard for those who do not keep in step with the dehumanizing accountability system that neoliberalism demands is as much at work within the culture of the university, as they are in the corporate world today.

There is no question that we are in the midst of a disastrous internationalizing project of neoliberalism. As Michael Peters (2001) argues, neoliberalism has attempted to provide "a Universalist foundation for an extreme form of economic rationalism," which can be regarded as the latest political–economic formation of advanced capitalism in the West. Furthermore, he insists, "such a philosophy is ultimately destructive of any full-fledged notions of community—national or international, imagined or otherwise" (117). Collective social action, accordingly, is considered a gross obstacle to the freedom of individuals and corporations, with their implacable drive to privatize all that, in another time in our history, would have been protected as a public good. The rampant individualism of neoliberal interests functions as a means to end state regulation and control, considered to be the major culprit in stifling the free-market's ability to flourish and its capacity to protect private interests—namely the interests of the ruling class.

As such, the logic of neoliberalism provides an intellectual anchor from which *mega-rich* ultraconservatives, conservatives, and liberals alike collaborate together for control of not only the marketplace, but all public and private institutions, including higher education. And even more to the point, as Jodi Melamed (2006) argues in *The Spirit of Neoliberalism: From Radical Liberalism to Neoliberal Multiculturalism*, "Neoliberal policy engenders new racial subjects, as it creates and distinguishes between newly privileged and stigmatized collectivities; yet multiculturalism codes the wealth, mobility, and political power of neoliberalism's beneficiaries to be the just desserts of 'multicultural world citizens,' while representing those neoliberalism dispossesses handicapped by their own 'monoculturalism' or other historico-cultural deficiencies" (1).

Economic Darwinism and the University

Henry Giroux (2011) identifies economic Darwinism "as a theater of cruelty and mode of public pedagogy ... [that] extends its reach throughout the globe, under mining all forms of democratic solidarity and social structures" (165). He contends that the notion of economic Darwinism well-illustrates the manner in which neoliberal policies within higher education have functioned, overtly and covertly, to support the survival of the fittest. In this instance, policies of deregulation, privatization, and lack of concern for the public good have rendered democratic education an endangered species. Key to this analysis is the manner in which the culture of higher education, today more than ever, functions in the interest of the plutocratic state, by securing the hegemonic consent of professors who, despite their expressed liberal ideals, practice a conservative culture that supports both the corporatization and instrumentalization of higher education. Implicated here, as Giroux (2012) notes, are the values of "unchecked competition, unbridled individualism, and a demoralizing notion of individual responsibility" (16), culprits in the legitimation crisis and moral impoverishment of neoliberal academic players, steeped to the gills in a homogenizing logic that threatens to obstruct the possibility of any genuine form of cultural democracy in the United States.

This disabling logic of neoliberalism has become well-entrenched across the university, but is most evident within graduate school education, where future academics and public intellectuals are initiated into careerist orientations that alienate them not only from one another and from the world, but also from the critical foundations necessary for the construction of democratizing knowledge—knowledge with the potential to challenge advancing inequalities orchestrated by the wealthy elite. Hence, from the moment that graduate students and young professors are initiated as tenuous agents of the neoliberal academy, they are conditioned into a culture of antidemocratic values that shape the expectations of their teaching, research, and tenure process. Similarly, an infantilizing culture of institutional surveillance, carried out by loyal gatekeepers, is rendered commonplace at every level of the enterprise. As a consequence, many graduate students and junior faculty are counseled to abandon their formerly idealistic progressive intentions and position themselves competitively within the knowledge marketplace, in ways that, on one hand, gain them recognition as so-called innovative thinkers; while on the other, they become willing agents of the university, positioning themselves as a good fit within the institution's neoliberal purpose.

This pernicious contradiction has become ever more intense in the last decade, as colleges and universities have instituted expectations that professors from all disciplines prove themselves to be effective grant writers and fundraisers in their quest for the golden ring of tenure. As a consequence, a good deal of the formation and energies of young professors in major public research universities today is not directed toward teaching nor public engagement (despite the rhetoric), but rather toward becoming published within refereed journals; getting publicly noticed as stars in the academic conference circuit; and developing effective grant writing skills—all the while, competitively shaping their research agendas in ways that will procure them greater access to private and public funds, along with the institutional benefits and privileges that these resources afford them. This phenomenon of professorial formation is, as one might expect, also accompanied by junior faculty (particularly those of color and working class) who are either left isolated to clumsily navigate their way through the constantly shifting minefields of the tenure-track process or forced into the mind-bending authoritarian dynamics of junior–senior faculty mentorship relationships, often fraught with deep anxieties and traditional expectations that junior faculty accommodate or suffer rejection at the time of tenure.

Although this dynamic has long existed within academe, the decreasing number of new tenure-track positions in the last decade and the increasing competition among new doctoral graduates has proven especially treacherous. Moreover, with the exaggerated emphasis placed on the hard sciences and technology, this has made young faculty in the humanities, social sciences, and education particularly susceptible to conforming to neoliberal priorities. Meanwhile, many senior faculty members, who entered the academy prior to the advent of neoliberalism, can also become targets of academic punishments, if they refuse to acquiesce on reform to neoliberal expectations— irrespective of the quantity, quality, or intellectual reach of their scholarship. It is a new money game, where the high stake of accountability rears its head in disturbing ways, particularly with respect to university labor. Nowhere is this more evident than for radical education scholars who, in the Gramscian sense, define their teaching and scholarship organically, within the critical moral precepts of social equality, economic justice, and universal human rights.

Neoliberal Multiculturalism

In the midst of the antiwar movement and civil rights struggles of the 1960s and early 1970s, the American university was challenged to break with its elite, lily-white, patriarchal tradition. The seeds of the current neoliberal assault on the academic borderlands began with a long-term strategy put in place by conservatives seeking "to win an ideological war against liberal intellectuals, who argued for holding government and corporate power accountable as a precondition for extending and expanding the promise of an inclusive democracy" (Giroux, 2007, p. 142). Those working to democratize the university called for inclusion of more women, as well as working class, and students and faculty of color. Alongside this call for inclusive admissions and hiring practices, pressure was placed upon colleges and universities to transform their curriculum in ways that would not only be culturally relevant, but that would engage the longstanding historical inequalities and social exclusions that persisted in US society. Hence, the call for a policy of democratic inclusion was also the result of a variety of public struggles that demanded the university make good on its promise of democracy, particularly to those who resided in the margins of mainstream opportunities.

Many of the multicultural gains of the time, made within the larger society of the university, were more consistent with liberal Keynesian-inspired economics still at work during that era, which recognized the importance of federal investment in social welfare programs, in order to stave off the downside of corporate capital investments. However, the conservative ideas of classical macroeconomic, which began to gain public currency with the deregulatory policies of Reaganomics, became the powerful precursor to the era of the *New Economy*, with its dramatic economic shift to the current neoliberal values and the ruthless consequences of inequality that we are grappling with today.

More to the point, as a larger number of border intellectuals from cultural, racialized, economic, gendered, and sexual borderlands began to penetrate graduate education, the entrance of their politically distinct voices and dissonant perspectives began to cause a clear backlash, whose consequence is being felt forcefully today. This phenomenon is juxtaposed with the ascendance of neoliberalism and the predominance of the economy as the most worthy concern of the nation. In concert, profit-logic not only shaped the priorities of capital, but also began to recast the very purpose of higher education.

Some of the most potent first public stirrings of neoliberalism's creep into educational policies and practices can be found in *A Nation at Risk*, a national report issued by Ronald Reagan's National Commission on Excellence in Education in 1983. The proposed recovery for the doom and gloom of public education and the forging of global economic superiority were best articulated in the report's assertion that the American public school system should function as an economic engine. The sprouting neoliberal vision of the ruling elite who manned the Reagan commission, including then Secretary of Education William Bennett, began to also forcefully tug at diversity debates that were underway within higher education. Thus, it's not surprising that by the early 1990s, the politics of difference had suddenly become well entrapped in the hyperbolic discourse of political correctness.

Within the university, growing conservative backlash to the politics of difference extended beyond simply ethnic studies faculty, but also to women and gender studies, sexuality studies, Marxists, structuralists, and poststructuralist scholars who, according to Roger Kimball (1990), in *Tenured Radicals: How Politics Has Corrupted Our Higher Education*, had become the new "establishment." Similar public assaults on higher education were found in Allan Bloom's (1987) *Closing of the American Mind* and Dinesh D'Souza's (1991) *Illiberal Education: The Politics of Race and Sex on Campus* that alleged liberal bias at the university and pointed to the destructive impact of multiculturalism to the integrity of the Western canon and the whole of American society.

Mean-spirited attacks associated with such politically repressive rhetoric began to gnaw away at the evolving counter-hegemonic visions of equality and inclusion within the university—visions that had been inspired by the civil rights movements and anti-imperialist struggles for self-determination. A variety of legal battles also ensued over three decades, beginning with the Bakke decision in 1978, eroding the delicate fabric of university affirmative action practices meant to remedy the historical impact of discrimination on communities of color. In concert, political correctness debates across the university underhandedly promoted an adherence to both a whitewashed and politically lukewarm scholarship, seeking to snuff out the dissenting voices of critical academics whose work aimed to critique, challenge, and transform the intellectual life of higher education, as well as the traditional academic formation of university students.

In place of values rooted in a critical vision of difference, the conservative multicultural proponents of economic Darwinism focused attention on the beneficiaries of neoliberalism in such a way that the formerly unattended inequalities associated with racism and other social exclusions were negated, ignored, or sidelined. This gave rise to the phenomenon that some scholars in the field now refer to as *neoliberal multiculturalism* (Fisk, 2005; Melamed, 2006, 2011; Darder, 2011), a conservative ideology of multiculturalism that deploys a meritocratic justification, linked principally to economic benefit, to justify inequalities. As such, those who practice neoliberal multiculturalism enact a structure of public recognition, acknowledgment, and acceptance of multicultural subjects, based on an ethos of self-reliance, individualism, and competition, while simultaneously (and conveniently) undermining discourses and social practices that call for collective social action and fundamental structural change.

Accordingly, in a culture where punitive values of victim-blaming readily adorn the scholarship of economist, social scientists, and educational theorists alike, decolonizing discourses that emphasize the recognition and complexity inherent in a politics of difference, along with the amelioration of poverty and other forms of social, political and economic inequalities, are deemed disruptive to the prevailing neoliberal order of the university. This is particularly so, when progressive efforts by border scholars become too closely aligned with larger social movement struggles for democratic public life and universal human rights. As a consequence, many border intellectuals who entered the academy during the *multicultural era* have found themselves further marginalized and derailed, at the very moment when their scholarly and political maturity could serve to more effectively challenge the forces of neoliberalism, as well as forge a more promising democratic vision. In light of this homogenizing neoliberal impetus, serious public pedagogical efforts for transformation are not only seen as professionally suspect, but politically dangerous.

By the late 1990s, major economic booms were the daily fare of morning newscasts, as the push toward the internationalization of capital became the universal magic bullet of the new era—as the gap between the rich and the poor began to quickly widen. Within higher education, this shift in the economy also led to several major shifts in the labor of academics, in a variety of ways. The globalization discourse permeated the halls like wildfire, as universities began to fashion themselves like multinational corporations and the use of computerized technology became a mandatory facet of academic life. The first served nicely to undermine gains made in the nation's multicultural arena by diverting resources and attention away from domestic diversity demands to the global, while the second initiative further intensified the labor of academics across the university, despite the time-saving rhetoric that promised greater efficiency.

Key to this discussion, as Giroux repeatedly asserts, is the political and economic tyranny that neoliberalism incarnates, through policies and practices that seized control of higher education and bludgeoned a critical multicultural vision of university formation, along with critical pedagogical efforts to cultivate and nurture values tied to social justice, economic democracy, universal human rights, and the political self-determination of oppressed populations. Not surprisingly, the educational advances of the era of difference proved to be but a short-lived moment in the history of American higher education, for as more students and faculty from the margins began to find their way into the seats of university classrooms, faculty meetings, and governance tables, the more aggressive conservative and neoliberal forces became in their efforts to swing the pendulum back to a more homogenous cultural moment, where an economically driven meaning of freedom and justice prevailed and the marketplace was heralded as the only true purveyor of equality.

Whitewashing the Borderlands

By now it should be no surprise to learn that neoliberal multiculturalism, with its economic Darwinist bent and incessant drive to quantify worth, value, or fit by perceived capital return, did not prove friendly to the academic borderlands—that intellectual terrain of struggle where the mixing of cultures, philosophies, histories, spiritualities, and everyday practices of life defied "the transcendent character of the traditional canon's exclusion—notably of women and people of color—marked as the product of the white male imagination" (Aronowitz, 1991, p. 205). Two of the most significant juxtapositions to the aforementioned economic shifts of the 1980s and '90s were the increasing number of women and students of color entering colleges and universities and, as a consequence, the quick flourishing of critical scholarship from borderland intellectuals. Much of this liberatory-inspired scholarship—tied to concerns generated by the civil rights movement, anti-imperialist struggles, the politics of difference, and feminist discourses of intersectionality—pushed forcefully against centuries of racializing patriarchal values and bourgeois priorities so prevalent in higher education.

Hence, a notable feature of the academic borderland was the overwhelming presence and alliances of dissenting voices calling for greater transparency of government and greater avenues for public democratic action, both within and outside of the university. The contentiousness this created resulted in the mean-spirited conservative attacks to the academic borderland, mentioned earlier. Attacks against border academics often centered on both administrative and disciplinary efforts to delegitimize cultural-centric philosophies and oppositional discourses, as well as stifle the tendency of many border intellectuals to gravitate toward unorthodox research designs, whose validity was often seen as highly questionable. In response, border intellectuals pushed more forcefully for community-centered participatory approaches or critical ethnographic and narrative designs, more closely aligned to political struggles for voice and democratic participation. As would be expected, this rankled mainstream faculty, including those from the hard sciences, who privileged quantitative approaches to knowledge construction. Some complained bitterly about the lack of objectivity and hard empirical evidence, as well as the sloppiness of investigations executed by border academics.

Meanwhile, as border intellectuals were transgressing positivist boundaries in a variety of traditional disciplines, rising neoliberal imperatives were making their way into the university just in time to conveniently push back, fiercely, against critical interventions initiated by radical intellectuals—whose projects were precisely designed to challenge the structures of inequality and reinvigorate the democratic potential of higher education. In many colleges and universities, administrators strategically defused so-called *cultural wars* and attempted to whitewash the borderlands by imposing cries of fiscal exigencies to cut programs, institute hiring freezes, harass tenured radical faculty, reject tenure cases, and move to eliminate entire departments.

Despite the struggle to build counter-hegemonic spaces, academic legitimacy, and greater culturally democratic solidarity within the academy, neoliberalism's world-flattening force worked to undermine discourses of difference—whether these were predicated on class, skin color, ethnicity, gender, sexuality, religion, physical ability, or political ideology. Through neoliberalism's neat and orderly morality of the marketplace and its professed cultural superiority, all historical forms of political-economic inequalities and social exclusions seemed washed away in the pristine belief in the sanctity of individual private interests and the doctrine of free enterprise, within a political system that has long equated capitalism with democracy. Faculty resistance to enter or defend this totalizing neoliberal vision of the marketplace was often met with slanderous character attacks that sought to brand radical scholars, whose scholarship and pedagogy countered allegiance to the status quo, as egotistical or narcissistic, or of questionable intellect or moral ineptitude.

As the liberal democratic purpose of higher education became more and more obfuscated, universities across the country became more deeply aligned with the narrow rationality of neoliberal objectives. Accordingly, border intellectuals teaching against the grain were pushed further and further into the margins with respect to their teaching, research, participation in the life of their departments, and the governance of the university. High-level administrators, now functioning like corporate CEOs, were less and less concerned with past ideals of liberal educational leadership as they spent more of their time hobnobbing with corporate executives, foundation officials, and other big business advocates, who potentially could assist these university presidents to make up for the increasing cuts in public monies. In the process, the values, priorities, and private interests of those who held the reins to research dollars also began to redefine the purpose of higher education, heavily tilting the public enterprise toward the neoliberal mission. With respect to the construction of knowledge, this turn has been attached to an over-dependence on scientific interpretations, evidence-based rhetoric, and overarching imperatives strategically deployed to sustain the legitimacy of neoliberal ideals.

In the alluring economic fumes of a commonsensical rhetoric that equates profit, progress, and prestige with policies and practices of deregulation, privatization, competition, and bootstrap economics, universities have been too easily herded into the fold with promises of dollars to build new facilities, shore up technology, support homogenizing curriculum, and hire faculty that could carry out the aggressive neoliberal agendas of public and private funders, whose primary vested interest in difference has been motivated by expanding markets and the management of workers at home and abroad. With a sharp eye toward profit and the control of resources—including people as reserve armies—the neoliberal rhetoric of difference functioned strategically as a means to increase production, maximize commerce, and support the growing needs of US militarization worldwide. Hence, through both covert and overt means, the political values and financial priorities of a neoliberal world began to seek greater control of the intellectual formation of graduate students and young faculty, who represent the legitimating research pool for the successful mobilization of new enterprises.

As would be expected, the widening impact of neoliberalism also made its way into the academic borderlands. Some ethnic studies programs, for example, were forced to dodge efforts of university administrators to terminate or undermine their future influence on the campus by compromising the historical vision and integrity of their emancipatory intellectual agenda. In some instances, faculty in the borderland jumped on to the neoliberal bandwagon, moving toward scholarship considered more acceptable, legitimate, and fundable by university officials. Oftentimes, this required a shift to research interests aimed toward more traditional interpretation of scholarship and research design, in ways that permitted them to more successfully pursue science, technology, engineering, and mathematics (STEM) monies—which currently postures as the new panacea for recovery of global educational and economic superiority.

In concert, funding for faculty positions and research projects that might serve as countervailing forces has become scarce. This resulted in radical intellectual projects being pushed further into the margins. Fewer opportunities and resources were to be found for studies that sought to examine public social issues, such as the democratic responsibility of the welfare state, policies of wealth redistribution, impact of the corporatization of the media, educational benefits of bilingual education, or disabling impact of high-stakes testing on the education of working class and students of color, just to name a few. In fact, funding waned across the board for critical scholars, even those working within area studies where borderland intellectuals were once more able to enjoy some political respite. Where monies were attained for such research, the language and political center of gravity of the discourse had to remain so camouflaged within neoliberal objectives that the actual conditions and data derived from these studies became distorted to unrecognizable proportions, by conclusions that ignored longstanding structural inequalities.

In a similar vein, border scholars are now expected to align themselves more staunchly within their particular disciplines of study, whether history, anthropology, sociology, or economics, in contrast to the more revolutionary ideals that were once at the heart of teaching and scholarship in the borderlands. It seems that in the world of economic Darwinism the disciplinary tradition provides a much neater and tidy picture of intellectual alliances, than does the messiness of transdisciplinary or even post-disciplinary border scholarship, often associated with ethnic, feminist, postcolonial, and queer sensibilities. In contrast, the traditional disciplinary mechanism works well to police and monitor the scholarship of exiled intellectuals, by means of disciplining values at work, particularly in the evaluation and credentialing of graduate students and junior faculty. This process serves well to weed out those considered not to be a good fit. And as previously noted, a good fit today is strongly associated with the capacity of junior faculty to bring in dollars. This newly instituted requirement of tenure in many universities serves to ensure that nonconforming academics, whose scholarship exists outside the priorities of state and federal agendas and the guidelines of public and private funding sources, will experience a difficult time remaining viable candidates for tenure.

Similarly, as targeted scholarships and fellowships for underrepresented students and faculty have dwindled, opportunities for working-class students and faculty from underrepresented communities have become fewer and fewer. In concert, border intellectuals who persist in their work with disenfranchised communities, or anchor their teaching and research on questions of social inequalities, or push against the boundaries of traditional methodologies and epistemologies are often marginalized and derisively dubbed as *activist* scholars. As such, radical scholars can find themselves exiled from meaningful participation in the evolution of university programs and departments by an antidemocratic wave that silences and banishes their contributions to the wasteland of irrelevancy. In a climate where the international control of knowledge and the maximization of profits are the greatest concern, public universities seem to have fully surrendered to the siren call of neoliberalism.

Critical Pedagogy and the Struggle for Democratic Public Life

In *Academic Labor in Dark Times*, Giroux (2009) argues that:

> At the very least, academics should be more responsible to and for a politics that raises serious questions about how students and educators negotiate the institutional, pedagogical, and social relations shaped by diverse ideologies and dynamics of power, especially as these relations mediate and inform competing visions regarding whose interests the university might serve, what role knowledge plays in furthering both excellence and equity, and how higher education defines and defends its own role in relation to its often stated, though hardly operational, allegiance to egalitarian and democratic impulses.

With this, he insists that a political project of democratic public life must be central to our efforts to defy the impact of neoliberalism. Also significant here is concern over the potential of critical pedagogy to serve as an effective educational force in the emancipatory struggle for universal human rights. For without the presence of a larger social struggle for change and a critical pedagogical space to engage our lived histories, many border intellectuals—born and reared in the margins of a classed, racialized, gendered, and heterosexist borderlands—would have been excluded, given that the politics of difference and dissent often predominate our scholarly projects. Many are, in fact, children of dissent, for our presence in the university was spawned directly by counter-hegemonic struggles that pushed against the once impenetrable walls of its discriminatory orthodoxy.

For critical intellectuals living in the borderlands of academe, the classroom represents a significant terrain of struggle and a key political space in the forging of a public pedagogy. This is often directly tied to critical pedagogical efforts by professors who seek to create political links between the classroom, campus, and community, in ways that foster a more seamless political democratic understanding of theory and practice. As such, critical pedagogical approaches are effective in creating emancipatory conditions within the classroom that support meaningful critical reflection and dialogue, the development of alternative and dissenting voices, collective participation, and the building of solidarity among university students.

In fact, as just mentioned, if it were not for critical pedagogy, many scholars of color sitting in this room today would not have found a place to flourish in the academy, despite legitimate critiques that have been launched and the need for ongoing interrogation. It has been through classroom practices firmly anchored upon critical principles—where transdisciplinary and postdisciplinary understandings are sought, through engaging simultaneously questions of culture, history, economics, politics, hegemony, critique, dialogue, and consciousness—that critical educators have worked with students to not only engage conditions of exploitation and alienation academically, but also cultivate intimate relationships of teaching and learning that break through the *violence of abstraction* (Neary, 2005) so prevalent in university classrooms.

A critical pedagogy requires that we create the conditions for university students to grapple rigorously not only with theories and practices of democratic life as cognitive phenomena, but also to tackle in the flesh the meaning and consequences of material and social conditions of exploitation and domination. From this place, the possibility of constructing grounded knowledge and integrating practices of social activism can emerge, as critical reflections and dialogues evolve organically in the process. However, there is no question that this pedagogical potential to support the exercise of dissent, through the political evolution of student voice and social agency, can also easily become a point of contention within the neoliberal university. This is so, not only because the ethical values of a critical democratic praxis are in conflict with the underlying ethos of neoliberalism, but also because there is far more utility in the domesticating pedagogy that Paulo Freire (1971) terms *banking education*—an appropriate pseudonym for neoliberal academic formation.

In the last three decades, we have seen neoliberalism steadily negate the hard-earned opportunities of disenfranchised people in this nation. Economic Darwinism has endangered species of education and the public good, leaving borderland intellectuals scrambling to regain political equilibrium, following repeated assaults. Unfortunately, the presidency of Barack Obama did not turn out to be the great panacea that so many had imagined. Instead, the Obama administration's policy decisions on public education, the economy, health care, and the military, to name a few, have left many feeling disappointed and betrayed. Nevertheless, or because of it, everywhere there are struggles being waged for dignity, freedom, and democratic life.

Across the country, thousands of people have congregated in a new show of collective dissent. Occupy Wall Street has inspired a movement of people who are quickly expanding and creating new forms of both communal and autonomous formations of dissent. This has left ample room for regional groups to bring specific attention to local issues in ways that are meaningful to its members. In New Mexico, for example, activists call themselves *(Un)occupy* Albuquerque and *(Un)occupy* Sante Fe, which speaks more accurately to the realities of Indigenous history and politics in the region. No matter the case, this national movement is spreading organically and in numbers that we have not seen since the civil rights and antiwar movements of the 1960s and 1970s took to the streets. And despite regional differences, this burgeoning social movement is calling for solidarity across the nation, as everyday folks join to push back the ruling class.

The Motive Force of Revolution

History confirms that democracy is never guaranteed, even during great movements of people. As such, we are reminded that democracy is never a given, but rather entails an ongoing emancipatory struggle for political voice, participation, and social action. With this in mind, higher education continues to exist as a formative contested terrain of struggle, given the potential of public education to serve as a democratizing force for the evolution of critical consciousness and democratic public life.

Yet, in light of the furtive nature of neoliberalism within higher education, border intellectuals cannot challenge its perils and pitfalls, if our work is not firmly grounded in a coherent and revolutionary political vision that critically embraces universal human rights—a vision that privileges the needs of the many, in place of the few. Hence, our struggles against all forms of inequality must recognize that *there is no liberation without a revolutionary transformation of the class society*. Which, incidentally, is exactly what the Occupy movement is demanding!

C. L. R. James, writing in *At the Rendezvous of Victory*, speaks dialectically of capitalism and its impact on the intellectual.

> Production, which should be [our] most natural expression of [our] powers, becomes one long murderous class conflict in which each protagonist can rest not for a single minute. Political government assumes totalitarian forms and government by executive decree masquerades as democracy. … The Intellectual is cut off from the world of physical production and the social organization of labor. The divorce between physical and mental labor is complete. The Individual, worker or Intellectual, is no more than the sport of vast forces over which he [or she] has no control. The senses of each are stimulated without possibility of realization. The resentments, the passions of frustrated social existence take revenge in the wildest of individual aberrations. Before these forces psychoanalysis is powerless, and voting every four years becomes a ghastly mockery. Facing the disintegration of society, capital mobilizes all available forces for the suppression of what is its own creation—the need for social expression that the modern productive forces instill into every living human being. The explosion of this suppression is the motive force of revolution.
>
> (James, 1984, p. 69)

How do we nurture "the motive force of revolution" in our everyday lives, pedagogy, and scholarship? How do we bring this dialectical dynamism to bear in our scholarship? How do we remain consistently committed to not only speaking and writing about these issues, but immersing ourselves in collective social movement work? These fundamental questions must inform the labor of all border intellectuals—questions that require our labor within the university to be informed and aligned to the material and social conditions at work in the communities in which we live and teach; and to connect these conditions to the life conditions of workers around the world.

Moreover, in contrast to neoliberal multiculturalism, we must consistently struggle for a notion of social recognition that embraces a revolutionary understanding of equality, with grounded political projects of action within and across communities. This entails a critical democratic process that encompasses, as Milton Fisk (2005) so rightly argues, "a social recognition … beyond the cultural recognition promoted by neoliberalism and its international institutions. It leads to a struggle from below [and in the flesh] for equality. This struggle engages the cooperation of each of the various components of a diverse society. The struggle becomes a common effort to establish public goods that reduce poverty and inequality" (28); and while doing so, confront uncompromisingly racism and other social crimes against humanity.

Raya Dunayevskaya (1989) wrote in *Philosophy and Revolution*: "Thought can transcend only other thought; but to reconstruct society itself, only actions of men and women, masses in motion, will do the 'transcending,' and thereby 'realize' philosophy, make freedom, and whole men and women, a reality" (415). It is this unquestionable Marxist ethos of equality and human rights that must continue to inform our labor within and without the university.

References

Aronowitz, S. (1991), "Review of Tenured Radicals: How Politics Has Corrupted Our Higher Education." *Teachers College Record* 93: 204–7.
Bloom, A. (1987), *The Closing of the American Mind*. New York, NY: Simon & Schuster.
Darder, A. (2011), *A Dissident Voice: Essays on Culture, Pedagogy and Power*. New York, NY: Peter Lang.
D'Souza, D. (1991), *Illiberal Education: The Politics of Race and Sex on Campus*. New York, NY: Simon & Schuster.
Dunayevskaya, R. (1989), *Philosophy and Revolution: From Hegel to Sartre and from Marx to Mao*, 3rd ed. New York, NY: Columbia University Press.
Fisk, M. (2005), "Multiculturalism and Neoliberalism." *Praxis Filosofica* 21: 21–8. http://www.miltonfisk.org/writings/multiculturalism-and-neoliberalism/.
Freire, P. (1971), *Pedagogy of the Oppressed*. New York, NY: Seabury Press.
Giroux, H. (2007), *The University in Chains*. Boulder, CO: Paradigm.
Giroux, H. (2009), "Academic Labor in Dark Times." *Counterpunch* (March 11). http://www.counterpunch.org/2009/03/11/academic-labor-in-dark-times/.
Giroux, H. (2011), "The Disappearing Intellectual in the Age of Economic Darwinism." *Policy Futures in Education* 9(2): 163–71.
Giroux, H. (2012), "Higher Education, Critical Pedagogy, and the Challenge of Neoliberalism: Rethinking the Role of Academics as Public Intellectuals." *Revista Aula de Encuentro*. Numero Especial. Andalucia, Espana: Servicio de Publicaciones e Intercambo Científico Universidad de Jaen.
James, C. L. R. (1984), *At the Rendezvous of Victory*. London: Allison & Busby.
Kimball, R. (1990), *Tenured Radicals: How Politics Has Corrupted Our Higher Education*. Chicago, IL: Ivan R. Dee.
Melamed, J. (2006), "The Spirit of Neoliberalism: From Racial Liberalism to Neoliberal Multiculturalism." *Social Text* 89(24): 1–24.
Melamed, J. (2011), *Represent and Destroy: Rationalizing Violence in the New Racial Capitalism*. Minneapolis, MN: University of Minnesota Press.
Neary, M. (2005), "Renewing Critical Pedagogy: From Popular Education to Academic Activism—Teaching as a Site of Struggle." Unpublished paper presented at The Higher Education Academy: Sociology, Anthropology, Politics (C-SAP) International Conference at the University of Birmingham, Birmingham.
Peters, M. (2001), *Postructuralism, Marxism, and Neoliberalism: Between Theory and Politics*. Lanham, MD: Rowman and Littlefield.
U.S. Department of Education (1983), *The National Commission on Excellence in Education*. A Nation at Risk: The Imperative for Educational Reform (April).

Part 3

Decolonizing Interpretive Methodology

Introduction

Darder has been writing and researching, knowing clearly for whom she does her work for. The birth of one of her latest works centering on the methodology of *Decolonizing Interpretive Research* is the culmination of over thirty-five years of incisive analysis around the dehumanizing conditions for doctoral students, subaltern researchers, and cultural workers throughout the world. This work is reminiscent of Freire's notion of liberation as a painful childbirth, in that the journey to birth this work was deeply rooted in the struggles of subaltern students, researchers, and her personal lived experiences within the academy and beyond. Decolonizing interpretive research as an evolving methodology is part of her larger political project of liberation that has spanned over three decades. Whereas Paulo focused on a *methodology of the oppressed* (Darder, 2024), Darder in her synthesis of years of work and reinvention of Freire's ideas through decolonizing interpretive research offers a *methodology of the subaltern*. This methodology is linked at the same time to her early work and dissertation on *Culture and Power* which also uses an interpretive methodology. Thus, returning to her earlier work and in its current iteration, decolonizing interpretive methodology offers a roadmap for readers to trace the evolution of Darder's body of work through a decolonizing lens.

Summary of Articles

This section opens with one of Darder's (1992) earlier works, "Problematizing the Notion of Puerto Ricans as 'Underclass': A Step Toward a Decolonizing Study of Poverty," a writing that names the dehumanizing use of the term "underclass" in social sciences research through the wisdom and lived experiences she uses to ground this critique. Similar to current articulations of inferiorizing and demeaning buzzword terms used today, during the time this work was first written, Darder (1992) brings to the forefront the problematics of the usage of "underclass," particularly as it is applied to Puerto Ricans, as well as contextually and then offers a decolonizing framework for understanding it. Through this process, we bear witness to the method behind a decolonizing methodology in the making. We become privy to the reality that a decolonizing methodology unfolds through an autoethnographic dimension linked to historical analysis, evident as Darder tells the story of a young social science researcher's unawareness of the degradation, historical linkages, and politics of the use of the term. As will be explored in other texts, according to Darder, much of what gives life to the work of decolonization can be linked to the body and its sensations or the feelings that something is just not quite right which often leads to further problematizing.

The body has always been a central aspect of Darder's work and in how she engages with those around her. The piece "Decolonizing the Flesh: The Body, Pedagogy, and Inequality" awakens us to the way in which the body holds so much power and is fundamentally part of how we engage in the world, especially through material relationships. In her teaching, Darder has recognized that the body must be part and parcel in that the physical sensations of the body are part of the learning where teaching to the flesh is integral to the intellectual formation of students. In her work, the body is an important piece of knowing intimately the world. This counters traditional forms of education that disrespect the body, rarely acknowledge the body, and even trap the body in educational spaces. This lack of body knowledge and wisdom is part of what must be decolonized to offer a critical praxis which Darder recognizes is key to a pedagogy of the body that honors how students show up in spaces and works to counteract the repressive conditions of schooling through honoring wisdom and voice. This vision for a critical praxis of the body is what Darder offers as an emancipatory vision grounded in love, ethics, and the body.

The final offering of this section, "Decolonizing Interpretive Research: Subaltern Sensibilities and the Politics of Voice," is a later piece in the Darderian corpus that synthesizes years of struggle, writings (including those above), love, and research as she further analyzes the possibilities of a decolonizing research methodology. This particular piece is in conversation with Gayatri Spivak's 1988 piece, "Can the Subaltern Speak?," in which Darder centers the subaltern and decolonizing aims given the impact of the Western gaze and epistemologies which Darder and Spivak critique. Grounded in subaltern sensibilities and the authority of lived experience, Darder lays out central tenets for the qualitative labor of decolonizing interpretive research to radically shift in both theory and practice the ways we engage fundamental issues of difference within the world. In this body of decolonizing interpretive methodology research, Darder highlights the struggle to wrestle away the decolonizing sensibilities at work that are often forced to grapple with the diabolical Western stronghold in place with respect to research and dominant epistemologies. It is this offering to subaltern researchers who sensibilities yearn to deny these dominant frameworks in favor of a liberating knowledge that emanates from within and with community. This is a praxis and a methodology of liberatory dreams.

7

Problematizing the Notion of Puerto Ricans as "Underclass": A Step Toward a Decolonizing Study of Poverty

Whereas the perceived problems of groups cannot be ignored, neither can the interest groups that define their membership and deviance .... Once a concept is incorporated in general perceptions and becomes a guide for program development, it is almost impossible to eradicate. Social scientists, who are often active members of the labeling professions, may ... exhibit insensitivity to political consequences. The result of their giving the intellectuals imprimatur to a concept is often the creation of a convenient terminology that unwittingly reinforces existing stereotypes and prejudices.
—Stafford and Ladner (1990, p. 140)

For those of us who have grown up as members of a subordinate culture and class in the United States, the words of Stafford and Ladner strike deep chords. Many of us are quite conscious of the effects that social science language and practices have had on our own lives. An effect that is often not dispelled by our own professional socialization into the social sciences. As a consequence, I am intimately linked to the following discussion in two very significant ways.

The first link is my birth. I am a Puerto Rican woman who was born, grew up, and lived through my early adulthood in conditions that are currently described by social scientists as "underclass." And even today as I write this article as a scholar and researcher, I am acutely conscious of the many stored memories of suffering, humiliation, and despair experienced by my family as a result of poverty.

The second link is an incident that I experienced with my students at a Community Fellows seminar.[1] A young social science researcher was invited to present his work on the current trends in the labor market and its impact on communities of color. Repeatedly, he used the term "underclass" to refer to those who live in poverty. Each time he spoke the term, the room grew increasingly tense and the silent resistance of the participants became quite noticeable. Finally, several of the students who could no longer contain their distress stated that they did not appreciate having the people in their communities referred to as underclass and that the term was demeaning and degrading to their human dignity.

The researcher, a well-meaning white, middle-class male, who considers himself very politically conscious, became quite confused by the anger of the group. And despite the students' objections, he could not stop using the term. It was as if the term "underclass" had become tenaciously embedded and intertwined into the linguistic structure that represented his thoughts. Even after several efforts by the group to bridge the gap for him, his comments inadvertently expressed suspiciousness as to the validity of the group's response. This caused him to become even more abstracted and encapsulated in the content of his presentation and hopelessly distanced from any possibility of dialogue with the group.

Hence, it is from the context of these two separate but related experiences that I will briefly discuss the problems inherent in the notion of Puerto Ricans as "underclass" and some beginning steps toward a decolonizing study of poverty.[2]

Underclass: Its Origins, Meaning, and Usage

Although there are a variety of ways in which the term "underclass" was used in the past, the most recent meaning emerged out of Gunnar Myrdal's (1962) text, *The Challenge to Affluence*, where he described an "underclass" that was cut off from society. He described the group as lacking the necessary education, skills, and personality traits required to integrate successfully into the modern economy. Myrdal's definition focused primarily on economics. Douglas Glasgow (1981) provided the earliest of the underclass formulations in the 1980s. He proposed that the underclass emerged from a combination of institutional racism and structural changes in the economy that produced and reinforced a cycle of poverty in the Black community.

As a result of the work of social scientists such as these, the use of the term "underclass" has spread like wildfire during the past two decades. So much so that it is now readily used by economists, political scientists, social scientists, and policymakers to refer to a group of people perceived as untouchable. And despite the claims of scholars such as Glasgow (1981) who deny that the term connotes "moral or ethical unworthiness" (p. 8), the term has, in fact, conveyed pejorative images of human beings as underlings, deficient, inferior, disadvantaged, and deprived.

From a historical context, it is significant to note that most of the descriptive categories used in reference to people who live in poverty have been derived primarily from research pertaining to the African American community. Yet much of the contemporary poverty metaphors in the social sciences can be readily traced to Oscar Lewis's (1963; 1968) "culture of poverty" arguments based on his study of Puerto Ricans and ghetto life. Prior to this time, those who lived in poverty were generally referred to as the poor by the well-meaning and as paupers or rabble by others not so empathetic to the plight of those who lived in impoverished conditions.

I believe that it is also of particular interest to note that social science christenings of the poor with such terms as the "culturally deprived," "disadvantaged," and later the "underclass" just happened to coincide with a historical period when communities of color were most actively involved in group struggles for self-determination. The introduction of such terminology in reference to communities of color at such a critical emancipatory period in their history leaves one open to speculate about the underlying motivations that may have informed the introduction of such terms in the first place.

It is also significant to mention that the contemporary use of the term "underclass" has come into vogue at a time when a major attitude of retrenchment is taking place with respect to questions of cultural diversity in the academy. Presently, a debate that is quickly gaining ground, and to a certain extent is supported by the work of William Wilson (1978), is shaped around questions related to the significance of race as a legitimate research category in the study of poverty. The underclass metaphor conveniently permits social science researchers to return to the politically disguised language of universalism by disengaging with subordinate cultural questions in their studies.

Although the term "underclass" may be considered to have a variety of meanings, there currently exists enough agreement in the social sciences to prompt the United States Accounting Office to issue a staff study entitled "The Urban Underclass: Disturbing Problems Demanding Attention" (U.S. General Accounting Office, 1990). To one extent or another, this study has accepted the primary characteristics described in much of the current literature on the underclass (i.e., Glasgow, 1981; Auletta, 1982; Kasurda, 1983; Murray, 1984; Lemann, 1986; Danziger & Gottshalk, 1987; Wilson, 1987; Ellwood, 1988; Jencks, 1988; Ricketts & Sawhill, 1988; Mincey, Sawhill, & Wolf, 1990). More specifically, the document assigns the following characteristics to the underclass (U.S. General Accounting Office, 1990, p. 1):

- They are permanently without connection to the legitimate labor force.
- The women in the group are likely to be persistently poor, to experience prolonged welfare dependency, and to experience high rates of out-of-wedlock births, often starting in their teen years.
- The children in the group are likely to be persistently poor and to experience high drop-out rates.
- Some people in the group exhibit disproportionately high rates of criminal behavior; others experience high rates of criminal victimization.

Furthermore, it states that "those discussing the underclass are usually referring to people who are concentrated in urban neighborhoods and who are predominantly black and Hispanic" (p. 1).

Puerto Ricans as Underclass

To engage in a discussion of a subordinate culture in the United States without examining the historical events that have shaped the group's presence in this country is to ignore the historicity of common day experiences and hence, to be in danger of perpetuating group misrepresentations. Social science misrepresentations inadvertently arise as a consequence of decontextualizing the realities of people's lives by thrusting them carelessly into the realm of universalism and ahistorical analysis. Such has been the experience of African Americans, Native Americans, Puerto Ricans, Chícanos, Mexicanos, Japanese, Chinese, and other people of color in the United States.

To better understand the Puerto Rican reality in the United States requires an understanding of two significant conditions—colonization and immigration. These two social forces have contributed greatly to the realities faced by Puerto Rican people in this country today. On one hand, Puerto Ricans have been forced to accept foreign political conquest and economic control of their native land, along with the cultural domination inherent in a colonized existence. On the other hand, they have had to contend with the forces of racial and economic discrimination and the pressure of assimilation as colonized immigrants in the United States (Blauner, 1987).

The majority of Puerto Rican immigrants landed in New York City, where even today, the largest population of Puerto Ricans living off the island reside. Most arrived with a limited knowledge of English, few skills, and very few financial resources. As a consequence, Puerto Rican communities were established wherever extended familial survival strategies could be established and the national cultural identity affirmed. In many cities, community-based organizations were created during the late 1960s and early 1970s in efforts to struggle for Puerto Rican political rights and self-determination through participation in local politics as well as state and national efforts to impact public policy.

But despite poverty programs that have resulted in modest socioeconomic gains for other communities of color, Puerto Ricans today are the most economically depressed group in the United States, with a poverty rate that has remained unchanged in the last decade. In New York City alone, over 45 percent of all Puerto Rican families live in poverty. In 1987, the median family income for Puerto Ricans was less than half of whites (Center on Budget and Policy Priorities, 1988). In addition, studies indicate that the number of Puerto Rican students dropping out of high school has increased as has the number of female-headed households.

This highly vulnerable status is coupled with labor statistics that show lower rates for Puerto Ricans' labor participation than for any other group, with those employed working fewer hours on the average (Borjas, 1985). It is this picture of not only persistent but increasing economic disenfranchisement that has caused some researchers to foster "considerable speculation that Puerto Ricans have become part of the urban underclass" (Tienda, 1989, p. 105).

But despite the speculation of social scientists such as Marta Tienda (1989) about the Puerto Rican population, the term "underclass" has been widely criticized by Puerto Rican researchers (Bonilla, 1989; Hernandez, 1990; Torres & Rodriguez, 1991). Here I would like to turn to the critique of Torres and Rodriguez (1991). Specific research areas addressed in their critique include the use of inadequate data, inadequate models, and the inaccessibility of the indigenous factor. In the first area, they point to the dearth of specific data on Puerto Ricans and problems with conclusions based on data derived from labor market studies concerning African Americans and Mexican Americans. The second area specifically critiques the use of statistical models for labor research that do not fit Puerto Ricans. Torres and Rodriguez (1991) explain:

> Key differentiating factors may be at work, which have not been effectively incorporated into the models thus far developed. These include: the multiracial character of the Puerto Rican population and the difficulties this presents vis a vis the racial dichotomy in U.S. society; the status of Puerto Ricans as colonial

immigrants; the influence of long-term structural regional change on Puerto Rican communities; the excessively high levels of urbanization and the impact of housing abandonment in areas of high Puerto Rican concentration. In addition, these models fail to capture the positive effect of a functional dual migration.

Third, Torres and Rodriguez (1991) address the problem related to the accessibility of understanding the indigenous factors that constitute the cultural values and social practices at the heart of the Puerto Rican community. They also argue against ignoring prior studies. An act that permits researchers to make, for example, frivolous claims about "a new poverty" and to ignore that it is, in fact, "the same poverty that originated in the 50s; it is a continuation of the same trend; it has just been given a new appearance and a new name (i.e., 'underclass')" (Torres & Rodriguez, 1991). Instead, they call for research that "builds on the historically unique and multifaceted reality of the group" which incorporates indigenous input. More specifically, Torres and Rodriguez (1991) further warn against the consequences of omitting the "indigenous factor." Here, they explain that this increases the possibility of producing research that "may be seen as alien to the self-defined needs of the community."

On the specific use of the term "underclass," Torres and Rodriguez (1991) examine several points. One of these specifically relates to methodological disputes over measurement and causality. Also of concern is the impact of the term with respect to the Puerto Rican community as a whole. They emphasize that "it is disparaging and stigmatizing; this makes it both offensive and impractical." From the pragmatic side, they question "who is and who is not a member of the underclass?" And last, Torres and Rodriguez criticize the indiscriminate manner in which the term is being used in the literature. They specifically cite Tiendas (1989) article entitled "Puerto Ricans and the Underclass Debate."

> It is of interest to note that the article refers to what is a prevailing conception in many circles: That is, *not* that there is a growing sector within the Puerto Rican community which evidences a persisting disadvantage, but rather that the *whole* group is becoming an underclass.
> (Torres & Rodriguez, 1991)

The Colonizing Impact of Social Science Language

In a variety of ways, the Torres and Rodriguez critique makes inference to what is essentially the potential colonizing impact of social science language on the Puerto Rican community. In this particular case, the focus is on the use of the underclass concept to describe a human phenomenon that on one hand is extremely complex and distant from most researchers, and on the other hand instills a fear of disorientation and loss of control that could result from the mere thought of confronting the unpredictable nature of the group in the concrete. This dilemma intensifies the potential for projections and distortions that can function to distance the researcher from the people being discussed. Often the mechanism by which one distances oneself from unacceptable conditions or human affliction is to formulate language that permits one to more rationally engage with realities of an unknown and highly feared situation.

Hence, social science language can serve the purpose of constructing artificial boundaries in order to make physical phenomena controllable to the mind of the researcher. It is through this process by which social scientists create terms for human conditions they wish to control. In this way, a categorical term functions to facilitate the ability to refer to a specific condition, quantify the condition, identify particular aspects of the condition, see the condition with respect to cause, set goals with respect to it, and even believe that the condition is understood. Unfortunately, it is often this scientifically sanctioned process of masking reality that can inadvertently "lead to human degradation" (Lakoff & Johnson, 1980, p. 236).

Paulo Freire (in Shor & Freire, 1987) addresses the standardization of language and social science constructs from the standpoint of "political and ideological foundation." A major concern is centered on the action of those in a society who use their position of power to assign meaning, determine values, set criteria, and standardize phenomena.[3]

> The question of power is there, enveloping our idioms and the problem of language even though we don't always perceive this power …. The dominant class has the power to establish its language [and values] as the standard.
> (Shor & Freire, 1987, p. 149)

At issue here is the question of who is doing the naming? In a culture that places great value on the notion of absolute truths such as that which generally gives structure to social science research, the people who impose their language on subordinate groups also have the power to define that which is considered "absolute and objective" truth in the society-at-large.

In their reference to the "politics of definition," Stafford and Ladner (1990) note that language plays "a critical role not only in the analysis of social problems but in the determination of power relationships" between groups in society (p. 143). Given the manner in which this operates, it is clear to see how language can function in the interest of social empowerment or in the interest of social domination. One of the most significant ways in which this occurs is where language is used to highlight properties of injustice or to shift our attention away from these properties.[4]

The colonizing influence of terms such as "the underclass" on the members of a particular subordinate group cannot be ignored. In many instances, when a group is labeled, the members of such a group learn to perceive themselves as persons who deserve the label and, hence, come to act accordingly. Herbert Gans (1990) in his critique of the underclass concept speaks to the danger of its widespread legitimation on those who live in poverty:

> Insofar as poor people keep up with the labels the rest of society sticks on them, they are aware of the latest ones. We do not all know the "street level" consequences of stigmatizing labels, but they cannot be good. One of the likely, and most dangerous, consequences of labels is that they can become self-fulfilling

prophecies. People who are described as members of the underclass may begin to feel that they are members of such a class and are therefore unworthy in a new way. At the least, they now have to fight against yet another threat to their self-respect, not to mention another reason to feel that the society would just soon have them disappear.

(p. 274)

In an effort to summarize the colonizing impact of the underclass concept, it is useful to refer to Gans's (1990) discussion on "deconstructing the underclass." In his work, Gans lists ten dangers inherent in the use of the underclass concept for naming the reality of people who live in poverty. These include:

1. Its unusual power as a "buzzword"
2. Its use as "a racial code word that subtly hides anti-black and anti-Hispanic feeling"
3. Its "flexible character" that allows wider and wider use for more and more people
4. Its use as a "synthesizing notion" that permits the lumping together and labeling of different people
5. The terms interference with antipoverty policy and other kinds of planning
6. The persuasive capacity of the underclass concept to serve as a reified definition of groups that can lead to moralistic victim-blaming notions
7. The manner in which the underclass has been analyzed in terms of neighborhoods or regions
8. The "concentration and isolation" hypothesis
9. The term itself "sidesteps" issues of poverty
10. The danger of inventing new unnecessary words which further marginalize subordinate groups

Finally, it is worth noting that a number of social scientists have addressed the colonizing impact of social science language on subordinate cultural groups (Memmi, 1965; Fanon, 1967; Freire, 1970; O'Neill, 1985; Freire & Macedo, 1986; Bosmajian, 1990). In particular, their work speaks to the tragic consequences of social science language with respect to the ways in which it often functions to silence and perpetuate the alienation of those groups who are perceived as deviant and, hence, excludes them from a social process where they can name their own experiences and actively participate in changing the conditions in which they live.

Toward a Decolonizing Social Science Study of Poverty

Kenwyn Smith (1990) asserts that "when we notice that our social institutions are driven by the larger political contexts in which they are embedded, we are forced to acknowledge that the content of our research and the methods we use are likewise subject to the prevailing political forces" (p. 121). As such, social science researchers must acknowledge the colonizing impact of traditional social science research language and methodology—a language and methodology which have often perpetuated elitist, authoritarian, fragmented, and hence, disempowering notions of poverty.

In efforts to overcome such a legacy, any social scientist who authentically seeks to participate on behalf of those who live in poverty must, first and foremost, enter into a relationship with the people. As a consequence of ignoring many of the issues discussed above, traditional social science has failed to function as a tool for empowerment and transformation in the lives of those who live in poverty. Instead, it has served to sustain the interests of a few, at the expense of the many. There is no place where this is more evident than in the outcome of thirty years of compensatory education, social welfare reform, and "war on poverty" programs—programs that were born of paternalistic notions of poverty or abstract liberal notions of generosity sustained by traditional forms of poverty research. Freire (1970) addresses the failure of such programs in the following manner:

> The task implies that ... leaders do not go to the people in order to bring them a message of "salvation," but in order to know through dialogue with them their objective situation and their awareness of that situation—the various levels of perception of themselves and of the world in which they exist. One cannot expect positive results from an educational or ... action program which fails to respect the particular view of the world held by the people. Such a program constitutes cultural invasion, good intentions notwithstanding.
>
> (p. 84)

What is clear from what we have seen in the past is that social scientists need a different vision of the world if we are to truly comprehend the nature of poverty in this country. This vision must incorporate a perception of human beings as having the capacity to overcome those social forces that function to dehumanize and disempower them. It is a vision that must define all human beings within the context of the social, political, economic, and historical forces at work in their lives—a view of human beings that refuses to separate them from nature or to decontextualize them from the reality of the power relationships that give shape to their world. And clearly it is a vision that supports the notion that people must actively participate in the process of their emancipation from those adverse social conditions that threaten their self-determination.

If we are to move toward a praxis of decolonization as researchers, we must be willing to embrace dialogical principles—that is, critical principles that position us to move contextually in communion with communities, rather than in opposition to their right to control their lives. In such an approach we are called to use our knowledge, resources, and influence to unmask those conditions and social forces that strip people of their humanity and perpetuate their suffering.

From the standpoint of overcoming forms of linguistic colonization, it requires that we examine carefully, in both theory and practice, the manner in which particular terms such as "underclass" work to perpetuate the social oppression of particular groups and to sustain the interest of the dominant culture. More specifically, this requires that such a term as "underclass" be problematized through a dialogical exercise in which the social reality is deconstructed, in order to fully unveil the overdetermination of the word by the structures of power that have imposed it upon the people.

John O'Neill (1985) describes a "praxis of conscientization" as an alternative approach to social science research. It is an approach that begins and ends with those who are the subjects of the study. That is, the participants are actively involved in the planning and development of the study, the collection of data, the final analysis of the information gathered, and the development of a set of recommendations for action. This suggests a form of study that carries a vision of empowerment through returning to the people what truly belongs to them. Inherent in this approach is not an attempt to learn about the people but to come to know with them the reality that challenges them and through this process to discover those actions that will function to transform the conditions that limit their lives.

As it might be evident even by this brief description of a dialogical research approach, the process requires time and cannot be accomplished simply through the quasi-involvement of the researchers nor solely quantifiable data. It is a form of research grounded in relationships that can move all the participants of a study through those critical steps that truly permit us to actively learn from one another, in order that we might transform our world together.

Quantitative descriptions coupled with disembodied terminology will only function to deepen the colonizing structures that permeate the lives of all people. Let us instead work toward participatory social science research efforts that can begin to answer honestly the many long-standing questions of poverty. It is this kind of research that we need in the Puerto Rican community.

Notes

1   The Community Fellows Program, established by Mel King in 1971, is a unique community development program of the Massachusetts Institute of Technology's Department of Urban Studies and Planning. The program brings together community-based people of color from major cities in the country who are specifically grappling with issues related to youth who live in poverty. Many of the Fellows were actually born and raised in the same communities in which they live and work.
2   A similar discussion can be waged for other terms such as "culturally deprived," "disadvantaged," "minority," and even the now common label of "Hispanic," which emerged into being as a governmentally assigned classification in the 1970s.
    It is particularly important to keep in mind that these all represent terms that emerged outside of the context of the communities or groups for which they are currently still used.
3   As with the use of the term "underclass," the "feminization of poverty concept" also serves as a means of perpetuating middle-class societal norms in order to dominate the lives and self-image of women, rather than to engage directly with the realities faced by women who parent children alone (Zinn, 1989). In both instances, the process constitutes an abuse of power that is executed through research language and methods that decontextualize or compartmentalize the experiences of those who live in poverty.

4   This brings the discussion back to the earlier concern regarding the current use of the term "underclass" as a deliberate or inadvertent shift away from engaging with questions of race as legitimate social science category in the study of impoverished communities. It is impossible for social science researchers to fully comprehend the realities that exist in the lives of Puerto Ricans or any other subordinate cultural group that lives in poverty without a willingness to engage critically with the intersection of race, class, and gender in the study of poverty. The complexity of these relationships cannot be addressed through research language and methods that artificially reduce or simplify what constitutes a complex entanglement of social, political, and economic relations of power.

References

Auletta, K. (1982), *The Underclass*. New York, NY: Random House.
Blauner, R. (1987), "Colonized and Immigrant Minorities," in R. Takaki (ed.), *From Different Shores*. New York, NY: Oxford University Press, 149–60.
Bonilla, F. (1989), *Breaking Out of the Cycle of Poverty*. Washington, DC: National Puerto Rican Coalition.
Borjas, G. (1985), "Public Spending for the Poor: Trends, Prospects, and Economic Limits," in S. Danziger and D. Weinberg (eds.), *Fighting Poverty: What Works and What Doesn't*. Cambridge, MA: Harvard University Press (is 1–64).
Bosmajian, J. (1990), *The Language of Oppression*. Lanham, MD: University Press of America.
Center on Budget and Policy Priorities (1988), *Shortchange: Recent Developments in Hispanic Poverty, Income, and Employment*. Washington, DC: Center on Budget and Policy Priorities.
Danziger, S., and Gottshalk, P. (1987), "Earning Inequality: The Spatial Concentration of Poverty and the Underclass." *American Economic Review* 77(2): 211–15.
Ellwood, D. (1988), *Poor Support*. New York, NY: Basic Books.
Fanon, F. (1967), *Black Skin, White Masks*. New York, NY: Grove Press.
Freire, P. (1970), *Pedagogy of the Oppressed*. New York, NY: Seabury Press.
Freire, P., and Macedo, D. (1986), *Literacy: Reading the Word and the World*. South Hadley, MA: Bergin and Garvey.
Gans, H. (1990), "Deconstructing the Underclass: The Term's Dangers as a Planning Concept." *Journal of the American Planning Association* 56(3): 271–7.
Glasgow, D. (1981), *The Black Underclass*. New York, NY: Vintage Books.
Hernandez, J. (1990), Latino Alternatives to the Underclass Concept. *Latino Studies Journal* 1(1): 95–105.
Jencks, C. (1988), "Deadly Neighborhoods." *New Republic* (June 13): 23–32.
Kasurda, J. (1983), "Caught in the Web of Change." *Society* 21(1): 41–7.
Lakoff, G., and Johnson, M. (1980), *Metaphors We Live By*. Chicago, IL: University of Chicago Press.
Lemann, N. (1986), "The Origins of the Underclass." *Atlantic Monthly* (June): 54–68.
Lewis, D. (1963), "The Culture of Poverty." *Scientific American* 215: 19–25.
Lewis, D. (1968), *La Vida: A Puerto Rican Family in the Culture of Poverty in San Juan and New York*. London: Panther Books.
Memmi, A. (1965), *The Colonizer and the Colonized*. Boston, MA: Beacon Press.

Mincey, R., Sawhill, I., and Wolf, D. (1990), "The Underclass: Definition and Measurement." *Science* 248(4954): 450-2.
Murray, C. (1984), *Losing Ground: American Social Policy, 1950-1980*. New York, NY: Basic Books.
Myrdal, G. (1962), *The Challenge to Affluence*. New York, NY: Pantheon.
O'Neill, J. (1985), "Decolonization and the Ideal Speech Community: Some Issues in the Theory and Practice of Communicative Competence," in Inj. Forrester (ed.), *Critical Theory and Public Life*. Cambridge, MA: MIT Press, 57-76.
Ricketts, E., and Sawhill, I. (1988), "Defining and Measuring the Underclass." *Journal of Policy Analysis and Measurement* 7(2): 316-25.
Shoř, I., and Freire, P. (1987), *A Pedagogy for Liberation*. Westport, CT: Bergin and Garvey.
Smith, K. (1990), "Notes from the Epistemological Corner: The Role of Projection in the Creation of Social Science." *Journal of Applied Behavioral Science* 26(1): 19-27.
Stafford, W. W., and Ladner, J. (1990), "Political Dimensions of the Underclass Concept," in H. Gans (ed.), *Sociology in America*. Newbury Park, CA: Sage, 138-55.
Tienda, M. (1989), "Puerto Ricans and the Underclass Debate: Evidence for Structural Explanations of the Labor Market Performance." *Annals of the American Academy of Political and Social Science* 501(1): 105-19.
Torres, A., and Rodriguez, C. (1991), "Latino Policy: Problems, Debates, and Prescriptions," in E. Melendez, C. Rodriguez, and B. Barry Figueroa (eds.), *Hispanics in the Labor Force*. New York, NY: Plenum, 247-63.
U.S. General Accounting Office (1990), "The Urban Underclass: Disturbing Problems Demanding Attention" (GAO/HRD-90-52). Annapolis, MD: U.S. General Accounting Office.
Wilson, W. J. (1978), *The Declining Significance of Race: Blacks and Changing American Institutions*. Chicago, IL: University of Chicago Press.
Wilson, W. J. (1987), *The Truly Disadvantaged: The Inner City, the Underclass, and Public Policy*. Chicago, IL: University of Chicago Press.
Zinn, M. B. (1989), "Family, Race, and Poverty in the Eighties." *Signs: Journal of Women in Culture and Society* 14(4): 856-74.

8

Decolonizing the Flesh: The Body, Pedagogy, and Inequality

The Body is our medium for having a world.

—Merleau-Ponty, 2002

[T]he body is also directly involved in a political field; power relations have an immediate hold upon it; they invest it, mark it, train it, torture it, force it to carry out tasks, to perform ceremonies, to emit signs.

—Foucault, 1995

I know with my entire body, with feelings, with passion and also with reason. It is my entire body that socially knows. I cannot, in the name of exactness and rigor, negate my body, my emotions and my feelings.

—Freire, 1995

Our bodies constitute primacy in our material relationships with the world. Without considering the materiality of the body, all notions of teaching and learning are reduced to mere abstractions. This represents a misguided attempt to situate the mind as an independent agent, absent of individual and collective emotions, sensations, yearnings, fears, and joys. Nevertheless, it is the body that provides the medium for our existence as subjects of history and politically empowered agents of change. But, as Peter McLaren (1998) reminds us, "bodies are also the primary means by which capitalism does its job" (p. xiii). We are molded and shaped by the structures, policies, and practices of domination and exclusion that violently insert our bodies into the alienating morass of an intensified global division of labor.

In *Pedagogy and the Politics of the Body*, Sherry Shapiro (1999), as other feminist theorists before her, contends that "any approach committed to human liberation must seriously address the body as a site for both oppression and liberation" (p. 18). Yet, seldom is the significance of the body made central to discussions of emancipatory pedagogy. Educational efforts to reinvent the social and material conditions in classrooms are often devoid of close consideration to the significance of the flesh in mediating conditions of teaching and learning, that is, unless the discussion turns to "classroom management," a convenient euphemism for the covert and overt regulation and control of students' corporeality.

Meanwhile, the classroom exists as an arena where abstract knowledge and its construction are objectified, along with the students expected to acquiesce to its alienating function, limiting rationality, and technocratic instrumentalism. Hence, the production of knowledge is neither engaged nor presented as a historical and collective process, occurring in the flesh and its sensual capacities for experiencing and responding to the world, instead, as Christopher Beckey (2000) argues in *Wicked Bodies*, "the flesh, the material aspect of the body, is seen as a hindrance which must be overcome, negated, and transcended" (p. 71), as if it were not involved in the act of knowing at all.

We as teachers know that teaching and learning can invoke a multitude of sensations and responses, including excitement, pain, joy, anger, pride, and frustration. Paulo Freire (1998) refers to these human responses when he considers the process of studying: "Studying is a demanding occupation, in the process of which we will encounter pain, pleasure, victory, defeat, doubt and happiness" (p. 78), all physical sensations of the body.

Students as Integral Human Beings

The notion of students as embodied and integral human beings has received limited attention in discussions of classroom praxis in the United States (Darder, 2002). Missing even in multicultural discussions of pedagogy is a more complex understanding of humanity and the significance of the body to intellectual formation. Such discussions have been left to educators whose tendency has been to overemphasize the role of subjectivity or fall into an overpsychologizing of the self. No matter how well meaning, this view often fails to address the material conditions and issues of power and privilege at work in the lives of historically disenfranchised students.

The reticence in education to engage issues of the body also has been tied to scholarly tendencies to ignore material analysis of societal structures and the political apparatus of public schooling that shapes classroom life. The historical absence of the body has been so because "bringing the body into critical discussion is ... [considered] potentially disruptive and subversive" (Levy, 2000, p. 82) to the social order of schooling. Grounded in such a worldview, many educators assume that teaching and learning are solely cognitive acts. As such, teachers do not concern themselves with the physical nature of their students, unless one is deemed as "inappropriate," at which time administrators or psychologists are summoned to evaluate and hopefully "fix the problem."

To support students in becoming *full subjects of history*, Freire urges teachers to grapple with the fact that students construct knowledge through the multitude of collective interactions of the body with the world. Amanda Sinclair (1999) reminds us that

> the immediate impact of a person's body on another is profound. A great deal happens before a person opens their mouth. Emotions are aroused, judgments are made. Comfort or discomfort levels are established well in advance of verbal

communication. We unconsciously or consciously register and make judgments about stature and voice. Bodies elicit feelings of excitement and admiration, attraction and desire, envy and distaste.

(p. 3)

The material conditions and histories of students are made visible by their bodies. Their histories of survival are witnessed in their skin, teeth, hair, gestures, speech, and even the movement of their arms and legs. If "bodies are maps of power and identity" (Haraway, 1990, p. 2), then teachers must work to engage students' physical realities more substantively, in an effort to forge an emancipatory practice of education. It is not enough to rely on abstract learning processes, where only the analysis of words and texts is privileged in the construction of knowledge. Such an educational process of estrangement functions to alienate students from the world around them, from themselves, and from each other.

Thus, teachers and students must labor in the flesh: teaching and learning must be anchored in a material understanding of our human existence, as a starting place for classroom praxis and our struggle to reinvent the world. Freire (1993) posits this as vital to critical pedagogy, in that

> We learn things about the world by acting and changing the world around us. It is [in] this process of change, of transforming the world from which we emerged, [where] creation of the cultural and historical world takes place. This transformation of the world [is] done by us while it makes and remakes us.
>
> (p. 108)

However, there is nothing automatic or "natural" about social change. Nor is it a process that can solely rely on calculating logic or cold rationality, given the manner in which the body's sentient forces overwhelmingly shape human experiences and responses to social structures. Struggles in the name of social justice must, then, hold steadfast the fullness of our human existence if we are to craft truly emancipatory ways of teaching and learning.

Schooling and the Flesh

In our efforts to understand the process of schooling, teaching and learning have to be acknowledged as human labor that take place within our bodies and incorporate, consciously or unconsciously, the totality of our being. The corporeal phenomenon is always at work as we strive to make sense of the material conditions and social relations of power that shape our particular histories. In *Teaching to Transgress*, bell hooks (1994, in Kazan, 2005, p. 379) describes an awareness of her body within the traditional classroom:

> I have always been acutely aware of the presence of my body in those settings that, in fact, invite us to invest so deeply in a mind/body split so that, in a sense,

you're almost always at odds with the existing structure, whether you are a black woman student or professor. But if you want to remain, you've got, in a sense, to remember yourself- because to remember yourself is to see yourself always as a body in a system that has not become accustomed to your presence or to your physicality.

Through such awareness of presence, teachers can begin to build a practice of education where students are not being asked to confront themselves and each other as strangers, but rather as fully embodied human beings from the moment they enter the classroom. A critical praxis of the body must seek to contend in the flesh with the embodied histories of the disenfranchised, as well as the social and material forces that shape the conditions in which we teach and learn.

Freire (1993) speaks to the undeniable centrality of the body in the act of knowing:

> The importance of the body is indisputable; the body moves, acts, rememorizes, the struggle for its liberation; the body in sum, desires, points out, announces, protests, curves itself, rises, designs and remakes the world ... and its importance has to do with a certain sensualism ... contained by the body, even in connection with cognitive ability .... [I]t is absurd to separate the rigorous acts of knowing the world from the [body's] passionate ability to know.
>
> (p. 87)

This sensualism, with its revolutionary potential to nurture self-determination and the empowerment of students as individuals and social beings, is systematically stripped away from the educational process of public schooling. Most teachers "already well-versed in maintaining a grey world of unsexy knowing ... are well placed to take up the challenge" (McWilliams, 2000, p. 29) of policing expressions of passion, excitement, and physicality within the classroom, particularly when working with youth.

Conservative ideologies of social control, historically linked to Puritanical views of the body as evil, sensual pleasure as sinful, and passions as corrupting to the sanctity of the spirit, continue to be reflected in the narrow, rule-based pedagogical policies and practices of schooling today. The sensuality of the body is discouraged in schools through the prominent practice of immobilizing students' bodies within hard chairs and desks that contain and restrict their contact with one another and the environment around them. Viviane Laroy (2002) contends that

> The body is not usually granted a lot of space in our educational system; it is nothing more than what allows us to remain seated for hours and to move from one classroom to another and to meet the requirements ... 90% of the time spent in schools is typically in a state of immobility. Learning is reduced to an airborne exchange of knowledge between different minds: the knowledge in the teacher's mind is transmitted to the learners, defined as minds able to receive new knowledge or not.
>
> (p. 1)

Laroy argues that this tradition of fettered bodies is anchored in three classical paradigms, Socrates, Christianity, and Pavlov's dog. In the classical tradition, the sensual body is quickly subordinated to the mind and intellect is privileged over the senses (Seidel, 1964). In Christianity, the separation between the body and the soul constitutes an essential pedagogical concern in preserving purity of thought. In the Pavlovian model, the body is transformed into an instrumentalized object to be manipulated and controlled through external stimulus in the process of learning.

Such views of teaching and learning ultimately lead to pedagogical practices that do emotional and psychological violence through their erasure of the body and the annihilation of the flesh in the traditional rubric of classroom life. Accordingly, inequalities are reproduced in class through racialized, gendered, and homophobic perceptions and distortions of male and female bodies, embodied within the pedagogy of even the most well-intentioned teachers. Consequently, students from communities where the body with its senses and spontaneities is given greater primacy in the act of knowing and being are often coerced into sacrificing their knowledge of the body's sensuality, creativity, and vitality, in favor of an atomized, analytical, and instrumental logic of being. In light of such tendency, we as teachers need "to reflect on what bodies we give 'permission' to in our classrooms and the extent to which we let those bodies speak" (Kazan, 2005, p. 394) or move freely. Reflections may prove, for example, significant to explaining the overwhelming tendency of teachers and school officials to label African American and Chicano boys as hyperactive or attention deficit when they find it difficult to comply with common expectations of immobility.

Similarly, Susie O'Brien (2000) argues that "the corporeal, physical and sexual realms are unwelcome intrusions" (p. 46) into the everyday world of the classroom. The systematic disembodiment of students in the process of learning begins early in their academic formation. Despite child development theories asserting that human beings are sexual beings even before birth, sexuality as an ever-present phenomenon is repressed and denied within the four walls of the classroom. This is the case at puberty when adolescent bodies are sensitive to heightened and confusing sensations. Seldom do teachers, many of whom are not comfortable with their own sexuality, critically engage questions of sexuality beyond the often repeated cliché of "raging hormones" to connote teenage sexuality. Meanwhile, students are not only pedagogically abandoned, but also left at the mercy of media and corporate pirates that prey upon the bodily sensations, emotions, and stirrings of youth (Rushkoff, 2001). Henry Giroux (1998) argues:

> In the slick world of advertising, teenage bodies are sought after for the exchange value they generate in marketing an adolescent sexuality that offers a marginal exoticism and ample pleasures for the largely male consumer. Commodification reifies and fixates the complexity of youth and the range of possible identities they might assume while simultaneously exploiting them as fodder for the logic of the market.
>
> (p. 41)

Frightened by their own corporeal ambivalence and the physicality of students' bodies, education policymakers institute practices that coerce teachers into silence, limiting any discussion about one of the most significant aspects of humanity. The message is clear: everyone, especially youth, is expected to check their sexuality (along with other aspects of their lived histories) at the door prior to entering school. Despite the difficulties and hardships that such silence portends for many students, such as isolation and increasing rates of suicide among gay youth, schools act as moral leaders, much like churches, policing and repressing the body's participation.

The minimalism of US schools in the area of human sexuality can be contrasted with other parts of the world where straightforward facts about the "birds and bees" are considered a pedagogical imperative. In Sweden, for example, compulsory sex education has been in place since 1956, given their recognition of sex as a natural human act and the frank acknowledgment that most people become sexually active before they are twenty years old. Students learn at an early age about sexuality, reinforcing a more open and positive view of sex and the body. Curriculum begins at age six with anatomy and from age twelve on, topics are more geared toward developing tools for taking responsibility for their sexual lives. The outcome is that Sweden's rate of teen pregnancy and sexually transmitted diseases is among the lowest in the world (Grose, 2007).

The issue of teen pregnancy also illustrates how school practices and policies associated to the body are inextricably tied to gendered ideologies of power and control. Sinclair (1999) reminds us that schools, like most institutions, are only able to "assimilate women's bodies so long as they conform to a neutral or desexualized form." Young teen mothers violate the norm by "drawing attention to their femaleness, their sexuality, and difference from the male norm" (p. 5). Hence, teen pregnancy is addressed by "excommunicating" and exiling young expectant mothers from the school campus while young fathers are left virtually untouched by the same system.

Missing, even in the university, is the willingness to contend with the sexuality of students in their process of academic formation despite the fact that "intense desires are played out in the university classroom" (O'Brien, 2000, p. 49). In keeping with the mind/body split, educators ignore the manner in which learning is both visceral and sensual. Consequently, the severing of the body's desires and sensations from the construction of knowledge interferes with students' capacity for self-knowledge. Such practices also thwart our knowledge of "the other," rendering us alienated and estranged to any human suffering that exists outside of the particular and limited scope of our identities, whether linked to gender, ethnicity, sexuality, skin color, ability, or spirituality. Spender (1995) argues that the absence of pedagogical engagement with the body inhibits the development of empathy and respect for those deemed as "the other." Thus, it should be no surprise to learn that many traditional curricular policies and practices, which reinforce abstract, fragmented, and decontextualized theories of teaching and learning, seldom function in the interest of oppressed populations. Instead, students are objectified, alienated, and domesticated into passive roles. Schools discourage us from thinking about ourselves as bodies (Kazan, 2005). This not only interferes with student achievement, but also sabotages social agency and the evolution of consciousness. This is visible when emotional and physical needs of students are ignored in an overriding effort to obtain their obedience and conformity.

In spite of major institutional efforts to control the body's desires, pleasures, and mobility in the classroom, students seldom surrender their bodies completely or acquiesce readily to authoritarian practices, providing the impetus for resistance (Shapiro, 1999). Many students engage in the construction of their cultural forms of resistance that may or may not always function in their best interest. Paul Willis (1977/1981) exposes this phenomenon in his ethnography of working-class kids in England. Then as it is today, expressions of youth resistance are enacted through counterculture alterations of the body, including clothing, hairstyle, posturing, manner of walking, way of speaking, piercing, and tattooing. They represent not only acts of resistance but also alternative ways of experiencing and knowing the world that are generally perceived by school officials as both transgressive and disruptive to the social order. Such views of students are exacerbated by what Giroux (1998) contends is a "new form of representational politics [that] has emerged in media culture fueled by degrading visual depictions of youth as criminal, sexually decadent, drug crazed, and illiterate. In short, youth are viewed as a growing threat to the public order" (p. 29).

Teachers, whose bodies are similarly restricted, alienated, and domesticated by their workplace, are under enormous pressure to follow strict policies and procedures for classroom conduct, while expected to dispense prepackaged curriculum, instead of employing more creative and critical approaches that are grounded in the actual needs of students. Given the impact of disembodied practices, teachers experience an uphill battle in meeting standardized mandates that extricate students' bodies from the equation of their learning. Nowhere is this more apparent than in low-income schools across the nation where teaching-to-the-test fronts as the "rigorous" and "scientific" curriculum of choice, even in many colleges and universities.

Along with teaching-to-the-test, there exists what Katherine Hayles (1999) terms as *incorporated knowledge*, notions of gender, sexuality, and "race" that are "deeply sedimented into the body and ... highly resistant to change" (p. 205). It constitutes knowledge that is generally beyond the reach of conscious view, given its habitual and ritualized nature. Its outcomes include repressive educational policies and practices that marginalize the knowledge and languages of oppressed populations, infantilize adult students, criminalize youth of color, and render suspicious any ideas or uses of the body that are perceived as existing outside of narrow mainstream views of normalcy. Incorporated knowledge associated with classroom management reproduces a variety of authoritarian classroom practices through teachers' efforts to maintain physical control of students. Even when teachers struggle within the classroom to implement more liberating strategies, they are often forced to become masters of deception, saying what the principal or district office wishes to hear, while doing behind closed doors what they believe is in concert with a democratic vision of education. Having to shoulder the hidden physical burden of such duplicity can drive some of the most effective teachers out of their chosen vocation, irrespective of their political commitment. Their experience of alienation and stress often becomes intolerable. Those who begin to feel defeated may in frustration begin to adopt more authoritarian approaches to manipulate and coerce "cooperation," while justifying the means in the name of helping students succeed academically.

What cannot be overlooked is the manner in which authoritarian practices are designed not only to "blindfold students and lead them to a domesticated future" (Freire, 1970, p. 79), but also to alienate and estrange teachers from their labor. Concerned with the need to restore greater freedom, joy, and creativity in the classroom, Freire (1998) urges teachers to reject their domesticating role and work to challenge the authoritarianism of standard policies and practices of pedagogy, curriculum, and school administration, which require an open process of dialogue, for "in classrooms, with the doors closed, it is difficult to have the world unveiled" (p. 9).

A critical praxis of the body is salient to rethinking university education, where there seems to be little pedagogical tolerance for the emotional needs of adult learners. "Somewhere in the intellectual history of the West there developed the wrongheaded idea that mind and heart are antagonists, that scholarship must be divested of emotion, that spiritual journeys must avoid intellectual concerns" (Lifton, 1990, p. 29). Such tradition sets an expectation, for example, that professors and students compartmentalize themselves within the classroom without any serious concern for the manner in which the essence of university education is tied to major moments of life transitions. Students are asked to make major intellectual commitments and material investments related to the direction of their uncertain futures. They also are expected to engage their studies and research as objective, impartial observers, even when the object of their study is intimately linked to conditions of human suffering.

Moreover, Freire (1993) argues that the traditional academic expectations of the university reinforce pedagogical myths. These include that feelings corrupt research and its findings; intuition should be feared; emotion and passion must be negated; and science and technology rule. These myths "end in convincing many that, the more neutral we are in our actions, the more objective and efficient we will be [in our knowing]" (p. 106). Hence, students are slowly but certainly socialized to labor as uncritical, descriptive, "neutral" scholars who are dispassionate and disembodied in their intellectual constructions of the world. The outcome is scholarship conceived through a deeply estranged way of knowing where values are restricted to scientific definitions and knowledge is divorced from human emotions and connections. Seldom does such an approach to knowledge guide or encourage students to grapple with moral questions that challenge the social and material relations of inequality that function to sustain human suffering in the first place.

Critical Principles for a Pedagogy of the Body

As our consciousness becomes more abstracted, we become more detached from our bodies. One could say that a hidden function of public schooling is to initiate and incorporate poor, working class, and students of color into social and material conditions of labor that normalize their alienation and detachment from the body. Such function is absolutely necessary for social control and the extraction of surplus labor, given that the body is the medium through which we wage political struggle and through which we transform our historical conditions as individuals and social beings (Eagleton, 2003). Hence, the perception of students as integral human beings is paramount to both questions of ethics and the development of critical consciousness. All aspects of our humanity, with their pedagogical needs, are present and active at all times; that is to say, all aspects of our humanity are integral to the process of teaching and learning. To perceive students in terms of only the mind or only one way of knowing can translate into an objectifying and debilitating experience for students, despite the intellectual and cultural strengths they bring to their education.

Students must therefore be acknowledged, respected, and treated as entering the classroom as whole persons. The degree to which this is possible is linked to the skill of teachers to be fully present, to negotiate the process of learning *with* their students, and to establish meaningful interactions in the classroom community. Such a horizontal view of student-teacher relationships goes hand in hand with obliterating the myth that an impersonal and emotionally distant approach to engaging students is professionally and pedagogically correct. It also counters beliefs among elitist mentors who brutalize their students through humiliation and cultivation of self-doubt, insisting that it engenders rigorous scholarship. What we often find is a reproduction of pedagogical brutality in their mentees who, having survived the hazing of privilege, now feel special and entitled. They defend dehumanizing pedagogical relations of power as they become the new gatekeepers of the discipline. Nowhere is this condition more devastating to watch than in students from oppressed communities who, "earning" entry into the elite group, embrace their position as a sign of "empowerment."

At issue is the reproduction of veiled class distinctions that educators enact in the classroom and in the "real world." Ira Shor and Paulo Freire (1986) insist that

> What we do in the classroom is not an isolated moment separate from the "real world." It is entirely connected to the real world and it is the real world which places both powers and limits on any critical course. Because the world is in the classroom, whatever transformation we provoke has a conditioning effect outside our small space. But the outside has a conditioning effect on the space also, interfering with our ability to build a critical culture separate from the dominant mass culture.
>
> (p. 26)

Nathan Snaza and Timothy Lensmire (2006) likewise argue that "we must cease to think of our lives separate from the operations of capital …. School *and* society *is* a false dichotomy: school is society" (p. 15, italics in original text).

Accordingly, critical principles that support a pedagogy of the body oblige educators to be cognizant of the larger social, political, and economic conditions that shape their lives and the lives of their students. In brief, the following provides a summary of important pedagogical considerations related to decolonizing the body within the context of teaching and learning:

- Teachers must engage the emotional and physical responses and experiences of students in the process of teaching and learning. Their responses and experiences are recognized as meaningful indicators of strengths and limitations that students face in the process of their intellectual formation and social consciousness.

- Knowledge must be understood as a historical and collective process emanating from the body's relationship to the world. The body is primary in the construction of knowledge and development of moral thought or, as Connell (1987) reminds us, "in the reality of practice, the body is never outside history" (p. 87).
- The mind and its cognitive capacities have to be understood as only one medium for the construction of knowledge. Hence, students are seen as integral human beings whose minds, bodies, hearts, and spirits are implicated in the process of teaching and learning. Our practices must reach into the students' innermost emotional and psychic centers if we are committed to a pedagogy of emancipation.
- The knowledge derived from the body's interactions with the world constitutes a significant dimension of a critical educational praxis. Classroom and community relationships, materials, and activities must reflect this knowledge through cultural integrity with the communities in which students reside.
- Teaching and learning must be understood as a process of human labor that is tied to the material conditions and social relations of power that shape classroom life. Hence, the question of power and the uses of authority must be interrogated consistently.
- Knowledge construction has to be seen as a collective, historical phenomenon that takes place continuously within and outside of school. To privilege school knowledge and ignore the knowledge and power of lived experiences, limit students' social agency and diminish important opportunities for active participation in their process of learning.
- Teachers must create meaningful interactions and activities in classrooms and communities that support students to grapple honestly with the tensions of differences in worldview, whether related to class, race, gender, sexuality, ability, or culture, and their consequences within contexts of inequalities.
- The knowledge that teachers have of their own bodies, including their sexuality, is an important aspect in their ability to effectively interact with and competently educate diverse student populations.
- Acts of resistance connected to the body can signal meaningful alternative ways of knowing and relating to the world. Opportunities must be created for students to reflect, affirm, and challenge the meaning of acts of resistance in their lives.
- Opportunities must be created in classrooms and communities that permit students to control aesthetic and physical conditions, including the definition and execution of knowledge construction, aesthetics, politics, fashion, voice, and participation.

The above principles for a critical praxis of the body are linked to decolonizing the body from educational and social constraints that repress the development of voice, disrupt democratic participation, and thwart the self-determination of disenfranchised populations. Educators must work together with students, parents, colleagues, and the community to challenge the conditions of their labor in schools that render them passive and domesticate their dreams.

Forging an Emancipatory Vision: Love, Ethics, and the Body

Forging an emancipatory vision of schooling calls us back home to our bodies in a world where all aspects of our daily life, such as birth, death, marriage, family, school, work, leisure, parenthood, spirituality, and even entertainment, are monitored and controlled (Lefebvre, 1971). The historical colonization of our bodies has left many of us numb, alienated, fragmented, defenseless, and at the mercy of capital. The consequence, as Richard Brosio (1994) reminds us, is a deep sense of personal and collective dissatisfaction generated by a marketplace that cannot satisfy the human needs of the body, needs that can only be met through relationships that break the alienation and isolation so prevalent in our lives today. Through integrating principles that sustain a critical praxis of the flesh, teachers can begin to create a space in which emotional intimacy can thrive, nourishing academic development and human connection among students. Terry Eagleton (2003) urges us to recognize that the origin of emancipatory possibility and human solidarity resides squarely in the body. For it is through the collective interactions of integral bodies in the classroom that the possibility of moral thought can be awakened. This constitutes a very important aspect of pedagogy since, as Eagleton suggests, it is moral thought that places our bodies back into history and creates a place for us to grapple with the impact of structural inequalities, social and economic injustice, and the curtailing of human rights.

Moreover, it is the absence of a truly democratic moral language and practice of the body that stifles our capacity for social struggle today. Many educators across the country bemoan, justifiably so, the conditions created by high-stakes testing and other accountability measures that negatively impact their labor. However, despite their frustration, educators have struggled for the past eight years to communicate a clear and coherent emancipatory moral message to challenge the shallow economistic moralism of the Bush administration's educational panacea, No Child Left Behind (Karp, 2003). Some would argue that the lack of a coherent political project is a direct result of teachers' alienated complicity with the status quo and the contradictions inherent in their lack of politics within a highly charged political arena. Rather than exercising a language of economic efficiency and neoliberal accountability, life in schools and society requires the development of a moral political language that can safeguard the dignity and integrity of all human differences that are intrinsic to a pluralistic nation. Genuine democracy requires the body's interaction with the social and material world in ways that nurture meaningful and transformative participation. It must exist as a practice in which human beings can interact individually and collectively as empowered subjects of their lives.

Freire emphasizes the significance of love and the importance of ethics in education. He embraces love as an emancipatory and revolutionary principle, compelling us to become part of a new decolonizing culture that nurtures human connection, intimacy, trust, and honesty from the body out into the world. In the same vein, Shapiro (1999) writes, "With love we affirm and are affirmed. In the sociopolitical struggle against death from hunger, disease, exploitation, war, destruction of the earth, and against hopelessness, there is a great and growing need for our capacity to become 'body-full' with love" (p. 99). For Eagleton (2003), love means to comprehend the moral and the material as inseparably linked. It constitutes an essential ingredient of a just society and the political principle that must motivate struggles for social justice and human rights. It is grounded in the mutuality and interdependence of human existence. Also inherent is the understanding that we as educators are never at liberty to be violent, cruel, brutal, or authoritarian in the name of being pedagogically rigorous or scientific, actions that belie an ethos of democracy or enlightenment.

Freire (1993, 1995, 1998) contends that ethics is a significant point of departure for our private and public lives. It constitutes a political and moral question. Without morality, our politics and pedagogy can result in an instrument of oppression. Eagleton (2003), however, reminds us that morality cannot be confused with moralism. Morality in a critical pedagogical context entails exploring deeply the quality of our sensations, ideas, and practices, a process that teachers and students cannot accomplish by abstracting life from our social surroundings, from our cultures, or from our histories of survival. It requires educators to bring together in their teaching the moral and political as well as the particular and universal, acknowledging that nothing can survive in isolation. Through collective struggles to decolonize our bodies, consciousness is born. Through collective actions with students, colleagues, and communities, we can work together for the shifting of consciousness and for the transformation of material conditions. They require our participation in the actual settings in which we live and work. To not act in the immediacy of our workplace or lived environment can place us in danger of living out an abstracted or "false consciousness," one that can cause us to lose touch with the grief or empathy for others that human oppression stirs in the human soul.

Muriel Rukeyser (1996) writes, "a true consciousness is the confession to ourselves of our feelings; a false consciousness disowns them" (p. 49). Ultimately it is this disowning that leads to the corruption of the mind and the body. It is the outcome of an overabundance of contrived representations and images in schools, society, and the media that repeatedly tell poor, working class, and racialized populations that our lives are worthless, beckoning us to abandon ourselves daily in the name of capital. At a time when our civil liberties are being undermined, great moral courage is required to voice our dissent against policies and practices that betray the oppressed, rendering them disposable and expendable. To counter debilitating conditions in classrooms and society, we need a revolutionary pedagogy committed to the unfettering of the body by embracing the liberation of humanity as sensual, thinking, knowing, and feeling subjects of history. It entails rewriting the body into our understanding of pedagogy by calling forth the establishment of new social, political, and economic conditions that can reap new possibilities for public schooling. For classroom conditions that begin with the primacy of the body carry radical possibilities for reconnecting students deeply to their development as fully integral human beings. Most importantly, since the body is the material foundation of our yearning for human liberation, it is only in our bodies that we can ultimately enact a revolutionary love, a love grounded in shared human kinship, political self-determination, and economic justice.

References

Beckey, C. (2000), "Wicked Bodies: Toward a Critical Pedagogy of Corporeal Differences for Performance," in C. O'Farrell, D. Meadmore, E. McWilliam, and. C. Symes (eds.), *Taught Bodies*. New York, NY: Peter Lang, 57–80.
Brosio, R. (1994), *A Radical Democratic Critique of Capitalist Education*. New York, NY: Peter Lang.
Connell, R. (1987), *Gender and Power*. Cambridge: Polity.
Darder, A. (2002), *Reinventing Paulo Freire: A Pedagogy of Love*. Boulder, CO: Westview Press.
Eagleton, T. (2003), *After Theory*. New York, NY: Basic Books.
Foucault, M. (1995), *Discipline and Punish*. New York, NY: Vintage Books.
Freire, P. (1970), *Pedagogy of the Oppressed*. New York, NY: Seabury Press.
Freire, P. (1993), *Pedagogy of the City*. New York, NY: Continuum.
Freire, P. (1995), *Pedagogy of Hope*. New York, NY: Continuum.
Freire, P. (1998), *Teachers as Cultural Workers*. Boulder, CO: Westview Press.
Giroux, H. (1998), "Teenage Sexuality, Body Politics and the Pedagogy of Display," in Epstein (ed.), *Youth Culture: Identity in a Postmodern World*. Maiden, MA: Wiley-Blackwell, 24–55.
Grose, T. K. (2007), "Straight Facts about the Birds and Bees. U.S. News and WorldReport (March 26)." Retrieved September 20, 2008, from http://www.usnews.com/usnews/news/articles/070318/26sex.htm.
Haraway, D. (1990), "A Manifesto for Cyborgs," in L. Nicholson (ed.), *Feminism/postmodernism*. New York, NY: Roudedge, 190–233.
Hayles, K. (1999), *How We Become Posthuman: Virtual Bodies in Cybernetics, Literature, and Informatics*. Chicago, IL: University of Chicago Press.
hooks, b. (1994), *Teaching to Transgress*. New York, NY: Routledge.
Karp, S. (2003), *Equity Claims Don't Pass the Test*. Rethinking Schools Online (Spring). Retrieved ESEA173.shtml.
Kazan, T. (2005), "Dancing Bodies in the Classroom: Moving toward an Embodied Pedagogy." *Pedagogy* 5(3): 379–408.
Laroy, V. (2002), "The Body in a Pedagogy of Being." *Humanizing Language Teaching* 4(6). Retrieved September 20, 2008, from http://www.hltmag.co.uk/nov02/mart.htm.
Lefebvre, H. (1971), *Everyday Life in the Modern World*. London: Penguin.
Levy, B. (2000), "Pedagogy: Incomplete, Unrequited," in C. O'Farrell, D. Meadmore, E. McWilliam, and C. Symes (eds.), *Taught Bodies*. New York, NY: Peter Lang, 81–90.
Lifton, R. (1990), "The Genocidal Mentality." *Tikkun* 5(3): 29–32, 97–8.
McLaren, P. (1998), "Foreword," in S. Shapiro (ed.), *Pedagogy and the Politics of the Body: A Critical Praxis*. New York, NY: Garland, ix–xviii.
McWilliams, E. (2000), "Stuck in the Missionary Position," in C. O'Farrell, D. Meadmore, E. McWilliam, and C. Symes (eds.), *Taught Bodies*. New York, NY: Peter Lang, 27–37.
Merleau-Ponty, M. (2002), *The Phenomenology of Perception*. New York, NY: Routledge.
O'Brien, S. (2000). "The Lecherous Professor," in C. O'Farrell, D. Meadmore, E. McWilliam, and C. Symes (eds.), *Taught Bodies*. New York, NY: Peter Lang, 39–55.
Rukeyser, M. (1996), *The Life of Poetry*. Ashfield, MA: Paris.
Rushkoff, D. (2001), "The Merchants of Cool: A Report on the Creators and Marketers of Popular Culture for Teenagers." Retrieved September 20, 2008, from http://www.pbs.org/wgbh/pages/frontline/shows/cool/.

Seidel, G. (1964), *Martin Heidegger and the Pre-Socratics*. Lincoln, NE: University of Nebraska Press.

Shapiro, S. (1999), *Pedagogy and the Politics of the Body: A Critical Praxis*. New York, NY: Garland.

Shor, I., and Sl Freire, P. (1986), *A Pedagogy for Liberation: Dialogues for Transforming Education*. South Hadley, MA: Bergin and Garvey.

Sinclair, A. (1999), "Body and Pedagogy." Retrieved September 20, 2008, from http://www.mbs.edu/index.cfm?objectid=951E3441-123F-A0D842535588B213E90B.

Snaza, N., and Lensmire, T. (2006), "Abandon Voice?: Pedagogy, the Body and Late Capitalism." *InterActions: UCLA Journal of Education and Information Studies* 2(2). Retrieved September 20, 2008, from http://repositories.cdlib.org/gseis/interactions/vol2/iss2/art3.

Spender, D. (1995), *Nattering on the Net: Women, Power and Cyberspace*. Melbourne: Spinifex.

Willis, P. (1977/1981), *Learning to Labour: How Working Class Kids Get Working Class Jobs*. New York, NY: Columbia University Press.

9

Decolonizing Interpretive Research: Subaltern Sensibilities and the Politics of Voice

Sensitive to the way in which colonialism produced powerful stereotypes of the people it colonised, the [subaltern scholar] is continually attentive to the way anyone is characterized, aware that fixed definitions can produce distorting blind spots, which carry a cost in the real world.

For us, to learn is to construct, to reconstruct, to observe with a view to changing—none of which can be done without being open to risk, to the adventure of the spirit.

(Freire, 1989)

Decolonizing interpretive research is uncompromisingly committed to creating counterhegemonic intellectual spaces in which new readings of the world can unfold, in ways that lead us toward possibilities of social and material change. True to this underlying revolutionary aim, many subaltern researchers have drawn heavily from the transgressive traditions of post-colonial theorists to forge inroads into the contentious terrain of our intellectual borderlands. The voices of subaltern scholars like Gayatri Chakravorty Spivak (1988) in "Can the subaltern speak?" have challenged the epistemic violence of Western academics. In particular, Spivak takes to task even the stalwart Western leftist theorists such as Foucault and Derrida, confronting the underlying economic interests that surround academic research as commodity—generally constructed in the absence of subaltern sensibilities.

Spivak, moreover, shatters neutral claims in Western representations of the subaltern, suggesting a need for decolonizing engagements that defy the hegemonic traditions of the Western interpretive lens. At the core of Spivak's acerbic critique is the incapacity of Westerners to listen or hear the other, beyond enforcing and projecting their own Eurocentric sensibilities upon them—rendering the subaltern unseen and unheard. Hence, despite a variety of strident critiques issued over the years regarding Spivak's abstracting language, "pretentiously opaque" disconnection from her readers, "bewildering eclecticism," exceeding focus on epistemology, and her retreat from political activism and the universal socialist project (Eagleton, 1999; Wallace, 1999), Spivak's willingness to risk stepping into "ways of thinking outside the European context that were discredited when capitalism became the most powerful imperialist force" (Spivak cited in Wallace, 1999) offered subaltern scholars inspiration to explore and voice the particularities of our lived experiences; and, by so doing, unveil colonizing and erroneous Western pronouncements of subaltern conditions.

Beyond Western Epistemologies

Sensitivity to the history of colonialism could be an important corrective to the presentism and Eurocentrism of most analyses [...] with their propensity to overstate the singularity of the present and to posit a radical discontinuity between contemporary social life and the recent past.
(Boaventura de Sousa Santos, 2007)

The political sensibilities from which decolonizing interpretive research emerges must then be understood as both highly diverse and resistant to an absolute universalizing epistemological language—a language of empirical inquiry that has been predominantly anchored in fixed Western epistemologies of patriarchal dominance, class divisions, heterosexism, abled bodies, and racializing reproduction. Accordingly, these have resulted in the subordination of subaltern voices often deemed suspect and, at times, dangerous to the veracity of so-called objective claims. It is important then to recognize that this discussion, true to its decolonizing intent, seeks to advance an evolving and itinerant—that is an epistemologically fluid and flexible means of knowing the world that deterritorializes and destabilizes the fixity of knowledge (Paraskeva, 2011)—redefinition of Western notions of qualitative research that typically have led to abstract formulations devoid of both the internal and social negotiations that shape subaltern existence, particularly with respect to the most impoverished.

Herein lies the rationale for a decolonizing interpretive research methodology, in that, subaltern intellectuals working to critique, redefine, and reinvent dominant readings of oppressive social phenomenon have struggled to infuse transgressive epistemological sensibilities, which defy the embedded conquering drive of the Eurocentric imagination. Accordingly, the subaltern interpretive voice has emerged through a courageous and yet risky, itinerant inquiry process that brushes Western traditional notions of culture, knowing, and society against non-Western epistemological sensibilities—transgressive sensibilities that unfold beyond the colonizing abyssal divide (Santos, 2005) and are anchored to subaltern lived histories of struggle and survival.

Hence, it is not incidental that theorists, such as Spivak who have issued fundamental challenges to Western epistemologies, have emerged from historically colonized populations. In that, we have arrived to our scholarly inquiries anchored to a decolonizing sensibility of subaltern existence—that is, we have been forced to navigate across the dialectical terrain of what Paulo Freire termed the oppressor/oppressed contradiction, as part of our process of social and academic survival as subaltern cultural citizens and borderland intellectuals (Darder, 1991/2012). Furthermore, navigating the ravaging tensions and struggles of our subaltern positionality has also shaped us as the makers of meaning who have elected, painstakingly so, to ground our interpretive research efforts within anti-colonial traditions. As such, the underlying ethos of our intellectual labor has brought about, in deliberate and meaningful ways, fundamental epistemological shifts in the production of knowledge and, in doing so, has sought to offer a more just and emancipatory political vision of scholarship within both the academic borderlands and practical everyday struggles for liberation.

Toward a decolonizing end, subaltern researchers have chosen to engage colonizing theories of subalternity in ways that treat these ideas as desacralized texts, ripe for deconstruction, to be systematically and qualitatively analyzed, based upon our own lived subalternity, as both self-determined historical subjects and subordinated intellectuals capable of voicing and living our commitment to an anti-colonial vision of the world. Therefore, to perceive decolonizing interpretive research, which emerges within these instances, as solely an abstract theoretical endeavor is to ignore and undermine the powerful decolonizing voice that we, as subaltern researchers, employ in our production of counterhegemonic inquiry, claims, and subsequent conclusions and the political intent that fuels our endeavors. As such, decolonizing interpretive approaches must be understood as itinerant subaltern forms of qualitative research that seek to formidably challenge and disrupt the one-dimensionality of Eurocentric epistemicides prevalent in traditional theories of research and society (Paraskeva, 2011).

A Decolonizing Ethical Stance

Context matters when we look at ethics. The long view of colonialism has taught us to be cautious when making universal claims given the brutal consequences for those who don't fit within the universal who could be subsequently de-humanized.
(Samek & Shultz, 2017)

Beyond decolonizing epistemological concerns is also the humanizing endeavor to reinvent a decolonizing ethical stance for our participation in the larger political project for social transformation. There is, then, a significant qualitative dimension at work here, in that it is precisely from what hooks (1994) calls an "authority of lived experience" and our subaltern sensibilities—generally rendered marginal and irrelevant to mainstream thought—that our decolonizing voices find the veracity to speak, to question, to transgress, and to reinvent the distorting discourses of the powerful, along with conditions of material and social inequality that have perpetuated the political and economic demise of subaltern populations.

Central to the qualitative labor of decolonizing interpretive research are found radical processes of social inquiry, critique, and cultural reformulations (or reinventions, as Freire would say) that strike at the very heart of dominant ideologies linked to persistent asymmetrical practices—practices that, wittingly or unwittingly, reproduce classed, racialized, gendered, heterosexual, abled, religious, and other formations that sustain recalcitrant inequalities, intractable social exclusions, and the persisting political disaffiliation of the subaltern. This interpretive process entails then a multitude of careful (re)readings of the world and of subaltern histories, in ways that critically and openly challenge what Freire referred to as the "tragic dilemma of the oppressed" (Darder, 2018). More importantly, subaltern relationships in the world, as they emerge between the subject and object or signifier and signified, must be understood as dialectically mediated within the social and material contexts of capitalist production. As such, mainstream theories of subalternity, as Spivak argued, are rooted in assimilative official transcripts of society, generally governed by the interests of the wealthy and powerful. More specifically, decolonizing interpretive researchers labor under a set of significant philosophical and political assumptions of difference:

> [...] that are fundamentally mediated by power relations that are socially and historically constituted; that facts can never be isolated from the domain of values or removed from some form of ideological inscription; that the relationship between concept and object and between signifier and signified is never stable or fixed and is often mediated by the social relations of capitalist production and consumption; that language is central to the formation of subjectivity (conscious and unconscious awareness); that certain groups in any society and particular societies are privileged over others and, although the reasons for this privileging may vary widely, the oppression that characterizes contemporary societies is most forcefully reproduced when subordinates accept their social status as natural, necessary, or inevitable; that oppression has many faces and that focusing on only one at the expense of others (e.g. class oppression versus racism) often elides the interconnections among them; and, finally, that mainstream research practices are generally, although most often unwittingly, implicated in the reproduction of systems of class, race, and gender oppression.
>
> (Kincheloe & McLaren, 2005)

With all this in mind, decolonizing interpretive research, as discussed here, must be understood as not only about a process of empowerment of individuals but, more importantly, as an ethical and political effort to shift in both theory and practice the ways in which we comprehend issues of difference, as well as our place in the world with respect to others. Or as Spivak asserts, "Politics is other people, not just me, me, me" (cited in Wallace, 1999). Hence "she invites one to look at one's own context, positioning and complicities, to unlearn one's privilege, to establish an ethical relationship to difference and to learn to learn from below" (Andreotti, 2007). This entails a decolonizing ethical sensibility of difference that centers the subaltern voice as communal, demythologizes commonsensical notions of knowledge production, exposes the coloniality of power, disrupts Eurocentric epistemicides, and provides itinerant rereadings of subalternity.

Furthermore, the intentionality of interpretive research is also fundamentally grounded in what Enrique Dussel (2013) called an ethics of liberation, with "a rethinking of the totality of moral problems from the point of view and the demand of 'responsibility' for the poor" (p. 142). This multidimensional interpretive ethos of research seeks to redefine and rearticulate historical and contemporary claims made of subalternity and provide decolonizing strategies of engagement for altering the current hegemonic discourses and practices in the world that perpetuate colonizing aberrations.

Subaltern researchers who embark upon such a process are uncompromisingly committed not only to reinterpreting the world, but to the struggle for the reinvention of social and material conditions of everyday life. Inherent here is a dynamic and evolutionary promise of knowledge production informed by the radicalization of consciousness—a revolutionary social process, anchored both within histories of survival and the contingencies of everyday life (Darder, 2015). Moreover, there is no illusive ethical claim of neutrality from a decolonizing interpretive lens, in that its fundamental purpose and aim are to serve as an emancipatory epistemological tool in the expression and participation of subaltern voices in the larger on-going political project of decolonizing society.

Politics of the Subaltern Voice

You who understand the dehumanization of forced removal-relocation-reeducation-redefinition, the humiliation of having to falsify your own reality, your voice— you know. And often cannot say it. You try and keep on trying to unsay it, for if you don't, they will not fail to fill in the blanks on your behalf, and you will be said.
(Minh-Ha, 2009)

The politics of the subaltern voice engages forthrightly with the phenomenon of human oppression and its debilitating historical impact upon the identities, social location, representations, and material conditions of oppressed populations. Accordingly, subaltern voices emerge from tenacious and tireless navigation through the dehumanizing forces of silence, as Minh-Ha (2009) suggests, in a quest to unsay the distorted Eurocentric representations placed upon us. This notion recalls the epistemicidal assertions of Boaventura de Santos Souza (2005) and Paraskeva (2011), which point to a phenomenon in which voices that emerge from the knowledge outside the Western purview are not only rendered silent and invisible, but are often absorbed or destroyed, as is precisely the case with the culture of forgetting (Darder, 2014) prompted by colonializing epistemologies. This further points to that repressive epistemological region that Santos (2007) calls the abyssal divide, where the voices of the Other are rendered irrelevant or nonexistent. Of this, Santos writes:

> What most fundamentally characterizes abyssal thinking is thus the impossibility of the co-presence of the two sides of the line. To the extent that it prevails, this side of the line only prevails by exhausting the field of relevant reality. Beyond it, there is only nonexistence, invisibility, non-dialectical absence.
> (p. 1)

It is also worth noting that racializing class formations and implicit beliefs, attitudes, and values shaped by the impact of this abyssal divide persist in adherence to a global coloniality of power (Quijano, 2000; Grosfoguel, 2011) that further subjugates subaltern voice even within the geographic, academic, and political contexts of its formation. As such, colonizing expectations of knowledge production continue to be defined by the ruling interests of the economically and politically powerful. In response, subaltern voices call for a reading of history and the economy that profoundly critique and challenge official scripts of colonization around the world and their post-colonial celebrations, exposing that the colonial matrix of power (Tlostanova and Mignolo, 2009)—which encompasses economic control, control of authority, control of the public sphere, and ideological control and legitimation of knowledge—persists long after colonial political rule ceases (Wanderley and Faria, 2013). From this vantage point, our subaltern voices fueled by decolonizing interpretive sensibilities shed light on the whitewashed partiality and limitations of recorded accounts of knowledge, revealing the absence of subaltern voices that remain exiled and suppressed by the power of epistemicides.

Politically speaking, subaltern voices must often undertake oppositional interrogations of official claims that emerge from those sanctioned mainstream intellectuals who purport expertise in the production and navigation of explanatory knowledge about the lives and survival of those deemed as other—knowledge about which they themselves are tragically ungrounded and inexperienced. A central concern here, of course, is the extent to which a colonizing or what Edward Said (1978) called "orientalist" gaze is implicated in the Western production of research expertise about the other. Thus, an accompanying question is to what extent do Western political and economic interests distort the perceptions of the other, where an underlying hidden curriculum is the assimilation of the other, in order to preserve the classed, racialized, gendered, abled, sexual, and religious hierarchies or supremacies of Western cultural domination around the globe.

Hence, it is not surprising, for example, to uncover that "the deep underlying assumption that emerges in [traditional] studies is the physical and mental laziness of 'non-Westerners' as an immanent quality that makes them unproductive" (Frenkel and Shenhav, 2003). Such studies derived from an all-too-common deficit perspective— despite well-meaning intentions—ultimately work to undermine the social and material well-being of the oppressed, often leaving us further marginalized, exploited, disempowered, and excluded from participation in decision-making about our own lives and access to the benefits enjoyed freely by the wealthy and privileged. In response, subaltern voices brush fiercely across dominant interpretations in an effort to halt the assault, struggle to decolonize knowledge, and work to (re)produce knowledge forms that are in sync with the histories, cultures, languages, and cosmologies of the oppressed.

Fraser's (1990) concept of subaltern counterpublics is useful here in that she speaks to the concept of "arenas where members of subordinate social groups invent and circulate counterdiscourses, which in turn permit them to formulate oppositional interpretations of their identities, interests, and needs" (p. 56). Herein is found the counterhegemonic dimension essential to decolonizing interpretive research; for without the "formulation of oppositional interpretation" or itinerant quality of subaltern voices, born of the deep dialectical tension between hegemonic and subaltern knowledge that must be courageously navigated, a genuinely decolonizing interpretive would be impossible. It is for this reason that decolonizing interpretive analyses draw heavily on subaltern historical and cultural sensibilities. This is in line with Frantz Fanon's insistence that as colonized subjects liberate themselves from the colonizing frameworks that have constricted their voices and consciousness, they "are all the time adding to their knowledge in the light of experience, [and] will come to show themselves capable" (p. 141) of speaking the unspeakable.

It is, therefore, important to note that despite conventional qualitative research efforts to expand the positivist norms of scientific interrogation, the qualitative research arena still constitutes a space of knowledge construction dominated by an elite few and, thus, generally exists as a more benevolent colonizing expertise that, wittingly or unwittingly, still represses and marginalizes the deeper sensibilities inherent in the subaltern voice. This is carried out "by making statements about it, authorizing views of it, describing it, by teaching it, settling it, ruling it: in short, [Western research has functioned as a hegemonic apparatus] for dominating, restructuring, and having authority over" (Said, 1978, p. 3) subaltern knowledge production.

Interpretive studies conducted by subaltern theorists such as Spivak and others, whether stated to be so or not, illustrate attempts to decolonize the interpretive, in that subaltern voices bring their histories as colonized subjects to bear on the manner in which the theories of decolonizing researchers engage philosophically, historically, and qualitatively the lives of oppressed populations. I also want to emphasize that a decolonizing interpretive dynamic is at work in many of the writings of subaltern researchers throughout the last century, although this phenomenon has seldom been noted in the manner offered in this discussion. Hence, there are now subaltern sociologists, psychologists, political scientists, anthropologists, and literary writers from racialized and oppressed communities that have employed a decolonizing interpretive lens, in their efforts to extend and redefine our understanding of oppression and its impact on our lives and the lives of our peoples. Again, as members of oppressed communities and intimately grounded in the histories of oppression of which we write, the sensibilities of subaltern voices can offer epistemological breakthroughs necessary to forging transformative political praxis linked to bringing together decolonizing theories and practices within our fields of study and out in the world.

It is also telling that subaltern scholars have not always been aware of one another, since they have emerged within differing intellectual traditions and from a variety of historical contexts and geographical locations. Yet, there seems, nonetheless, to be an underlying similarity in the oppressor-oppressed dialectic often expressed in their works, which gives credence to both Santos and Paraskeva's claims related to epistemological differences inherent to subaltern sensibilities. This, of course, in no way implies that the subaltern voice exists as an essentialized phenomenon—or as Spivak (as cited in Wallace, 1999) asserts, "I do not think that just being in India is a union ticket to authenticity"—but rather to suggest that despite the many differences at work in its expression, there is indeed an epistemological thread of subalternity at work that offers sufficient continuity to speak across conditions of oppression. This is indeed a juncture where the edges of my analysis brush countercurrent to Spivak's defensive retorts against the existence of any stability across subaltern voices beyond strategic essentialism. In contrast, the argument here contends, without essentializing, that there exist decolonizing epistemological resonances that arise directly from one's social location within the colonial matrix of power. And that it is, in fact, these decolonizing resonances mitigated by political commitments that create possible fields for dialogue across subaltern differences, as well as guide our decolonizing responses amid interactions with Western intellectuals that profess to be allied to the struggle for human liberation.

Hence, decolonizing intentions have opened the way for counterhegemonic considerations that critically privilege the cultural histories and experiences of oppressed peoples and further contribute to reinventing false and debilitating notions of subalternity. The autoethnographic episteme from whence subaltern voices partly emanate, therefore, sits subtlety but powerfully beneath—suggesting a decolonizing episteme at work in the research finding, claims, and conclusions of subaltern scholars from different parts of the world. Furthermore, had Scholars such as Fanon, Memmi, Nyerere, Cabral, Bhabha, Spivak, and others not found the courage and intellectual wherewithal to follow the inner stirrings of their subaltern sensibilities, the decolonizing interpretive perspectives they have produced—centered on the lives of formerly colonized, enslaved, and genocided populations—would have remained ever silenced within the hegemonic abyssal divide of Western epistemological traditions.

Decolonizing Methodologies

Decolonizing Methodologies [...] provoke revolutionary thinking about the roles that knowledge, knowledge production, knowledge hierarchies and knowledge institutions play in decolonization and social transformation.

(Smith, 1999)

Decolonizing methodologies begin with the view that all human beings participate actively in producing meaning, irrespective of their social location. Subaltern researchers involved in conducting decolonizing interpretive study do not simply see their work as an academic exercise in knowledge construction, but as part of a larger imperative for liberating subaltern meaning and provoking revolutionary thought. In this sense, decolonizing researchers recognize themselves as cultural workers and, thus, their intellectual efforts are understood as deeply political projects of contestation. Therefore, they do not enter the arena as impartial and neutral observers or solely objective thinkers but, rather, as transformative intellectuals, grounded in a humanizing emancipatory political vision of inquiry. Hence, decolonizing researchers who seek to (re)create knowledge must labor consistently to be cognizant of the histories, lived experiences, cultural realities, and economic plights of the communities that inspire their research not solely as academic initiative, but as an intimately experienced and lived political commitment.

Decolonizing methodologies then encompass a rigorous process of study that helps to expand the limits of rationality and, by so doing, supports the development of counterhegemonic forms of thinking and reflecting upon the world, so to better grasp the impact of current social and material relations of power at work in the lives of subaltern populations. In turn, decolonizing interpretive research designs aim to demystify the artificial limits of racialized formations and economic hierarchies of domination, viewing all cultures and linguistic systems as significant to our planetary survival. In the process, subaltern sensibilities serve to support the epistemological creativity, imagination, questioning, doubting, and risk-taking so necessary to this approach. And, as inferred earlier, this decolonizing process of study signals a research design that incorporates the subaltern researcher as an unapologetic political participant, whose knowledge is understood a priori as partial, unfinished, and deeply informed by the particular historical, economic, and cultural configurations of the times.

I would be remiss to not mention that there are those who openly discredit decolonizing interpretive research as highly subjective abstraction that fails to produce practical or useful knowledge they bemoan the absence of voices (as legitimated by the mainstream). About the first line of critique, decolonizing interpretive studies are absolutely by no means a lesser alternative in research design or less rigorous than other forms of research designs, in that it requires rigorous engagement and rereadings of official discourses on histories, politics, economics, geographies (i.e., land-based), psychologies, spirituality, and so on. This in itself points to a profound intellectual challenge as well as an enormous possibility for producing counterhegemonic readings of the world that lead to the construction of decolonizing theories—theories anchored in subaltern sensibilities.

About specious concerns that decolonizing interpretive methodologies are less scientifically rigorous due to intentional integration of subaltern sensibilities, there are a few things that must be noted. Rigor is the outcome of developing an intellectual capacity to engage critically and move with depth into different aspects and dimensions of an issue or problem that one is studying and to do this both systematically and creatively. Within the context of a decolonizing interpretive analysis, subaltern researchers must enact these itinerant analytical skills in a manner that consistently contends with the link between theory and practice within their own labor as educators and researchers out in the world. Academic rigor within the context of a decolonizing interpretive research must be understood then as not only a cognitive or abstract process of analysis. Rather, it also entails a deeply physical, emotional, and spiritual activity of communal solidarity, which, when practiced consistently, allows subaltern researchers to become more integral human beings, through a creative and itinerant epistemological process of problematization and radicalization (Darder, 2015)—an empowering process of knowledge construction that although deeply rooted within the researchers' worldview, also crosses frontiers to evoke the common humanity of all.

On the criticism relative to practicality or usefulness, a decolonizing interpretive design is meant to both recover and generate new insights and theories from the richness of detailed comparisons of the existing literature related to subaltern theories and practices—comparisons deeply grounded within the decolonizing sensibilities of the researcher's political intent. This is essential, if subaltern voices are to disrupt and deliberately shift and shatter the hegemonic reasoning ascribed to social phenomena and move us beyond the traditional views of knowledge and society. This inherently implies that a very different practice must ensue, given shifts in epistemological frameworks that both define the problem and posit alternatives for future liberatory possibilities. For example, this signals decolonizing approaches that move us beyond the deceptive quantophrenia of positivism countering the unrelenting tendency to seek quantification of all human phenomena and rely on the tyrannous discourses of so-called evidence-based, even among qualitative researchers. The privileging of this Western hallmark of knowledge production anchored in a longstanding quest for mastery over nature, wittingly or unwittingly, interrupts our ability to delve deeper into contestations of human meaning and deep asymmetries of power responsible for disastrous consequences among subaltern populations.

In contrast, decolonizing methodologies are counterpunctal to the Eurocentric aesthetics of traditional research. It is for this reason that Fanon (1967) insisted, "But the native intellectual who wishes to create an authentic work [...] must realize that the truths of a nation are in the first place its realities. [They] must go on until [they have] found the seething pot out of which the learning of the future will emerge" (p. 223). This learning of the future that Fanon refers to is precisely that decolonizing knowledge that can support a shift in dominant social relationships and material structures, in the interest of economic and cultural democracy.

And lastly, there is the often-voiced and well-meaning concern about the "absence of voices." Decolonizing interpretive research signals an analysis that requires inherently a formidable process of simultaneous itinerancy and deductive analysis. This entails an inferential analysis that is deeply grounded in the a priori subaltern sensibilities of the researcher—sensibilities culturally groomed and sharpened within the subaltern context in which they labor (Darder, 2012). That is, to "know an area of inquiry inside out and [be] intimately familiar with the issues and controversies" that exists within the communal cultural context. Accordingly, research conclusions, traditionally assumed to be derived from purely individual production or a unilateral voice—true to the individualistic assumptions of a western episteme—can, in fact, only be derived from subaltern researchers' consistent and on-going engagements with the communal voices of fellow subaltern subjects. Hence, decolonizing interpretive research is inextricably tied to communal subaltern voices (or the "I am because we are" voice) and sensibilities, which sit and remain ever at the center of this intimate form of qualitative analysis. In many ways, this dialectical understanding of the subaltern voice echoes Freire's (1970) notion that the emancipatory knowledge of the researcher must emerge from an intimate understanding of "the empirical knowledge of the people" (p. 181).

All this, of course, entails a grueling and precarious process in the reformulation of existing hegemonic conceptualizations based on epistemologies of the subaltern. As such, colonizing knowledge must be systematically deconstructed by way of the wisdom of decolonizing epistemologies brought to light by an itinerant practice of analysis, critique, and reformulation. It is from whence that decolonizing interpretive methodologies can advance renewed emancipatory insights and new decolonizing perspectives. These perspectives, anchored to a priori knowledge of lived histories and an immense field of non-Western epistemologies, are exercised in the contestation and reinvention of hegemonic practices, within both the research arena and the larger field of political struggle. This points to a significant dialectical understanding within radical subaltern sensibilities—our individual voice exists dialectically to the larger communal expressions of voice. It is, again, important not to essentialize the meaning of what has just been stated, in that decolonizing theorists are subaltern researchers who recognize they are deeply accountable for the exercise of their individual voices, but who are keenly aware that the subaltern voice also emerges inherently from the devastation of communities—communities historically subordinated by genocide, slavery, colonization, and impoverishment to conserve economic apartheid, domestically and internationally.

Hence, the overarching purpose of a decolonizing methodology is to provide an emancipatory reformulation of the conceptual or ideological interrelationships that exist between theoretical explanations and practical applications within specific fields or areas of study and struggle. In light of this underlying purpose, the development of decolonizing theories must be understood as deeply integrative. This to say, it will either produce a new or reformulated decolonizing framework for consideration within some aspect of human phenomenon or demonstrate ways in which existing hegemonic proclamations of counterhegemonic theoretical perspectives (i.e., critical, feminist, queer, etc.) can be practiced in the world. Important to this rearticulation is a sound decolonizing analysis and interpretation that seek to demonstrate clearly the theoretical, structural, and practical transformations necessary to effectively integrating, in practice, conclusions that arise from decolonizing interpretive studies. As such, decolonizing forms of understanding that emerge here aim to further knowledge practices, pedagogical interventions, and political strategies that can move us toward more humanizing ways of being, feeling, thinking, speaking, and knowing the world.

Decolonizing Inquiry as Humanizing Praxis

For apart from inquiry, apart from the praxis, individuals cannot be truly human. Knowledge emerges only through invention and re-invention, through the restless, impatient, continuing, hopeful inquiry human beings pursue in the world, with the world, and with each other.

(Freire, 1970)

For Freire (1970), the construction of knowledge—particularly by and with oppressed populations—must unfold organically through a humanizing praxis that is grounded in the voices and sensibilities of subaltern researchers, both within the academy and out in the larger society. This calls for a decolonizing research process that situates subaltern sensibilities at the epicenter, driving and producing research that speaks to the specificities of their subalternity. Significant decolonizing human inquiry is an understanding of the interpretive research process as also tied to the expression of what Freire (1970) called our true vocation: to be human. As such, when communal and individual processes of inquiry are stifled or squelched—as these have been for so long among the subaltern—results are often conditions of dehumanization that deactivate the social agency, voice, and political self-determination of racialized and economically impoverished communities. For Freire (1970), "coming to voice and democratic participation then are inextricably linked to an evolving praxis of *naming the world* and cultivating the power to *denounce injustice* and *announce justice*." This is central to the discussion here, in that "oppressive reality absorbs those within it and thereby acts to submerge [...] consciousness" (p. 51), by way of everyday practices that blunt subaltern sensibilities and silence our unruly voices seeking to bear witness to conditions of subjugation that persists in the world today:

> In direct contrast, decolonizing interpretive research is intent on creating counterhegemonic spaces for human inquiry that openly unveil human subjugation and its consequences, motivated by radical compassion and the transformative power of communal solidarity. About this, the subaltern Maori scholar, Linda Tuhiwai Smith (1999) asserts, The intellectual project of decolonizing has to set out ways to proceed through a colonizing world. It needs a radical compassion that reaches out, that seeks collaboration, and that is open to possibilities that can only be imagined as other things fall into place.
>
> (p. xii)

Furthermore, Freire asserts, "While the problem of humanization has always, from an axiological point of view, been humankind's central problem, it now takes on the character of an inescapable concern" (p. 43). Inescapable concern, indeed, given the current disastrous conditions produced by globalized neoliberal interests that have hardened exclusions based on economic greed, wrongheaded notions of privilege, deviant ideologies of race, patriarchal dominance, and other forms of social exclusion, with an unrelenting push to further the disaffiliation subaltern populations.

Counter to political exploitation, domination, disempowerment, false generosities, and violence against the oppressed, decolonizing interpretive knowledge challenges forthrightly the persisting coloniality of power, to put in place liberatory ways of knowing and being that can potentiate our revolutionary dreams. Moreover, as revolutionary praxis, the restoration of our humanity is paramount to decolonizing research approaches, where the subaltern scholar engages systematically in sustained practices of transformative problem-posing inquiry (Freire, 1970), so as to articulate new truths in line with emancipatory possibilities. It is precisely through this rigorous and sustained progression of problematization that subaltern researchers arrive to decolonizing conclusions—conclusions embraced as legitimate and vital dimensions of our evolving sensibilities as empowered subjects of history, despite our legacies of social and material subordination.

Posited throughout this discussion has been a way of knowing that considers transformation and empowerment only possible through a sustained decolonizing process that faithfully and consistently acknowledges, draws on, and gives expression to subaltern sensibilities and itinerant epistemologies of the south (Santos, 2007) that invoke a larger emancipatory project—one that derails the social and material exclusions of subalternity. As such, this heralds a humanizing practice of research and politics linked to an underlying radical and transformative ethos of interpretive research, fueled by our political commitment to construct together the knowledge, structures, institutions, and relationships necessary to forging culturally democratic and economically just futures.

References

Andreotti, V. (2007), "An Ethical Engagement with the Other: Spivak's Ideas in Education." *Critical Literacy: Theories and Practices* 1(1): 69–79.
Darder, A. (1991), *Cultural and Power in the Classroom*. Westport, CT: Bergin & Garvey.
Darder, A. (2012), *Cultural and Power in the Classroom*, 2nd ed. Boulder, CO: Paradigm.
Darder, A. (2014), "Cultural Hegemony, Language, and the Culture of Forgetting: Interrogating Restrictive Language Policies," in P. Orelus (ed.), *Affirming Language Diversity in Schools and Society: Beyond Linguistic Apartheid*. New York, NY: Routledge, 35–53.
Darder, A. (2015), *Freire and Education*. New York, NY: Routledge.
Darder, A. (2018), *A Student Guide to Freire's Pedagogy of the Oppressed*. London: Bloomsbury.
Dussel, E. (2013), *Ethics of Liberation: In the Age of Globalization and Exclusion*. Durham, NC: Duke University Press Books.
Eagleton, T. (1999), "In the Gaudy Supermarket." *London Review of Books* 21(10): 3–6.
Fanon, F. (1967), *The Wretched of the Earth*. New York, NY: Grove Press.
Fraser, N. (1990), "Rethinking the Public Sphere: A Contribution to the Critique of Actually Existing Democracy." *Social Text* (25/26): 56–80.
Freire, P. (1970), *Pedagogy of the Oppressed*. New York, NY: Seabury Press.
Freire, P. (1989), *Pedagogy of Freedom*. New York, NY: Continuum.
Frenkel, M., and Shenhav, Y. (2003), "Decolonizing Organization Theory: Between Orientalism and Occidentalism," available at: www.mngt.waikato.ac.nz/ejrot/cmsconference/2003/proceedings/postcolonial/Frenkel.pdf.
Grosfoguel, R. (2011), "Decolonizing Post-Colonial Studies and Paradigms of Political Economy." *Transmodernity* 1(1), available at: http://escholarship.org/uc/item/21k6t3fq.
hooks, b. (1994), *Teaching to Transgress*. New York, NY: Routledge.
Kincheloe, J. L., and McLaren, P. (2005), "Rethinking Critical Theory and Qualitative Research," in N. Denzin and Y. Lincoln (eds.), *The Sage Handbook of Qualitative Research*, 3rd ed. Thousand Oaks, CA: Sage Publications.
Mignolo, W. (2007), "Delinking: The Rhetoric of Modernity, the Logic of Coloniality and the Grammar of De-coloniality." *Cultural Studies* 21(2/3): 449–514.
Minh-Ha, T. T. (2009), *Women, Native, Other*. Bloomington, IN: Indiana University Press.
Paraskeva, J. (2011), *Conflicts in Curriculum Theory*. New York, NY: Palgrave.
Quijano, A. (2000), Coloniality of Power, Eurocentrism, and Latin America. *Napantla: Views from the South* 1(3): 533–80, available at: http://iss.sagepub.com/content/15/2/215.short?rss=1&ssource=mfr.
Said, E. (1978), *Orientalism*. New York, NY: Vintage Books.
Samek, T., and Shultz, L. (2017), *Information Ethics, Globalization and Citizenship*. Jefferson, NC: McFarland, 37.
Santos, B. de Sousa (2005), *Democratizing Democracy: Beyond the Liberal Democratic Canon*. London: Verso.

Santos, B. de Sousa (2007), *Another World Is Possible: Beyond Northern Epistemologies*. London: Verso, 71.
Smith, L. T. (1999), *Decolonizing Methodologies*. London: Zed Book.
Spivak, G. C. (1988), "Can the Subaltern Speak?" in C. Nelson and L. Grossberg (eds.), *Marxism and the Interpretation of Culture*. Urbana, IL: University of Illinois Press, 271–316.
Tlostanova, M. V., and Mignolo, W. (2009), "Global Coloniality and the Decolonial Option," Kult 6: Special Issue on Epistemologies of Transformation, Department of Culture and Identity, Roskilde University, 130–47.
Wallace, J. (1999), Deconstructing Gayatri. The Higher Education, July 30, available at: www.timeshighereducation.com/features/deconstructing-gayatri/147373.article.
Wanderley, S., and Faria, A. (2013), "Border Thinking as Historical Decolonial Method: Reframing Dependence Studies to (Re)connect Management and Development. EnANPAD," available at: www.anpad.org.br/admin/pdf/2013_EnANPAD_EOR2021.pdf.

Part 4

Toward a Critical Theory of Racism

Introduction

Antonia Darder's (and her longtime collaborator Rodolfo Torres) understanding of "race" as a paper tiger construct that must be "shattered" has urged educators to examine the ways in which a commonsensical notion of "race" has become part of everyday discourse without question. As a result, this "make-believe" concept has infiltrated the way many come to comprehend racialized communities and acts of racisms linked to class. While this analysis may be relegated to mere semantics, the depth of this argument has put forth a much-needed rupture in the ways in which the discourse of race is carried forth in education and society. Darder's incisive and courageous critique of race is fundamental to her scholarship.

Darder and Torres posit a critical theory of racism in their study of marginalized and racialized populations in the United States. In the process of focusing on understanding the material conditions of racialized groups in the United States, their work is undeniably historical and comparative—both within and beyond its national and geographical border.

Summary of Articles

In this incisive article, "Shattering the 'Race' Lens: Toward a Critical Theory of Racism," Darder and Torres call for a critical theory of racism in understanding contemporary debates on the study of race and racism in the United States. They pursued this line of thinking to assist us in understanding the complicated, and at times, contradictory issues on "race" as common-sense discourse in US culture and society. Darder and Torres are concerned that critical scholars and educators are overly consumed with the use of "race" as a central category of analysis for interpreting social exclusion, marginalization, and racialized inequalities. In the process, this approach explains away the very idea of capitalism—and the ways in which political economic questions are deemed secondary and/or afforded the same equivalence to other units of analysis. Hence, it is not surprising to find that theories, practices, and policies are deeply rooted in the politics of identity and representation. Darder and Torres are further concerned that an approach focused primarily on "race" and representation might potentially do away with the imperatives of capitalist accumulation in both the United States and beyond. It ignores the existence of class divisions within racialized populations (p. 95).

A critical theory of racism and political economy-inspired class analysis might be useful here. Parochial notions of "race," firmly anchored in the civil rights and black power rhetoric, while instructive and necessary for the time, are unable to comprehend the plurality of racisms and differentiated class relations in the contemporary context. Drawing from political theorist Ellen Meiksins Woods, Darder and Torres see racism as integral to the process of capital accumulation. Following Wood's (1995) lead in thinking about the relationship between democracy and capitalism, they are also not interested in conflating the "plurality of human experience and social struggles with a complete dissolution of historical causality, where there is nothing but diversity, difference, and contingency, no unifying structures, no logic of process, no capitalism and therefore no negation of it, no universal project of human emancipation" (Wood in Darder, p. 97).

In "What's So Critical about Critical Race Theory: A Conceptual Interrogation," Darder and Torres acknowledge and commend on the scholarly works done in understanding "race" within the United States. However, they are interested in raising a different set of questions—fundamentally grounded in a political economy of racism and migration. Darder and Torres see the analytical limitations of "race" when thinking about the formation of a critical social science, and perhaps more importantly, the implementation of progressive social and educational policies that impact working-class and racialized populations in the United States. A key point for them is the use of critical race theory (CRT) to "buttress" educational-political debates of racism with the utility of "race" as the central unit of analysis. Darder and Torres recognize that the language of "class" and "capitalism" are used in some of the scholarship from critical race theorists, but more often than not, the works are generally "vague and undertheorized" when attempting to provide a critique of capitalism. They make it clear that their analyses of racism in the contemporary context start with the capitalist mode of production, class relations, and class struggle.

In this short article "Racism in a Medically Segregated World," Darder starts by citing Dr. Martin Luther King's quote from the *Medical Committee for Human Rights Convention* in 1966 where he sees injustice in health as the "most shocking and inhumane of all inequalities." Darder evokes King's words in thinking about the persistence of racism in a medically segregated world. She uses the (il)logic of neoliberalism which at one point historically offered a "safety net" to some social welfare protection against the "excesses to capital." As a way to comprehend oppression in medicine, she offers a grounded analysis in thinking about the relationship between racism and the medical profession. Darder attempts to understand racism as a structural phenomenon—an apparatus tied to power and state control. She points to white physicians, in particular, who work within a Eurocentric analytic frame based on their own history and background, and their inculcation into the field itself. To be sure, medical schools (not unlike other educational institutions) are a by-product of ethnocentrism that produces and perpetuates a certain set of standards and protocols that are generally based on "implicit cultural assumptions that function to preserve and protect the privilege, power and wealth of a ruling class." Hence, white physicians, similar to white teachers, are not taught to understand racism as a structural phenomenon.

According to Darder, racialized assumptions work to "normalize, justify, and reproduce biases" held by many doctors and medical school professors—based on their own inherent racist ideologies and practices with working-class medical students of color. The medical field, not surprising, has a long and problematic history toward people of color in the United States. For good reason, the Western field of medicine and its concomitant institutions are not trusted by those most oppressed in society. In articulating a medical apartheid, Darder points to (1) the eugenics movements in the United States in the 1920s and (2) the sterilization of Puerto Rican women in the 1960s as two prime examples of structural racism. She sees the exigency of coherence and vigilance in what we say and do in response to creating a cultural democracy in medicine.

In "A Marxist Challenge to the Concept of 'Race,'" Darder and Torres (2023) returned to their central arguments from their instructive work in *After Race: Racism after Multiculturalism* (2004). Some two decades later, they continue to be consistent and principled in their political and theoretical intervention in the study of racism—working within the Marxist tradition in their attempt to understand racism within the United States and beyond the nation-state. They go beyond the worn-out "race-versus-class" argument that has been central to US sociological and educational discourse for many decades. Darder and Torres point to the "insidious racializing logic of capital or capitalism as an ideology" that makes it extremely difficult for scholars to come together to speak and work across differing perspectives. Here, they speak squarely to the tensions between Marxists and critical race theorists writing and thinking in those fields, including education. Darder and Torres point to how scholars and activists have "overlooked or ignored among race-based theories that tend to discount the ways in which the material conditions of impoverished white populations around the world are more similar to impoverished populations of color than to their more affluent counterparts" (p. 93).

They see the organizing potential missed or lost when its politics and pedagogy are not grounded in anti-capitalism. For Darder and Torres, the insistence on a liberal, rights-centered political agendas serve to undermine a coherent working-class movement in the United States. In addition, the contemporary writings on "race" obscure class struggle, class conflict, and generally lack a systematic critique of capitalism. Darder and Torres are worried that some four decades later, much of the critiques done by Marxist scholars in understanding racism are just as compelling, relevant, and necessary, but maligned and conspicuously absent from contemporary debates on race and racism in the United States and beyond.

10

Shattering the "Race" Lens: Toward a Critical Theory of Racism

Race has become the lens through which is refracted all of society's problems.
—KENAN MALIK (1996)[1]

The truth is that there are no races .... The evil that is done by the concept and by easy-yet impossible-assumptions as to its application. What we miss through our obsession is, sim-ply, reality.
—KWAME ANTHONY APPIAH (1995)[2]

In recent years, "race"[3] has been the focus of theoretical, political, and policy debates. Dramatic national and international changes, both economic and political, have created conditions in which, on the one hand, racialized structures, processes, and representations are more intricate and elusive; yet, on the other hand, the historically entrenched inequalities persist. The changing socioeconomic conditions in the United States present immense challenges and opportunities for anti-racist activists and social science scholars to rethink the nature of contemporary racialized inequality. With President Bill Clinton's recent "race initiative" commencement address at the University of California, San Diego, and the acrimonious debates on affirmative action, language policy, and immigration, it is more evident now than ever before that there is a need for a critical theory of racism that can assist us to better understand the complex issues associated with the increasing racialization of American society.

"Race," though a key concept in sociological discourse and public debate, remains problematic. Policy pundits, journalists, and conservative and liberal academics alike all work within categories of "race" and use this concept in public discourse as though there is unanimity regarding its analytical value. However, like all other component elements of what Antonio Gramsci[4] called common sense, much of the everyday usage of "race" is uncritical. Gramsci argues that human beings view the world from a perspective that contains both hegemonic forms of thinking and critical insight. As such, notions of common sense are "rooted in cultural folklore but at the same time are enriched with scientific ideas and philosophical opinions, which enter into ordinary daily life."[5] Racialized group conflicts are similarly advanced and framed as a "race relations" problem, and presented largely in Black/white terms.

A prime example of this confusion is the analysis of the causes of the 1992 Los Angeles riots. In the aftermath of the riots, academics and journalists analyzed the riots as a matter of "race relations"—first it was a problem between Blacks and whites, then between Blacks and Koreans, and then between Blacks and Latinos, and back to Blacks and whites. The interpretation of the riots as a "race relations" problem failed to take into account the economic restructuring and the drastic shifts in demographic patterns that have created new dynamics of class and racialized ethnic relations in Los Angeles[6] These new dynamics include increasing changes in the ethnic composition of the city and a dramatic shift from a manufacturing-centered economy to one based on light manufacturing, service industries, and information technologies-urban dynamics intricately linked to "the globalizing pressure of capitalism to abandon the will to social investment within the national-domestic sphere."[7]

The Question of Identity Politics

[W]e work with raced identities on already reified ground. In the context of domination, raced identities are imposed and internalized, then renegotiated and reproduced. From artificial to natural, we court a hard-to-perceive social logic that reproduces the very conditions we strain to overcome.

—JON CRUZ (1996)[8]

Over the last three decades, there has been an overwhelming tendency among social science scholars to focus on notions of "race." Over the last three decades, there has been an overwhelming tendency among a variety of critical scholars to focus on the concept of "race" as a central category of analysis for interpreting the social conditions of inequality and marginalization.[9] As a consequence, much of the literature on subordinate cultural populations, with its emphasis on such issues as "racial inequality," "racial segregation," "racial identity," has utilized the construct of "race" as a central category of analysis for interpreting the social conditions of inequality and marginalization. In turn, this literature has reinforced a racialized politics of identity and representation, with its problematic emphasis on "racial" identity as the overwhelming impulse for political action. This theoretical practice has led to serious analytical weaknesses and absence of depth in much of the historical and contemporary writings on racialized populations in this country. The politics of busing in the early 1970s provides an excellent example that illustrates this phenomenon. Social scientists studying "race relations" concluded that contact among "Black" and "white" students would improve "race relations" and the educational conditions of "Black" students if they were bused to "white" (better) schools outside their neighborhoods.[10] Thirty years later, many parents and educators adamantly denounce the busing solution (a solution based on a discourse of "race") as not only fundamentally problematic to the fabric of African American and Chicano communities, but an erroneous social policy experiment that failed to substantially improve the overall academic performance of students in these communities.

Given this legacy, it is not surprising to find that the theories, practices, and policies that have informed social science analysis of racialized populations today are overwhelmingly rooted in a politics of identity, an approach that is founded on parochial notions of "race" and representation which ignore the imperatives of capitalist accumulation and the existence of class divisions within racialized subordinate populations. The folly of this position is critiqued by Ellen Meiksins Wood[11] in her article entitled "Identity Crisis," where she exposes the limitations of a politics of identity which fails to contend with the fact that capitalism is the most totalizing system of social relations the world has ever known.

Yet, in much of the work on African American, Latino, Native American, and Asian populations, an analysis of class and a critique of capitalism is conspicuously absent. And even when it is mentioned, the emphasis is primarily on an undifferentiated plurality of identity politics or an "intersection of oppressions," which, unfortunately, ignores the overwhelming tendency of capitalism to homogenize rather than to diversify human experience. Moreover, this practice is particularly disturbing since no matter where one travels around the world, there is no question that racism is integral to the process of capital accumulation. For example, the current socioeconomic conditions of Latinos and other racialized populations can be traced to the relentless emergence of the global economy and recent economic policies of expansion, such as the North American Free Trade Agreement (NAFTA). A recent United Nations report by the International Labor Organization confirms the negative impact of globalization on racialized populations. By the end of 1998, it was projected that one billion workers would be unemployed. The people of Africa, China, and Latin America have been most affected by the current restructuring of capitalist development.[12] This phenomenon of racialized capitalism is directly linked to the abusive practices and destructive impact of the "global factory"—a global financial enterprise system that includes such transnational corporations as Coca-Cola, Walmart, Disney, Ford Motor Company, and General Motors. In a recent speech on "global economic apartheid," John Cavanagh,[13] co-executive director of the Institute for Policy Studies in Washington, D.C., comments on the practices of the Ford Motor Company.

> The Ford Motor Company has its state-of-the-art assembly plant in Mexico ... where because it can deny basic worker rights, it can pay one-tenth the wages and yet get the same quality and the same productivity in producing goods The same technologies by the way which are easing globalization are also primarily cutting more jobs than they're creating.

The failure of scholars to confront this dimension in their analysis of contemporary society as a racialized phenomenon and their tendency to continue treating class as merely one of multiplicity of (equally valid) perspectives, which may or may not "intersect" with the process of racialization, are serious shortcomings. In addressing this issue, we must recognize that identity politics, which generally gloss over class differences and/or ignore class contradictions, have often been used by radical scholars and activists within African American, Latino, and other subordinate cultural communities in an effort to build a political base. Here, fabricated constructions of "race" are objectified and mediated as truth to ignite political support, divorced from the realities of class struggle. By so doing, they have unwittingly perpetuated the vacuous and dangerous notion that the political and economic are separate spheres of society which can function independently—a view that firmly anchors and sustains prevailing class relations of power in society. Ramon Grosfoguel and Chloe S. Georas posit that "social identities are con-structed and reproduced in complex and entangled political, economic, and symbolic hierarchy."[14] Given this complex entanglement, what is needed is a more dynamic and fluid notion of how we think about different cultural identities within the context of contemporary capitalist social formations. Such a perspective of identity would support our efforts to shatter static and frozen notions that perpetuate ahistorical, apolitical, and classless views of culturally pluralistic societies. How we analytically accomplish this is no easy matter. But however this task is approached, we must keep in mind Wood's concern:

> We should not confuse respect for the plurality of human experience and social struggles with a complete dissolution of historical causality, where there is nothing but diversity, difference and contingency, no unifying structures, no logic of process, no capitalism and therefore no negation of it, no universal project of human emancipation.[15]

Hence, if we are to effectively challenge the horrendous economic impacts of globalization on racialized communities, we must recognize that a politics of identity is grossly inept and unsuited for building and sustaining collective political movements for social justice and economic democracy. Instead, what we need is to fundamentally reframe the very terrain that gives life to our political understanding of what it means to live, work, and struggle in a society with widening class differentiation and ever-increasing racialized inequality. Through such an analytical process of reframing, we can expand the terms by which identities are considered, examined, and defined, recognizing racialized relations of power are fundamentally shaped by the profound organizational and spatial transformations of the capitalist economy.

A Critique of Race Relations

If "race relations" are a feature of contemporary society, it seems obvious that academics should study them. But the casual observer could equally well conclude from personal observation that it is "obvious" that the sun circulates around the earth. In order to believe otherwise, it is necessary to confront personal experiences with analytical reasoning and forms of rational measurement. In other words, "obviousness" is a condition which depends upon the location of the observer and the set of concepts employed to conceive and interpret the object.

—ROBERT MILES (1993)[16]

There has been a tendency in postmodern and poststructuralist views of the anti-racism project and "race relations" to neglect or ignore profound changes in the structural nature and dynamics of US capitalism in place of obvious or common-sense appraisals of racialized inequality. This same tendency is also evident in much of the recent scholarship on cultural politics and social difference. At a time when a historical materialist analysis of capitalism is most crucially needed, many social theorists and radical educators seem reticent to engage the very idea of capitalism with any analytical rigor or methodological specificity. Yet, recent structural changes in the US political economy and the increasing cultural diversity of America have made the issue of racism much more complex than ever before.

Rather than occupying a central position, these historical socioeconomic changes serve merely as a backdrop to the contemporary theoretical debates on the meaning of "race" and representation in contemporary society, debates that, more often than not, are founded on deeply psychologized or abstracted interpretations of racialized differences and conflicts. This constitutes a significant point of contention, given the dramatic changes in US class formation and the demographic landscape of major urban centers. These changing conditions have resulted in major shifts in perceptions of social location, prevailing attitudes, and contemporary views of racialized populations. More so than ever, these socioeconomic conditions are linked to transnational realities shared by populations of Mexico, Taiwan, the Caribbean, and other "developing" countries, despite specific regional histories which gave rise to particular sociocultural configurations, configurations that are fundamentally shaped within the context of the ever-changing global economy.

Recent works in cultural studies, multicultural education, and critical pedagogy have brought new critical perspectives to the study of racism and cultural differences within society. US scholars such as Cornel West, Michael Omi, Howard Winant, bell hooks, Henry Giroux, and others have attempted to recast the debate on the nature of "race" and racism and its implications for social change and educational reform. More specifically, these scholars discuss the concept of "race" within the larger context of changing social and economic conditions and posit "race" as both a social construct and fluid analytical category, in an effort to challenge static notions of "race" as a biologically determined human phenomenon. Although it cannot be denied that these provocative and eloquent works represent a challenge to the mainstream analysis of "race relations" and have made contributions to our understanding of the significance of racism and anti-racist struggles, they have failed to reconceptualize the traditional social science paradigm that relies on the reified category of "race." In the final analysis, the conceptual framework utilized by these scholars is entrenched in the conventional sociology of "race relations" language.

Nowhere has this theoretical shortcoming been more evident than in the contemporary multicultural education debate—a debate that has widely informed the development of postmodern educational theory today. Despite an expressed "transformative" intent, much of the multicultural education literature has only peripherally positioned public education within the larger context of class and racialized class relations. Noticeably absent from much of the writings of even critical multicultural educators is a substantial critique of the social relations and structures of capitalism and the relationship of educational practices to the rapidly changing conditions of the US political economy. The absence of an analysis of the capitalist wage-labor system and class relations with its structural inequalities of income and power represents a serious limitation in our efforts to construct a theory and practice of democratic life.

A lack of imagination in multicultural education discussions is also highly evidenced by a discourse that continues to be predominantly anchored in the Black-white framework that has for over a century shaped our thinking and scholarship related to social group differences. One of the most severe and limited aspects of the Black-white framework to the future of the anti-racist project is its tendency (albeit unintentionally) to obstruct or camouflage the need to examine the particular historical and contextual dimensions that give rise to different forms of racisms around the globe. Furthermore, the conflation of racialized relations into a Black-white paradigm, with its consequential rendering of other subordinate cultural populations to an invisible or "second-class oppression" status, has prevented scholars from engaging with the specificity of particular groups and delving more fully into the arena of comparative ethnic histories of racism and how these are ultimately linked to class forms of social inequalities.

The habitual practice of framing social relations as "race relations" in discussions of students from subordinate cultural communities obfuscates the complexity of the problem. Here educational theorists assign certain significance to "racial" characteristics rather than attributing student responses to school conditions and how these are shaped by the structure of society and the economic and political limitations which determine the material conditions under which students must achieve. The unfortunate absence of this critique veils the real reasons why African American, Latin American, and other "minority" students underachieve, perform poorly on standardized tests, are over-represented in remedial programs and under-represented in gifted programs and magnet schools, and continue to drop out of high school at alarming rates. As a consequence, educational solutions are often derived from distorted perceptions of the problem and lead to misguided policies and practices. The politics of busing in the early 1970s discussed earlier in this chapter provides an excellent example of this phenomenon of distortion.

Although some would be quick to object to our critique, we can see the above also at work in the manner in which many education scholars have focused their studies in racialized communities. Overall, studies with minority students have placed an overwhelming emphasis on cultural and linguistic questions tied to academic achievement. This is illustrated by the large body of education literature that focuses on the cultural difference of "language minority" students, while only marginally discussing the impact of racialized inequality and class position on identity and cultural formations, as if somehow the problems of African Americans, Latinos, Native Americans, and other students from subordinate cultural populations can be resolved simply through the introduction of culturally relevant curriculum or the enactment of language policy. Moreover, it is this limited view of the problem that most informs the recent political debates between supporters of bilingual education and California's Proposition 227 (also known as the Unz Initiative or English for the Children).

From "Race" to Racialization

For three hundred years black Americans insisted that "race" was no useful distinguishing factor in human relationships. During those same three centuries every academic discipline ... insisted that "race" was the determining factor in human development.

TONI MORRISON (1989)[17]

As Morrison implies, unproblematized "common sense" acceptance and use of "race" as a legitimate way to frame social relations have been highly prevalent in the social sciences. The use of this term, for example, among Chicano scholars in the 1960s can be linked to academic acts of resistance to the term "ethnicity" and theories of assimilation which were generally applied to discuss immigration populations of European descent. In efforts to distance Chicano scholarship from this definition and link it to a theory of internal colonialism, cultural imperialism, and racism, Chicanos were discussed as a colonized "racial" group in much the same manner that many radical theorists positioned African Americans. Consequently, the term's association with power, resistance, and self-determination has veiled the problematics of "race" as a social construct. Protected by the force of cultural nationalist rhetoric, "race" as an analytical term has remained a "paper tiger"—seemingly powerful in discourse matters but ineffectual as an analytical metaphor, incapable of moving us away from the pervasive notion of "race" as an innate determinant of behavior.

In these times, we would be hard-pressed to find a progressive scholar who would subscribe to the use of "race" as a determinant of specific social phenomena associated with inherent (or genetic) characteristics of a group. Yet the use of "race" as an analytical category continues to maintain a stronghold in both academic and popular discourse. What does it mean to attribute analytical status to the idea of "race" and use it as an explanatory concept in theoretical discussions? The use of "race" as an analytical category means to position it as a central organizing theoretical principle in deconstructing social relations of difference as these pertain to subordinate cultural populations.

Notwithstanding provocative arguments by left theorists such as Adolph Reed, Jr., who unequivocally assert that "Race is purely a social construction; it has no core reality outside a specific social and historical context its material force derives from state power, not some ahistorical 'nature' or any sort of primordial group affinities,"[18] there is an unwillingness to abandon its use. Yet, it is this persistent use of "race" in the literature and research on African Americans, Latinos, and other culturally subordinated populations that perpetuates its definition as a causal factor. As such, the notion of "race" as a social construction "only leads us back into the now-familiar move of substituting a sociohistorical conception o race for the biological one that is simply to bury the biological conception below the surface, not to transcend it."[19] Hence, significance and meaning are still attributed to phenotypical features rather than to the historically reproduced processes of racialization. This ultimately serves to conceal the underlying causes of material conditions experienced by racialized groups that are determined by complex social processes, one of which is premised on the articulation of racism to effect legitimate exclusion.[20]

This process of racialization is at work in the disturbing "scientific" assertion that "race" determines academic performance made by Richard J. Herrnstein and Charles Murray in their book *The Bell Curve*.[21] Their work illustrates the theoretical minefield of perpetuating such an analytical category in the social sciences and the potential negative consequences on racialized groups. The use of the term "race" serves to conceal the truth that it is not "race" that determines academic performance, but rather, that academic performance is the outcome of an interplay of complex social processes, one of which is tied to the articulation of racism (and its subsequent practices of racialization) to effect exclusion in the classroom and beyond.

It is within the historical and contemporary contexts of such scholarship that differences in skin color have been and are signified as a mark which suggests the existence of different "races." As a consequence, a primary response among many progressive activists and scholars when we call for the elimination of "race" as an analytical category is to reel off accusations of a "color-blind" discourse. This is not what we are arguing. What we do argue is that the fixation on skin color is not inherent in its existence but is a product of signification. This is to say, human beings identify skin color to mark or symbolize other phenomena in a variety of social contexts in which other significations occur. As a consequence, when human practices include and exclude people in light of the signification of skin color, collective identities are produced and social inequalities are structured.[22]

Moreover, it is this employment of the idea of "race" in the structuring of social relations that is termed *racialization*. More specifically, Miles in his book *Racism* defines this process of racialization as

> those instances where social relations between people have been structured by the significance of human biological characteristics in such a way as to define and construct differentiated social collectivities ... the concept therefore refers to a process of categorization, a representational process of defining an Other (usually, but not exclusively) somatically.[23]

Hence, to interpret accurately the conditions faced by subordinate cultural populations requires us to move from the idea of "race" to an understanding of racialization and its impact on class formations. This summons a bold analytical transition from the language of "race" to recognizing the centrality of racism and the process of racialization in our understanding of exclusionary practices that give rise to structural inequalities.

Toward a Plurality of Racisms

[T]he presumption of a single monolithic racism is being replaced by a mapping of the multifarious historical formulations of racisms.

—DAVID THBO GOLDBERG[24]

In order to address these structural inequalities, an analytical shift is required, from "race" to a plural conceptualization of "racisms" and their historical articulations with other ideologies. This plural notion of "racisms" more accurately captures the historically specific nature of racism and the variety of meanings attributed to evaluations of difference and assessments of superiority and inferiority of people. Conversely, to continue our engagement of racism as a singular ideological phenomenon fails to draw on the multiplicity of historical and social processes inherent in the heterogeneity of racialized relations. This is to say, for example, that the notion of "white supremacy" can only have any real meaning within populations whose exploitation and domination are essentialized based on skin color. As such, this view severs the experience of African Americans, for instance, from meaningful comparative analysis with those racialized populations whose subordination is predicated on other social characteristics.

Consequently, "white supremacy" arguments cannot be employed to analyze, for example, the racialization of Jews in Germany during the 1930s, or Gypsy populations in Eastern Europe, or the Tutsi population in the Congo. Closer to home, the concept of "white supremacy" sheds little light on what is happening in Watts and South Central Los Angeles between the Korean petite-bourgeoisie and the African American and Latino underclass or reserve army (to use a more traditional concept!). Instead, what we are arguing for is a plural concept of racism that can free us from the "Black/white" dichotomy and, in its place, assert the historically shifting and politically complex nature of racialization. More specifically, it is a pluralized concept of racism that has relevance and analytical utility in comprehending the political economy of racialized relations in South Central Los Angeles as well as the larger sociocultural landscape that can, beyond this analysis, link the economic structures of oppression in this local context to the global context of racialized capitalism. Most importantly, we argue that the problems in racialized communities are not about "race" but rather about the intricate interplay between a variety of racisms and class. It is for this reason that we do not believe that scholars should not be trying to advance a "critical theory of race."[25] A persistence in attributing the idea of "race" with analytical status can only lead us further down a theoretical and political dead end. Instead, the task at hand is to deconstruct "race" and detach it from the concept of racism. This is to say, what is essential for activists and social science scholars to understand that the construction of the idea of "race" is embodied in racist ideology that supports the practice of racism. It is racism as an ideology that produces the notion of "race," not the existence of "races" that produces racisms.[26]

Hence, what is needed is a clear understanding of the plurality of racisms and the exclusionary social processes that function to perpetuate the racialization of members from culturally and economically marginalized communities. Robert Miles convincingly argues that these processes can be analyzed within the framework of Marxist theory without retaining the idea of race as an analytical concept.

> Using the concept of racialization, racism, and exclusionary practices to identify specific means of effecting the reproduction of the capitalist mode of production, one is able to stress consistently and rigorously the role of human agency, albeit

always constrained by particular historical and material circumstances, in these processes, as well as to recognize the specificity of particular forms of oppression.[27]

Miles's work also supports the notion that efforts to construct a new language for examining the nature of differing racisms requires an understanding of how complex relationships of exploitation and resistance, grounded in differences of class, ethnicity, and gender, give rise to a multiplicity of ideological constructions of the racialized Other. This knowledge again challenges the traditional notion of racism as predominantly a Black/white phenomenon and directs us toward a more accurately constructed and, hence, more politically and analytically useful way to identify a multiplicity of historically specific racisms.

We recognize that there are anti-racist scholars who cannot comprehend a world where the notion of "race" does not exist. Without question, mere efforts to undo and eliminate the idea of "race" as an analytical category in the social sciences are insufficient to remove its use from the popular or academic imagination and discourse of everyday life. Moreover, in a country like the United States, filled with historical examples of exploitation, violence, and murderous acts rationalized by popular "race" opinions and scientific "race" ideas, it is next to impossible to convince people that "race" does not exist as a "natural" category. So, in Colette Guillaumin's words, "Let us be clear about this. The idea of race is a technical means, a machine, for committing murder. And its effectiveness is not in doubt."[28] But "races" do not exist. What does exist is the unrelenting idea of "race" that fuels racisms throughout the world.

The Need for a Critical Theory of Racism

Moreover, language presents us with resources for the construction of meanings which reach out towards the future, which point to possibilities that transcend our experience of the present. And those fighting for liberation from oppression and exploitation will invariably find within language words, meanings and themes for expressing, clarifying, and coordinating their struggle for a better world.
—DAVID MCNALLY (1997)[29]

In considering a shift from the study of "race" to the critical study of racism, what is clear is that we need a language by which to construct culturally democratic notions of sociopolitical theory and practice. This entails the recasting and reinterpretation of social issues in a language with greater specificity, which explicitly reflects an international anti-racist notion of society. Such a language must unquestionably be linked to global histories of social movements against economic inequalities and social injustice. Although we fully recognize that theoretical language alone will not necessarily alter the power relations in any given society, it can assist us to analytically reason more accurately and, thus, to confront more effectively how power is both practiced and maintained through the systematic racialization of subordinate populations. As such, a critical language of racism can provide the foundation for developing effective public policies that are directly linked to liberatory principles of cultural and economic democracy. In summary, we deny any place for the use of "race" as an analytical concept and support efforts to eliminate all conceptions of "race" as a legitimate entity or human phenomenon. We believe that the future struggle against racism and capitalism must at long last contend with the reality that there are no "races" and therefore no "race relations."

> There is only a belief that there are such things, a belief which is used by some social groups to construct an Other (and therefore the Self) in thought as a prelude to exclusion and domination, and by other social groups to define Self (and so to construct an Other) as a means of resisting that exclusion. Hence, if it is used at all ... "race" should be used only to refer descriptively to such uses.[30]

In light of this, we posit a critical conceptualization of racism with which to analyze both historical and contemporary social experiences and institutional realities. Insofar as such a concept, whether employed in social investigation or political struggle, reveals patterns of discrimination and resulting inequalities, it raises the question: What actions must be taken to dismantle these inequalities? This in turn requires nothing less than to confront racism in all its dimensions head-on. At the risk of being redundant, we must emphasize once again that rejecting "race" as having a real referent in the social world does not mean denying the existence of racism, or the denial of historical and cultural experiences predicated on a specific population's particular struggle against racism. Rather, a critical theory of racism represents a bold and forthright move to challenge common-sense notions of "race" that often not only lead to profound forms of essentialism and ahistorical perceptions of oppression but also make it nearly impossible to dismantle the external material structures of domination that sustain racialized inequalities in schools and the larger society.

Furthermore, we recognize the empirical reality that people believe in the existence of biologically distinct races. This can be captured analytically by stating that people employ the idea of "race" in the construction and interpretation of their social worlds. Similarly, we acknowledge that it is a common practice among the oppressed to invert the experience of exploitation. This is to say that negative notions of "race" linked to racist ideology are turned on their head and employed to fuel political movements among racialized populations. Social activists and scholars are not obliged to accept the common-sense ideas employed in the social world and use them as analytical concepts. The whole tradition of critical/ Marxist analysis highlights the importance of developing an analytical framework that penetrates the surface and reified realities of social relations. (See, for example, Marx's discussion of the distinction between phenomenal forms and essential relations, his discussion of reification, and his discussion of method in the Introduction to the Grundrisse der Kritik der politischen Okonomie[31] [1939].) In keeping with this tradition, we focus on racism as an analytical concept—a concept that has a real object in the social world, namely an ideology with a set of specific characteristics informed by economic imperatives—and we only refer to the idea of "race" when people use the notion in their everyday genres, utilizing it to make social distinctions based on the significance that is attached to differences between populations. Finally, unlike scholars who argue resolutely for a critical theory of "race," we seek a critical language and conceptual apparatus that make racism the central category of analysis in our understanding of racialized inequality, while simultaneously encompassing the multiple social expressions of racism. Undoubtedly, this entails the development of a critical language from which activists and scholars can reconstruct theories and practices of contemporary society that more accurately reflect and address capitalist forms of social and material inequities that shape the lives of racialized populations. Most importantly, we are calling for a critical theory of racism that can grapple with a radical remaking of democracy in the age of a globalized post-industrial economy. There are many who have proclaimed the death of the socialist project, but we argue that its renaissance is close at hand and will be articulated through a language that is fueled by the courage and passion to break with those hegemonic traditions on the left that fail to support a democratic vision of life for all people.

Notes

1   Malik (1996, p. 34).
2   Appiah (1995, p. 75).
3   Quotation marks are used around the word "race" not only to distinguish it as a social construct but to question the legitimacy of its descriptive and analytical utility. Following the example of British sociologist Robert Miles, we agree that the use of "race" as an analytical concept disguises the social construction of difference, presenting it as inherent in the empirical reality of observable or imagined biological differences. For more on this issue, see Miles (1989) and (1993). For an insightful note on the use of quotation marks and the "racial" logic of the practice itself, see Jacobson (1998_1, pp. ix, x).
4   Gramsci (1971).
5   Darder (1991, p. 42).
6   Valle and Torres (1995, pp. 139–53).
7   Cruz (1996, p. 29).
8   Ibid., 35.
9   Some contemporary examples of this scholarship can be found in West (1993); hooks (1996); Omi and Winant (1993); and Gates, Jr. (1992).
10 Gordon Allport's (1954) and Kenneth Clark's (1955) strongly influenced the intellectual rationale and public policy decisions that instituted the busing solution in the United States.
11 Wood (1994, pp. 28–9).
12 Associated Press, Geneva, report released by the United Nations' International Labor Organization, entitled "Unemployment Will Reach 1 Billion Worldwide by Year's End," on Sunday, September 28, 1998.
13 Cavanagh, "Global Economic Apartheid" (1996, p. 2), available through Alternative Radio. Boulder, Colorado. Dr. Cavanagh is a specialist in international trade, economics, and development and is coauthor with Barnet (1994).
14 Grosfoguel and Georas (1996, pp. 193).
15 Wood (1995, p. 263).
16 Miles, *Racism after "Race Relations,"* 1.

17 Morrison (1989, p. 3).
18 Reed Jr., (1998, p. 22).
19 Appiah, "The Uncompleted Argument," 74.
20 Miles and Torres (1996, p. 32).
21 Herrnstein and Murray (1994).
22 Miles and Torres, "Does 'Race' Matter?," 75.
23 Miles (1989).
24 Goldberg (1990, p. xiii).
25 For recent scholarly works that focus on "critical theories of race," see Delgado (1995); Crenshaw, et al. (1995); and Wing (1997); as well as writings by Winant (1994).
26 Guillaumin (1995).
27 Miles, *Racism after "Race Relations,"* 52.
28 Guillaumin, *Racism, Sexism, Power, and Ideology*, 107.
29 McNally (1997, pp. 40–1).
30 Miles, *Racism after "Race Relations,"* 42.
31 Marx (1939).

References

Anthias, F., and Yuval-Davis, N. (1992), *Racialized Boundaries: Race, Nation, Gender, and Color and Class and the Anti-racist Struggle*. New York, NY: Routledge, 15.

Appiah, K. A. (1995), "The Uncompleted Argument: Du Bois and the Illusion of Race," in L. Bell and D. Blumenfeld (eds.), *Overcoming Racism and Sexism*. Lanham, MD: Rowman and Littlefield, 75.

Baldwin, J. (1998), "On Being White … and Other Lies," in David Roediger (ed.), *Black on White: Black Writers on What It Means to Be White*. New York, NY: Schocken, 178.

Barnet, R. J. (1994), *Global Dreams: Imperial Corporations and the New World Order*. New York, NY: Simon and Schuster.

Cavanagh, J. (1996), "Global Economic Apartheid." Alternative Radio (September 19). Takoma Park, MD. www.alternativeradio.org.

Crenshaw, K., Gotanda, N., Peller, G., and Thomas, K. eds. (1995), *Critical Race Theory: The Key Writings That Formed the Movement*. New York, NY: New Press.

Cruz, Jon (1996), "From Farce to Tragedy: Reflections in the Reification of Race at Century's End," in A. F. Gordon and C. Newfield (eds.), *Mapping Multiculturalism*. Minneapolis, MN: University of Minnesota Press, 29.

Darder, A. (1991), *Culture and Power in the Classroom*. Westport, CT: Bergin and Garvey, 42.

Davis, A. (1996), "Gender, Class, and Multiculturalism: Rethinking Race Politics," in A. F. Gordon and C. Newfield (eds.), *Mapping Multiculturalism*. Minneapolis, MN: University of Minnesota Press, 43.

Delgado, Richard, ed. (1995), *Critical Race Theory: The Cutting Edge*. Philadelphia, PA: Temple University Press.

Gates Jr., H. L. (1992), *Loose Canons: Notes on the Culture Wars*. New York, NY: Oxford University Press.

Gilroy, P. (1991), *"There Ain't No Black in the Union Jack": The Cultural Politics of Race and Nation*. Chicago, IL: University of Chicago Press, 9.

Goldberg, D. T. (1990), *Anatomy of Racism*. Minneapolis, MN: University of Minnesota Press, xiii.

Gordon Allport's (1954), *The Nature of Prejudice*. Reading, MA: Addison-Wesley.

Gramsci, A. (1971), *Selections from the Prison Notebooks*. New York, NY: International Publications.
Grosfoguel, R., and Georas, C. S. (1996), "The Racialization of Latino Caribbean Migrants in the New York Metropolitan Area." *Centro: Focus en Foco* 1–21(8): 193.
Guillaumin, C. (1995), *Racism, Sexism, Power, and Ideology*. London: Routledge.
Harris, C. (1998), "Whiteness as Property," in David Roediger (ed.), *Black on White: Black Writers on What It Means to Be White*. New York, NY: Schocken, 107.
Herrnstein, R. J., and Murray, C. (1994), *The Bell Curve: Intelligence and Class Structure in American Life*. New York, NY: Free Press.
hooks, b. (1989), *Talking Back*. Boston, MA: South End Press, 112–13.
hooks, b. (1996). *Killing Rage: Ending Racism*. New York, NY: Henry Holt and Company, Inc.
Jacobson, M. F. (1998), *Whiteness of a Different Color: European Immigrants and the Alchemy of Race*. Cambridge, MA: Harvard University Press, ix, x.
Kenneth Clark's (1955), *Prejudice and Your Child*. Boston, MA: Beacon Press.
Malik, K. (1996), *The Meaning of Race: Race History, and Culture in Western Society*. New York, NY: New York University Press, 34.
Marx, K. (1939), *Grundrisse der Kritik der politischen Okonomie*. Moskau: Verlag fur Fremdsprachige Literatur.
McNally, D. (1997), "Language, History, and Class Struggle," in E. M. Wood and J. B. Foster (eds.), *In Defense of History: Marxism and the Postmodern Agenda*. New York, NY: Monthly Review Press, 40–1.
Miles, R. (1989), *Racism*. London: Routledge.
Miles, R. (1993), *Racism after "Race Relations"*. London: Routledge.
Miles, R., and Torres, R. D. (1996), "Does 'Race' Matter? Transatlantic Perspectives on Racism after 'Race Relations,'" in V. Amit-Talai and C. Knowles (eds.), *Re-situating Identities: The Politics of Race, Ethnicity and Culture*. Peterborough: Broadview Press, 32.
Mills, C. W. (1997), *The Racial Contract*. Ithaca, NY: Cornell University Press, 76.
Morrison, T. (1989), "Unspeakable Things Unspoken: The Afro-American Presence in American Literature." *Michigan Quarterly Review* 28(1) (Winter): 3.
Omi, M., and Winant, H. (1993), *Racial Formation in the United States: From the 1960s to the 1980s*. New York, NY: Routledge.
Reed Jr., A. (1998), "Skin Deep." *Village Voice* 24 (September): 22.
Valle, V., and Torres, R. D. (1995), "The Idea of Mestizaje and the 'Race' Problematic: Racialized Media Discourse in a Post-Fordist Landscape," in A. Darder (ed.), *Culture and Difference*. Westport, CT: Bergin and Garvey, 139–53.
West, C. (1993), *Race Matters*. Boston, MA: Beacon Press.
Wieviorka, M. (1997), "Is It Difficult to Be an Anti-Racist?" in P. Werbner and T. Modood (eds.), *Debating Cultural Hybridity: Multicultural Identities and the Politics of Anti-Racism*. London: Zed Books, 40.
Winant, H. (1994). *Racial Conditions: Politics, Theory, Comparisons* (NED-New edition). Minneapolis, MN: University of Minnesota Press. http://www.jstor.org/stable/10.5749/j.ctttss2b.
Wing, A. K. (1997), *Critical Race Feminism: A Reader*. New York, NY: New York University Press.
Wood, E. M. (1994), "Identity Crisis." *In These Times* (June): 28–9.
Wood, E. M. (1995), *Democracy against Capitalism: Renewing Historical Materialism*. New York, NY: Cambridge University Press, 263.

11

What's So Critical about Critical Race Theory? A Conceptual Interrogation with Rodolfo Torres

Racism as it operates socially, in no way assumes an explicit theory of "race."
—PIERRE-ANDRE TAGUIEFF, 2001, p. 197

Over the last half-century considerable attention has been paid to issues related to "race" and "race relations" in the social sciences, humanities, and legal studies. The debates intensified first with the groundbreaking *Brown v. Board of Education* case in 1954 and then again with the civil rights movements of the 1960s. The current debates are beginning to intensify once more as critical race theorists[1] not only retain the idea of "race" but further entrench it as a central category of analysis. Hence, the early "race" paradigm has become the new orthodoxy, retaining symbolic and political utility for many. This is evident in even more progressive articulations of "race" such as *The Miner's Canary*, a highly acclaimed book by Lani Guinier and Gerald Torres (2002) that enlists race as a political space within the context of what they term "a political race project."

Before continuing any further, we wish to acknowledge and commend such efforts to make sense of the problematics associated with "race" within U.S. society. However, we seek to raise different questions regarding the foundational theories that shape these arguments and, more importantly, to question the analytical limitations of "race" with respect to the formation of a critical social science and execution of progressive social policies.

Critical race theory emerged as an offshoot of critical legal theory. Legal scholars in this tradition argued that legal theory had historically failed to engage in a critical analysis of society and, by so doing, continued to function as a fundamental tool of oppression that ultimately benefited the state. Not long after, critical legal theory was critiqued by black critical legal scholars such as Derrick Bell, Patricia Williams, Randall Kennedy, Lani Guinier, and others who pointed to the failure of critical legal scholars to engage questions of "race" within the framework of the alternative views they posited. The result was the forging of a subdivision of critical legal theory that is now called critical race theory.

Latino critical legal scholars such as Gerald Torres and Richard Delgado, in concert with Latino scholars in education and other disciplines, followed suit by developing a field of study today known as Latino critical race theory, or LatCrit, to address similar issues within the context of Latino life in the United States. Similar critical race theory began to evolve among Asian American scholars with the work of Mari Matsuda, often considered one of the founders of the field.

Grounded in the belief that "much of the national dialogue on race relations takes place in the context of education" (Roithmayr, 1999, p. 1), African American and Latino scholars such as Gloria Ladson-Billings, Daniel Solorzano, Dolores Delgado Bernal, and Laurence Parker began to infuse their arguments in education policy with critical race theory. Their key argument was the uncompromising insistence that "race" should occupy the central position in any legal, educational, or social policy analysis. Given the centrality assigned to "race," "racial" liberation was embraced as not only the primary but as the most significant objective of any emancipatory vision of education or the larger society.

The Centrality of "Race"

There is no question but that the issues raised by critical race theorists in education, policy studies, and the social sciences are significant to our understanding of the conditions that plague racialized student populations in US schools today. However, one of our major concerns with the use of critical race theory to buttress educational-political debates of racialized oppression or racism is directly linked to the use of "race" as the central unit of analysis. Coupled with an uncompromising emphasis on "race" is the conspicuous absence of a systematic discussion of class and, more importantly, a substantive critique of capitalism.

Let us be more specific here. In contending with questions of "race" and institutional power, references are indeed made to "capitalism" or "class"[2] in some works by critical race theorists and, in particular, Latino critical race theorists, who acknowledge that "attention to class issues has been … a pending, but as yet underdeveloped, trajectory in the future evolution of LatCrit theory and the consolidation of LatCrit social justice agendas" (Iglesias, 1999, p. 64).[3] However, these efforts to explore the ways in which socioeconomic interests are expressed in the law or education are generally vague and undertheorized. Because of this lack of a theoretically informed account of racism and capitalist social relations, critical race theory has done little to further our understanding of the political economy of racism and racialization. In addition, much of critical race theory's approach is informed by ambiguous ideas of "institutional racism" or "structural racism," which, as Miles (1989) points out, are problematic due to the danger of conceptual inflation.

Our aim here is not to dismiss this important body of work but to point out an important analytical distinction we make in our intellectual and political project. Our analysis of racism in contemporary society begins with the capitalist mode of production, classes, and class struggle. The mode of production, which is the site of class relations, is the point of departure in our interrogation of racism as an ideology of social exclusion. In contrast, critical race scholars attribute constitutive power to the American legal system itself. Hence, the "relative autonomy" of legal institutions is invoked to stress the power of "race" and to set their work apart from critical legal scholars, who "could not come to grips with the continuing problems of deeply embedded racism" (Guinier and Torres, 2002, p. 34). We maintain that the legal system (the state) is located in a given economic context and is shaped by the imperatives of capital.[4]

Our critique, then, is tied to the continued use of the traditional language of social theory, which has always been inadequate in problematizing notions of "race" in both research and popular discourse. In essence, we argue that the use of "race" has been elevated to a theoretical construct, despite the fact that the concept of "race" itself has remained under-theorized. Hence, to employ alternative constructs derived from legal theory to shape arguments related to educational policy and institutional practices, although well meaning and eloquent, is like beating a dead horse. No matter how much is said, it is impossible to enliven or extend the debate on educational policy with its inherent inequalities by using the language of "race."

Even a brief overview of the most prominent writings in critical race theory shows how little movement there has been in furthering our understanding of the concept or redirecting the debate. Overall, most of the work is anchored in the popular intersectionality argument of the poststructuralist and postmodernist era, which maintains that "race," gender, and class should all receive equal attention in our understanding of society and our development of institutional policies and practices. More recently, Guinier and Torres (2002), in an apparent effort to push through the limits of the intersectionality argument, proposed to advocate for what they term "racial literacy" from which "to identify patterns of injustice that link race to class, gender, and other forms of power." (29) Despite their innovative use of "race," its traditional analytical use remains intact.

Our concerns with critical race theory go beyond the desire to construct intellectual abstractions. Rather, our concerns are grounded in political questions such as: Where exactly does an anti-race theory of society lead us in real political struggles for social justice, human rights, and economic democracy? How do we launch a truly universal emancipatory political project anchored primarily upon a theory of "race"? Where is a critique of capitalism or an explicit anti-capitalist vision in a critical theory of "race"? Can we afford to overlook the inherent existence of a politics of identity in the foundational views that led to the construction of critical race theory? We are also troubled by the confusion with respect to the terms critical race theorists use to frame their analysis.

In this context, it is important to distinguish between how we understand the construct of "race" and its genesis. In our analysis, "race," simply put, is the child of racism. That is to say, racism does not exist because there is such a thing as "race." Rather, notions of "race" are a fundamental ideological construction of racism or a racialized interpretation of phenotypically and, may we add, regionally different human beings. The process of racialization, then, is at work in all relations in a capitalist society. Alternatively, we might say that the empire is not built on "race" but on an ideology of racism—this being one of the primary categories by which human beings are sorted, controlled, and made disposable at the point of production.

Hence, the experience of alienation is shaped along a variety of variables, one of which is that of racialization or racialized class relations. Racism is one of the primary ideologies by which material conditions in society are organized and perpetuated in the service of capitalist accumulation. This is why, to repeat, the empire is not built on "race" but on a variety of ideologies (of which racism is one) that justify the exploitation and domination of populations deemed as "Other" so as to conserve the capitalist social order.

We also seek to interrogate the idea of "race" as culture. For example, instead of linking the notion of culture to class relations which emerge at the point of production, or to the relations of production in which human beings exist and survive, critical race theorists link culture to the idea of "race"—an idea that historically has been associated with phenotypical traits. In the new "race" orthodoxy, phenotypical traits remain central to social construction, shared histories, and social narratives defined by experiences that are phenotypically determined. Miles (1989) associates this discourse of "race" to the process of signification:

> [W]hen the idea of "race" is employed, it is the result of signification whereby certain somatic characteristics are attributed with meaning and are used to organise populations into groups which are defined as "races." People differentiated on the basis of the signification of phenotypical features are usually also represented as possessing certain cultural characteristics, with the result that the population is represented as exhibiting a specific profile of biological and cultural attributes. The deterministic manner of this representation means that all those who possess the signified phenotypical characteristics are assumed to possess the additional characteristics.
>
> (p. 71)

Narrative and Storytelling as Method

The process of signification is at work in the emphasis that critical race theory places on "experiential knowledge" (Delgado, 1995; Ladson-Billings, 1999). Robin Barnes (1990) notes that "Critical race theorists … integrate their experiential knowledge, drawn from a shared history as 'Other' with their ongoing struggles to transform a world deteriorating under the albatross of racial hegemony" (1864–5). In concert with this privileging of experience, critical race theory employs narratives and storytelling as a central method of inquiry to "analyze the myths, presuppositions, and received wisdoms that make up the common culture about race and that invariably render blacks and other minorities one-down" (Delgado, 1995, p. xiv). The results of this storytelling method are theorized and then utilized to draw conclusions meant to impact public policy and institutional practices.

The narrative and storytelling method employed by critical race theorists sought to critique essentialist narratives in law, education, and the social sciences. In place of a systematic analysis of class and capitalist relations, critical race theory constructs "race"—centered responses to Eurocentrism and white privilege. Delgado Bernal (2002) affirms the validity of this position, arguing that

Western modernism is a network or grid of broad assumptions and beliefs that are deeply embedded in the way dominant Western culture constructs the nature of the world and one's experiences in it. In the United States, the center of this grid is a Eurocentric epistemological perspective based on White privilege.

(111)

The narrative method based on this perspective "has become especially successful among groups committed to making the voice of the voiceless heard in the public arena" (Viotti da Costa, 2001, p. 21). However, despite an eagerness to include the participation of historically excluded populations, scholars who embrace the poetics of the narrative approach often "fail to challenge the underlying socioeconomic, political and cultural structures that have excluded these groups to begin with and have sustained the illusion of choice" (Watts, 1991, p. 652). Thus, the narrative and storytelling approach can render the scholarship antidialectical by creating a false dichotomy between objectivity and subjectivity, "forgetting that one is implied in the other, [while ignoring] a basic dialectical principle: that men and women make history, but not under the conditions of their own choosing" (Viotti da Costa, 2001, p. 20).

We agree that "cultural resources and funds of knowledge such as myths, folk tales, *dichos, consejos,* kitchen talk, [and] autobiographical stories" (Delgado Bernal, 2002, p. 120) employed by critical race theory can illuminate particular concrete manifestations of racism. However, we contend that they can also prove problematic in positing a broader understanding of the fundamental macrosocial dynamics which shape the conditions that give rise to the "micro-aggressions" (Solorzano, 1998) of racism in the first place. In an incisive critique of the narrative approach, Emilia Viotti da Costa (2001) argues,

The new paths it opened for an investigation of the process of construction and articulation of multiple and often contradictory identities (ethnic, class, gender, nationality and so on), often led to the total neglect of the concept of class as an interpretive category .... What started as ... a critique of Marxism, has frequently led to a complete subjectivism, to the denial of the possibility of knowledge and sometimes even to the questioning of the boundaries between history and fiction, fact and fancy.

(19)

Robin Kelley, in his book *Yo' Mama's DisFUNKtional* (1997), offers the following illuminating and sobering commentary regarding the limits of personal experience and storytelling:

I am not claiming absolute authority or authenticity for having lived there. On the contrary, it is because I did not know what happened to our world, to my neighbors, my elders, my peers, our streets, buildings, parks, our health, that I chose not to write a memoir. Indeed, it relied on memory alone. I would invariably have more to say about devouring Good and Plentys or melting crayons on the radiator than about economic restructuring, the disappearance of jobs, and the dismantling of the welfare state.

(4–5)

Hence, we believe the use of critical race theory in education and the social sciences in general, despite authors' intentions, can unwittingly serve purposes that are fundamentally conservative or mainstream at best. Three additional but related concerns with the storytelling narrative method are also at issue here. One is the tendency to romanticize the experience of marginalized groups, privileging the narratives and discourses of "people of color," solely based on their experience of oppression, as if a people's entire politics can be determined solely by their individual location in history. The second is the tendency to dichotomize and "overhomogenize" both "white" people and "people of color" with respect to questions of voice and political representation (Viotti da Costa, 2001). And the third, anticipated by C. L. R. James in 1943,[5] is the inevitable "exaggerations, excesses and ideological trends for which the only possible name is chauvinism" (McLemee, 1996, p. 86). Unfortunately, these tendencies, whether academic or political, can result in unintended essentialism and superficiality in our theorizing of broader social inequalities as well as the solutions derived from such theories.

Yet, truth be told, prescribed views of humanity are seldom the reality, whatever be their source. Human beings who share phenotypical traits seldom respond to the world within the constraints of essentialized expectations and perceptions. Hence, any notion of "racial" solidarity "must run up against the hard facts of political economy ... and enormous class disparities" within racialized communities (Gates, 1997, p. 36). This is why Gilroy (2000) warns against "short-cut solidarity" attitudes that assume that a person's political allegiance can be determined by his or her "race" or that a "shared history" will guarantee an emancipatory worldview. For this reason, we argue that such declarations, though they may sound reasonable, commonsensical, or even promising as literary contributions, have little utility in explaining "how and why power is constituted, reproduced and transformed" (Viotti da Costa, 2001, p. 22).

Identity Politics and the Mantra of Intersectionality

Since the 1970s, much of the progressive literature on subordinate cultural populations has utilized the construct of "race" as a central category of analysis for interpreting social conditions of inequality and marginalization. In turn, this literature has adhered to a perspective of "race" as identity. This "raced" identity has received overwhelming attention in both the sociological and political arenas. Unfortunately, the unrelenting emphasis on "identity" unleashed a barrage of liberal and conservative political movements that unwittingly undermined the socialist project of emancipation in this country and abroad. Radical mass organizations that had once worked to spearhead actions for economic democracy, human rights, and social justice were crippled by the fury. In the midst of the blinding celebratory affirmations of identity, neoliberal efforts to seize greater dominion over international markets proliferated, and globalization became the policy buzzword of US economic imperialism at the end of the twentieth century. Given this legacy, it is not surprising that many of the theories, practices, and policies that inform the social science analysis of racialized populations today are overwhelmingly rooted in a politics of identity. Consequently, this approach—steeped in deeply insular perspectives of "race" and representation—has often ignored the imperatives of capitalist accumulation and the presence of class divisions among racialized populations, even though, as John Michael (2000) reminds us, "identity categories and groups are always [racialized] and gendered and inflected by class" (29).

As we have previously stated, much of the literature on critical race theory lacks a substantive analysis of class and a critique of capitalism. And when class issues are mentioned, the emphasis is usually on an undifferentiated plurality that intersects with multiple oppressions. Unfortunately, this "new pluralism" fails to grapple with the relentless totalizing dimension of capitalism and its overwhelming tendency to homogenize rather than to diversify human experience (Wood, 1994).

Strongly influenced by a politics of identity, critical race theorists incorporate the intersectionality argument[6] to refer to their examination of race, sex, class, national origin, and sexual orientation and how the combination of these identities plays out in various settings (Delgado and Stefancic, 2001). This school of thought, common to progressive scholarship, generally includes a laundry list of oppressions (race, class, gender, homophobia, and the like) that are to be engaged with equal weight in the course of ascribing pluralized sensibilities to any political project that proposes to theorize social inequalities. Hence, inadvertently in the name of recognizing and celebrating difference and diversity, this analytical construct reduces "the capitalist system (or the 'economy') to one of many spheres in the plural and heterogeneous complexity of modern society" (Wood, 1995, p. 242).

Wood argues that the intersectionality argument represents a distorted appropriation of Antonio Gramsci's notion of "civil society," which was explicitly intended to function as a weapon against capitalism by identifying potential spaces of freedom outside the state for autonomous, voluntary organization and plurality. However, as used by many on the left to link multiple oppressions to specific plural identities, the concept has been stripped of its unequivocal, anticapitalist intent. Wood speaks to the danger inherent in this analytical twist.

> Here, the danger lies in the fact that the totalizing logic and the coercive power of capitalism is reduced to one set of institutions and relations among many others, on a conceptual par with households or voluntary associations. Such a reduction is, in fact, the principal distinctive feature of "civil society" in its new incarnation. Its effect is to conceptualize away the problem of capitalism, by disaggregating society into fragments, with no overarching power structure, no totalizing unity, no systemic coercion-in other words, no capitalist system, with its expansionary drive and its capacity to penetrate every aspect of social life.
>
> (Wood, 1995, p. 245)

This denial of the totalizing force of capitalism does not simply substantiate the existence of plural identities and relations that should be equally privileged and given weight as modes of domination. The logic of this argument fails to recognize that "the class relation that constitutes capitalism is not, after all, just a personal identity, nor even just a principle of stratification or inequality. It is not only a specific system of power relations but also the constitutive relation of a distinctive social process, the dynamic of accumulation and the self-expansion of capital" (Wood, 1995, p. 246).

Furthermore, such logic ignores the fact that notions of identity result from a process of identification with a particular configuration of historically lived or transferred social arrangements and practices tied to material conditions of actual or imagined survival. The intersectionality argument fails to illuminate the manner in which commonly identified diverse social spheres or plural identities exist "within the determinative force of capitalism, its system of social property relations, its expansionary imperatives, its drive for accumulation, its commodification of all social life, its creation of the market as a necessity, and so on" (Wood, 1995, p. 246).

There is no question but that racism as an ideology is integral to the process of capital accumulation. The failure to confront this dimension in an analysis of contemporary society as a racialized phenomenon or to continue to treat class as merely one of a multiplicity of (equally valid) perspectives, which may or may not "intersect" with the process of racialization, is a serious shortcoming. In addressing this issue, we must recognize that even progressive African American and Latino scholars and activists have often used identity politics, which generally glosses over class differences and/or ignores class contradictions, in an effort to build a political base. Constructions of "race" are objectified and mediated as truth to ignite political support, divorced from the realities of class struggle. By so doing, race-centered scholars have unwittingly perpetuated the vacuous and dangerous notion that politics and economics are two separate spheres of society which function independently—a view that firmly anchors and sustains prevailing class relations of power in society.

Separation of the Political and Economic

One of our greatest concerns with the way notions of "race" and "race relations" have evolved over time, including the most recent arguments for a critical race theory, is the fact that political and economic spheres continue to remain separate in traditional analytical treatments of "race." In shedding light on the impact of such a practice, we turn once again to the work of Wood (1995) who argues that "there has been a tendency to perpetuate the rigid conceptual separation of the 'economic' and 'political' which has served capitalist ideology so well ever since the classical economist discovered the 'economy' in the abstract and began emptying capitalism of its social and political content" (19).

In essence, Wood attempts to reveal the way this false separation of the political and economic has served to obscure and distort our understanding of the fragmentation of social life within capitalism. Michael Parenti's (1995) work similarly exposes the class-driven interests of the economy hidden under its abstraction.

> The economy itself is not a neutral entity. Strictly speaking, there is no such thing as "the economy." Nobody has ever seen or touched the economy. What we see are

people engaged in the exchange of values, in productive and not such productive labor, and we give an overarching name to all these activities, calling them "the economy," a hypothetical construct imposed on observable actualities. We then often treat our abstractions as reified entities, as self-generating forces of their own. So we talk about the problems of the economy in general terms, not the problems of the capitalist economy with a specific set of social relations and a discernable distribution of class power. The economy becomes an embodied entity unto itself.

(81)

Traditional and popular conceptual formations utilized down to the present day to define "race" within the United States have likewise concealed the deeply embedded relationship between racism and class. For this reason, Miles and Brown (2003) assert that one of the major analytical tasks before us is "the historical (as opposed to abstract theoretical) investigation of the interpolation of racialisation and racism in political and economic relations" (137).

The separation of economic and political spheres was underscored in the civil rights movements of the 1960s and 1970s. Although these movements sought to address the impoverished material conditions of African Americans and other economically oppressed populations, their emphasis on a liberal, rights-centered political agenda undermined the development of a coherent working-class movement in the United States. Unfortunately, the opposition to a class-based politics, resulting from an ideological separation of economic and political spheres, solidified the division between economic and political action—a division inherent in capitalist appropriation and exploitation. As Wood (1995) suggests, "This 'structural' separation may, indeed, be the most effective defense mechanism available to capital" (20).

Our opposition to the separation of political and economic spheres is in concert with Marx's notion that the ultimate secret of capitalist production is a political one. The key to Marx's argument is that the well-camouflaged continuity between what we term "economic" and "political spheres" be exposed. In Marxist analysis, the economy is viewed as a set of social relations. This view is in sharp contrast with classical views of the economy that "fail to treat the productive sphere itself as defined by social determinations and in effect deal with society 'in the abstract'" (Wood, 1995, p. 22). Consequently, when theories of "race," racism, and other forms of inequality are informed by liberal perspectives of the economy, their critical edge is eroded, and they are easily assimilated into mainstream ideologies that retreat from class concerns.

Contrary to such perspectives, we argue for a materialist understanding of the world in which we grapple forthrightly with the impact of racism upon our lives. This entails understanding two significant principles of analysis. The first requires us to engage the social relations and practices by which human beings interact with nature and which are thereby implicated in producing the life conditions we are seeking to remedy. And second, we seek a historical understanding of human life that recognizes all products of social activity and all social interactions between human beings as material forces. All social forms, including those that sustain racism, as well as other forms of social inequalities, are products of a particular social system of production.

Wood (1995) sheds light on this relationship by linking the mode of production to questions of power relations and exploitation.

> A mode of production is not simply a technology but a social organization of productive activity, and a mode of exploitation is a relationship of power. Furthermore, the power relationship that conditions the nature and extent of exploitation is a matter of political organization within and between contending classes. In the final analysis the relation between appropriators and producers rests on the relative strength of classes, and this is largely determined by the internal organization and the political forces with which each enters into the class struggle.
>
> (27)

Hence, all forms of social inequality are defined by class relations or motivated by the persistent drive to perpetuate class inequality within the context of the capitalist state, a phenomenon perpetuated by the ongoing construction and reconstruction of capitalist class relations. Thus, racism is operationalized through racialized class relations. Sexism is operationalized through gendered class relations. Heterosexism is operationalized through homophobic class relations. All these function in concert to sustain cultural, political, and economic stratification within societies at large.

To reiterate, everything functions within the context of material conditions—whether one is talking about psychological, corporeal, or spiritual dimensions of culture. We understand culture as a social phenomenon produced at the point of production through the particular configuration of social-material relations found within the nation-state, which include the particularities of the region's historical, social-material arrangements and organization.

Given this perspective, class is implicated in all social arrangements of oppression, including racism. Nothing occurs without implicating the material conditions that shape the way individuals and groups locate themselves (and are located) in the context of the body politic of the nation-state. What, then, is the motivating force for the construction of particular social arrangements, whether these are marked by physical, national, or ideological signifiers? Simply put, it is the exploitation and domination of the majority of the population in the interest of sustaining the power of capital. This is inextricably tied to retaining dominion over the world's populations and natural resources by the ruling elite.

Capitalist class relations, both anchored in and camouflaged by the precepts of modernity, are constructed in the historical, social-material milieu of each nation-state at the moment of colonization, by way of the introduction of capitalist modes of production into each region. Consequently, questions of the economy and politics are inextricably linked and cannot be separated. Hence, to speak of the political sphere as being separate from the economic is to create a false abstract notion that fundamentally serves the interests of capitalist relations and the accumulative drive for capital and power by the few. This abstract separation conceals the unjust accumulation of capital and power—an accumulation sustained by asymmetrical relations tied to class and firmly anchored to the social practices of racism, sexism, homophobia, ethnocentrism, and other forms of social inequality.

White Supremacy and the Intractability of Racism

James Baldwin argues, in his 1984 essay "On Being 'White' ... and Other Lies," "No one was white before he/she came to America. It took generations, a vast amount of coercion, before this became a white country" (Baldwin, 1998, p. 78). Baldwin's words clearly point to the artificial construction of a "black-white" paradigm for organizing power in America. We argue that this racialized construction of power was (and continues to be) predicated upon the political economic imperatives of capitalism, rather than an essentialized and intractable white supremacy.

Although a goal of critical race theory is to eliminate "racial oppression" as part of a larger effort to end all forms of oppression (Tate, 1997), a central tenet of this perspective is that "race" is an essential reality of life and racism a permanent feature of social relations in the modern world. Hence, critical race theorists and their supporters uncompromisingly adhere not only to a belief in the existence of "races" but also to the "normalcy" of racism. For example, Ladson-Billings (1999) explains that critical race theory begins with the view that

> racism is "normal, not aberrant, in American society" (Delgado, 1995 p. xiv) Indeed, Bell's major premise in *Faces at the Bottom of the Well* (1992) is that racism is a permanent fixture of American life. Thus, the strategy becomes one of unmasking and exposing racism in its various permutations.
>
> (12)

This belief in the permanence of racism is coupled with the notion of white supremacy in the literature on critical race theory. Major writings in the field (Bell, 1992; Crenshaw, et al., 1995; Delgado, 1995; Wing, 1997) highlight two central unifying ideas. The first is to understand how a "regime of white supremacy and its subordination of people of color have been created and maintained in America" (Crenshaw, et al., 1995, p. xiii), and the second is "to change the bond that exists between law [or institutions] and racial power" (Ladson-Billings, 1999 p. 14). It is important to note that, although mention is made of changing the law and other societal institutions such as schools, the change is first and foremost concerned with the idea of "racial power," preserving the centrality of "race."

Hence, in their efforts to sort out the complexities of "race" problems in America, critical race theorists and many prominent intellectuals place an emphasis on the notion of white supremacy. For example, Villenas, Deyhle, and Parker (1999) speak of education as "the greatest normalizer of White supremacy" (48). The writings of bell hooks illustrate the common use in critical race theory of the term "white supremacy" when addressing the racialized inequalities suffered by African Americans. In *Talking Back* (1989) hooks explains the shift in her language.

> I try to remember when the word racism ceased to be the term which best expressed for me the exploitation of black people and people of color in this society and when I began to understand that the most useful term was white supremacy ... the

ideology that most determines how white people in this society perceive and relate to black people and other people of color.

(112–13)

hooks's explanation illustrates both her belief in the existence of a "white" ideology that has "black" people as its primary object (despite her mention of "people of color") and the reification of skin color as the most active determinant of social relations between "black" and "white" populations. The persistence of such notions of racialized exploitation and domination privileges one particular form of racism while ignoring the historical and contemporary oppression of populations who have been treated as distinct and inferior "races" without the necessary reference to skin color.

Moreover, white supremacy arguments essentialize "black-white" relations by inferring that the inevitability of skin color ensures the reproduction of racism in the "postcolonial" world, where "white people" predominantly associate "black people" with inferiority. Delgado Bernal (2002) expresses this view in her discussion of a "Eurocentric perspective" when she writes: "Traditionally, the majority of Euro-Americans adhere to a Eurocentric perspective founded on covert and overt assumptions [of] White supremacy" (111).

This view fails to recognize the precolonial origins of racism, which were structured in Europe by the development of nation-states and capitalist relations of production. "The dichotomous categories of Black as victims, and Whites as perpetrators of racism, tend to homogenize the objects of racism, without paying attention to the different experience of men and women, of different social classes and ethnicities" (Anthias and Yuval-Davis, 1992, p. 15). As such, there is little room to link, with equal legitimacy and analytical specificity the continuing struggles against racism by Jews, Romas, the Irish, immigrant workers, refugees, and other racialized populations of the world (including Africans racialized by Africans) to the struggle of African Americans.

Theories of racism based on racialized ideas of "white supremacy" ultimately adhere to a "race relations" paradigm. Thus, these theories anchor racialized inequality to the alleged "nature" of "white people" and the psychological influence of "white ideology" on both "whites" and "blacks" rather than to the complex nature of historically constituted social relations of power and their material consequences. In light of this, hooks's preference for "white supremacy" (although, more recently, she links it to both patriarchal and capitalist formations) represents a perspective that, despite its oppositional intent and popularity among activists and critical race scholars, fails to advance an understanding of the debilitating structures of capitalism and the nature of class formations within a racialized, gendered world. More specifically, the struggle against racism and class inequality cannot be founded on either academic or popularized notions of "race" or "white supremacy"—notions that ultimately reify and "project a 'phantom objectivity,' an autonomy that seems so strictly rational and all-embracing as to conceal every trace of its fundamental nature" (Radin, cited in Harris, 1998, p. 07). Rather than working to invert racist notions of racialized inferiority, antiracist scholars and activists should seek to develop a class-based critical theory of racism.

Our contention with the critical race theorists is that they remain silent about capitalist production relations in the midst of their often-repeated intersectionality mantra of class, race, and gender. However, it is not our intention to resurrect the race-versus-class debate of the last several decades. Instead, we seek to place the political, economic, and ideological process of capitalist social relations at the center of an understanding of racialized inequalities. Moreover, we find no theoretical or empirical reasons for legitimizing the ideological notion of "race" or "white supremacy" by promoting these ideas as central analytical categories. On the contrary, as Balibar (1991) suggests, an "after race" position must be something more substantial. It must challenge "the idea that there is *no end to racism* in *history*" (18).

Reframing the Politics of Racism

In order to begin reframing the politics of racism, it is necessary to construct a new language with which to articulate the conditions of exclusion, exploitation, and domination in the world. As activists and social scientists, we must begin this effort in our scholarship and our political practice by deconstructing "common sense categories and [setting] up rigorous analytic concepts in their place. Here, it appears to us that an excessively vague use of the vocabulary of race should be rejected, and that one should resist the extensions which banalise the evil, or remove its specificity" (Wieviorka, 1997, p. 40). More specifically, we must begin by shattering our "race fixation."

However, despite the dangerous distortions that arise from the use of "race" as a central analytical category, most scholars seem unable to break with the hegemonic tradition of its use in the social sciences. Our efforts to problematize the reified nature of the term "race" and eliminate it as a metaphor in our work are met with resistance, even by progressive intellectuals of all communities. This resistance is expressed through anxiety, trepidation, and anger. Even merely questioning the existence of "races" is often met with greater suspicion than liberal notions that perpetuate a deficit view of "race."

Oliver Cox, in his 1948 treatise on "race relations," for example, posits that "it would probably be as revealing of [negative] interracial attitudes to deliberate upon the variations in the skeletal remains of some people as it would be to question an on-going society's definition of a race because, anthropometrically speaking, the assumed race is not a *real* race" (Cox, 1959, p. 319).[7] Similarly, in a more recent work, *The Racial Contract,* Charles Mills (1997) argues that "the only people who can find it psychologically possible to deny the centrality of race are those who are racially privileged, for whom race is invisible precisely because the world is structured around them, whiteness as the grounds against which the figures of other races-those who, unlike us, are raced-appear" (76).

Inherent in these commentaries is the refusal to consider that the denial of "races" does not imply the denial of racism or the racist ideologies that have been central to capitalist exploitation and domination around the globe. The failure to grasp this significant analytical distinction ultimately stifles the development of a critical theory of racism, one with the analytical depth to free us from a paradigm that explains social subordination (or domination) by the alleged "nature" of particular populations.

Visceral and uncritical responses to eliminating the concept of "race" are often associated with a fear of delegitimizing the historical movements for liberation that have been principally defined in terms of "race" struggles, or progressive institutional interventions that have focused on "race" numbers to evaluate success. Although understandable, such responses demonstrate the tenacious and adhesive quality of socially constructed ideas and show how these ideas, through their historical usage, become commonsense notions that resist deconstruction. The dilemma for scholars and activists in the field is well articulated by Angela Davis (1996).

> "Race" has always been difficult to talk about in terms not tainted by ideologies of racism, with which the notion of "race" shares a common historical evolution. The assumption that a taxonomy of human populations can be constructed based on phenotypical characteristics has been discredited. Yet, we continue to use the term "race," even though many of us are very careful to set it off in quotation marks to indicate that while we do not take seriously the notion of "race" as biologically grounded, neither are we able to think about racist power structures and marginalization processes without invoking the socially constructed concept of "race."
>
> (43)

Consequently, "race" has been retained as "an analytical category, not because it corresponds to any biological or epistemological absolutes, but because of the power that collective identities acquire" (Gilroy, 1991, p. 9). This power requires that racialized identities be accepted as commonplace and as central to political struggle, despite the constructed limitations that belie their utility.

Terry Eagleton (2000) asserts, "There can be no political emancipation for our time which is not at some level indebted to the Enlightenment" (65). In agreement, we posit that reframing a politics of racism requires us to rethink one of the fundamental critiques of the Enlightenment made by many progressive theorists, including those at the forefront of critical race theory. The demise of the meta-narratives in the late twentieth century cleared the way for the "new pluralism." Tied to this politics of diversity was the eradication of any assumptions that supported the existence of universal principles of rights sufficiently undifferentiated to accommodate diverse identities and lifestyles. The increasing fragmentation of social relations and personal identities was thought to require more complex pluralistic principles that recognized the plurality of oppressions or forms of domination. The socialist emancipatory project was rejected in favor of what was considered to be the more inclusive category of democracy, a concept that essentially treats all oppressions equally. These theories were posited as being more in tune with the complexity of human diversity than those that "privileged" class relations or "reduced" all oppressions to class struggle.

However politically progressive such a view might seem, its results were disastrous to the development of a truly expansive emancipatory movement and the forging of an economically democratic society. As Eagleton (2000) reminds us,

A classless society can be achieved only by taking class identifications seriously, not by a liberal pretense that they do not exist. The most uninspiring kind of identity politics are those which claim that an already fully fledged identity is being repressed by others. The more inspiring forms are those in which you lay claim to an equality with others in being free to determine what you might wish to become. Any authentic affirmation of difference thus has a universal dimension.

(66)

In the absence of this "universal dimension," social movements principally grounded in identity politics—despite appalling material inequalities—resulted in an uncritical acceptance of capitalist expansion.

Consequently, the final years of the twentieth century were marked by one of the greatest moments of capitalist expansion, shrouded in the rhetoric of globalization—an economic expansionism carried out with few political restraints or legal reprisals by the myriad of identity movements all busy vying for their piece of the pie. While the new pluralism aspired to create a democratic community that could embrace and celebrate all social formations of difference—with its mantra of "race, gender, and class"—it failed to acknowledge the possibility that these differences could also encompass relations of exploitation and domination. Thus, advocates of the "new pluralism" failed to recognize several deadly fundamental realities of class relations: (1) it can exist only within structures of inequality; (2) all social oppressions are fundamentally linked to class within the context of capitalist relations of power; and (3) differences within groups also "proliferate along the obvious axes of division: gender, age, sexuality, region, class, wealth and health … [challenging] the unanimity of racialized collectivities" (Gilroy, 2000, p. 24).

The "new pluralism" opened the door to the carte blanche dismissal of class analysis and the unbridled impact of capitalism on people's lives. In its place, hidden narratives of distinct collectivities evolved along with essentialized notions that often shaped new forms of social tyranny for those perceived as "Other" within the context of antiracism. In the name of conserving the right to difference and oppositionality, such narratives also eroded the sustained solidarity of diverse sectors of the population both from within and without. Underpinning these movements was the goal of stripping away the Enlightenment metanarrative of universal humanity. Without this metanarrative, as Jeffrey Isaac (1992) argues, theory lost its sense of purpose:

If there are no metanarratives, no underlying reasons for us to do what we should do then the theorist or political writer is under no obligation to offer such reasons in support of his or her proposal. Theory then becomes rhetoric, or poetry, or perhaps a game in which the writer's will to power or self-expression becomes his or her primary motivation.

(8–9)

Instead, we firmly believe that to reframe the politics of racism in society today requires a willingness to resurrect the Enlightenment tradition within a historical process as posited by Marx. "By putting a critique of political economy in place of uncritical submission to the assumptions and categories of capitalism, he made it possible to see within it the conditions of its suppression by a more humane society" (Wood, 1995, p. 177). These categories of political economy devised and articulated by Marx are requisite conceptual tools in understanding racism in contemporary capitalist societies. One of the major objectives of this volume and in particular this chapter has been to show that the retention of "race" as a discursive or analytic category is seriously problematic. Moreover, an attempt to develop a "critical theory of race" or a LatCrit methodology will in effect reproduce a specious concept which has no theoretical or analytical value. Also, the widely employed notion of *intersectionality* is equally problematic where a multitude of oppressions and identities are assigned "equivalent" explanatory power outside class relations. As we posit in our introduction, to treat the category of class as just another "ism" as many LatCrit writers do is simplistic and misguided. The concept of class is located within production relations and represents a very different and unique structural feature in a capitalist political economy.

As we have attempted here, the terrain occupied by critical race and LatCrit scholars must and can be contested. The task for all anti-racist scholars is to focus on *racism as an ideology* and *racism as a relation of production*. Such an interrogation requires a renewed historical materialist method informed by Marx's writings, most notably the preface to *A Contribution to the Critique of Political Economy*. Thus, this analysis leads us to locate the capitalist mode of production at the center of a theory of racism and class inequality. Finally, the theoretical argument that we offer is that any account of contemporary racism(s) and related exclusionary practices divorced from an explicit engagement with racialization and its articulation with the reproduction of capitalist relations of production is incomplete. The continued neglect by critical race theorists to treat with theoretical *specificity* the political economy of racialized class inequalities is a major limitation in an otherwise significant and important body of literature.

Notes

1   For scholarly works that focus on "critical race theories," see Richard Delgado, *Critical Race Theory: The Cutting Edge* (1995); Kimberle Crenshaw, Neil Gotanda, Gary Peller, and Kendal Thomas, eds., *Critical Race Theory: The Key Writings That Formed the Movement;* Mari Matsuda, Charles Lawrence, Richard Delgado, and Kimberle Crenshaw, *Words That Wound: Critical Race Theory, Assaultive Speech, and the First Amendment* (1993); as well as writings by Michael Omi and Howard Winant, including *Racial Conditions* (Winant 1994).

2   Recent efforts to bring "class" into the debate are a positive conceptual and theoretical development. But we caution our colleagues not to fall into the trap of just adding "class" to the equation of other identities. As we argue in this volume, there is a need to sort out the salient theoretical underpinnings of an approach to class-based analysis that recognizes struggle and conflict as a means of social change. In these chapters, we attempt to specify the meaning of a Marxist-informed class-based approach that views class and classes in capitalist society in terms of their structural position within production relations. The Marxist theory of modes of production is central and necessary to this project of deracialization in capitalist society.

3   Also see the article by Elizabeth M. Iglesias (1999), "Out of the Shadow: Marking Intersections in and between Asian Pacific American Critical Legal Scholarship and Latina/o Critical Theory," where she issues a call "for LatCrit theory to move beyond abstract race/class debates by centering political economy and the production of class hierarchies" (95).
4   Care must be taken not to speak of the state and capital in monolithic terms, as they are sometimes at odds. See Ralph Miliband's (1998) *Divided Societies: Class Struggle in Contemporary Capitalism* and Nico Poulantzas's (1973) *Political Power and Social Classes* for competing views of the state in capitalist societies, though both would agree on the heterogeneity of capital and the state.
5   C.L.R. James addresses the "Negro Question" in the "Historical Developments of the Negroes in American Society" (1943), which was originally circulated within the Workers' Party as a memorandum dated December 30, 1943. It was submitted to the 1944 National Convention of the Workers' Party, and first published as "Negroes and the Revolution: Resolution of the Minority" in the *New International*, January 1945 (McLemee, 1996, p. 149). Although James identifies the "dangers" of the "chauvinisms of the oppressed" in this essay, he makes a case that "the only way to overcome them is to recognize its fundamental progressive tendency and to distinguish sharply between chauvinisms of the oppressed and the chauvinism of the oppressor" (McLemee, 1996, p. 86). However, more than sixty years later, what we have learned from a myriad of antiracism struggles, rooted in nationalism and identity politics is that chauvinism of any persuasion ultimately confines, restricts, and delimits the political solidarity required to challenge the totalizing impact of capitalism in this country and around the world.
6   One of the most significant theoretical contributions made during the post-civil rights era regarding questions of racialized identities was formulated by radical feminists of color who presented the most sophisticated articulations of the intersectionality argument, with its often cited mantra of "race, class, and gender."
7   More than fifty years after the publication of *Caste, Class and Race* by Doubleday in 1948, many scholars continue to attribute Marxist analytical status to the work of Oliver Cox. We argue that this is misleading because Cox, who retained "race" as the central category of analysis in his work, remained staunchly anchored in a "race relations" paradigm.

References

Anthias, F., and Yuval-Davis, N. in association with H. Cain (1992), *Racialized Boundaries: Race, Nation, Gender, and Color and the Anti-racist Struggle*. London: Routledge.

Baldwin, J. (1998), "On Being White ... and Other Lies," in D. Roediger (ed.), *Black on White*. New York, NY: Schocken, 177–80.

Balibar, E. (1991), "Es gibt keinen Staat in Europe: Racism and Politics in Europe." *New Left Review* 186: 5–19.

Barnes, R. (1990), "Race Consciousness: The Thematic Content of Racial Distinctiveness in Critical Race Scholarship." *Harvard Law Review* 103: 1864–71.

Bell, D. (1992), *Faces at the Bottom of the Well*. New York, NY: Basic Books.

Cox, O. (1959), *Caste, Class and Race: A Study in Social Dynamics*. New York, NY: Monthly Review Press.

Crenshaw, K., Gotanda, N., Peller, G., and Thomas, K., eds. (1995), *Critical Race Theory: The Key Writings That Formed the Movement*. New York, NY: New Press.
Davis, A. (1996), "Gender, Class and Multiculturalism," in Avery F., Gordon and C. Newfield (eds.), *Mapping Multiculturalisms*. Minneapolis, MN, and London: University of Minnesota Press, 40–8.
Delgado, R. (1995), *Critical Race Theory: The Cutting Edge*. Philadelphia, PA: Temple University Press.
Delgado, R., and Stefancic, J. (2001), *Critical Race Theory*. New York, NY: New York University Press.
Delgado Bernal, D. (2002), "Critical Race Theory, Latino Critical Theory, and Critical Raced-Gendered Epistemologies: Recognizing Students of Color as Holders and Creators of Knowledge." *Qualitative Inquiry* 8(1): 105–26.
Eagleton, T. (2000), *The Idea of Culture*. Oxford: Blackwell.
Garcia, I. (1997), *Chicanismo: The Forging of a Militant Ethos among Mexican Americans*. Tucson, AZ: The University of Arizona Press.
Gates, H. L., Jr. (1997), *Thirteen Ways of Looking at a Black Man*. New York, NY: Random House.
Gilroy, P. (1987), *"There Ain't No Black in the Union Jack": The Cultural Politics of Race and Nation*. London: Hutchinson.
Gilroy, P. (1991), *"There Ain't No Black in the Union Jack": The Cultural Politics of Race and Nation*. Chicago, IL: University of Chicago Press.
Gilroy, P. (2000), *Against Race: Imagining Political Culture beyond the Colorline*. Cambridge, MA: Harvard University Press.
Guinier, Lani, and Torres, G. (2002), *The Miner's Canary: Enlisting Race, Resisting Power, Transforming Democracy*. Cambridge, MA: Harvard University Press.
Harris, C. (1998), "Whiteness as Property," in D. Roediger (ed.), *Black on White: Black Writers on What It Means to Be White*. New York, NY: Schocken Books.
hooks, bell (1989), *Talking Back*. Boston: South End Press.
Iglesias, Elizabeth M. (1999), "Out of the Shadow: Marking Intersections in and between Asian Pacific American Critical Legal Scholarship and Latina/o Critical Theory." *Third World Law Review* 19: 349–83.
Isaac, J. C. (1992), *Arendt, Camus, and Modern Rebellion*. New Haven, CT: Yale University Press.
Kelley, R. (1997), *Yo' Mama's DisFUNKtional*. Boston, MA: Beacon Press.
Ladson-Billings, G. (1999), "Just What Is Critical Race Theory, and What's It Doing in a Nice Field Like Education?" in D. Deyhle, L. Parker, and Sofia Villenas (eds.), *Race Is-Race Isn't: Critical Race Theory and Qualitative Studies in Education*. Boulder, CO: Westview Press, 7–30.
Marx, A. W. (1998), *Making Race and Nation: A Comparison of South Africa, the United States, and Brazil*. Cambridge: Cambridge University Press.
McLemee, S. (1996), *C.L.R. James on the Negro Question*. Jackson, MS: University Press of Mississippi.
Michael, J. (2000), *Anxious Intellects*. Durham, NC: Duke University Press.
Miles, R. (1989), *Racism*. Key Ideas series. London: Routledge.
Miles, R., and Brown, M. (2003), *Racism*, 2nd ed. London: Routledge.
Mills, C. (1997), *The Racial Contract*. Ithaca, NY: Cornell University Press.
Parenti, M. (1995), *Against Empire*. San Francisco, CA: City Lights Books.

Roithmayr, D. (1999), "Introduction to Critical Race Theory," in L. Parker, D. Deyhle, and S. Villenas (eds.), *Race Is-Race Isn't: Critical Race Theory and Qualitative Studies in Education*. Boulder, CO: Westview Press, 1–6.

Solorzano, D. (1998), "Critical Race Theory, Race, and Microaggressions, and the Experience of Chicana and Chicano Scholars." *International Journal of Qualitative Studies in Education* 11(1): 121–36.

Taguieff, P. (2001), *The Force of Prejudice: On Racism and Its Doubles*. Minneapolis, MN: Minnesota University Press.

Tate, W. F., and Apple, M. (1997), "Review of Research in Education." *Review of Research in Education* 22(1): 195–247.

Villenas, S., Deyhle, D., and Parker, L. (1999), "Critical Race Theory and Praxis: Chicano(a)/ Latino(a) and Navajo Struggles for Dignity, Education Equity, and Social Justice," in L. Parker, D. Deyhle, and S. Villenas (eds.), *Race Is-Race Isn't: Critical Race Theory and Qualitative Studies in Education*. Boulder, CO: Westview Press, 31–52.

Viotti da Costa, E. (2001), "New Publics, New Politics, New Histories: From Economic Reductionism to Cultural Reductionism-In Search of Dialectics," in G. M. Joseph (ed.), *Reclaiming the Political in Latin American History: Essays from the North*. Durham, NC, and London: Duke University Press, 17–31.

Watts, S. (1991), "The Idiocy of American Studies: Poststructuralism, Language and Politics in the Age of Self-Fulfillment." *American Quarterly* 43(4) (December): 652.

Wieviorka, M. (1997), "Is It Difficult to Be an Anti-Racist," in P. Werbner and T. Modood (eds.), *Debating Cultural Hybridity: Multicultural Identities and the Politics of Anti-Racism*. Atlantic Highlands, NJ: Zed Books, 139–53.

Wing, Adrien K. (1997), *Critical Race Feminism: A Reader*. New York, NY: New York University Press.

Wood, E. M. (1994), "Identity Crisis." *In These Times* (June): 28–2.

Wood, E. M. (1995), *Democracy against Capitalism: Renewing Historical Materialism*. New York, NY: Cambridge University Press.

12

Racism in a Medically Segregated World

Medical students and patients of color are more likely to have their concerns invalidated by the medical establishment.
 Of all the forms of inequality, injustice in health is the most shocking and the most inhuman.

—Martin Luther King Jr., Medical Committee for
Human Rights Convention (1966)

Just as in education and other areas of social welfare in the United States, the inequalities that Dr. Martin Luther King Jr. was raising in 1966 about health care have continued to persist in today's medically segregated world. In our fast-moving culture and with the increasing virtualization of social relations, the concentration of poverty and its consequences may not always be so apparent to those who live in neighborhoods of greater affluence. Yet, this invisibility must be understood in the context of neoliberalism's dismantling of the safety net, which once offered some semblance of social welfare protection against the excesses of capital. A disgraceful consequence of neoliberalism has been precisely the rising segregation of poor people, particularly people of color, associated with a growing centralization of wealth among the few and deepening structures of economic apartheid within both urban and rural areas across the United States.

The current neoliberal disregard for the impoverishment of large sectors of the population has left millions in extreme poverty around the globe, without access to adequate health care. Just as we can conceptualize education with respect to segregation, so too the history of medicine and health care abuses must be understood in these terms as well. Similarly, issues of racism in medicine must be engaged within the realities of absurd contradictions of a political economy devoid of a moral compass. Hence, racism or any other form of inequality or social exclusion within medicine, education, or the wider society can never be effectively ameliorated without attending to the underlying structural causes.

Comprehending Racism

In a recent national poll sponsored by CNN and the Kaiser Family Foundation, almost half of all the participants stated that racism is a "big problem" in the United States today. This figure constitutes a significant shift from just four years ago, when slightly more than a quarter of Americans described racism in this way. It goes without saying that racism constitutes one of the most violent and insidious forms of human oppression. Yet, racism still seems to be one of the most difficult social phenomena for members of the dominant culture to both see and comprehend.

Often the difficulty with comprehending racism arises from a legacy of faulty perceptions and assumptions that persist in the perceptions of white folks. In addition to ethnocentric values, much of the difficulty is also related to a pervasive and commonsensical ideology of race, coupled with an epistemology that effectively stifles the ability of white physicians to move from an individual perception of bias, prejudice, and discrimination to an understanding of racism as a structural phenomenon, which is perpetuated by an institutional apparatus of power and control. This becomes even more complicated when conditions of racism commingle with other forms of oppression to intensify and amplify the lives of patients from subaltern populations. Nevertheless, what is key here is that the ability to comprehend racism, as an institutional phenomenon, is essential to both its amelioration and eradication.

Ethnocentrism in medicine is most often manifested through institutional standards and protocols of behavior by which all in the profession are judged and compared. These standards and protocols are generally based on implicit cultural assumptions that function to preserve and protect the privilege, power, and wealth of a ruling class. This phenomenon, for example, is at work in expressed colorblind views, which prevail in medicine and medical schools today. Colorblindness as an ideology tends "to individualize conflicts and shortcomings, rather than examine the larger picture of cultural difference, stereotypes, and values placed in context" (Williams, 2011). In the process, both the normalizing and naturalizing of white superiority and chauvinism function to effectively silence the voices of medical students and patients of color, by ignoring or silencing their concerns or experiences related to racism.

As such, racialized assumptions work to normalize, justify, and reproduce biases held by many doctors and medical school professors who fail to perceive the racism inherent in their conditioned inclination to judge and compare the success of poor and working-class medical students of color, for example, against that of affluent white students. Furthermore, it is worth noting here that the notion of a universal ranking of humanity in a hierarchical order that privileges the dominant culture is well integrated across our society, including in the practice of medicine. As such, the Western notion of social Darwinism reflects a prime example of an ideology that wittingly or unwittingly reinforces cultural racism in the sciences, and today sustains the ravenous neoliberal culture of economic Darwinism (Giroux, 2010).

Unfortunately, doctors from the dominant culture, more often than not, tend to misperceive and misinterpret cultural values, beliefs, and ways of knowing that are not their own. Numerous studies have shown the presence of such implicit bias among physicians. According to a study published in the *American Journal of Public Health* in March 2012, a staggering two-thirds of doctors exhibited racial bias toward patients of color. Moreover, white and Asian physicians overall held more pro-white attitudes on both measures than did African American physicians, whose scores were largely neutral with respect to racial bias. Another study (Chapman, Kaatz, and Carnes, 2013) concluded, "cultural stereotypes may not be consciously endorsed, but their mere existence influences how information about an individual is processed and leads to unintended biases in decision-making" (p. 1504). With this in mind, John Hoberman (2012), in *Black and Blue: The Origins and Consequences of Medical Racism*, laments that most studies of medical racism do not address the racially motivated thinking and behaviors of physicians practicing today. Within the private sphere of physicians, "racial fantasies and misinformation distort diagnoses and treatments" (p. 2).

Doctors' attitudes, just like the rest of the population's, are mired in racial stereotypes and folkloric beliefs about racial differences that permeate the general population. Hoberman (2012) further contends that within the world of medicine this racial folklore has shaped perceptions within all medical subdisciplines, from cardiology to gynecology to psychiatry. In the process, doctors have imposed white or Black racial identities upon every organ system of the human body, along with racial interpretations of Black children, Black seniors, the Black athlete, Black musicality, Black pain thresholds, Black lung capacity, and other aspects of Black minds and bodies. This misreading and distortion of bodies of color have extended across other racialized populations, as well.

Despite the long-term persistence of racialization in medicine, the medical establishment seldom engages substantively with either historical or contemporary information about medical racism. For this reason, a deeper understanding of the pervasiveness of racism is unlikely to reach medical schools until the current curriculum is transformed and a new historical and sociopolitical view of medicine is embraced. Until then, university professors in schools of medicine or doctors from the dominant culture are more likely to misread the essence, nuances, and inner complexities inherent to living with racism, and thus will tend to invalidate or overly question concerns or the lived experiences of medical students or their patients of color. This is particularly the case with white male doctors or professors who exist in the confines of a mainstream life, where they do not need to be conscious of the profound privilege they enjoy simply because of their skin color, affluence, gender, and profession.

The Legacy of Medical Apartheid

Structural racism, in the context of capitalism, constitutes one of the most pervasive forces at work in the history of medicine and as such constitutes the wretched cornerstone upon which a medically segregated world has been constructed. The persistent racialization of patients of color throughout history and today reflects enduring and deeply rooted prejudices of the dominant culture that work to justify and sustain political, social, and economic inequity. Racial stereotypes and depictions fuel misconceptions of Black people, Latino people, Native Americans, Muslims, and other subordinate cultural groups as inferior, stupid, undeserving, or violent—portrayals that imprison communities of color within reified images of the white imagination that often determine the manner in which we are treated, whether in medical schools, doctor's offices, or society at large. The persistent difficulty of the dominant society, and by association with the medical profession, to accept the lives and struggles of people of color, with dignity and as legitimate, is intensified by repressive contradictions that have persisted throughout the history of medicine in the United States.

Harriet Washington (2006) rightly declares that medical apartheid has been a hidden dimension of medicine, from colonial times to the present. Throughout, it has been customary to employ so-called scientific criteria for classification, as a means to predict and determine the health, mental health, and future human value of poor and working-class populations to the project of US capitalist accumulation. In many ways, the same deficit mentality at work in the justification of genocide, slavery, and colonization around the world has persisted (albeit camouflaged) throughout our institutions, including in the study and practice of medicine.

During the US Civil War, for example, a major study was launched to quantify the differences in lung capacity of Union soldiers. According to Lundy Braun (2014), the study concluded that white soldiers had a higher lung capacity than those labeled "Full Black" or "Mulatoes." The study relied on the spirometer, an instrument used to measure the capacity of the lungs, which had been formerly used by plantation doctors to make the same assertions; however, with the added caveat that due to poor lung capacity, Black bodies were made for the fields and little else—where their forced labor was said to "revitalize the blood" of a flawed Black physiology. Today, doctors still examine our lungs using spirometers that are "race corrected" and normal values for lung health are reduced for Black patients.

Moreover, as Braun correctly notes, "Not only might this practice mask economic or environmental explanations for lower lung capacity, but the logic of innate, racial difference is built into things like disability estimates, pre-employment physicals, and clinical diagnoses that rely on the spirometer. Race has become a biologically distinct, scientifically valid category despite the unnatural and social process of its creation." Unfortunately, the accumulation of one-dimensional medical research over the years (such as lung capacity in Black patients) makes it very difficult to dislodge racialized assumptions, particularly when the problematic nature and assumptions of quantitative data go unquestioned and the absence of environmental or socioeconomic context go unnoticed.

The early 1900s initiated the modern era of scientific research, where subjects were seen as objects whose conditions could not only be measured but also manipulated. At that time, measuring and comparing cranium sizes to determine morality and intelligence were commonplace. This form of evaluation was considered to be fully scientific, objective, controlled, reproducible, and statistically accurate—in other words "evidence-based." This led (not surprisingly) to a taxonomy that "objectively and scientifically" ranked the racial group of the early psychometrists as superior in human intelligence, with other "races," of course, hierarchically lagging behind.

One of the most notorious studies in medicine was conducted in Tuskegee, Alabama. The forty-year Tuskegee syphilis study, which took place from the 1930s through the 1970s, serves as a profound metaphor for "medical racism, government malfeasance, and physician arrogance" (Reverby, 2009). The study focused on untreated syphilis among African American men of the region. During the study, US Public Health Service doctors told participants that they were being treated for their disease. Instead, a control group was being inoculated with a placebo, while doctors observed, callously, as the participants suffered through the progression of late-stage syphilis until their painful death.

In the 1930s, the eugenics movement in the United States, with Margaret Sanger as one of its most ardent supporters, began to focus almost exclusively on eliminating what the group termed the negative traits of society. Not surprisingly, the traits considered "undesirable" were to be found predominantly in poor and uneducated populations and populations of color. In an effort to prevent these groups from propagating, the eugenicist movement helped to drive legislation to support forced sterilization (Norrgard, 2008). Thirty-one states, including California, enacted sterilization laws. These laws resulted in the forced sterilization of over 64,000 women (Black, 2003).

Initially, sterilization efforts focused on the disabled but later grew to include people whose only "crime" was poverty. These medically executed sterilization programs received legal support from the US Supreme Court. In the ruling of *Buck v. Bell* (1927), Supreme Court Justice Oliver Wendell Holmes argued, "It is better for all the world, if instead of waiting to execute degenerate offspring for crime, or to let them starve for imbecility, society can prevent those who are manifestly unfit from continuing their kind ... Three generations of imbeciles are enough." The court decision legalized sterilization laws in the United States. California's program was so robust that the Nazis turned to California for advice in perfecting their efforts. Hitler proudly admitted to following the laws of California and several other states, which allowed sterilization, without consent, for prevention of the reproduction of the "unfit" (Kühl, 1994).

Women of color in US urban settings and on reservations were specifically targeted for sterilization without consent or under questionable circumstances. In Puerto Rico, under the auspices of Operation Bootstrap, the medical and government establishment targeted poor, working-class women for sterilization, supposedly to reduce the island's population and unemployment rate (Briggs, 2002). In the 1960s, Puerto Rico earned the dubious distinction of having the highest sterilization rate in the world, with women of childbearing age in Puerto Rico ten times more likely to be sterilized than white women in the United States. By 1965, over 30 percent of Puerto Rican women had been sterilized.

My mother was among these women sterilized, after being asked to sign consent while in the middle of labor with her second child. Puerto Rico was also the site where human trials of the birth control pill were conducted prior to prescribing it to women on the mainland. In the 1970s, Native American women reported being sterilized at Indian Health Service hospitals after going in for routine medical procedures such as appendectomies. In 1975, in *Madrigal v. Quilligan*, Mexican immigrant mothers sued doctors, the state, and the US government after they were sterilized while giving birth at Los Angeles County General Hospital (Tajima-Peña, 2015).

More recently, in 2013, concerns over sterilization abuse were raised by a study that found that almost 150 women had been illegally subjected to sterilization in California prison medical facilities, from 2006 to 2010 (Johnson, 2013). As this demonstrates, women of color were heavily singled out for sterilizations because the largely white medical establishment believed that lowering birth rates in communities of color would better society—since the cause for the problems people experienced was considered to be located within the people themselves. Moreover, such abuses continue to demonstrate the manner in which sterilization and incarceration have been used effectively as means for social containment of impoverished populations of color, overwhelmingly represented in US prisons.

Most disturbing then is the manner in which the legacy of medical apartheid and its structural causes persist today. This phenomenon manifests itself across the medical-industrial complex through the culture of health care, within doctor's offices, clinics, and hospitals alike. Medical researchers too perpetuate racism in medicine when they fail to interrogate commonsensical ideas that racialized bodies of color, whether intentional or not. However, strongly implicated in the perpetuation of this legacy is the traditional formation of medical students, which prepares both medical researchers and clinicians to see the world through the narrow and privileged lens of biomedicine.

Racialization and Medical School Formation

Schools of medicine have, unfortunately, been slow or reticent to reorient the field, beyond cosmetic curricular initiatives or well-intentioned efforts to bring more students of color into the fold. The traditional, one-dimensional, curative focus, and vertical structure of medicine can be linked to ideological beliefs and institutional practices that have, as Braun argues, perpetuated plantation structures of racialization within impoverished communities. In many Black, Latino, and Native American communities, the hospital essentially became "the big white house" where racism and other forms of societal inequalities were enacted through a racializing and paternalistic health care culture that exclusively privileged a Western scientific epistemology of disease that rejected as mere superstition the health epistemologies of curanderos, santeras, sobadores, medicine people, naturalists, and Chinese medicine.

At times, rejection of such alternative modalities has been made on the premise that alternative health care approaches are either not scientifically proven or that practitioners do not practice in sterile conditions. Yet, it is interesting to note that these claims seldom go beyond the anecdotal and that the medical establishment is resistant to acknowledge that millions of people over the years have experienced success with alternative health approaches, when conventional medicine failed. Hence, underneath such debates exist deep epistemological tensions and ideological questions related to power, authority, and conquest that seldom are addressed (Saks, 2005).

Consequently, poor and working-class communities of color have been subjected to health disparities tied to medical issues of authority and control, and afforded none or little voice or authority in their own health care decision-making, whether at the national or local level. In many instances, low-income patients of color only receive palliative care, due to either lack of access to state-of-the-art medical treatment or the fact that they do not come in for treatment until the late stages of an illness. My aunt who died of breast cancer is sadly an example of this latter phenomenon. The distrust of doctors and hospitals she had developed over her lifetime fueled a stubborn reticence that led to her demise at only sixty-six years old.

The Western epistemological propensity of "scientifically" reducing, fragmenting, and disembodying knowledge has also led to a health care system, particularly in communities of color, which has focused on one set of symptoms or disease at a time, ignoring the interactions among diseases, overall cultural and social dimensions of health, and an integral approach to medicine that could access the strengths and wisdom that patients possess with respect to their own participation in their health care. Similarly, the medical field and the formation of physicians are still plagued by the legacy of scientific racism and ethnocentric beliefs in the superiority of Western medicine, medical school formation, and health care. The neoliberal era has only solidified and intensified these beliefs, despite the rhetoric of inclusion and occasional cultural competency modules that might be added to the medical school curriculum. In some cases, views of culture, ethnicity, or race only reinforce dominant social constructions of particular races, normalizing economic and political hierarchies by conserving stereotypes and myths of superiority that justify inequalities.

Moreover, in the contemporary neoliberal quest for measurable data and "evidence-based" legitimacy, medical assessment and standardized protocols are constructed under a rubric of objective knowledge, where medicine is treated as an objective and external body of information, as if produced independent of human beings and independent of culture, time, and place. Meanwhile, little attention or relevance is given to the fact that a stubborn logic of innate racial differences continues to drive research, health protocols, assessment criteria, and the treatment provided within communities of color today. In 2011, a John Hopkins study suggested that medical students may "learn" to treat nonwhite patients differently than white patients, which impacts health disparities. It goes without saying that these dynamics can have negative impacts on the education and experience of medical students; but, in particular, for the patients of color they will eventually treat, care may be compromised by such views.

Brian McKenna (2011), a medical anthropologist, contends that professors in medical schools by in large uphold a carte blanche adherence to the educational practice of meritocracy—a practice that functions as one of the primary socialization and sorting mechanisms, implicated in the difficulties many working-class students of color face in medical school. Through everyday practices of meritocracy, an unjust distribution of wealth and power, both in the field and society, is justified. First, this is done by establishing the merit of the medical elite as legitimate heirs to power, privilege, and wealth. And second, meritocratic logic persists in blaming those who cannot "pull themselves up by their bootstraps," by implying they don't have the necessary intelligence, motivation, or drive to partake of the health care offered them by the medical establishment.

Money as the Driving Force

In today's world, money is the overarching driver of biomedicine, as the commercial and market interests of medicalization expand their jurisdiction. Medical officials, government agencies, and Big Pharma corporate leaders perpetuate a voracious appetite for (ever-changing) accountability measures in exchange for federal funding and corporate contributions to medical research, tax initiatives in support of medical education and research, and state budget increases for public health initiatives. In addition, major medical research institutions rake in billions of dollars in expenditures for medical research that often simply perpetuates the distorted and racialized notions of patients of color from working-class communities.

Consistent with the neoliberal education agenda, schools of medicine also have become part of the corporate system of education. At the administrative level, medical schools are expected to function with the breadth and efficiency of large corporations, where medical students are more like consumers than cultural citizens who must grapple ethically with their world; knowledge is more like a commodity for the marketplace; and teaching, clinical in focus and technical in orientation, is more obsessed than ever with data collection, performativity and accountability. As such, medical education is rigidly hierarchized and instrumentalized to better serve the interests of the medical-industrial complex and its segregated world. The consequence is that teaching cultural diversity in medical schools not only remains fragmented, with uncertainty about what it means to be "culturally competent" (Siraj, 2011), but there is a glaring scarcity in the number of lectures and courses offered to medical students (Horowitz, 2005).

Scholarships to medical school—albeit helpful to individuals and in making a small dent in the dearth of Black and Latino medical school enrollments across the United States—unfortunately, do little to undo or cast away the legacy of 500 years of segregated medicine in this country. More to the point, such efforts alone do not attend to the structural root of a medically segregated world, which can only be understood by connecting social and material conditions of oppression to the commonsensical manner in which power and privilege are reinforced, reproduced, and distributed among a tiny elite. Hence, to transform medicine and the culture of medical school requires full reinsertion into the very social fabric of society, the place where the genuine transformation of oppressive values and beliefs can be identified, challenged, and reinvented, in the interest of a truly democratic system of medicine and society—where the lives of everyday people are inextricably linked to an emancipatory understanding of medicine.

In the current context, it is not surprising to find professors of medicine who exhibit dehumanizing acts of power in their responses to medical students, most particularly those from working-class communities of color. Such relationships bear severe consequences upon the lives of medical students, who are not yet fully indoctrinated into the hierarchical sanctum, so they are still able to call into question the racializing injustices and authoritarian nature of this pedagogical domestication and elitist formation. Studies, however, have shown that as medical students don their white coats, along with the veil of silence and subordination expected of them, they soon find themselves only too well disciplined in both accepting Western science as God and the authority of a homogenizing medical world as superior (McKenna, 2011).

This process of formation, unfortunately, often leaves young doctors impoverished by a contrived professional arrogance that deliberately alienates them from their own capacity to know the world as integral human beings—where heart, body, and spirit complement the mind in a multidimensional and emancipatory dance of healing. The larger implication of this professional formation, of course, is that once students leave medical school the tendency is to reproduce what they experienced and were taught—not only with respect to content, but also the manner in which doctors perceive their entitlement and privilege, in comparison to those outside the medical field.

More and more, doctors are converted from actively engaged healers to passive medical technicians who toe the line. As an affluent and compliant workforce of the medical-industrial complex, doctors often become involuntary agents of an immoral free-market economy that has transformed medicine into a commodity for profit, to be bought and sold to the highest bidder. Health management organizations on steroids are the new phenomenon, as smaller practices and hospitals are swallowed up, and doctors try to stem the tide of the receding humanistic vision that once beckoned them to embrace medicine as a vocation.

Protests and Mobilization

It is worth noting here that during the 1960s and 1970s, many medical students across the country did mobilize to support the antiwar and civil rights movements and to denounce, for example, the repression of the Black Panthers—who considered the fight against medical discrimination as central to their politics (Nelson, 2013). Medical student demands centered on culturally relevant curriculum and responsive medical school governance policies, along with efforts to gain an equal voice in decisions of admissions, promotions, and graduation standards. As a direct outcome of progressive efforts by medical students in that era, some important changes were accomplished.

In *White Coat, Clenched Fist*, Fitzhugh Mullan (2006) speaks to his own politicization and that of many other medical students and residents during the 1960s. He explains how their work became the starting point for many discussions among the medical left during the era of the Vietnam War, a period which coincided with the introduction of the modern concept of family medicine into health care policy and medical education. Regrettably, the contemporary neoliberal medical establishment has unabashedly picked apart many of the community practices associated with that era, in the quest to squeeze out greater profits from the illnesses and health problems of the population, as well as the labor of physicians working with the most needy patients.

More recently, Jennifer Tsai (2015), a medical student at Brown University's Warren Alpert Medical School, noted, in the White Coat Die-In demonstrations orchestrated by medical students across the nation, aspiring physicians displayed solidarity with the message that racial injustice is a public health concern that merits the attention and efforts of health care professionals. It is clear from the mobilization and investment of our medical community that there is a desire to engage in clearer articulation and understanding of the health disparities landscape.

Unfortunately, in the midst of these expressions of solidarity among medical students today, many are entering into clinical practice at the very moment when past advances associated with civil rights, in both education and medicine, have been eroded or abandoned in the absence of a robust emancipatory ethics to guide the way.

An Ethics for Liberation

The erosion of a humanizing ethics in medicine is profoundly responsible for the growing inequities in health care today—inequities perpetuated most often through a false dichotomy that separates clinical competency from the capacity of doctors to also become self-reflective in their practice (McDermott, 2012). Hence, prior to positing questions of health care allocation, we should be considering fundamental questions about how we define health, and how health should be inextricably linked to our personal and communal liberation. This is to say that we need ethical standards of medicine in the United States that begin with a deep sense of faith in others and a solid commitment to political solidarity. In addition, there is a need for a critical ethics of medicine, one capable of infusing criticality into medical research, formation, practice, and community health practices—a criticality that holds medicine's moral obligation to the people at the very center of discourses on health care.

In today's world, physicians have a responsibility to both ask and answer difficult questions about racism and its impact on medicine and society. Yet ongoing public opportunities for tackling hard questions generally remain in the hands of a tiny elite, while, as McKenna (2011) reminds us, the hidden curriculum of medical school socializes students to be quiet in the face of unethical behavior, as they undergo cultural indoctrination. In the process, medical students move from being reluctant to speak out against injustices in their first year to not even hearing the injustice in the third. This dynamic is further intensified by the fact that medical students must eventually compete for internships and residencies, requiring strong recommendations from professors. The consequence here is that there is an interlocking system of hierarchical expectations that reinforce and perpetuate the strict hegemony of biomedicine. So even when questions of bioethics are raised, for example, seldom are the issues framed around the pernicious impact of material inequality, the historical legacy of racism in medicine, or the longstanding consequence of these on the lives of the most vulnerable.

Nevertheless, even in the midst of this hidden curriculum, medical students are introduced to four ethical precepts during their medical formation: beneficence (do the right thing); non-maleficence (do no harm); respect for autonomy; and the exercise of justice. But given the stubborn persistence of racism in medicine, these have proven to be miserably insufficient. Hence, if medicine is to genuinely support just and democratic life, there are at least three additional ethical principles that must be at the forefront of medical school formation and medical practice. The first is to *honor all life*; the second is *community care*; and the third is to *speak truth to power*.

To honor all life is to fundamentally enter into a relationship with living beings with a sense of respect, faith, and kinship. Emerging from African wisdom, the principle of *Ubuntu*, "I am because we are"; and the Maya adage, "*In Lak'ech: Tu eres mi otro yo*: You are my other me," reminds us of our fundamental connection to all life. Both these non-Western notions constitute the heart from which all interactions between living beings must proceed, so that no person or living being is left outside the circle of life. This speaks to a sensibility that goes beyond the Western epistemological notions of "Do onto others as you would have them do onto you." Or "I think, therefore I am." Both *In Lak'ech* and *Ubuntu* begin with the essence of honoring the shared life and connection between us. It is only through beginning with such an ethical sensibility that we can move to an ethics of community care.

The ethics of community care points to an underlying recognition that medicine began and must return to its communal origins of caring for one another, if it is to serve as an emancipatory force in our society. And as such, medical care is not an object to be reformed, but rather a relationship between human beings for the benefit of both the patient and the physician. With this thought in mind, John McKnight (1995) argued,

> Service systems can never be reformed so they will 'produce' care. Care is the consenting commitment of citizens to one another. Care cannot be produced, provided, managed, organized, administered, or commodified. Care is the only thing a system cannot produce. Every institutional effort to replace the real thing is a counterfeit. Care is, indeed, the manifestation of community … And it is at this site that the primary work of a caring society [and a caring medical community] must occur (p. x).

Furthermore, an ethics of community care also values, supports, and promotes patient participation and decision-making in the process of a liberatory health care—an ethos of health care that unfolds *with* communities.

Lastly is the ethical principle of speaking truth to power. Speaking truth to power is not about moral superiority. It is about the willingness to move beyond disabling attitudes of denial, neutrality, and silence. It is about the courage and strength (both personal and political, individual and communal) to stand up in opposition to policies and practices within medicine, the university, and the larger society that continue to reproduce pernicious structures of racism and inequalities in medicine today.

To speak truth to power requires that we live our lives with the same truth we expect, and, most importantly, that we cultivate coherence so that the gap between the words we speak and the actions we take becomes less and less each day. It is through such coherence that we might finally begin to undo not only the silences of the past, but also the silences of today. Over fifty years ago, James Baldwin wrote, "We live in an age in which silence is not only criminal but suicidal." Nowhere are these words more applicable than in the medically segregated world that continues to exist today.

References

Black, E. (2003), "Eugenics and the Nazis—The California Connection." *San Francisco Chronicle* (November 9).

Braun, L. (2014), *Breathing Race into the Machine: The Surprising Career of the Spirometer from Plantation to Genetics*. Minneapolis, MN: University of Minnesota Press.

Briggs, L. (2002), *Reproducing Empire: Race, Sex, Science, and US Imperialism in Puerto Rico*. Berkeley, CA: University of California Press.

Chapman, E. N., Kaatz, A., and Carnes, M. (2013), "Physicians and Implicit Bias: How Doctors May Unwittingly Perpetuate Health Care Disparities." *Journal of General Internal Medicine* 28(11) (November): 1504–10.

Giroux, H. (2010), "The Disappearing Intellectual in the Age of Economic Darwinism." *Global Research*. See: https://www.globalresearch.ca/index.php?context=va&aid=20112.

Hoberman, J. (2012), *Black and Blue: The Origins and Consequences of Medical Racism*. Berkeley, CA: University of California Press.

Horowitz, S. (2005), "Cultural Competency Training in US Medical Education: Treating Patients from Different Cultures." *Alternative and Complementary Therapies* 11(6): 290–4.

Johnson, C. G. (2013), "Female Inmates Sterilized in California Prisons without Approval." *The Center for Investigative Reporting*. https://cironline.org/reports/female-inmatessterilized-california-prisons-without-approval-4917.

Kühl, S. (1994), *The Nazi Connection: Eugenics, American Racism, and German National Socialism*. New York, NY: Oxford University Press.

McDermott, D. (2012), *Can We Educate Out of Racism*? MJA (1) July (15).

McKenna, B. (2011), "Medical Education under Siege: Critical Pedagogy, Primary Care, and the Making of 'Slave Doctors.'" *International Journal of Critical Pedagogy* 4(1): 95–117.

McKnight, J. (1995), *The Careless Society: Community and Its Counterfeits*. New York, NY: Basic Books.

Mullan, F. (2006), *White Coat, Clenched Fist: The Political Education of an American Physician*. Ann Arbor, MI: University of Michigan Press.

Nelson, A. (2013), *Body and Soul: The Black Panther Party and the Fight against Medical Discrimination*. Minneapolis, MN: University of Minnesota Press.

Norrgard, K. (2008), "Human Testing, the Eugenics Movement, and IRBS." *Nature Education* 1(1): 170.

Reverby, S. (2009), *Examining Tuskegee: The Infamous Syphilis Study and Its Legacy*. Chapel Hill, NC: The University of North Carolina Press.

Saks, M. (2005), *Professions and the Public Interest: Medical Power, Altruism, and Alternative Medicine*. New York, NY: Routledge.

Shaban, H. (2014b), "How Racism Creeps into Medicine." *The Atlantic*. See: https://www.theatlantic.com/health/archive/2014/08/howracism-creeps-into-medicine/378618/.

Siraj, H. H., Zamzam R., Ismail J., and Mohamad N. (2011), "Managing Diversity: A 'Must Have' Skill for Medical Students." *Procedia: Social and Behavioral Sciences*.18: 379–83.

Tajima-Peña, R. (2015), *No Mas Bebes*. Good Docs. See: https://www.gooddocs.net/?utm_source=Good+Docs+Outreach&utm_campaign=a2d6bc9e47-NMB_Womens_Studies_12_8_2015&utm_medium=email&utm_term=0_226baca2d6bc9e47-108886969#!no-mas-bebes/c1s3b.

Tsai, J. (2015), "How Racism Makes Us Sick: The Medical Repercussions of Segregation." *In-Training*. See: https://intraining.org/racism-make-us-sick-part-onemedicalrepercussions-segregation-8302.

Ture, K., and Hamilton, C. (1992), *Black Power: The Politics of Liberation*. New York, NY: Vintage Books.

Washington, H. (2006), *Medical Apartheid: The Dark History of Medical Experimentation on Black Americans from Colonial Times to the Present*. New York, NY: Anchor Books.

Williams, M. T. (2011), "Colorblind Ideology Is a Form of Racism." *Psychology Today* (December 27). See: https://www.psychologytoday.com/blog/culturallyspeaking/201112/colorblind-ideology-is-form-racism.

Young, I. M. (1990), *Justice and the Politics of Difference*. Princeton, NJ: Princeton University Press.

13

A Marxist Challenge to the Concept of "Race"

Antonia Darder and Rodolfo D. Torres

In short, we need to study each domain in which corrective action is to be undertaken in detail, so that we can identify the real sources of disadvantage suffered by the relevant individuals and groups. By using the shorthand of "race"… we also entrench—avoidably—the very racial categories that undermine the possibility of attaining a truly non-racial democratic [society].
—Neville Alexander (2006, p. 11)

Howard Ryan's essay featured in this volume represents an excellent contribution to the kind of comprehensive analyses still required within the field, in order to more deeply engage the relationships, contradictions, and questions that exist between the categories of class, "race," and school reform. And, as such, it provides a compelling beginning from which to launch a variety of responses speaking to the purpose and aims of this book. However, despite sharing a Marxist lens of analysis, there are a few significant points of departure in our work, which we began almost twenty years ago with our book, *After Race: Racism after Multiculturalism* (2004). For example, although Ryan speaks definitively about the retreat from class in many perspectives related to "race," we argue that it is not solely a retreat from class but also the insidious racializing logic of capital or capitalism as an ideology that makes it difficult and at times even impossible for scholars and activists to speak across our differing perspectives. In fact, our longstanding efforts to enter constructive exchanges across differing perspectives of class and "race"/racism in education and society have nearly always proven futile, given the highly contentious nature of the debate.

Nevertheless, we believe it important to point to the myriad ways in which capitalism occupies a very distinct analytical space, in that all structures and social phenomena are directly shaped by the totalizing logic of capital and capitalism as a system of economic, political, and social life. From this vantage point, it is difficult to imagine that we can reach an understanding of globalized conditions of inequality created by capital without the existence of a grand theory to bring together our engagements with what remains an internationalized system of capitalist oppression. Most recently, we've witnessed the destructive impact of globalized conditions as put into motion by the political economy of the pandemic and the disparate responses of governments around the world. Consequently, already existing conditions of extreme inequality have been severely exacerbated by the pandemic. For example, Oxfam (2021; 2017) reports that eight men now own more wealth than 3.6 billion people. The richest 1 percent have more than twice as much wealth as 6.9 billion people, while almost half of humanity survives on $5.50 a day.

As would be expected, poor and racialized populations globally have faced overwhelming negative consequences associated with Covid-19 and its variants, with statistics showing staggering disparities in infection rates and death rates (Booth and Barr, 2020). However, despite arguments that suggest "race" is the primary cause of widespread poverty and health disparities among oppressed populations, it has been people with disabilities who have had the highest rates of Covid-19 deaths (Clegg, 2020). In an effort to address harmful racializing notions, Chowkwanyun and Reed (2020) argue that disparity figures without explanatory context can erroneously suggest that certain problems are "primarily racial" and, thus, undermine efforts to eliminate inequities. So, whether we are focusing on health or educational disparities, their analysis points to an urgent need for a social critique that is explicitly grounded in unpacking the unrelenting impact of the structural dynamics and material consequences of capitalism in the world today.

At the core of our response is the belief that a Marxist class-conflict analysis is indispensable to understanding not only racism but all forms of human oppression in society. Due to the nature of the task at hand, we are unable to respond to Ryan's essay in a complete and comprehensive manner. So, in an effort to be concise, we focus on several salient points that we believe are significant to scholarly or community efforts to engage in comradely dialogue across differing viewpoints. These include the retreat from class, concerns tied to perpetuating the concept of "race," the importance of understanding racism (not "race") and racialization, some underlying concerns with race-based theories, and a note regarding the need for a socialist perspective in progressive discussions of educational reform.

Retreat from Class

In his excellent and well-researched discussion, Ryan unapologetically critiques the retreat from class in scholarly discussions of both "race" and educational reform—a phenomenon that has prevailed across the literature during the past three decades. In agreement with his concern, we reassert the importance of class and production relations, particularly with respect to the process of racialization within education, despite tendencies to interpret our position as an attempt to return to an outdated paradigm of economic determinism. Yet, Marxism has been an important site of conflicting and competing readings of Marx, and also of its various interpretations of "race," as Ryan has noted.

Our position here is to draw attention to the importance of class in any educational analysis that positions itself as contributing to a political project of liberation, in that the majority of racialized students continue to be differentially located within the structures of capitalist social relations of production. Hence, their experiences of alienation and repression cannot be definitively characterized as being fundamental or intrinsic across class, skin color, or gender. This is generally overlooked or ignored among race-based theories that tend to discount the ways in which the material conditions of impoverished white populations around the world are more similar to impoverished populations of color than to their more affluent counterparts (Moss, 2003). To not acknowledge this shared condition of economic, political, and societal oppression in schools and on the streets is to ignore the organizing potential of bringing together subaltern populations across differences and diverse perspectives. In the final analysis, the project of liberation must be inherently anti-capitalist and seek to reimagine the meaning of a democratic socialism in the twenty-first century.

Furthermore, one of our concerns with the way notions of "race" and "race relations" have been deployed over time, by critical race theorists and other race-based scholars, is the manner in which the political and economic spheres are theorized as separate spheres in their treatments of "race." This is to say that notions of "race" or "race relations" in traditional discourses, more often than not, fail to systematically counter the racializing logic of capital, where such ideas are mobilized insidiously and invisibilized within education and other social contexts by way of neutral, common-sense, and meritocratic rationales. In *Democracy against Capitalism*, Wood (1995, p. 19) argues that this practice serves the deeply anti-democratic aims of capitalism by transfiguring the "economy" into an abstract entity and "emptying capitalism of its social and political content." What Wood seeks to reveal is the manner in which the false separation of the political and the economic obscures and distorts the fragmenting nature of social life within capitalism. Hidden behind this abstraction, as Parenti (1995, p. 81) asserts, are the class-driven interests of the economy. Yet, frequently, when the "problem of the economy" is mentioned in academic and even activist discourses, it is spoken of in generalized terms that render it a neutral entity, not as "the problems of the capitalist economy with a specific set of social relations and a discernible distribution of class power." Along with this retreat of class politics, there has also been a "licensed disregard and, in some cases, outright contempt for working-class and poor people irrespective of race" (Reed, 2020, p. 162).

These critiques serve to highlight that the act of simply referring to a population's economic status or social class in discussions of "race" and racism does not constitute employing a political-economic lens of analysis in one's interpretation of social phenomenon, nor does it entail challenging the logic of capitalist ideology. It is interesting to note that even Ryan, who carefully moves to challenge race-based theories, does not foreground this issue in his treatment of Cedric Robinson's (2019) implicitly race-based criticism of Marx's anti-Eurocentric argument. Given Ryan's central concern with a return to class, he could have offered a more robust challenge in his analysis of Robinson's work. For example, in "Rethinking Black Marxism: Reflections on Cedric Robinson and Others," Meyerson (2000, p. 2) critiques theorists like Robinson who enable the relative autonomy of "race" through a reductionist and distorted analysis of class and its primacy. He counters this tendency by noting that an emphasis on the primacy of class and the working class as revolutionary agent does not "render women and people of color 'secondary'" in Marxist analyses. Rather, he argues,

> The primacy of class means that building a multiracial, multi-gendered international working-class organization or organizations should be the goal of any revolutionary movement: the primacy of class puts the fight against racism and sexism at the center. The intelligibility of this position is rooted in the explanatory primacy of class analysis for understanding the structural determinants of race, gender and class oppression. Oppression is multiple and intersecting but its causes are not.

The bottom line of this analysis is a focus on the manner in which the logic of capital and the primacy of class fuel racism, in contrast to an analysis that focuses on the socially constructed and fictitious phenotypical category of "race," an idea grounded in an oppressive dualistic epistemology that ultimately bolsters conditions of racialized oppression. This exacerbation occurs through the pernicious process of racialization, an underlying belief system that equates the color of people's skin—including those labeled as white—with essential or intrinsic group characteristics. As Alexander (2006) notes, this system of "race" categorization functions to undermine democratic life. It is, therefore, not surprising to find that within schools and society more broadly there is a deeply imbedded or implicit ideological structure of thought that is enacted materially, attributing to particular groups (depending on who is doing the signification) an inherently evil or dangerous nature, along with judgments made about their innate intellectual inferiority or superiority. For this reason, we insist that unjust capitalist relations are perpetuated not by "race" but by the ideological institutionalization of racism, whose true constitutive foundation is unquestionably tied to material subjugation.

Materiality of Racism

Traditional and popular conceptual formations utilized up to the present day to define "race" within the United States have generally concealed the deeply embedded relationship that exists between racism and class. For this reason, Miles and Brown (2003, p. 137) assert that one of the major analytical tasks before us is "the historical investigation of the interpolation of racialization and racism in political and economic relations." Regrettably, despite the contemporary glut of literature on critical race theory (CRT), it remains the case that there are few treatments of "race" that offer a systematically grounded and theoretically informed account of the intricate relationship at work between racism, power, and class and its articulation within capitalist social relations. In considerable part, this is because there remains a conventional separation of economic and political spheres in both theory and practice. To Ryan's credit, we believe he attempts, through his discussion, to break with this duality, but because of his sympathy with the category of race, the separation persists.

Historically, the separation of economic and political spheres has been underscored in the United States since the civil rights movements of the mid-twentieth century. Although these movements sought to address the impoverished material conditions of African Americans and other economically oppressed populations, their persistent emphasis on a liberal, rights-centered political agenda served to undermine the persistent development of a coherent working-class movement in the United States, as it has in other parts of the world. Unfortunately, opposition to a class-based politics, resulting from an ideological separation of the economic and political spheres, reinforces a division between economic and political action—a division inherent in capitalist appropriation and exploitation. In fact, as Wood (1995, p. 20) argues, "This 'structural' separation may, indeed, be the most effective defense mechanism available to capital," in its perpetuation of economic inequalities and its longstanding assault on working people.

Our rejection of the separation of political and economic spheres echoes Marx's notion that the ultimate aim of capitalist production, with its incessant focus on capital accumulation, is political control. A central claim of this argument is that the well-camouflaged overlap that exists between what we term economic and political spheres must be exposed with specificity and commitment. In Marxist analysis, the economy is viewed as a set of social relations. This view is in sharp contrast with classical views of the economy that "fail to treat the productive sphere itself as defined by social determinations and in effect deal with society 'in the abstract'" (Wood, 1995, p. 22). Consequently, when theories of "race," racism, and other forms of inequality and oppression (no matter how progressive or radical such theories claim to be) fail to counter the oppressive structures of capitalism, their critical edge is assimilated by mainstream ideologies that categorically obscure class struggle.

In contrast, we argue for a materialist understanding of the world in which we grapple forthrightly with the impact of racism upon our material lives. This entails two significant principles of analysis. The first requires us to engage in the social relations and practices by which human beings interact with the world and which are thereby implicated in producing the life conditions we are seeking to remedy. And second, we argue for a historical understanding of human life that recognizes that all products of social activity and all social interactions between human beings are manifested as material forces of production. By all social forms, that is, all products of social activity and all social interactions between human beings, we mean to encompass all ideologies and practices that sustain and perpetuate racism and other forms of human inequalities as direct products of a particular social system of production.

Wood (1995, p. 27) sheds light on this relationship by directly linking the mode of production to questions of power relations and exploitation.

> A mode of production is not simply a technology but a social organization of productive activity, and a mode of exploitation is a relationship of power. Furthermore, the power relationship that conditions the nature and extent of exploitation is a matter of political organization within and between contending classes. In the final analysis the relation between appropriators and producers rests

on the relative strength of classes, and this is largely determined by the internal organization and the political forces with which each enters into the class struggle.

As such, we argue that all forms of social inequality are defined by class relations and, in other respects, motivated by the persistent drive to perpetuate class inequality within the context of the capitalist state, a phenomenon of social class warfare that is perpetuated by the ongoing construction and reconstruction of capitalist class relations. Thus, racism, in the form of social policies and practices, is operationalized through racialized class relations. Sexism is operationalized through gendered class relations. Heterosexism is operationalized through homophobic or transphobic class relations. Islamophobia is operationalized through Judeo-Christian class relations. In turn, all of these inequalities function to sustain cultural, political, and economic stratification within societies at large.

To reiterate, everything functions within the context of material conditions—whether one is talking about corporeal, psychological, or spiritual dimensions of culture. We understand culture as a social phenomenon produced at the point of production through the particular configuration of social-material relations, which include the particularities of the region's historical and social-material arrangements and organization. Hence, we argue that class is implicated across all social arrangements of oppression, including racism. Nothing occurs without implicating the material conditions that shape the way individuals and groups locate themselves (and are located) in the context of the body politic of the nation-state. What, then, is the motivating force for the construction of particular social arrangements, whether these are marked nationally or internationally by physical, social, or ideological signifiers? Simply put, it is the exploitation and domination of the majority of the population in the interest of sustaining unequal capitalist accumulation—an accumulation that sustains extreme disparities of wealth and power between the haves and have-nots. This is inextricably tied to elite dominion over the majority of the world's populations and natural resources. The global pandemic fiasco of inequality tied to (in)adequate access to vaccination, for example, well illustrates the manner in which this phenomenon is systematically enacted and extended, even during moments of world crisis.

The origin of nation-states must be understood within the wider history of capitalism and colonialism (Berger, 2001), in that racialized class relations, anchored within and camouflaged by historical and contemporaneous events, were constructed within the social-material milieu of nation-states, at the moment of colonization (Blaut, 1989). Furthermore, Virdee (2019, p. 3) reminds us that within the processes of colonialism an "intimate relationship between capitalism, class struggles and racism" was forged—a relationship solidified through the forceful introduction of capitalist modes of production into each region. Moreover, we cannot overlook the interdependency of nation-state formation and capitalist formation in our conceptualization of inequalities—along with the manner in which liberalism "served as capitalisms humane face, made to conceal capitalism's inhumane aspects" (Hadžidedić, 2022, p. 3) including genocide, colonization, and slavery. Hence, to speak of the political sphere as being separate from the economic sphere is to create an illusion that fundamentally serves the interests of capitalist exploitation and the accumulative drive for capital and power by the few. This abstract separation conceals unjust processes of capitalist accumulation, of both material and political power—an accumulation sustained by asymmetrical class relations firmly anchored to social practices of racism, sexism, homophobia, ethnocentrism, and other forms of social inequality and exclusion.

A central tenet of contemporary capitalism as a global system, now vastly intensified under the neoliberal offensive and underpinning reform efforts, is the aggressive dismantling of the welfare state, with major cuts made to all public services. During the Covid-19 pandemic we have witnessed this phenomenon just about everywhere, to varying degrees. Responses to the pandemic must be understood as based on particular histories, including constructed social, cultural, and political traditions, and nation-state locations, within global production chains embedded in the capitalist world economy. In broad terms, this has resulted in the failure of state revenues to keep up with the costs of publicly funded health services due to reduced tax revenues from capital, and in many cases also political pressures to lower income tax rates under the neoliberal logic of individuals choosing and purchasing services, rather than relying on public provisions (Wallerstein, 2013).

However, it must also be clearly noted that poorly resourced nation-states often cannot afford to adequately fund health and other public services; while wealthier nations—the United States and the UK as two prominent examples—clearly choose not to—yet, also disingenuously citing lack of state revenues for public services. One clear example is the increasing amount of taxpayers' money funneled into the military, while support for public services dwindles. Furthermore, over the last three decades, the pressure on public expenditure has been exacerbated by capital's demands for increased public spending on private ventures that subsidized corporate activities, including for-profits education, health, and prison initiatives. Wallerstein (2013) elaborates this tension as one of several "secular tendencies" of the capitalist world economy approaching absolute limits and contributing to systemic pressures on capitalism's intrinsic requirement of endless accumulation of capital. During the pandemic, the global production and distribution of ventilators, personal protection equipment, and vaccines to the majority of the world's most impoverished populations were negatively affected as a result.

Under conditions of seemingly permanent budget crises of national governments, impelled and reinforced by market-inspired "solutions" to problems that the neoliberal offensive to restore profits has created, the provision of public education was also flung into a permanent crisis. Neoliberal educational "solutions," as is well explicated by Ryan in his chapter, leaned heavily on the application of market principles for the provision of education, which in policy terms favored ostensibly diverse and competing, public and private, and increasingly specialized, educational providers. This firmly established market premise was tied to the notion that diversity and competition would lead to more efficient and higher-quality education. This market-driven approach has been consistently employed in response to education's move to virtual education in Covid-19 pandemic contexts, which was responsible for creating a learning crisis for almost half of all students globally (World Economic Forum, 2022), particularly where students not only had limited access to computer technology but were unprepared to contend with the isolation and demands of online instruction. This has often been spoken of as technological inequities based on students' race (Rafalow, 2020). Again, we strongly disagree, arguing that to understand the gross inequalities visible in health care and education during the pandemic, for example, requires a serious engagement with the materiality of racism within capitalist rule, which simultaneously produces conditions that perpetuate sexism, disablism, and other forms of social inequalities as well.

Racisms NOT "Race"

Another epistemological duality in Ryan's work that needs to be challenged, also present across much other work whose intent is to address the phenomenon of racism, is the unproblematized acceptance of "race" as a legitimate category to frame social relations. Its expression is prevalent in schools, as much as it is prevalent in discourses related to educational reform. Since education mirrors the ideological and material structures of the larger society, schools and other institutions powerfully socialize and condition students' perceptions of themselves by way of the hidden racialized perspectives that inform the curriculum, textbooks, and classroom life. These racialized perceptions are projected and internalized by both students of subordinate and dominant populations and, in turn, are used to reach conclusions about social relationships, including how students define racism and how they perceive and respond to racialized discourses and events that involve racialized populations.

In the early 1980s, Robert Miles (Miles, 1993) blew open the debate concerning the analytical utility of "race" as a suitable construct for the sociological analysis of human populations. He also called into question the "race-relations" paradigm that dominated the field at that time. His efforts aided Marxist scholars in recovering class analysis as a significant analytical tool in the examination of racism, at a time when postmodern theories had begun to severely curtail and erode the analytical power of class in scholarly examinations of culture (Wood, 1998). Miles also pointed to the need for scholars to engage historical specificity, rather than adhere to a view of singularity, in theorizing racism. He argued that historically specific racisms possess their own "effectivity" and, as such, could operate as a constitutive (determinant) force in shaping the ideologies of the time. Four decades later this critique remains compelling and instructive but is still conspicuously missing as we navigate through contemporary debates.

Today, as then, traditional arguments about "race" dominate the educational literature and debates tied to educational reform, wherein primary analytical status is attributed to the idea of "race." The use of "race" as an analytical category, here, refers to the practice of positioning "race" as the central organizing principle in explanatory deconstructions of social relations in the world. For several decades, our work has challenged schools of thought that employ this idea of "race" within the social sciences. Similarly, we disagree with the traditional use of "race relations"—the social relations between people of different "races"—as the object of study (for many of the reasons noted earlier), in that we consider the use of these terms as the primary locus for the analysis of racism ineffective in moving toward a more materially and politically just world. Instead, we employ the concept of racism and recognize a plurality of historically specific racisms, unhinged from the idea of the existence of such a thing as "race."

Unfortunately, the persistent use of the notion of "race" in educational practice and educational reform discussions serves in consequence, if not necessarily intent, to uphold a definition of "race" as a causal factor. In other words, meaning and significance are attributed to phenotypical features, rather than the relationship of difference with respect to the historically reproduced complex processes of racialization, predicated on its materiality. For generations, disturbing "scientific" assertions, based on biological claims found on notions of genetic superiority or inferiority, well illustrate the theoretical minefield of perpetuating "race" as an analytical category in the social sciences, and the attendant negative consequences this has had on students from racialized groups. The use of "race," in fact, serves to hide the truth; that it is not a person's skin color that determines academic performance but rather the interplay of complex social processes, one of which is premised on the articulation of racism in order to perpetuate the exclusion of populations deemed as deficit and inferior.

This habitual practice of framing social relations as "race relations" in educational discussions of racialized groups both compounds and obscures the complexity of the problem. Here, educational theorists assign significance to "racial" characteristics or behaviors rather than connecting student responses to the economic and political limitations that determine the unequal material realities in which students strive to achieve educational success. The unfortunate persistence of "race" interpretations inadvertently veils the real reasons why racialized students in the United States, for example, underachieve, perform poorly on standardized tests, are overrepresented in remedial programs, underrepresented in AP courses, and continue to drop out of high school at alarming rates (Darder, 2012).

Accordingly, educational reform solutions are often derived from distorted perceptions of the problem. The politics of busing in the early 1970s and the multicultural debates of the 1980s, spearheaded by social scientists and educators utilizing a "race relations" paradigm, provide excellent examples of race-centered reform efforts that have failed to effectively ameliorate racism within schools or society. Yet, despite the distortions that arise from the use of "race" as a central analytical category in educational reform efforts, scholars, reformers, and policymakers have been unable to break with the hegemonic tradition of its use. Moreover, efforts to problematize the reified nature of the term "race" and consider its elimination as metaphor in our work have been quickly greeted with major resistance, even among progressive educators across all communities—a resistance expressed through responses of anxiety, trepidation, fear, and even outrage. So much so that critical conversations related to differences that exist in framing racism are seldom possible. Instead, responses to such efforts frequently evidence a fear of delegitimating historical movements that have principally been defined in terms of "race" struggles. Undoubtedly, there is a tenacious and adhesive quality at work in socially constructed or fabricated ideas, which through their historical usage become so fixated and commonsensical that they resist not only deconstruction but even serious dialogical efforts.

What cannot be missed here is that to combat racism we must contend with both the ways in which it is informed and through which it manifests as both ideology and institutional practices. About this, Graves Jr. and Goodman (2022, p. 242) argue, in their book *Racism Not Race*:

> Racism has its origins in the worldview that races are biologically real and differ in abilities. The view of humankind provided false justification for enslavement and colonization. It still functions in providing cover for police violence and countless everyday acts that promote that status quo. The most important step to combat racism, therefore, is to expose racial ideology to the light of facts and science.

To do this requires a willingness to shift our thinking from talking about "race" to talking about racism (and, we would insist, racisms in the plural), and to employ the concept of racialization as a historically specific ideological process. In other words, we maintain that what is needed is not a critical theory of "race," for this can only leave us stuck in an intellectual quagmire, and further disillusioned by our failure to effectively organize a political offensive against conditions of racism in this country and abroad. Instead, efforts with an anti-racism intent should embrace a global perspective of historically defined racialized relations and acknowledge the conceptual and material plurality of racisms at work across societies. This is anything but a matter of mere semantics; rather it is a call for a new analytic framework from which to identify those structures and representations that preserve racialization—the latter being a process that infuses an essentialized racial character to particular group phenomenon, by categorizing, marginalizing, or regarding certain outcomes as "race" determined.

To construct a new language for examining the nature of racisms requires an understanding of how complex relationships of exploitation and resistance, grounded in differences of class, gender, and ethnicity, give rise to a multiplicity of ideological constructions meant precisely to racialize the other. This knowledge challenges traditional notions of racism as solely a Black/white dichotomous phenomenon and directs us toward a more accurately constructed, and hence more politically useful, idea of racism as a plural construct. In this way, we can contemplate more earnestly radical calls for educational reform, where the relations of power that shape the institutional relations that racialized students must face in schools and society are engaged straightforwardly through the materiality that gives rise to their everyday experience of racism in schools and in the world.

Toward a Democratic Vision of Educational Reform

In the sphere of US education today, we believe there is a dire need to provide an ideological critique of educational reform and the role of the state in systematically perpetuating inequality. That said, Ryan's chapter is an excellent treatise that correctly touches on this need, through his comprehensive discussion of class, race, and education reform. More critiques, similar to his contribution, are required, critiques that can assist us to recast, in more inclusive and contextual ways, educational debates related to public schooling and the academic achievement of students from subaltern communities. By so doing, educational reform discussions about the curriculum, textbooks, teacher education, and classroom initiatives can be directly linked to political power and its material consequence to students and their communities. Hence, as Ryan argues, debates related to educational reform cannot be single-issue oriented, in that, when we treat questions of educational reform in isolation, we are unable to effectively mobilize a political project that supports educational justice and democratic schooling, precisely because the question of economic democracy is left off the table.

Instead, the relationship between a variety of educational reforms must be addressed contextually with respect to the oppressive structural conditions that impact all working people within the US political economy. What underpins the necessity for such an approach is the recognition that similar hegemonic forces of social control move across all public reform arenas. This reinforces the need for coalition and social movement building across cultural, ethnic, and national ties, in efforts to address the social inequities inherent in the educational experience of students from racialized populations. This, of course, requires that questions of racism and other forms of social inequalities be integrated, explicitly as constitutive of all platforms associated with educational reform.

Central to this vision of educational reform is a reconceptualization of the role of the state, in ways that expand the boundaries of participatory democracy, cultivate a genuine sense of the commons across our differences, and initiate organization structures that promote a genuine spirit of collective ownership of schools within communities. This is truer today than ever before, as we contend with the troublesome impact of almost two years of virtual education during the pandemic and the serious consequences resulting for working-class students and, in particular, racialized students. This articulation calls for infusing educational reform debates with a new set of frameworks from which to embark on a genuinely radical democratic educational project. More specifically, this points to a political process that incorporates a radical understanding of social change, political practices of teacher unions, community movements for social justice, structural educational reform efforts, and an overall commitment to genuine equality across American society. Furthermore, education reform debates must be formulated in conjunction with a clearly focused social change strategy, given that ongoing contemporary reform programs are devoid of a politics of social change and a theory of social movements and thus constitute a limited approach toward democratizing education.

Unfortunately, most educational reform efforts today are predominantly grounded in a neoliberal reform paradigm. This inevitably leads to limited reform outcomes, due to the failure to challenge fundamentally the long-standing and persistent economic and political practices of the ruling class. Furthermore, despite the contribution of identity politics to rethinking "race" and schooling, educational reform efforts informed by decontextualized, homogeneous, and homogenizing, static, and monolithic views of racialized subjects inadvertently function as analytical and political traps that can lead to a dead-end system of reform. That being the case, despite decades of educational campaigns for reform, an educational system of inequalities persists, excluding genuinely diverse perspectives (despite more than fifty years of institutional rhetoric supporting multiculturalism, diversity, social justice, and more recently decolonization), and reproducing a discriminating structure of rewards and punishment, all of which serve to perpetuate repressive and dehumanizing conditions for all students and teachers, but in particular working-class students from economically impoverished, racialized communities.

Unfortunately, as Ryan implies in his work, the majority of current reform efforts in the United States are not linked to social justice practice or community movements for educational equity, let alone concerted efforts to end racism. Instead, most are overwhelmingly driven by the political and economic interests of the existing social order, which most often places them in direct opposition to radical social movements striving to democratize public institutions, including public education. Although it can be said that in recent years the work of social movements, most recently that of Black Lives Matter, has indeed generated increasing numbers of conversations concerning "race" and some changes in institutional practices, these reforms have been limited and have failed to transform the fundamental nature of structural inequalities in the United States—attributable to deeply rooted structures that are overwhelmingly steeped in the logic of capital. There is no question that educational policy reform efforts need to be radically democratized. However, to accomplish this, educational reformers must acknowledge and incorporate, in concrete ways, the political concerns and economic realities of communities and social movements in their articulation and redesign of the policies and practices advocated. Along the same lines, community and social movements must acknowledge the political centrality of their role in shifting educational reform debates away from the hands of elite policymakers and toward radical political processes and practices of democratic participation.

The absence of a systematic analysis of class and its antagonisms, along with its inequalities of material and political power, represents a serious shortcoming of contemporary educational reform efforts. Given the absence of more substantive analysis, it is imperative that educational movements for social justice be uncompromisingly committed to the goals of structural economic reform. An understanding of the political economy of schooling and the history of current educational practices can better enable educators to reconceptualize the roles of public policy reform, the systematic rethinking of education, and the reconstruction of an educational political project anchored to principles of social justice and economic democracy. This implies conceptualizing the classroom as a powerful political arena of production, along with the integration of cooperative structures of communal school ownership, leadership, teaching, and learning. This rethinking of schools is essential to any critically economic and democratic political vision of education.

Furthermore, to fully understand embedded inequalities, particularly racialized inequalities in education today, requires that we comprehend educational institutions as the direct result of inherent structural features, themselves shaped by macroeconomic forces and trends. Tackling the problems of educational reform, understood as rooted in profound structural inequalities of class and power, also requires the marshaling of new social formations and movements across society with a consciously articulated democratic agenda to end not only racism but every other form of human oppression perpetuated within schools and society.

We believe it is time to seriously consider socialist alternatives that ask tough questions concerning: What works and what doesn't? Who benefits and who does not? How can we create a just system of education within inherently unjust economic conditions of the state? How do we contend with the debilitating antagonisms fueled by identity politics? How do we confront openly recalcitrant practices and policies of meritocracy that perpetuate racism? How can we build a common vision across our differences, despite differing discourses and interpretation of racism? And, in so doing, how do we build the kind of critical solidarity that can contend with the intellectual tensions of differing interpretations of "race," while keeping focused on our shared political vision?

The urgency we are facing today—given the certainty of Covid-19 becoming endemic with more pandemics expected in the future and the consequences of ineffective educational policies over the last two years (Asher, 2022)—requires that such questions be widely discussed and linked to political struggles focused on the radical democratization of education. Ryan's work highlights key concerns, particularly with respect to contestations at work across class and racialized debates. About this, Reed (2020, p. 14) rightly argues that "a policy agenda that seeks only to redress disparities will be incapable of ending precarity for the masses of Black and brown workers." The bottom line concerns the urgency of a return to a public-good model of governance, which requires going beyond solely anti-discrimination policies, toward "a robust public sector and direct state intervention" to support a just educational system. This is fully in line with a Marxist call for educational reforms founded on principles of class struggle—where racism and other forms of human oppression are engaged consistently. This would entail the status quo conceding reforms, obviously to its hegemonic disadvantage, by way of pressures from educational and wider societal struggles focused on establishing conditions for economic democracy and educational justice in this country and abroad, as a vital aspect of realizing the potential for wider transformative economic and democratic possibilities.

References

Alexander, N. (2006), "Racial Identity, Citizenship and Nation Building in Post-Apartheid South Africa." Lecture delivered at East London Campus, University of Fort Hare. March 25. Available online: https://www.marxists.org/archive/alexander/2006-racial-identity-citizenship-and-nation-building.pdf.

Asher, G. (2022), "Working, in, against and beyond the Neoliberal University: Critical Academic Literacies as a Pedagogical Response to the Crisis of the University," in G. Asher, S. Cowden, A. Maisuria, and S. Housee (eds.), *Critical Pedagogy and Emancipation: A Festschrift in Memory of Joyce Canaan*. Oxford: Peter Lang, 89–116.

Berger, M. T. (2001), "The Nation-State and the Challenge of Global Capitalism." *Third World Quarterly* 22(6): 889–907.

Blaut, J. M. (1989), "Colonialism and the Rise of Capitalism." *Science and Society* 53(3): 260–96.
Booth, R., and C. Barr (2020), "Black People Four Times More Likely to Die from Covid-19, ONS Finds." *The Guardian* (May 7).
Chowkwanyun, M., and Reed, A. (2020), "Racial Health Disparities and Covid-19: Caution and Context." *New England Journal of Medicine* 383(3): 201–3.
Clegg, R. (2020), "Covid: Learning Disability Deaths Rates 'Six Times Higher.'" *BBC News* (November 13).
Darder, A. (2012), *Culture and Power in the Classroom*, 2nd ed. Boulder, CO: Paradigm Press.
Darder, A., and Torres, R. D. (2004), *After Race: Racism after Multiculturalism*. New York, NY: New York University Press.
Graves, J. L., Jr., and Goodman, A. H. (2022), *Racism Not Race*. New York, NY: Columbia University.
Hadžidedić, Z. (2022), *Nations and Capital*. London: Routledge.
Meyerson, G. (2000), "Rethinking Black Marxism: Reflections on Cedric Robinson and Others." *Cultural Logic* 6: 1–48.
Miles, R. (1993), *Racism after "Race Relations"*. London: Routledge.
Miles, R., and Brown, M. (2003), *Racism*, 2nd ed. New York, NY: Routledge.
Moss, K. (2003), *The Color of Class: Poor Whites and the Paradox of Privilege*. Philadelphia, PA: University of Pennsylvania Press.
Oxfam International (2017), "Just 8 Men Own Same Wealth as Half the World." Available online: https://www.oxfam.org/en/press-releases/just-8-men-own-same-wealth-half-world.
Oxfam International (2021), "5 Shocking Facts about Extreme Global Inequality and How to Even it Up." Available online: https://www.oxfam.org/en/5-shocking-facts-about-extreme-global-inequality-and-how-even-it.
Parenti, M. (1995), *Against Empire*. San Francisco, CA: City Lights Books.
Rafalow, M. H. (2020), *Digital Divisions: How Schools Create Inequality in the Tech Era*. Chicago, IL: University of Chicago Press.
Reed, T. F. (2020), *Toward Freedom: The Case against Race Reductionism*. London: Verso.
Robinson, C. J. (2019), *On Racial Capitalism, Black Internationalism, and Cultures of Resistance*. London: Pluto Press.
Virdee, S. (2019), "Racialized Capitalism: An Account of Its Contested Origins and Consolidation." *The Sociological Review* 67(1): 3–27.
Wallerstein, I. (2013), "Structural Crisis, or Why Capitalists May No Longer Find Capitalism Rewarding," in I. Wallerstein, R. Collins, M. Mann, G. Derlugian, and C. Calhoun (eds.), *Does Capitalism Have a Future?* Oxford and New York, NY: Oxford University Press, 9–35.
Wood, E. M. (1995), *Democracy against Capitalism: Renewing Historical Materialism*. New York, NY: Cambridge University Press.
Wood, E. M. (1998), *The Retreat from Class: A New "True" Socialism*, 2nd ed. New York, NY: Verso.
World Economic Forum (2022), "The Global Education Crisis Is Even Worse than We Thought: Here's What Needs to Happen." Available online: https://www.weforum.org/agenda/2022/01/global-education-crisis-children-students-covid19/.

Part 5

Interrogating Latino Studies

Introduction

Darder (and her comrade Rodolfo Torres) makes a significant contribution to the field of Latino Studies and more specifically, Latino (Latinx) education in the United States. They bring a political economy-inspired class analysis in their understanding of a very diverse group, with particular histories from their country of origin and its relationship to the US hegemonic state. In many ways, they are calling for a renewal to radical class/internationalist politics of the 1960s and 1970s—returning to the central premise of the field and the formation of ethnic studies more broadly. While recognizing the important work done in cultural studies, social sciences, the humanities, and other related fields under the rubric of Latino studies, they call for a return to historical materialism for understanding identity, culture, and difference. This is done so in light of major demographic changes and shifting class relations for Latinos over the last five decades, both in the US metropoles and in more rural spaces. They critically engage the relationship between Latinos and (1) political economy, (2) globalization, (3) difference, and (4) education. Darder and Torres also see the significance of transnational (and hence multi-directional and multi-dimensional) and internationalist approaches and perspectives to Latino studies and pedagogy.

Summary of Articles

In the 2003 article "Mapping Latino Studies: Critical Reflections on Class and Social Theory," Darder and Torres provide a critical reflection of theoretical strands in understanding both social theory and the pedagogical question when engaging with the ever-growing field of Latino Studies. Looking backward (thirty years to be precise) to look forward, Darder and Torres are concerned that Latino Studies as a field of study and political project has gotten away from its original emancipatory intent of class struggle—and to forthrightly understand the ravages of capitalism on poor and working-class Latinos in the United States. While speaking specifically to Latino Studies, they addressed larger theoretical, philosophical, and pedagogical concerns on and about academic programs that were on the margins of the university. Over time, such programs (including Black Studies, Native American Studies, Asian American Studies, and Latino Studies) have been, in many ways, institutionalized. They have since been incorporated into the liberal wing of the university.

In "Radicalizing the Immigrant Debate in the United States: A Call for Open Border and Global Human Rights in New Political Science," Darder calls for a paradigmatic shift in our thinking about the immigrant debate, especially as it relates to the US/Mexico border. She frames the immigration phenomenon in the context of the internationalization of capital as poor and working-class people and their racialized bodies are part and parcel of capital accumulation in the US metropole. Darder (2011) insists that we "jettison stereotypical attitudes and ignorance of immigrant populations" and to see that immigrants are not only essential but necessary to the US wage-labor system (p. 281). Anti-immigrant policies and practices are issues not to be "solved," but rather to understand that immigration is a necessity in and for the system. Hence, there is a need for a reserve army of workers that can be exploited and used to control and police other laborers and workers.

As Darder makes clear, and drawing from Marxist geographer David Harvey, the internationalization of capital with neoliberal "solutions" does and will not help to sustain poor and working-class people politically and economically. Similar to the first two readings in this section, Darder (2011) points to the implications and consequences of "exclusionary identity politics based on race, ethnicity, and religion" that yet again allow for the state to flourish. Darder puts a face to the debate by engaging with various "on-the-ground" examples. She describes the various anti-immigrant campaigns happening at the time (and as it continues to persist two decades later) at the El Paso-Juarez and San Diego-Tijuana borders, the "build-a-wall" rhetoric that is exacerbated by xenophobic neoconservative politics at both the local and national levels. The impact on poor and working-class women and their racialized bodies—a phenomenon Darder refers to as "the politics of colonized wombs" (p. 290)—is absolutely real. Darder calls for a radical possibility of open borders and sees that the "freedom of movement has always been seen as a natural right and a universal aspiration." Ultimately, she is calling for globalizing human rights—in the process of creating a global citizenship.

In "Latinos, Education, and the Church: Toward a Culturally Democratic Future," Darder returns to the concept of cultural democracy as an important philosophical analytic in her engagement with the education of Latino students within US Catholic schools (K-12 and the university) and beyond to understand the role of the Church in responding to social and economic inequalities. For Darder, there is a larger ecumenical dialogue to be had in establishing a more "humanizing structures and practices of formal and informal learning" (p. 20). She provided data (acquired from the US Census) that is instructive in understanding Latino students: (1) by 2026, Latino children are projected to comprise one-third of all children in the United States, (2) nearly one in three Latinos lives in poverty, (3) one in five Latinos is unemployed, and (4) one in six Latino boys born in 2001 are considered of risk of going to prison during their lifetime. These data speak to the enduring legacy of *Brown* (1954), *Lemon Grove School District* (1941) and *Mendez v. Westminster* (1946), to name a few of the landmark decisions that still impact Latino students today.

The data also speaks to a widening class/socioeconomic gap within the Latino population. Darder's call for a "cultural democracy of schooling" critically engages with the relationship between culture and power. She reminds us that Catholic schools, like most educational institutions, can inadvertently reproduce that structure and logic of assimilative schooling that can be detrimental for Latino students and undermine their cultural strengths and ways of knowing and being in the world. Darder reminds us of the genesis of Catholic schooling (in response to the oppression imposed on them) by mainstream US educational institutions. She closes the piece by engaging with liberation theologian Gustavo Gutierrez's "theology as a love letter" and reminds us of the Church's commitment to a socially just world.

14

Mapping Latino Studies: Critical Reflections on Class and Social Theory

Antonia Darder and Rodolfo D. Torres

> *When you say "America" you refer to the territory stretching between the icecaps of the two poles. So to hell with your barriers and frontier guards!*
>
> —Diego Rivera[1]

The conservative climate befalling universities across the United States raises serious concerns for the future of Latino Studies. This is particularly true where university discourse, victim to its own political retrenchment, wrongly concludes that questions of culture, race, diversity, and multiculturalism were sufficiently attended to in the post-civil rights era. Correspondingly, as the multicultural or diversity rhetoric wanes in the marketplace of ideas, raising dollars emerges as the top priority for universities nationwide—a feat accomplished primarily by adjusting faculty scholarship and research agendas to coincide with the priorities and mandates of the corporate world. In the main, many academic departments and university policy centers or "think tanks" are almost entirely dependent on corporate monies, advanced research priorities, and policy "solutions" that, in the final analysis, are commensurate with the needs of capital. The impact of such measures is, unfortunately, to render most Latino Studies scholars virtually invisible, stifling our efforts to influence the course of public policy or political direction toward greater democratic and participatory solutions.

The social project of Latino Studies has been deemed intellectually suspect, as original analysis and innovative research and teaching approaches are sharply eclipsed by a revamped emphasis on traditional pedagogy and positivist scientific methods. Here we are referring to reductionistic, instrumentalized, and fragmented methods of research and teaching that, historically, have been most responsible for promoting intellectual parochialism (i.e., teacher-centered lecture format or the dominance of psychology paradigms in education). Critical comparative studies and collaborative interdisciplinary efforts to construct a full-bodied knowledge of Latino life and thought are thus often discouraged by those who continue to privilege the narrow rationality of quantitative enthusiasts.

As a consequence, Latino studies scholarship within the humanities, for example, can seldom forge a solid relationship with the social sciences; nor can either field readily establish a foothold within the "hard" sciences of physics, mathematics, or the "applied" disciplines. Hence, despite recent seismic paradigm shifts that have challenged positivist claims regarding a single, fixed truth or scientific recourse to grand narratives, there still exists a real need to break down the strictures of discipline-specific knowledge construction. To accomplish this, we argue that Latino Studies needs to move more vigorously toward what Bob Jessop and Ngai-Ling Sum (2001) term a post-disciplinary approach to our teaching and research in the field.

This is not to suggest that we reject the wealth of information that can be gleaned from well-designed quantitative studies. Rather, our concern is linked to the preferential and exclusive legitimacy frequently assigned to the use of quantitative methods. When taken solely on their own merit, the latter fail to render the complexity of the racialized cultural experience and cannot provide the analytical richness required to transform our scholarship into a truly emancipatory political project. In contrast, Latino Studies scholarship needs to be independent, critical, and infused with what C.W. Mills (2002) terms "sociological imagination"—a pedagogical and investigative discourse that provides us with an agenda of policies and practices that can assist Latino Studies scholars to map out the possibilities for economic democracy and social justice, particularly in the face of neo-liberal excess and scientism.

Critical Scholarship

What we choose to emphasize in this complex history will determine our lives.
—Howard Zinn[2]

Our discussion of Latino Studies is forthrightly directed toward promoting critical scholarship—scholarly work carried out with the expressed intent of challenging the current nature of economic inequality and social oppression. This approach is particularly significant to how we participate in the construction of knowledge in our classrooms and as public intellectuals out in the world. As such, a critical Latino Studies program must begin with a clear vision of our work and its relationship to the world. This is no easy task, given that Latino Studies is not monolithic and that we all work within the contested terrain of both multidisciplinary expectations and community exigencies. Nevertheless, what allows us to struggle together across our differences is the fact that social justice and economic democracy are central to the political project that first inspired the scholarly formation of the field. With this as our starting point, there are several issues that need to be consistently revisited in the course of Latino Studies research. In the spirit of W.E.B. Du Bois, we need to "return to the basics" history, political economy, and public policy—in our efforts to effectively challenge racism and class inequality within education. Greater focus must be placed on comparative work in the field (i.e., studies which compare different marginalized groups or studies which compare the US Latino experience with that of the populations in Latin American countries). In doing so, we can develop not only knowledge of how we are similar, but also of how we are different. This knowledge can help build a robust field of Latino Studies that is usefully complex and needfully inclusive. A key criticism of Latino Studies to date is that much of the research within the field is "fuzzy" and overly concerned with texts. In response, we need to move beyond merely descriptive, anecdotal accounts of Latino life in the United States, if we are to provide greater analytical specificity and rigor to our construction of theories that examine the dynamics of exploitation and domination.[3]

Currently, there are a variety of theoretical debates influencing both research and pedagogy within Latino Studies. It is important for us to be consistently cognizant and engaged in these debates. For example, feminist theories are vital to our knowledge of Latinas and their location within our communities and the larger social context. This is particularly significant for understanding how Latinas move across contested terrain to give meaning to their racialized, gendered identities. The work on Latino masculinities seeks to provide a more complex understanding of Latino men, their identities, and subjectivities, in an effort to disrupt commonly held assumptions that make homogenous and reify the experience of Latino males within US contexts. Postmodern theories, with their emphasis on fragmentation and difference, the rupture of meta-narratives, and engagement with identity politics have also had an influence on how issues of culture and identity are approached within the classroom and community. In contending with questions of "race," Latino critical race theory, or LatCrit (Crenshaw, Gotanda, Peller, & Thomas, 1995; Delgado, 1995; Wing, 1997; Gunier & Torres, 2002) has left its mark in the field. Using this approach, legal scholars whose work represents theoretically diverse perspectives ascribe primary explanatory power to the concept of "race." Similarly, post-colonial theories have contributed to our understanding of human agency, the politics of location, and the struggle for decolonization—all key concepts in understanding the complexity of Latino lives in the United States.

At the same time that Latino Studies is experiencing something of a renaissance within the academy, there has been a renewed intellectual and political interest in historical materialism. Unlike Latino Studies scholars who impertinently deride Marxist methodology as unfashionable and obsolete, we welcome its renewal. In the past, the retreat from political economy and class within African American and Latino Studies scholarship was stirred by a response to the narrowness of reductionist economic arguments. And rightly so, for many of the early Marxist scholars tended to focus on class, without rigorous attention paid to questions of racism, sexism, or heterosexism. However, today we dispute post-Marxist claims that classical Marxism hinders engagement with important issues of racialized identities and inequalities. Instead, we contend that it is not a feat of economic reductionism to treat with analytical specificity, the notion of class as a relationship and as a means for examining inequalities of power and wealth. Nor is it reductive to understand how class relations of power lead us to organize our work and political involvement in particular ways; or guide our practical consideration as to the strategies we use to struggle for workers' rights, housing, education, immigration, and health care. Instead, such forms of analysis engage class as intrinsic to all social relations, and thus, view all social arrangements as configured, dialectically, within the context of contemporary capitalist social formations.

As Latino Studies scholars strive to make sense of the current political economy operating locally and globally, theories of globalization also surface in discussions of late capitalism and the rapid movement and exploitation of labor, resources, as well as the economic and political power wielded by multinational corporations.[4] However, these arguments have generated considerable debate among many progressives, educators, and theorists. While there are those who have incorporated theories of globalization in their critiques of contemporary social problems, others argue that it is just the same old capitalism working as usual—the same old capitalism that must be fiercely challenged.[5] This latter view seeks to reintroduce a class analysis to the construction of social theory and public policy and, by so doing, make central a critique of capitalism.

Ellen Meiksins Wood (1994) explains succinctly what it means to challenge capitalism. "Addressing capitalism means considering it as a historically specific system of social relations, a social form with its own logic and its own laws of motion the imperatives of competition, profit maximization, 'productivity,' 'growth,' and 'flexibility' with all their social and ideological consequences" (28). Wood clearly calls for scholarship that engages with how power is tied to external conditions; the social impact of changing modes of production upon workers; the political economy and the ways it structures the social conditions of institutions and community life, to impact on class formations; the increasing significance of class; and the specificity of capitalism as a totalizing system of social and political domination and exploitation. In concert with this view, we argue that to ignore this dimension has far-reaching political implications for the future, particularly during a time of dramatic demographic shift.

The Changing Demographics

Official celebratory pronouncements hardly conceal diffused anxieties about the impending impact of projected demographic changes in the Latino population of the United States.

—Renato Rosaldo (1993)

In January 2003, the US Census Bureau estimated the Latino population to be 37 million, constituting 13 percent of the total population. With these new numbers, Latinos have the dubious distinction of being the nation's largest minority group, surpassing African Americans with an estimated population of 36.2 million. To make sense of the current conditions, we must remain attentive to the impact of such changes in the regions where large Latino populations reside and what these changes mean to the local, national, and international political economy. For example, it is impossible to ignore what many are calling the "browning" or "Latinization" of vast metropolitan areas in the United States. This phenomenon is vividly exemplified in the current population of Los Angeles County where, of the 9.8 million residents, over 4.2 million are Latinos.

Population projections claim that by the year 2005, "minority" residents are expected to become the majority in most large urban centers. Already, today, in many large neighborhoods of Los Angeles, New York, Chicago, Dallas, and Miami, Latino residents comprise the majority. In fact, according to Jorge Mariscal (2003), this phenomenon is even beginning to occur in the deep South where "Latino immigrants have moved in large numbers into the old confederacy." Indeed, within the past decade, the national census documented a dramatic increase in the Latino population of North Carolina (393.9 percent), Arkansas (323.3 percent), Georgia (299.6 percent), and Tennessee (278.2 percent).

Important to understanding the evolving public needs of these cities is recognizing the migratory patterns that give shape to the shifting landscape of many working-class Latino neighborhoods. For example, more than 50 percent of all Latinos in California are foreign born, over 700,000 of whom have their origins in Central America. The significance of this statistic cannot be downplayed, since many have come to California in response to regional wars and impoverishment spurred on by historical and contemporary US economic policies in Latin America. The growing number of diverse Latino immigrants poses a positive challenge to our scholarship and pedagogy, pushing against the grain of traditionally defined notions of Latino identities from the more obvious political concerns related to how we label Latino populations to the more complex issues of redefining ideas of citizenship (Oboler, 1995).

We maintain that complex ideas such as citizenship need to be contested concepts, precisely because they are interrelated with wider cultural and social issues of racialized class identities. Such issues have often been sidelined or neglected by research and practices anchored in Latino identity politics. This is particularly the case when there is failure to engage the complexity of histories, cultures, and regional economies that inform the construction of diverse Latino identities. This is well-illustrated by many US-born and immigrant Latinos, who not only identify with indigenous or mestizo roots, but who identify themselves as Afro-Latinos. This complexity was clearly evident in the 2000 Census, where Latinos were asked to claim a particular "racial origin." "Some of the nation's 35 million Latinos scribbled in the margins that they were Aztec or Mayan. A fraction said they were Indian. Nearly 48% described themselves as white, and 2% as black. Fully 42% said they were 'some other race'"(Fears, 2002: A1). Accounts such as this clearly point to the need for careful analytical attention to be paid to racialized constructions of identities in these times of major demographic shifts, changing class formations, and new forms of global dislocation. Minimally, they serve to explain why one-size-fits-all responses to Latino education, citizenship, and well-being within the United States will always be insufficient.

The Limits of Identity Politics

We work with raced identities on already reified ground. In the context of domination, raced identities are imposed and internalized, then renegotiated and reproduced. From artificial to natural, we court a hard-to-perceive social logic that reproduces the very conditions we strain to overcome.

—Jon Cruz (1996)

Over the last three decades, there has been an overwhelming tendency among Latino Studies scholars to focus on notions of "race" in ways that draw directly on the intellectual and political tradition of many African American scholars. The use of "race" among Chicano scholars of the 1960s can be linked to academic acts of resistance to the term "ethnicity," and theories of assimilation, which were generally applied to immigrant populations of European descent. In efforts to distance Chicano history from this concept and link it to a theory of internal colonialism, cultural imperialism, and racism, Chicanos were discussed as a colonized "racial" group in much the same manner that many radical theorists positioned African Americans within the US political economy. As such, association of the term "race" with power, resistance, and self-determination has veiled the problematics of "race" as a social construct. Protected by the force of cultural nationalist rhetoric, "race" as an analytical term has remained a "paper tiger" seemingly powerful in discourse matters but ineffectual as an analytical metaphor, incapable of moving us away from the pervasive notion of "race" as an innate determinant of behavior.

Consequently, much of the past literature on Latino populations, with its emphasis on such issues as "racial inequality," "racial segregation," "racial identity," "racial consciousness," has utilized the construct of "race" as a central category of analysis for interpreting the social conditions of inequality and marginalization. In turn, this literature has reinforced a racialized politics of identity and representation, with its problematic emphasis on "racial" identity as the overwhelming impulse for political action (Darder & Torres, 1999).

Given this legacy, it is not surprising to discover that the theories, practices, and policies that have informed social science analysis of racialized populations today are overwhelmingly rooted in a politics of identity—an approach that is founded on parochial notions of "race" and representation, which ignore the imperatives of capitalist accumulation and the existence of class divisions within Latino communities. The folly of this position is critiqued by Wood (1994), when she exposes the limitations of a politics of identity which fails to contend with the fact that capitalism is the most totalizing system of social relations the world has ever known. Yet despite this fact, in much of the work on Latino, African American, Native American, and Asian populations, a systematic analysis of class and a critique of capitalism is often conspicuously absent. And even when class is mentioned, the emphasis is primarily on an undifferentiated plurality of identity politics or an "intersection of oppressions," which, unfortunately, ignores the overwhelming tendency of capitalism to homogenize rather than to diversify human experience.

This practice is particularly disturbing since no matter where one travels in the world, there is no question that racism as an ideology is integral to the process of capital accumulation. The failure of Latino Studies scholars to confront this dimension in their analysis of contemporary society as a racialized phenomenon or to continue treating class as merely one of a multiplicity of (equally valid) perspectives, which may or may not "intersect" with the process of racialization, is a serious shortcoming.[6] In addressing this issue, we must recognize that identity politics, which generally glosses over class differences and/or ignores class contradictions, has often been used by even radical scholars and activists within African American, Latino, and other racialized communities, in efforts to build strong political bases that distinguish Latino Studies from other fields of inquiry. Here, constructions of "race" are objectified and mediated as truth to ignite political support, divorced from the realities of class struggle.

Hence, if we are to effectively challenge the horrendous economic impact of globalization on racialized and other marginalized communities, we must recognize that a politics of identity is grossly inept and unsuited for building and sustaining collective political movements for social justice and economic democracy. Instead what we need is fundamentally to reframe the very terrain that gives life to our political understanding of what it means to struggle against widening class differentiation and ever-increasing racialized inequality.

Class Matters

One of the main reasons for studying class structure is because of its importance in explaining other elements of class analysis, especially class formation, class consciousness and class struggle.

—Erik Olin Wright (1997)

Central to our comprehension of pedagogy and research in Latino Studies is our ability to engage class not as an identity or a phenomenon equal to other forms of oppression, but rather as relations of power that encompass social processes that reproduce structural inequality. From this standpoint then, we can consider how the relationship between culture, class, power, and ideology impacts the construction of knowledge; how we might move toward dismantling the structures of racialized inequality which persist in society today, as opposed to reform efforts; and how we contend with political efforts to completely dismantle the remnants of progressive health, education, and welfare policies.

The collapse of the Soviet Union in the 1980s in conjunction with the shift toward postmodern paradigms of knowledge and theoretical orientations, resulted in a retreat from class analysis. As mentioned earlier, Latino Studies was no exception. Hence, we are well aware that to reassert the importance of class analysis in our discussion of Latino Studies scholarship may be viewed by some as a return to an outdated theoretical paradigm. However, Marxist theory has always been a site of conflicting and competing perspectives. Moreover, our concern with the question of class analysis is far beyond simple ideological contestation. For us, class is tied intrinsically to material conditions within society and how we understand the manner in which relations of production and asymmetrical structures of power are at work in very concrete ways within the daily life of Latino populations.

For example, there is no doubt that large numbers of African American, Latino, and Native American workers fail to ever find long-term or substantial employment in the labor market. In fact, Latino and other racialized minorities are disproportionately represented in low-income jobs and state unemployment rolls. Moreover, an inter-relationship clearly exists between Latin American migration to the United States and exclusionary processes which ensure that the ranks of the small entrepreneurs include Latino immigrants who sustain a complex of financial and cultural ties with their countries of origin. These are but two simple examples that speak to the significance of class, in the structural conditions and social realities that impact Latino communities today.

A class analysis must also be central to our efforts to better understand Latino communities and issues of education; otherwise, we risk reinscribing existing inequities pertaining to educational attainment and achievement opportunities. For example, the digital divide within the United States is no longer concerned primarily with describing inequitable physical access to computers at school for certain marginalized, low-income groups. Instead, it is increasingly used to describe inequitable differences in the quality of new technology use in schools (Cuban, 2001). As we move from living and working in an industrial to a "postindustrial" society, there remain fundamental questions still to be answered concerning the "proper" relationships among education, work, and new technologies. These include: Which groups have the most ready access to effective uses of new technologies in schools, and why? What is (or what should be) the emancipatory role of technology within schools, colleges, and universities (i.e., distance learning, flexible course offerings, small- and large-scale activism, and access to vital information)? What are the consequences of technology-rich education in relation to Latino students' social and academic development—particularly when these students have historically had far less access to new technologies than their white or Asian counterparts (Tornatzky, Macias, & Jones, 2002)? What social and moral values does technology-driven education cultivate, and what might this mean for Latino students currently enrolled in US public schools, in terms of current and future conceptions of and practices associated with "being a good citizen?"

To engage such questions effectively requires that we recognize that class and "race" are concepts of a different sociological order. Class and "race" do not occupy the same analytical space and, thus, cannot constitute explanatory alternatives to each other. Class is a material space, even within the mainstream definition that links the concept to occupation, income status, and educational attainment—all of which, in turn, reflect the materiality of class, though not with any analytical specificity. Hence, the significance of class can be rigorously considered only through an approach that recognizes the social relations of production as germane to any social justice or emancipatory political project.

By posing critical questions that interrogate the power relations that condition and structure the nature and extent of exploitation across classes, Latino Studies scholars can unveil the internal organization and social relations at work between contending classes. In the final analysis, the relationship between appropriators and producers rests on the relative strength of classes and the manner in which these are thrust into the political arena of class struggle (Wood, 2000). True to this view, we challenge the post-Marxist dismissal of class as an analytical category. Instead, we reaffirm class analysis in Latino Studies research and pedagogy as essential, in the face of staggering economic inequality.

Inequality in the "New Economy"

We are all living through an unprecedented situation marked by dramatic new developments, including not only the New Economy boom and bust, but also an unheard of polarization of wealth ... a phenomenon of capital accumulation and crisis –hence class struggle.

—Monthly Review[7] (Eds., 2001)

The growing gap between the rich and the poor is one of the most compelling issues in the United States, particularly when we consider the overwhelming concentration of wealth and income that remains in the hands of a few. In spite of this, it is commonplace for educators to consider questions of pedagogy in the absence of fundamental social questions related to economic inequality. Yet, we cannot gain a better understanding of what is driving many of the difficulties Latinos are facing in this country today without addressing the changing nature of the capitalist economy. By grounding our work in material concerns, we are intellectually and politically motivated to consider, at the very least, such questions as: Who is working? And who is not? Who is gaining economic ground? And, who is losing ground?

It is imperative that Latino Studies scholars investigate more seriously changing conditions of labor and the consequences of "globalization." In so doing, we must recognize that there is considerable theoretical debate over how best to describe the changing nature of work and the direction of the modern capitalist economy. Competing opinions abound as to the extent and meaning of these changes, and whether they represent a new kind of epochal shift in the basic logic of capitalist accumulation. Once again, the city of Los Angeles can provide a worthy illustration as to why we raise this particular issue.

As a consequence of the de-industrialization of Los Angeles, thousands of workers have experienced, first hand, what it means to see work disappear and to contend with the accompanying structural conditions that have created deep-seated class divisions in the region. As a direct outcome, Los Angeles unemployment was higher at the end of the century, than it was in 1969 (Scott & Soja, 1996). Similarly, it is these conditions that have had a perilous effect on the city's diverse populations. It is not surprising then to discover that the 1992 uprising in South Central Los Angeles, contrary to portrayal by the media and many academics, resulted largely from high rates of joblessness, rather than issues of "race relations" between Blacks and whites. In fact, over 60 percent of those arrested were Latinos. By characterizing this event as a crisis in "race relations"—first, between Blacks and Koreans; then between Blacks and Latinos; and finally, back to Blacks and whites—the media both avoided and prevented any substantive inquiry into the structural economic problems of the city and region. Moreover, the interpretation of the riots as a "race relations" problem failed to take into account the drastic shifts in demographic patterns which have created new dynamics of class and racialized relations in Los Angeles (Valle & Torres, 2000).

This perspective is further sustained by an analysis of the problems inherent in contemporary capitalist restructuring. The reindustrialization of large urban centers with light manufacturing, for example, represents an urban development strategy that is partly responsible for stagnant wages, given the abundance of surplus labor owed to increasing rates of unemployment and cheap immigrant labor. Undoubtedly, this has contributed to further economic decline of many working-class neighborhoods in the large and densely populated inner cities. Similarly, the closing of heavy manufacturing production plants (such as automotive and aerospace factories) across the nation has had a deleterious effect on Latino and African American workers, in particular. Such closures, along with the negative repercussions of NAFTA on workers, have contributed to the phenomenon discussed openly by even the dismantling of the middle class and the increasing polarization of wealth. In addition, the economic instability of many working-class Latino communities has been further exacerbated by the replacement of union labor by non-union labor, and the reduction of benefits and real wages over the last decade (Darder & Torres, 1997).

Although these conditions are tremendously detrimental to the quality of life for Latino populations in the United States, we believe it is important for Latino Studies scholars to also take note of positive grassroots efforts to strike back against the ravages of deepening economic inequality. For example, recent neighborhood efforts in Latino communities have resulted in the introduction and passage of Living Wage ordinances. Latino youth involved with Californians for Justice have been instrumental in the *Schools Not Prisons* community organizing campaign for democratic schooling. Such community-wide efforts represent a significant and tangible possibility for the implementation of structural reforms at the local efforts that can only be successful when structural inequalities are intricately linked with the process of racialization.

From "Race" to Racialization

For three hundred years black Americans insisted that "race" was no usefully distinguishing factor in human relationships. During those same three centuries every academic discipline insisted that "race" was the determining factor in human development.

—Toni Morrison (1989)

Everywhere we look, policy pundits, journalists, and academics alike, all continue to work within categories of "race" as though there is unanimity regarding their analytical value. Like all other components of what Antonio Gramsci called common sense, much of the everyday usage of "race" is uncritical. This phenomenon, of course, is no different within the context of Latino populations. Yet, some would argue that there exists more fluidity in the manner in which Latinos relate to the issue of "race," than is the case with other racialized groups. This is said to be reflected in the various terms used to describe a person through the signification of his or her skin color (i.e., mestizo, morena, trigueno, mulata, etc.). However, this fluidity, albeit a legacy of Spanish colonization and carefully constructed social and exclusionary hierarchies, does not find a home within US bureaucratic structures. It is not unusual to find that dark-skinned Latino immigrants from Brazil, Colombia, Panama, and other Latin American countries are surprised to learn that they are categorized as Black within the context of the US racialized gaze. Hence, there are those who might conclude that "race matters in Latin America, but it matters differently" (Fears, 2002; A1). This may well be related to the historical fact that, until recently, questions of class have foregrounded most liberatory struggles, despite the obvious fact that racism has long been at work in all Latin American countries. In the most simple terms, this is reflected by the typically light-skinned phenotypical characteristics of the elite class, as compared with the generally darker-skinned features of most members from poor and working-class populations. So, although the notion of race may be engaged differently by Latino immigrants, there is no question that their perceptions are, nevertheless, linked to the particular processes of racialization inherent in the histories of Latin American conquest and slavery.

In these times, we would be hard-pressed to find scholars who would subscribe openly to the use of "race" as a determinant of any specific social phenomena associated with inherent genetic characteristics. Even the American Anthropological Association in 1997 issued a recommendation that the US government scrap the term "race" on official forms, since it held no scientific justification in human biology. More recently, human genome research supports the fact that "race" has no biological foundation. However, such events have done little to challenge or erase such disturbing "scientific" assertions as those made by Richard Hernstein and Charles Murray (1994) in their book, *The Bell Curve*.

It is within the historical and contemporary contexts of such scholarship that differences in skin color are signified as marks suggesting the existence of different "races." As a consequence, a primary response among many progressive activists and scholars when we call for the elimination of "race" as an analytical category is to reel off accusations of a "color-blind" discourse. This is not what we are arguing. What we do argue is that the fixation on skin color is a product of signification, rather than a product of some "truth" concerning some essential relationship between skin color and inherent abilities. This is to argue that people identify skin color as marking or symbolizing other phenomena in a variety of social contexts in which other significations occur. As a consequence, when social practices include and exclude people in light of the signification of skin color, collective identities are produced and social inequalities are structured (Miles & Torres, 1996).

"Racialization" is the term we give to the use of "race" in structuring social relations. More specifically, Robert Miles (1982, 1989, 1993) in his book *Racism* defines this process of racialization as "those instances where social relations between people have been structured by the signification of human biological characteristics in such a way as to define and construct differentiated social collectivities the concept therefore refers to a process of categorization, a representational process of defining an Other (usually, but not exclusively) somatically" (75). Hence, to interpret more lucidly the conditions faced by Latino populations require us to move beyond the idea of "race" to an understanding of racialization and its impact on class formations. To continue using the concept of "race" as an analytic term is to affix and essentialize skin color characteristics in relation to certain groups, in a way that elides the processes involved in the social construction of "race." The former holds no hope of change or reform (i.e., skin color is something to be "worked around"); while the latter concept is far more dynamic, in that it offers possibilities for challenging categories that serve to undermine the agency of many marginalized groups. As such, this summons a bold analytical transition from the language of "race" to recognizing the centrality of racism and the process of racialization in our understanding of exclusionary practices that give rise to structural inequalities.

Central to this discussion is also the manner in which social theories of racism are predominantly anchored in the Black-white paradigm of "race relations," which severely limit our efforts in Latino Studies to speak to the complexity of Latino racialization. One of the most limiting aspects of the Black-white framework is its tendency to obstruct or camouflage the need to examine particular histories and contextual dimensions that give rise to different forms of racisms around the globe. The subsequent conflation of racialized relations into a Black-white paradigm has often functioned to render Latino populations invisible or to a "second-class oppression" status. This has prevented Latino studies scholars from engaging with significant differences among Latino populations and from delving more fully into comparative histories of racism and how these are linked to class inequalities.

If we are then to theoretically grasp the complexity of contemporary Latino life, the racialized language of "Black" and "white" must be dispensed with and replaced by a new conceptual language rooted in, but not determined by, the political economy of labor migration, and capitalist social and class relations.[8] Mariscal (2003) alludes to this need with respect to Latino immigrant workers in the deep South, where demographic changes reflect the historical nature of the racialization process. "They have little knowledge of the struggles for equal rights and the history of anti-Mexican racism in the Southwest. As they enter a culture based on black/white relations, these workers are unaware of regional histories, past labor struggles and the persistence of long-standing 'southern values.' In effect, they walk into a black/white universe like virtual aliens from another planet." Furthermore, he reminds us that the recent media coverage of the Trent Lott affair reveals that the discussion of race in this country "is still firmly grounded in a narrow and antiquated black/white reality."

Toward a Critical Theory of Racism

The idea of "race" has profound meanings in the everyday world, but these have no scientific credibility and I can therefore find no reason why those who write in the Marxist tradition should wish to legitimise an ideological notion by elevating it to a central analytical position.

—Robert Miles (1984)

Recent structural changes in the US political economy and the increasing diversity within Latino communities have made the issue of racism more complex than ever before. But rather than occupying a central position, these historical socio-economic changes have served merely as a backdrop to the contemporary theoretical debates on the meaning of "race" and representation in the US today, debates that, more often than not, are founded on deeply psychologized or abstracted notions of racialized differences and conflicts. This constitutes a significant point of contention, generating many questions yet to be answered regarding the continued use of the idea of race in theorizing the Latino life condition. What does it mean to utilize "race," in light of the growing complexities we are facing, within both social and political arenas? What are the strengths and limitations of "race-centered" politics? How is racism structured within the context of advanced capitalist relations of power?

Such inquiry into the analytical utility of "race" in Latino Studies scholarship is, by no means, meant to negate the worthiness of on-going work on racialized inequalities or obstruct the struggle against racism or deny that "race" is a social construction. Rather, it represents an effort to seek greater analytical clarity in how we make sense of cultural, historical, and political differences. Moreover, there remains a need to expose critically, and with greater specificity, the manner in which the ideology of racism produces notions of "race," as opposed to the popular belief that the existence of "races" produces racism.

This highlights the need for Latino Studies scholars to interrogate with greater analytical depth the terms we use and the concepts we commonly uphold. For example, it is not uncommon to find the interchangeable use of "race" and "culture" in discussions of Chicanos, Puerto Ricans, and other Latino populations. It is significant to note, for instance, that instead of linking the notion of culture to class relations which emerge at the point of production (or social relations of production), most scholars link culture to the notion of "race"—a concept associated with phenotypical traits, but now linked to the notion of social construction, shared histories, and narratives associated with the racialized category of Latino.

Meanwhile, the habitual practice of framing social relations as "race relations" continues to obscure material conditions of inequality. This is exemplified by educational theories that assign significance to "racial" characteristics, rather than attributing student responses to school conditions, historically shaped by structural inequalities that determine the context in which students must achieve. This unfortunate absence of class analysis veils the real reasons why so many Latino, African American, and other racialized students fare poorly on standardized tests, are over-represented in remedial programs, and continue to drop out of high schools and universities at alarming rates. As a consequence, educational solutions are often derived from distorted perceptions of the problem and lead to misguided policies and practices.

The previous example points to the manner in which racialized constructs of culture can obscure the reality that class is intrinsic to all social arrangements—including racism. To conceal this fact makes it more difficult to address effectively the motivating forces for the construction of particular social arrangements, whether these be marked by physical, geographical, or ideological signifiers. Hence, an interrogation of the use of "race" is tremendously important within Latino Studies, given that nothing occurs without implicating the material conditions that shape how individuals and groups locate themselves within the context of the larger society (Torres & Darder, Forthcoming 2004).

Yet, we recognize that mere efforts to undo and eliminate the idea of "race" as an analytical category in our scholarship are insufficient to remove its use from the popular imagination and the discourse of everyday life. Moreover, in a country like the United States, filled with historical examples of exploitation, violence, and murderous acts justified by both popular opinions and scientific ideas of "race," it is next to impossible to convince people that "race" does not exist as a "natural" category. So in Colette Guillaumin (1995, p. 107) words "let us be clear about this. The idea of race is a technical means, a machine for committing murder. And its effectiveness is not in doubt." But "races" do not exist. What exists is the tenacious and unrelenting idea of "race" that fuels racism throughout the world.

Hence, the future struggle against the ravages of racism and capitalism must at long last contend with the reality that there are no "races" and therefore no "race relations." In light of this view, we call for a critical reconceptualization of racism with which to analyze the historical and contemporary social experiences and institutional realities faced by Latino communities and other racialized populations. Insofar as such a concept, whether employed in social investigation or political struggle, reveals patterns of discrimination and resulting inequalities, it also helps us to grapple more specifically with those actions that must be taken to dismantle the structural inequalities we encounter in our everyday lives. Such a critical theory of racism represents a bold and forthright move to challenge commonsense notions of "race" that often lead to profound forms of essentialism and ahistorical perceptions of oppression. Moreover, these notions make it nearly impossible to dismantle the external material structures of exploitation and domination that sustain racialized inequalities within the body politic of the capitalist state.

The Nature of the Capitalist State

A theory of the state is always a theory of society and of the distribution of power in that society.
—Ralph Miliband (1969)

The nature of the capitalist State is another important issue so often ignored in the bulk of Latino Studies scholarship. Yet, this is a serious omission when we consider current material conditions of contemporary society. During the last decade alone, the State has been seized on the one hand by neoliberal capitalist interests of the likes of Bill Gates; and on the other, by the politicians—whether they be weak-willed Democrats the likes of Clinton or reactionary Republicans like George W. Bush. As a consequence, State policies, which have ushered in significant welfare cutbacks, corporate corruption, the war in Afghanistan, "homeland security," and now the war on Iraq, have also fueled the anti-intellectual fervor of the popular media. Meanwhile, news reports of the atrocities of US oil companies in Nigeria, the unabashed sale of obsolete US weapons to impoverished developing nations, and the role of the United States in the creation of instability and unrest in the Middle East remain almost non-existent in world reports on the evening news.

With the unbridled ferment and advancement of capital, the safety net of the Welfare State is quickly being eroded. As conservative interests flagrantly channel massive expenditures toward the military and prison industrial complex, support for health, education, and housing for the poor continues to wane in comparison. The recent projections for California's budget reflect this unfortunate trend in the distribution of public expenditures. The yearly allocation for state prisons was the only line-item in the budget to increase for 2004. In addition, popular conservative campaigns over the last twenty years have also done their part to destroy the power of unions, abolish immigrant rights, privatize education and health services, eradicate affirmative action, and dismantle bilingual education.

How then do we come to understand the nature and impact of such State policies and campaigns upon Latino populations? To best respond, we argue that we must recast our scholarship and pedagogy in more rigorous analytical ways, so that we might better understand how State policies and practices have historically functioned to reproduce inequalities. Although, for the most part, this critical analysis of the capitalist State and its class structure remains conspicuously absent in much of the research in Latino Studies, one notable exception is the neo-Marxist-inspired work of Mario Barrera (1979). In his seminal volume, *Race and Class in the Southwest*, Barrera provided a formidable class analysis of racialized class inequality and the positioning of the capitalist State in Chicano economic history.

What we are suggesting here is that the nature of the State be fully interrogated as a site of conflict and counter-hegemonic struggle. As such, questions that must be engaged include: What is the role of the capitalist State in the reproduction of inequality? To what extent are racialized relations a sphere of action autonomous from State-structured economic relations? In what ways are class, gender, and racialized relations structured by policies of the State? How do class, gender, and racialized relations structure each other? Hence, we argue that research on the accumulation and legitimation needs of the capitalist State (Jessop, 2003) can provide needed clarity in understanding Latino conditions of racialized class inequality. Such research can also point to the kinds of public policies that can function to restructure conditions of social and economic exploitation in a liberal capitalist democracy.

Critical Policy Studies

The Promise of the social sciences is to bring reason to bear on human affairs.
—C. Wright Mills (2002)

More than ever, there is a need to consider issues of pedagogy and research in Latino Studies with respect to public policy and the conditions of everyday life. It is disheartening to find that Latino Studies scholars often ignore, in both their teaching and research, the particulars of public policy and its impact on communities. And when policy is engaged, there is often a lack of specificity and rigor in their theoretical understanding of what constitutes public policy. To address both these concerns requires us to shift toward both a social theory and community-informed public policy discourse, and away from the limits of traditional quantitative policy interventions that have historically been highly technical and grounded in normative political science, a perspective typically anchored in either statistical or descriptively anecdotal approaches to frame public policy debates.

In response to traditional policy approaches, there are those in the field of Latino Studies who advance the human capital model in public policy recommendations as a solution to structural inequalities. However, this model of analysis provides only a narrow view of production and an even more limited understanding of social reproduction in the political economy. Hence, left to its own devices, the human capital model can inadvertently lead to victim-blaming interpretations in which Latinos are ultimately held responsible for institutional failures to provide adequate schooling, job opportunities, and optimal health care within Latino communities.

Instead, we would argue that critical policy approaches to class/structural analysis provide greater possibilities for comprehending and transforming the social and economic inequalities faced by Latinos today. From this perspective, income inequalities result from the normal operation of the capitalist economy. That is, income inequality is a structural aspect of the capitalist economy and does not derive from individual differences in skills and competencies. More importantly, class is defined within the social relations of production, giving it a central role in mediating income inequalities in US society.

For years, the hope of social change was founded on possibilities of litigation to correct social wrongs. But today, the terrain of social change is shifting as the role of litigation for social change seems to be declining and the role of public policy, increasing. This is particularly evident in states like California, where the initiative process seems to have run amuck[9] and litigation is too slow a process to counter the wave of right-wing corporate interests that dominate the political scene especially within the context of education. Thus, fifty years after the monumental victory in *Brown vs. The Board of Education*, it is strikingly evident that the traditional approach to framing public policy is insufficient to effectively address racialized, gendered, and class inequalities.

Moreover, constructing public policy formulated on political sound-bites tied merely to number crunching or limited personalized accounts has failed to provide Latino scholars and activists with the necessary mechanisms to dismantle the pervasive structures of inequalities. There is a dire need then to engage not only with the technical dimensions of public policy (i.e., initiatives, referendums, and the ballot box), but also with its conceptual ideological apparatus. This requires us to question more deeply the philosophical dimensions and political interests that undergird public policy discourse. It also demands that our work focus on "the things people see everyday, around issues that touch people's daily lives, like health and work, the environment and housing, and the education of their children" (Marable, 1998).

For these reasons, we insist that our work must not stay hidden within the safety of the classroom nor remain invisible and excluded within the realm of policy discourse. We need a proactive approach to public policy within the field of Latino Studies— an approach that advances empirically rich and theoretically bold policy alternatives. Through combining our pedagogy, research, and activism, Latino Studies scholars can begin to draw up alternative city, state, and federal budgets that target health, education, and welfare spending. In so doing, our scholarship can be used widely to help lay out alternative strategies that support the practice of anti-corporate and democratic social action. Such efforts are not meant to serve primarily the interests of policymakers and government agencies, but rather to support independent and critical research in Latino Studies that scrutinizes policy in relation to its actual consequences for equality, social justice, and economic democracy.

In these times of political unrest and economic uncertainty, we need our scholarship to be tied to a moral imperative of policy and social reconstruction. Public policy initiatives that are grounded in social movements and the changing class realities of Latino communities are urgently needed. However, such a daunting task cannot be accomplished without working together to build coalitions (Valle and Torres, 2000). In practice, this requires that we become more creative about how we utilize both institutional and community resources. In addition, it requires that we work to acknowledge the existence of racialized class divisions within our communities, in order to advance and support greater democratic participation within the context of public policy debates.

All this is to argue that we must work to participate more openly in the arena of public policy, in order to challenge the policy pundits and political sycophants who exploit and repress community political development. In an age where urban legends, public relations schemes, and manufactured perceptions can often yield greater currency than the facts, there is a real need for critical scholars in Latino Studies to speak truth to power. This implies a willingness to use our academic pursuits in ways that publicly expose the corrupt corporate politics of urban development, the contradictions of labor leadership, the racialized policies and practices of public education, the inhumanity of the prison industrial complex, the atrocities of war, and other obstructions to democratic life.

In a world that is becoming fiercely polarized, Latino Studies scholars must use their influence to establish and participate in policy forums that support cross-dialogues among people in labor, education, community organizing, religion, health care, and public office. Here again, the community must serve as an indispensable site for the construction of knowledge and political action, upon which to anchor our theoretical endeavors to actual events and conditions we find in the world. By connecting our teaching practice and research to a larger social democratic project, the classroom becomes a workplace for both professors and students. In doing so, we can expand our influence in the field in ways that can effectively contribute to our struggle against racism and economic injustice, while we infuse our pedagogy and scholarship with individual passion, political commitment, and sociological imagination.

Notes

1   Cited in Davis (2001).
2   Cited in Leob (1999).
3   A good example is found in the work of Mary Pardo (1990) with the "Mothers of East L.A.," where she provides both a class and gender critique of women workers.

4   For an excellent review of contemporary debates on globalization see David Held & Anthony McGrew, *Globalization/Anti-Globalization, Polity* (2002).
5   In the last decade, *Monthly Review* has published some of the most incisive critiques and formidable interrogations into the globalization debate. Some of these authors included Ellen Meiksins Wood, Harry Magdoff, Frances Fox Piven, Robert McChesney, Peter Meiksins, Bill Tabb, and Istvan Meszaros.
6   One of the most significant theoretical contributions made during the post-civil rights era regarding questions of racialized identities was formulated by radical feminists of color who rendered the most sophisticated articulations of the intersectionality argument, with its often cited mantra of "race, class and gender."
7   See "The New Economy: Myth and Reality" by the *Monthly Review* editors (2001), Vol 52, No. 11, April 2001.
8   The groundbreaking work of Robert Miles has strongly influenced our views on the question of "race." See Racism and Migrant Labor, (1982); Racism (1989); and Racism After Race Relations (1993). We would also like to note that Paul Gilroy, an early critic of Miles, recently has advanced in his new book, *Against Race: Imaging Political Culture Beyond the Colorline* (Gilroy, 2000), a similar position.
9   During the 1990s, the initiative process (once envisioned as a legislative vehicle for the masses) became co-opted as an effective tool for neoliberal interests in California. Several conservative initiatives were successfully passed by voters, including Proposition 227, which called for the elimination of bilingual education in public schools; Proposition 187, which called for the elimination of health, education, and welfare benefits to undocumented immigrants; and Proposition 209, which called for the elimination of race as a determinant of educational admission to state colleges and universities.

References

Barrera, M. (1979), *Race and Class in the Southwest*. Notre Dame, IN: Notre Dame Press.
Crenshaw, K., Gotanda, N., Peller, G., and Thomas, K., eds. (1995), *Critical Race Theory: The Key Writings That Formed the Movement*. New York, NY: The New Press.
Cruz, J. (1996), "From Farce to Tragedy: Reflections in the Reification of Race at Century's End," in G. Allen and C. Newfield (eds.), *Mapping Multiculturalism*. Minneapolis, MN: University of Minnesota Press, 29.
Cuban, L. (2001), *Oversold and Underused: Computers in Classroom*. Cambridge, MA: Harvard University Press.
Darder, A., and Torres, R. D. (1997), *The Latinos Study Reader: Culture, Economy and Society*. Boston, MA: Blackwell.
Darder, A., and Torres, R. D. (1999), "Shattering the 'Race' Lens: Toward a Critical Theory of Racism," in R. Tai and M. Kenyatta (eds.), *Critical Ethnicity: Countering the Waves of Identity Politics*. New York, NY: Rowman and Littlefield, 173–92.
Davis, M. (2001), *Magical Urbanism: Latinos Reinvent the US City*. New York, NY, and London: Verso Books.
Delgado, R., ed. (1995), *Critical Race Theory: The Cutting Edge*. Philadelphia, PA: Temple University Press.
Editors (2001), "The New Economy: Myth and Reality." *Monthly Review* 52(11): 15.

Fears, D. (2002), "People of Color Who Never Felt They Were Black: Racial Labels Surprises Many Latino Immigrants." *Washington Post* (December 26, A1).
Gilroy, P. (2000), *Against Race: Imaging Political Culture Beyond the Colorline*. Boston, MA: Harvard University Press.
Guillaumin, C. (1995), *Racism, Sexism, Power and Ideology*. London: Routledge.
Gunier, L., and Torres, G. (2002), *The Miner's Canary: Enlisting Race, Resisting Power, Transforming Democracy*. New York, NY: New York University Press.
Hernstein, R. J., and Murray, C. (1994), *The Bell Curve Intelligence and Class Structure in American Life*. New York, NY: The New Press.
Jessop, B. (2003), *The Future of the Capitalist State*. UK: Polity.
Jessop, B., and Sum, N.-L. (2001), "Pre-disciplinary and Post-disciplinary Perspectives." *New Political Economy* 6(1): 89–101.
Leob, P. (1999), *Soul of a Citizen: Living with Conviction in a Cynical Time*. New York, NY: St. Martin's Press.
Marable, M. (1998), "Being Left: A Humane Society Is Possible through Struggle." *Z Magazine* interview with Manning Marable. www.znet.org.
Mariscal, J. (2003), "A Chicano Looks at the Trent Lott Affair." *La Prensa*, San Diego (January 3).
Miles, R. (1982), *Racism and Migrant Labour*. London: Routledge.
Miles, R. (1984), "Marxism versus the Sociology of 'Race Relations'?" *Ethnic and Racial Studies* 7(2): 232.
Miles, R. (1989), *Racism*. London: Routledge.
Miles, R. (1993), *Racism after "Race Relations"*. London: Routledge.
Miles, R., and Torres, R. D. (1996), "Does 'Race' Matter? Transatlantic Perspectives on Racism after 'Race Relations'," in V. Amit-Talai and C. Knowles (eds.), *Re-situating Identities: The Politics of Race, Ethnicity, and Culture*. Ontario, Canada: Broadview Press, 24–46.
Miliband, R. (1969), *The State in Capitalist Society*. New York, NY: Basic Books.
Mills, C. W. (2002), *The Sociological Imagination*. London: Oxford University Press.
Morrison, T. (1989), Unspeakable Things Unspoken: The Afro-American Presence in American Literature. *Michigan Quarterly Review* 28(1): 1–34.
Oboler, S. (1995), *Ethnic Labels, Latino Lives: Identity and the Politics of (Re)Presentation in the United States*. Minneapolis, MN: University of Minnesota Press.
Pardo, M. (1990), Mexican American Women Grassroots Community Activist: Mothers of East Los Angeles. *Frontiers* 11(1): 1–7.
Rosaldo, R. (1993), *Culture and Truth: The Remaking of Social Analysis*. Boston, MA: Beacon Press.
Scott, A., and Soja, E. (1996), *The City: Los Angeles and Urban Theory and the End of the Twentieth Century*. Berkeley, CA: University of California Press.
Tornatzky, L., Macias, E., and Jones, S. (2002), *Latinos and Information Technology: The Promise and the Challenge*. Claremont, CA: The Tomas Rivera Policy Institute.
Torres, R. D., and Darder, Antonia (Forthcoming 2004), *After Race: Essays on Racism, Class and Inequality*. New York, NY: New York University Press.
Valle, V., and Torres, R. D. (2000), *Latino Metropolis*. Minneapolis, MN: University of Minnesota Press.
Wing, Adrien K., ed. (1997), *Critical Race Feminism: A Reader*. New York, NY: New York University Press.
Wood, E. M. (1994), "Identity Crisis." *In These Times* (June): 28–9.

Wood, E. M. (2000), *Democracy against Capitalism: Renewing Historical Materialism*. New York, NY: Cambridge University Press.
Wright, E. O. (1997), *Class Counts: Comparative Studies in Class Analysis*. New York, NY: Cambridge University Press.

15

Radicalizing the Immigrant Debate in the United States: A Call for Open Borders and Global Human Rights

For what was once hailed as a human right is now opposed as an economic liability. Our governments are trapped in a morally warped and ideologically unsustainable paradigm. They applaud the free movement of capital; while they abhor the free movement of labor.

—Human Rights Watch[1]

When you say "America" you refer to the territory stretching between the icecaps of the two poles. So to hell with your barriers and frontier guards!

—Diego Rivera[2]

The US border with Mexico constitutes one of the most bloody and contentious geopolitical arenas in the world. Since its inception in 1948, increasing violence and conflict, varying in nature according to political and economic pressures, has plagued the border.[3] In the last decade, active campaigns for the militarization of the border by both official border patrol agents and border vigilantes have prevailed. Many of the names of some these campaigns—Operation Rio Grande at the Brownsville-Matamoros border, Operation Hold the Line at the El Paso-Juarez border, and Operation Gatekeepers and the Minuteman Project at the San Diego Tijuana border—attest to the war-like mentality.[4]

In the midst of this intensification of border security, there are now an estimated 12 million undocumented immigrants in the United States. Of those unable to enter successfully, 3,000 have died in the last five years. The unsolved murders of almost 400 young maquiladora workers in the border cities of Juarez and Chihuahua are considered by some to be directly linked to the ongoing contested border politics of the region.[5] Over a thousand would-be immigrants are deported or detained each month—a number that actually tripled in the last year, despite the raging national debate on immigration. The US Citizenship and Immigration Services (USCIS), under the auspices of the Department of Homeland Security, has in custody more than 15,000 detainees in detention centers and jails across the country.

The same anti-immigrant sentiments that have historically fueled US-Mexico border conflicts are also brewing in Washington today, where the contentious debate on US immigration reform threatens to become the most important national issue of the 2008 presidential campaign. Over the last year, Congress Democrats and Republicans have debated furiously over the best approach to address the issue of "illegal immigration." In May 2007, the debate resulted in the introduction of numerous measures to intensify enforcement of anti-immigrant policies, including a "compromise bill" touted to ease the path toward legalization for many immigrants. However, immigrant rights groups vehemently protested proposed legislation, which is expected to turn as many as 12 million immigrants into "guest workers" and dissolve family reunification laws, creating greater hardship for undocumented immigrant families.

Such policies and practices surrounding immigration blatantly reflect an ideologically unsustainable paradigm. Thus, I wish to argue for the need to transform the US immigration debate from one that primarily demonizes and criminalizes Mexicans as violent smugglers of drugs and people to one that forthrightly focuses on the underlying forces of capital that thwart global sustainability. Hence, this essay seeks to link issues of local concern with the historical phenomenon of migration and capital. By doing so, local immigration debates can more effectively create the political space for discussing questions of education, youth unemployment, labor abuses, housing shortages, transportation needs, police abuses, and social tensions related to immigrant communities, beyond nativist notions that position immigrants as the problem to be solved.

This, of course, does not mean that we should be blind to the particular problems faced daily by immigrants or the difficulties experienced by those living in previously homogeneous communities who are unprepared to negotiate the local conditions that result from US economic folly abroad. So, yes, local communities must work together with new immigrant residents to address the class conflicts associated with immigrant life and labor in the United States. There is a need to jettison stereotypical attitudes and ignorance of immigrant populations. It requires negotiating differences in culture, aesthetics, uses of space, and tolerance for more intimate living arrangements. In addition, class issues, camouflaged behind a discourse of racialization, must be weeded out and transformed.

The realities of the changing economy in many cities and rural communities must be renegotiated. Downtown areas that once were abandoned have taken on new life in the presence of immigrant residents. New enclaves of immigrants have developed and new businesses inspired by immigrant consumer patterns have begun to be frequented by the larger community. Often these factors stimulate tremendous economic revitalization in blighted communities, but are generally ignored or even maligned in mainstream immigration debates.

But other factors are also ignored. For example, with almost 12 million undocumented people in the United States, how can we, by any stretch of the imagination, speak about immigration as an aberration? Instead what seems clear here is that immigration is a necessity of the system. It results from the policies and practices tied to the current political economy—including the culture of business and government—and the economic imperatives of the nation-state. We must speak to what exists in this country as an exploitive de facto guest worker system, integral to the US wage-labor system. And as de facto guest workers, undocumented immigrants labor without equal rights, labor without representation, subsist on meager wages, suffer medical neglect, are consistently subjected to oppressive institutional conditions, and are denied *carte blanche* recognition of the important economic role they play in this society. Meanwhile, the differences in the conditions between men and women immigrants are generally overlooked, while the emotional needs of families living in exile do not even make it on the radar screen.

Yet immigrants from Mexico, Latin America, and the Caribbean continue to make the arduous journey northward seeking a better quality of life for themselves and their families. Their trek northward is the most logical response to the global structures of inequality. They move from geographical regions where wealth concentrations are low to the empire of capital—the United States—where concentrations of capital are high and density is still low by many world standards. They move to the region of the world that has the highest consumption rate of all industrialized nations. Hence, what cannot be denied is that the decision to emigrate is overwhelmingly one of economics.[6]

Nevertheless, the aspiration for survival and a better quality of life—oftentimes cited by immigration advocates and neoconservative alike—is not the root cause of immigration. For people have been on the move since the beginning of time and had it not been for this phenomenon, with its economic imperatives and the dispossession of lands from Native American nations, the United States would not exist today. Thus, the politics of immigration has always been tied to the prevailing politics of capital accumulation. For example, since 2001 the United States has effectively capitalized on the tragedy of September 11[7] to exacerbate hostilities against those perceived as outsiders and step up the regulation and monitoring of the movement of people on US territory. Moreover, conflicting and contradictory national efforts, which "on one hand, advocate for the open and unrestricted movement of commerce, trade, finance capital, technology, and ideas; and on the other, [install] deeply isolationist policies to restrict the movement of people and workers across its borders,"[8] function to intensify the anti-immigrant debate. As the Iraq situation has become more and more volatile, the media's anti-immigrant fervor has been heightened, obscuring more important reasons for the current economic instability.[9]

Yet, despite the intensification of anti-immigrant backlash, millions of immigrants and their supporters took to the streets during Spring 2006 to effectively protest against the Sensenbrenner bill.[10] Key provisions of this broad-reaching legislation call for the building of 700 miles of walls and fences along the US-Mexico border; call for the mandatory federal custody of illegal aliens detained by local authorities; and make mandatory employer verification of legal status of workers through electronic means. In addition, the bill criminalizes as a felony anyone remaining in the United States without proper documentation, as well as those who provide assistance to undocumented immigrants.

During summer 2006, the action of Elvira Arrellano became an important symbol of immigrant resistance against the inhumanity of both federal and local anti-immigrant policies and practices. Arrellano, seeking to resist her deportation, took refuge in a Chicago church so she could remain in the country with her seven-year-old son, Saul, who is a US citizen. Her action powerfully defied the powers of the Department of Homeland Security combined. Her courageous act of resistance helped to put a human face on national immigration debates. In fact, in November 2006, Saul addressed the Mexican Congress pleading for help in stopping the deportation of his mother. As a result, the Mexican government passed a resolution against deportations, appealing to humanitarian principles of family cohesion. Yet despite this action, the Mexican government is as much responsible for the reasons that Mexican citizens find little recourse for their lives than to an existence as undocumented immigrants.

Challenging Nativism in the Face of Poverty

People hunger for modernity and they gamble. Knowing full well that the odds are stacked against them ... they move ... if they sense there is even a small chance of advancement and a new life.

—Mike Davis[11]

A long history of impoverished people on the move calls into question nativist condemnations of neoconservatives like Samuel P. Huntington who bemoan the cultural wars and the clash of civilization. He argues:

The persistent inflow of Hispanic immigrants threatens to divide the United States into two peoples, two cultures, and two languages. Unlike past immigrant groups, Mexican and other Latinos have not assimilated into mainstream U.S. culture, forming instead their own political and linguistic enclaves—from Los Angeles to Miami—and rejecting the Anglo protestant values that built the American dream. The United States ignores this challenge at its peril.[12]

In this alarmist attack of Latino immigration, Huntington invokes racialized images of despicably deficient Latino immigrants who defy democratic values, are responsible for lowering US wages, harbor contempt for US culture, and stubbornly insist on retaining their culture and language. The danger of such ruthless anti-immigrant rhetoric is that it functions to not only distort the relevance of necessary debates, but unfortunately also makes its way into the arena of public policy, where restrictive immigration policies in the name of sustainability camouflage a deeply entrenched egoistic defense of privilege.[13]

This was most recently apparent when the city council of Farmers Branch, a town located just north of Dallas, Texas, unanimously approved some of the most daunting anti-immigrant measures in the nation, first in November 2006, requiring all property owners and employers to report illegal immigrants, then again in May 2007, passing the first ordinance in the nation barring undocumented immigrants from renting apartments.[14] The Farmers Branch proposal followed similar legislation passed in Escondido, California, and Hazleton, Pennsylvania, to fine property owners who rent to illegal immigrants, deny business permits to companies that employ or do business with undocumented workers, and require tenants to register and pay for rental permits.[15]

Almost as problematic are the rhetorical responses of some Latino officials and national publications—responses that lacked the depth of analysis to counter the obstructive vitriolic of anti-immigrant backlash. Typical responses of such publications as *Hispanic Business*, for example, assert that "The majority of immigrants arrive in the United States in search of the *American Dream*."[16] In concert, the publication has gone to great lengths to showcase the entrepreneurial qualities of Latino immigrants, along with their contribution to the economy.[17] Unfortunately, these responses to the anti-immigrant backlash degenerate into superficial and defensive posturing, which fails to interrogate the political economy of migration and its roots in imperialism.

Hence, Mexican migration must be traced historically to imperial rule in the last century, a dynamic that predates the "globalization" debate. Implicit here is a critique of contemporary notions of globalization, such as Thomas Friedman's celebration of globalization in *The World is Flat* or Michael Hardt and Antonio Negri's argument in *Empire*, that classical imperialism has disappeared and along with it both powers of the nation-state and the working class.[18] Both these views fail to prove out in today's world and steer observers away from the salient question that must be asked: What is the underlying structural root of increasing immigration?

Both Friedman's and Hardt and Negri's arguments seem to dismiss or ignore the implications of the movement of people and their relationship to the accumulation of wealth, on one hand, and the global dispossession of large populations, on the other. For example, the conditions of northward migration are intimately linked to the participation of ruling elites of countries such as Mexico, which has a long historical connection to US imperial policies and practices. For over a century, the Mexican government and capitalists have partnered with the United States in pursuit of their own self-interests, while neglecting the needs of the majority of the Mexican people. For example,

> in 1991, the Salinas government passed a reform law that both permitted and encouraged privatization of the ejido lands. Since the ejido provided the basis for collective security among indigenous groups, the government was, in effect, divesting itself of its responsibilities to maintain the basis for that security. This was moreover, one item within a general package of privatization moves under Salinas which dismantled social security protections in general and which had predictable and dramatic impacts upon income and wealth distribution.[19]

Hence it should be no surprise that many indigenous communities in opposition to these reforms joined the Zapatista rebellion in January 1994 against the Mexican government, on the very day that the NAFTA agreement went into enforcement.

However, it must be repeated that even these contributing factors predate the contemporary globalization debate and entail a long history of US capital relations with members of the Mexican ruling class, via the nation-state apparatus, irrespective of which party has been in office. Hence, immigration reforms must take into account the trends of migration tied to US economic and political interests in the southern hemisphere and the need for cheap labor to carry out dispossessing strategies of accumulation.

Another distortion in the current debate is that immigrants live at the margins of our nation's economy. Nothing is further from the truth. In fact, immigrants are strategically integrated into the US class-wage system and exploited as cheap labor. To ignore the implications of this reality is to be duped by the ruse that somehow immigrants are extraneous to the class-wage system when they are undeniably integral to sustaining its vitality.

Moreover, it is seldom noted that Huntington's lamentations—including Latino immigrant concentration in particular areas, their cultural and linguistic influence on social formations, and their impact on the economy—are the result of the very neoliberal policies he has advanced. Global neoliberal policies have led to a widening gap worldwide between rich and poor, resulting in unbridled migration to this country, not only from Latin America.

Also often ignored are the actual hardships of migration and the fact that most people would much prefer to remain in their own countries, on their own land, in familiar surroundings, providing their children and families a decent quality of life. When this possibility becomes more and more difficult, in the wake of neoliberal accumulation by dispossession, people are left little choice than to endure the hardships of staying or risk the hardships of leaving for a potentially better life. Immigrants repeatedly mourn leaving their families behind and living a life of exile in order to ensure economic subsistence. Yet US ethnocentrism, with its smug arrogance, is often at work in the criminalization of immigrants, preventing the empire's pampered citizens understanding life beyond material comforts.

Meanwhile, the increasingly unfettered movement of capital helps create the poverty that prompts economic migration from the so-called "developing" countries. Structural adjustment programs, imposed on countries by the International Monetary Fund and the World Bank in return for loans, generally lead to cuts in health, education, and welfare spending and to mass privatization, with people pushed out of their exploitable lands to serve the interests of capital. To illustrate the enormous impact of these policies on the world's disenfranchised population, consider the following facts and statistics on poverty:[20]

- half the world—nearly 3 billion people—live on less than $2 a day
- the GNP (Gross National Product) of the poorest forty-eight nations (25 percent of the world's countries) is less than the wealth of the world's three richest people combined
- less than 1 percent of what the world spent every year on weapons was needed to put every child into school by the year 2000, but it did not happen
- the wealthiest nation on earth (the United States) has the widest gap between rich and poor of any industrialized nation
- 20 percent of the population in the wealthiest countries consume 86 percent of the world's goods
- a few hundred millionaires now own as much wealth as the world's 2.5 billion people
- approximately 790 million people in the developing world are still chronically undernourished

- a mere 12 percent of the world's population uses 85 percent of water resources
- 1.7 million children will die this year alone due to poverty.

Hence, anti-immigration reform policies must be challenged in ways that both expose and disrupt institutional practices anchored in neoliberal orthodoxy—draconian reforms that result in great metropolises of capital, expanding an economics of poverty that give rise to global slums.[21] And the building of a 700-mile border wall between the United States and Mexico[22] will certainly not ameliorate these conditions. For a border wall cannot contain the political mendacity, exploitative labor practices, and shameful poverty tied to the unchecked excesses of capital and efforts to safeguard capitalism from impending crisis. On another note, we cannot ignore that these are the same interests that proclaim the virtues of accountability, yet wash their hands of responsibility for the forced migration created by unrelenting policies of accumulation.

Global immigration today is inextricably tied to a historical context in which the internationalization of capital does not work to dismantle the nation-state, but rather is legitimated through its apparatus. Instead of the demise of the working class, this mechanism has solidified class divisions by placing greater power in the hands of the state to regulate (or deregulate) the affairs of capital. While, simultaneously, utilizing the media and other cultural and technological means of ideological control to undermine the powers of mass protest along with the movement of people—whether that is by control of migration patterns or the mass incarceration of impoverished populations.

Immigration and the New Imperialism

A never-ending accumulation of property must be based on a never-ending accumulation of power.
—Hannah Arendt[23]

The difficulty in addressing the question of immigration in the United States is sifting through all the sources of misinformation and constantly shifting rhetoric. Moreover, there is a need to counter the othering of immigrants as "evil," criminals, or demons who are wickedly threatening the well-being and stability—or sustainability—of the American Dream. To do this requires understanding that increasing immigration is not rooted in the wayward individual aspirations of illegal immigrants. Instead, as David Harvey argues in *The New Imperialism*, it is rooted in the:

> uneven geographical conditions that arise out of the uneven patterning of natural resource endowments and locational advantages, but, more importantly, are produced by the uneven ways in which wealth and power themselves become highly concentrated in certain places by virtue of asymmetrical exchange relations.[24]

Moreover, for the United States to maintain its political dominance and its relentless strategies of capital accumulation, it has extended its military, political, and economic power (most notably in Iraq) to the point that the dangers of overreach are undeniable. Today's so-called "immigration problems" constitute only the tip of the iceberg of the enormous global chaos being created by ruthless forces of capital excess. Current efforts to control or "liquidate" immigrants, then, must be tied to the overreaching of US power worldwide. Hence, the threat to this nation is not increasing immigration, but the destructive impact of "accumulation by dispossession."[25] This refers to the wide range of processes by which the United States has made major economic gains through:

> the commodification and privatization of land and the forceful expulsion of peasant populations; the conversion of various forms of property rights (common, collective, state, etc.) into exclusive private property rights; the suppression of rights to the commons; the commodification of labour power and the suppression of alternative (indigenous) forms of production and consumption; colonial, neo-colonial, and imperial processes of appropriation of assets (including natural resources [such as water and air]); the monetization of exchange and taxation, particularly of land; the slave trade; and usury, the national debt, and ultimately the credit system as radical means of accumulation.[26]

Such forms of accumulation worldwide have been carried out with little regard to the destructive outcome of neoliberal policies and practices on impoverished populations. Moreover, the elimination of regulatory statutes designed to protect labor and the environment from degradation must also be seen as a loss of human rights. And the reversion of hard-won common property (i.e., state pensions, health insurance, etc.) to the private domain constitutes one of the most flagrant policies of dispossession to come out of neoliberal orthodoxy.

Unfortunately, the rogue nature of such economic imperialism is not new to the United States, despite the culture of denial that has prevailed among a large portion of the US population. In fact, Harvey argues that the United States "has a history of ruthlessness that belies its attachment to its constitution and the rule of law." More specifically, he cites:

> McCarthyism, the murder or incarceration of Black Panther leaders, the internment of Japanese in the Second World War, surveillance and infiltration of opposition groups of all kinds, and now a certain preparedness to overthrow the Bill of Rights by passing the Patriot and Homeland Security Acts. It has been even more significantly ruthless abroad in sponsoring coups in Iran, Iraq, Guatemala, Chile, and Vietnam (to name a few) in which untold thousands died. It has supported state terrorism throughout the world wherever it has been convenient. CIA and Special Forces units operate in innumerable countries. Study of this record has led to paint a portrait of the US as the greatest "rogue state" on earth.[27]

Xenophobic neoconservative rhetoric blatantly accuses immigrants of (1) being a drain to the economy, (2) being the cause of mass unemployment, and (3) threatening the course of "sustainable development." Yet the real culprit is the internationalization of capital with its neoliberal solutions. For example, capitalists use technological changes and speculative investment to induce unemployment, thus creating an industrial reserve army of unemployed workers. Rather than immigrants, it is this deliberate creation of unemployment that has exerted a downward pressure on wage rates, thereby creating new opportunities for profitable deployment of capital. This exploitive process of capital accumulation at the expense of workers has been responsible for stagnant and declining real wages over the last fifteen years. In fact, it must be noted that this form of othering of both immigrants and unemployed workers has been necessary to the stabilization of capitalism.

Meanwhile, the liberalization of the market has served to produce greater levels of social and economic inequality. Within this dynamic, the "predatory" rhetoric of immigration serves to effectively camouflage capitalism's predatory practices, which have created the impetus for increasing immigration to the centers of concentrated wealth in the United States—whether that be their movement to global cities or promising rural communities. Moreover, it cannot be left unsaid that "the State, with its monopoly of violence and definitions of legality plays a crucial role in both backing and promoting"[28] the predatory rhetoric of immigration.

So, the so-called "problems of immigrants" must be linked to the over-extension of political economic power abroad, which results in "chronic insecurity at home." In response, Harvey argues, the middle classes took to the defense of territory, nation, and tradition, mobilizing the territorial logic of power to shield themselves against the alienating forces of neoliberal capitalism. The racism and nationalism that had once bound nation-state and empire together re-emerged among the working class, and blaming the problems on immigrants became a convenient diversion for elite interests. As a consequence, exclusionary identity politics based on race, ethnicity, and religion again flourished.[29]

Moreover, the inflammatory rhetoric toward immigrants, with its focus on building a border wall, works to effectively camouflage the current vulnerability of the US economy, by deflecting attention from burgeoning corporate debt, US dependence on foreign investment inflow to cover foreign debts, and the increasing devaluation of the US dollar. Furthermore, blaming immigrants for social and economic ills puts window-dressing on the vast drain created by the turn to a permanent war economy—a desperate attempt by US interests to conserve political and economic dominance worldwide.

The Rhetoric of Population Control

From Nazi-era eugenics to forced sterilizations, the population [control] framework is indelibly linked to colonial paternalism.

—Adam Werbach[30]

Many anti-immigration debates are firmly anchored in a discourse of human overpopulation.[31] Leading anti-immigrant policy institutes, including *NumbersUSA* and *Center for Immigration Studies*, wield arguments about the negative impact of immigrants on community sustainability and resource depletion. The environmental wing of anti-immigrant forces, which emerged from the zero-population movement of the 1960s and 1970s, includes members of such organizations as *Environment-Population Balance, Carrying Capacity Network*, and *Negative Population Growth*. These organizations point to immigration as the most incorrigible factor in US population growth.[32]

Public figures such as former governor of Colorado, Richard Lamm, co-author of *Immigration Time Bomb: The Fragmenting of America*,[33] suggest that "uncontrolled immigration" will be the peril of the United States if strict measures to curb immigration are not enforced. Meanwhile, anti-immigrant zero-population advocates contend that the current population of the Earth, now over 7 billion, is simply too many people for our planet to sustain at current consumption levels. However, this challenge for sustainability is distributed unevenly, given the fact that the so-called first world consumes over 86 percent of the world's resources. But rather than move toward changing consumption and redistribution patterns, a campaign to stop population growth is their major concern. Hence, it is not surprising that aggressive population control efforts in disenfranchised communities have led to human rights violations—violations directly linked to the involuntary sterilization of Puerto Rican, African American, and Mexican immigrant women in the United States.

Xenophobic attitudes linked to population growth are also used as a rationale for the establishment and enforcement of anti-immigrant public policies. Here, the principal cause for poverty in the world is attributed to the reproductive function of poor and immigrant women; a phenomenon I refer to as "the politics of colonized wombs."[34] That is, the cause of social and economic ills among immigrants becomes defined as a question of reproductive control. The racialization and sexism inherent in this biologically determinist view of the problem also preclude, unfortunately, an examination of the predatory nature of capitalism as enumerated earlier.

More recently, for example, the reactionary reproductive rhetoric of immigration took a new spin. On November 14, 2006, a Missouri Republican-led panel on immigration asserted that abortion is partly to blame for increasing immigration, because it has caused a shortage of American workers. According to David Lieb:

> The report from the House Special Committee on Immigration Reform says that liberal social welfare policies have discouraged Americans from working and have encouraged immigrants to cross the border illegally.
>
> The statements about abortion and welfare policies, along with a recommendation to abolish income taxes in favor of sales taxes, were inserted into the immigration report by Rep. Edgar G.H. Emery (R), the panel's chairman … who equates abortion to murder.
>
> [Emory asserted that] "We hear a lot of arguments today that the reason that we can't get serious about our borders is that we are desperate for all these workers,"

he said. "You don't have to think too long. If you kill 44 million of your potential workers, it's not too surprising we would be desperate for workers."

"Suggestions for how to stop illegal hiring varied without any simple solution," the report states. "The lack of traditional work ethic, combined with the effects of 30 years of abortion and expanding liberal social welfare policies have produced a shortage of workers and a lack of incentive for those who can work."[35]

What is clear here is (1) pro-life neoconservatives are primarily concerned with life that looks like them, while calling for population control of immigrants; and (2) the long historical tradition to blame women's reproduction for the ills of the world is still alive and kicking. The misogyny of the latter view seems to trump the plethora of research and United Nations reports[36] that repeatedly argue that the most important factor in reducing population increase around the world is the improvement to quality of life and economic well-being of impoverished communities. Incidentally, it is also considered the quickest road to full citizenship and democratic participation in the political affairs of any society.

Open Borders: A Radical Possibility

In all, the irrepressibility of movement seems a powerful argument against state efforts to suppress it.

—Alan Dowty[37]

The radical possibility of open borders is in concert with a United Nations proclamation that "the right to leave or stay [is] nothing less than a right of personal self-determination."[38] Moreover, given the current struggles of millions of people on the move having to contend with the hostility of border enforcement and anti-immigrant views, the right to remain or return constitutes one of the major problems faced by immigrant populations. Coercive migration policies, as we are currently witnessing in the United States, place immigrant populations often in harm's way.

Yet what cannot be denied is that whether in indigenous contexts around the world or the ancient civilizations of Greece and Egypt, the freedom of movement has always been seen as a natural right and a universal aspiration. In Greece, for example, the Delphi priests regarded the right of unrestricted movement as one of the four freedoms that distinguished liberty from slavery.[39] Moreover, the insuppressible nature of human movement alone seems to fly in the face of current coercive efforts to control immigration.

In the current hostile climate of border policy debates, the issue of immigration (entering the country) also becomes an issue of emigration (leaving the country). Often temporary undocumented immigrant workers are prevented from leaving given the hostile border conditions, which would require them to make another dangerous and costly journey back into the United States. Or, should they be detained at the border, this can mean the revocation for ten years of all legal rights to visit, with the threat of incarceration should one be caught attempting to cross the border during the time period. As a consequence, many workers become stuck in the United States and are forced to remain permanently, rather than solely during periods of seasonal work.

Increased surveillance and the building of a 700-mile wall at the border will only exacerbate the problems that it portends to solve. Along these lines, an *Albuquerque Tribune* editorial argued that "History has shown that border fences and walls, from the Berlin Wall to the Great Wall of China, have done little to improve relations or security between nations. That is best done not by building walls but by building trust and respect through diplomacy, economic development and common labor, environmental and social agreements."[40]

Stephen Castles contends that "barriers to mobility contradict the powerful forces which are leading toward greater economic and cultural interchange."[41] Rather than shut people out, the United States should adopt the same policy for the movement of people that it adopts for the movement of capital. Instead of archaic policing methods at the border that intensify animosities and violence, the United States should open up the borders and move toward greater economic integration with Mexico and Latin America. Such a move could potentially open opportunities to pursue investment policies that support the democratization of the economy by way of cooperative economic ventures rooted in the material and social needs of all people, rather than the narrow accumulative pursuits of transnational corporations.

Instead of blaming immigrants for the difficulties communities encounter in creating sustainable development, let's point the finger where it belongs: the ruthless neoliberal policies of privatization that have pillaged and plundered the world's resources. The historical record speaks volumes and we don't have to look very far for examples. The devastating impact of NAFTA in Mexico and the Caribbean alone (and more recently CAFTA in Central America[42]), where wages have fallen and people have less access than ever to the goods they produce, is a stark example. On the agricultural front, the subsequent lowering of import barriers allowed the entrance of extremely cheap imports from the highly subsidized agribusiness in the United States, driving down the prices of produce to a level that small, local agricultural producers could not rival. People who found themselves close to starvation, as a result, were forced to leave their lands and join the ranks of unemployed workers in large urban cities. This pattern of dispossession has been repeated among rural populations worldwide. And although some neoliberal analysts might point to a few exceptions of job creation or the increased flow of certain goods to support the legitimacy of their claims, the historical record belies their hypocrisy.

Hence, despite neoconservative alarmist rhetoric to the contrary, some of the potential benefits of open borders might include:

- the democratization of border culture
- the increasing possibility of economic justice through mutual efforts to meet the material needs of all people
- the growth of opportunities for a more equitable distribution of wealth and increasing reciprocity of natural resources

- a more tension-free atmosphere for cultural exchange
- an expanding interaction and flow of ideas across the border
- a decrease in the social tensions and animosities reinforced by rigid "closed border" beliefs and practices
- increasing responsiveness to the welfare of both US and Mexican citizens
- stopping all punitive actions sanctioned against immigrants and their families
- ending the border abuse of immigrants and would-be immigrants
- dismantling the exploitive underground economy of border-crossing
- releasing all those who are currently incarcerated for crossing the border without documents
- and finally, creating a global citizenship that both respects cultural sovereignty and yet functions in concert with global human rights.

Globalizing Human Rights

Of all human rights failures today, those in economic and social areas are by far the larger numbers and are the most widespread across the world.
—Human Rights Watch[43]

Given widespread human rights failures in both economic and social arenas, what we need at this historical juncture are coherent counter-hegemonic strategies to interrupt international imperialist practices that have precipitated forced immigration to the centers of concentrated wealth. We need an ethics of sustainable development that functions at the local level, in concert with the global struggle for emancipation from the devastating impacts of the new imperialism, with its dispossession of three-quarters of the world's population. Such a politics must be firmly grounded in both a critical analysis of the political economy of migration and the aggressive efforts toward globalizing human rights. If we were to begin with an understanding that the freedom of movement constitutes a fundamental human right, then the integration of a globalizing human rights agenda, within debates on immigration policy and reform, can be understood as a most reasonable and logical conclusion.

In 2003, the Immigrant Workers Freedom Rides campaign made four central demands that must be integrated into any globalizing human rights agenda: (1) legalization and a "road to citizenship"; (2) family reunification; (3) immigrants' rights in the workplace; and (4) civil rights and civil liberties for all.[44] Thus if we were to take these four demands, we can begin to craft a preliminary global agenda of human rights for immigrants around the world. The sense that all human beings should be acknowledged as legitimate and legal subjects, irrespective of where they reside, goes without saying. Moreover, citizenship must be redefined within a global context, opening the road to the creation of societies that function in the interest of the collective global good, rather than in the interests of a few.

The issue of family reunification dramatically exposes the manner in which current neoconservative immigration policies betray the so-called family values of their architects. It seems that family values in this context are only legitimate if they are about white Christian US citizens. However, globalizing the right of family reunification can serve to shift the dynamics of political and economic abuses suffered by immigrants worldwide.

Globalizing worker rights for all workers, irrespective of national documentation, is a central concern that cannot be overlooked. Policies and practices that stop labor abuses of immigrant workers, as with all workers, must be forthrightly addressed within a human rights agenda. The failure to address labor issues in connection to immigrant populations is an egregious offense that places state officials in complicity with the injustice of unfair and dangerous labor practices, which dehumanize and strip workers of their dignity.

Lastly, the struggle for civil rights and civil liberties must be a central tenet of a globalizing human rights agenda. In a time when we are witnessing our civil liberties quickly eroding, political debates on immigration must be inextricably linked to the unveiling of neoliberal policies and practices and their subsequent impact on civil liberties of undocumented populations in the United States.

Closing the border cannot solve the problems attributed to immigration. The flow of immigrants is the expression of a long set of political economic arrangements that have created huge economic needs and conditions that provoke movement to the empire. To transform these conditions requires a major disruption of neoliberal policies and practices that reproduce savage inequalities along with despicable forms of human rights violations that guarantee their preservation. To counter this dehumanizing trend also calls for a bold and aggressive move toward a fundamental political commitment and solidarity with those who are weary and dispossessed by the ravages of capital. It embodies nothing less than an uncompromising commitment to become citizens of the world and join in the dismantling of neoliberal abuses that threaten not only all our lives, but the very sustainability of the planet.

Notes

1. Human Rights Watch, http://www.hrw.org.
2. Cited in Davis (2001).
3. Hernandez (2000).
4. Lee Siu Hin, "Violence, Killing, Life and Rape on the U.S.-Mexico Border: Can a Conscience Human Being Ignore the Facts?" *Human Rights Watch*, June 1998, http://www.change-links.org/Violence.html.
5. Livingstone (2004, pp. 59–76).
6. See Castles (2000, pp. 269–81) for a discussion of definitions and causes of migration.
7. On September 11, 2001, the twin towers of the World Trade Center in New York City were destroyed when two passenger airliners were hijacked and diverted to crash into each tower. The September 11 attacks generated xenophobic and anti-immigrant violence in some US communities.

8   See Sassen (2005, pp. 49–86).
9   Darder and Torres (2004).
10 The Border Protection, Anti-terrorism, and Illegal Immigration Control Act of 2005 (H.R. 4437)—or the Sensenbrenner bill, after its sponsor, Wisconsin Republican, Jim Sensenbrenner—was passed by the House of Representatives and includes the following provisions (see http://thomas.loc.gov/cgi-bin/bdquery/z?d109:h.r.04437):
    - Requires up to 700 miles (1,120 km) of fence along the US-Mexican border at points with the highest number of illegal border crossings (House Amendment 648, authored by Duncan Hunter (R-CA52)).
    - Requires the federal government to take custody of undocumented aliens detained by local authorities. This would end the practice of "catch and release," where federal officials sometimes instruct local law enforcement to release detained undocumented aliens because resources to prosecute them are not available. It also reimburses local agencies in the twenty-nine counties along the border for costs related to detaining undocumented aliens (Section 607).
    - Mandates employers to verify workers' legal status through electronic means, phased in over several years. Also requires reports to be sent to Congress one and two years after implementation to ensure that it is being used (Title VII).
    - Eliminates the Diversity Immigrant Visa (also known as Green Card Lottery) program (House Amendment 650, authored by Bob Goodlatte).
    - Prohibits grants to federal, state, or local government agencies that enact or maintain a sanctuary policy (House Amendment 659, authored by Thomas Tancredo, withdrawn December 16, 2005, by unanimous consent).
    - Incorporates satellite communications among immigration enforcement officials (House Amendment 638, authored by John Carter).
    - Requires all US Border Patrol uniforms to be made in the United States to avoid forgeries (House Amendment 641, authored by Rick Renzi).
    - Institutes a timeline for deployment of US-VISIT to all land-based checkpoints (House Amendment 642, authored by Michael N. Castle).
    - Requires the Department of Homeland Security (DHS) to report to Congress on the number of Other Than Mexicans (OTMs) apprehended and deported and the number of those from states that sponsor terrorism (Section 401).
    - Formalizes congressional condemnation of rapes by smugglers along the border and urges Mexico to take immediate action to prevent them (House Amendment 647, authored by Ginny Brown-Waite).
    - Requires all undocumented aliens, before being deported, to pay a fine of $3,000 if they agree to leave voluntarily but do not adhere to the terms of their agreement. The grace period for voluntary departure is shortened to sixty days.
    - Requires DHS to conduct a study on the potential for border fencing on the US-Canada border.
    - Sets the minimum sentence for fraudulent documents at ten years, fines, or both, with tougher sentencing in cases of aiding drug trafficking and terrorism.
    - Establishes a Fraudulent Documents Center within DHS.
    - Increases penalties for aggravated felonies and various frauds, including marriage fraud and document fraud.
    - Establishes an eighteen-month deadline for DHS to control the border, with a progress report due one year after enactment of the legislation.
    - Requires criminal record, terrorist watch list clearance, and fraudulent document checks for any illegal immigrant before being granted legal immigration status.

- Reimburses states for aiding in immigration enforcement.
- Causes housing of a removed alien to become a felony and sets the minimum prison sentence to three years.
- Allows deportation of any undocumented alien convicted of driving under the influence (DUI). Adds human trafficking and human smuggling to the money-laundering statute. Increases penalties for employing undocumented workers to $7,500 for first-time offenses, $15,000 for second offenses, and $40,000 for all subsequent offenses.
- Prohibits accepting immigrants from any country which delays or refuses to accept its citizens who are deported from the United States (Section 404).

11 "Mike Davis in *Planet of Slums*," *Socialist Worker*, June 24, 2006, http://www.socialistworker.co.uk/article.php?article_id ¼ 9073.
12 Samuel P. Huntington, "The Hispanic Challenge," *Foreign Policy*, March/April 2004.
13 Røpke (2006, pp. 191–4).
14 See Jim Lane, "Unbridled Anti-immigrant Racism in Texas," *People's Weekly World*, 2006, http://www.pww.org/article/view/10161 and Stephanie Sandoval, "FB Immigration Law Wins Easily," *Dallas News*, May 13, 2007, http://www.dallasnews.com/sharedcontent/dws/news/politics/local/stories/051307dnmetfarmersbranch.621241fe.html.
15 In several cases where challenges have been brought against local ordinances, the courts have found that the cities had over-reached when trying to pass a law that is preempted by federal immigration laws, and agreed to temporarily block their implementation. Nearly twenty of the laws that have passed have been tabled or defeated. In December 2006, the city of Escondido, California, agreed to a permanent injunction against enforcement of its anti-immigrant ordinance, http://www.aclu.org/immigrants/discrim/29164prs20070322.html.
16 See "Immigrants Gain Power," *Hispanic Business*, May 30, 2006.
17 See "Immigrants Are Behind One Quarter of Startups," *Hispanic Business*, November 15, 2006.
18 Friedman (2005); Hardt and Negri (2001).
19 Harvey (2005, p. 160).
20 See Anup Shah, "Causes of Poverty," http://www.globalissues.org/TradeRelated/Facts.asp.
21 See Davis (2006).
22 A House bill, passed on a 239–182 vote, includes a proposal to build 700 miles of additional fence through parts of California, Arizona, New Mexico, and Texas, at a potential cost of $7 billion. The government will also enlist military and local law enforcement to help stop illegal entrants. See Jamie Reno, "Is U.S-Mexico Border Wall a Good Idea? Border Expert David Shirk Discusses Controversial Border Fence Legislation," *Newsweek*, October 12, 2006.
23 Arendt (1968, p. 23).
24 Harvey (2005, p. 32).
25 See discussion of accumulation by dispossession and the issues of chronic insecurity in Harvey (2005, pp. 137–82).
26 Ibid., p. 145.
27 Ibid., p. 28, 38.
28 Ibid., p. 145.
29 Ibid., p. 188.

30 Adam Werbach, "The End of the Population Movement," *The American Prospect*, October 2005, http://findarticles.com/p/articles/mi_hb3463/is_200510/ai_n18248157.
31 See Christopher Hayes, "Round Population Numbers Fuel the Immigration Scare," *The Nation*, October 24, 2006.
32 See Tom Barry, "Immigration Debate: Politics, Ideologies of Anti-Immigration Forces," *IRC Americas Program Special Report*, June 17, 2005, http://www.americas.irc-online.org/am/652.
33 Lamm and Imhoff (1985).
34 Darder (forthcoming).
35 See report by David A. Lieb, *Associated Press*, November 14, 2006.
36 See Røpke (2006); *United Nations, Population, Gender and Development: A Concise Report*, ST/ESA/SER.A/193, 2001; and Pinstrup-Andersen and Pandya-Lorch (2001).
37 Dowty (1987, p. 13).
38 Ibid., p. 4.
39 Ibid., p. 11.
40 "The Border Wall: Who Will Build It?" *People's Weekly World Newspaper*, November 2, 2006, http://www.pww.org/article/articleprint/10093.
41 Castles (2000, p. 279).
42 See "Coalition Mourns One Year of CAFTA; Calls for Trade with Justice" and other articles on the negative impact of the Central American Free Trade Agreement; http://www.stopcafta.org.
43 Shah (2014).
44 See "The Immigrant Workers Freedom Ride," *The Free Press Journal* 33:5 (September–October 2003), http://www.freepress.org/departments.php/display/20/2003/182/1/ 23; also see report on Voices of The Immigrant Workers Freedom Ride in New York, *Amsterdam News*, October 9–15, 2003. For more organizational information on The Immigrant Workers Freedom Ride, http://www.iwfr.org/.

Reference

Arendt, H. (1968), *Imperialism*. New York, NY: Harcourt Brace Janovich, 23.
Castles, S. (2000), "International Migration at the Beginning of the Twenty-First Century: Global Trends and Issues." *International Social Science Journal* 52(3): 269–81.
Darder, A. (forthcoming), *Forging a Puerto Rican Feminism: The Poetics of Consciousness and Embodied History*. New York, NY: Routledge.
Darder, A., and Torres, R. (2004), *After Race: Racism after Multiculturalism*. New York, NY: New York University Press.
Davis, M. (2001), *Magical Urbanism: Latinos Reinvent the U.S. City*. New York, NY: Verso.
Davis, M. (2006), *Planet of Slums*. London: Verso.
Dowty, A. (1987), *Closed Borders: The Contemporary Assault on Freedom of Movement*. New Haven, CT: Yale University Press, 13.
Friedman, T. L. (2005), *The World Is Flat: A Brief History of the Twenty-First Century*. New York, NY: Farrar, Straus and Giroux.
Hardt, M., and Negri, A. (2001), *Empire*. Boston, MA: Harvard University Press.
Harvey, D. (2005), *The New Imperialism*. New York, NY: Oxford University Press, 160.

Hernandez, R. D. (2000), "Violence, Subalternity, and El Corrido Along the U.S.-Mexico Border." *The Berkeley McNair Research Journal* 8 (Winter): 136–52.

Lamm, R., and Imhoff, G. (1985), *The Immigration Time Bomb: The Fragmenting of America*. New York, NY: EP Dutton.

Livingstone, J. (2004), "Murder in Juarez: Gender, Sexual Violence, and the Global Assembly Line." *Frontiers: A Journal of Womens Studies* 25(1): 59–76.

Røpke, I. (2006), "Migration and Sustainability—Compatibility or Contradictory." *Ecological Economics* 59(2): 191–4.

Sassen, S. (2005), "The De Facto Transnationalizing of Immigration Policy," in C. Joppke (ed.), *Challenge to the Nation-State*. Oxford: Oxford University Press, 49–86.

Shah, A. (2014), Causes of Poverty [Online]. Available at: http://www.globalissues.org/issue/2/causes-of-poverty.

16

Latinos, Education, and the Church: Toward a Culturally Democratic Future

The article provides a comprehensive critical analysis of key issues that are deeply salient to an examination of the relationship of Latinos, education, and the Church. The status of Latinos and their educational participation in the US is systematically presented through a critical theoretical lens that brings questions of historical, political, and economic inequalities and their consequences to the center of this interpretive interrogation. With this foundational piece in place, the article moves to the concept of cultural democracy as an important philosophical principle in our work to transform the education of Latino children within Catholic schools and beyond. The role and responsibility of the Church is linked here to proclamations offered by Pope Francis toward revolutionizing the labor of the Catholic Church and Catholic education in an effort to more effectively engage with the pedagogical needs of Latino communities. Moreover, the discussion employs a much needed critical philosophical lens that defies the presentation of recipes or prescriptions for how emancipatory education will look when achieved, but rather invites Catholic educators, scholars, and the leadership of the Church into deeper reflection and consideration of the culturally democratic dimension that must be integrated into Catholic social teaching, if we are to genuinely achieve the necessary structural changes required to ensure educational justice for all Latino students.

School broadens not only your intellectual dimensions, but also the human one … School can and should function as a catalyst, being a place of encounter and convergence of the entire educational community with the single objective of shaping and helping [students] to grow as mature, simple, honest, and competent persons who know how to love faithfully, who know how to live their lives as a response to God's call and their future professions as a service to society.

—Pope Francis[1]

Pope Francis's powerful words about the function of schooling coincide well with the ideas of the late Brazilian education philosopher Paulo Freire, in their underlying intent to inspire societies toward a more loving and humanizing educational purpose. Freire insisted that our historical vocation as subjects of history and, thus, by extension the purpose of schooling, should be that "of becoming more fully human" (Freire, 1970, p. 84). This points to salient issues that must be at the forefront of our consciousness, as we move to examine the role of Catholic educators in supporting Latino students across all communities and educational settings. To do so, however, means a careful rethinking of the Church's vision for education today beyond solely Catholic school formation and Church affiliation.[2] Instead, there is a need for greater critical engagement with the lives of Latino children and their families, within the everyday places where we struggle to survive and make a place for ourselves, in these times of change and great uncertainty. This requires that the labor of Catholic educators engage with the historical, social, and material conditions that shape the lives of Latino communities in the US today. With this, there must be a decisive recognition that the education of Latino students matters and that there is serious urgency for proactive responses by the Church on this question.

Similarly, this raises the need for more deliberate engagement within future practices of Catholic educators, in ways that can play important public pedagogical roles, particularly with respect to the need of the most impoverished Latino communities. This to highlight that a renewed Catholic vision of emancipatory education could potentially help lead the larger society toward establishing more humanizing structures and practices of formal and informal learning, which can in turn support the development of social consciousness, democratic voice, and community participation in the daily culture of neighborhood churches and schools—a process that is necessary to reinventing a more just world.

However, any humanizing vision for democratic education and the transformation of social inequalities will be, indeed, fully contingent on educational priorities, ethical concerns, and curricular approaches that fundamentally impact the social and intellectual formation of Latino students. Inherent to this process must be emancipatory values of community that can sustain a universal understanding of human kinship and solidarity, within and across cultural communities. However, it should be noted that relying solely on a liberal universal human rights notion of human existence as a primary philosophical foundation for diversity practice within churches, schools, and communities is insufficient to meeting the educational needs of working-class Latino students. Traditional mainstream efforts to conflate cultural differences and erase or revise histories of genocide, slavery, and colonization have often been carried out in the name of universality. This has led to an overarching tendency to deny the destructive and persistent impact of racializing and economically induced historical violence upon oppressed Latino populations. Basic to the politics and practices of racialization, impoverishment, and social exclusion, US schooling and other social institutions have perpetuated deficit discourses that reinforce the angst and frustration of Latino populations—populations that historically have looked to the Church for respite from inequality, seeking a more just vision and greater acceptance of cultural difference.

Yet, just as poverty and institutional racism have remained pervasively embedded in contemporary life, so too has the Church perpetuated a hidden curriculum of assimilation, reinforcing structures of inequality and social exclusion, whether by deliberate design, unfortunate ignorance, or dire neglect. This debilitating phenomenon has often led to conditions that have failed to address cultural differences, within and outside the Church, while professing to bestow generosity onto impoverished and racialized communities. This is particularly the case with Latino immigrant populations, the majority of whom profess to be Catholic and, as such, today provide the US Church with a lion's share of its newest and most devout congregants.

If the future work of Catholic educators in the United States is to evolve in ways that can contend seriously with the educational needs of Latino communities, then it will require that the societal forces that reverberate harshly in the hardships faced by Latinos and Latinas become part-and-parcel of a larger ecumenical dialogue for the future. This is essential to the contribution of our labor in Latino communities, given that the status of education in our communities is in crisis. Moreover, we must acknowledge this educational crisis as a human rights issue—one that requires closer interrogation of the social dilemmas and contradictions it poses for any institution publicly committed to the dignity and well-being of the most vulnerable populations.

The Status of Latino Education

A change of attitude towards [Latinos][3] is needed on the part of everyone, moving away from attitudes of defensiveness and fear, indifference and marginalization—all typical of throwaway culture—towards attitudes based on a culture of encounter, the only culture capable of building a better, more just and fraternal world.

—Pope Francis[4]

Educators across the country continue to grapple with the failure of mainstream education to meet the needs of Latino students, especially of Latino immigrant students. In the last two decades, a variety of federal and state policy initiatives have supported culturally assimilative and linguistically restrictive educational policies. As a consequence, the right to bilingual education for language minority students was abolished, while practices tied to federal mandates of *No Child Left Behind* (NCLB) and *Race to the Top* (RTTT) reinforced high-stakes testing, standardization of the curriculum, and the privatization of education. In Arizona, mean-spirited policy initiatives against Chicanos and Mexican immigrants encompassed nativist efforts to restrict the use of Spanish in schools and the workplace, the elimination of Mexican American studies at the secondary level, and the banning of books considered to be subversive by conservative proponents of curricular and textbook reforms (Aguirre, 2012; Darder, 2012).

Yet, despite the repressive intent of such policies, demographers across the nation are forecasting that by 2050, populations of color will be the majority in the United States and Latinos will comprise the largest of these populations (Passel & Cohn, 2008; Krogstad, 2014).[5] In fact, according to statistics released in July 2015, Latinos already outnumber whites in California (Panzar, 2015). Hence, these changing demographics are a factor that all US institutions, including the Church and Catholic education, must consider seriously with respect to future planning, if they are to remain relevant and effective to an increasingly Latino populace.

Latino Demographics

According to the most recent US Census data, the Latino population today is nearly 52 million and the largest and youngest ethnic minority population in the United States. The Mexican-origin population is estimated to comprise 67 percent of the total Latino population. Moreover, one in five schoolchildren and one in four newborns are Latino. Never before in the nation's history has an ethnic minority group made up so large a share of the youngest population; numbers expected to triple in the next three decades (Passel & Cohn, 2008). By 2036, Latino children are projected to comprise one-third of all children, ages 3–17 (U.S. Census Bureau, 2008). Among the 30 million young people, ages 18–24, living in the United States today, 6 million (20 percent) are Latino youth. By the sheer force of numbers, the education that Latino students undergo will dramatically shape both the future of the Church and the history of this nation.

It is against the backdrop of intense national debate about the looming specter of the "browning of America," that we must work to grapple with the impact of demographic change. The subject of Latinos as a growing diaspora has also gained considerable attention in policy circles and theoretical discussions. Projections by the Pew Hispanic Center[6] showed that 82 percent of the future Latino population increase will be due to immigrants from Latin America, with the majority being their US-born descendants (Taylor, Gonzalez-Barrera, Passel, & Lopez, 2012). Currently, 93 percent of all Latinos living in the United States are under the age of eighteen and born in this country. The trends in population shifts also show a declining white population, while there has been a steady Latino population increase in the last three decades. It is also worth noting, as the percentage of the white population decreases in number—for they will still hold the majority of national wealth, power, and privilege—new waves of political suppression may arise. In fact, the last decade of political turmoil in Arizona, including the passage of Proposition 200 in 2004 that introduced a voter ID Law as an explicit attempt at political suppression (Deutsch, 2011), may be a bellweather of future backlash, as the white population loses the security of its former majority status.

Moreover, given rising Latino immigration to the United States, it is important to note that our well-being is also tied to the well-being of workers in the Caribbean, Mexico, and Latin America. Many of the difficult economic conditions and political ramifications faced by Latino workers in their countries of origin—many that were historically provoked by US economic policies and targeted investments—have served as a catalyst for Latino immigration. Ana Maria Pineda (2005) reflects on this phenomenon:

> The colonization of the Americas by Spain has negatively marked the history of Latinos/ Hispanics in the United States. We continue to live out the consequences of a history of conquest and colonization. Five hundred years later, the lives of the Hispanic community has not greatly improved. This is true of the Latino reality on both sides of the border. What is experienced in Latin America is shared in similar ways by the Hispanic/Latino community in the United States. The constant migration of Latinos from south and north of the U.S. border makes this a local

and global reality for Sisters of Mercy. The Catholic Church has not given this
migrant group the pastoral attention it needs.

(p. 15)

Similarly, commonplace practices of US labor exploitation have stirred the undocumented movement of workers across the US/Mexico border. However, although demographically more significant today, the political economy of the border has been a longstanding phenomenon, one that historically also prompted Puerto Rican, Dominican, and other Latin Americans workers to trek north for better-paying jobs and to secure a more promising educational future for their children.

Latino Enrollment and Graduation Rates

In the nation's schools, Latino students have today reached a new milestone. For the first time, one in four (24.7 percent) public elementary school students are Latino, following similar milestones reached recently by Latinos among public kindergarten students (in 2007) and public nursery school students (in 2006). Among all pre-K through 12th grade public school students, a record 23.9 percent are Latino. And for the first time, the number of 18- to 24-year-old Latino youth enrolled in college exceeded 2 million, reaching a record 16.5 percent of all college enrollments (Fry & Lopez, 2012). As students in nursery school progress through kindergarten and into elementary school and high school, Latino students are expected to become an even larger share of all school enrollments, including Catholic schools—where today only 15 percent of the students are identified as Latino (McDonald & Schultz, 2015) and only 3 percent of all Latino students enrolled in elementary and secondary education attend Catholic schools (Suhy, 2012).[7]

In the last decade, the graduation rates for Latino students across the country have improved. Recent data indicates that Latino students are much less likely to drop out of high school than they were a decade ago. A recent study of high school graduation rates found that 78 percent of Latino students graduated from high school in 2010, an increase from 64 percent in 2000 (Murnane, 2013). Similarly, the number of Latino students in the United States earning associate and bachelor's degrees has improved dramatically since 1977. However, despite these impressive gains, Pew Research Center data indicates that of all students completing Bachelor's degrees, only 11 percent were conferred on Latino students, despite the much-touted fanfare about their increase in college enrollment. In fact, as Kelly, Schneider, and Carey (2010) state,

> across the country, 51% of Hispanic students who start college complete a bachelor's degree in six years, compared to 59% of White students. That disparity holds true no matter the ability of the students or the reputation of the schools: Hispanic students graduate at lower rates than their White peers across similarly ranked colleges, from the nation's least selective to its most selective colleges and universities.

(para. 3)

This discrepancy clearly points to a high attrition rate for Latino college students, which spurs concerns about the institutional commitment of universities and colleges in ensuring that Latino students are served effectively.

The Teaching Workforce

Despite the increasing number of Latino students in US schools, 2010 national student enrollment in public schools when compared to the teaching force by race/ethnicity showed the overwhelming percentage of teachers educating Latino and other children of color are white. In fact, according to the National Center for Education Statistics (2008), 83 percent of the teaching force nationally is white, while only 7 percent of all classroom teachers are of Latino descent. This absence is also echoed in Catholic schools, where Latino educators comprise only 6.3 percent of the workforce (Ospino, 2014).[8]

This fact alone is of dire concern, given the growing number of Latino students in large urban centers such as Los Angeles, Chicago, and New York, where they are already the majority and a rapidly growing percentage of new students who will matriculate into all systems of schooling, in the next decade. This cultural discrepancy in the teaching force brings to mind the idea posed by Antonio Gramsci (1971)—teachers, consciously or unconsciously, serve as conserving moral agents of the state. This factor cannot be ignored in light of more than four decades of research on culture and education, which has shown repeatedly that when Latino students are educated with culturally and linguistically responsive curriculum that positively engages their cultural strengths; are taught by Latino bicultural educators; and their parents are invited to participate in their school in meaningful ways, their academic achievement improves, irrespective of income level (Moll, Amanti, Neff, & González, 1992; Nieto, 2009; Diaz-Soto & Haroon, 2010; Darder, 2012).

Yet, unfortunately, the glaring over-representation of white teachers in all schools is an issue typically dismissed by the neoliberal culture of schooling today, with its "neutral" claim about the standardization of knowledge and overwhelming emphasis on science, technology, engineering, and mathematics (STEM)—an emphasis that is often utilized to sideline the messiness of a humanities curriculum that places greater attention on the larger social and ethical questions of human existence. Accordingly, there is widespread negation of the histories, cultural traditions, and indigenous beliefs of Latino communities—knowledge that could well strengthen a sense of self-determination, social agency, academic confidence, and political empowerment, when cultivated among both Latino teachers and students. Instead, the views and perspectives of our teachers and students are often over-surveilled, their voices silenced, and cultural protocols marginalized, by authoritarian policies and practices of accountability that seek to homogenize Latino populations into a mainstream where deep structural inequality and poverty persist.

The Persistence of Poverty

As long as the problems of the poor are not radically resolved by rejecting the absolute autonomy of markets and financial speculation and by attacking the structural causes of inequality, no solution will be found for the world's problems or, for that matter, to any problems.

—Pope Francis[9]

True to Pope Francis's critique of the absolute autonomy of the market, one of the most distinctive features of the US economy is its widening gap in income distribution. In fact, inequality has become so extreme in the United States that it resembles the class-stratified societies of early twentieth-century Europe. The US economy continues to generate tremendous wealth, but the wealth does not reach working families, remaining concentrated at the top. Those in most need go without health care, quality education, or a living wage. One of the striking features of the growing significance of inequality in the United States seems to be our lack of financial knowledge—in a society, where more and more, decisions are predicated on the whims of the marketplace.

Yet, inequality matters and tackling its persistence is a matter of local, regional, and national importance. This is particularly the case for impoverished Latino communities, who comprise one of the most economically and socially disenfranchised populations in the United States today. Hence, as Pope Francis contends, seeking solutions to poverty should become central to all facets of society. His words also reinforce the tremendous need for the Church to take a more robust interest in the education of poor Latino communities. This is particularly so given that the lack of both educational and labor opportunities is associated with incapacitating life conditions, including an excess of social and material stressors that can result in poor health and increased mortality. While solutions often seem elusive, the Church and the nation ignore poverty at its own peril.

Comprehensive data from 2011 showed that over 50 million people in the United States are living in poverty and this rate is now higher than it was in 1970. In the Latino community, the child poverty rate is 35 percent, in comparison to 12 percent of their white peers. The total raw number of Latino children living in poverty, however, is higher than the number for any other minority ethnic group in the United States (Lopez & Velasco, 2011). Among them, the children of Latino immigrants are most likely to face dire conditions of poverty, in comparison to other US children (Aizenman, 2009). And although the poverty rate among all Latinos is 25 percent, Puerto Rican and Chicano/Mexicano populations—the two largest Latino populations in the United States—have rates closer to 30 percent (Motel & Patten, 2012). Hence, nearly one in three Latinos today lives in poverty.

Poverty rates, moreover, are also closely tied to unemployment, with more than one in ten Latinos currently jobless. The joblessness amongst Latino youth is even worse. One in five young Latinos is unemployed. In certain cities across the United

States, nearly 50 percent of all youth of color cannot find jobs. Chicago, for example, is one of those cities with one of the highest metropolitan youth unemployment rates in the country. Of course, the overall joblessness is compounded by the historic loss of wealth in Latino communities, due to the recession in 2007. The unprecedented loss of homes and property fueled by the foreclosure crisis sent Latino net worth to an all time low. According to the 2010 census, the median wealth of white households is eighteen times that of Latino households. Wealth inequalities by ethnicity are the largest recorded, since the government began publishing this data a quarter century ago (Domhoff, 2013); and it is a phenomenon that still appears to be growing, according to a December 2014 Pew Research Center report on widening inequality along racial/ethnic lines since the end of that recession (Kochhar & Fry, 2014).

The lack of jobs and other financial resources is making it much harder for communities to recover. Economists predict that it will take at least a full generation before Latino and Black communities regain what was lost in this last decade. And although the number of Latinos receiving a college degree (9 percent) has risen (Fry & Taylor, 2013), not only does the number of degrees conferred on Latinos still trail that of most other ethnic groups in the nation, there is also an increasing joblessness rate reported even among college graduates. So, despite reported increases in high school and college graduation rates, Latino youth are still experiencing conditions of persistent inequality in a worsening economic climate.

Conditions Faced by Latino Youth

Although young Latino and Latina students tend to express optimism about their futures and place a high value on education, hard work, and educational success, national studies indicate that they are much more likely than white youth to drop out of school, become teenage parents, live in poverty, have higher levels of exposure to gang activity, experience higher incidences of police profiling and incarceration, and are more apt to be targeted for military recruitment, which is justified by military recruiters given that Latinos are considered to be underrepresented in the armed forces (Ash, Buck, Klerman, Kleykamp, & Loughran, 2009).

Furthermore, a national report released in 2012 by the Social Science Research Council reported that 5.8 million young people, age 16–24, are living on the margins without even part-time jobs. Low-income African American and Latino youth nationally are most likely to be labeled "disconnected," a term used to refer to a lack of participation in school or work life (Burd-Sharps & Lewis, 2012).

This signals a difficult passage to adulthood for many Latino youth, who must already contend with higher rates of poverty and school dropout. Teen pregnancy among young Latinas places them in greater conditions of disadvantage than their male counterparts, making their conditions more similar to Black males. Hence, more young Latinas (20.3 percent)—many already young mothers—than young men (16.8 percent) are considered disconnected. And this phenomenon of youth disconnection is most prevalent in communities where older adults have persistently struggled with high unemployment and economic instability. Hence, with vanishing opportunities in the labor market, it is not surprising that low-income Latino youth are more apt to respond affirmatively to military recruitment efforts, in the hopes of securing future financial stability for themselves and their families. Unfortunately, the impact of military service can be wrought with its own set of difficulties, once Latino and Latina soldiers return to civilian life.

The issue of incarceration also merits a brief note here, in that Juvenile Justice population comparisons show alarming disparities in youth incarceration. According to the Annie E. Casey Foundation Report *Reducing Youth Incarceration in the United States* (Annie E. Casey Foundation, 2013),

> Large disparities remain in youth confinement ... African-American youth are nearly five times more likely to be confined than their white peers. Latino and American Indian youth are between two and three times more likely to be confined. The disparities in youth confinement rates point to a system that treats youth of color, particularly African Americans and Latinos, more punitively than similar white youth.
>
> (p. 2)

And according to the Children's Defense Fund (CDF), one in six Latino boys born in 2001 are considered at risk of going to prison during their lifetime (CDF, 2007).

Concerned with staggering rates of school suspensions that criminalize youth, community advocates across the nation draw parallels with high dropout and unemployment rates for youth of color with the "school to prison pipeline" (Knefel, 2013). Along similar lines, 1.7 percent of the white population is incarcerated, as compared to more than 10 percent of the population of color in the United States. This alarming disparity of incarceration, particularly for working class men of color, suggests imprisonment may be employed as a de facto means for mass containment and regulation of impoverished populations. Moreover, poverty, poor literacy rates, and high dropout rates have all been correlated with probability of incarceration (Hammond, Linton, Smink, & Drew, 2007). And while school dropout, unemployment, and incarceration are typically blamed for poor social mobility among the poor, an education, more often than not, does prove to be the ticket to social mobility that most believe it to be.

Myth of Social Mobility

Both the historical record and current statistical data confirm the persistence of Latinos among the nation's most educationally and economically disenfranchised populations. But why have these conditions changed so little over the last five decades, despite an unprecedented number of well-educated Latinos? Efforts to critically examine the persistence of Latino poverty and academic underachievement point to a powerful contradiction. On one hand, referring back to Pope Francis's words, most educational institutions are market-driven and tend to reproduce, often without intent, racialized class formations. This dynamic is perpetuated by way of recalcitrant structures of assimilative schooling that overtly or covertly function to undermine the cultural strength that Latino students bring to the classroom. As such, these students are expected to not only embrace the dominant cultural values of rugged individualism and competition, but also accept victim-blaming notions that put responsibility for poor social mobility squarely back on the shoulders of the most disenfranchised.

There is no question that education is widely upheld within the Church and the larger society as the great promise of upward social mobility, along with the many privileges this supposedly bestows. College graduation then is promulgated as the determining vehicle for both social and material success. In concert with the myth of the American dream, long held as the national ethos, this hidden curriculum encompasses a set of ideals that bolster a meritocratic system that claims to guarantee equal opportunity for prosperity and success. From this vantage point, upward mobility can readily be achieved through exhibiting individual hard work, personal perseverance, and a competitive spirit. In the process, education is lauded as the great democratizing process in action, where all can become educated and economically successful, if only they can persevere and excel according to an assimilationist ideal. In the process, not only does this view justify and shroud existing inequalities, but establishes the superior "merit" of the people at the top as the main criterion for success. Meanwhile, the blame for poverty is assigned to the poor themselves, inferring that they do not possess—genetically, culturally, or spiritually—the sufficient mettle to avail themselves of what is being offered.

This all-too-common notion obscures the structural origin of the difficult conditions faced by Latino students and their communities, as well as obstructs access to effective solutions that would invite a more communal approach to the problem and a genuine commitment to transforming the values, structures, and relationships of exclusion that predominate across societal institutions, including the Church and Catholic education. Social mobility rhetoric, laced in bootstrap values of rugged individualism and "race to the top" perseverance, belies the fact that poverty trumps social mobility, with few exceptions.

Recent studies conclude that it is not only more difficult for poor Americans to rise up from the lower economic rungs, but that US social mobility is actually lower than that of Canada and Western Europe (DeParle, 2012). In fact, a 2013 study by the Brookings Institution found inequality is rising against a background of low social mobility and a growing gap between families at the top and the bottom of income distribution. This raises concerns about the ability of today's impoverished class to work their way up the economic ladder; concluding that "upward social mobility is limited in the United States" (Greenstone, Looney, Patashnik, & Yu, 2013). This phenomenon is well-illustrated by income data from the Brookings Institution associated with parent's income levels, which dramatically show that children born into low-income families are significantly more likely to remain stuck at the low-end of the income distribution as adults (Reeves & Howard, 2013).

Yet, despite the difficulties and contradictions at work, Latino educators, parents, and community organizations have worked, for almost a century, to support the education of their children—both within the Church and their communities. Two often cited school desegregation cases that predate *Brown v. Board of Education* (1954) are *Roberto Alvarez v. the Board of Trustees of the Lemon Grove School District* (1941) and *Mendez v. Westminster* (1946). These efforts were grounded in parental belief that education can play a pivotal role in improving the future of their children and their community. These efforts, along with many others since then, reveal the importance that Latino communities attach to education, as well as the political agency and solidarity required to effect meaningful change. It has been through sustained communal efforts over the past five decades that Latino parents, teachers, and students have enacted their social agency and collective consciousness to interrogate inequalities and work for educational justice. This is a phenomenon that has taken place within the context of Catholic education, as it has in the larger society.

Today, we see those efforts at work in Latino pro-immigrant struggles, where undocumented Latino immigrant youth and their allies have willingly put their personal security and lives on the line, in the struggle for both their cultural citizenship and immigrant educational rights. Their courageous efforts over the last decade have prompted heated national debates and expanded dialogues about the rights of undocumented immigrants. And although pro-immigrant efforts have infused new life into this important issue, these have not yet led to the passage of the Dream Act, which would provide immigration benefits to those who arrived in the United States as children, before the age of sixteen and who resided in the United States continuously, for at least five years prior to the bill being enacted into law. While recognizing the political possibilities of such movements, it is essential to also acknowledge the failure of many such efforts to integrate a substantive critique of structural economic inequalities, beyond the reach of individual academic effort. Even the campaign for the Dream Act has often been couched around a limited notion of individual rights and access to the American dream, which speaks simply to a pathway or entrance into a system of growing injustice, without linking the work to the need for a more egalitarian society.

Education and community practices then must move beyond notions of "social mobility" that have proven miserably inadequate, in that this approach has failed to contend with those institutional policies and practices that reproduce conditions of economic apartheid, racism, and social alienation, in the lives of Latino communities. From the standpoint of a serious historical analysis, it is glaringly obvious that widespread educational restructuring can not possibly be accomplished without sustained dialogue and genuine participatory efforts for social and economic reform, grounded in what it means to exist within a genuinely democratic society. This said, it would do well for the Church and Catholic education, in specific, to take a more grounded and substantive approach to Latino education questions, by both entering into larger Latino educational debates and supporting community efforts to transform the schooling of all Latino students. Such an effort would, of course, demand that Catholic educators teaching within Latino communities critically challenge and transform deficit notions that bankrupt our emancipatory efforts, within the Church and the larger society.

Challenging Deficit Notions

One of the most pervasive aspects of unacknowledged racism is the manner in which Latino students continue to be perceived as intellectually and culturally deficient. Longstanding perceptions and preconceptions of Mexican children as a "Mexican Problem" have been well documented by historian Gilbert G. Gonzalez (2013). Today, deficit notions still shape the pedagogy, curriculum, and classroom life of Latino students, particularly those from poor working-class communities. In the twenty-first century the "Mexican Problem" has become the "Hispanic Problem," in which notions of cognitive deficiencies pervade public debates on Latino immigration reform.[10] The disabling impact of deficit notions is readily apparent by the huge number of Latino students who sincerely believe that the reason they do poorly academically is because they are just too "dumb." As a consequence, the victim-blaming ideology associated with processes of racialization in schools becomes well internalized, resulting in the often-touted achievement gap with its alarming disparities. An internalized belief of intellectual inferiority among Latino students can negatively impact in very real ways their educational progress and their aspirations for the future.

Even more disconcerting is the manner in which disparities in achievement are attached to "evidence-based" measures that negate the impact of assimilative learning conditions, with respect to both language and culture. Consequently, on measures of reading and writing proficiency, for example, Latino students are almost twice as likely as their White peers to score below basic levels (The Nation's Report Card, 2013). These test scores are, nonetheless, liberally employed to legitimate the achievement gap, without critically questioning the problematic classroom conditions that lead to poor performance among Latino students. Hence, it is not surprising that across all categories, students of color are found to lag behind.

Similarly, as mentioned earlier, suspension and expulsion rates for Black and Latino students are deplorable. According to the study *Out of School & Off Track: The Overuse of Suspensions in American Middle and High Schools* (Losen & Martinez, 2013), the rate of secondary school suspensions for Black (24 percent) and Latino students (12 percent) has doubled since 1972, while that of white peers only slightly increased. In the same study, the breakdown for secondary school data for Latino English Language Learners revealed a serious increase in their risk for suspension, particularly among males. The severity of the issue prompted not only a nationwide call for a moratorium on the use of expulsion and suspensions, but also a recent Department of Justice investigation into discriminatory policies in Florida's Palm Beach County, where ELL students were not being allowed to enroll in the county's public schools, and those who did were found to have much higher suspension and expulsion rates compared to other students (Losen & Martinez, 2013). This increasing use of suspensions and expulsion, as mentioned earlier, is strongly linked to an increase in high school dropout rates, which remain stubbornly high with more than 40 percent of Latino youth over the age of nineteen failing to earn a high school diploma (Cardenas & Kirby, 2012). These disturbing statistics point to not only untenable circumstances faced by Latino students, but also the failure of many schools to support their social and academic well-being.

The New Face of Segregation

Despite hopeful desegregation reform efforts initiated by the Brown v. Board of Education decision in the 1950s, the proportion of Latino students attending segregated schools has actually increased in the last two decades, particularly in large urban school districts, where Latino student enrollments are now heavily concentrated. A report released by the Civil Rights Project, *E Pluribus ... Separation: Deepening Double Segregation for Students* (Orfield, Kucera, & Siegel-Hawley, 2012), "shows that segregation has increased seriously across the country for Latino students, who are attending more intensely segregated and impoverished schools than they have for generations" (p. 1). Student enrollment by ethnicity in high-poverty versus low-poverty schools shows an inverse relationship, particularly for low-income Latino elementary students who attend not only the poorest schools but some of the most segregated in the nation. Accordingly, Latino students have become the new face of segregation. In concert, the proportions of Latino students who graduate from high school prepared for college admission and then enroll in college or university still remain low. And despite increases in educational attainment in recent years, the body of research in the field well attests that educational conditions for Latino and Latina students have remained chronic, over the last fifty years (Darder & Torres, 2013).

In challenging deficit notions, it is important that the persistence of low achievement and failure not be explained away by discriminatory views that see the problem as housed in the nature or culture of Latino communities or the lack of intellectual potential of our children. In the past, such victim-blaming perspectives were the most common conclusions drawn from social science research on the academic failure of Latino students. Too often culturally deterministic views that engender such research reinforce racialized perceptions that further disenfranchise Latino students, most who are already struggling with challenging circumstances of life. Although we can find a plethora of research on the education of Latino students today, mainstream educational policies and practices often still echo, albeit in more sophisticated terms, a belief in the cultural inferiority of Latino children. In contrast, seldom do we find sustained public proclamations for structural change in the schooling of Latino students, beyond neoliberal solutions that commodify knowledge, instrumentalize teaching, and convert students into clients and parents into stakeholders—as if they genuinely held decisive power to educational decisions, within the existing structures of inequity that persist.

Despite a history that reveals the persistence of discrimination, the struggle for educational justice persists. In response, Latinos have used political pressure and the legal system to struggle for equal education. A poignant example is found in the struggle of Mexican Americans in the Southwest who, despite a shared belief in the value of education, faced major obstacles (San Miguel, 2013). As economic conditions permitted, these parents presented their children for enrollment, but often their children were either not accepted or segregated and, more often than not, provided only a substandard education. In frustration, some Latino parents turned to Catholic schools, in the hopes that this would afford their children a better opportunity. However, since only a limited number of children were accepted into parochial schools—which often also reflected racializing deficit notions—Latino parents fought difficult uphill battles to advocate on behalf of their children. For example, inspired by the educational efforts of the Chicano Movement, Católicos Por La Raza (CPLR) organized and held a demonstration and a mass in downtown Los Angeles in 1968 to call attention to conditions of Catholic education (Acuña, 2013). Catholic High School students rose up for change in the Church, calling upon the Church leadership to use its wealth to help solve the poor educational conditions of Chicano and Chicana students in Catholic schools (Sánchez Walsh, 2013)[11]. Beyond building of new parish schools, which more recently have been rapidly closing, seldom has the Church, as an institution, stood officially on the side of cultural democracy, as Latino parents fought for the education of their children and the dignity of our humanity. And when this has been the case, it generally has been due to the efforts of individual priests, religious, or members of the Hispanic Ministry.

Cultural Democracy: Beyond One-Dimensional Humanity

We need ... to counter the dominance of a one-dimensional vision of the human person, a vision that reduces human beings to what they produce and to what they consume. This is one of the most insidious temptations of our time.

—Pope Francis[12]

The concept of cultural democracy[13] is introduced here precisely as a pluralistic means to counter the one-dimensionality associated with ethnocentric schooling. Generally speaking, cultural democracy is conceptualized through related communal commitments that include: (a) protection and promotion of the integrity of cultural worldviews, cultural difference, and the cultural rights of all people; (b) encouragement of active participation in the cultural life of the community and society; (c) social and material structural conditions that enable all cultural communities to participate in decisions that affect the quality of our lives; and (d) consistent and on-going policies and practices to ensure just and equitable access to cultural and material resources and institutional support (Adams & Goldbard, 1995).

With these communal commitments in mind, the inclusiveness and socially just emphasis of a culturally democratic philosophy of education functions to counter persistent colonizing values of the past, which have become normalized within most US mainstream institutions, including the Church and Catholic education, and imposed on Latino, Black, and indigenous communities and additional populations perceived as "others." In response, values and attitudes that require rethinking include commonsensical beliefs in progress that privilege the dominant epistemology and culture as superior and enact ethnocentric policies and practices to dominate and control those perceived as less worthy of opportunities or less capable of self-governance. These values inherent to dominant discourses of modernity prevail within Catholic schools and other societal institutions, steeped in values that celebrate self-reliance and bootstrap individualism over communal values of interdependence and cooperation, more prevalent in the epistemological worldview of working-class Latino communities.

Central to the concept of cultural democracy is a fundamental relationship that exists between culture and power. By culture, this refers here to all the relational and organizational structures—historically, socially, and materially situated—around which relations of power are organized within institutions, communities, and societies. Embedded within cultural relationships of individual and communal life are the underlying philosophical and epistemological assumptions about that world and the different configurations of power relations that conserve ways of being considered legitimate and superior (Darder, 2012). It is precisely this relationship between culture and power and its movement within the context of a dominant culture that subordinates those considered "other," which is usually missing from mainstream discourses of multiculturalism or cultural inclusivity. Instead, there is political pretense that when any two cultures come in contact, they are on an equal playing field. History plainly demonstrates that nothing could be farther from the truth. The consequence then is that, without addressing the deeper oppressive structures predicated on Eurocentric cultural notions of truth, structural inequalities remain untouched in society, the Church, and schools.

Hence, in order to understand and critically engage the relationship between culture and power, Catholic educators must also comprehend the dynamics that exist between what is considered truth (or knowledge) and power—for it is this relationship that must be questioned with respect to its ethnocentric impact on schooling and control over what constitutes knowledge in Catholic schools today.

> Truth ... is produced only by virtue of multiple forms of constraint. And it induces regular effects of power. Each society has its regime of truth, its "general politics" of truth: that is, the types of discourse which it accepts and makes function as true; the mechanisms and instances which enable one to distinguish true and false statements; the means by which each is sanctioned; the techniques and procedures accorded value in the acquisition of truth; the status of those who are charged with saying what counts as true.
>
> (Foucault, 1977, p. 131)

As such, those in power shape our understanding of the world. So, while individuals shape their own identities, the power relations that determine what constitutes legitimate truths are also shaping us. Joe Kincheloe (2008), for example, explained that in the 1700s, Western societies came to see that it was far more efficient to utilize power to influence individual consciousness in ways that supported the interests of the powerful, rather than to resort to brutal force in seeking compliance. "Power connects with the heart and soul of individuals, disciplines their bodies, shapes their attitudes, their language, the ways they learn, and their phenomenological level of existence. In such a disciplined society, power wielders would not have to use violence as often, as they could count on the citizen's individual consciousness to mold their behaviors" (p. 219). An implicit but important assumption here is that, if the process of schooling is to be informed by cultural democracy, Catholic educators must recognize that the inability of Latino communities to express our cultural truths is directly tied to asymmetrical relations of power that subordinate the expression of our cultural knowledge, wisdom, and ways of being.

Dominant and Subordinate Cultures

A dialectical or relational view of culture and its link to social power is essential to understanding the dominant cultural logic that upholds culturally subordinate or repressive power relations that exist in American society and, thus, can be tenaciously embedded in Catholic Church and school policies and practices. Culture then does not function in a vacuum, but rather as a social system characterized by social stratification and tensions (Freire & Macedo, 1987). It is also significant to note that subordinate cultures are marginalized not only through the dominant culture's function to legitimate the interests and values of dominant groups, but also through an ideology that invalidates Latino cultural values, heritage, language, knowledge, and lived experiences that fall outside the purview of the Western gaze—this points to significant human dimensions that are essential for the survival of subordinate cultures. Keeping this in mind can help us understand how Latinos, for example, are situated and recreated within social and material processes of society that are, in fact, inextricably shaped by a politics of assimilation. And this is only perpetuated through a hidden curriculum that obscures relations of power and decultures those students considered inferior or problematic to the dominant ethos.

Cultural Invasion

Throughout American institutions, including the Church, the dominant culture employs dominant practices that exert control over working-class racialized populations and, by so doing, perpetuates a condition that Freire (1970) called *cultural invasion*. This speaks to antidialogical processes that sustain social, political, and economic oppression of subordinate groups. Freire (1971) described cultural invasion as a process by which

> The invaders penetrate the cultural context of another group, in disrespect of the latter's potentialities; they impose their own view of the world upon those they invade and inhibit the creativity of the invaded by curbing their expression .... The invaders act; those they invade have only the illusion of acting through the action of the invaders .... All domination involves invasion ... a form of economic and cultural domination.
>
> (p. 150)

Given the impact of schooling processes shaped by the subordinating forces of cultural invasion, any attempt to create an effective educational foundation for Latino students must also challenge ethnocentric ideologies and practices that result in further domination of students, based on the color of their skin and the language they speak. Understanding, therefore, how the dominant culture perpetuates the internalization of inferiority, language domination, racism, and the debilitating impact of these on the academic formation of Latino students is key to breaking free from culturally invasive dynamics that betray our well-meaning efforts to serve Latino communities.

Internalization of Inferiority

One of the most insidious aspects in how the process of cultural invasion functions is through the internalization of inferiority, which is then often perpetuated by Latinos students and their families. So often this results from a process of schooling that has systematically conditioned Latino students to identify with the assumed superiority of the dominant culture to the extent that they participate in their own cultural negation. About this, Freire (1970), argued,

> for cultural invasion to succeed, it is essential that those invaded become convinced of their intrinsic inferiority ... The more invasion is accentuated and those invaded are alienated from the spirit of their own culture and from themselves, the more the latter want to be like the invaders: to walk like them, dress like them, talk like them.
>
> (p. 161)

This is precisely what a culturally democratic educational practice seeks to transform, so that Latino students within Catholic education and beyond can truly find the place to be themselves and to exercise their cultural knowledge and language as an asset to their academic formation, rather than a hindrance.

Language Domination

Language domination is sustained via a twofold process. First, the language that many bicultural students bring to the classroom is systematically silenced and stripped away, through values and beliefs that render it inferior to Standard English. Second, the traditional literacy process in US schools perpetuates subordinate social relations through an instrumental approach that functions to discourage the development of critical literacy among working-class Latino students (Nieto, 2009; Diaz-Soto & Haroon, 2010). Accordingly, many Latino students are forced to contend with institutional negation and disrespect of their linguistic codes. In many Catholic schools, Latino students are not only discouraged but also actively prevented from speaking their native language. Catholic educators often justify these practices with concerns that Spanish will interfere with the student's intellectual and emotional development (Ramirez, Castaneda, & Herold, 1974; Grande, 2004; Diaz-Soto & Haroon, 2010). No matter how well-meaning, Freire and Macedo (1987) point to the xenophobic beliefs that undergird this view, which

> blindly negates the pluralistic nature of U.S. society and falsifies the empirical evidence in support of bilingual education, as has been amply documented. These educators ... fail to understand that it is through multiple discourses that students generate meaning in their everyday social context.
>
> (p. 154)

Therefore, it is critical that Catholic educators recognize the role language plays as one of the most powerful transmitters of culture and, as such, its central role to both intellectual formation and the survival of subordinate cultural populations. Within a student's primary language is contained the codification of lived experiences that provide avenues for students to express their own realities and to question the wider social order. Similarly, the primary language holds huge significance with respect to learning and brain development (Lipina & Colombo, 2009) and to children's formation of self-confidence and sense of intimacy and security within their own cultural community—both hugely significant to the academic formation of Latino children. Catholic school practices that ignore the significance of students' primary language unwittingly hinder students' critical capacities and prevent the development of understanding necessary to their intellectual development and social empowerment.

Racism

Racism represents one of the most pervasive forms of human oppression in US society today and yet, it seems one of the most difficult for individuals of the dominant culture to comprehend. Often the difficulty arises in faulty perceptions and assumptions that persist in the epistemological framework of Euroamericans. In addition to strong ethnocentric values, much of the difficulty here is related to a pervasive and commonsensical ideology of race, with its hierarchical view of races, coupled with a worldview that effectively obstructs the ability of most Euroamericans to move from an individual perception of bias and prejudice to an understanding of racism as a structural phenomenon associated with institutional power and control and perpetuated through the process of schooling. This is particularly so when questions of inequalities are simultaneously tied to class privilege. Yet, the ability to comprehend racism as an institutional phenomenon is essential to addressing educational policies and practices of inequality in Catholic schools (McCarthy, et al., 2005).

Racism in the form of ethnocentrism most often manifests in standards of behavior considered color-blind, by which everything is judged and compared. These standards are based on the implicit assumptions of the dominant culture that retains power within a multicultural society (Phillips, 1979; Parker, Deyhle, & Villenas, 1999). This phenomenon is particularly prevalent in color-blind views that persist in Catholic schools today. The hidden curriculum of white superiority silences the voices of Latino students, by ignoring their experiences of racism. Hence, unexamined racialized assumptions support an assimilative bias held by many Catholic educators—well-meaning and devout teachers who too often fail to perceive the racism embedded in their tendencies to judge and compare the success of poor and working-class Latino students against that of more affluent students from the dominant culture.

However, most Catholic educators seem genuinely unaware of their unexamined expectations and everyday practices that loudly signal to Latino students that in order to "succeed," they must adopt dominant cultural values as their own. Well-meaning Catholic educators often, similarly, express that they "love all their students" or that they believe "all people are the same," or that they "treat all students the same," without acknowledging either the cultural differences or the asymmetrical relations of power at work within their classrooms. The most damaging consequence of this approach, of course, is that Catholic educators can fail to see that Latina and Latino students already possess cultural values and community knowledge that are not only essential to their learning, but to their survival—given their community histories of struggle in the face of gross inequalities and social exclusions. Many Catholic educators can, therefore, easily miss the essence, nuances, and inner complexities that are inherent to being bicultural; and, thus, inadvertently invalidate the lived experiences of Latino students by rejecting the definitions and meanings that Latino students and parents offer about their own lives and their communities.

Important to this discussion is also the distinction between individual racism and institutional racism. "The first consists of overt acts by individuals ... the second type is less overt, far more subtle, less identifiable in terms of specific individuals committing the acts. But it is no less destructive of human life" (Ture & Hamilton, 1992, p. 4). Some concrete examples may help to shed some light on this distinction. When a teacher consistently nags and humiliates Latino students because they do not speak "proper" English, this is an act of individual racism. But when a community of Latino parents complains to the principal or parish priest and no action is taken to halt the teacher's actions, then, it becomes a form of institutional racism. When a social studies teacher glosses over the impact of colonization and presents the story as one of benevolence, this is an act of individual racism. That this teacher is knowingly permitted by school administrators to perpetuate this discourse in the classroom is an act of institutional racism. What is most significant here is that both forms of racism result from deep-rooted prejudices and stereotypes. But institutional racism is a form of racialized discrimination that is woven into the fabric of the power relations, social arrangements (i.e., school policies), and practices through which collective actions result in the use of a racialized criterion to determine who is inequitably rewarded in schools (Knowles & Prewitt, 1969). Institutional racism can only result when it is, knowingly or unknowingly, bolstered by institutional resources, power, and authority.

In direct opposition, a culturally democratic practice can only be accomplished when institutional resources, power, and authority are utilized in the interest of genuinely democratic attitudes and relationships with respect to differences. Hence, in the same spirit of institutional justice and human equality forged in John Dewey's (1916) education writings or Paulo Freire's (1970) *Pedagogy of the Oppressed*, the concept of cultural democracy seeks to function here as an educational perspective, in concert with Catholic social teachings, that can transform the ethnocentric constriction of mainstream classroom life. Above all, it represents a concerted effort to awaken and cultivate the voices and participation of Latino students as active social actors within the Church, their education, and in the world.

Rethinking the Role of the Church

Today, we need a Church capable of walking at people's side, of doing more than simply listening to them; a Church which accompanies them on their journey; a Church able to make sense of the 'night' contained in the flight of so many of our brothers and sisters from Jerusalem; a Church which realizes that the reasons why people leave also contain reasons why they can eventually return. But we need to know how to interpret, with courage, the larger picture.

—Pope Francis[14]

What does this extensive discussion mean for the role of the Church and Catholic education in Latino communities? Latinos, as the country's fastest-growing ethnic population, now make up nearly 40 percent of all Catholics and this number is expected to grow in the coming years, as the birthrate of Latinos exceeds all other ethnic populations in the United States. Today, approximately 60 percent of all Latinos identify as Catholic; and Latino immigrant populations are said to be "contributing significantly to the stability of American Catholicism" (Shrank, 2013, n.p.). Hence, there is no doubt that the Church continues to serve as an important hub for Latino community life and particularly for Spanish-speaking congregants; and, as such, can play a pivotal role in supporting the educational advancement of Latino communities in this country.

Typically, however, the Church has taken a more passive role on educational debates seen as outside the purview of Church orthodoxy. Yet, today, even within the Church, there is growing concern with decreasing enrollment in Catholic schools. In the past decade, 16 percent of Catholic schools across the nation closed. Enrollment nationwide declined 23 percent, driven by a variety of factors, including changes in demography. Nevertheless, only about 4 percent of all Latino children currently attend Catholic schools. This suggests that if the Church is to support Latino communities, its exclusive focus on parochial education must be rethought, along with any deficit perspectives that might betray the emancipatory interests of Latino children.

For example, Catholic education within the Latino community has often played a paradoxical role. The commonsense belief in the superiority of Catholic private education inadvertently has served to reinscribe a meritocracy of class privilege and power. Historically, Catholic students who were admitted and whose parents could afford to pay for tuition were considered an exclusive group, seen as deserving of greater privilege and opportunities, than the excluded. Meanwhile, students who did not pass the entrance exam or whose family could not afford the tuition were considered justifiably excluded. Seldom questioned were the politics of testing or culturally oppressive practices or the material conditions of inequality that influenced the academic performance of excluded students. Some of these attitudes, unfortunately, persist even today with authoritarian proponents that advocate for steeper practices of competition as the solution to effective intellectual formation.

Whether one agrees with this view or not, the question remains: What of the other 96 percent of Latino students who attend other systems of education? The question is a legitimate one to consider here, given that educational rights have been a central concern of the Church in the United States. In fact, Catholic schooling began "in a spirit of protest," when Church leaders of the mid-1800s protested the discrimination of Catholic children, who were forced to read Protestant texts. Ignored and maligned by state legislatures, the Church turned to its congregations, demanding that every parish build and support a school and that all Catholic families enroll their children in a Catholic school. The result was the largest private school system in the world, entirely supported by a largely working-class minority population. Moreover, sisters from religious orders predominantly staffed Catholic schools[15] during this era—an exceedingly important factor in the growth of the parochial school system in this country.

It is this same spirit of protest that now must ignite Church concerns related to the material and cultural discrimination of Latino communities today. The Church cannot afford to see the issue of education within solely a Catholic vacuum, but rather must see it as a larger community question, deserving of the Church's attention and investment. This to suggest that the Church must take a proactive leadership role in creating the conditions by which Latino communities can reflect and act upon the importance of education. This echoes Pope Francis' sentiment in *Apostolic Letter to All the Consecrated People on the Occasion of the Year of Consecrated Life*, "I also expect from you what I have asked all the members of the Church: to come out of yourselves and go forth to the existential peripheries" (2014, No. 4). Such a process of going forth entails working with communities in ways that support a shared vision and humanizing purpose for education. Moreover, this work must be understood in concert with the Church's responsibility to act in solidarity with the most vulnerable populations, in order to transform the discriminatory conditions of their lives. This idea is clearly in sync with the tenets of Catholic social teaching, which views the work with the most vulnerable populations as central to the Church's mission in the world.

Here Church authority and Catholic school leadership must move to abandon authoritarian postures, in order to cultivate greater possibilities for ecumenical dialogue and solidarity with and among disenfranchised Latino populations. Accordingly, the establishment of liberatory relationships with formerly colonized populations such as Latino in the United States must also encompass a commitment to the process of decolonization. This to say, the Church's relationship with Latino populations must go beyond traditional missionary paradigms, which have oftentimes reinscribed deficit notions. Instead, ministerial and pedagogical relationships with Latino communities must be anchored to the concrete experiences and conditions of our everyday lives. The Church can work through its Catholic educational leaders to consider larger questions of schooling, in ways that promote the social agency, responsibility, and consciousness of the Church, school, and community, in the interest of greater educational justice for Latino students—within and outside the traditional scope of the Church. Just as Catholic congregants are expected to bring our faith to all secular arenas, so too should the Church be a living example of struggle for the most vulnerable in the world today—but not in ways that perpetuate a view of the vulnerable as welcomed outsider, but rather as members of the human family that must also have a place at the table of decision-making and the future evolution of both the Church and society. Beyond its powerful pedagogical role at the pulpit, the Church must then take up Pope Francis's edict to walk alongside Latino communities and accompany us on our journey toward building a better world.

Catholic Education as Revolutionary Labor

I ask you, instead, to be revolutionaries, to swim against the tide; yes, I am asking you to rebel against this culture that sees everything as temporary and that ultimately believes that you are incapable of responsibility, that you are incapable of true love.

—Pope Francis[16]

In many of his recent public proclamations, Pope Francis has called upon the clergy, the faithful, and the world to not only reinstate our concern for the poor, but also to be revolutionaries and rebels in this time of crisis, against the loveless forces of oppression that spiritually and materially impoverish us all. The "true love" that Pope Francis references above is reminiscent of Paulo Freire's pedagogy of love and Gustavo Gutierrez's "theology as a love letter." This is a love for the Divine that goes beyond dogma, disembodied theory, or affiliations, to unite the love of the Church and the people in action within community, for the well-being of our brethren and the world. This declaration of love by the Pope must fully inform Catholic education in the Latino community and the Church's commitment to a socially just world.

Similarly, through integrating the seven principles of Catholic social teaching—life and dignity of the human person; family, community and participation; rights and responsibilities; option for the poor and vulnerable; dignity of work and rights of workers; solidarity; and care for God's creation (USCCB, 2005)—in conjunction with cultural democracy, a more justly grounded sense of well-being and community can potentially evolve, through fostering authentic relationships of participation between Latino communities and the Church. Moreover, through culturally democratic strategies founded on Catholic social teaching (Heft, 2006), policies and practices of inequality that interfere with the spiritual and educational formation of Latino communities within the Church, Catholic schools, and the larger society can be better challenged and transformed, with greater coherence to principles of social justice. This entails recognition that in order to bring about both attitudinal and structural change requires the combined efforts of all, working as both individuals and in community. This is particularly salient for Latino communities which will be most affected by the new conditions that should emerge. Ultimately, social change requires commitment, faith, and personal strength by Church leadership and Catholic educators to work with parishioners in the world.

This revolutionary labor encompasses a deep and humble commitment to communal participation and an underlying faith in the capacity of the people to evolve and reinvent together structures that can meet the essential needs of their lives. This, undoubtedly, encompasses a dramatic shift in the exercise of power and the establishment of more horizontal relationships that open the epistemological field for the evolution of consciousness and the transformation of education. Catholic education by this definition must welcome the Latino community itself, with policies and practices enacted in our primary culture and language. By so doing, a powerful praxis, founded on love and dignity, can support the critical dialogue required to reflect, to name, to critique, and to learn together, so that our teaching can work to dismantle the injustice that chokes off our existence, as Catholics and citizens of the world. In his address from the pastoral visit to Cagliari in September 2013, Pope Francis asserts, "All the wars, all the strife, all the unresolved problems over which we clash are due to the lack of dialogue" (as cited in Birch, 2015). His uncompromising faith in the power of dialogue, rooted in love, serves then as an indispensable ethical foundation for a humanizing pedagogy for Church ministry and for Catholic education.

Pope Francis calls for a transformation of consciousness for Catholics and non-Catholics alike; and that we take on this challenge with courage, commitment, and resolve. Hence, the Church too must change in its practice and aspire more fully to stretch beyond the boundaries of its place of sanctuary and security, as we must all. And this we must do in order to work together in the mundane world of our everyday lives—where quotidian forms of educational injustices have become most normalized and persistent. It is here that a culturally democratic form of Catholic education can best cultivate and nurture a place for on-going public dialogue for social justice. A revolutionary labor of Catholic educators then is one that focuses consistently on the establishment of humanizing relationships within the classroom and communities—relationships linked to the development of consciousness and social responsibility.

Through creating culturally democratic conditions of Catholic education, that center on dialogue and democratic participation in the life of the larger society, educational issues of Latino students can be linked effectively to the overall well-being of Latino families and their dreams of a better life for their children. The underlying assumption here is that the Church and Catholic education have a moral responsibility to be responsive to the needs of Latino populations, who constitute one of the most faithful populations in the Church. However, tending to the spiritual needs of a community, without serious regard for their culture or the larger societal forces that negatively impact their personal freedom and social development is not only shortsighted, but unconscionable in light of the radical commitment to the poor expressed by the Holy Father. Catholic Social Teaching anchored in culturally democratic principles—with an interest in both Church and community—seems an ideal place from which to tackle more substantive ethical and practical concerns with respect to the education of Latino students.

Through the integration of the cultural and linguistic knowledge of Latino communities within parochial education, Catholic educators committed to cultural democracy can also generate a deeper sense of familiarity, more fluidity in communication, and enter into communal solidarity with an oppressed population, who to this day remains in the process of democratic formation within the Church and beyond. Through encompassing an understanding of the culture, language, history, and the difficult conditions faced by Latinos in this hemisphere—along with a vision of faith, hope, and possibility—the work of Catholic educators for social justice can move toward a more participatory practice of education in Latino communities today.

Through its prominent intermediary role between Church and community, Catholic educators possess a vital opportunity to participate with Latino populations in the process of their democratic formation within the United States, many who may have had few opportunities for political participation in their lives, but yet yearn for a more just future for their children. By effectively interpreting, with courage and resolve, the oppressive conditions at work in the lives of Latino students, Latino Catholic educators, in particular, can serve as a viable humanizing force in this work. Anchored in an intimate knowledge of culture, history, language, and the biculturation experience, the Church in general and Catholic education in particular can begin to enter into a new relationship with Latino communities—one in which the voices and participation of Latino students reside at the center of the educational discourse, rather than ignored or forgotten on the margins.

Notes

1 Vatican Information Service (2013).
2 The US Council of Catholic Bishops' writing on Catholic education provides some thoughtful discussions on Church school formation and Church affiliation. See: http://www.usccb.org/beliefs-and-teachings/how-we-teach/catholic-education/
3 "Latinos" is inserted here in the place of "migrants and refugees," in that many of the issues faced by impoverished Latino communities in the United States echo concerns expressed by the Pope in this message. This is true for Latino immigrant populations, which now comprise an increasingly larger sector of the US Catholic Church.
4 Francis (2013b).
5 Although earlier projections for 2050 forecasted even more robust growth in the Latino population, projections in the last year indicate that, although the Latino population is expected to double to about 106 million, this is nearly 30 million lower than earlier projections published by the Census Bureau.
6 Founded in 2001, the Pew Hispanic Center is a nonpartisan research organization that seeks to improve understanding of the US Hispanic population and to chronicle Latinos' growing impact on the nation. See: http://www.pewhispanic.org/
7 Student diversity in Catholic schools has increased significantly in the past forty years. It is worth noting that when data were first collected, the Hispanic/Latino population was included and the reports listed non-whites as "minorities." In 1970, the diversity percentage was 10.8 percent, in 1980 it had increased to 19.4 percent and by 2010 was 29.8 percent. In 2015, the racial diversity was 20.4 percent and Hispanic/Latino was 15.3 percent (McDonald & Shultz, 2015).
8 It is worth noting that Ospino's (2014) report *Hispanic Ministry in Catholic Parishes* also illustrates the significance of Latino presence. In parishes with active Hispanic Ministries, both the number of Latino teachers and the enrollment of Latino children in parochial schools were considerably higher.
9 As cited in O'Leary (2013, n. p.).
10 This issue of deficient intelligence among Latino immigrant resurfaced in 2013 public debates spurred on by Harvard graduate Jason Richwine, whose doctoral dissertation advanced the notion that Hispanic populations have lower IQs than whites (Richwine, 2009). This argument is in the tradition of scientific racism formerly advanced by *Bell Curve* co-author Charles Murray (Herrnstein & Murray, 1996), Richwine's mentor at Harvard. This came to public attention after Richwine coauthored an immigration policy report (Rector & Richwine, 2013) for the

conservative think tank, the *Heritage Foundation*. For several thoughtful critiques of racism and intelligence testing, see *Chicano Education in the Era of Segregation* (Gonzalez, 2013) and *Culture and Power in the Classroom* (Darder, 2012).

11 See Acuña (2013) and Sánchez Walsh (2013) for images of the Católicos Por La Raza activities.
12 Francis (2013a).
13 This brief discussion of the concept of cultural democracy is based on earlier work that has appeared in *Culture & Power in the Classroom* (Darder, 1991). For a more substantive discussion of this topic see the 2nd edition of the text (Darder, 2012).
14 (Francis, 2013d).
15 National Catholic Educational Association report, *U.S. Catholic Elementary and Secondary Schools 2014–2015* (McDonald & Shultz, 2015) confirms the dramatic shift, where 97.2 percent of full-time professional staff is Laity, while today only 2.8 percent is Religious/Clergy.
16 Francis (2013c).

References

Acuña, R. F. (2013). "Católicos por la raza: 'God is beside you on the picketline' [Weblog post] (July 11)." Retrieved from http://www.notesfromaztlan.com/2013/07/11/catolicos-por-laraza-god-is-beside-you-on-the-picketline/.

Adams, D., and Goldbard, A. (1995), *Cultural Democracy: Introduction to an Idea*. Retrieved from http://www.wwcd.org/cd2.html.

Aguirre Jr., A. (2012), "Arizona's SB1070, Latino Immigrants and the Framing of Anti-immigrant Policies." *Latino Studies* 10(3): 385–94. doi:10.1057/lst.2012.28.

Aizenman, N. C. (2009), "Children of Illegal Immigrants Twice as Likely as Other Kids to Be Poor." *The Washington Post* (December 9). Retrieved from http://www.washingtonpost.com/wp-dyn/content/article/2009/12/08/AR2009120804446.html.

Annie E. Casey Foundation (2013). *Reducing Youth Incarceration in the United States* [Data snapshot report] (February). Retrieved from http://www.aecf.org/m/resourcedoc/AECF-DataSnapshotYouthIncarceration-2013.pdf.

Ash, B., Buck, C., Klerman, J. A., Kleykamp, M., and Loughran, D. S. (2009), *Military Enlistment of Hispanic Youth: Obstacles and Opportunities*. Retrieved from Rand Corporation website: http://www.rand.org/content/dam/rand/pubs/monographs/2009/RAND_MG773.pdf.

Birch, D. (2015), *The Wisdom of Pope Francis*. New York, NY: Skyhorse Publishing.

Burd-Sharps, S., and Lewis, K. (2012), *One in Seven: Ranking Youth Disconnection in the 25 Largest Metro Areas*. Retrieved from http://www.measureofamerica.org/one-in-seven/.

Cardenas, V., and Kirby, S. (2012), *The State of Latinos in the United States*. Retrieved from Center for American Progress website: https://cdn.americanprogress.org/wp-content/uploads/issues/2012/08/pdf/stateoflatinos.pdf.

Children's Defense Fund (2007), *America's Cradle to Prison Pipeline Report*. Retrieved from http://www.childrensdefense.org/programs-campaigns/cradle-to-prison-pipeline/.

Darder, A. (1991), *Culture and Power in the Classroom: A Critical Foundation for Bicultural Education*. Westport, CT: Bergin & Garvey.

Darder, A. (2012), *Culture and Power in the Classroom: Educational Foundations for the Schooling of Bicultural Students*, 2nd ed. Boulder, CO: Paradigm.

Darder, A. (2014), *Freire and Education*. New York, NY: Routledge.

Darder, A., and Torres, R. D. (2013), *Latinos and Education: A Critical Reader*. New York, NY: Routledge.

DeParle, J. (2012). "Harder for Americans to Rise from Lower Rungs." *New York Times* (January 4). Retrieved from http://www.nytimes.com/2012/01/05/us/harder-for-americans-to-risefrom-lower-rungs.html?pagewanted=all&_r=0.

Deutsch, L. (2011), "Arizona Voter ID Law Challenged in Court." *The Huffington Post*. Retrieved from: http://www.huffingtonpost.com/2011/06/22/arizona-voter-id-lawcourt_n_881957.html.

Dewey, J. (1916), *Democracy and Education*. New York, NY: MacMillan.

Diaz-Soto, L., and Haroon, K. (2010), *Teaching Bilingual/Bicultural Children*. New York, NY: Peter Lang.

Domhoff, D. W. (2013), "Wealth, Income, and Power [Web log post]." Retrieved from http://whorulesamerica.net/power/wealth.html.

Fix School Discipline (2012), "Los Angeles students, parents, and teachers call for national moratorium on out-of-school suspensions [Web log post] (August 21)." Retrieved from http://fixschooldiscipline.org/los-angeles-students-parents-and-teachers-join-nationalsolutions-not-suspensions-campaign-to-halt-out-of-school-suspensions/.

Foucault, M. (1977), *Discipline and Punish: The Birth of the Prison*. New York, NY: Pantheon Books.

Francis (2013a), "Audience with Representatives of the Churches and Ecclesial Communities and of the Different Religions: Address of the Holy Father Pope Francis." Retrieved from http://w2.vatican.va/content/francesco/en/speeches/2013/march/documents/papafrancesco_20130320_delegati-fraterni.html.

Francis (2013b), "Meeting with the Bishops of Brazil: Address of Pope Francis." Retrieved from https://w2.vatican.va/content/francesco/en/speeches/2013/july/documents/papafrancesco_20130727_gmg-episcopato-brasile.html.

Francis (2013c), "Meeting with the Volunteers of the XXVIII WYD: Address of Pope Francis." Retrieved from http://w2.vatican.va/content/francesco/en/speeches/2013/july/documents/papa-francesco_20130728_gmg-rio-volontari.html.

Francis (2013d), "Message of His Holiness Pope Francis for the World Day of Migrants and Refugees 2014." Retrieved from https://w2.vatican.va/content/francesco/en/messages/migration/documents/papa-francesco_20130805_world-migrants-day.html.

Francis (2014), "Apostolic Letter to All the Consecrated People on the Occasion of the Year of Consecrated Life (November 21)." Retrieved from https://w2.vatican.va/content/francesco/en/apost_letters/documents/papa-francesco_lettera-ap_20141121_lettera-consacrati.html.

Freire, P. (1970), *Pedagogy of the Oppressed*. New York, NY: Seabury Press.

Freire, P. (1998), *Pedagogy of Freedom: Ethics, Democracy and Civic Courage*. Lanham, MD: Rowman & Littlefield Publishers.

Freire, P., and Macedo, D. (1987), *Literacy: Reading the Word and the World*. New York, NY: Praeger.

Fry, R., and Lopez, M. H. (2012), *Hispanic Student Enrollments Reach New Highs in 2011*. Retrieved from Pew Hispanic Center website: http://www.pewhispanic.org/2012/08/20/hispanicstudent-enrollments-reach-new-highs-in-2011/.

Fry, R., and Taylor, P. (2013), "Hispanic High School Graduates Pass Whites in Rate of College Enrollment (May 9)." Retrieved from Pew Hispanic Center website: http://www.pewhispanic.org/2013/05/09/hispanic-high-school-graduates-pass-whites-in-rate-ofcollege-enrollment/.

Gramsci, A. (1971), *Selections from the Prison Notebooks*. New York, NY: International Publishers.

Greenstone, M., Looney, A., Patashnik, J., and Yu, M. (2013), "Thirteen Facts about Mobility and the Role of Education." Retrieved from the Brookings Institute website: http://www.brookings.edu/research/reports/2013/06/13-facts-higher-education.

Gonzalez, G. G. (2013), *Chicano Education in the Era of Segregation*, 2nd ed. Denton, TX: University of North Texas Press.

Grande, S. (2004), *Red Pedagogy: Native American Social and Political Thought*. New York, NY: Rowman & Littlefield.

Hammond, C., Linton, D., Smink, J., and Drew, S. (2007), *Dropout Risk Factors and Exemplary Programs*. Retrieved from National Dropout Prevention Center website: http://www.dropoutprevention.org/resource/major_reports/communities_in_schools/Dropout%20Risk%20Factors%20and%20Exemplary%20Programs%20FINAL%205-16-07.pdf.

Heft, J. (2006), "Catholic Education and Social Justice." *Catholic Education: A Journal of Inquiry and Practice* 10(1): 6–23.

Herrnstein, R. J., and Murray, C. (1996), *Bell Curve: Intelligence and Class Structure in American Life*. New York, NY: Free Press.

Kelly, A., Schneider, M., and Carey, K. (2010), *Rising to the Challenge: Hispanic College Graduation Rates as a National Priority*. Retrieved from American Enterprise Institute website: http://www.aei.org/files/2010/03/18/Rising-to-the-Challenge.pdf.

Kincheloe, J. (2008), *Knowledge and Critical Pedagogy: An Introduction*. New York, NY: Springer.

Knefel, M. (2013), *The School-to-Prison Pipeline: A Nationwide Problem for Equal Rights*. Retrieved from http://www.rollingstone.com/music/news/the-school-to-prison-pipeline-anationwide-problem-for-equal-rights-20131107.

Knowles, L. L., and Prewitt, K. (1969), *Institutional Racism in America*. Upper Saddle River, NJ: Prentice Hall.

Kochhar, R., and Fry, R. (2014), *Wealth Inequality Has Widened along, Racial, Ethnic Lines since the End of Great Recession*. Retrieved from Pew Research Center website: http://www.pewresearch.org/fact-tank/2014/12/12/racial-wealth-gaps-great-recession/.

Krogstad, J. M. (2014), *With Fewer New Arrivals, Census Lowers Hispanic Population Projections*. Retrieved from Pew Research Center website: http://www.pewresearch.org/facttank/2014/12/16/with-fewer-new-arrivals-census-lowers-hispanic-populationprojections-2/.

Lipina, S. J., and Colombo, J. A. (2009), *Poverty and Brain Development during Childhood: An Approach from Cognitive Psychology and Neuroscience*. Washington, DC: American Psychological Association.

Lopez, M. H. (2009), *Latinos and Education: Explaining the Attainment Gap*. Retrieved from Pew Hispanic Center website: http://www.pewhispanic.org/2009/10/07/latinos-andeducation-explaining-the-attainment-gap/.

Lopez, M. H., and Velasco, G. (2011), *Childhood Poverty among Hispanics Sets Record, Leads Nation* (September 28). Retrieved from Pew Hispanic Center website: http://www.pewhispanic.org/2011/09/28/childhood-poverty-among-hispanics-sets-record-leads nation/.

Losen, D. J., and Martinez, T. E. (2013), *Out of School & Off Track: The Overuse of Suspensions in American Middle and High Schools*. Los Angeles, CA: The Center for Civil Rights Remedies. Retrieved from the Civil Rights Project website: http://civilrightsproject.ucla.edu/resources/projects/center-for-civil-rights-remedies/school-to-prison-folder/federal-reports/out-of-school-and-off-track-the-overuse-of-suspensions-in-americanmiddle-and-high-schools/OutofSchool-OffTrack_UCLA_4-8.pdf.

McCarthy, C., Giardina, M., Harewood, S., and Park, J. (2005), "Contesting Culture," in C. McCarthy et al. (eds.), *Race, Identity and Representation*, 2nd ed. New York, NY: Routledge, 307–17.

McDonald, D., and Schultz, M. (2015), *United States Catholic Elementary and Secondary Schools, 2014–2015: The Annual Statistical Report on Schools, Enrollment, and Staffing*. Arlington, VA: National Catholic Education Association. Retrieved from https://www.ncea.org/datainformation/catholic-school-data.

Moll, L. C., Amanti, C., Neff, D., and González, N. (1992), "Funds of Knowledge for Teaching: Using a Qualitative Approach to Connect Homes and Classrooms." *Theory into Practice* 31(2): 132–41. doi: 10.1080/00405849209543534.

Motel, S., and Patten, E. (2012). *The 10 Largest Hispanic Origin Groups: Characteristics, Rankings, Top Counties* (June 27). Retrieved from Pew Hispanic Center website: http://www.pewhispanic.org/2012/06/27/the-10-largest-hispanic-origin-groups-characteristicsrankings-top-counties/.

Murnane, R. J. (2013), *U.S. High School Graduation Rates: Patterns and Explanations*. National Bureau of Economic Research (Working Paper No. 18701). Retrieved from http://www.nber.org/papers/w18701.pdf.

National Center for Education Statistics (2008). "The Condition of Education 2008 (NCES 2008-031)." Washington, DC.

The Nation's Report Card (2013), 2013 "Mathematics and Reading". Retrieved from http://www.nationsreportcard.gov/reading_math_2013/#/student-groups.

Nieto, S. (2009), *Culture, Language and Teaching: Critical Perspectives*. New York, NY: Routledge.

O'Leary, N. (2013), "Pope Francis Attacks 'Tyranny' of Unfettered Capitalism, 'Idolatry of Money' (November 26)." Retrieved from http://worldnews.nbcnews.com/_news/2013/11/26/21623507-pope-francis-attacks-tyranny-of-unfettered-capitalismidolatry-of-money?lite.

Orfield, G., Kucera, J., and Siegel-Hawley, G. (2012), *E pluribus … Separation: Deepening Double Segregation for Students: Executive Summary*. Retrieved from the Civil Rights Project website: http://civilrightsproject.ucla.edu/research/k-12-education/integration-anddiversity/mlk-national/e-pluribusseparation-deepening-double-segregation-formore-students/.

Ospino, H. (2014), *Hispanic Ministry in Catholic Parishes: A Summary Report of Findings from the National Study of Catholic Parishes with Hispanic Ministry*. Boston, MA: Boston College. Retrieved from http://www.bc.edu/content/dam/files/schools/stm/pdf/2014/HispanicMinistryinCatholicParishes_2.pdf.

Panzar, J. (2015), "It's Official: Latinos Now Outnumber Whites in California." *Los Angeles Times* (July 8). Retrieved from http://www.latimes.com/local/california/la-me-census-latinos20150708-story.html.

Parker, L., Deyhle, D., and Villenas, S. (1999), *Race Is … Race Isn't: Critical Race Theory and Qualitative Studies in Education*. Boulder, CO: Perseus Books Group.

Passel, J., and Cohn, D. (2008), *U.S. Population Projections: 2005–2050*. Retrieved from Pew Hispanic Center website: http://www.pewhispanic.org/2008/02/11/us-populationp rojections-2005-2050/.

Phillips, C. (1979), "Rethinking the Study of Black Behavior," in *Collective Monographs I: Toward a Black Perspective in Education*. Pasadena, CA: Stage 7, 11–30.

Pineda, A. M. (2005), *The History and Experience of Latinos/Hispanics in the United States*. Retrieved from http://www.mercyworld.org/_uploads/_ckpg/files/mirc/papers/pinedaA4.pdf.

Ramirez, M., Castaneda, A., and Herold, P. L. (1974), "The Relationship of Acculturation to Cognitive Style among Mexican Americans." *Journal of Cross-Cultural Psychology* 5(4): 424–33.

Rector, R., and Richwine, J. (2013), "The Fiscal Cost of Unlawful Immigrants and Amnesty to the U.S. Taxpayer (Report No. 133) (May 6)." Retrieved from Heritage Foundation website: http://www.heritage.org/research/reports/2013/05/the-fiscal-cost-of-unlawfulimmigrants-and-amnesty-to-the-us-taxpayer.

Reeves, R. V., and Howard, K. (2013), "The Glass Floor: Education, Downward Mobility, and Opportunity Hoarding." Retrieved from the Brookings Institution website: http://www.brookings.edu/research/interactives/2013/income-mobility-and-education.

Richwine, J. (2009), *IQ and Immigration Policy* (Doctoral dissertation). Available from ProQuest Dissertations and Theses database (UMI No. 3365409).

San Miguel Jr., G. (2013), *Those Who Dared: Ethnic Mexican Struggles for Education in the Southwest since the 1960s*. College Station: Texas A&M University Press.

Sánchez Walsh, A. (2013), "Catolicos por la raza & remembering the Chicano moratorium [Web log post]." Retrieved from http://usreligion.blogspot.com/2013/08/politicalcatholics-catolicos-por-la.html.

Shrank, A. (2013), "Dwindling Catholic Schools See Future in Latino Students. *Catholic News Service* (February 28)." Retrieved from http://www.religionnews.com/2013/02/28/catholic-schools-seek-out-latino-students/.

Suhy, T. (2012), "Sustaining the Heart: Attracting Latino Families to Inner-City Catholic Schools." *Catholic Education: A Journal of Inquiry and Practice* 15(2): 270–94.

Taylor, P., Gonzalez-Barrera, A., Passel, J. S., and Lopez, M. H. (2012), *An Awakened Giant: The Hispanic Electorate Is Likely to Double by 2030*. Retrieved from Pew Hispanic Center website: http://www.pewhispanic.org/2012/11/14/an-awakened-giant-the-hispanicelectorate-is-likely-to-double-by-2030/.

Ture, K., and Hamilton, C. V. (1992), *Black Power: The Politics of Liberation*. New York, NY: Vintage Books.

U.S. Census Bureau, Population Division (2008), "Projected Population by Single Year of Age, Sex, Race, and Hispanic Origin for the United States." July 1, 2000 to July 1, 2050. Retrieved from https://www.census.gov/population/projections/data/national/2008.html.

USCCB (2005), Seven Themes of Catholic Social Teaching (Publication No. 5-315). Retrieved from http://www.usccb.org/beliefs-and-teachings/what-we-believe/catholic-socialteaching/seven-themes-of-catholic-social-teaching.cfm.

Vatican Information Service (2013), "Pope, in Dialogue with Students of Jesuit-run Schools, Affirms That Poverty in the World Is a Scandal (June 7)." Retrieved from http://visnews-en.blogspot.com/2013/06/pope-in-dialogue-with-students-of.html.

Antonia Darder holds the Leavey Endowed Chair of Ethics and Moral Leadership at Loyola Marymount University and is Professor Emerita of the University of Illinois, Urbana Champaign.

Part 6

Critical Pedagogy, Social Justice, and the Politics of Difference

Introduction

Considered the "father" of critical pedagogy, Paulo Freire has undoubtedly left his influence on critical pedagogues and scholars. In a similar fashion, Antonia Darder, a critical pedagogy elder and multidimensional thinker, has arguably had a similar impact within the field of critical pedagogy and social justice. This section intends to offer a more expansive view of Darder's oeuvre in ways that illustrate her contributions and impact on the field of critical pedagogy and the struggle for social justice. In these times of watered-down interventions, miseducative practices, and attacks on critical theoretical frames, Darder's writings and life have offered a grounding and recentering of the essence of what it means to be committed to an opening of our consciousness through a critical pedagogical stance. The sampling of texts in this section offers a mere glimpse into the depth and power of her work. We invite readers to continue to visit and revisit her work with the same opening and expansiveness required of one's politics to continuously grapple with a changing world and a necessary reinvention of it.

Summary of Articles

In "Critical Leadership for Social Justice," Darder explicates the notion of leadership for social justice within the structures and logics of the neoliberal university. She points out the tensions and contradictions by unveiling the "hidden curriculum of patriarchy, racism, class apartheid, homophobia, and ableism that persist tenaciously within the traditional epistemological spheres and cultural practices of universities today" despite the rhetoric of diversity, equity, inclusion, and justice (DEIJ). This nauseating appropriation and expropriation of language within and beyond the university speak to public discourses that have very little interest in real institutional, structural, and material change, but rather a façade of quick-fixes and band-aid-like remedies to appease the mass. It is used as a tool for promotion and recruitment of student tuition and the almighty dollar—under the rubric of inclusivity. As Darder rightfully notes, the university today (more so than ever) exists as a "disturbing battleground, where ideas and practices can easily degenerate into a nightmare of undemocratic repression and bureaucratic madness." In light of this, notions of equality, public responsibility, and the common good have been undermined by the neoliberal ethos of greed, materialism, individualism, and competition.

Darder unveils some of the most pervasive "dirty little secrets" by systematically examining power and privilege at its core. She looks into the logic of neoliberalism within university life and where it is most impacted: graduate school education. Future academics and public intellectuals are inculcated into careerist orientations that police and discipline them (body, spirit, and mind) from the kind of transformative and critical knowledge needed to change the institution (and in the process, to change themselves). This is done so by directing (both implicitly and explicitly) young scholars to move away from emancipatory politics and ways of knowing and being—to a more narrowly defined knowledge construction and scholarly formation that "fit" neatly within the institution. By the time scholars and professors come to intellectual and political maturity (which takes vigilance, time, and tremendous energy), they have already been pushed to the margins of university life, departmental and governance decisions, and dustbins of history. Drawing on Peggy McIntosh's (1988) work on white privilege, Darder develops a set of critical principles that speak forthrightly to power and privilege. These principles and ethical commitments include the notion of critical leadership as (1) pedagogical, (2) a moral commitment, (3) a political act, (4) not a neutral affair, (5) purposeful, and (6) a dialectical process. Other indispensable qualities for critical praxis of leadership include (by not limited to) dialogue, conscientization, democratic negotiation, understanding context, question of ethics, and the notion of unfinishedness.

Darder's body of work is so expansive that we had to create a space for it to be honored. Whether it is writings and work within the medical field, on war, politics, bioethics, religion and/or spirituality, Darder is one of the powerful multidimensional thinkers of our time. In "Political Grace and Revolutionary Critical Pedagogy," Darder takes up the notion of spirituality and more critically the possibilities of political grace as a necessary component for our revolutionary movements for a more just world. Referred to as a communal dance of people yearning for freedom, political grace pushes back against the Western forms of spirituality that can strip away its power; it is force. Influenced by the expansiveness of critical pedagogy, her writings reflect a commitment to critical pedagogical formation that continues to evolve not only the field but the world which represents political grace as she writes about here as a form of love. Thus, to embrace a revolutionary critical pedagogy that is infused with political grace is to fight communally for freedom across our differences.

Another integral dimension of Antonia Darder's life is her artistry and how it is interwoven into all that she does in life. The piece "Radio and the Art of Resistance: A Public Pedagogy of the Airwaves" offers a small glimpse into Antonia Darder the artist. In this work, she offers community radio as a public pedagogical space that can support marginalized community voices. As a testament to her work and analyses, Darder offers a historical understanding of the airwaves and media in the age of neoliberalism to set the context for community radio as public pedagogy. *Liberacion!* as a radio collective represents critical pedagogy in public action that is tied to the needs of the oppressed and offers a counter-hegemonic space for community voice and alternative readings of the world. A public pedagogy coupled with the art of resistance represents for Darder a much-needed communal embodiment and understanding of knowledge that is transformative and life-affirming.

17

Political Grace and Revolutionary Critical Pedagogy

Political grace insists on an ethic of radical risk because the times require it, because the divine plane of creation that offers life is at risk itself from the holocaust of global plunder.

—Wes Rehberg (2012)

The risk of global plunder is evident around the globe, as corporations exert their rule over the material world, poverty intensifies, and complicit governments justify the denial of social welfare to oppressed populations. We live in an era where neoliberalism has made kowtowing to the interests of the wealthy and powerful above reproach and few courageous oppositional forces have garnered the means or public will to persist in campaigns of public protest. In many instances, the lethal combination of oppressive neoliberal policies and the veneration of technology has effectively ushered in the disposability of a lion share of the working class. No longer are the liberating promises of the enlightenment project, which sought to overcome the tyrannies of autocratic rule and incontrovertible abuses of professed Divine authority able to interrupt the ravages of capitalism at any level. Ecologically, the planet is suffering from what may well be irreparable colonization of the life's sphere, with its unmerciful and heedless destruction of forests, wildlife, soil potency, and water supplies. This ravaging of the earth, indeed, only echoes the violent estrangement and domestication of our own colonization, as the cultures and languages of subaltern populations are rapidly disappearing.

It is in the midst of grave economic exploitation and rampant disregard for the lives of the many that Freirian educators, scholars, and activists are called to risk a liberating praxis that embodies a new sense of revolutionary subjecthood and challenges our domesticated tolerances for societal injustice and human oppression. Simultaneously, emancipatory objectives of our pedagogical labor call for building a political solidarity that acknowledges the spiritual oneness of our humanity, while embracing the cultural differences in our expressions, as necessary biodiversity for our human survival and evolution. This entails that, rather than falling into us/them binaries that demonize and segment, we seek to retain the dialectical tensions that forever persist between the universalism of our humanity and the particularisms born from the survival of distinct cultural communities within different histories, material conditions, gendered and racialized relations, religious beliefs, and sexual orientations—all that deeply influence our various spiritual expressions and political sensibilities. Moreover, emancipatory struggles that affirm life necessitate we work to dismantle reified ideologies of capital, born of a mind that objectifies human spirituality, converting religious dogma into an instrument of exploitation and oppression.

As critical educators working to create pedagogical spaces for learning within what Paulo Freire (1998a) termed *unity within diversity*, we are obliged to create those necessary conditions within schools and society for communal openness, compassion, faith, and visionary hope that allow us to rethink spirituality, in our quest for freedom. For it is, indeed, within a politically thoughtful and compassionate arena of struggle that solidarity can unfold and liberating practices within schools and communities become possible. In essence, this signals recognition of a collective spiritual dimension that must manifest and unfold within our pedagogical and political praxis of community, if we are to genuinely extend our criticality beyond limiting and narrow allegiance to Western precepts of rationality. Herein then lies the extraordinary function of political grace as an integral spiritual force within the commons that can serve to better propel revolutionary movements for a more just world.

Political Grace: A Communal Dance of Revolution

If I can't dance, I don't want to be part of your revolution.
—Emma Goldman (1931)

Emma Goldman's often-repeated phrase serves as a useful metaphor for conceptualizing political grace as a revolutionary process that emerges precisely from a communal dance of people yearning for freedom. McLaren draws also on the power of this metaphor when he writes, "Knowing is a type of dance, a movement, but a self-conscious one. Criticality is not a line stretching into eternity, but rather it is a circle. In other words, knowing can be the object of our knowing, it can be self-reflective, and it is something in which we can make an intervention" (Mclaren, 2008, p. 476). There is no question that in our world today, there exists the pedagogical and political imperative for this communal dance, for this intervention, as a means for exercising the committed political interventions of radically motivated human beings who embody the class consciousness, liberatory spirituality, and critical praxis necessary to contend with the messiness, multiplicity, uncertainty, and ambiguity of our contemporary existence. At a time when so many people are historically disaffiliated from any emancipatory ethics of social struggles or have been usurped into a virtualized world that not only deceptively imprisons their sensibilities and manufactures their desires, grounded emancipatory political formation among teachers and students is urgently needed—a formation that recognizes the undemocratic fusion of transnational state interests with the transnational capitalist class (Robinson, 2014).

In Freire's writings, he repeatedly insisted that education is not only an essential political project for our liberation, but education must first and foremost serve as a humanizing endeavor, if just ideals are to be materialized. With this in mind, critical educators are compelled to labor with students and communities in integral ways that support the formation of consciously loving and engaged citizens—citizens who can challenge and transgress the asymmetrical relations of power and debilitating institutional structures in schools and communities that threaten democratic life. This signals an emancipatory educational process that prepares students, particularly from oppressed communities, for the expression of voice, participation in civil society, and ethical decision-making in all aspects of their life. A central political aim of this humanizing endeavor is to support the evolution of class consciousness with an explicit aim toward the establishment of a more harmonious and peaceful world. In this evolution of class consciousness, the communal spiritual dimension cannot be negated or ignored, given its constitutive potential to initiate and sustain committed revolutionary action.

This spiritual dimension of political grace is conceived here as a deeply multidimensional human phenomenon that counters the limiting ontological (beingness) and epistemological (knowingness) values at the heart of Western psychology, theology, and pedagogy interrogating the "normative premises upon which knowledge judgments are made" (Bekerman & Zemblayas, 2014, p. 53). It also "involves a larger epistemological fight against neoliberal and imperial common sense, and a grounding of our critical pedagogy in a concrete universal that can welcome diverse and particular social formations joined in class struggle" (McLaren, 2016, p. 37). This also draws on Boaventura de Sousa Santos' (2007) critique of the *abyssal divide*—where the cultural ways of knowing and the languages of "the other" are rendered irrelevant or outside the boundaries of legitimate rationality. Of this, Santos writes, "What most fundamentally characterizes abyssal thinking is thus *the impossibility* (italics added) of the co-presence of the two sides of the line. To the extent that it prevails, this side of the line only prevails by exhausting the field of relevant reality. Beyond it, there is only nonexistence, invisibility, non- dialectical absence" (1). So, whereas positivist psychology as well as the banking model of education (Freire, 1970) reduces the individual to an atomized object to be filled, fixed, or controlled, a critical pedagogical translation of political grace is rooted instead in the dialectic of the human being, as always *both* individual and communal entity, integrally immersed (as part of the human condition) within an evolving spiritually of both the individual and the world, simultaneously.

As such, political grace defies Calvinistic notions of monastic self-abnegation, that demand the individual transcendence from the lesh—in that "the children of God are shut with the prison of this mortal body" (Boer, 2009, p. 102). In contrast, a critical pedagogical understanding of political grace does not theorize human spirituality as either passive or depoliticized phenomenon, devoid of the lesh and its connection to the material world. Nor is the emergence of political grace dependent on official structures of organized religion, per se, although this view of spirituality may exist within such contexts if grounded in a communal liberatory intent (i.e., Liberation theology). However, this argument should not be mistakenly interpreted along the line of today's New Age obsession with Eastern meditation, for example, that attempts to make distinctions between religion and spirituality, as Slavoj Žižek (2011) warns.

Spiritual medication in its abstraction from institutionalized religion, appears today as the zero-level undistorted core of religion: the complex institutional and dogmatic edifice which sustains every particular religion is dismissed as a contingent secondary coating of this core. The reason for this shift of accent from religious institution to the intimacy of spiritual experience is that such a meditation is the ideological form that best its today's global capitalism. (28)

With this in mind, what is proposed here is a pedagogical understanding of spirituality that cannot be separated, objectified, or dehumanized, in that it exists as an integral force of humanity, enacted upon the world through communal engagement. This to say, an emancipatory expression of spirituality, as conceived here, eschews the notion that somewhere is found "a pure, universal core of 'undistorted' spirituality" (Anderson, 2013), but rather categorizes spirituality comparable to intellect or emotion—a human interactive faculty with the potential to express itself across the dialectical continuum of oppression and liberation. Hence, in this discussion of political grace, spirituality is grounded to a communal exercise of justice, which intrinsically seeks to counter what Žižek calls the "mad dance" of capitalism, the monstrosity of the globalized infrastructure of capitalist greed, and the deliberate destruction of the commons.

Perhaps more to the point, revolutionary social transformations are impossible without the active and organic participation of the people, who generate together, through their collective yearnings, labors, and struggles, the political force that ultimately makes possible the reinvention of the world. This can result, however, as much from a process of thoughtful deliberation as it can occur from a spontaneous communal response to the unbearable pressure of brutal repression over time. Political sociologist, George Katsiaficas (1989), terms this phenomenon *the Eros effect* in his study of social movements, where he draws on the work of Herbert Marcuse to define the underlying dialectical intent of his theory of Eros: "to reintegrate the emotional and the rational at a level on which emotional and irrational are not synonymous in their usages nor derogatory in their characterizations. I seek to affirm the emotional content of social movements as erotic action, action which may be considered collective liberatory sublimation—a rational way of clearing collective psychological blockages" (Katsiaficas, 1989, p. 2–3). This call for integration of the emotional and rational echoes Freire's (1993) insistence that educators acknowledge and contend with the totality of the human being; in that we come to know and *read the world* not only through the faculty of the mind, but also through the vital discernments of the heart, body, and spirit. To subjugate any of these dynamic human faculties can result in deeply flawed pedagogical and political efforts that will fail to grapple with the oppressor/oppressed contradiction, leaving the underlying structures of oppression unchanged.

More importantly, in the struggle for our liberation, critical pedagogical formation must support the ability to engage the complexity of our existence beyond the restrictive hegemonic arbitrations of the good/ bad or positive/negative splits. This is particularly so, in that major historical changes have seldom resulted without counterhegemonic acts of resistance and dissent being judged by the powerful as vulgar, wrongheaded, impulsive, violent, deceitful, and evil. Hence, to promote a concept of spirituality promulgated on an ontological dualism of good/bad humanity, wittingly or unwittingly, smothers the very ire necessary for democratic life. The consequence is a hegemonic political culture that infantilizes humanity, squelches dissent, and narrows rationality in ways that veil the wretched inequalities that persist in every aspect of our lives—whether these are linked to racism, class privilege, gendered relations, sexual politics, disablism, and so forth.

So whether one speaks of political grace or the Eros effect, both constructs are philosophical attempts to counter transcendental notions that objectify and individuate the power of love and binarize the relationship between matter and spirit, while exteriorizing the phenomenon of spirituality as something that exists separate and apart of the body, to which one must either surrender or master. Consequently, rather than comprehend love as the inherent force of life generated through our shared oneness (or spirituality), the communal understanding or manifestation of love remains shrouded in a discourse of individual yearnings and ego-driven aspirations of the Western imaginary. In contrast, it is precisely when the spiritual solidarity of a people is asserted organically in response to collective suffering and in the name of revolutionary action—breaking down the barriers of our atomized domestication—that political grace unfolds to support acts of resistance and dissent. About this, Rehberg (2012) writes in *Political Grace: The Gift of Resistance*:

> Political grace suffuses and infuses both person and community, relationally and individually together, thus ethically and in transintuitive and transreflexive ways, especially in conditions of extreme estrangement, and estrangement that results from radical suffering. It helps empower persons and communities to respond to the conditions which cause suffering, via resistance and revolutionary transformation ...
>
> (p. 31).

This dance of political grace constitutes then a collective human phenomenon that counters the "civilizing" and colonizing intent of the hegemonic order, defying paradigms of oppression—across class, gender, race, sex, religion, and bodily ableness—which brutally objectify, pacify, and ravage subaltern populations around the world with an ideologically pretentious and opportunistic rhetoric of progress and profit. In response to such conditions, the communal dance of political grace, engendered by criticality, openness, faith, and humility, is generated through the loving interaction of communities immersed in the materiality of the body and their organic relationships in the world.

And, thus, it is political grace that emerges from and through emancipatory communal life, where *love as a political force* (Darder, 2015) makes possible genuine transformative acts by those who on the surface might seem independent, neutralized, or disaffiliated.

Love as a Political Force

I have a right to love and to express my love to the world and to use it as a motivational foundation for struggle.

—Paulo Freire (1998a)

In his writings, Freire made references to the political nature of love and its significance to the revolutionary project. He elucidated on this love born of collective consciousness that emerges from our shared curiosity, creativity, and imagination, and that extends meaning to our resistance and counterhegemonic practices in schools and communities. This love is conceived as a powerful motivational foundation for revolutionary struggle, from which we as educators and cultural workers gain the courage to risk uncertainty, welcome our unfinishedness, and embrace indescribable possibilities as markers of liberatory life. Comprehending love as a political force is also essential to understanding Freire's revolutionary vision of consciousness and transformation (Darder, 2015). The inseparability with which he theorized the political significance of love in the evolution of consciousness and political empowerment is key here to grasping the meaning of political grace.

Drawing from Eric Fromm's (1956) contribution to this question, expressed so formidably in his book *The Art of Loving*, love is catapulted beyond mere sentimental exchanges between individuals, but rather constitutes an intentional spiritual force and act of consciousness, with the potential to emerge and mature through our social and material practices, as we work to live, learn, labor, and transform the world together. This critical communal view of love as both political and spiritual is, unfortunately, often ignored, maligned, and glossed over, even on the left, by the very people who most need to comprehend its humanizing and transformative potential. Moreover, in contexts where we are forced to counter daily institutional structures and practices that repress our humanity, this revolutionary, spiritual, and communal sense of love can act as a profoundly humanizing force in our lives, despite the difficulties we face.

Freire wrote of the politics of love by engaging foremost with the pedagogical exchanges he considered important to relationships between teachers and students. In particular, he sought to articulate indispensable qualities of teaching (Freire, 1998b), anchored in our humanity, that worked to cultivate greater intimacy with self, others, and the world, believing that "living with [democracy] and deepening it so it has real meaning in people's everyday lives" (Carnoy, 1987, p. 12) had to be a significant political concern of educators committed to overcoming injustice in the world. Critical democracy and the solidarity necessary for its evolution are made possible through a liberatory pedagogy fortified by a universal regard for the dignity and humanity of all people, no matter their differences or circumstances. The view of love as a dialectical force simultaneously unites and respects difference, while it supports a revolutionary sense of lived kinship, vital to our political efforts if we are to effectively transform the social and material conditions of inequality and disaffiliation that are the hallmark of capitalism.

Revolutionary Critical Pedagogy

> [Revolutionary] critical pedagogy is a reading and an acting upon the social totality by turning abstract "things" into a material force for liberation, by helping abstract thought lead to praxis, to revolutionary praxis, to the bringing about of a social universe that is not based on the value form of labor and financial gain but based on human need.
>
> —Peter McLaren (2016)

Inherent to revolutionary praxis is a pedagogical commitment to critically engage the deceptive domestication of the hidden curriculum—that begins in preschool with fairy tales, progresses to college readiness discourse in high school, and extends to the careerism of university formation—and unveil with students the prevailing injustices that have become normalized in their psyches. For McLaren, this impels critical educators "to challenge this natural attitude of capitalist schooling and its moralizing machinery by climbing out of our spiritually dehydrated skin and re-birthing ourselves into relations of solidarity and [community]" (2016, p. 19). This, in essence, delimits, in brief, the meaning of political grace, as discussed throughout this essay.

A revolutionary critical pedagogy imbued with political grace also heralds a radically human understanding of oppression and transformation, capable of witnessing and contending with the most tragic human circumstances and, yet, not fall prey to helplessness and despair. Given our labor within school and community conditions wrought in the impoverishment and violence of social inequalities and human exploitation, we cannot seek to avoid pain and suffering nor the impact of oppression upon our own lives and the lives of students, their parents, and communities. For suffering, in a revolutionary sense, can only be transfigured through an open and honest praxis that, without condoning, seeks the underlying possibilities or "roses in the concrete" (Duncan-Andrade, 2009) that might be garnered from our collective tragedies and suffering—even if only as an impetus to break free from the confines of our suffering.

At the heart of a revolutionary critical pedagogy sits an uncompromising commitment to fight with the oppressed not only for transcending those "dehumanizing conditions of human life under capitalism but also going beyond the given to create the conditions of possibility for individuals to shape their own destiny" (McLaren, 2016, p. 30). This entails merging our communal yearning for freedom, the power of our criticality to reimagine the world, and the spiritual force of political grace to fight together in ways that will reinvigorate—*across our differences*—the unrealized potential of socialist class consciousness.

References

Anderson, A. G. (2013), "Žižek and the Ideology of 'Religionless Spirituality'. The Grand Ampersand." Retrieved at: https://grandampersand.wordpress.com/2013/01/21/zizek-and-the-ideology-of-religionless-spirituality/.

Bekerman and Zemblayas, M. (2014), "Some Reflections on the Links between Teacher Education and Peace Education: Interrogating the Ontology of Normative Epistemological Premises." *Teaching & Teacher Education* 41: 52–9.

Boer, R. (2009), *Political Grace: The Revolutionary Theology of John Calvin*. Louisville, KY: Westminster John Knox Press.

Carnoy, M. (1987), *Foreword to Pedagogy of the Heart*. P. Freire. New York, NY: Continuum, 7–19.

Darder, A. (2015), *Freire & Education*. New York, NY: Routledge.

Duncan-Andrade, J. M. R. (2009), "Note to Educators: Hope Required When Growing Roses in Concrete." *Harvard Education Review* 79(2): 1–13.

Freire, P. (1970), *Pedagogy of the Oppressed*. New York, NY: Seabury Press.

Freire, P. (1993), *Pedagogy of the City*. New York, NY: Continuum.

Freire, P. (1998a), *Pedagogy of Freedom: Ethics, Democracy and Civic Courage*. Lanham, MD: Rowman & Littlefield Publishers.

Freire, P. (1998b), *Teachers and Cultural Workers: Letters to Those Who Dare to Teach*. Boulder, CO: Westview Press.

Fromm, E. (1956), *The Art of Loving*. New York, NY: Harper & Row.

Goldman, E. (1931), *Living My Life*. New York, NY: Alfred A, Knopf, Inc.

Katsiaficas, G. (1989), "The Eros Effect." Paper presented at the 1989 meeting of the American Sociological Association. San Francisco.

McLaren, P. (2008), "This Fist Called My Heart: Public Pedagogy in the Belly of the Beast." *Antipode* 40(3): 472–81.

McLaren, P. (2016), "Revolutionary Critical Pedagogy: Staking a Claim against the Macrostructural Unconscious." *Critical Education* 7(8): 1–41.

Rehberg, W. (2012), *Political Grace: The Gift of Resistance*. Chattanooga, TN: Wild Clearing.

Robinson, W. I. (2014), *Global Capitalism and the Crisis of Humanity*. New York, NY: Cambridge University Press.

Santos, B. de Sousa (2007), "Beyond Abyssal Thinking." *Eurozine*. See: http://www.eurozine.com/pdf/2007-06-29-santos-en.pdf.

Žižek, S. (2011), *The Monstrosity of Christ: Paradox or Dialectic?* Boston, MA: MIT Press.

18

Radio and the Art of Resistance: A Public Pedagogy of the Airwaves

The time has come for educators to develop more engaged systematic political projects in which power, history, and social movements can play an active role in constructing the multiple and shifting political relations and cultural practices necessary for connecting the construction of diverse political constituencies to the revitalization of democratic public life.

(Henry Giroux, 2003, p. 13)

The revitalization of public democratic life, as articulated in these words by Henry Giroux, speaks to the heart of all critical pedagogical efforts within and outside classroom life. In contrast, it is through both the silencing and the dismantling of democratic participatory rights that we are rendered most vulnerable to the destructive impact of neoliberal forces in the world today. At a time when public mainstream discourse touts its self-congratulatory "post-racial" declarations, the policies and practices of the State continue to harshly impact the lives of poor African Americans and Latinos, as well as other working-class people in the United States and abroad. Moreover, their disempowering impact within the public sphere is particularly felt among those who can find little relief from the poverty, surveillance, and injustice that thwart their community participation.

In Champaign-Urbana, the twin-city Midwest university town where I live and teach, community participation is further complicated by the rhetoric of corporate interests which effectively shrouds the neoliberal objectives of small university town governance. Within this context, calls for institutional change and municipal reform must be made by community residents who depend on nomadic, albeit progressive, student and faculty participation. This aspect unfortunately serves as a double-edged sword, in that there is a transient quality to public life and the body politic of this Midwest community. Such a politically unstable context requires creative pedagogical interventions by those who will eventually move on, in concert with those who call these twin cities home. In an effort to support the tenuous nature of community relationships within the confines of a neoliberal university agenda, public pedagogical projects can serve as alternative venues for supporting civic participation and a critical form of public engagement.

Critical public interventions are of particular importance within an increasingly conservative culture of scholarship, where neoliberal interests are neatly concealed within an academic rhetoric that furiously prioritizes global concerns over the needs of local communities. This is the case, particularly, in the current climate of "economic decline," where university "shock doctrine" solutions conveniently signal retrenchment among administrators, faculty, and students through institutional reliance on "color blind" neoliberal policies that effectively reinforce traditional structures of privilege and power.

The Media in the Age of Neoliberalism

Understood as one of neoliberalism rather than simply globalization, the current era seems less the result of uncontrollable natural forces and more as the newest stage of class struggle under capitalism.

(McChesney, 2001)

It is impossible to speak of the media in the age of neoliberalism without engaging its power to exercise a homogenizing impact on social, political, and economic relations at a global level. McChesney insists that *neoliberalism* is a more accurate explanatory term from which to discuss the overwhelming control of the corporate sector over the public sphere. From this standpoint, "governments are to remain large so as to better serve the corporate interests, while minimizing any activities that might undermine the rule of business and the wealthy ... The centerpiece of neoliberal policies is invariably a call for commercial media and communications markets to deregulate" (http://www.monthlyreview.org/301rwm.htm). Moreover, given its privatizing propensity, ownership of the airwaves has become consolidated among a few corporate giants, including General Electric, Time Warner, Univision Communication, and Viacom, who now monopolize the ideological architecture and design of US radio programming.[1]

This power over the airwaves was consolidated following the passage of the Telecommunications Act of 1996, which was the first major reform in the telecommunications law since the act of 1934. Supposedly, the law was to create greater access to the communications industry by fostering increased market competition for the airwaves. But in reality, the act radically restructured regulations in such a way as to intensify the market's rule, rather than benefit consumers, as its proponents claimed. As large corporations fought behind the scenes over the wording of the act, citizen consumers were left completely out of the picture, the majority unaware of the corporatized politics that threaten the democracy of telecommunications in this country. So, although it is true that the Telecommunications Act indeed required a radical overhaul given the dramatic changes in digital technology since 1934, McChesney (1998) argues that the result of the Act of 1996 was a complete disaster.

> The results of the Telecommunications Act, with its relaxation of ownership restrictions to promote competition across sectors, have been little short of

disastrous. Rather than produce competition, a far-fetched notion in view of the concentrated nature of these markets, the law has paved the way for the greatest period of corporate concentration in US media and communication history. The seven Baby Bells are now four—if the SBC Communications purchase of Ameritech goes through—with more deals on the way. In radio, where ownership restrictions were relaxed the most, the entire industry has been in upheaval, with 4,000 of the 11,000 commercial stations being sold since 1996. In the 50 largest markets, three firms now control access to over half the radio audience. In 23 of those 50 markets, the three largest firms control 80 percent of the radio audience. The irony is that radio, which is relatively inexpensive and thus ideally suited to local independent control, has become perhaps the most concentrated and centralized medium in the United States.

(http://bostonreview.net/BR23.3/mcchesney.html)

In line with this unprecedented corporate control of the airwaves, radio, in conjunction with other media outlets, delivers the hidden curriculum of a de facto neoliberal public pedagogy—one that, Giroux (2004a) contends, "has become thoroughly reactionary as it constructs knowledge, values, and identities through a variety of educational sites and forms of pedagogical address that have largely become the handmaiden of corporate power, religious fundamentalism, and neo conservative ideology" (p. 497). Hence, in contrast to the old belief that the media should function as a neutral sphere in which different ideas and perspectives can be engaged and interrogated within a democratic context, the mainstream media now, more than ever, is a powerful hegemonic tool that functions in the overriding justification and legitimation of societal inequalities, political exclusions, and environmental demise.

Thus, efforts to counter the pervasiveness of oppression—whether tied to racism, class and gendered inequalities, or stifling homophobic representations—must contend with neoliberal distortions that create confusion and contradictions among even well-meaning people. In the homogenizing script of neoliberal existence, bootstrap accountability returns as a central value of the "good society." Therefore, the stories that move across the mainstream airwaves embrace again notions of self-reliance and self-made individualism. Accordingly, a "rugged individualism" is venerated, and social action, outside the marketplace or neoliberal dictates, is deemed either suspect or the product of the weak and whining.

Moreover, Giroux (2004b), in *Dissident Voice*, condemns neoliberal ideology for its dehistoricizing and depoliticizing of society, as well as "its aggressive attempts to destroy all of the public spheres necessary for the defense of a genuine democracy, neoliberalism reproduces the conditions for unleashing the most brutalizing forces of capitalism. Social Darwinism has been resurrected from the ashes of the 19th century sweatshops and can now be seen in full bloom." As such, neoliberal sensibilities turn a blind eye to the suffering of the oppressed through a systematic denial of their dehumanizing propensities—propensities that privilege profit and material gain over even the essential human needs of the most vulnerable. The stories of the disenfranchised are systematically silenced and maligned, while their truths are relegated to the political waste basket of corporate dominion. This consistent denial or marginalization of stories that unveil injustice prevents any possibility of truly becoming a democratic society, in that the strength, knowledge, and wisdom of those subjugated are rendered unavailable or nonexistent. This further prevents the genuine integration of disenfranchised populations into the decision-making life of the community. Instead, neoliberalism leaves us all at the mercy of the marketplace, restricting the nature of our very existence, as it unmercifully seeks to shrink and contort our definitions of self and humanity.

In response to the limiting neoliberal priorities of both public universities and municipalities, many communities have begun to explore the use of community radio, in an effort to both counter the silences and revitalize solidarity across cultural, class, gendered, and sexual differences. Early proponents of the use of community radio include the founders of Pacifica in California, which later merged with KPFK, one of the strongest public radio stations in the western United States.[2] KPFK has been a leader in the use of the airwaves as public pedagogy, regularly airing programming produced by David Barsamian[3] of *Alternative Radio* and Amy Goodman and Juan Gonzalez of *Democracy Now!* KBOO community radio in Portland, Oregon has been broadcasting to diverse communities for over forty years.[4] In a city that is predominantly white, the station focuses its programming *by and for* marginalized communities in the area. Since 1979, WMNF has brought alternative music, arts, and public affairs programming to the region.[5]

Independent Media Centers around the country have also played an important role in championing more democratic access and control for media resources, including the establishment of low-wave radio stations to serve their local and surrounding communities. One excellent example is the work of the Grand Rapids Community Media Consortium[6] which, for over twenty-five years, has maintained technology tools and created media services and community venues to benefit the larger community. Here in the Midwest—just as with the Zapatistas' "Voice of the Voiceless" and other community-based radio projects around the world—the use of alternative media has shown the potential to enhance communication and social action among disenfranchised communities. WRFU[7], a project of Champaign-Urbana Independent Media Center[8], has been an important resource for the airing of alternative voices.

An important thread that weaves through the mission of most community radio stations is an emphasis on critical engagement with controversial, neglected, and non-mainstream perspectives, as well as an expressed commitment to social justice and democratic life. No doubt that without community stations such as these, the airwaves would remain completely in the hands of corporate media moguls, eliminating the possibility for alternative programming and dissenting views. Moreover, in light of the growing international consolidation of control over the media, community radio creates an important political space where hegemonic belief systems can be challenged and alternative views can be mobilized for social action. In his writings about community radio in South Africa, Eronini R. Megwa (2007) asserts:

> Community radio gives listeners a sense of community and identity and creates action space for people to have both direct and indirect link with community power structures as well as to have access to resources. Community radio is an integral

part of the community in which it is located. It is acceptable to the community as a development tool. Community radio can mobilize communities to act as change agents by engaging groups and organizations to direct their resources in order to actualize strategies at individual, group, and organizational levels.

(p. 53)

Community Radio as Public Pedagogy

I attended to the public pedagogy of the free radio airwaves. Between belting out oldies lyrics along with the station disc jockeys who populate the dial, I listened to National Public Radio in its various forms across two time zones. Within one 13-hour jaunt, I learned four lessons that make me a modern American:

Lesson One: Consume above all else, consume,

Lesson Two: Believe experts,

Lesson Three: Romanticize the past, and

Lesson four: Civic life is boring.

(Shannon, 2007)[9]

In 1941, twenty years after the first radio news program was aired, George V. Denny, executive director of the League for Political Education, enthusiastically declared that *radio builds democracy*. As a device designed to attract attention and stimulate interest in social and political problems, radio, he surmised, could function as an effective medium of public instruction within a democratic society. Hence, the interrogation of radio as a public sphere for democratic participation has a long history within the educational field. However, initial perspectives were generally grounded upon a modernist assumption that a "neutral" discourse, which presented a variety of sides, was in the best interests of genuine democracy.

Peter G. Mwesige (2009), who studied the promise and limits of radio programming in Uganda, strongly disagrees with any view that essentializes radio as a democratizing public sphere. He argues instead that

radio also appears to peddle misinformation and distortions; to invite adulterated debate that excites and inflames rather than informs; to give the public the illusion of influence; and, arguably, to lead to political inertia. At the group level, talk radio may have created an illusion of competition to the extent that it provided voice to oppositional political groups that were otherwise not fully free to participate in the political process. What we have, then, is an imperfect public sphere – but a sort of public sphere nonetheless.

(p. 221)

Similarly, critical education theorists (Freire, 1993; Kellner, 1995; McLaren, 1997; Apple, 2004; Giroux, 2004a) have indeed shattered the assumption of neutrality attached to public media production. Instead, they unveil the hidden curriculum of wealth and power, embedded in discourses of neutrality and meritorious solutions thought to "naturally" arise from the "fair airing" of all sides. In concert, the four lessons garnered by Patrick Shannon during his thirteen hours of "free" radio listening shed light not only on the overwhelming adherence of radio to values that bolster neoliberal society, but also on the deceptive manner in which the notion of neutrality operates amidst the public airwaves. And, despite claims that listeners are not passive agents, constant repetition of embedded values appears to erode the human agency of unsuspecting audiences, while simultaneously conditioning and priming the mind (Croteau & Hoynes, 1994; 2002), as Shannon notes, to equate consumption with freedom; to believe in the power of experts over one's own knowledge; to objectify the past as romantic ideal; and to readily abdicate our right to civic participation in search of pleasure and entertainment. In the midst of convoluted discourses that legitimize and perpetuate the interests of the powerful and wealthy, critical educators and community activists are challenged to establish spaces for counter-hegemonic dialogue and alternative public engagement. This entails the development of a critical public pedagogy in which social agency is nurtured and critical faculties of political discernment are activated and stretched, in the interest of social justice and public democratic life.

With this intent, the *Liberacion!* [10] radio collective was established in 2005 as a means to apply critical academic knowledge to the practice of a public pedagogy within the public sphere of radio programming. Critical public pedagogy is defined here as a deliberate and sustained effort to speak through a critical lens of society in such a way as to inform (and transform) mainstream public discourses and community political practices, in the interest of the disenfranchised. This is of particular significance, as previously noted, within the contemporary neoliberal context in which we struggle to live and resist the market forces of privatization and "accountability" that are ever encroaching upon our daily lives. More specifically, the work here points to a political process within the public life of a small rural university town in the Midwest—a context in which the power of conservative ideologies pushes forcefully against the forces of difference—forces which call for systematic and structural institutional change, predicated upon the politics of social justice, human rights, and economic democracy.

Nowhere is the battle to control the minds and hearts of the populace as contentious and strained as it is within small rural communities, where notions of "tradition" and "insider" entitlement are given free rein over political and cultural forces that seek social inclusion within the fabric of democratic life. More specifically, this means that forces for democratic inclusion must engage within a community context where neoliberal values and the rhetoric of impending economic collapse now offer respite from the "bothersome" politics of diversity. Within this deeply entrenched conservative public arena, community radio plays a significant role in countering the official transcript of "whiteness," privilege, and conserving ideals of tradition, so blindly embedded in the dominant relationships and discourses of both the university and the larger municipal landscape.

It is precisely in the midst of such a politic that critically engaged radio pedagogy, with an eye toward participation within the public sphere, has been forged. This entails a pedagogical process that makes central the significance of public life and recognizes the importance of creating alternative venues for democratic participation, especially for those who have been historically silenced and relegated to the margins of municipal existence. It was through a sustained commitment to combine graduate intellectual formation, collective media production, and critical community engagement that the *Liberacion!* radio collective was born. Its impetus emerged from an acceptance that democracy is never guaranteed and that inherent in its possibilities is the need for ongoing interaction and engagement with public issues that require the silences to be broken and the voices of the voiceless and unattended to find themselves at the center of the airwaves.

Hence, progressive, independent media production, tied foremost to the needs of the disenfranchised and oppressed within neoliberal society, encompasses a counter-hegemonic alternative for community expression and dialogue, as well as political engagement. That is, it involves a form of public engagement that places public media "at the heart of a democratic society" (Aufderheide & McAfee, 2005)—one that "treats people as active learners in and builders of society … [where] people can assert themselves not only as individuals but also, if they work with others, as decision-makers and mobilizers of the public will."

It is with these key elements in mind that the radio collective was established, to function principally as an avenue for alternative readings of the world, as well as a means to document ongoing political struggles—struggles that, although they might seem unrelated and disparate, are fundamentally interconnected with the subordination of populations deemed disposable and problematic to neoliberal capitalist dictates. Within small communities, such efforts are especially significant in that fewer public pedagogical venues are available for challenging the distortions and false readings which flourish about the "Other," who remains underserved and only minimally acknowledged within the public life of the twin cities.

This is important here, in that the radio collective exists within a context where the airwaves, just as the streets, are dominated and policed through a racialized victim-blaming rhetoric that belies the impoverished conditions and lack of opportunities available to marginalized populations in the region. This home of the diehard Indian mascot "tradition" is also home to poor Black and Latino families who contend daily with the impact of poor schooling, high unemployment, lack of health care, poor housing, and increasing homelessness and incarceration. Moreover, it is the site where racialized policing has led, for example, to numerous police shootings of unarmed Black youth; where corporate-inspired relationships permitted a twenty-year cover-up of an abandoned toxic waste site in a poor Black community; and where deep homophobic culture has resulted in violent attacks on working-class gay and transgendered people in the campus town area.

A recent incident serves as an illustration of the difficulties and tensions at work in this small rural college town. In October 2009, police shot to death Kiwane Carrington, a fifteen-year-old poor Black youth who had lost his mother to cancer two months earlier. The youth, who had forgotten his key to the house in which he was staying, was apprehended when attempting to enter the home through a rear window. Within minutes of the arrival of an officer and the Chief of Police, the boy was gunned down, allegedly for trying to flee from the scene. Although Kiwane was unarmed and there was no evidence of the youth resisting arrest, police entered the scene with pistols drawn—an action which is considered a violation of their own protocols for handling juvenile encounters. Official action taken after the death of Kiwane and the arrest of the other youth who accompanied him met with a community outcry.

A community coalition formed in response to the shooting was circulated and then presented to the City with over 1,700 signatures from individuals calling for an investigation into the death and the dismissal of a criminal case filed against the other youth. Despite this and a variety of other concerted community efforts, the shooting was ruled "accidental" by the State's Attorney (whose husband is a Champaign police officer). During the months that followed the shooting, the local "news" venues ran stories that seem to both support police actions in the case and belittle community participation in the matter. One editorial that appeared in the *New Gazette* on March 3, 2010, again maligned the community coalition's persistent public involvement:

> The incident is a tragedy both for Carrington's friends and family members as well as the community, and *the event has become a cause celebre for local residents* who feel the shooting reflects an institutional bias by police against members of minority groups. So they have taken up [the arrested youth's] cause, insisting that the charge against him be dismissed. But the [State's Attorney], quite correctly, refused to do so, *explaining that public opinion plays no role in prosecuting cases ...* The justice system would be a shambles *if the prosecution of criminal cases became the subject of popularity contests ...* That's why the petition drive ... is not just naive, but a*n assault on the entire concept of the rule of law ...* [The youth being charged] is represented by a lawyer who is working with [the State Attorney's] office to resolve this case *based on its merits.* That is how it has to be. To handle it any other way would turn the entire concept of the judicial system upside down.
> (My emphasis)

Members of the *Liberacion!* radio collective, as an active independent community radio project, gathered to produce and air two community radio programs on the Kiwane Carrington case as a contribution to the collective action and an effort to bring alternative voices to bear on the official transcript being circulated by the mainstream media, the courts, and the police department. The radio segments were archived on the *Liberacion!* website [11] and copies were made and distributed within the community as part of an educational campaign. It is important to note at this juncture that the effectiveness of the *Liberacion!* radio efforts on this issue was only possible given preestablished working relationships with community residents, members of the Independent Media Center's newspaper, the community group *Citizens for Peace and Justice,* and the Solidarity Committee of the Graduate Employees Organization (GEO) on campus. Key to this discussion is the impact of the radio production. The two segments on the case were played on both community radio stations and on a variety of other public affairs programs. CD copies were burned and circulated widely in the community for use in stimulating further dialogue on the issue at community meetings. Needless to say, the use of radio programming here functioned effectively to expand community awareness about the case and to consolidate the voices of community members in calling for a fundamental change in the policing of African American youth.

What must be underscored here is that public pedagogical actions are most powerful and effective when linked to larger social movement efforts, which support and sustain one another in the collective endeavor of creating public spaces for alternative political discourses. And although the theoretical lens that best informs the praxis of the radio collective is that of a critical public pedagogy, the production process by which mainstream airwaves are disrupted and redefined is firmly anchored upon an art of resistance, with its multiplicity of voices and methods for naming the world.

The Art of Resistance and Multidimensionality

> *"We chose the title 'The Art of Resistance' as a way of communicating to fans and listeners to stop and think about their lives and the world around them,"* Cunningham says. *"I'm not a teacher or a politician; I'm an artist, writer and musician, and this is my way of expressing what's on my mind and how I think I can impact people's lives. I've learned over the years that music can be as powerful a force as politics to bring out issues that need to be addressed, and the things like what we touch on here, like the prison industry and the way children are being raised, will open eyes."*
>
> (Caleb Cunningham, 2009, Hip-Hop Collective Project Lionheart)[12]

The art of resistance, as described by the Project Lionheart band member above, is shaped by struggles to address in multidimensional ways the underbelly of economic and cultural domination as it manifests itself within disenfranchised communities, while simultaneously seeking critical solutions that might potentially disrupt its negative impact. There's no doubt that the art of resistance encompasses a deep faith in humanity and the profound capacity of human beings for creativity and resilience, even in the face of suffering and adversity. The art of community resistance, then, implies that there is an organic and collective quality to the manner in which issues are undertaken and to the participatory processes by means of which the design of *Liberacion!* radio programs is carried out. This posits a formulation of community resistance that inherently redefines the potential power of the airwaves within the public arena, from being solely entertainment to having public pedagogical significance for democratic life. In the Gramscian sense, then, this public media production by the radio collective functions, uncompromisingly, as a counter-narrative to hegemonic discourses of the neoliberal State. It is precisely this quality of counter-narration that supports a space in which dominant political, economic, cultural, and ideological interests and their consequences can be interrogated, unveiled, and potentially transformed.

True to the radio collective's critical foundation, *Liberacion!* radio segments focus consistently on emancipatory themes and issues raised by community participants themselves, in which multidimensional aspects of social issues can be engaged by a variety of spokespersons representing both academic and non-academic praxis. Hence, for example, an interview with a professor who can provide a critical theoretical analysis of incarceration is woven together with an interview of a parent of an incarcerated youth, and with a commentary of an educator who teaches in a prison program, as well as with the poetry of inmates and the music of *Dead Prez* that challenges the politics of incarceration in the Black community. Through the use of what I term a *multi-intellectual design*, this form of community resistance as public pedagogy is shaped, simultaneously, through multidimensional discursive forms which break with the tradition of isolated, one-dimensional approaches generally utilized even among progressive radio programmers.

This form of multidimensional community engagement is important to building greater fluidity and a more expansive understanding of political participation and community resistance. Thus, a capacity to willingly and legitimately integrate vastly different perspectives and different articulations of similar societal mechanisms and oppressive structures cannot be undermined or ignored within critical media production or community resistance efforts. Through multiple discursive engagements with a variety of social and political issues, new public discourses organically emerge to forge new avenues and possibilities for dissent.

From the experiences of the radio collective, new avenues for dialogue, solidarity, and dissent are best achieved through dismantling false competing perspectives that privilege either academic knowledge over the community or community knowledge over the academic. This calls for releasing the objectifying strictures perpetuated by anti-intellectual views of disenfranchised community members, as well as debilitating criticisms of elitism projected on to formally educated comrades. Moreover, it is only through the courage to enter into such a multidimensional praxis of public pedagogy, with humility, dignity, and respect, that new relationships of solidarity can be built, anchored upon ongoing genuine exchanges of both lived and formally studied knowledge, technical skills, historical understandings, and community resources— all deeply valuable and vital to the interrogation and transformation of racialized inequalities, class and gendered formations, heterosexist ideations, and other forms of social exclusions in the world.

This is the kind of public pedagogy that embraces an integrated and communal understanding of knowledge—one that is guided by life-affirming principles of social justice, human rights, and economic democracy. The intentionality behind this public pedagogical approach with students is fundamentally linked to creating the conditions, through dialogue, reflection, and action, for the development and evolution of political consciousness—a consciousness grounded in organic community relationships and joint political labor. Effectively integrating public pedagogical projects, such as the *Liberacion!* radio collective, into the intellectual formation of graduate students demands that our teaching be rooted in a political process of critical academic praxis.

Within this perspective, the privilege of an education is not predicated upon competing against one another for individual rewards or privileged institutional status. Rather, university education is a politicizing context in which faculty and students must consistently (re)learn together to read the shifting cultural landscapes of power, so that we might sharpen our understanding of institutional constraints that thwart community self-determination. Such formation also challenges deeply held bourgeois notions of "professionalism"¹³ tied to traditional academic preparation and, instead, asks students to consider how their intellectual preparation will function in the service of justice.

Within such a context, academic "success" is no longer attached to the material ambitions of individuals and their contribution to bolstering capitalist democracy; rather, it is linked to generating academic resources and technical skills that can be shared and utilized in the collective interest of community solidarity and democratic participation. And all of this can only be generated and sustained through the unambiguous cultivation of a revolutionary love—a love that enhances our solidarity and commitment to one another, as kin and comrades, in our struggle to overcome the debilitating forces of human oppression through the daily revitalization of democratic public life.

Notes

1 Who Owns the News Media (http://www.stateofthemedia.org/2010/media ownership/dashboard.php). *Fear and Favor in the Newsroom*, produced by Beth Sanders and Randy Baker in 1996 and narrated by Stud Terkel, provides one of the most powerfully incisive critiques of corporate control of news reporting in the United States. Unfortunately, the documentary was "turned down by virtually every entity in the PBS system. Frontline, Point of View, PBS's independent documentary series, and PBS itself all refused to give the show a national broadcast. Indeed, after viewing an early sample clip of the show, Mark Weiss, the Executive Producer of Point of View, told us P.O.V. would not be interested, because the show would not be well received in venues such as Redbook." (Sanders & Baker). To learn more about the story of the documentary, see http://www.albionmonitor.com/9804b/copyright/fearfavor.html and listen to a Democracy Now! segment about the film at http://www.democracynow.org/1997/11/18/fear_and_favor_in_the_newsroom.
2 Pacifica was established in the late 1940s out of the peace movement surrounding the Second World War. In 1949 KPFA went on the air from Berkeley, California. KPFK, in Los Angeles, was the second of what would eventually become five Pacifica Stations to go on the air. See http://www.kpfk.org/aboutkpfkpacifica-.html.
3 Alternative Radio, established in 1986, is dedicated to the founding principles of public broadcasting, which urge that programming serve as "a forum for controversy and debate," be diverse, and "provide a voice for groups that may otherwise be unheard." The project is entirely independent, sustained solely by individuals who buy transcripts and tapes of programs. See http://www.alternativeradio.org/.
4 See http://kboo.fm/node/34.
5 See http://www.wmnf.org/station/about.
6 To learn more about the work of the Grand Rapids Community Media Center, see http://www.grcmc.org/.
7 See http://www.wrfu.net/.
8 The Urbana-Champaign Independent Media Center is a grassroots organization committed to using media production and distribution as tools for promoting social

and economic justice in the Champaign County area. See http://www.ucimc.org/content/about-uc-imc.
9   See http://www-rohan.sdsu.edu/~rgibson/rouge_forum/shannon.htm.
10 I established the Liberacion! radio collective with graduate students and community members. The intent was to create a space where students could be involved in the practice of public pedagogy, in conjunction with community members. For more information on the program and our radio archives, see http://www.radioliberacion.org/.
11 To access the radio segment of The Police Shooting of Kiwane Carrington 1 & 2, see http://www.radioliberacion.org/audio/Kiwane.mp3; http://www.radioliberacion.org/audio/Kiwane2.mp3.
12 See http://www.prlog.org/10436445-seattlebased-hiphop-collective-project-lionheart-makes-sound records-debut.html.
13 For an excellent historical discussion and critique of "professionalism," see *The Culture of Professionalism: The Middle Class and the Development of Higher Education in America* by Burton Bledstein (1978).

References

Apple, M. W. (2004), *Ideology and Curriculum*. London: Routledge & Kegan Paul.
Aufderheide, P., and McAfee, N. (2005), What Makes Pubcasting Public Is Engagement, Current.Org. http://www.current.org/why/why0517aufdermcafee.shtml.
Bledstein, B. (1978), *The Culture of Professionalism: The Middle Class and the Development of Higher Education in America*. New York, NY: W. W. Norton.
Croteau, D., and Hoynes, W. (1994), *Invitation Only: How the Media Limit Political Debate*. Monroe, ME: Common Courage Press.
Croteau, D., and Hoynes, W. (2002), *Media Society: Industries, Images, and Audiences*. Los Angeles, CA/London: Pine Forge Press.
Denny, G. (1941), "Radio Builds Democracy." *Journal of Educational Sociology* 14(6): 370–7. http://dx.doi.org/10.2307/2262537.
Freire, P. (1993), *Pedagogy of the City*. New York, NY: Continuum.
Giroux, H. (2003), "Public Pedagogy and the Politics of Resistance: Notes on a Critical Theory of Educational Struggle." *Education Theory* 35(1): 5–16. http://dx.doi.org/10.1111/1469-5812.00002.
Giroux, H. (2004a), "Public Pedagogy and the Politics of Neo-liberalism: Making the Political More Pedagogical." *Policy Futures in Education* 2(3–4): 494–503. http://dx.doi.org/10.2304/pfie.2004.2.3.5.
Giroux, H. (2004b), "Neoliberalism and the Demise of Democracy: Resurrecting Hope in Dark Times, Dissident Voice." http://dissidentvoice.org/Aug04/Giroux0807.htm.
Kellner, D. (1995), *Media Culture: Cultural Studies, Identity and Politics between the Modern and the Postmodern*. London: Routledge. http://dx.doi.org/10.4324/9780203205808.
McChesney, R. (1998), "Making Media Democracy." *Boston Review* (Summer). http://bostonreview.net/BR23.3/mcchesney.html.
McChesney, R. (2001), "Global Media, Neoliberalism, and Imperialism." *Monthly Review* 52(10): 1–19. http://www.monthlyreview.org/301rwm.htm.
McLaren, P. (1997), *Revolutionary Multiculturalism: Pedagogies of Dissent for the New Millennium*. Boulder, CO: Westview Press.

Megwa, E. R. (2007), "Community Radio Stations as Community Technology Centers: An Evaluation of the Development Impact of Technological Hybridization on Stakeholder Communities in South Africa." *Journal of Radio Studies* 14(1): 49–66. http://dx.doi.org/10.1080/10955040701301847.

Mwesige, P. (2009), "The Democratic Functions and Dysfunctions of Political Talk Radio: The Case of Uganda." *Journal of African Media Studies* 1(2): 221–45. http://dx.doi.org/10.1386/jams.1.2.221_1.

Shannon, P. (2007), "Pedagogies of the Oppressors: Critical Literacies as Counter Narratives." Speech Presented at the Rouge Forum on March 2.

19

Critical Leadership for Social Justice: Unveiling the Dirty Little Secret of Power and Privilege

The more radical the person is, the more fully he or she enters into reality so that, knowing it better, he or she can transform it. This individual is not afraid to confront, to listen, to see the world unveiled. This person is not afraid to meet the people or to enter into dialogue with them. This person does not consider himself or herself the proprietor of history or of all people, or the liberator of the oppressed; but he or she does commit himself or herself, within history, to fight at their side.
—Paulo Freire (1971)

The university today exists as a disturbing battleground, where ideas and practices can easily degenerate into a nightmare of undemocratic repression and bureaucratic madness. This phenomenon is fueled by wholesale abandonment of the public good and a full-fledged institutional divestment from the welfare of the commons. In the process, liberal values of equality and public responsibility have been precariously undermined by an unrelenting neoliberal culture of rampant greed, racism, increasing public surveillance, and the social regulation and containment of subaltern populations. In the wake of this fiasco, critical notions of multiculturalism and diversity within the university, along with scholarship anchored in community concerns, have been rampantly undermined by an economic ethos that has rendered difference a whore to its own utilitarian pursuits.

It is thus impossible to speak about critical leadership for social justice without attempting to systematically unveil the manner in which neoliberalism has eroded culturally democratic possibilities within the US academy. The all-too-common institutional bypassing of complex moral and ethical questions tied to diversity and emancipatory struggles for social justice has resulted in economic policies and practices in higher education that, wittingly or unwittingly, reproduce racialized structures and relationships, despite rhetorical claims to the contrary. This constitutes one of the most pervasive "dirty little secrets" behind the exercise of power and privilege in the academy.

Much of this article is composed of the text from the social justice keynote address presented at the University Council for Educational Administration annual convention on November 20, 2015, in San Diego, California.

In today's corporatized university, college students have become consumers who can now choose across a variety of educational products, rather than cultural citizens who must grapple to understand themselves and their world, as both individuals and participants in the welfare of the commons. Knowledge has been reduced to a market commodity, to be bought and sold to the highest bidder. Teaching in many classrooms now resembles a market "quality-controlled" operation driven by standardization and a banking pedagogy (Freire, 1971), overwhelmingly obsessed with the use of expensive and ever-changing technology. Assessment of students has also become more and more tied to the evaluation of faculty through the use of commonsensical matrices of product satisfaction.

Incessant data gathering and the expansion of accountability regimes substitute for critical engagement with real concerns that shape students' classroom experiences, particularly for racialized working-class students, and all this is accompanied by an epistemicidal curriculum that, for the most part, has become deeply instrumentalized and narrowly defined by a logic that too quickly circumvents questions of criticality (Paraskeva, 2011). Within such a context, the troubled conditions of our world are easily skirted or obscured, despite growing repression of democratic rights, increasing poverty in the midst of obscene wealth accumulation, a nation perpetually at war, the proliferation of police shootings of youth of color, the unprecedented incarceration of subaltern populations, and state-sanctioned attacks against public education by unaccountable billionaires, corporate foundations, and the media (Burns, 2015).

With few instances of courageous university leadership in opposition to the culture of corporatization, often the only form of dissent remaining is public resistance or mass protest, as we witnessed recently at the University of Missouri. Yet even the resignation of Tim Wolfe was an economic decision rather than a moral or ethical one, for had Wolfe stayed and football players continued to strike, the university would have lost millions of dollars (Green, 2015).

There is no question, then, that higher education today is deeply mired in a culture of economic rule, often shrouded by conservative rhetoric that seeks to delimit genuine struggles for social justice in academia and the larger society. Glimpses of this rhetoric are apparent in conservative responses to university protests across the country. Harvard professor of law Alan Dershowitz, in a recent interview, sternly asserted: "The last thing these students want is diversity. They want superficial diversity of gender; superficial diversity of color; but the last thing they want is diversity of ideas. We're seeing a curtain of Mccarthyism descend over many college campuses."[1] He went on to compare the "tyrannical students" involved in campus protests to Nazi book burners of the 1930s.[2]

However, it is precisely this rhetorical call for the "diversity of ideas" that has been used ad nauseam in diversity debates to subterfuge pressing concerns over social and material inequalities and institutional disregard for establishing a cultural democratic environment—concerns that time and again have been belittled or vilified or simply ignored by an economic rationality that undermines their legitimacy. With this in mind, Wendy Brown (2006) asserts that the American nightmare today constitutes an indefensible alliance of neoliberalism, conservatism, and the undoing of democratic life. Brown rightly argues that neoliberalism and neoconservatism are two distinct and contradictory political rationalities that converge in their devaluation of political liberty, equality, substantive citizenship, and the rule of law, in favor of market-driven governance and institutional policies on the one hand, and valorization of state power for moralistic ends on the other. This convergence results in undemocratic institutional forms that, despite social justice or diversity claims, are indifferent to veracity and accountability and to political freedom and equality, defying even liberal ideals of the academy—so much so that Brown (2015) warns, "neoliberal reason ... is converting the distinctly political character, meaning, and operation of democracy's constituent elements into *economic ones*. Liberal democratic institutions, practices and habits may not survive this conversion. Radical democratic dreams may not either" (p. 17).

Thus, it should not be surprising to learn that transformative notions of multiculturalism and diversity tied to community concerns have been effectively derailed by an aggressive and virulent economic ethos of the university. Accordingly, scholarship, leadership, and activism for structural change, political inclusion, economic access, and human rights have given way to multicultural market niches, the management of an international workforce, a colonizing paradigm of international education, and the portrayal of happy colored faces on public relations pamphlets and websites. Yet in this efficient and cost-effective neoliberal world, where difference is well rhetorized and "celebrated," those considered to be "deficient" subjects, unable to march to the homogenizing and bootstrap neoliberal refrain, are cast aside to the margins of society, left abandoned, impoverished, criminalized, and jailed behind iron bars, with little concern for their numbers or well-being. Blatant disregard for those unable to keep in step with the dehumanizing accountability culture that neoliberalism promotes is, sadly, as much at work today within the culture of the university as within the corporate world. Accordingly, universities have become overwhelmingly driven by an economic rationalism, where the financial bottom line capsizes any full-ledged notion of social justice, democratic participation, or community life.

The term "neo-liberalism," coined in the late 1930s, did not actually come to serve "as shorthand for the valorization of the minimal state and deregulated market" (Bell, 2014, p. 502) until the 1970s. Michael Peters (2001) argues that "neoliberalism has attempted to provide a Universalist foundation for an extreme form of economic rationalism ... and a philosophy that is ultimately destructive of any full-ledged notions of community—national or international, imagined or otherwise" (p. 117). Collective social action is thus considered a gross obstacle to the freedom of individuals, unless collective action serves the interests of the military or corporate elite. This point is best illustrated by the politics of the Trans-Pacific Partnership (or TPP)—a wide-reaching trade and investment agreement involving twelve countries. The collective global corporatization TPP not only portends a further erosion of nation-state regulation, but also privileges the rights of corporations over the rights of workers (Gearhart, 2015). As such, neoliberal policies, grounded in this limiting economic rationalism, provide the legitimizing anchor from which "mega-rich" conservatives and liberals alike co-conspire for control of not only the labor force and marketplace, but all public and private institutions, including the university.

Economic Darwinism and the University

As a theater of cruelty and mode of public pedagogy, economic Darwinism extends its reach throughout the globe, undermining all forms of democratic solidarity and social structures that depend on long term investments and are committed to promoting the public and common good.

—Henry Giroux (2010a)

Henry Giroux's use of *economic Darwinism*—drawing on the notion of social darwinism—serves as an accurate term to describe the manner in which neoliberal policies within higher education function, overtly and covertly, to support the *survival of the fittest*. In such a world, the wealthy, white, male, and able still overwhelmingly prevail over the university's resources and decision-making arenas. Furthermore, Giroux points to policies of deregulation, privatization, and a lack of concern for the public good, rendering both democratic education and the social welfare of the nation's endangered species. In this analysis, he implicates the values of "unchecked competition, unbridled individualism, and a demoralizing notion of individual responsibility" (Giroux, 2012, p. 16) as major culprits in the legitimation crisis and ethical impoverishment of neoliberal academic leaders who ascribe to a profit logic that undermines possibilities for culturally democratic life.

This disabling logic of neoliberalism, entrenched across the university, is most evident within graduate school education, where future academics and public intellectuals are initiated into careerist orientations that disconnect them not only from one another and the world, but also from the critical engagement necessary for the construction of disruptive and transformative knowledge—knowledge with the potential to challenge advancing inequalities orchestrated by the wealthy elite. From the moment that graduate students and young professors are initiated as tenuous agents of the neoliberal academy, they are conditioned into a culture of anti-democratic values that shapes expectations of their teaching, research, and tenure process as it erodes their intellectual freedom. Similarly, an infantilizing culture of institutional surveillance is carried out by complicit and loyal gatekeepers of all colors, genders, and sexualities.

The latter point helps to illustrate the limitations of a politics of identity, which often "ignores issues of unequal distribution between identities and ultimately issues of the underlying economic structure, which betray democratic ideals" (Fraser, 1997; Fisk, 2005). Hence, a politics of identity alone cannot forge democratic leadership, particularly within the context of the neoliberal university. Rather, what is indispensable is a coherent and lived emancipatory politics, enacted through a critical praxis of leadership (to be discussed later) that can extend courageously "beyond the common sense of official power and its legitimating ideologies" (Giroux, 2010b).

This is also important given the disabling structures of accountability, bolstered by bureaucratic regimes of power and hegemonic ideologies that have become more solidified in the last decade. Accordingly, colleges and universities have instituted greater expectations that, for example, professors from all disciplines become effective grant writers and fundraisers in their quest for the security of tenured employment.

Hence, a great deal of the energy of graduate students and young professors in major public research universities today is directed away from emancipatory efforts and community commitments and toward becoming published in refereed journals, getting publicly noticed as "rising stars" on the conference circuit, and developing effective grant-writing skills, while competitively shaping their research agendas to garner private and public funds. This narrow culture of professorial formation, as one might expect, has also been accompanied by tenure-track faculty who are left to navigate clumsily through the constantly shifting minefield of the tenure process or forced to contend with the mind-bending authoritarian dynamics of faculty mentorship, often fraught with deep anxieties and traditional expectations that young faculty either accommodate or suffer rejection at the time of tenure.

Although this dynamic has long existed within academia, the last two decades have witnessed a decreasing number of new tenure-track positions and an increase in casual employment, along with increasing competition among new doctoral graduates. This has proven especially treacherous for those now saddled with unprecedented debt upon completion of their degrees (Meyer, 2015). Moreover, with an exaggerated emphasis placed on STEM, this has made graduates in the humanities and social sciences particularly vulnerable to current neoliberal priorities within higher education. Yet it is worth noting not only that STEM-tenured faculty posts are not plentiful, but also that half of the jobs in the field do not even require a bachelor's degree (Rothwell, 2013).

Conditions of Power and Privilege

I decided to try to work on myself at least by identifying some of the daily effects of white privilege in my life. I have chosen those conditions that I think in my case attach somewhat more to skin-color privilege than to class, religion, ethnic status, or geographic location, though of course all these other factors are intricately intertwined.

—Peggy McIntosh (1988)

In the face of dwindling academic posts, young graduate students who seek to become tenured faculty or university administrators are counseled to abandon their "idealistic" intentions and to position themselves competitively for a job in ways that will, on the one hand, gain them recognition as "innovative" thinkers while, on the other, make them a "good institutional fit." This generally points to possessing an academic pedigree; an entrepreneurial predisposition; core values of individualism and competition; a naïve, centrist, or conservative political orientation; a subdued social justice outlook; and malleability to hierarchical leadership structures. Unfortunately, a "good institutional fit" is too often linked to the subtle (or not-so-subtle) manner in which classism, racism, patriarchy, disablism, homophobia, and religious chauvinism coalesce to preserve institutional conditions of privilege. Drawing on Peggy McIntosh's (1988) work on white privilege—where she openly acknowledges that she was not taught to see the "invisible systems conferring dominance on [her] group"—one can point to numerous university conditions of privilege sanctioned by the official power of the university and its Western ideology of domination. A few of these can be briefly expressed in the following ways:

1. I can critique my institution and talk about how much I dislike its policies and behavior without being seen as a cultural outsider.
2. I can feel like I am an authority on social justice even if I have never lived in poverty, experienced racism, or studied the scholarly literature in the field.
3. I look for grants and research that provide me the most acclaim or funding, rather than those tied to emancipatory objectives.
4. My expertise in my field of study is rarely questioned or criticized—in fact, it is valued and often gains me entrance into committees, task forces, etc.
5. I don't worry about being a token scholar, trotted out primarily for diversity initiatives.
6. I can be sure that because of my race, my research will not be questioned as to its legitimacy, limited scope, or if it is a "good fit."
7. I do not have to contend with people constantly mispronouncing my name.
8. I don't worry about being constantly challenged or racialized by affluent students.
9. I don't worry about being perceived as suspect or "second class" in the institutional setting.
10. I don't worry about being labeled as angry when I speak my mind at department meetings or in other university settings.
11. I can be sure that I will not be seen as a numeric minority or ever have to contend with the expectations or distortions this elicits.
12. I can be pretty sure that most of my colleagues will be neutral or pleasant to me.
13. I can conduct my research without undue surveillance or the need to provide an overabundance of proof of its legitimacy.
14. I can, if I wish, arrange to be in the company of students or colleagues of my race most of the time, without due concern from others.
15. My perspective is widely represented in journal articles across all fields of study.
16. When I read books on national heritage or civilization, I am most often shown that people of my skin color are the heroes.
17. I can be sure that my name or skin color won't count against me when applying for jobs.
18. I can swear, get angry, or not respond to emails without having people attribute these to my lack of civility, bad morals, or anger because of my race.
19. I can speak in public to a powerful dominant white audience without putting my race on trial or receiving hostile critiques if there is disagreement with my perspective.
20. I am never asked to speak for all the people of my racial group.
21. I can remain oblivious of the language and customs of others in my society, without experiencing any real penalty for such oblivion.
22. I can be sure that if I ask to talk to the dean, Program director, or chair of the department, I will most often be facing a person of my color.
23. If I am called into the office for one of my actions, I can be sure I haven't been singled out because of my race or my politics.

24. The pictures placed on the walls of my institution do not reflect stereotypical representations of people of my color.
25. I can go home from most university meetings feeling connected, rather than isolated, out of place, outnumbered, unheard, held at a distance, or feared.
26. I can take a job at any institution without having coworkers on the job suspect that I got it to fill a quota, rather than because of my qualifications.
27. I can be absent from department meetings without fearing that people of my color will be mistreated or issues will be discussed that negatively impact people of my community.
28. When things go badly, I don't need to reflect on each negative episode or situation to decipher whether I am being racialized.

These conditions of privilege are, more often than not, carried out unintentionally by well-meaning subjects, but are nevertheless enacted daily as microaggressions (which must also be linked, however, to macroaggressions) in university relationships with students, faculty, and administrators who persist on the borders. Institutional conditions of privilege are enacted through attitudes and practices of individuals shaped by embedded asymmetrical relations of power—persistent attitudes and practices of privilege that betray the promises of diversity of another time. The outcome of conditions of privilege—reflective of structural inequalities and enacted through institutional relationships by individuals—is that there has been little to no challenge to the oppressive structures of power within the university. As such, we are left to contend with a neoliberal multiculturalism that systematically negates the power of our political agency of difference to challenge racialized inequalities and other social exclusions, whether within the classroom or beyond.

Neoliberal Multiculturalism

Neoliberal policy engenders new racial subjects, as it creates and distinguishes between newly privileged and stigmatized collectivities; yet multiculturalism codes the wealth, mobility, and political power of neoliberalism's beneficiaries to be the just desserts of "multicultural world citizens," while representing those neoliberalism dispossesses handicapped by their own "monoculturalism" or other historico-cultural deficiencies.

—Jodi Melamed (2006)

In the midst of the anti-war movement and civil rights struggles of the 1960s and 1970s, the American university was challenged to break with its lily-white, male, and class-privileged tradition. The seeds of the current neoliberal assault on the academic borderland, as Giroux (2007) suggests in *The University in Chains*, can be found in the long-term authoritarian strategies put in place by conservatives who sought "to win an ideological war against liberal intellectuals, who argued for holding government and corporate power accountable as a precondition for extending and expanding the promise of an inclusive democracy" (p. 142). Those working to democratize the university called for inclusion of more students and faculty of color. Alongside this call for inclusive admissions and hiring practices, pressure was placed on colleges and universities to transform the curriculum in ways that would not only be culturally relevant, but also would engage the longstanding historical inequalities and social exclusions that persisted. Multicultural gains made within the larger society and the university at the time were more consistent with the liberal Keynesian-inspired economics, which recognized the importance of using systematic government intervention (Bell, 2014) to alleviate the downside of corporate capital investments. However, conservative *laissez-faire* views of classical macroeconomics, which began to regain currency with the deregulatory policies of Reaganomics, became the powerful precursor to the era of the "New Economy" and its ruthless consequences of inequality. The era was punctuated by a national report issued by Ronald Reagan's National Commission on Excellence in Education in 1983. This federal report was an aggressive political move by neoliberal conservatives to redefine the purpose and practice of public education. *A Nation at Risk's* proposed antidote for both the doom and gloom of public education and our diminishing global superiority was the assertion that the American public school system should function as an economic engine. The sprouting neoliberal educational vision of the ruling elite who manned the Reagan commission also began to forcefully tug at diversity debates underway within higher education.

As a greater number of intellectuals from the cultural, economic, gendered, and sexual margins began to enter graduate education, the presence of their politically distinct voices and transgressive views began to rouse backlash in the academy. It's not surprising, then, that by the early 1990s, the politics of difference had become mired in the hyperbole of political correctness, as mean-spirited attacks began to gnaw away at multicultural visions of equality and inclusion within the university—visions inspired by struggles for self-determination. Conservative backlash within the university also extended beyond ethnic studies faculty, targeting women and gender studies, sexuality studies, Marxists, and poststructuralist scholars who, according to Roger Kimball in *Tenured Radicals: How Politics Has Corrupted Our Higher Education* (1990), had become the new "establishment." Similar public assaults on higher education were at work in Allan Bloom's *The Closing of the American Mind* (1987) and Dinesh D'souza's *Illiberal Education: The Politics of Race and Sex on Campus* (1991), which alleged liberal bias at the university and pointed to the destructive impact of multiculturalism on the integrity of the Western canon and American society.

In place of more culturally democratic values, the proponents of economic Darwinism proposed a focus on entrepreneurship, derailing attention from social and material inequalities. As Brown (2006) has noted, "class and other impediments to servicing the entrepreneurial self are radically depoliticized, what the neoliberals call 'the equal right to inequality' is newly legitimated, thereby tabling democracy's formal commitment to egalitarianism. a permanent underclass, and even a permanent criminal class, along with a class of ... non-citizens are produced and accepted as an inevitable cost of such a society" (p. 695). It is, moreover, this cockeyed and insipid conservative platitude of "the equal right to inequality" that has been utilized to justify and rationalize a political economy that requires an immoral concentration of global wealth among a few. Subsequently, over 50 percent of the global wealth today is held in the hands of 1 percent of the population, while over 70 percent of the world's population scrap over a mere 3 percent of the global wealth (Treanor, 2015).[3]

It is precisely this political culture of greed that has given rise to a toothless "neoliberal multiculturalism" (Fisk, 2005; Melamed, 2006; Darder, 2011)—a conservative ideology of difference that deploys meritocratic justification to explain and legitimate inequalities. Adherents to this ideology enact a structure of public recognition, acknowledgment, and acceptance of multicultural subjects based on an ethos of self-reliance, individualism, and competition, while simultaneously (and conveniently) rendering suspect or irrelevant social justice discourses and practices aimed at the redistribution of power and wealth.

In a culture where a victim-blaming and stigmatizing ideology drives the institutional solutions of university leaders, culturally democratic efforts to contend with the oppressor/oppressed contradiction (Darder, 2015), and the complexities inherent in a politics of difference are often judged as disruptive, divisive, or offensive. This is so even today, when border academics such as Steven Salaita, considered too closely aligned with anti-imperialist struggles, are chastised, while repressive conditions within the university remain intact. Similarly, more progressive thinkers and leaders who entered the academy during the "diversity era" find themselves today more marginalized at the very moment when their scholarly and political maturity might serve to more effectively challenge current inequalities, as well as forge a more promising democratic vision. This phenomenon may also be associated with an appetite for so-called originality and innovativeness of scholarship—a neoliberal academic expectation that inadvertently stiles the evolution of substantive diversity critiques within the university and the larger society.

Not surprisingly, the educational advances of the "diversity era" proved to be a short-lived moment in the history of American higher education, for as more subaltern students and faculty began to find their way into university classrooms, faculty meetings, and governance tables, the more aggressive both conservative and neoliberal forces became in an effort to swing the pendulum back to a more homogenous cultural moment when an economically driven meaning of freedom and justice prevailed and the marketplace was heralded as the true purveyor of equality.

Assault on the Borderlands

To survive the Borderlands you must live sin fronteras[4] be a crossroads.
—Gloria Anzaldúa (1987)

It should not be surprising to learn that the incessant neoliberal drive to quantify worth, value, or fit it by perceived capital return did not prove friendly to university diversity or the *academic borderlands*—a term that draws on Anzaldúa's (1987) revolutionary concept of the Borderlands to refer to an intellectual terrain of struggle where the mixing of cultures, philosophies, theories, spiritualities, and everyday practices of life defies "the transcendent character of the traditional canon, because its exclusion—notably of women and people of color—marked it as the product of the white male imagination" (Aronowitz, 1991, p. 205). Significant features of the academic borderlands during the era of diversity included the increasing number of women and students of color entering colleges and universities, the vast flourishing of non-traditional scholarship, and the overwhelming presence of dissident voices calling for cultural, political, and economic change, while pushing forcefully against centuries of racializing and heteronormative patriarchal values (Darder, 2011).

As border intellectuals were transgressing the traditional boundaries of a variety of disciplines, rising neoliberal imperatives were making their way into the university just in time to conveniently push back fiercely against critical interventions designed to challenge the one-dimensionality of inequality in order to reinvigorate the democratic potential of higher education with a quest for borderless possibilities. At many colleges and universities, traditional administrators worked strategically to defuse what they referred to as the "cultural wars" by imposing austerity measures and fiscal pressures to cut programs, institute hiring freezes, harass noncompliant faculty, reject tenure cases, and even move to merge or eliminate entire departments.

As liberal ideals of higher education receded more and more, universities across the country became more deeply aligned with the narrow rationality of neoliberal objectives. Border intellectuals were pushed further into marginal spaces that served to limit their participation in the life of departments and the governance of the university. High-level administrators, now functioning like corporate CEOs, were less and less concerned with past promises of diversity, as they spent more time hobnobbing with corporate executives, foundation officials, and other big business advocates who could potentially help them recover the loss of public monies. In the process, the values, priorities, and private interests of those who held the reins to research dollars more tightly redefined the purpose of higher education, heavily tilting the enterprise with incentives to support economic self-sufficiency, unfettered deregulation, unrelenting privatization, marketplace competition, accountability schemes, technological supremacy, and maximizing economic profit. Economic incentives became tied to an overdependence on quantitative scientific interpretations fueled by a science paradigm that privileged a longstanding "evidence-based" discourse.

Despite protests against priorities that equated profit, progress, and prestige with policies of deregulation, privatization, free-market competition, and bootstrap economics, university administrators have been too easily herded into the fold with promises of dollars to build new buildings, expand our dependency on technology, support conservative curricula, and hire faculty ready to carry out the political agendas of public and private funders. Hence, through both covert and overt means, the political values and financial priorities of corporate rule have sought greater control of student intellectual formation, the labor of academics, and research agendas in order to legitimate transnational enterprises. With a keen eye on profit, control over resources, and the use of working-class communities for warfare, the neoliberal rhetoric of difference has functioned strategically to increase production, maximize commerce, and support the growing needs of US militarization and sustain the economic impact of global violence.

In fact, a recent report entitled "The Most Militarized Universities in America" noted that "Seventeen powerhouse research universities traditionally supporting the military-industrial complex rank in the top 100" (Arkin & O'Brian, 2015). Among those included in this elite group are Johns Hopkins (#7), Penn State (#15), Georgia Tech (#26), Harvard, Stanford, the Massachusetts Institute of Technology (#47), and the University of Southern California (#21). The federal government awarded over $3 billion last year to these schools alone. And rather than study traditional weapons systems, these universities primarily carry out classified research on intelligence technologies, cyber security, and big-data analytics. Also noteworthy here is the fact that most common academic concentrations for military workers are found in the STEM field. The unbridled advance of STEM education must be understood in concert with expanding militarization rather than superficial interpretations of science as "the new frontier," which fail to question the heavy promotion of STEM as an area of study and "career" choice.

As funding sources have diminished for faculty positions and research in the humanities and social sciences that could serve as a countervailing force, fewer resources are available for research that critically examines issues tied to social and material inequalities. A larger consequence here is that the university, now fully in bed with corporate interests, has systematically eroded the potential "to cultivate the next generation of critical scholars and leaders who can offer a counter narrative to the national security state" (Arkin & O'Brian, 2015). Thus, critical scholars and leaders in the borderland today are expected to align themselves more narrowly within particular disciplines of study, whether history, anthropology, sociology, or economics, in contrast to transdisciplinary or *sin fronteras* approaches that have been at the heart of teaching and research for social change.

In a world where economic Darwinism prevails, traditional disciplinary approaches provide neater and tidier intellectual alliances than does counterhegemonic scholarship produced by scholars in ethnic, feminist, postcolonial, and queer studies. This tyranny of strict disciplinary boundaries has also worked well to police and monitor the scholarship of more mature border intellectuals, as well as discipline current efforts of graduate students and young faculty from subaltern communities. Similarly, faculty and university leaders of color who persist in their advocacy for community-based research and participatory approaches in the interest of oppressed communities are often marginalized and derisively dubbed "activists," their scholarly work and emancipatory efforts challenged as mere "opinion" and subjected to excessive requests for proof, despite historical evidence and bountiful research to substantiate their conclusions.

Unfortunately, at the moment when they are most needed, critical scholars and potential leaders for social justice are often exiled from meaningful participation by an anti-democratic conservative wave that banishes formidable findings tied to social justice, human rights, and economic democracy to the wasteland of irrelevancy. In a climate where the international control of knowledge and the maximizing of profits are the greatest concerns, university administrators have often served—wittingly or unwittingly—as gatekeepers, through a banking form of leadership that thwarts the critical praxis needed for social change.

Critical Praxis of Leadership

For apart from inquiry, apart from the praxis, individuals cannot be truly human. Knowledge emerges only through invention and re-invention, through the restless, impatient, continuing, hopeful inquiry human beings pursue in the world, with the world, and with each other.

—Paulo Freire (1971)

The dehumanizing impact of social and material inequalities perpetrated by hierarchical and undemocratic forms of university leadership impels us to unveil the hidden curriculum, with its anti-dialogical values and practices, in an effort to move toward a decolonizing vision of leadership and a more just social order. By so doing, our task is to counter traditional social arrangements of accountability and institutional priorities that thwart social justice aims as we work to create a critical praxis of leadership to support self-determination and culturally democratic life. This begins with the willingness to disrupt epistemologies that exclusively privilege Western assumptions—assumptions attached to classed, racialized, patriarchal, and heterosexist codes of conduct that result in what Boaventura de Sousa Santos (2007) calls an *abyssal divide*—where the other is rendered irrelevant or nonexistent. Of this Santos writes: "What most fundamentally characterizes abyssal thinking is thus the impossibility of the co-presence of the two sides of the line. To the extent that it prevails, this side of the line only prevails by exhausting the field of relevant reality. Beyond it, there is only non-existence, invisibility, non-dialectical absence" (p. 1). The challenge that Santos poses—moving beyond the abyssal divide—constitutes one of the most difficult epistemological challenges faced by critical leaders for social justice in trying to establish alliances across dominant/subordinate cultural divides.

Principles and Ethical Commitments

I am speaking of a universal human ethic, an ethic that is not afraid to condemn the kind of ideological discourse I have just cited. Not afraid to condemn the exploitation of labor and the manipulation that makes a rumor into truth and truth into a mere rumor. To condemn the fabrication of illusions, in which the unprepared become hopelessly trapped and the weak and the defenseless are destroyed. To condemn making promises when one has no intention of keeping one's word, which causes lying to become an almost necessary way of life. To condemn the calumny of character assassination simply for the joy of it and the fragmentation of the utopia of human solidarity. The ethic of which I speak is that which feels itself betrayed and neglected by the hypocritical perversion of an elitist purity, an ethic affronted by racial, sexual, and class discrimination.

—Paulo Freire (1998a)

What is most evident for those who have felt betrayed by the very issues Freire raises, yet have remained in this intractable emancipatory struggle, is this: if there is to be a genuinely emancipatory approach to university educational leadership, it demands a decolonizing approach that fully supports both individual and community empowerment. This signals an emancipatory vision that embraces the indigenous call of "idle no more" and extends beyond the academy, where the insights and participation of administrators, faculty, students, and community members from historically oppressed communities are central to any leadership for social justice in education. Inherent in such an emancipatory vision are principles and ethical commitments that can inform a critical praxis of leadership for social justice. The following section offers a very brief summary and preliminary discussion of some of the vitally important critical principles and ethical commitments.

Critical Leadership Is Pedagogical

This notion of critical leadership as a pedagogical practice moves us beyond the traditionally hierarchical and individualistic banking model of leadership. Instead we are drawn toward an understanding of leadership as a social phenomenon that must exist communally and evolves pedagogically, through open structures of participation. The vision here is to *learn together* as a way of life in which we transform the world as community through a humanizing praxis of inquiry and decision-making, where the common good stretches across our differences and our institutional priorities.

Critical Leadership as Moral Commitment

In *Pedagogy of Freedom*, Freire (1998a) wrote: "Human existence is, in fact, a radical and profound tension between good and evil, between dignity and indignity, between decency and indecency, between the beauty and the ugliness of the world" (p. 53). Yet it has been the stubborn unwillingness to contend with institutional tensions and difficult moral questions within the university and the larger society that has resulted in an oppressive bureaucratic system of leadership—ruled by absolute, top-down, and expedient policies—that ignores conditions of human suffering and material oppression. In the wake of such neglect, the tensions and their consequences are seldom unaddressed. Instead, a conserving bureaucratic culture of control, contradictions, distortions, denial, manipulation, and hostility permeates the university environment, often tangibly experienced in ways that further alienate and isolate students, faculty, and administrators from their labor and consigns them to institutional lives of banality and routinized existence.

Critical Leadership Is a Political Act

Inherent in a critical theory of leadership for social justice is the understanding that if, as Freire proposed, education is political, then leadership, too, is a political act. As such it is informed by a question posing pedagogy of leadership that recognizes that culture and power are inextricably linked to any system of organization. That said, there must be consistent and humanizing protocols for examining, in an ongoing and organic manner, the consequences of decisions that are made and their impact upon the most disenfranchised, as the consequences of those decisions unfold. Through such a process, a critical leadership for social justice must create the conditions to question why—to question the conditions in which we exist, how they came to be this way, and, more important, how we can work together in the interest of democratic life.

Critical Leadership Is Not a Neutral Affair

A critical leadership for social justice is never a neutral affair. During the struggle against apartheid in South Africa, Desmond Tutu asserted: "If you are neutral in situations of injustice, you have chosen the side of the oppressor."[5] As such, a critical vision of leadership exposes the illusion of neutrality by examining the asymmetry of power relations in the face of oppressive policies and practices. Instead of neutrality, a dialogical process of leadership opens the way for honest questioning, open exercise of voice, multiple forms of participation, and genuine structures of democratic decision-making, guided by a moral imperative inextricably tied to the consequences of policy decisions and practices, particularly upon the most vulnerable.

Critical Leadership Is Purposeful

The purposefulness of critical leadership thus echoes a humanizing intent that informs our critical pedagogical practice. First and foremost, this approach to leadership encompasses an uncompromising commitment to conditions of our labor and of life that create opportunities for collective empowerment and self-determination—with a particular focus on those who most experience conditions of disempowerment, alienation, or isolation. This purpose signals the transformation of undemocratic relationships, institutional structures, and material conditions that perpetuate domination and reproduce material inequalities and social exclusions. Moreover, the underlying purpose of such a critical approach encompasses an ethos of leadership that openly nurtures and cultivates loving, hopeful, ethical, and committed relationships of solidarity with others and the world.

Critical Leadership as a Dialectical Process

To understand critical leadership as a dialectical process is to recognize that the needs of individuals and those of the community are always causing dialectical tension within the competing dimensions of our humanity. Hence, the tension is embraced as a human creative force that permits individual participation in the evolution of a collective process of self-determination without degenerating into moral relativism, even in the midst of resistance. Instead, our comfort with an emancipatory dialectics allows us to more fully embrace our social agency, the unfolding of social consciousness, and our resistance and that of others as a meaningful and potentially humanizing moral compass. This dialectical process of leadership can also help us to better unveil, challenge, and reinvent together those forms of injustice that are driven by apolitical and ahistorical readings of the world.

Dialogue

In this critical vision of leadership, dialogue is not only essential but also serves as the political means by which we forge relationships of empowerment and establish participatory communities for social change. The process of dialogue within this context entails purposeful communication that leads to self-determination and political action; a collective process of conscientization; communal labor that supports the development of solidarity; and an open and humanizing process of inquiry. For Freire, dialogue constitutes a way of knowing and being rather than a tactic or skill to be used to persuade others. Our dialogical engagements, then, must be understood not merely as individual exchanges but collective processes from whence we are able to both know and act upon our world in order to change it (Darder, 2015). As such, dialogue constitutes an indispensable component of a critical praxis of leadership.

Conscientization

As would be expected, the Freirean principle of conscientization, or *conscientização*, again defines here the ongoing aim and practice of critical leadership for social justice. This requires us to remain ever vigilant in our continuing evolution as cultural workers as we seek to practice and develop together a greater sense of critical social consciousness that encompasses the needs of individuals and the commons. This points to an awareness of our consciousness as individuals, as well as the conditions and social location we hold; consciousness about the social structures that limit us and potentiate our labor and relationships; an understanding of how these two intersect; an awareness of the power relations that inform cultural, political, social, and economic conditions; and acceptance of our individual and social responsibility as cultural citizens and subjects of history to live our pedagogy.

Critical Democratic Negotiation

However, none of the above is possible without an ongoing process of critical democratic negotiation. This speaks to the process of engaging organically with the dialectical tension between authority and freedom, within the actual contexts and relationships in which tensions and struggles arise. The dialectical tension between authority and freedom is understood as a significant and necessary aspect of our human condition that cannot be avoided without sacrificing democracy. Regarding this, Freire (1998a) posited: "It is not possible to have authority without freedom or vice versa" (p. 21). Hence we must be willing to practice a critical form of leadership that demands our presence in the interest of democratic life, beyond vulgar competition, infantilizing micromanagement, egotistical ambitions, or careerist pursuits of recognition.

Ideological Intersections

A critical leadership for social justice calls for personal vigilance and political groundedness within the context of our labor within organizations and communities. These critical qualities assist us in reading the world more accurately, particularly with respect to the ideological intersections at work in all organizational structures where humans exist. We can think of this as an axis relationship in which there is an intersection between the continuum of tyranny and powerlessness, on the one hand, and the continuum of absolute authority and absolute freedom on the other. Contending dialectically with the meaning of these ideological intersections is paramount to our struggle for social justice, precisely because people in any and all organizations will exhibit different response patterns across these continuums, depending on histories, political coherence, grounded knowledge, cultural worldviews, and the depth of their personal and communal commitment to an emancipatory political project.

The Cultural Context as Essential

In concert with Freire's philosophy, the cultural context constitutes an essential dimension of critical practice. This is particularly significant given that the hegemony of the dominant worldview often functions systematically to marginalize other ways of being and knowing. A deep recognition of the fundamental role that the cultural context plays in this work and the lives of the oppressed prompted Freire (2005) to argue, "one cannot expect positive results from an educational or political action program which fails to respect the particular view of the world held by the people. Such a program constitutes cultural invasion, good intentions notwithstanding" (p. 95).

Integration of Our Human Faculties

Another significant aspect of a critical theory of leadership is a commitment to relationships of solidarity, which—through the integration of our human faculties—nurtures the evolution of social agency and collective agency or political grace. Collective agency or political grace refers to that collective force generated by those who, committed together to struggle for a more just world, seek to connect and labor in communal relationships of struggle. Moreover, given its emancipatory purpose, a critical praxis of leadership requires the exercise of this integral process—where mind, heart, body, and spirit are fully welcome in the service of liberation. This integral dynamic generates the conditions for individual and collective empowerment and generates the creative force, through our communal exchanges, that mobilizes us toward emancipatory possibilities and social transformation. As such, a critical theory of leadership encompasses a political intent that rebels against the fragmenting and fracturing of our humanity and, instead, aims to prepare and support us all to live with a greater sense of love as a political force that can connect us to the truth of our material conditions that surround us, alerts us to the possibilities, and propels us more openly toward relationships of solidarity and social justice.

A Question of Ethics

For Freire, a question of ethics was always at the forefront of his thinking on education, politics, and social transformation. This point is crystallized in *Pedagogy of Freedom: Ethics, Democracy, and Civic Courage* (1998a), where he forthrightly takes up ethical dilemmas and concerns at the heart of a pedagogy for liberation. Four significant needs that can further inform a critical praxis of leadership for social justice include: (1) the need to counter determinism; (2) the need to assume responsibility for our lives as individuals and communal beings; (3) the need to carry out our practices through fellowship and solidarity; and (4) the need to understand and embrace our unfinishedness.

Critical Leadership as Unfinishedness

Paulo Freire (1998a) wrote: "If this world were a created finished world, it would no longer be susceptible to transformation. … This unfinishedness is essential to our human condition. Wherever there is life, there is unfinishedness" (p. 32). At the heart of this notion of unfinishedness is the recognition that oppression is never a permanent condition, and it is precisely because no human condition is ever absolute or finished that the struggle remains viable and hope fertile, even within political moments that may appear desolate and barren. An understanding of unfinishedness can also nurture and sustain a critical utopian vision that defies both a politics of prescription and determinism and allows us to remain in a permanent state of discovery, creativity, and epistemological curiosity (Freire, 1998a).

Indispensable Qualities of Leadership for Social Justice

There is no question that a critical leadership for social justice requires a fundamental shift in how we define our labor and how we understand our purpose as cultural citizens. This calls on us to shed our internalized oppression, eject colonizing ideologies of domination, establish solidarity with others, recognize ourselves as subjects of history, garner the courage to speak out when necessary, and cultivate a strong sense of social agency in order that we can name, critique, decolonize, and reinvent our world anew, in the interest of a just and democratic future. Drawing inspiration from Freire's (1998b) indispensable qualities for those who *dare to teach*, I want to try to quickly summarize many of the points included above by offering two sets of indispensable qualities for those who *dare to lead*.

    The first group of ethical qualities points to those associated with political struggle and the second to those associated with personal struggle. However, given the nature of the work and the critical values and principles that inform these qualities, there is much overlapping of points, thanks to the ongoing dialectics between the public and personal conditions of our everyday lives. This phenomenon is readily apparent as one engages these two sets of indispensable qualities, which are not meant to serve as any sort of taxonomy or prescription, but rather as a politically inspired suggestion or reminder of the complexity and multidimensionality of the principles and commitments that we must assume in our emancipatory quest to redefine the ways we think and practice a critical praxis of leadership in the world.

Ethical Qualities of Political Struggle for Social Justice

- Understands the link between culture and power
- Engages consistently with political questions of the economy
- Rooted in a historical understanding of our collective existence
- Knowledge of micro and macro systems and their connection
- Knowledge of overarching social and political contradictions at work
- Comprehends the underlying dynamics of material inequalities and social exclusions
- Recognizes the inextricable connections between all forms of oppression
- Reads both formal and impersonal power relations
- Conscientious language use and knowledge of its relationship to power
- Emphasis on voice, democratic participation, and collaborative decision making
- Consistently moves toward dialogue as the means for transformative action
- Accepts the meaningfulness and necessity of resistance
- Enacts a critical sense of authority in the interest of freedom
- Politically strategic, choosing battles tied to the greatest common benefit
- Commitments to solidarity and community self-determination
- Understands political change as part of the ongoing process of life
- Acknowledges the power and ongoing nature of unfinishedness
- Embodies radical hope and possibility
- Embraces a historical view (long view) of revolutionary struggle for social justice

Ethical Qualities of Personal Struggle for Social Justice

- Knowledge of one's personal demons, struggles, and limitations
- Self-vigilant in one's attitudes and behaviors toward self, others, and the world
- Commitment to our kinship and common good—*Tu eres mi otro yo*
- Practices with confidence and humility (comfortable with knowing and not knowing)
- Expresses faith and respect for others, in words and deeds
- Embodies presence and an engaged style of communication and participation
- Enacts courage and thoughtfulness when challenging others
- Exercises a collective sensibility in decision-making with others
- Impatiently patient—respect for the process
- Commitment to living, working, and loving with a critical integrity
- Focus on nurturing relationships rather than simply being right
- Grounded in a revolutionary love, anchored in justice and humanity
- Forgiveness for one's own and others' limitations and shortcomings
- Compassion for struggles faced in our efforts to become more socially conscious

- Embraces humor, joy, and the sensual dimensions of our humanity
- Respect for the preciousness of all life

The Struggle for Democratic Public Life

At the very least, academics should be more responsible to and for a politics that raises serious questions about how students and educators negotiate the institutional, pedagogical, and social relations shaped by diverse ideologies and dynamics of power, especially as these relations mediate and inform competing visions regarding whose interests the university might serve, what role knowledge plays in furthering both excellence and equity, and how higher education defines and defends its own role in relation to its often stated, though hardly operational, allegiance to egalitarian and democratic impulses.

—Henry Giroux (2010a)

For those who embrace this praxis of critical leadership, the university continues to represent an important terrain of struggle and key public pedagogical space from whence we can strive to continue forging democratic public life. This notion is often directly tied to critical educational efforts by critical professors and leaders from the borderlands, who seek through their praxis to establish political links among the classroom, college campus, the community, and the larger society, in ways that can foster and support the university as a site of culturally democratic possibility.

A praxis of critical leadership for social justice seeks to create emancipatory conditions within the university that support meaningful dialogue for seriously questioning the status quo and the ideologies, policies, and practices that betray earlier liberal democratic ideals of intellectual freedom. This, however, requires a sound pedagogical engagement that can move us beyond the conservative rhetorical refrains of a "diversity of ideas." Rather, what is needed are critically communal relationships of leadership that can infuse our labor with the courage and epistemological flexibility to embrace—or at least be open to—difference, even when it may seem incomprehensible and we are readily tempted to eliminate it, particularly when it makes us anxious, uncertain, or insecure. In the process, we must become more conscious of those historical moments when liberal ideals of the university prevailed, so that we might explore together those critical possibilities that can propel us beyond the current neoliberal nightmare. In fact, if it were not for the work of critical scholars in the academic borderlands, many of us would never have found an opportunity to flourish in the academy despite the underlying oppressive nature of higher education, both in this country and in other parts of the world. Since democracy is never a given, the political project for democratic public life must be understood as an ongoing one rather than a determined destination. As such, the struggle for social justice necessitates courageous forms of leadership that can remain ever vigilant to inequalities and exclusions, constantly pushing against reified boundaries of legitimacy that prevent our movement toward a genuinely humanizing culture of the university and society.

A critical leadership for social justice that supports public democratic life and political dissent creates the conditions for university administrators, faculty, and students to not only grapple rigorously with theories and practices of democratic life as cognitive phenomena, but also ask them to tackle rigorously and in the flesh the meaning and consequences of material inequalities and ideologies of racism, orientalism, Islamophobia, sexism, homophobia, heterosexism, disablism, and other prevailing forms of social exclusion with respect to their everyday lives and the larger societal conditions in the world.

In the last three decades, we have seen neoliberalism steadily negate the hard-earned opportunities gained by earlier civil rights struggles. Yet what is made only too clear by this history is that democracy is never guaranteed, which is truer today than ever. And as such, we must keep in mind that democracy necessitates an ongoing emancipatory historical and international struggle for political voice and participation. Higher education, then, persists as a contested terrain of struggle, given the potential of education to function as a democratizing force. However, we cannot overcome the perils and pitfalls of current conditions of injustice that exist all around us if our work is not firmly grounded in an imaginative and creative political vision that requires us to consistently reach beyond the comprehensibility of this unjust and racialized economic order.

There is no question that an imaginative, fluid, and grounded political vision of struggle is especially necessary within the context of leadership today, in that our labor for social change is, indeed, made more difficult in this historical moment when neoliberalism has made a farce of the democratic ideal of "civic engagement," undermining the public good and the power of our differences. To counter this travesty, we must move, in *theory and practice*, beyond the usual reformism and embrace in our daily praxis wider political possibilities that might allow us, in a Deleuzian sense, to "bring something incomprehensible into the world!" (Deleuze & Guattari, 1987, p. 78). For this is the truly creative substance from whence genuine social and political transformation is born.

This demands from us a more profound sense of our human affiliation, the evolution of consciousness, and a reinvestment in the collective power of social movement and political encounters across our differences. Toward this end, we can strive to become more politically vigilant in our responses to the world so that we do not fall prey to the commonplace contradictions of either neoliberalism or academic elitism, which easily betray our liberatory dreams. This requires that we understand that *no one exists outside the system* (Darder, 2015) and that none of us is free of contradiction; furthermore, a purity of politics or sectarianism is not the answer to the suffering and alienation we are facing today. This speaks to a political vision where uncertainty, ambiguity, discomfort, and incomprehensibility exist in dialectical alliance with their negation.

Through the latitude that such political awareness affords us, we can more easily enter into critical engagement with the complexities and nuanced ways in which hegemony impacts our lives as educators and world citizens, as well as the many differences that exist among us as a consequence of our different cultural histories and material conditions of survival.

At the heart of such awareness must also be the recognition that liberation, whether in the university, our communities, or the larger world, can only be enacted through a radically imaginative, hopeful, and loving political vision where neither diversity nor unity is sacrificed. And, most important, to persist in this long historical struggle for justice requires that we, as individuals and collective beings, face daily our deeply conditioned fear of freedom and dare to be powerful together. To use Audre Lorde's (1997) words, "*When [we] dare to be powerful—to use [our] strength in the service of [our emancipatory] vision, then it becomes less and less important whether [we are] afraid*" (p. 13). In our personal and political struggles as leaders, scholars, and activists for social justice, let us work to echo the strength and commitment of the many freedom fighters across our histories who committed their lives to that incomprehensible possibility of collective freedom, and *dare to be powerful together*.

Notes

1   See: http://video.foxnews.com/v/4610150912001/alan-dershowitz-students-dont-want-diversity-of-ideas/?#sp=show-clips.
2   Ibid.
3   See Jill Treanor's article for a stark rendition of *The Global Wealth Pyramid*, a graph derived from research conducted by Credit Suisse and data collected by the Swiss Global Wealth Databook.
4   *Sin fronteras* translation: without borders.
5   See: http://organizingchange.org/here-is-how-moral-leaders-approach-neutrality/.

References

Anzaldúa, G. (1987), *Borderlands/La frontera: The New Mestiza*. San Francisco, CA: Aunt Lute.
Arkin, W. M., and O'Brien, A. (2015), "The Most Militarized Universities in America: A VICE News Investigation." *Vice News*. Retrieved from https://news.vice.com/article/the-most-militarized-universities-in-america-a-vice-news-investigation.
Aronowitz, A. (1991), "[Review of the Book Tenured Radicals: How Politics Has Corrupted Our Higher Education, by R. Kimball.]" *Teachers College Record* 93(1): 204–7.
Bell, E. (2014), "There Is an Alternative: Challenging the Logic of Neoliberal Penalty." *Theoretical Criminology* 18(4): 489–505.
Bloom, A. (1987), *The Closing of the American Mind*. New York, NY: Simon & Schuster.
Brown, W. (2006), "American Nightmare: Neoliberalism, Neoconservatism, and De-democratization." *Political Theory* 34(6): 690–714.
Brown, W. (2015), *Undoing the Demos: Neoliberalism's Stealth Revolution*. New York, NY: Zone Books.
Burns, J. (2015), "The Moral Bankruptcy of Corporate Education." *Teachers College Record* (September 1). http://www.tcrecord.org.
Darder, A. (2011), *A Dissident Voice: Essays on Culture, Pedagogy, and Power*. New York, NY: Peter Lang.

Darder, A. (2015), *Freire and Education*. New York, NY: Routledge.
Deleuze, G., and Guattari, F. (1987), *A Thousand Plateaus: Capitalism and Schizophrenia*. Minneapolis, MN: University of Minnesota Press.
D'souza, D. (1991), *Illiberal Education: The Politics of Race and Sex on Campus*. New York, NY: Simon & Schuster.
Fisk, M. (2005), "Multiculturalism and Neoliberalism." *Praxis Filosofica*: 21–8. Retrieved from http://www.miltonisk.org/writings/multiculturalism-and-neoliberalism/.
Fraser, N. (1997), "Multiculturalism, Antiessentialism, and Radical Democracy," in N. Fraser (ed.), *Justice Interruptus: Critical Reflections on the "Postsocialist" Condition*. New York, NY: Routledge.
Freire, P. (1971), *Pedagogy of the Oppressed*. New York, NY: Seabury Press.
Freire, P. (1998a), *Pedagogy of Freedom: Ethics, Democracy, and Civic Courage*. Lanham, MD: Rowman & Littlefield.
Freire, P. (1998b), *Teachers as Cultural Workers: Letters to Those Who Dare Teach*. Boulder, CO: Westview Press.
Freire, P. (2005), *Pedagogy of the Oppressed (30th anniversary ed.)*. New York and London: Continuum.
Gearhart, J. (2015), "TPP Ignores Worker's Weeds and Fails to Address Weaknesses from Past Trade Agreements." *The World Post*. Retrieved from http://www.hufington post.com/judy-gearhart/tpp-ignores-worker-needs_b_8537878.html.
Giroux, H. (2007), *The University in Chains*. Boulder, CO: Paradigm.
Giroux, H. (2010a), "The Disappearing Intellectual in the Age of Economic Darwinism. *Global Research*." Retrieved from http://www.globalresearch.ca/index.php?context=va&aid=20112.
Giroux, H. (2010b), "Rethinking Education as the Practice of Freedom: Paulo Freire and the Promise of Critical Pedagogy." *Truthout* (January 1). Retrieved from http://www.truth-out.org/archive/item/87456:rethinking-education-as-the-practice-of-freedom-paulo-freire-and-the-promise-of-critical-pedagogy.
Giroux, H. (2012), "Higher Education, Critical Pedagogy, and the Challenge of Neoliberalism: Rethinking the Role of Academics as Public Intellectuals," in *Revista Aula de Encuentro, Número especial*. Andalucía, España: Servicio de Publicaciones e Intercambio Científico Universidad de Jaén, 15–27.
Green, A. (2015), "The Financial Calculations: Why Tim Wolfe Had to Resign." *The Atlantic* (November 9). Retrieved from http://www.theatlantic.com/business/archive/2015/11/mizzou-tim-wolfe-resignation/414987/.
Kimball, R. (1990), *Tenured Radicals: How Politics Has Corrupted Our Higher Education*. Chicago, IL: Ivan R. dee.
Lorde, A. (1997), *The Cancer Journals*. San Francisco, CA: Aunt Lute.
McIntosh, P. (1988), "White Privilege: Unpacking the Invisible Knapsack." Excerpted from *White Privilege and Male Privilege: A Personal Account of Coming to See Correspondences through Work in Women's Studies*. Working paper 189. Wellesley, MA: Wellesley College Center for Research on Women.
Melamed, J. (2006), "From Racial Liberalism to Neoliberal Multiculturalism." *Social Text* 89(4): 1–24.
Meyer, J. (2015), "The Unprecedented Debt Burdens Facing Millennials." *The Manhattan Institute*. Retrieved from http://www.economics21.org/iles/pdf/HBc%20Testimony%20Meyer.pdf.
Paraskeva, J. (2011), *Conflicts in Curriculum Theory*. New York, NY: Palgrave.

Peters, M. (2001), *Postructuralism, Marxism, and Neo-Liberalism: Between Theory and Politics*. Lanham, MD: Rowman & Littlefield.

Rothwell, J. (2013), *The Hidden STEM Economy*. Washington, DC: The Brookings Institution.

Santos, B. de Sousa (2007), "Beyond Abyssal Thinking." *Eurozine*. Retrieved from http://www.eurozine.com/pdf/2007-06-29-santos-en.pdf.

Treanor, J. (2015), "Half of World's Wealth Now in Hands of 1% of Population. *The Guardian* (October 13)." Retrieved from http://www.theguardian.com/money/2015/oct/13/half-world-wealth-in-hands-population-inequality-report.

Afterword: The Darder Question: "To End the World as We Know It"

João M. Paraskeva

University of Strathclyde

Will the theoretical needs be immediate practical needs?

—Marx, 1843

In his hiking toward a revolution, penciled in the "Critique of Hegel's Philosophy of Right," Karl Marx insightfully highlighted a major obstacle faced by a(ny) needed successful radical German revolution. As he (1843, p. 27) argued, it was necessary to see that "theory is actualized only in so far as it is an actualization of the people's need." The theoretical backbone for a drastic change needed to be magnetized through people's needs and desires. Karl Marx wrangles with "theory and people's needs" cataphorically describes Antonia Darder's entire intellectual footprint. As this reader accurately shows, Darder's *jouissance* is a spitting image of Marxist and neo-Marxists—of a neo-*Gramscian* bent. Echoing Marx, she is quite aware that "theory is fulfilled in a people only insofar as it is the fulfillment of the needs of that people" (Marx, 1843, p. 27), or "people's everyday creations" as Oliveira (2024) would put it.

It is not an easy affair to "excavate" (Mignolo, 2018) and to *palavrar* (Pessoa, 2002)[1] the work and thought of a heavy-weight public intellectual such as Antonia Darder, who is simply one of the brightest neo-*Gramscians*—with strong decolonized *Freirean* impulses currently in the field of education and curriculum within and beyond the Global North. As this reader attests, an arduous, laborious, meticulous, creatively conceived, and meritorious testimony that reinforces existing challenges and accomplishments and helps to plow new "unknown" epistemological rivers in the field. Darder's legacy is so intricate and eclectic that it is impossible to do justice to all her rich thesaurus in a single volume—much less in a brief afterword. Darder's linguistic tessiture epitomizes Fanon's (1963, p. 188) claims that "everything can be explained to the people, on the single condition that you want them to understand." She is a superb speaker, swimming conformably through the complex denotative and connotative intricacies of the deep structures of the dominant *"langue-parole"* wrangles of coloniality, and a superlatively gifted writer. And as if that wasn't enough, a rebel visual arts master with oils reminding us of the utopia crafted by world icons of resistance, through plastic arts as subversive acts of speech and as sharped weapons against systems of domination and oppression—such as the awe-inspiring surrealism of Magdalena Carmen Frida Kahlo y Calderón or the inspiring *transculturation* impulses of Carlos Irizarry. With Darder, we learn, among other crucial issues, how ideology is eloquently vocal within the Freudian hysterical silences of any discursive forms (Eagleton, 2003; Jal, 2023). As I had the opportunity to document in another space (Paraskeva, 2023), her multifarious heritage re-affirms her sublime standing as second to none among the radical critical public neo-*Gramscian* intellectuals within what I called the rich generation of the utopia (Paraskeva, 2021).

Antonia Darder's *thesaurus* is a complex political project whose polychromatic and dense nerves make it very difficult to establish well-defined boundaries throughout the successive phases. I would prefer to frame it as "dynamics" that she went through over decades. The reader thoroughly mines such dynamics around the political economy, culture and power, Latino studies, class, race, and gendered theoretical analyses within and beyond Western epistemological hemispheres. Such different dynamics of her long and intense radical *poiesis*, well genealogically "exfoliated" (Gil, 2018) in this reader become irremediably mutually contaminated. They talk to each other, and challenge the readers to take control, to take positions, to situate themselves in the text and context. She thus exhibits rigid structural and post-structural veins that announce the "death of the author" (see Foucault, 1973; Barthes, 1977; Blanchot, 1989). Darder advances a language limitedness enriched by the reader. She builds a very rich conceptual skein that embodies the solidity of what I call the "Darder question," synthesized in her commitment "to end the world as we know it"—a question that, despite appearing in her last metamorphoses in a more evidently explicit way, always hovered throughout her entire political pedagogical treatise. Darder's question, which erupts out of the reader's labor, and the dynamics that are inherent to it, overcomes Feuerbach's eleventh thesis (Marx, 1976), transcoding it by advocating that the transformation of the world implies not just the end of the world as it exists but as we think of it. Darder (2016; 2019) was one of the first, and clearly the first Freirean scholar to realize that there was a severe problem with the critical matrix, deeply mortgaged to the Cartesian cogito, which in many ways sank into arguments as reactionary as those they criticized.

However, as her journey demonstrates and this comprehensive manuscript exemplifies accurately, Darder's question is just the beginning of another set of dynamics. Her work reveals a constant uphill struggle of an intellectual situated at the core of the neo-*Gramscian* republic, aware that the way to answer the question posed goes through the same path that led precisely to the emergence of such a question. Thus, while on the one hand, it matters to unpack "the end of the world as we know it," on the other hand, such a move toward *il nuovo ordine*[2] through education implies precisely what we lack(ed) as a field, which is a theory that addresses people's endless diverse and different needs or "everyday creations" (Oliveira, 2024). To craft such a theoretical platform, Darder untiringly pushed for "alternative ways to think [and] to conceptualize education and curriculum alternatively" (Paraskeva, 2011; Santos, 2014). To labor on Darder's matrix is to be committed to acknowledging the field's "involution and imparity" (Paraskeva, 2021; 2022; 2023; 2024) in which "the old world is dying, and the new world struggles to be born," as Gramsci (1990) would have phrased it and be capable of addressing one of the best Marxist impulses that run deep through her Neo-*Gramscian* veins: "Will the theoretical needs be immediate practical needs?" (Marx, 1843). In her neo-*Grasmcian* terms, the utopia toward *di un nuovo ordine*,[3] a world we all wish to see (see Amin, 2008) is possible as long as critical theorists and pedagogues act "not as vanguard but as rearguard organic intellectuals" (Santos, 2018) to understand that theory and practice are not parallel paths. She pushes us all into a zone of theoretical trepidation that will only ease through a commitment to conscientização' (Freire, 1990) or conscienscism (Nkrumah, 1964), helping to perceive how societal needs are intimately connected to "social, political, and economic oppressive dynamics and contradictions and to take action against the oppressive elements of reality." (Freire, 1990)

Among the different dynamics that work in a spiral underpinning Darder's intellectual footprint, I highlight two for their importance given the regressive moment in which humanity finds itself, namely her critique of the Prosperous reason and the (self) critique of the dogmatic reveries that flood the counter-hegemonic platform drowning into a functionalist and deterministic swamp, as reactionary as the functionalism of the dominant theories that they had always and rightly so criticized (Paraskeva, 2019; 2021; 2022). While in the latter, Darder echoes Amilcar Cabral's motto—showing not courage but intellectual honesty, alerting for the dangers constructed within her very own counter-hegemonic republic, in the former, she greatly helps better to unpack the field's original sin, eugenics, and its epistemicidal nature (Paraskeva, 2011; 2014; 2016a; 2018; 2022). In doing so, she transmutes the *Freirean* legacy to another, much more, radical level[4] and openly calls for a commitment to a non-derivative "transcritique" (Karatani, 2003; Paraskeva, 2024). That is, she avoids exploring "dialectical syntheses of opposites and antagonistic positions" (Zizek, 2004, p. 121) and reads the word and the world "neither from one's viewpoint, nor from the viewpoint of others, but to face the reality that is exposed through difference (parallax)" (Zizek, 2004, pp, 121–2; Karatani, 2003). In so doing, Darder epitomizes the call for an itinerant educational/curriculum theory (ICT), viewed as a political praxis that "is both epistemologically fierce and deeply anchored in the sensibilities of our 'subalternities'—the only place from which we can truly rid ourselves of the heavy yoke of Western sanctioned tyranny, which has wrought bitter histories of impoverishment, colonization, enslavement, and genocide" (Darder, 2016, p. x)

As this volume shows, echoing Paulo Freire's (1990)[5] diegeses, Antonia Darder (2022, p. 3) helps one to understand how the epistemicidal nature of white reason saturates our educational institutions any coarcting and "political vision and it is out of sync with the human needs of the massive majority." The yoke of Modern Western Eurocentric epistemologies frames the eugenic supremacy of a Prosperous reason—as Paget Henry (2000) would certainly prefer to put it, one that was able to unleash and legitimize what Paulo Freire called cultural invasion through "the construction and imposition of deceptive myths and deficit views of subordinate cultural populations abound, a reason that preserves and perpetuate unequal institutional structures associated with oppressive forms of social and material control of subaltern populations" (Darder, 2022, p. 2). Darder (2022, p. 4) is quite aware of the eugenic nature of such invasions. She writes:

> An anti-dialogical process that reproduces the social, political, and economic oppression of subordinated populations through silencing the cultural values, lived histories, and voices of subaltern populations. Freire (1970) describes cultural invasion as a process by which "the invaders penetrate the cultural context of another group, in disrespect of the latter's potentialities; they impose their view of the world upon those they invade and inhibit the creativity of the invaded by curbing their expression" (p. 150). The consequence is that those who are invaded are left believing that their survival is predicated on assimilating the ways of their colonizers.

Darder (2011, 2012) ferociously counterattacks by placing the power of biculturalism/ty at the center of the debates. In doing so, she challenges celebratory multicultural impulses. She tries not only to deconstruct the false monumentality of an abyssal eugenic reason (Santos, 2018), thus denouncing the epistemicidal nature of the field—both theoretical and practical (Paraskeva, 2011) but also proposes a path that responds to the legitimacy of the alternative views of the "word and the world" of the oppressed. She dared to do what no *Freirean* had done until then and did what Freire would probably have done in her place and time. She tore a non-derivative *Freirean* river. She hasn't reinvented Paulo Freire—a "cult" so worn in certain Freirean territories that it already creates nausea. She grabs Freire non-derivatively and concomitantly produces a non-derivative *Freirean* river. The metamorphoses inherent to the decolonial hermeneutical dynamics, deeply rooted in the struggles of subaltern students, researchers, and personal lived experiences speak volumes to such a river.

Such a *Darderian* move does not happen overnight, though. Although such a move is quite visible in her most contemporary theoretical decolonial "hermeneuticity," where she crafts a non-derivative philosophy of praxis, the fact is that it permeates her entire trajectory and explains her coherent take when she assumed a ballistic antagonistic posture toward some of the arguments framed within the very counter dominant platform. Her commitment to a "non-derivative philosophy of praxis"—thus refining and complexifying one of the noblest postulates of *Gramscianism*. On one hand, this makes her critique of dominant models more scathing and destructive; and on the other hand, it leaves her no other option than to move away from dogmatic and reactionary counter-hegemonic positions entirely out of touch from the actual colors structuring the dynamics of inequality and social injustice that frame reality triggering endless "people's needs" (Marx, 1843).[6]

Darder's question implies a parallax commitment that she sublimely accomplishes. For example, when she (together with Rodolfo Torres) (2004) counters "backward" takes advanced by some of the heralds of critical race theory. While this was not the only "lethal purge" within the counter-hegemonic planisphere, one should not ignore, for example, Ellsworth's (1989) devastating critique on the reactionary nature of the critical—the truth is that Darder and Torres' (2004) critique was politically chirurgical and impacted a crucial dynamic within the central nervous of coloniality system: "race/

ism." Contrary to Ellsworth (1989), undeniably, Darder and Torres (2004) persistently pushed the debate into a radically different epistemological orbit, denouncing the racialization of critical race theory as fundamentalist at its best and reactionary at its worst.

While they (2004) concur with critical race theorists that capitalism was and remains a racialized political project and that race should be framed as the very core of such a eugenic project impacting the daily life experiences of people of color (Bernal, 1987; Ladson-Billings & Tate IV, 1995), Darder and Torres (2004) argue that poverty, exploitation, and segregation dynamics are structural within the curriculum epistemicide (Paraskeva, 2016a) and cannot be detached from the capitalist modes of production and stripped from its ideological bone. They alert about the dangers of the use of "race as the central unity of analysis of racialized oppression and racism" (Darder & Torres, 2004, p. 98). Such centrality quashes ideological dynamics that manure capitalism's unequal social structures. That is, "the failure to engage the political economy and its impact on class formations" (hooks, 2000; Darder & Torres, 2004, p. 4) situates the debates around critical issues involving class, race, ethnicity, and gender in a dangerous vacuum—what one would call autonomy nullification, a kind of perpetual short circuit in agency dynamics— for any counter-hegemonic agenda. The fallacy not of the centrality of race but of placing race as the only category at the center of the dynamics of inequality and exploitation, Darder and Torres (2004, p. 5) claim, in examining the eugenic bone of the curriculum epistemicide (Paraskeva, 2016a) produces a "circularity of race logic" that legitimizes the erroneously cult that "racism exists because there such thing as race" (p. 100). Concomitantly, they (2004, p. 100) add, such circularity not only ignores that "notions of racism are fundamental ideological constructions of race," but also attempts to weave (and in so many ways successfully) what I would coin as zero-ideological ideology orbit which fertilizes the coloniality zone that "obscures and disguises class interests behind the smokescreen of multiculturalism, diversity, difference, and more recently whiteness" (Darder & Torres, 2004, p. 1). They (2004) pushed the debate to the aeropaus of the dynamics of ideological production (Apple & Weis, 1983), placing "race" with relative autonomy.

While race frames the logic underpinning the capitalist "unreason of reason" (Mbembe, 2017) and was created "to justify a racially exploitative economic system and invented to lock people into the bottom of it" (Oluo, 2018, p. 12), capitalism and its oppressive and exploitive dynamics "does not *just* refer to a racial classification" (Lugones, 2008, p. 2). For example, as I had the opportunity to explain in another context, caste dynamics, while preceding coloniality and the Empire and quite structural during coloniality tenure (Ambedkar, 2018; Teltumbde, 2018; 2010; Paraskeva, 2023), constitute one of the most dangerous forms of segregation. Unfortunately, it is wholly produced as non-existent in our field (Paraskeva, 2023).

Coloniality and its capitalist nerve thus need to be perceived as "an encompassing eugenic phenomenon having 'race' one of the axes of the system of power and as such it permeates all control of sexual access, authority, labor, subjectivity/inter-subjectivity, and the production of knowledge from within these inter-subjective relations." Or all control over "sex, subjectivity, authority, and labor" (Lugones, 2008, p. 2) and I would add class, race, gender, ethnicity, and caste are "articulated around it" (Lugones, 2008, p. 2). That is,

> understanding these features of the organization of gender in the modern/colonial gender system—the biological dimorphism, the patriarchal and heterosexual organizations of relations—is crucial to an understanding of the differential gender arrangements along "racial" lines. Biological dimorphism and heterosexual patriarchy are all characteristics of what I call the 'light' side of the colonial/modern organization of gender. Hegemonically, these are written large over the meaning of gender.
>
> (Lugones, 2008, p. 2)

The Eurocentric Empire of "un/reason," a full-blast "colonization of the culture" (Quijano, 2000, pp. 189–90) is too complex to be explained solely based on the construction of a racialized subject. Such colonization fosters "the elaboration of a Eurocentric perspective of knowledge to legitimize ideas and practices of relations of superiority and inferiority between dominant and dominated" (Quijano, 2000, p. 188). Coloniality is an epistemological beast that "puts all the eggs in one basket, and racial oppression will interact with many other *divisive social categories*, privileges, and disadvantages to produce a myriad of effects" (Oluo, 2018, p. 17). Coloniality and modernities relate to race, class, gender, ethnicity, and caste material as well as inter-intra-subjective social dynamics (Lugones, 2008) not just granting systemic inequality to the social system and its social apparatuses (Althusser, 1971), but also paving the way for an abyssal reason (Santos, 2007) eugenically at its very core.

Darder's *oeuvre*—as this reader demonstrates—is a marvelous journey "through deep differences" (see Karatani, 2003) or "radical differences" (see Jameson, 1991) that helps to move the debate to a non-derivative zone that paves the way to get us out of the straitjacket created not only by deterministic dominant and counter dominant hemispheres, but also by projected antinomies between "extreme, reconstructive postmodern and critical" rivers and face the differences and diversities that arise from them through difference and diversity (Best & Kellner, 1991, p. 257) thus creating pluri-diverse decolonial standpoints toward a just critical approach so needed in our field (Paraskeva, 2024). Darder's question calls for a parallax transcritique (Karatani, 2003), escalates Gramsci's (1990) calls against "indifference as the deadweight of history," and incarnates the non-abyssal ethos of the itinerant educational and curriculum theory (Paraskeva, 2011, 2016, 2022; Jupp, 2017, 2023) that aims "a general epistemology of the impossibility of a general epistemology" (Santos, 2007, p. 67); helping one to understand the impossibility of ending the world as it is without ending the dominant Eurocentric way of mining the meaning (Williams, 2013). Echoing Proust (2003), Darder helps us to understand that such a decolonial move implies "not necessarily seeking new landscapes but having new eyes." As this volume shows, the future of the field certainly needs to go beyond Darder's legacy. However, it cannot avoid going through it.

To be continued.

Notes

1. A decolonial reading of reality implies a unique *Pessoanian* process of "palavrar," that is, the creation of "palavras" (words) so that they say things that no other says, as crafted by the great Mozambican novelist Mia Couto.
2. New order.
3. Of a new order.
4. There is a hasty tendency to treat critical intellectuals and pedagogues as a monolithic group. What I have framed in other contexts as a critical river running within a generation of utopia (Paraskeva, 2011, 2016b, 2018, 2021, 2022) is a diverse and complex group of intellectuals. They all play an important role in the political-pedagogical project of critical theory and pedagogy. However, some take more progressive stances; others subscribe to more left-centrist dynamics (in the United States with liberal impulses); others are committed to radical perspectives, and others to dynamics more aligned with anarchist impulses. Even though these distinctions are not so fixed, static, and objective (just within the Marxist, Neo-Marxist, and Neo-Gramscian "republics," there are infinite and antagonistic dynamics), I think it is crucial to understand the commonalities and differences within and beyond such "rivers," which in the case of Antonia Darder help to situate and understand better her radical critical streak.
5. It is obvious that Paulo Freire was a prolific writer, and his entire intellectual production is extremely important. But it is also true that he will go down in history for having written one of the most insightful books of humanity and certainly the most remarkable piece in the field of critical pedagogy, *Pedagogy of the Oppressed*. This volume is Paulo Freire's book, *the* hallmark of Critical Pedagogies.
6. On this position also see Darder, Antonia, Mayo, Peter and Paraskeva, João M. (2017).

References

Althusser, L. (1971), "Ideology and Ideological State Apparatuses," in L. Althusser (ed.), *Lenin and Philosophy and Other Essays*. New York, NY: New Left Books, 85–126.

Ambedkar, B. (2018), *The Annihilation of Caste*. Triplicane, Chennai: MJ Publishers/Moven Books.

Amin, S. (2008), *The World We Wish to See: Revolutionary Objectives in the Twenty-First Century*. New York, NY: Monthly Review Press.

Apple, M., and Weis, L. (1983), *Ideology and the Practice of Schooling*. Philadelphia, PA: Temple University Press.

Barthes, R. (1977), *The Death of the Author*. London: Fontana.

Bernal, M. (1987), *Black Athena: The Afroasiatic Roots of Classical Civilization*. New Brunswick, NJ: Rutgers University Press.

Best, S., and Kellner, D. (1991), *Postmodern Theory: Critical Interrogations*. London: Bloomsbury Publishing.

Blanchot, M. (1989), *The Space of Literature*. Lincoln, NE: University of Nebraska Press.

Cabral, A. (1973), *Return to the Source: Selected Speeches of Amilcar Cabral*. New York, NY: Monthly Review Press.

Darder, A. (2011), *A Dissident Voice*. New York, NY: Peter Lang.

Darder, A. (2012), *Culture and Power in the Classroom*, 2nd ed. Boulder, CO: Paradigm.

Darder, A. (2016), "Foreword. Ruthlessness and the Forging of Liberatory Epistemologies: An Arduous Journey," in J. M. Paraskeva (ed.), *Curriculum Epistemicides*. New York, NY: Routledge, ix–xvi.

Darder, A., ed. (2019), *Decolonizing Interpretive Research: A Subaltern Methodology for Social Change*. New York, NY: Routledge.

Darder, A. (2022), "Reflections on Cultural Democracy and Schooling," Target article for the Special Issue on "Cultural Democracy and Social Justice in the Classroom". *Aula de Encuentro* 24(1): 39–89.

Darder, A., and Torres, R., D. (2004), *After Race: Racism after Multiculturalism*. New York, NY: New York University Press.

Darder, A., Mayo, P., and Paraskeva, J. M. (2017), "Introduction," in A. Darder, P. Mayo, and J. M. Paraskeva (eds.), *International Critical Pedagogy Reader*. New York, NY: Routledge, 13–36.

Dussel, E. (1984), *The Underside of Modernity*. New Jersey, NJ: Humanities Press.

Dussel, E. (1995), *Philosophy of Liberation*. Eugene, OR: Wipf & Stock.

Dussel, E. (2013), *Ethics of Liberation: In the Age of Globalization and Exclusion*. Durham, NC: Duke University Press.

Eagleton, T. (2003), *After Theory*. New York, NY: Basic Books.

Ellsworth, E., (1989), "Why Doesn't This Feel Empowering? Working through the Repressive Myths of Critical Pedagogy," Harvard Educational Review, 59, 297–324.

Fanon, F. (1963), *Wretched of the Earth*. New York, NY: Penguin Books.

Foucault, M. (1973), *The Order of Things*. New York, NY: Vintage Books.

Freire, P. (1970), *Pedagogy of the Oppressed*. New York, NY: Continuum.

Freire, P. (1990), *Pedagogy of the Oppressed*. New York, NY: Continuum.

Gil, José (1998), *Metamorphoses of the Body*. Minneapolis, MN: University of Minnesota Press.

Gil, J. (2018), *Caos e Ritmo*. Lisboa: Relógio D'Água.

Gramsci, A. (1990), *Selections from Prison Notebooks*. New York, NY: International Publications.

Henry, P. (2000), *Caliban Reason*. New York, NY: Routledge.

hooks, b. (2000), *Where We Stand: Class Matters*. New York, NY: Routledge.

Jal, M. (2023), "Epistemological Untouchability: The Deafening Silence of Indian Academics," in J. M. Paraskeva (ed.), *Critical Perspectives on the Denial of Caste in Educational Debate Towards a Non-derivative Curriculum Reason*. New York: Routledge, 188–239.

Jameson, F. (1991), *Postmodernism or the Cultural Logic of Late Capitalism*. Durham, NC: Duke University Press.

Jupp, J. (2017), "Decolonizing and De-canonizing Curriculum Studies: The Contribution of João M. Paraskeva's Works." *Journal of the American Association for the Advancement of Curriculum Studies* 12(1): 1–25.

Jupp, J. (2023), *Itinerant Curriculum Theory: Decolonial Praxis, Theories, and Histories*. New York, NY: Peter Lang.

Karatani, K. (2003), *Transcritique: On Kant and Marx*. Cambridge, MA: MIT Press.

Ladson Billings, G., and Tate, W. (1995), "Toward a Theory of Critical Race Theory in Education." *Teachers College Record* 97(1): 47–68.

Lugones, M. (2008), "Coloniality of Gender." *Worlds and Knowledges Otherwise* 2(Spring): 1–17.

Marx, K. (1843), "Critique of Hegel's Philosophy of Right." New York, NY: New Comb Livraria Press.

Marx, K. (1976), *Karl Marx: Thesis of Feuerbach*. http://www.marx2mao.com/M&E/TF45.html.
Mbembe, A. (2017), *A Critique of White Reason*. Durham, NC: Duke University Press.
Mignolo, W. (2018), "The Invention of the Human and the Three Pillars of the Coloniality Matrix of Power," in C. Walsh and W. Mignolo (eds.), *On Decoloniality: Concepts, Analytics, Praxis*. Durham, NC: Duke University Press, 153–76.
Nkrumah, K. (1964), *Consciencism*. New York, NY: Monthly Review Press.
Oliveira, I. (2024), "ICT and Curriculum as Everyday Creation: A Doable Possibility of the Emancipation of Curriculum Theory," in J. M. Paraskeva (ed.), *Itinerant Curriculum Theory: A Declaration of Epistemological Independence*. London: Bloomsbury, 143–160.
Oluo, I. (2018), *So You Want to Talk about Race?* New York, NY: Seal Press.
Paraskeva, J. M. (2011), *Conflicts in Curriculum Theory*, 1st ed. New York, NY: Palgrave.
Paraskeva, J. M. (2014), *Conflicts in Curriculum Theory*. Paperback 1st ed. New York, NY: Palgrave.
Paraskeva, J. M. (2015), "The Curriculum: Whose Internationalization?," in J. M. Paraskeva (ed.), *The Curriculum: Whose Internationalization?* New York, NY: Peter Lang, 1–12.
Paraskeva, J. M. (2016a), *Curriculum Epistemicides*. New York, NY: Routledge.
Paraskeva, J. M. (2016b), "Opening Up Curriculum Canon to Democratize Democracy," in J. M. Paraskeva and S. Steinberg (eds.), *Curriculum: Decanonizing the Field*. New York, NY: Peter Lang, 3–38.
Paraskeva, J. M., ed. (2018), *Towards a Just Curriculum Theory: The Epistemicide*. New York, NY: Routledge.
Paraskeva, J. M. (2019), "What Happened to (Curriculum) Critical Theory? The Need to Go above and beyond Neoliberal Rage without Avoiding It." *Linguagens, Educação e Sociedade* 24(41): 58–94.
Paraskeva, J. M. (2021), *Curriculum and the Generation of Utopia*. New York, NY: Routledge.
Paraskeva, J. M. (2022), "Introduction. The Original Sin. A Critique of the Curriculum Reason: Towards a 'Non-Derivative' Critical Curriculum Reason," in J. M. Paraskeva (ed.), *The Curriculum: A New Comprehensive Reader*. New York, NY: Peter Lang, 1–60.
Paraskeva, João M. (2023), *Critical Perspectives on the Denial of Caste in Educational Debate: Towards a Non-Derivative Curriculum Reason*. New York, NY: Routledge.
Paraskeva, João M. (2024), *Itinerant Curriculum Theory: A Declaration of Epistemological Independence*. London: Bloomsbury.
Pessoa, Fernando (2002), *The Book of Disquiet*. New York, NY: Penguin Books.
Proust, M. (2003), *In Search of Lost Time*. New York, NY: Penguin Books.
Quijano, A. (1991), "Colonialidad y Modernidad/Racionalidad." *Perú Indígena* 29(1): 11–21.
Quijano, A. (2000), "Coloniality of Power and Eurocentrism in Latin America." *International Sociology* 15(2): 215–32.
Santos, B. de Sousa (2007), *Another Knowledge Is Possible*. London: Verso.
Santos, B. de Sousa (2014), *Epistemologies from the South*. Boulder, CO: Paradigm Publishers.
Santos, B. de Sousa (2018), *The End of the Cognitive Empire*. Durham, NC: Duke University Press.
Teltumbde, A. (2010), *The Persistence of Caste: The Khairlanji Murders and India's Hidden Apartheid*. New York, NY: Zed Books.

Teltumbde, A. (2018), "Umar Khalid and the Hate Republic." *Economic and Political Weekly* 53(36) (September 8): 1–3.
Williams, R. (2013), *Long Revolution*. London: Verso.
Žižek, S. (2004), "The Parallax View." *New Left Review* 25: 121–34.

Epilogue: Teaching for the End of the World (As We Know It): Decolonizing the Curricular Limits of Modernity

As we consider the conditions that exist around the globe, what has become increasingly obvious is the unsustainability and unprecedented irrationality of today's world. Vanessa Machado de Oliveira (2021) suggests "although modernity always sees itself and behaves as if 'young,' it has grown old and is facing its end" (p. xxii). The world in which most of us reside has emerged directly from the greed and impunities associated with the principles of modernity—principles that fiercely uphold the structures of patriarchy, colonization, and capitalism despite progressive proclamations to the contrary. My aim here is to briefly unpack institutional patterns related to the curriculum that are ensconced in the logic of modernity—patterns that camouflage, negate, and refute a worldview that sustains the impoverishment of the majority of the world's population. This speaks to conditions carried out through an unsustainable global system of human exploitation and resource extraction. Inherent to this analysis is the very epistemicidal nature of the curriculum—its theories, research, design, and development—paving the way for particular principles of schooling framed within the logic modernity, which, as we will see later, constitutes an abyssal divide (Santos, 2007). Such divisive reason normalizes, disciplines, conditions, oppresses, and anesthetizes students at every level of the enterprise to perceive social injustices, epistemological apartheid, and human suffering as commonsensical phenomena while dehumanizing and blaming the oppressed for their own misfortunes.

Fundamental to this discussion are the ways in which curricular patterns, shaped by the epistemicidal logic of modernity, have failed to create the conditions for the development of the full potential of students, particularly of working-class and racialized students. So, while some may argue that education has made significant advancements in terms of accessibility and knowledge dissemination globally, colonizing structures, policies, and practices of schooling have consistently placed an overemphasis on the standardization of dominant knowledge and the uniformity of processes, procedures, and outcomes in sync with the advancement of capitalism. Hidden in this blatant fallacy of uniformity as a guarantor of equality is the systematic refusal to acknowledge the impossibility of social policies that deter just access. Furthermore, policies and discursive practices of equality thrown into inequitable curricular structures only serve to multiply inequalities and social injustices. This approach, primarily driven by a focus on individualism, competition, efficiency, meritocracy, and accountability, has failed to address the larger collective needs of students and their formation as culturally democratic citizens. By narrowing the focus solely on measurable outcomes and overemphasizing individual needs instead of social collective needs, as has been so prevalent in the last four decades of neoliberal rule, Western educational institutions have neglected the critical democratic formation of students, prioritizing the instrumentalization and marketization of knowledge production. Under the auspices of modernity, educational structures, including those of curriculum development, constitute the lab through which regulatory forms of knowledge and cultural production have been developed and legitimized.

This narrow focus has limited the abilities of teachers, students, parents, and the community to engage in effective transformative and emancipatory practices that are so essential to challenging oppressive social structures and fostering institutional practices that engender social justice, collective human rights, and economic democracy. Accordingly, incessant data gathering and the expansion of meritocratic accountability regimes substitute for critical engagement in the real concerns that shape students' classroom experiences, particularly of racialized, working-class students. This signals the perpetuation of an epistemicidal curriculum that too quickly circumvents questions of criticality (Paraskeva, 2011). Within such a context, the troubled conditions of our world are easily skirted or obscured despite growing repression of democratic rights; increasing poverty amid obscene wealth accumulation; a nation perpetually at war; environmental havoc; the proliferation of police shootings of youth of color; massive waves of immigration that are addressed inhumanly; the unprecedented incarceration of subaltern populations; and state-sanctioned attacks against public education by unaccountable billionaires, corporate foundations, and the media (Burns, 2015).

With this in mind, our work must encompass interdependent and multidimensional lenses that engage more substantively conditions associated with the social, material, emotional, and spiritual dimensions of our shared humanity. Such an integral approach can assist us in disrupting modernity's ideological prison, in ways that can make clearer what it means *to teach for the end of the world as we know it*. This also entails deliberating on what it means to teach both within the midst of a process of chaotic transition, while we simultaneously prepare ourselves, our students, and our communities in ways that can help us embrace new possibilities in how we define humanity, education, justice, and collective existence in the years to come. It entails a non-derivative itinerant pedagogy (Paraskeva, 2016) to "discover not what we are but to refuse what we are" (Foucault, 1980, p. 216). In essence, this speak to a curricular process of unlearning oppressive and conditioned notions of learning and being in the world, while simultaneously encompassing the multidimensionality of life and the interdependence and inseparability of our humanity.

What Machado de Oliveira (2021) makes painfully clear in her treatise on *Hospicing Modernity* is that this process cannot be undertaken effectively without thoughtful efforts to demythologize the values of modernity, which requires from us all a critical examination of modernity's assumptions, power dynamics, and consequences. By naming, challenging, and deconstructing the institutional mechanisms and relationships that perpetuate the ideological reproduction of modernity's entrenched apparatus, anticolonial and decolonial paradigms can unfold organically in ways that can assist us to shift our collective consciousness toward a more just future.

Demythologizing Modernity

As Paulo Freire (1971) understood, "[A] critical and dynamic view of the world strives to unveil reality, unmask its mythicization, and achieve a full realization of the human task: the permanent transformation of reality in favor of the liberation of people" (p. 102). Whether we are examining levels of growing economic inequality in the world, massive waves of immigration, forecasting future pandemics, reemergence of dangerous nationalists and populist with overt eugenic impulses, or evaluating the devastating impact of climate change, what is increasingly observable is the destruction of the liberal social contract of the past, echoed by the deterioration of the power of civil society, including human relationships at every level. Of this, Fraser (2013) has argued that the social contract, which establishes the rights and responsibilities between citizens and the state, has been eroded in contemporary society. The rise of neoliberalism (as a global expression of advanced capitalism) and its prioritization of market forces have served to divide and aggravate the lack of collective solidarity, widening social inequalities around the world. Similarly, the global proliferation of Western education has failed to be the great panacea in that "the world has greater access to formal educational opportunity than ever before, yet many of the individual and collective benefits education promises are falling further and further out of reach" (Toukan, 2023, p. 1). And, despite looming signs of societal collapse, twenty-first-century institutions remain as normative, disciplinary apparatuses (Foucault, 1980) blocking any anti-dialectical (Deleuze, 1989) and emancipatory praxis (Santos, 2007) and stubbornly adhered to a logic of modernity—a debilitating logic of power consolidation and material accumulation that has conditioned us all to horde as much as possible, instead of facing the deeper personal, relational, structural, and spiritual traumas that incapacitate and disrupt possibilities for genuine democratic life.

In order to demythologize modernity, we must consistently question its foundations, challenge its established norms, and disrupt the prevailing power structures that perpetuate its deceptive logic of human advancement and progress. Toward this end, Machado de Oliveira and others have argued that the one-story line of modernity has been essential to justifying institutional structures that, wittingly or unwittingly, perpetuate poverty, racism, sexism, and other brutal forms of inequalities worldwide. Moreover, we cannot deny modernity's role in propagating government initiatives and business policies and practices of expropriation, extraction, exploitation, militarization, dispossession, destitution, genocides, and ecocides worldwide. Internationally, it has bolstered a system of economic domination by the Global North over the Global South in that the majority of the wealth of the Global North has been proliferated and sustained "by historical and systemic processes of exploitation, resource extraction, land-grabbing, unfair trade, enforced debt, and tied aid"(Machado de Oliveira, 2021, p. 67).

Within the United States, this is made apparent by the ways in which oppressed populations are systematically arranged and divested (or "planned," particularly within urban contexts) through policies and practices that produce and reproduce social and material inequalities related to housing, labor, education, health care, and transportation, alongside one of the largest and brutal racialized incarceration systems in the world. Conditions tied to global economic apartheid must be recognized then as part of a deeper structural and epistemic political project that shapes the conditions of people's lives, both domestically and internationally. As such, what happens locally within schools and communities is always connected to international structural forces related to labor and the marketplace—forces generally obscured by the mythical rhetoric of modernity. And despite the many social and technological advances that have transpired in the last century, humanity still remains deeply divided between the haves and have-nots. Humanity as we know it is only possible through its sub-humanity (Santos, 2014). The majority of the world's countries are governed by the law of profit and greed, which normalizes the economic precarity created by the financial anarchy of the wealthy and powerful. Hence, the logic of modernity bolsters sweeping controls over the internationalization of capital, as well as narrowly defines the culture of knowledge production, which sustains the concentration of power and wealth among a very small percentage of the world's population. The neoliberal cult of "profit over people" (Chomsky, 1999), more than simply consolidating and worsening the poverty of the working class, actually triggers the formation of a new class—the precariat (Paraskeva, 2024).

Over the last decade, a variety of Oxfam[1, 2] reports have outlined the shocking facts about global poverty. Eight men own more wealth than 3.6 billion people (that's half of the world's population). The collective wealth of the world's five wealthiest men more than doubled between 2020 and the end of 2023, ballooning from an already staggering $405 billion to $869 billion.[3] The wealthiest 1 percent own more than twice as much wealth as 6.9 billion people. Meanwhile, poverty continues to take a devastating toll on the lives of more than 700 million people who live in extreme poverty. Closer to home, US data show that the top 10 percent of the population own 70 percent of the country's wealth.[4] Moreover, The US Census Bureau reports that more than 40 million people in the United States live in poverty, including one child in every six. Growing income inequality and the toxic combination of tax breaks for the rich, unemployment and unstable employment, increasing indebtedness, and devastating cuts to the social safety net have served to not only bankrupt promises of equity touted across educational institutions, but also make clear that modernity is indeed in decay.

With this is mind, it is imperative that we confront the greed, lovelessness, and immorality of those who perpetuate conditions of economic and cultural apartheid, through the use of a Cartesian rationality that separates, marginalizes, invisibilizes, and exterminates those perceived as enemies or obstructions to modernity's project of progress (Leitão, 2018), in many cases producing them as "non-existent" (Santos, 2018). With this in mind, decolonizing efforts must counter commonsense myths such as "the poor will always be with us"; or that "the poor are poor because of their own doing"; or that oppressed populations are culturally and intellectually deficient, and thus require fixing; or that we are all on a level playing field and those who "win" or prosper are the natural heroes. To demythologize modernity's commonsensical categories implies a commitment to a non-derivative epistemology of "countersense" (Paraskeva, 2024).

It is astonishing that so many who live in the Global North seem blatantly unaware that most of their comforts, freedoms, and rights have been and continue to be built on the backs of oppressed populations. As such, they remain unaware of the ways in which projected myths of scarcity perpetuate commonsensical beliefs that there are not enough resources for all; that having more is better; and that the current state of massive global inequality is simply the outcome of Social Darwinism; that is, a survival of the fittest. Needless to say, such unawareness is not innocent at all, in that mainstream myths conveniently justify modernity's rationale for perpetual accumulation in the name of progress, obscure conditions of oppression, and deflect responsibility away from those responsible for global poverty and human suffering in the first place.

The construction and imposition of colonizing myths and deficit views reinforce what the late Brazilian educational philosopher Paulo Freire (1971) termed *cultural invasion*—a social instrument of domination that arises out of a deliberate and planned intention to forge social, political, and economic control. Accordingly, the ancestral wisdom, knowledge, and ways of existence of the oppressed are rendered marginal. Within universities, for example, there is "much ambivalence about the legitimacy of indigenous knowledge and the role of indigenous intellectuals" (Mutua & Swadener, 2004, p. 10). Hence, there has always been an implicit (or explicit) demand placed on subaltern populations to abandon our cultural ways of being, our language, and our cultural wisdom, in order to belong or succeed within mainstream institutions. Diversity and difference on these grounds are akin to a derivative and representational politics of tolerance, where different-colored individuals are allowed, as long as we embrace the fundamental ideals of modernity that perpetuate the dominant social order.

To contend with institutional dynamics that sustain such expectations requires a critique that moves beyond typical discussions of "race" or racism or identity politics, in order to unveil the dehumanizing structural forces of modernity's nerve center—namely, capitalism. This signals a critique that challenges steadfastly the colonizing forces linked to class, race, gender, disability, sexuality, and other markers of social inequality—forces that function to sustain the suppression of oppressed populations deemed problematic to capitalist accumulation. Furthermore, the inclination to overlook poverty as a *necessary prerequisite* of capitalism in discussions of material and social exclusion, within education and beyond, is hugely responsible for perpetuating ineffective focalized views of the problem—where the problem and its corresponding solutions are treated as independent from its underlying systemic origin. Here, we can point to the manner in which the standardized curriculum and the accompanying system of meritocracy and accountability within schools and universities are shaped by modernist principles of individualism and competition in ways that frame reality as a totality. Consequently, institutions overlook or ignore not just the deeper social and material realities that impact student learning but also how different and diverse such realities actually are.

It is essential then to unveil the pedagogical dynamics within schools and universities that provoke social reification and alienation, reinforcing a deep sense of estrangement of students from nature and from their own bodies. In *Pedagogy of the Oppressed*, Freire (1971) noted that forces of alienation within education serve to intensify student anxieties, insecurities, and their fear of freedom, given the manner in which social alienation and disaffiliation thwart epistemological curiosity and passion for learning, aspects important to intellectual and political formation. The consequence is that within the context of education, whether wittingly or unwittingly, the colonizing logic of modernity is upheld to the detriment of students and their communities, who, as Young (1990) argued, exist fettered by the five faces of oppression—namely, systemic violence, exploitation, marginalization, powerlessness, and cultural imperialism.

The Colonizing Logic of Modernity

To move beyond the limits of modernity, epistemicidal patterns of representation and relational engagement embedded in its colonizing logic must be unveiled—patterns that camouflage, negate, and refute its foundational role in perpetuating what Quijano (1992) terms as *el patron colonial de poder* or *colonial matrix of power*, which persists long after official colonial structures of governance have been dismantled (Mignolo, 2007). More specifically, this refers to enduring colonial relations of power linked to economic control, control of authority, control of the public sphere, and ideological control (or control of what knowledge is considered truth). As Mignolo (2007) recognized:

> [B]oth "liberation" and "decolonization" point toward conceptual (and therefore epistemic) projects of de-linking from the colonial matrix of power. Because of the global reach of European modernity, de-linking ... presupposes border thinking or border epistemology in the precise sense that the Western foundation of modernity and of knowledge is, on the one hand, unavoidable and, on the other, highly limited and dangerous.
>
> (p. 455)

Subsequently, we all continue to be mired in the legacy of colonialism, which gave rise to histories of patriarchy, slavery, apartheid, and genocide. Furthermore, colonialism as a global hegemonic project was essential to the historical proliferation of the modernist ethos, of which conquest and annihilation constitute the driving forces. Concurrently, modernity lays claim to values of benevolence and universality on one hand, while attempting to justify and conceal its violent forces of unsustainability, on the other.

Moreover, modernity has perpetuated an epistemology of war, conquest, and annihilation, where violence is carried out by the systemic objectification of the Other and the separation of human beings from their organic relationship to nature, the planet, and beyond. Modernity is not only related to the territorial occupation of individuals and communities considered inferior or sub-human, but in many cases their systematic extermination. Modernity then must be understood as an epistemicidal project, with an epistemic commitment to occupy and colonize the minds of those who manage to survive extermination (Cabral, 1973; Memmi, 1991; Césaire, 2000). In its wake, we have witnessed, for example, long-standing political tolerance for the displacement, segregation, and most recent genocide of more than 30,000 Palestinians by the Israeli government of Netanyahu (Batrawy, 2024). Attacks in the region have been carried out even as Israeli citizens themselves, along with millions of people around the world, continue to protest the inhumanity and injustices being perpetrated in their name—injustices tied to nearly eight decades of political and economic subjugation of a people within their own homeland. This is a contemporary example of how oppressed populations fighting for self-determination have been historically objectified, racialized, animalized, and demonized as deserving extermination. Ultimately, Palestinians have been denied the right to fight back against the structural traumas of occupation they have faced since 1948. The irony here is that conditions of apartheid and genocide are being enacted by a government whose people have historically known such oppression and genocide. Even more disconcerting is the manner in which any critiques of the Israeli government are quickly judged and interpreted as antisemitism, in an effort to silence dissent and delegitimate criticism of antidemocratic policies and military actions taken by Israel, as nation-state, against a sovereign people. What cannot be lost here is the limits of progressive politics in challenging and deterring Israel's growing authoritarianism and disdain for democracy (Hill & Plitnick, 2021).

Underlying this phenomenon are also an anthropocentric politics of absolutism and epistemic Eurocentric exceptionalism, in which modernity privileges and positions certain humans at the center, as both primary and separate from any significant relationship to the rest of existence. This is defended on the grounds that humans have the capacity to reason, while the intelligence of other life forms is considered inferior and without real consequence. In this way, the eugenic logic of modernity—so rooted in the struggles for the US curriculum—naturalizes, normalizes, disciplines, and justifies arbitrary categorizations, divisions, and hierarchies, including the racializing of human beings through the articulation of signifier/signified of supremacy or deficiency. This phenomenon is enacted by privileging the worth of dominant bodies and cultures, as well as their particular approach to knowledge production. This has served historically to defend cultural, racialized, gendered, and spiritual supremacy and absolutism, wherein certain people are considered to naturally embody authority, to be the legitimate arbiters of justice, and best suited to impose objective and universal parameters and protocols for morality, ethics, economy, politics, and science.

Another example here is the manner in which Christianity, a key player on the colonial stage, justified the murder and pillaging of indigenous populations by considering them to be beasts or without souls. Along these lines, the denial of the humanity of the Other has been central to modernity's political expression, where an implicit and explicit racialized hierarchy of humanity has prevailed for centuries. Within this one-dimensional story of progress, the oppressed are falsely assumed to be a uniform, monolithic category, or totalized entity in need of salvation. Western notions of "humanizing the oppressed" are, thus, rooted in a paternalistic benevolence that seeks to repair subaltern humanity or infuse humanity onto those who are deemed as inhuman or lesser humans. This is in contrast with decolonizing or anticolonial views of humanity or humanization, grounded in an understanding that we are all already human beings (it isn't a quality that needs to be bestowed upon us), that there is a myriad of human diversity and difference within and across oppressed communities, and that any humanizing project must fundamentally encompass a multiplicity of struggle to dismantle oppressive structures that deny us the diverse expression of our humanity.

Furthermore, the ethos of modernity is advanced as the only legitimate means for social mobility within education and society, where a one-dimensional story of human progress, development, and evolution has been naturalized and normalized through advancing a one-dimensional curriculum and system of evaluation, as well as a one-dimensional view of human beings (Marcuse, 1964). Traditional forms of curriculum theory and development, steeped in modernist principles, function not just to colonize student consciousness (including what they believe is possible for themselves and their communities), in conjunction with the ongoing economic and social colonization of the material world. In the process, the hegemonic values perpetuated within the traditional curriculum and its approach to knowledge production function to systematically perpetuate complacency and consensus, whilst concurrently suppressing the expression of dissent within the classroom and beyond.

In fact, traditional forms of curriculum theory and development, both dominant and counter-dominant, much more than relating to mechanisms of colonialization have committed themselves to blatant epistemicide (killing of knowledge) by proclaiming both scientific validity and historical legitimacy of Eurocentric epistemological platforms, to the detriment of those who exist beyond the Eurocentric matrix. Colonialism unquestionably has an epistemicidal nature in its genesis. In other words, the inculcation of modernity's ways of existing and thinking onto colonized individuals and communities simultaneously has implied, wittingly or unwittingly, an epistemological extermination of the ways of thinking and existing of the colonized. In fact, this is one of the most blatant blind spots of many counter-hegemonic intellectuals and movements. There seems to be an inability to understand that the dominant curriculum model cannot be transformed using the same Eurocentric epistemological tools that bog them down in a functionalist quagmire. These represent the same oppressive tools criticized as being the prerogative of conventional positivist and behaviorist movements (Paraskeva, 2016, 2022, 2023). The epistemicidal nature of the curriculum, therefore, cannot be fully understood or disrupted apart from struggles between hegemonic and counter-hegemonic movements within institutions and communities.

It is precisely with an eye toward disrupting the eugenic practices tied to the Western curriculum within educational institutions that Machado de Oliveira (2021) denounces the process of curricular colonization; and highlights how the epistemicidal process is accomplished through a series of institutional patterns of representation and engagement. These include:

- *Hegemonic practices* that reinforce and justify the status quo
- *Eurocentric projections* that present the dominant view as universal and superior
- *Ahistorical thinking* that forgets or denies the role of historical legacies and complicities

- *Depoliticized orientations* that disregard the impact of power inequalities and suppress dissent
- *Self-serving motivations* that are invested in self-congratulatory heroism or triumphalism
- *Uncomplicated solutions* that offer "feel good" quick fixes that leave the root of problems untouched
- *Paternalistic projections* that infantilize subaltern populations and seek or expect gratitude from those who have been "helped."

As might be obvious here, an ideological apparatus of denial within dominant social apparatuses (Althusser, 1971) is absolutely essential to perpetuating conditions that conserve these institutional patterns of representation and engagement. As such, Machado de Oliveira (2021) also argues that modernity constrains our consciousness through denials that serve to obscure institutional patterns of injustice, even in the midst of expressed commitments to diversity, equity, inclusiveness, or educational justice.

- Denial of systemic, historical, and ongoing violence and of complicity in harm
- Denial of the limits of the planet and of the unsustainability of modernity and coloniality
- Denial of entanglement: viewing human beings as separate from each other
- Denial of the magnitude and complexity of the problems we need to face together, by looking for simplistic solutions, generally aligned with the economic bottom-line

Machado de Oliveira's (2021) reasoning speaks volumes to the true nature of the epistemicidal denial that saturates the curriculum field (Darder, 2015, 2019; Paraskeva, 2016, 2022, 2023). In light of this discussion, the difficulties we face in our efforts to actualize change in the curriculum are linked to the ways in which educational institutions, domestically and internationally, uphold these denials—denials embedded in the prevailing logic of modernity that shapes the foundational character of the Western educational enterprise, which is mobilized worldwide. Anchored in modernist logic, epistemic cleansing can be denied and the divide between legitimate and delegitimate knowledge preserved by the use of textbooks and curricular materials within disciplines and fields of study that perpetuate and reinforce the dominant cultural and economic worldview.

In summary, the hegemony of modernity and the monumentalism of its epistemic empire (Santos, 2018) are upheld within curricular studies by: (1) defending the more benevolent expression of modernity, associated with progressivism, democracy, industrialization, secularization, humanism, individualism, scientific reasoning, and the conservation of the nation-state; (2) accommodating critiques, as long as the critiques are not conflictive and do not disrupt or shatter the epistemic lens of the dominant ideologies and its allegiance to capitalist life; (3) appropriating emancipatory cultural language, while stripping it of its emancipatory or revolutionary intent; and (4) weaving a very concrete discursive praxis that, through mechanisms of a derivative articulation and rearticulation of the commonsense, promotes a one-dimensional representational approach to reality (Hall, 1996). Hence, it is not surprising that since the 1960s civil rights era of the United States, for example, there has been much curricular posturing related to equal rights, diversity, and social justice, yet the perpetuation of alarming equity gaps in education and the economy within subaltern communities persists.

On Challenging Modernity

By opening the veins of modernity (Galeano, 1997), we create the opportunity to bring greater awareness to the oppressive conditions of our lives, under the politics of subalternity. In the process, we can also unveil how the logic of modernity has narrowed and twisted the lives of oppressed populations, while concurrently feigning ignorance about the consequences that colonialism (and capitalism) has had upon the contemporary issues that plague around the world (Leitão, 2018). This spirit is echoed in bell hooks's (1981) proclamation, "I will not have my life narrowed down. I will not bow down to somebody's else's whim or to someone else's ignorance" (p. 109). Nevertheless, challenging the culture of modernity is not an easy task, given the manner in which many educators safeguard their allegiance to privileges sustained by modernist principles. Thus, to challenge the logic of modernity requires great imagination, to consider what might actually be possible; as well as a great deal of curiosity about that which is yet to be imagined. Somehow, in the midst of modernist decay and its symptoms of collapse, those committed to justice will need to collectively garner the political will to consistently challenge systemic expressions of oppression that can strip us of our dignity and our right to be.

As noted earlier, this entails de-linking from the hegemonic cognitive empire (Mignolo, 2018; Santos, 2018) and concomitantly dismantling the myths that sustain, normalize, and naturalize the values of modernity. That is, that conserve our separation from nature, alleged universalism, default humanism, accumulation as aspirational goal, and the idea of "helping" others catch up with the knowledge of the West. At this juncture, the words by aboriginal activist, Lila Watson, expressed in her address at the 1985 United Nations Decade for Women Conference in Nairobi, in response to persisting colonial perceptions and attitudes in their offers of help, seems useful. "If you have come here to help me, you are wasting your time. But if you have come because your liberation is bound up with mine, then let us work together" (quoted in Sovereign Union, 2011). Lila's words challenge the hidden and not so hidden ways in which the logic of modernity advances cultural supremacy, as well as point to the radical shift in consciousness necessary to accomplish this task.

Thus, often underlying official interventions within oppressed individuals and communities are the belief that there is one superior way to learn, to work, to live, to feel, to listen, to look, to love, to think, and to exist. Similarly, we see the propensity for conquest and economic accumulation, carried out in the name of progress— progress as a totality, a monolithic destiny, an inevitable entity. Within schools, this is transmitted through a "neutral" curriculum that is tied to a so-called scientifically meritocratic cult (Young, 1958), which paves the way for a oppressive system of power and privilege. Within education, policies emphasize high-stakes testing, curricular standardization, and meritocratic accountability measures, in the midst of a precarious terrain of oppressive social policies. This also points to the debilitating use of labels and commonsense categorizations. Examples abound in the treatment of Attention-Deficit/Hyperactivity Disorder (ADHD), opioid dependency, and other addictions, ss well as in the (mis)perception and (mis)labeling of those whose treatments are co-opted by the haves and made unreachable to the overwhelming number of children, youth, and adults from oppressed populations who live as casualties of structural trauma [Maté, 2018]. Within communities, this phenomenon is also at work in the politics of gentrification and policing, enacted supposedly as a means for increasing the stability, well-being, and safety of neighborhoods, but usually results in pushing out working-class and racialized communities, whose members can no longer afford rents or local services. It does not require great stretch of the imagination to see all this is aligns with the interests of the ruling class.

To challenge the cultural roots of modernity and open the way toward the reinvention of institutional structures and practices, educators, students, activists, and researchers must recognize the link between culture and power and its role in the cultural, historical, and linguistic experiences of oppressed communities (Darder, 2012). This is essential to engaging school and community conditions of class inequality and racism, where the political dynamics between oppressed individuals and communities and mainstream institutions are often difficult, contentious, and strained. These dynamics are apparent wherever people of modest means must struggle for their sovereignty and recognition (Taylor, 1994; Fraser & Honneth, 2006), the integrity of their cultural beliefs, respect for their ways of life, and their collective right to self-determine their own destinies.

An often-ignored dimension of this struggle, as alluded above in hooks's (1981) words, is the burden of having to fit into the mainstream myth of normalcy; or having to present ourselves in a way that is comfortable to those who hold institutional authority and power over our destinies. This also illustrates some of the ways racism and the process of racialization are pervasively at work within oppressed individuals and communities, but also how class antagonisms impact formal and informal institutional structures and relationships that keep people divided into categories of superior/inferior, visible/invisible (Ellison, 1952), and existent/nonexistent (Santos, 2007). If certain populations, for example, are not seen or identified as part of the dominant culture or class, they can often be perceived as anti-intellectuals or inferior, justifying intervention by experts whose job it is to "save" oppressed populations from our backwardness. In an act that Freire (1971) called "false generosity," those from the dominant culture (even on the left) have intervened paternalistically into the lives of subaltern communities to "teach us" the proper way to be. This destructive symptom of epistemicide mines, contaminates, and saturates the curriculum field, including its theories, research, development, and practices (Jupp, 2017, 2023; Paraskeva, 2024).

In other instances, actions are taken in the name of equality and democracy; but this, more often than not, is a conditional democracy, based on our willingness to assimilate, acquiesce, or adhere to the dominant values and class priorities assigned by capitalist society. As such, our curricular and pedagogical work within schools and communities must cultivate a greater understanding about how conventional approaches to curriculum development remain harnessed to a culturally invasive project of modernity, as well as demonstrate that the successful alternative forms of praxis are indeed possible. A useful transformative example of such a praxis has been prominent in the pedagogy of the Highlander Folk School (now the Highlander Research and Education Center), whose work is described in a dialog between Myles Horton and Paulo Freire (1990) in *We Make the Road by Walking*.

For almost a century, Highlander has supported the leadership and efforts of labor activists, civil rights activists (including Rosa Parks), members of the Appalachian People's Struggles, and more recently Latino immigrants and young people, in developing new strategies and alliances to advance multiracial, intergenerational movements for social and economic justice. The Center's work has, moreover, supported genuine transformation in how communities see the Other. This is an essential question, given that our capacity to work together during difficult times can only be realized through our communal engagement of the realities, conditions, needs, and interests of the communities that we say we seek to serve—and this can only be accomplished *with* them. Such cultural transformation begins by disrupting modernity's ideological prison—a prison of exclusion reinforced by the belief that only the "experts" have the right to decide and self-determine their lives and the lives of others in society. It is this elitist belief, perpetuated by the colonizing culture of education, that has for centuries sought to stifle the intellectual and political formation of subaltern populations.

Decolonizing Curriculum Studies

Within education, as in other fields and disciplines, we need to commit to a decolonizing approach to curriculum studies—one where our particular ontological, epistemological, and methodological interventions are in sync with a just and liberatory intent. In *Decolonizing Methodologies*, Linda Tuhiwai Smith (2012, p. 11) argues that the word "research" "is inextricably linked to European imperialism and colonialism" that is, it is deeply ingrained within the very veins of coloniality. This means that not just the word itself but the entire research enterprise "is probably some of the dirtiest words and enterprises in the indigenous world's vocabulary" (1). Smith (2012) further argues:

> The intellectual project of decolonizing has to set out ways to proceed through a colonizing world. It needs a radical compassion that reaches out, that seeks collaboration, and that is open to possibilities that can only be imagined as other things fall into place.
>
> (p. xi)

Moreover, to decolonize curriculum studies implies decolonizing "its research," the material discourses that are crafted and crafted its theories. It implies decolonizing our interpretive approaches to our hermeneutical veins (Darder, 2019). Smith (2012) adds that our approach to decolonization must "provoke revolutionary thinking about the roles that knowledge, knowledge production, knowledge circulation, knowledge hierarchies, and knowledge institutions play in decolonization and social transformation" (1). With these words in mind, decolonizing curriculum studies entails a non-abyssal methodology that is unwaveringly committed to creating non-derivative counterhegemonic intellectual spaces where non-Eurocentric readings of the "word and the world" can unfold in ways that might lead us to rethink ways of existence and knowing that have been discarded in the past and, in so many cases, viewed as nonexistent (Santos, 2007; Paraskeva, 2016; 2023), as well as to create an openness of consciousness where unimagined possibilities of social and material change can materialize. Decolonizing curriculum implies a commitment to alternative ways of viewing, reading, and feeling (Santos, 2014).

Early decolonizing intellectuals or *early epistemologists of the south* (Santos, 2014), such as Frantz Fanon, Amilcar Cabral, Aquilino Ribeiro, Stuart Hall, Edward Said, Gloria Anzaldúa, Grace Boggs, Chandra Talpade Mohanty, Vine Deloria Jr., Audre Lorde, Shiv Visvanathan, bell hooks, and many others, have challenged the violence of *epistemic fascism* of Western academics. Through intellectual endeavors—keynote addresses, lectures, seminars, workshops, media engagement, and writings—decolonizing intellectuals have confronted the underlying economic interests that deem the academic curriculum as a commodity—a curriculum generally constructed in the absence of subaltern sensibilities. The works of oppressed educators, scholars, and activists, over the years, have shattered traditional curriculum claims of neutrality and homogeneity in Western representations of oppressed populations, suggesting the need for decolonizing engagements that defy the hegemonic curricular traditions of the Western interpretive lens. At the core of such critiques is the incapacity/inability of Westerners or those immersed in an ideology of whiteness to listen or hear or feel the Other, beyond enforcing and projecting their own Eurocentric sensibilities upon us—often leaving the subaltern unseen and unheard within the curriculum—even when included in reading lists.

Critical, anticolonial, and decolonial intellectuals have also alerted us to the functionalist nature that has contaminated many counterhegemonic intellectuals and movements and that ultimately, in their struggle against epistemicide, end up further deepening and worsening the epistemicidal nature of the field. Paraskeva (2016; 2022; 2023) denounced this contamination as *reversive epistemicide*. Darder and Torres decades earlier (2004) vehemently led the battle against the dangers of race essentialism in our analyses of power and domination. From this view, mechanical and dangerously Manichean efforts to replace "class" with "race" have not served to dismantle the oppressive matrix, which relies on the relative autonomy of various socially graded categories. As Huebner and Paraskeva (2022) assert, the so-called complicated curriculum conversation is manifestly and unapologetically eugenic and urgently needs to be decolonized.

When underrepresented perspectives are centered, there are often accusations of being biased or advocating "political correctness." Hence, despite such mainstream critiques, oppressed educators have had to risk stepping into "ways of thinking outside the European context that were discredited when capitalism became the most powerful imperialist force" (Spivak *quoted in* Wallace, 1999), gathering together inspiration to explore and voice the particularities of lived experiences; and, by so doing, unveil false

Western pronouncements about the historical and contemporary conditions that have shaped oppressed existences—pronouncements that fail to engage the persistence and impact of structural trauma associated with legacies of colonialism—patriarchy, slavery, economic exploitation, and genocide in the world today. Despite this neglect, what has become more apparent over the years is that sensitivity to the history of these conditions actually can serve as an important corrective to the Eurocentric bias that informs most analyses, with its curricular propensity to overstate the present by positing a radical discontinuity between contemporary social life and past histories of oppression (Santos, 2007).

The political sensibilities that best can inform the decolonizing of the curriculum generally emerge from the inclusion of highly diverse and multidimensional analyses, as well as resistance to an absolute or universalizing language. This is essential to knowledge production that seeks to defy the countless curricular practices aligned to patriarchal dominance, class divisions, racializations, linguistic genocide, heterosexism, abled bodies, and other markers of injustice enacted through an exclusionary politics of institutional fit or scientific validity. Of this Fanon (1963, p. 170) argued, "[C]olonization is not satisfied merely with holding a people in its grips and emptying the native's brain of all form and content. By a kind of perverted logic, it turns to the past of the oppressed people and distorts, disfigures, and destroys it!" Accordingly, the decolonizing of the curriculum aims to deconstruct and eliminate the subordination of oppressed voices, so often deemed suspect and, at times, dangerous to the veracity of objective knowledge. Such deconstruction debunks curriculum as knowledge regulation and constitutes the gateway toward curriculum as knowledge emancipation. There is no decolonization without an emancipated subject.

True to its political intent, decolonizing approaches to curriculum development advance an evolving and itinerant epistemology—that is an organic, fluid, discontinued, and flexible means of knowing the world that, according to Paraskeva (2011), destabilizes fixed knowledge forms and absolutes beliefs of our time. Such epistemology paves the way for an itinerant curriculum theory, a decolonial turn, challenging the epistemicidal nature of the field—its theory and research—in its dominant and counter-dominant forms (Paraskeva, 2011, 2016, 2022, 2023; Darder, 2015, 2019). The itinerant curriculum theory (ICT) is

> informed by its epistemological rupture from the coloniality of power and disaffiliation with hegemonic dogma, a process that liberates our field of consciousness, opening the way for resurgences of subaltern perspectives, new expressions of solidarity, and the powerful regeneration of that political force necessary for transforming the social and material conditions of our present existence—not only in the mind but also in the flesh
>
> (Darder, 2015, p. xiv).

ICT is a "deliberate disrespect of the canon, a struggle against epistemological orthodoxy" (Darder, 2015, p. xxv), and it attempts "to bring scientific knowledge face-to-face with nonscientific, explicitly local knowledges, knowledges grounded in the experience of the leaders and activists of the social movements studied by social scientists" (p. xxv).

Decolonizing the curriculum entails a redefinition of Western notions that bend toward abstract formulations, empty of both the personal and social negotiations that shape subaltern life, particularly concerning economically impoverished communities. This also attends to unveiling how mainstream (fundamentally Eurocentric) educational forms have ignored the tensions and its complicity with modernity's atrocities. About this Spivak (1999, p. 2) reminds us, "The mainstream, has never run clean, perhaps never can. Part of mainstream education involves learning to ignore this absolutely, with a sanctioned ignorance."

Herein lies the rationale for a decolonizing methodology of curriculum theory and development that critiques, redefines, and reinvents dominant readings of learning, teaching, and schooling in ways that counter what Freire (1971) called "banking education." In the process, educators must struggle to simultaneously transgress the sanctity of modernist values while working to infuse the curriculum with decolonizing epistemological sensibilities—sensibilities that defy the ruthless drive to conquer embedded in the Eurocentric imagination. Accordingly, indigenous voices and knowledge—within and beyond the Global South—can only arise through a courageous and yet risky, itinerant inquiry process that brushes hegemonic ideals against non-Western epistemological sensibilities—transgressive sensibilities that unfold when freed from the clutches of the coloniality of power.

It is not incidental that oppressed intellectuals who have issued fundamental challenges to Western epistemologies have come from historically colonized populations; in that we have entered the process of scholarly inquiries through a decolonizing sensibility of subaltern existence—that is, we have had to navigate across the dialectical discontinued terrains of the oppressor/oppressed conflicts and contradictions (Freire, 1971), as part of our process of social, political, spiritual, and academic survival as borderland intellectuals. Eugenics frames the oppressed experience (Smith, 2012; Santos, 2014). Thus, decolonizing the curriculum is impossible without the participation of members from oppressed communities, in that it is precisely the process of navigating the brutal epistemological tensions of subaltern positionality that has shaped us as makers of meaning who have elected, painstakingly so, to ground our pedagogical and curricular practices within anticolonial traditions. As such, the underlying ethos of our intellectual labor calls for decolonizing epistemological shifts in the production and circulation of knowledge forms, by offering a just and emancipatory political vision of the curriculum within both the academic borderlands and our practical everyday struggles for liberation.

Within this framework, as Tuck and Yang (2012) correctly argue, "decolonization is not a metaphor." Rather, it embodies a purpose to unsettle hegemonic and particular counter-hegemonic theories, policies, and practices, to disrupt settler colonialism, recover stolen lands, and effect concrete change to the daily conditions of suffering and injustice experienced by our communities. This points to the political power of disruption and deconstruction. As such, decolonizing educators and researchers have chosen to engage colonizing theories of subalternity in ways that treat these ideas as desacralized texts, ripe for deconstruction, to be systematically and qualitatively analyzed based upon our own lived subalternity, as self-determined historical subjects and empowered intellectuals, capable of voicing and living our commitment to an anticolonial vision of the world. But no decolonization is possible within the epistemological matrix of modernity and its colonizing logic. As such, decolonizing implies an ethical commitment to dismantle the logic of coloniality and its epistemic purpose.

A Decolonizing Ethical Stance

The process of decolonizing the curriculum necessitates an ethical stance that can disrupt the one-dimensionality of Eurocentric epistemicides prevalent in traditional theories of curriculum and society (Paraskeva, 2011, 2022). Sempere, Alliyu, and Bollaert (2022) posit that "[P]olitical limitations to conventional 'narrow' approaches to ethics refer to the lack of sensitivity towards (de)coloniality, the global inequalities that continue to shape the international development sector, and the historic call for epistemic, cognitive, or knowledge justice" (p. 3). With this in mind, Samek and Shultz (2017) warn that "context matters when we look at ethics. The long view of colonialism has taught us to be cautious when making universal claims given the brutal consequences for those who don't fit within the universal." Intellectuals such as Michel Foucault (1980) and Gilles Deleuze (1989), among others, insightfully alerted us to the dangers of derivative and representational interpretations of history that frame reality—coloniality, colonialism, modernity, and post-modernity inclusively—as a unified totalized matrix with predictable continual, stable, and fixed metamorphoses. The curriculum field is, in fact, one of the political arenas in and through which such erroneous interpretations are produced, legitimized, and normalized.

Beyond epistemological concerns, then, is also a humanizing endeavor to reinvent our expression and participation in the classroom and within the larger political project for social transformation. There is, then, a significant qualitative dimension at work here, in that it is from what hooks (1994) asserted, in *Teaching to Transgress,* as the "authority of lived experience" and our oppressed sensibilities—generally rendered marginal and irrelevant within the mainstream curriculum—that decolonizing voices find the veracity to speak, to question, to transgress, and to reinvent the distorting curricular discourses of the powerful that continue to wreak political and economic havoc in culturally, economically, and politically oppressed communities.

In concert, a decolonizing curricular educational praxis must be well-grounded in what Dussel (2013) called an *ethics of liberation* to assist us in rethinking the totality of moral problems more comprehensively, beyond the Eurocentric matrix. Briefly, this demands that we: (1) critique the system as a totality; (2) embrace a life-affirming vision; (3) disrupt the logic of capital; (4) unveil myths that perpetuate exclusions; (5) recognize oppression as a global phenomenon; (6) develop a multidimensional sensibility; (7) labor with the most oppressed; (8) challenge forces of alienation; and (9) seek new ways of thinking and being that dissolve our dependence on a logic of privilege, exclusion, and conquest; and (10) struggle collectively for a historical alternative. Embracing an ethics of liberation in curriculum development challenges, redefines, and rearticulates the blindness of historical and contemporary atrocities tied to settler colonialism and false claims about the colonized. Here, the aim is to develop curriculum strategies of engagement for challenging false discursive practices and disabling pedagogical practices that disaffiliate us from our humanity, from one another, and from our shared responsibility for the planet's well-being.

Also central to the labor of decolonizing the curriculum are radical processes of social inquiry, critique, cultural, and spiritual reformulations that strike at the very heart of dominant ideologies, and practices that, wittingly or unwittingly, reproduce classed, racialized, gendered, heterosexual, abled, religious, and other forms of inequity. Hence, a decolonizing curricular process constitutes a discontinued itinerant multitude of careful (re)readings of the world and of subaltern histories, in ways that critically address the world's endless difference and diversity, openly challenging what Freire referred to as the "tragic dilemma of the oppressed," a phenomenon that keeps us objectified and oppositionally defined (Darder, 2019). More importantly, in our efforts to decolonize the curriculum, class formations and antagonisms cannot be ignored; as these emerge within the social and material contexts of capitalist production of commodities, given its focus on the control of wealth, the extraction of labor, and the accumulation of wealth. In the absence of these considerations, mainstream curriculum theories of diversity fail to engage social and material inequalities rigorously and, thus, remain rooted in assimilative official transcripts of society that conserve the wealth and power of the ruling elite.

Decolonizing curriculum studies necessitates an ethical and political commitment to both confront and shift, in both theory and practice, the ways in which we comprehend issues of difference and diversity, as well as our place in the world with respect to others. This signals the important role played by the positionality of educators, students, activists, and communities. In this regard, critical pedagogues such as Michael Apple (1990) advocate "the need to situate" as a *sine qua non* condition in the struggle for a relevant curriculum. Decolonizing should be viewed as a non-derivative philosophy of praxis (Gramsci, 1990) occupying and saturating curriculum theory and development. This requires that we examine critically our own contexts, contradictions, and complicities *to learn to unlearn* (Tlostanova & Mignolo, 2012) our privilege, to establish an ethical relationship to difference, diversity—and our own ignorance—and to dissolve the arrogance of the academic expert gaze. This entails a decolonizing ethical sensibility of difference that centers subaltern voices, demythologizes commonsensical notions of knowledge production, exposes the coloniality of power, disrupts Eurocentric epistemicides, and provides itinerant or fluid re-readings (Paraskeva, 2011) of the historical beliefs, contemporary conditions, and the lived experiences that shape our world.

The Subaltern Voice

The subaltern eye, hearing, feeling, and voice demand that we engage seriously and forthrightly with the phenomenon of human oppression and its debilitating impact upon identities, social locations, and the material realities of subaltern life (Darder, 2015, 2019). Zuleika Bibi Sheik (2020) asks us to, [invoke] within us the connection to ourselves, our ancestors, the land, our bodies, and others, so that the knowledge that is inherent and deep within us may be cultivated. [This] asks, when we peel away the layers of scar tissue necrotized at the colonial wound through "epistemological deep listening" and heal all that has been erased, denied, shamed, negated, and exiled, what emerges?

(p. 2)

Accordingly, it emerges from a tenacious navigation to break through the personal and structural traumas caused by the *culture of silence* (Freire, 1971) or the *cult of absences* (Santos, 2018) and efforts to dismantle the distorting Eurocentric representations and engagements that have been projected upon oppressed individuals and communities. This brings to mind the impact of epistemicides, where voices that emerge from knowledge outside the Western purview are not only silenced or invisibilized but eradicated, as is the case of the *culture of forgetting* (Darder, 2014). This refers to a pedagogical space of banking education (Freire, 1971), where oppressed students are, wittingly or unwittingly, taught to reject the native tongue and uncritically adopt the hegemonic language and cultural system of the dominant culture of schooling— an outcome rooted in colonizing curriculum practices. This again points to that repressive epistemological region of the *abyssal divide*, where the voices of the Other are relegated to the consequences of marginal existence. Such an abyssal divide is a symptom of modernity reason. According to Santos (2007), modernity reason is an abyssal thinking. That is, "a system of visible and invisible distinctions, the invisible ones being the foundation of the visible ones. The invisible distinctions are established through radical lines that divide social reality into two realms, the realm of 'this side of the line' and the realm of 'the other side of the line'" (Santos, 2007, p. 45). Such abyssal lines constitute the very core of "the epistemological foundation of the capitalist and imperial order that the global North has been imposing on the global South" (ix). Invisibility and non-existence of the "one side" are the roots of visibility and existence of the "another side" (Paraskeva, 2016). With this in mind, "what most fundamentally characterizes abyssal thinking is thus the impossibility of the co-presence of the two sides of the line. To the extent that it prevails, this side of the line only prevails by exhausting the field of relevant reality. Beyond it, there is only nonexistence, invisibility, non-dialectical absence" (Santos, 2007, p. 1).

Within this repressive zone of coloniality, racializing class formations and implicit beliefs, attitudes, and values of ethnic cleansing and exclusion are hardened and reified by the agonizing tensions generated by the abyssal divide. Moreover, through curricular adherence to the *global coloniality of power* (Quijano, 2000; Grosfoguel, 2011), oppressed populations have been subjected to dehumanizing assumptions and deficit views, even within our own community contexts. Subsequently, the standardization of knowledge and the universal expectations of the curriculum continue to be "normalized, disciplined, uniformized" (Foucault, 1980), defined by the oppressive cultural values and market interests of the economically and politically powerful. In response, the decolonizing of the curriculum implies an epistemological shock (Paraskeva, 2023), paving the way for a multiplicity of readings of the materiality of history and the economy that interrupt the "natural order" of mainstream narratives.

Thus, to decolonize curriculum studies implies to detotalize and deterritorialize the field's theory, research, and development to move to an itinerant plateau, (Paraskeva, 2011; 2016) that recognizes, addresses, and engages with the world's endless different and diverse epistemological perspectives. Such *itinerantology* is a commitment to a cohabitus of both sides of the line, a post-abyssal path (Paraskeva, 2023)

Along these lines, the decolonial curriculum must mirror decolonial thinking, a decolonial way of existence, and a decolonial philosophy of praxis. It implies that a decolonizing curriculum is rooted in a critical approach that focuses on creating counterhegemonic intellectual spaces in which new readings of the world can unfold, in ways that lead us toward change, both in theory and practice (Darder, 2015, p. 63). True to these aims, a decolonizing curriculum encompasses a critical lens that expands the limits of rationality and, by so doing, supports the development of counterhegemonic forms of thinking and reflecting upon the world, in order to better grasp the impact of social and material relations of power at work in the lives of oppressed populations. In turn, a decolonizing curricular design aims to demystify the artificial limits of racialized formations and economic hierarchies of domination, viewing all languages and cultures as significant to our planetary survival. Furthermore, emancipatory principles serve to support the epistemological creativity, imagination, questioning, doubting, and risk-taking necessary to this approach (Darder, 2015).

Decolonizing curriculum studies entails verbalizing the historical critique, spirit of resistance, and cultural reclamation of Caliban reason (Henry, 2000), which encompasses a multiplicity of non-derivative post-abyssal efforts that serve to expose the *colonial matrix of power* (Quijano, 1992; Mignolo, 2007; Tlostanova & Mignolo, 2009b). This colonizing matrix encompasses economic control, control of authority, control of the public sphere, and ideological control and legitimation of knowledge, which persist long after official colonial political rule has ceased. In essence, this phenomenon is, above all, about control of the mind (Cabral, 1973; Césaire, 2000). Herein lies the pervasive mechanism by which knowledge forms are either judged legitimate, excluded, or even produced as non-existent (Paraskeva, 2011; 2016; Santos, 2014). Aligned with this point is the manner in which the global coloniality of power is masked by modernity's ideological apparatus, which deceptively normalizes and disciplines, on one hand, expressions of patriarchy, colonialism, capitalism, and globalization (Mohanty, 2003; Lugones, 2010; Grosfoguel, 2011; Mignolo, 2012; Smith, 2012), while on the other hand silences counternarratives generated by members of oppressed communities.

Correspondingly, the decolonizing curriculum undertakes oppositional interrogations of official claims that emerge from sanctioned elite intellectuals who purport expertise in the production and navigation of explanatory knowledge *abou*t the lives and survival of those deemed as Other—knowledge about which they themselves are generally ungrounded and inexperienced. Another central concern here, of course, is the extent to which a colonizing or what Said (1978) called an "orientalist" gaze is implicated in the Western production of curricular expertise. A critical question, then, is to what extent do mainstream political and economic interests distort perceptions of the Other/Othering/Otherness, preserving classed, racialized, gendered, abled, sexual, and religious hierarchies and supremacies around the globe? The answer can assist us in better understanding why school discourses about oppressed students around the world are still embedded with "deep underlying [modernist] assumptions about the physical and mental laziness of 'non-Westerners' as an immanent quality that makes us unproductive" (Frenkel & Shenhav, 2003).

In contestation, oppressed voices brush fiercely across colonizing interpretations in an effort to halt the assault, to struggle to decolonize knowledge, and to work to (re)produce knowledge forms that are in sync with the histories, cultures, languages, and cosmologies of racialized and working-class people. Fraser's (1990, p. 56) concept of *subaltern counterpublics* is useful here in that she speaks to the concept of "arenas where members of subordinate social groups invent and circulate counterdiscourses, which in turn permit them to formulate oppositional interpretations of their identities, interests, and needs." Here, we find another counterhegemonic dimension essential to decolonizing the curriculum. For without the formulation of oppositional interpretations or the itinerant dimension of subaltern voices, genuine decolonizing curriculum projects would be impossible.

In other words, although it is not the responsibility of subaltern faculty, students, and communities to decolonize the curriculum, it is impossible to decolonize the curriculum without their organic insights and active participation. Accordingly, the process of decolonizing the curriculum must draw effectively on subaltern historical and cultural sensibilities. This is in line with Fanon's (1963, p. 141) insistence that when historically colonized subjects work to liberate themselves from the colonizing frameworks that have constricted our voices and stifled our consciousness, we "are all the time adding to our knowledge in the light of experience [and] will come to show [ourselves] capable" of speaking the unspeakable and doing the unimaginable, in the midst of a crumbling world.

A Vision for "For the End of the World (As We Know It)"

"Teaching for the end of the world" makes fundamental the need for a radical shift in consciousness, the dismantling of old regimes of knowledge, and the building of new educational structures, relationships, and practices that promote democratic life and global justice. This radical shift required, as Amilcar Cabral (1970) stated, one to "tell no lies. Expose lies whenever they are told. Mask no difficulties, mistakes, failures. Claim no easy victories" (p. 72). As argued throughout this work, this requires decolonizing curricular approaches that can, simultaneously, disrupt the colonizing logic of modernity, challenge the immutability of capitalism, and unveil the myths that breed eugenics, exclusion, and suffering. To enact such approaches demands we pose tough provocative questions, enter into courageous dialogues, imagine radical solutions, and seek uncompromisingly genuine emancipatory forms of cultural, political, and economic life. This includes deliberating together on what it means to teach, learn, and dream within an era of turbulent historical transition.

To do this requires the forging of solidarity within and across communities and carving out adequate time to dream collectively visions of the world that will follow.

In the midst of the current mainstream culture of chaos, we must prepare ourselves, our students, and our communities to imagine and welcome "alternative ways to think education alternatively" (Santos, 2007), opening new possibilities in how we define our collective existence as living beings on this planet. Most importantly, as Freire implored us, we must begin the arduous labor wherever we find ourselves—for many of the solutions we seek are actually to be found under the rubble and decay of the present. This is to say that true societal transformation only advances on the heels of what came before. It is at once a process of building on our histories, as it is also an awakening of the unimaginable or yet nonexistent pieces of a just and loving future beckoning us forth.

Creating ample spaces and time for deep critical reflection and hard, honest dialogue with others across our agreements and disagreements is imperative to forging the solidarity necessary in undertaking the audacious task of teaching for the end of the world, toward the world we all wish to see (Amin, 2008)—given the ways modernity has made recalcitrant states of subalternity. To teach for the end of the world is to teach for a world converging in difference and diversity, capable of addressing oppositional approaches within and beyond the Global North (Amin, 2008).

Hence, the work calls us to grapple with how we are all positioned differently, and thus, we all possess wisdom, as well as blind spots. So, rather than succumbing to conventional educational dynamics of competition, coercion, manipulation, and disrespect, we must work to shatter the oppressor/oppressed contradictions that keep us trapped in colonizing dynamics tied to our positionality. Accordingly, comprehending how our positionality is implicated in our teaching enhances our capacity to engage more authentically within the classroom and beyond—an issue unfortunately marginalized in approaches that persist in distancing themselves from recognizing the interdependence of human existence or the broader social struggles at work. This demands that we be deeply self-reflective about our own complicity in perpetuating attitudes and relationships that betray our emancipatory aims, no matter our positionality. Disabling dynamics can also be found within highly sectarian arenas of identity politics, where the conditions of people's lives are rendered less important than vanguardist dogmas of a particular political, cultural, or religious sector.

Here, we would do well to be watchful when identity politics, rather than opening the door for greater dialogue and engagement, closes down crucial dialogue and becomes part of the problem. The capitalist system has historically taught us that the dynamics and social categories of oppression and resistance have relative autonomy. It is a dangerous mistake—as the most recent examples of genocide in Gaza demonstrate— to persist in privileging any category of domination or resistance (Darder & Torres, 2004). Arundhati Roy (2023) sheds light on the ways in which the *weaponization of identity as a form of resistance* has unfolded in the last few decades as the dominant response to the *weaponization of identity as a form of oppression*. The concern here is when the oppressor/oppressed contradiction becomes hardened and impenetrable. Moving away from this contradiction demands that we work consistently to dismantle binaries of identity that obstruct our capacity to grasp both the multidimensionality of our humanity and the unfinishedness of our existence. For if not, we can remain ever stuck in a modernist loop of superiority and hierarchical existence that impedes dialogue, leading us toward violent or warlike solutions that only perpetuate the toxic social disease of modernity.

To close, it seems fitting to offer questions that again draw from Machado de Oliveira (2021), to ponder as we grapple with the task of decolonizing the curriculum—questions that echo aspects of the issues posed earlier, but here are presented from the viewpoint that forces of human oppression are, in fact, social maladies that require our intervention.

- What if racism and colonialism and all other forms of toxic, contagious divisions are preventable social diseases? And there are strategies and relationship for contending with this phenomenon?
- What if the texts, education, and forms of organization used in planning that we revere have carried and spread the disease, but also contain latent parts of the medicine that can heal it? How can we begin to access those latent parts that can help us change the course of history?
- What if learning to activate this medicine requires coming to terms with our violent histories (as painful as they may be); learning to see the world through the eyes of others (as impossible as that sounds); and facing humanity (in our own selves, first) in its full complexity, affliction, and imperfection? How can we activate this medicine in the interest of our genuine transformation and liberation?
- What if the purging prompted by the medicine leads us to confront our traumas and to learn how to let go of fears of scarcity, loneliness, worthlessness, guilt, and shame? Are we willing to walk through the fire of those traumas within and outside of ourselves, in the interest of a more just and loving world?
- What if we must learn to trust each other without guarantees? What are the skills and commitments that we must bring to such a complex and humanizing political project for change? Are we willing to suspend our disbelief and conditioning, in order to learn new ways of being?
- What if the motivation to survive alongside one another in a finite planet in dynamic balance (without agreements, coercive enforcements, or assurances) will come through being taught collectively by the disease itself? Are we truly willing to study the manner in which each of us is complicit with the illness of oppression and the perpetuation of a way of life that is moving us rapidly toward extinction?
- What if collective healing will be made possible precisely by facing together the end of the world as we know it? Are we willing to abandon our denial, arrogance, competition, individualism, and false notions of humanity, in the interest of the greatest good—which is inextricably linked to the individual good of each of us?

Our ability to engage these questions is vitally important in these times. For without embracing an ethically informed decolonizing philosophy of praxis that overrides the mythology of modernity, no substantive institutional transformation is possible—leaving us to participate endlessly in an exercise of moving the furniture from here to there, but leaving the basic structure of the room unchanged. I am reminded, here of

Audre Lorde's (1984, p. 111) warning, *For the master's tools will never dismantle the master's house. They may allow us temporarily to beat him at his own game, but they will never enable us to bring about genuine change.* As long as we remain trapped in the epistemological prison of modernity, our effort to transform society will remain a dubious affair. This to say, the revolutionary change required will not emerge from bloody battlefields nor from the abstracted knowledge wars of academics, nor the old oppositional politics that often keeps us ideologically trapped in the oppressor/oppressed narrative. Revolutionary transformation of society can only emerge from an organic and dynamic process of human collaboration, where all have a meaningful place at the table, where the dignity of communities is unquestionably respected, and all life is deemed precious.

Hence, decolonizing the curriculum, like our struggles on the streets, must begin with a call for both disruption *and* openness; starting wherever we are at, with faith in one another and trust in our human creativity and resourcefulness, as well as our capacity to reflect, to voice, and to be consistently responsive to the difficult challenges that will arise in the years to come. More than ever, we are in need of decolonizing curricular approaches that emerge from shared life-affirming visions—collective visions that can bring us closer together, as courageous, committed, and loving human beings, who together rethink, reinvent, and recreate—in the midst of the chaos—liberating possibilities and undreamed of ways of being and knowing that reconnect us to the revolutionary essence of what it means to be fully alive and free, within the organic dynamics of our collective existence. This is a vision that denounces hatred, greed, and injustice and announces a wonderous loving field of collective human existence, from whence true power is generated, and authentic personal and collective freedom can unfold.

Notes

1. See: https://www.oxfam.org/en/5-shocking-facts-about-extreme-global-inequality-and-how-even-it.
2. See: https://www.oxfam.org/en/press-releases/just-8-men-own-same-wealth-half-world.
3. See: https://www.oxfamamerica.org/explore/research-publications/inequality-inc/.
4. See: https://www.statista.com/chart/19635/wealth-distribution-percentiles-in-the-us/.

Bibliography

Althusser, L. (1971), "Ideology and Ideological State Apparatuses," in L. Althusser (ed.), *Lenin and Philosophy and Other Essays*. New York, NY: Monthly Review Press, 85–126.

Amin, S. (2008), *The World We all Wish to See*. New York, NY: Monthly Review Press.

Apple, M. (1990), *Ideology and Curriculum*, 2nd ed. New York: Routledge.

Batrawy, A. (2024), "Gaza's Death Toll Now Exceeds 30,000. Here Is Why Its an Incomplete Count." *National Public Radio*. See: https://www.npr.org/2024/02/29/1234159514/gaza-death-toll-30000-palestinians-israel-hamas-war.

Burns, J. (2015), "The Moral Bankruptcy of Corporate Education." *Teachers College Record* (September 01). See: http://www.tcrecord.org.
Cabral, A. (1970), *Revolution in Guinea: Selected Texts*. New York, NY: Monthly Review Press.
Cabral, A. (1973), *Return to the Source: Selected Speeches of Amilcar Cabral*. New York, NY: Monthly Review Press.
Césaire, A. (2000), *Discourse on Colonialism*. New York, NY: Monthly Review Press.
Chomsky, N. (1999), "Language and Freedom." *Resonance* 4(3): 86–104.
Darder, A. (2011), *A Dissident Voice: Essays on Culture, Pedagogy and Power*. New York, NY: Peter Lang.
Darder, A. (2012), *Culture and Power in the Classroom*, 2nd ed. New York, NY: Paradigm.
Darder, A. (2014), "Cultural Hegemony, Language, and the Culture of Forgetting: Iinterrogating Restrictive Language Policies," in P. Orelus (ed.), *Affirming Language Diversity in Schools and Society: Beyond Linguistic Apartheid*. New York, NY: Routledge, 35–53.
Darder, A. (2015), "Decolonizing Interpretive Research." *The International Education Journal: Comparative Perspectives* 14(2): 63–77. Special *Edition: ANZCIES Conference Proceedings 2014.*
Darder, A. (2019), *Decolonizing Interpretive Research: A Subaltern Methodology for Social Change*. New York, NY: Routledge.
Darder, A., and Torres, R. D. (2004), *After Race: Racism after Multiculturalism*. New York, NY: New York University Press.
Deleuze, G. (1989), *Logic of Sense*. New York, NY: Columbia University Press.
Dussel, E. (2013), *Ethics of Liberation: In the Age of Globalization and Exclusion*. Durham, NC: Duke University Press Books.
Ellison, R. (1952), *Invisible Man*. New York, NY: Random House.
Fanon, F. (1963), *Wretched of the Earth*. New York, NY: Grove Press.
Fraser, N. (1990), "Rethinking the Public Schere: A Contribution to the Critique of Actually Existing Democracy." *Social Text* 25/26: 56–80.
Fraser, N. (2013), *Scales of Justice: Reimagining Political Space in a Globalizing World*. Cambridge: Polity Press.
Fraser, N., and Honneth, A. (2006), ¿*Reconocimiento o redistribución*? Madrid: Morata.
Freire, P. (1971), *Pedagogy of the Oppressed*. New York, NY: Seabury Press.
Frenkel, M., and Shenhav, Y. (2003), *Decolonizing Organization Theory: Between Orientalism and Occidentalism*. Accessed at: http://www.mngt.waikato.ac.nz/ejrot/cmsconference/2003/proceedings/postcolonial/Frenkel.pdf.
Foucault, M. (1980), *Power Knowledge*. New York, NY: Pantheon Books.
Galeano, E. (1997), *Open Veins of Latin America: Five Centuries of Pillage of a Continent*. New York, NY: Monthly Review Press.
Gramsci, A. (1990), *Selections from Prison Notebooks*. New York, NY: International Publications.
Grosfoguel, R. (2011), "Decolonizing Postcolonial Studies and Paradigms of Political-Economy: Transmodernity, Decolonial Thinking and Global Coloniality." *Transmodernity: Journal of Peripheral Cultural Production of the Luso-Hispanic World* 1(1): 1–38.
Hall, S. (1996), "The Problem of Ideology: Marxism without Guarantees," in D. Morley and K.-H. Chen (eds.), *Stuart Hall: Critical Dialogues in Cultural Studies*. New York, NY: Routledge, 24–43.

Henry, P. (2000), *Caliban's Reason: Introducing Afro-Caribbean Philosophy*. New York, NY: Routledge.

Hill, M. L., and Plitnick, M. (2021), *Except for Palestine: The Limits of Progressive Politics*. New York, NY: The Free Press.

hooks, b. (1981), *Ain't I a Woman: Black Women and Feminism*. Boston, MA: South End Press.

hooks, b. (1994), Teaching to Transgress: Education as the Practice of Freedom, New York, NY: Routledge.

Horton, M., and Freire, P. (1990), *We Make the Road by Walking: Conversations on Education and Social Change*. Philadelphia, PA: Temple University Press.

Huebner, D., and Paraskeva, J. M. (2022), "Curriculum Afterword," in J. M. Paraskeva. (ed.) *Conflicts in Curriculum Theory*, 2nd ed. New York, NY: Palgrave, 215–61.

Jupp, J. (2017), "Decolonizing and De-Canonizing Curriculum Studies." *Journal for the American Association for the Advancement of Curriculum Studies* 12(1): 1–22 (1–25).

Jupp, J. (2023), *Itinerant Curriculum Theory: Decolonial Praxis, Theories, and Histories*. New York, NY: Peter Lang.

Leitão, R. (2018), "Recognizing and Overcoming the Myths of Modernity," in C. Storni, K. Leahy, M. McMahon, P. Lloyd and E. Bohemia (eds.), *Design as a Catalyst for Change*—DRS International Conference 2018, 25–28 June, Limerick, Ireland. Retrieved from: https://dl.designresearchsociety.org/cgi/viewcontent.cgi?article=1592&context=drs-conference-papers.

Lorde, A. (1984), "The Master's Tools Will Never Dismantle the Master's House," in A. Lorde (ed.), *Sister Outsider: Essays and Speeches*. Berkeley, CA: Crossing Press, 110–14.

Lugones, M. (2010), "Toward a Decolonial Feminism." *Hypatia* 25(4): 742–59.

Machado de Oliveira, V. (2021), *Hospicing Modernity*. Berkeley, CA: North Atlantic Books.

Marcuse, H. (1964), *One-Dimensional Man: Studies in the Ideology of Advanced Industrial Society*. Boston, MA: Beacon Press.

Maté, G. (2018), *In the Realm of Hungry Ghosts: Close Encounters with Addiction*. Berkeley, CA: North Atlantic Books.

Maté, G. (with D. Maté) (2020), *The Myth of Normal: Trauma, Illness, and Healing in a Toxic Culture*. New York, NY: Avery.

Memmi, A. (1991), *The Colonizer and the Colonized*. Boston, MA: Beacon Press.

Mignolo, W. (2007), "Delinking: The Rhetoric of Modernity, the Logic of Coloniality and the Grammar of De-coloniality." *Cultural Studies* 21(2–3): 449–514.

Mignolo, W. D. (2012), *Local Histories/Global Designs: Coloniality, Subaltern Knowledges, and Border Thinking*. Princeton, NJ: Princeton University Press.

Mignolo, W. (2018), "The Invention of the Human and the Three Pillars of the Coloniality Matrix of Power," in C. Walsh and W. Mignolo (eds.), *On Decoloniality. Concepts, Analytics, Praxis*. Durham, NC: Duke University Press, 153–76.

Mohanty, C. T. (2003), *Feminism without Borders: Decolonizing Theory, Practicing Solidarity*. Durham, NC: Duke University Press.

Mutua, K., and Swadener, B. B. (2004), *Decolonizing Research in Cross-Cultural Contexts: Critical Personal Narratives*. Albany, NY: State University of New York Press.

Paraskeva, J. (2011), *Conflicts in Curriculum Theory*, 1st ed. New York, NY: Palgrave.

Paraskeva, J. M. (2016), *Curriculum Epistemicide*. New York, NY: Routledge.

Paraskeva, J. M. (2022), "The Generation of the Utopia: Itinerant Curriculum Theory towards a 'Futurable Future.'" *Discourses. Studies in the Cultural Politics of Education* 43(4): 347–66.

Paraskeva, J. M. (2023), *Critical Perspectives on the Denial of Caste in Educational Debate: Towards a Non-derivative Curriculum Reason*. New York, NY: Routledge.

Paraskeva, J. M. (2024), *Itinerant Curriculum Theory: Towards a Declaration of Epistemological Independence*. London: Bloomsbury.

Quijano, A. (1992), "Colonialidad y Modernidad/Racionalidad." *Perú Indígena* 29(1): 11–21.

Quijano, A. (2000), "Colonialidad del poder y classificacion Social." *Journal of World Systems Research* 6(2): 242–386.

Roy, A. (2023), "Approaching Gridlock: Arundhati Roy on Free Speech and Failing Democracy." Lit Hub. Retrieved from: https://lithub.com/approaching-gridlock-arundhati-roy-on-free-speech-and-failing-democracy/.

Said, E. W. (1978), *Orientalism: Western Concepts of the Orient*. New York, NY: Pantheon.

Samek, T., and Shultz, L. (2017), *Information Ethics, Globalization and Citizenship*. Jefferson, NC: McFarland, 37.

Santos, B. de Sousa (2007), *Another World Is Possible: Beyond Northern Epistemologies*. London: Verso.

Santos, B. de Sousa (2014), *Epistemologies of the South*. New York, NY: Routledge.

Santos, B. de Sousa (2018), *The End of the Cognitive Empire*. Durham, NC: Duke University Press.

Sempere, M. J. C., Alliyu, T., and Bollaert, C. (2022), "Towards Decolonising Research Ethics: From One-off Review Boards to Decentralised North-South Partnerships in an International Development Programme." *Education of Science* 12(4): 236. Retrieved from: https://www.mdpi.com/2227-7102/12/4/236.

Sheik, Z. B. (2020), "From Decolonising the Self to Coming to Voice." *Education as Change* 24(1–5): 1–5. Retrieved from: https://repub.eur.nl/pub/135071/Repub_135071_O-A.pdf.

Smith, L. T. (2012), *Decolonizing Methodologies: Research and Indigenous Peoples*. London: Zed Books.

Sovereign Union (2011), "'Liberation' and 'You Are on Aboriginal Land.'" Retrieved from: http://nationalunitygovernment.org/content/liberation-and-you-are-aboriginal-land.

Spivak, G. C. (1988), "Can the Subaltern Speak?" in C. Nelson, and L. Grossberg (eds.), *Marxism and the Interpretation of Culture*. Chicago, IL: University of Illinois Press, 271–316.

Taylor, Ch (1994), *Multiculturalism*. Princeton, NJ: Princeton University Press.

Tlostanova, M. V., and Mignolo, W. (2009a), Global Coloniality and the Decolonial Option. *Kult 6: Special Issue on Epistemologies of Transformation*. Department of Culture and Identity. Roskilde University, 130–47.

Tlostanova, M. V., and Mignolo, W. (2009b), *Learning to Unlearn: Decolonial Reflections from Eurasia and the Americas*. Columbus: Ohio State University.

Toukan, E. (2023), A New Social Contract for Education: Advancing a Paradigm of Relational Interconnectedness *Education Research and Foresight Working Paper 31*. Paris: UNESCO.

Tuck, E., and Yang, K. W. (2012), "Decolonization Is Not a Metaphor." *Decolonization: Indigeneity, Education, & Society* 1(1): 1–40.

Wallace, J. (1999), "Deconstructing Gayatri." *The Higher Education* (July 30). Retrieved from https://www.timeshighereducation.com/features/deconstructing-gayatri/147373.article.

Young, M. (1958), *The Rise of Meritocracy*. London: Thames & Hudson.

Young, I. M. (1990), *Justice and the Politics of Difference*. Princeton, NJ: Princeton University Press.

Index

academic borderlands 120, 122–5, 161, 343, 345–6, 385
African Americans 101–2, 134, 136, 178, 182–3, 185, 199, 229, 323, 331
  labor and wages 252, 288
  political economy 245, 248
  Tuskegee syphilis study 215
Alexander, N. 225, 228
algorithmic capitalism 58
Allende, S. 53
Alliyu, T. 386
Allport, G. 188 n.10
Alternative Radio 326, 333 n.3
American Anthropological Association 253
American Dream 266–7, 269, 290–1
American Journal of Public Health 213
Anglo conformity/assimilation ideology 83
Annie E. Casey Foundation Report, *Reducing Youth Incarceration in the United States* 289
anti-immigrant campaigns/policies 240, 264–5, 269, 272
anti-Mexican racism 254
anti-racist politics 5, 205
Anzaldúa, G. 97, 108, 110, 345
  Borderlands/La Frontera: The New Mestizo 109
  New Metizas 72
Appiah, K. A. 177
Apple, M. 387
Arblaster, A. 86
Arendt, H. 269
Aronowitz, S.
  class identity 104, 113 n.6
  The Politics of Identity 112 n.3
Arrellano, E. 265
art of resistance, radio and 312–13, 331–3
Assange, J. 59
authority
  of experience 72, 91, 101, 112 n.4, 132, 161, 386
  and freedom 29–30, 351–2

Baldwin, J. 222
  "On Being 'White' … and Other Lies" 201
Balibar, E. 203
banking education 24, 36, 52, 57, 127, 317, 338, 385, 388
Barnes, R. 194
Barrera, M., *Race and Class in the Southwest* 257
Barsamian, D. 326
Beckey, C., *Wicked Bodies* 146
Bell, D., *Faces at the Bottom of the Well* 201
Bennett, W. 121
Bhabha, H., third space 108–9
bicognitive development 77
biculturalism x, xiv, 3, 36, 74, 299, 364
  bicultural affirmation 81
  biculturality, theory 78
  bicultural voice 83, 89–92
  bilingualism and 3, 36, 102
  critical theory of 98–9
  cultural consciousness and decolonization 102–3
  cultural identity 81, 82, 108
  cultural response patterns 81, 82
  culture and power 79, 81
  dualistic and traditional/atraditional communities 77
  essentialism 100–1
  ethnicity and identity formation 99–100, 111
  of Mexican American children 76–7
  models and factors 76
  mode of engagement 81, 82
  philosophy of cultural democracy 83–5
  politics of 2, 71–2, 97, 111
  poverty and evasion of class 103–5

primary and dominant culture 79–82, 90
socialization process 74–6
sociocultural environments 3
solidarity of difference 110–11
sphere of 80
transborder experience 108–10
bilingual education 3, 36, 75, 80, 82–3, 102, 125, 182, 257, 283
Black Lives Matter movement 52, 59, 66, 236
Black Panthers, repression 219
Black/white phenomenon 177, 182, 185–6, 201, 234, 254
Bloom, A., *The Closing of the American Mind* 121, 344
body, pedagogy of the 132, 152–4
    consciousness 156
    critical principles 152–4
    love, ethics and 155–6
    schooling and 147–52
    students as integral human beings 146–7
Boggs, G. L. 2
Bollaert, C. 386
Bolsonaro, J. M. 51
The Border Protection, Anti-terrorism, and Illegal Immigration Control Act (2005) 277 n.10
borders/border security 263
    academic borderlands 120, 122–5, 161, 343, 345–6, 385
    assault on borderlands 345–7
    culture 108–10
    open borders, radical possibility of 273–5
    US-Mexico border conflicts 240, 263–5, 285
Braun, L. 214
Brazil
    banking educational approach 52
    national literacy campaign 48
Brosio, R. 155
Brown, M. 199, 228
Brown v. Board of Education 191, 258, 291, 293
Brown, W. 338–9, 344
Buck v. Bell 215

Cabral, A. 7, 363, 390
California's Proposition 227 182, 260 n.9
capital accumulation 55, 174, 179, 198, 229–31, 240, 248, 265, 270–1
capitalism 4, 8, 38–9, 49, 62–3, 71, 173, 179, 205, 207 n.5, 246, 320, 365, 375
    advanced 97–8, 103, 118, 373
    algorithmic 58
    anti-democratic aims 227
    as domination 20, 35, 47, 74
    global 18, 52, 55–6, 318
    intrinsic perversity 48
    mass production 33
    politics of reformism 34
    racism/democracy and 10, 124, 174, 179, 181, 185, 187, 197, 200, 225, 256, 365
    schooling and 9, 19, 31–5
    systematic prerequisite 104
    and technology 18, 34
Carey, K. 285
Carr, P., *Does Your Vote Count: Critical Pedagogy and Democracy* 85–6
Castañeda, A. 71, 73, 76–7, 83–5
Castles, S. 274
Catholic education/schooling 240–1, 281, 295, 298–9
    Catholic Social Teaching 281, 303
    Church and 283, 285, 290–1, 294, 296, 300–1
    as revolutionary labor 302–4
    student diversity in 304 n.7
    US Council of Catholic Bishops' writing on 304 n.2
Católicos Por La Raza (CPLR) 294
Cavanagh, J. 179
Chega Freire movement 52
Chicago Teachers Union (CTU) 62
Chicano movement 48, 294
Children's Defense Fund (CDF) 112 n.5, 289
Chomsky, N. 53
Chowkwanyun, M. 226
Citizens for Peace and Justice 330
Civil Rights Act (1964) 84
civil rights and social movement 36, 59, 121, 123, 127, 191, 199, 219, 229

Civil Rights Project, *E Pluribus ... Separation: Deepening Double Segregation for Students* 293
Clark, K. 188 n.10
class-conflict analysis (race), Marxist 225–6
  educational reform, democratic vision of 234–7
  materiality of racism 228–32
  race as legitimate category 232–4
  retreat from class 226–8
classrooms and communities 29, 154
climate change and pandemics 53
Clinton, B., race initiative 177
colonialism 160–1, 230, 376, 378, 380, 384, 386
community radio as public pedagogy 326, 327–31
compulsory sex education, Sweden 150
Connell, R. 154
conscientization 141, 351
CORE (Caucus of Rank-and-File Educators) 62
Covid-19 pandemic 18, 51, 53–4, 56, 226, 231, 237
Cox, O., on race relations 203, 207 n.7
critical democracy 71, 73, 85, 320
  and process of schooling 85–9
  and solidarity 320
critical leadership for social justice 312, 337
  conscientization 351
  critical democratic negotiation 351
  critical praxis of leadership 348
  cultural context as essential 352
  as dialectical process 350–1
  dialogue 351
  ethical qualities of personal/political struggle 354–5
  ideological intersections 352
  integration of our human faculties 352
  as moral commitment 349
  neutral affair, never 350
  pedagogical practice 349
  political act 349–50
  purposefulness 350
  question of ethics 353
  struggle for democratic public life 355–7
  as unfinishedness 353

critical legal theory 191
critical pedagogy xvii–xviii, 3, 5–6, 8, 92, 147, 181, 311, 313, 350, 367 n.5
  decolonizing analysis of society 11
  democratic public life, struggle 126–7
  genealogy of 6
  love as political force 319–20
  movement 48
  political grace 316–19
  revolutionary 321
critical race theory (CRT) xi, xiv, 3, 7–10, 173–4, 185, 191, 228, 254–6
  education policy with 192–3
  experiential knowledge 194
  identity politics and intersectionality 196–8
  LatCrit 191–2, 206, 207 n.3, 245
  narrative and storytelling method 194–6
  need for 186–8
  separation of political and economic 198–200, 229
  white supremacy and intractability 201–3
critical theory of education 5–7
  competition and individualism 7, 12, 28
  theoretical language 6
Cruz, J. 178, 247
cultural consciousness 100, 111
  affinity 102
  and decolonization 102–3
cultural context (knowledge production) 38–9, 102, 163–4, 167–8, 372, 374, 387
cultural democracy 3–4, 11, 71–3, 81, 83, 92, 119, 168, 175, 187, 294, 303, 305 n.13
  communal commitments 294
  critical theory of 71, 73, 75, 85, 89
  culturally democratic environment 84, 92, 281, 348
  educational theory of 3
  philosophy of 4, 73, 83–5
  of schooling 240–1, 295
cultural deprivation model 75
cultural difference model 75, 107–8
cultural invasion 3, 36, 39, 47, 74, 90, 296, 363, 375

internalization of inferiority 297
culture (cultural) 100, 122, 345, 366, 374
　alienation, biculturation 80–2
　border 108–10
　and decolonizing education 38
　and difference x, 2, 102, 111
　dominant and subordinate 296
　dualism, biculturation 80–1
　of forgetting 388
　imperialism 98–9, 248
　of poverty 134
　and power 1, 3–4, 11, 47, 71, 73–4, 79, 81, 85, 241, 295, 349, 381
　race and 194, 255
　separatism, biculturation 80–2
　of silence 29, 388
　as social phenomenon 200, 230, 349
　wars 123, 346

Darder, A. ix–xii, xv–xix, 2, 8–9, 13–14, 18, 71–2, 132, 173–4, 239–40, 311–13, 365, 383
　jouissance 361
　life of xiii, 1
　politics of colonized wombs 240
　politics of forgetting 7
　question 362, 364, 366
　relationship with Freire 18 (*see also* Freire, P.)
　thesaurus 362
　works of (*see* works of Darder)
Davis, A. 204
Davis, M. 266
deAnda, D. 71, 76
decolonization 102–3, 132, 245, 301
　curriculum studies 382–6, 389, 393
　ethical stance 386–7
　liberation and 376
　methodology of subaltern 131
　modernity (*see* modernity)
　social science study of poverty 139–41
　subaltern voice 387–90
decolonizing interpretive research 131–2, 159
　ethical stance 161–3
　inquiry as humanizing praxis 169–71
　methodologies 166–9
　politics of subaltern voice 163–6
　subalternity 161–3, 166
　Western epistemologies 160–1

dehumanization 30, 38, 40–1, 45, 54–5, 59–61, 117–18, 131, 153, 163, 170, 276, 321, 339, 348, 371, 388
Deleuze, G. 386
Delgado Bernal, D. 194, 202
Delgado, R. 191
democracy 33, 85–7, 89, 120, 127, 155–6, 188, 204, 235, 355–6. *See also* cultural democracy
　and capitalism 10, 124, 174
　intimacy with 49, 61
　as moral ideal 87
　radio builds democracy 327
　as site of struggle 85, 120
　and transitive consciousness 88
　values indispensable to 62–6
Denny, G. V. 327
Dershowitz, A. 338
Dewey, J. 299
　democracy, defining 87
　democratic schooling 71, 73, 86–7
Deyhle, D. 201
dialectical relationship 28–30, 45, 102
dialogue (schools and communities) 60, 88, 126–7, 152, 329
　bicultural 90
　critical leadership for social justice 351
　as epistemological practice 28, 30
　and solidarity 30, 41, 48, 332
Dowty, A. 273
Dream Act 291
D'Souza, D., *Illiberal Education: The Politics of Race and Sex on Campus* 121, 344
Du Bois, W. E. B. 244
Dunayevskaya, R. 72
　Philosophy and Revolution 128–9
Dussel, E., ethics of liberation 162, 386

Eagleton, T. 155, 156, 204
economic Darwinism 34, 117, 125, 127, 344, 347
　neoliberalism and 121, 212
　and university 118–20, 340–1
economic democracy 1, 4, 35, 45, 71, 111, 180, 187, 196, 235–7, 244, 249, 259, 372
economic inequality 35–6, 49, 104, 106, 122, 186, 229, 240, 244, 250–2, 258, 271, 373

economics 134, 198, 265, 269, 344, 347
educational reform, race and 181, 225–6, 233
   democratic vision of 234–7
   neoliberal educational solutions 231
e-learning. *See* virtual learning
Ellsworth, Elizabeth 364–5
emancipation of labor 21, 39, 42
emancipatory pedagogy x, 11, 21, 28–9, 65, 145, 147, 155, 192, 282, 317, 349, 385
England, working-class kids in 151
Enlightenment 204–5, 315
epistemological curiosity 57, 63–4, 376
Eros effect 318–19
ethics of community care 221
ethnicity 72, 286, 288, 293, 366
   and formation of identity 99–100
   and theories of assimilation 183, 248
ethnocentrism 20, 90, 174, 212, 268, 298
Euroamerican educator 91
Eurocentrism 159–60, 168, 194, 202, 366, 378, 388
   Eurocentric bias 384
   one-dimensionality 161, 386
Europe
   anti-austerity campaigns in 59
   immigration populations of 183, 248
evidence-based research x, 124, 168, 292, 346

faith, politics of 47, 64–5
Fanon, F. 41, 102, 165, 168, 361, 384, 390
Fisk, M., social recognition 128
Fordham, S., racelessness/acting white 83
Ford Motor Company 179
Foucault, M. 3, 145, 295, 386
Frankfurt School 6
Fraser, N., subaltern counterpublics 164, 373, 390
Freire, E. 46
Freire, N. 46
Freire, P. x, xiii–xiv, xvii, xix, 3, 9, 13, 17–18, 22, 33–4, 38, 45, 50, 60, 62, 64–6, 127, 131, 140, 145–7, 153, 168, 170, 281, 296–7, 311, 318, 320, 337, 348, 363, 367 n.4, 373, 382, 385, 391
   centrality of body 148
   consciousness and transformation, revolutionary vision 11
   denounced fatalism 47
   Education for Critical Consciousness 87
   ethics in education 155–6
   false generosity 40–1, 170, 381
   intimacy with democracy 49, 61
   language of historic possibility 52
   limit-situations 27, 29, 40
   pedagogical myths 152
   Pedagogy of Freedom 42, 46, 349, 353
   pedagogy of love 10, 65, 155, 302
   Pedagogy of the City 30
   Pedagogy of the Heart/Under the Shade of the Mango Tree 18, 48, 51, 55, 63
   Pedagogy of the Oppressed (*see Pedagogy of the Oppressed* (Freire))
   political and ideological foundation 138
   relationship with Darder 18
   suffering exile 52
   Teachers as Cultural Workers 41, 49
   "tragic dilemma of the oppressed" 162, 387
   unfinishedness xix, 3, 14, 39–42, 312, 353
   vision of world 2, 11, 23, 28
   We Make the Road by Walking. 382
Friedman, T. L., *The World Is Flat* 43 n.3, 267
Fromm, E., *The Art of Loving* 320
Fuss, D., *Essentially Speaking: Feminism, Nature, and Difference* 112 n.4

Gans, H., deconstructing the underclass 138–9
Georas, C. S. 180
Gilroy, P. 8, 196
Giroux, H. 6, 71, 122, 149, 151, 323, 325, 340, 355
   Academic Labor in Dark Times 126
   on critical democracy 73
   economic Darwinism 118
   neoliberal fascism 54
   Schooling and the Struggle for Public Life 73
   student voice 88–9
   The University in Chains 343
Glasgow, D. 134
global capitalism 18, 52, 55–6, 318
globalization 53, 117, 122, 179–80, 205, 246, 249, 251, 267

globalizing human rights xi, 240, 275–6
Global North 361, 373, 375, 388, 391
Global South 373, 385, 388
Goldberg, D. T. 184
Goldman, E. 316
Gomez-Pena, G. 97
    Warriors for Gringostroika 72, 109–10
Gómez-Quiñones, J. 4
Gonzalez, G. G., "Mexican Problem" 292
Gonzalez, J. 326
Goodman, A. 326
Goodman, A. H., *Racism Not Race* 234
Gorostiaga, X. 104
Gramsci, A. 13, 39, 45, 103, 177, 252, 286, 363
    civil society 9, 197
    indifference as the deadweight of history 366
Grand Rapids Community Media Consortium 326
Graves, J. L., Jr., *Racism Not Race* 234
Grosfoguel, R. 180
Grossberg, L. 109
Guillaumin, C. 186, 256
Guinier, L. 193
    The Miner's Canary 191
Gutierrez, G., "theology as a love letter" 241, 302
Gypsy populations, Eastern Europe 185

Hall, S. 105
    ethnicity 72, 99–100, 112 n.4
Hardt, M., *Empire* 267
Harvey, D. 240, 271
    The New Imperialism 269–70
Hayles, K., incorporated knowledge 151
hegemony 3, 90, 194, 203, 233, 331, 379
    belief systems 326
    and counter-hegemonic movements 378, 383, 389
    culture of schooling 23–4, 35, 63
    hegemonic power 38
    and subaltern knowledge 165
Henry, P. 363
Herrnstein, R. J., *The Bell Curve* 184, 253
heterosexism 39, 200, 230
higher education 118, 120–4, 126–7, 337–8, 340–1, 344–6, 355–6
Highlander Folk School (Highlander Research and Education Center) 382

historical process, knowledge as 26–8, 49, 64
Hoberman, J., *Black and Blue: The Origins and Consequences of Medical Racism* 213
Holmes, O. W. 215
hooks, b. 21, 63, 72, 105, 381
    authority of lived experience 161, 386
    "Essentialism and Experience" 101, 112 n.4
    Talking Back 201–2
    Teaching to Transgress 147, 386
hope as ontological requirement 65–6
Hopkins, J. 217
Horton, M., *We Make the Road by Walking.* 382
House Special Committee on Immigration Reform, report 272–3
Huebner, D. 383
human emancipation 71, 174, 180
humanity 14, 21, 37–40, 42, 45, 56, 59, 83, 146, 156, 170, 196, 294–5, 326, 350, 372, 374
    decolonizing 377–8
    fate of 53–5, 63
    "humanizing the oppressed" 377
humanization 21–2, 34, 170, 378
Human Rights Watch 263, 275
Huntington, S. P. 266, 268
hybridity 81, 108–9

identity politics 100, 104, 205, 235, 245, 375, 391
    Chicano movement 48
    and intersectionality 196–8
    limits of 9, 247–9, 340
    question of 178–80
illegal immigration 264
Immigrant Workers Freedom Rides campaign 275
immigration/immigrants 62, 76, 80, 135, 177, 183, 240, 284, 292
    border security 263 (*see also* borders/border security)
    challenging nativism, poverty 266–9
    coercive migration policies 273
    Farmers Branch proposal 266
    globalizing human rights 275–6
    guest workers 264–5
    illegal immigration 264

immigration problems 270-1
and new imperialism 269-71
Puerto Rican 136
rhetoric of population control 271-3
Sensenbrenner bill 265
US class-wage system 268
incarceration 36, 66, 216, 269, 274, 288-9, 329, 332, 338, 372, 374
incorporated knowledge 151
Independent Media Centers 326, 330, 333 n.7
inequalities xi, 2, 6, 10, 19, 23, 31, 35, 38-9, 42, 49, 66, 85-6, 104, 123, 125, 128, 187, 203, 230-1, 236, 287, 302, 375
  Brookings Institution on 290
  equal right to 344
  Latino conditions of racialized class 257
  and marginalization 178, 196, 248
  in new economy 251-2
  Pew Research Center report on 288
institutional racism 134, 192, 282, 299
integral human beings, students as 146-7, 152-3, 156, 167, 219
internationalization of capital 4, 122, 240, 269, 271, 374
International Labor Organization 179
International Monetary Fund 55, 268
intersectionality ix, 8-9, 39, 123, 193, 206, 207 n.6, 260 n.6
  identity politics and 196-8
Isaac, J. 205
Islamophobia 230
itinerant curriculum theory (ICT) 384

James, C. L. R. 196, 207 n.5
  At the Rendezvous of Victory 128
Jessup, B. 244
Jews, racialization 185, 202
Jordan, J. 100

Kahlo y Calderón, M. C. F. 362
Katsiaficas, G., the Eros effect 318
K-6 dual immersion language programs x
Kelley, R., *Yo' Mama's DisFUNKtional* 195
Kelly, A. 285
Kimball, R., *Tenured Radicals: How Politics Has Corrupted Our Higher Education* 121, 344

Kincheloe, J. 295
King, M., Community Fellows Program 141 n.1
King, M. L., Jr., *Medical Committee for Human Rights Convention* 174, 211
knowledge 63, 87, 126, 147, 154, 164-5, 169, 332, 348, 355, 375, 382-3
  democratizing 119
  dialectical understanding 29
  as historical process 26-8, 49, 64
  incorporated 151
  standardization 286
KPFK (public radio station) 326, 333 n.2

Ladner, J. 133, 138
Ladson-Billings, G. 201
Lamm, R., *Immigration Time Bomb: The Fragmenting of America* 272
Laroy, V. 148-9
Latina/o Studies xi, xiv, 2, 4, 239, 243
  capitalist State 256-7
  changing demographics 246-7, 284-5
  class 249-50
  critical policy studies 257-9
  critical scholarship 244-6
  critical theory of racism 254-6
  identity politics, limits of 247-9
  immigrants (*see* immigration/immigrants)
  persistence of poverty 287-8
  race to racialization 252-4
  second-class oppression 254
  technology-rich education 250
Latino critical race theory (LatCrit) 191-2, 206, 207 n.3, 245
Latino Question 4-5
Latino students, education 240
  Catholic education as revolutionary labor 302-4
  Catholic educators 282-3, 291, 297-8
  challenging deficit notions 292-3
  Church, role of 299-301
  conditions faced by youth 288-9
  cultural democracy 294-5
  cultural invasion 296
  dominant and subordinate cultures 296
  educational needs of working-class 282
  enrollment and graduation rates 285-6
  internalization of inferiority 297

language domination 297–8
myth of social mobility 289–91
new face of segregation 293–4
racism 298–9
status of 283
teaching workforce 286
Lensmire, T. 153
Lewis, O., culture of poverty 134
Liberacion! (radio collective) 313, 328, 332, 334 n.10
Kiwane Carrington case 329–30
liberation 11, 17, 27, 30, 49, 63–4, 156, 192, 204, 352–3, 373
and decolonization 376
ethics of 162, 220–2, 386
politics of 12, 61
unity within diversity 61, 316
Lieb, D. 272
Lorde, A. 13–14, 111, 357, 393
love 333
ethics and body 155–6
pedagogy of 10, 65, 155, 302
poetics and methodology of 3, 10–12
as political force 11, 319–20, 352
Luttwak, E., *The Endangered American Dream* 112–13 n.5

Macedo, D. 297
Machado, A. 61
Machado de Oliveira, V. 371–3
curricular colonization 378–9, 392
Hospicing Modernity 372
Madrigal v. Quilligan 215
Malik, K. 177
Manning, C. 59
Mariscal, J. 247, 254
Marxist theory 185, 206 n.2, 249
Marx, K. 5, 49, 56, 105, 199, 205–6
A Contribution to the Critique of Political Economy 206
"Critique of Hegel's Philosophy of Right" 361
Matsuda, M. 192
McCarthyism 270, 338
McChesney, R. 324
McIntosh, P. 312, 341
McKenna, B. 217, 220
McKnight, J. 221
McLaren, P. 145, 316, 321

Mcnally, D. 186
media and ideological distortions 105–6
medical racism 211
comprehending racism 212–13
ethics for liberation 220–2
family medicine 219
legacy of medical apartheid 213–16
medical school formation 216–17
money as driving force 218–19
protests and mobilization 219–20
Megwa, E. R. 326
Melamed, J. 343
The Spirit of Neoliberalism: From Radical Liberalism to Neoliberal Multiculturalism 118
Mendez v. Westminster 291
meritocracy 35, 217, 237, 300, 375
Merleau-Ponty, M. 145
Mexican American communities 4, 76–7, 136, 283, 293
Mexican migration 267
Meyerson, G., "Rethinking Black Marxism: Reflections on Cedric Robinson and Others" 227
Michael, J. 197
micro-aggressions 195
Mignolo, W. 376
Miles, R. 8, 180, 185, 188 n.3, 192, 194, 199, 228, 232, 254, 260 n.8
Racism After Race Relations 107–8, 184, 186, 253
Miliband, R. 256
Mills, C. W. 257
The Racial Contract 203
sociological imagination 244
Minh-Ha, T. 98, 163
displacing 109
modernity 294, 371–2, 391–2
on challenging 380–2
colonizing logic of 376–80
demythologizing 373–6
and monumentalism 379
morality 42, 156, 214
Morrison, T. 183, 252
"The Most Militarized Universities in America" (report) 347
motive force of revolution 127–9
Mullan, F., *White Coat, Clenched Fist* 219
multiculturalism 35–8, 48, 72, 181–2, 295

and diversity 339
neoliberal ix, 4, 37, 117–18, 120–2, 128, 343–5
Murray, C., *The Bell Curve* 184, 253, 304 n.10
Mwesige, P. G. 327
Myrdal, G., *The Challenge to Affluence* 134

National Center for Education Statistics 286
A Nation at Risk (report) 36, 120, 344
nation-states 200, 202, 230–1, 267, 339, 379
Neary, M., violence of abstraction 72
Negri, A., *Empire* 267
neo-*Gramscian* republic 361–3
neoliberalism (neoliberal) 36, 40, 43 n.3, 51, 53, 55–6, 313, 337, 356
  academic borderlands 122–5
  assault on borderlands 345–7
  critical pedagogy and democratic public life 126–7
  economic Darwinism and university 118–20, 340–1
  equal right to inequality 344
  fascism 54
  media in the age of 324–7
  motive force of revolution 127–9
  multiculturalism ix, 4, 37, 117–18, 120–2, 128, 343–5
  and neoconservatism 339
  policies and practices on labor, impact 72
  power and privilege 341–3
New Economy era 120, 251–2, 344
new pluralism 197, 204–5
No Child Left Behind (NCLB) 155, 283
North American Free Trade Agreement (NAFTA) 179

Obama, B. 127
O'Brien, S. 149
Occupy movement 59, 127–8
Omi, M. 98
  "By the Rivers of Babylon: Race in the United States (Part II)" 113 n.7
O'Neill, J., praxis of conscientization 141
open borders xi
  benefits of 274–5
  radical possibility of 240, 273–4

Operation Gatekeepers 263
Operation Hold 263
Operation Rio Grande 263
oppositional consciousness 106–7
oppression 19, 39–40, 42, 66, 83, 145, 162, 165, 196, 201, 228, 321, 325, 392
  faces of 30, 98, 376
  and genocide 377
  intersection of 179, 248
  poverty as 20
  second-class 254
  weaponization of identity 391
Orloeski, J., *The Social Dilemma* 58
Ospino, H., *Hispanic Ministry in Catholic Parishes* 304 n.8
Out of School & Off Track: The Overuse of Suspensions in American Middle and High Schools (study) 292
Oxfam International 226, 374

Pacifica, California 326, 333 n.2
Paraskeva, J. 163, 165, 383–4
Parenti, M. 198, 227
Parker, L. 201
Patterson, W. L. 8
pedagogy 11, 20, 31, 37, 90, 146, 239, 245, 249–50, 257
  of answers 63–4
  of the body (*see* body, pedagogy of the)
  of courage 3, 13–14
  critical (*see* critical pedagogy)
  of freedom 42, 46, 353
  of love 10, 65, 155, 302
  problem posing 36, 64
  public radio as public xi, 313, 324–31
  of question 57, 66
  of transgression 21
Pedagogy of the Oppressed (Freire) 1–2, 6, 19–21, 23, 36, 39, 51–2, 131, 160, 299, 367 n.4, 376
  cultural context 38–9
  dialectical relationship 28–30
  fear/love of freedom 19, 46–7, 63
  historicity of knowledge 26–8, 49, 64
  labor of love 46
  political resistance 25–6
  politics of education 22–6
  ruling class/oppressors 47
  transgression 21

Peru, Q'eros culture 112 n.2
Peters, M. 118, 339
Pew Hispanic Center 284, 304 n.6
Pineda, A. M. 28
political economy xi, 23, 30–2, 34–5, 47, 54, 182, 235–6, 246, 258, 264, 365
    of advanced capitalism 103
    inequalities and social exclusions 123
    of migration 275
    racism and racialization 174, 185, 192, 206, 227
political grace 312, 316
    love as 11, 319–20, 352
    monastic self-abnegation 317
    as revolutionary process 316–19
    spiritual dimension 317–19
politics of education 22–6
    classroom and community life 23
    classroom practices 24
    hegemonic culture of schooling 23–4
    reward and punishment, system 24–5
    standardized knowledge and curricula 24, 57
    teaching-to-the-test 24, 57
Pope Francis 281, 283, 287, 289, 294, 300, 302
    Apostolic Letter to All the Consecrated People on the Occasion of the Year of Consecrated Life 301
    transformation of consciousness 303
post-disciplinary approach 244
posthuman zone 59
postmodern educational theory 181
Poverty 19–20, 36, 51–3, 133, 135, 138, 142 n.4, 282, 289, 375
    challenging nativism in 266–9
    culture of 134
    economic migration 268
    and evasion of class 103–5
    facts and statistics on 268–9, 374
    Latinos 287–8
    as necessary prerequisite of capitalism 375
    social science study of 139–41
power 111, 204, 234, 246, 295–6, 343
    coloniality of 55, 162, 376, 388–9
    culture and 1, 3–4, 11, 47, 71, 73–4, 79, 81, 85, 241, 295, 349, 381
    epistemicides of 27, 164
    mode of production and 200, 229–30
    and privilege 85, 146, 218, 312, 324, 337, 341–3, 380
    relations and exploitation 200, 229–30
    truth and 3
problem posing pedagogy 36, 64, 170
pro-democracy movements 59
professionalism 333, 334 n.13
Proust, M. 366
public pedagogy, radio as xi, 312, 323
    art of resistance and multidimensionality 331–3
    community radio 326, 327–31
    critical 328
    Liberacion! 313, 328–30, 332, 334 n.10
    media in age of neoliberalism 324–7
    WMNF 326
public schools 25, 31, 73, 76–7, 83, 121
Puerto Ricans 13, 132, 287
    colonizing impact of social science language 137–9
    labor participation 136
    Operation Bootstrap 215
    sterilization, women 175
    as underclass 131–3, 135–7

question-posing pedagogies 57
Quijano, A., coloniality of power 55, 376, 388

race/racism 8, 12, 19, 36, 39, 47–8, 74, 78, 80, 101, 173, 188 n.3, 193, 375
    as analytical category 108, 181, 183–4, 186, 203–4, 232–3, 253, 256
    and capitalism 9–10, 20, 174, 179, 181, 185, 187, 197, 200, 225, 256, 365
    and class relations 10, 20, 107, 194, 199, 200, 205
    class struggle 47, 175, 229
    critical theory of (*see* critical race theory (CRT))
    and difference 107–8
    discrimination and 5, 47, 49, 212, 293, 299
    diversity and 49, 243
    in education and society 225–6
    identity politics 178–80, 196–8
    as ideology/relation of production 206
    institutional 134, 192, 282, 299

Latina and Latino students 298–9
media and ideological distortions of difference 105–6
and medical profession 174 (*see also* medical racism)
and nationalism 271
perversity 61
plurality of 9, 174, 184–6, 197, 234
race relations paradigm 9, 107, 177–8, 180–2, 191, 198, 201, 227, 232, 251, 254
to racialization 183–4, 252–4
reframing politics of 203–6
as structural phenomenon 174–5, 212, 298
Race to the Top (RTTT) 283
racial literacy 193
radical democratization of education 235, 237, 339
Ramirez, M. 71, 73, 76–7, 83–5
Rashid, H. 78
Reagan, R. 36, 55, 344
National Commission on Excellence in Education 121
Reed, A. 226
Reed, A., Jr. 5, 183
Reed, T. F. 237
Rehberg, W., *Political Grace: The Gift of Resistance* 315, 319
revolutionary critical pedagogy 312, 321
revolutionary praxis xi, 22–3, 26, 41, 170, 321
Rivera, D. 243, 263
Roberto Alvarez v. the Board of Trustees of the Lemon Grove School District 291
Roberts, S., *Who We Are: A Portrait of America* 112 n.5
Robinson, C. 227
Robinson, W. I. 55
Rodriguez, C. 136–7
Rosaldo, R. 246
Roy, A. 391
Rukeyser, M. 156
Ryan, H. 225–8, 231–2, 234–7

safety net 33, 36, 174, 211, 257, 374
Said, E. W., orientalist gaze 164, 389
Samek, T. 386

Sandoval, C., differential consciousness 82, 106–7
Sanger, M. 215
Santos, B. de S. 160, 165
abyssal divide 56, 163, 317, 348, 388
Santos, G. 99
Schneider, M. 285
schooling xi, 1, 3–4, 21, 83, 117, 132, 155–6, 281–2, 286, 294–6, 371, 388. *See also* Catholic education/schooling
and capitalism 3, 6, 9, 19, 31–5
critical democracy and 85–9
cultural democracy of 240–1, 295
democratic 49, 71, 73, 86–7, 235, 252
emancipatory vision of 155–6
hegemonic culture of 23–4, 35, 63
minimalism of US schools 150
racism in 234–5
teaching and learning 147, 149, 153–4, 385
traditional classroom 147–8
sectarianism 48, 61, 356
sterile and necrophilic 62
Sempere, M. J. 386
sexism 39, 48, 200, 228, 230, 245, 272, 356
Shakur, A. 42
Shannon, P. 327–8
Shapiro, S. 155
Pedagogy and the Politics of the Body 145
Sheik, Z. B. 387
Shor, I. 153
Shultz, L. 386
Sinclair, A. 146, 150
Smith, K. 139
Smith, L. T., *Decolonizing Methodologies* 170, 382
Snaza, N. 153
Snowden, E. 59
social class 5, 8, 20, 31, 42, 56, 85, 227, 230
social Darwinism 54, 212, 325, 340, 375
social justice ix, xiv, 1, 4, 13, 37, 71, 73, 147, 156, 196, 236, 311, 372
critical leadership for (*see* critical leadership for social justice)
and economic democracy 244, 249, 259
social media platforms 58

Social Science Research Council 288
social science study
    language, colonizing impact of 137–9
    of poverty 139–41
society, schooling and 4, 21, 34, 83, 85, 92, 153, 156, 173, 179, 193, 225, 228, 233–4, 237, 378
    analysis of 4, 11, 248
    Church and 295–6, 301–2
    civil 9, 21, 197, 373
    medicine and 218, 220
    negative traits of 215
    transformation of 2, 17, 61, 65, 80, 128, 391, 393
solidarity xi, xvii, 9, 11–12, 17–18, 39–40, 49, 56, 62, 64, 86, 91, 126, 196, 291, 316, 333, 352, 390–1
    critical democracy and 320
    dialogue and 30, 41, 48, 301, 332
    of difference 110–11
    multiethnic 47
    political 207 n.5, 220, 315
    student participation 85, 89
Solidarity Committee of the Graduate Employees Organization (GEO) 330
Solis, A., biculturality theory 78
Spender, D. 150
spirituality 29, 312, 316–19
Spivak, G. C. 160, 162, 165, 385
    "Can the subaltern speak?" 132, 159
Stafford, W. W. 133, 138
Steinberg, S. 5
structural racism 175, 192, 213
student-teacher relationships 153
student voice 3, 21, 64, 73, 83, 88
    and active citizenship 89
    and empowerment 73, 89–91
    and social agency 127
Sum, N.-L. 244
Sweden
    compulsory sex education 150
    rate of teen pregnancy 150

Taguieff, P.-A. 191
teacher authority 29
teen pregnancy 150, 288
Telecommunications Act (1996) 324
Thatcher, M. 55, 65

Tienda, M. 136
    "Puerto Ricans and the Underclass Debate" 137
Torres, A. 136–7
Torres, G. 193
    The Miner's Canary 191
Torres, R. D. xi, 7–9, 173–4, 239, 364–5
    After Race: Racism after Multiculturalism 10, 39, 175, 225
    Latinos and Education ix, 10
    The Latino Studies Reader 4, 10
transformation ix, xii, 21, 23, 25, 49, 140, 161, 169–70, 282, 350, 362, 382–3
    imposed 62
    revolutionary vision of consciousness and 11, 302–3, 320
    of society 2, 17, 61, 65, 80, 128, 391, 393
Trans-Pacific Partnership (TPP) 339
Trump, D. 53
Tsai, J. 219
Tuck, E. 385
Tutsi population, Congo 185
Tutu, D. 350

underclass 131–3, 141 n.3, 142 n.4, 185, 344
    characteristics 135
    colonizing impact of social science language 137–9
    deconstructing 139
    origins, meaning, and usage 134–5
    Puerto Ricans as 135–7
    social science study of poverty, decolonizing 139–41
unemployment crisis 33, 35, 105, 215, 251–2, 287–9, 374
    immigrants and 252, 271
    Los Angeles 251
The United States 25, 31–2, 87, 107, 119, 215, 265, 270, 380
    American pedagogy 11, 90
    bicultural individuals 3–4, 71, 81
    Civil War 214
    Covid-19 51, 226
    critical pedagogy movement 48
    cultural domination 103, 106
    eugenics movements 175
    imperialism 8, 196

incarcerations 36, 289
labor exploitation 285
Latino Question 4–5
minimalism of schools 150
politics of meritocracy 35
public school system 121
subordinate cultures 98–9, 102–3, 107, 112 n.1, 133, 135
"The Urban Underclass: Disturbing Problems Demanding Attention" (General Accounting Office) 135
Third World feminism 82, 106
working-class movement 175, 199, 229
universal human rights 120, 122, 127–8, 282
university education 152, 332, 349
economic Darwinism and 118–20, 340–1
(Un)occupy Albuquerque/Sante 127
The US Citizenship and Immigration Services (USCIS) 263

Valentine, C. 71
bicultural model of human development 75–6
Valverde, L., purposes for students/schools 84
Vargas, J. C. 14
Vietnam War 219
Villenas, S. 201
violence 41, 263, 295, 346, 376
of abstraction 72, 126
of colonialism 20
epistemic fascism of Western academics. 383
Kiwane Carrington case 329–30
McCarthyism 270
of oppression 20, 40–1, 377
physical and psychological 40, 103, 149
of social inequalities and human exploitation 321
spiritual 40
World Trade Center in New York City 276 n.7
Viotti da Costa, E. 195
Virdee, S. 230
virtual learning 54, 231, 235
opportunities 60
and technology 56–60

Wallerstein, I. 231
Washington, H. 214
Watson, L. 380
Werbach, A. 271
West, C. 106
Western modernism 195
white privilege 194–5, 312, 341
white supremacy 185
and intractability of racism 201–3
Willis, P. 151
Wilson, W. 135
Winant, H. 98
"By the Rivers of Babylon: Race in the United States (Part II)" 113 n.7
Winston, H. 8
Wood, E. M. 104, 174, 180, 197–8, 200, 229, 246, 248
civil society 9
Democracy against Capitalism 227
"Identity Crisis" 179
mode of production and power 200, 229–30
working-class communities/students xi, xviii, 11, 12, 19, 29, 32–3, 35, 42, 216, 218, 235–6, 297–8, 338, 371–2
bicultural x, 73, 78, 82–3, 88 (*see also* biculturalism)
bilingual education 125
deficit paradigm of difference 37
educational needs 282
incarcerations 36
kids, England 151
medical students 175, 212, 217–18
meritocratic process of class formation 36, 217
non-union labor 252
success 33
works of Darder 10
After Race: Racism after Multiculturalism 10, 39, 175, 225
The Critical Pedagogy Reader 6, 10
Culture and Power in the Classroom xvii, 1, 10–11, 71, 131, 305 n.13
Decolonizing Interpretive Research 10, 131
A Dissident Voice 5, 325
Freire and Education 17
The International Critical Pedagogy Reader 10

Latinos and Education ix, 10
The Latinos Studies Reader 4, 10
"rican woman madness is just another word for love" xiv–xv
The Student Guide to Pedagogy of the Oppressed 10
"Teaching as an Act of Love" 12, 18
World Bank 55, 268
Wright, E. O. 249

Yang, K. W. 385
Young, I. M. 376
   Justice and the Politics of Difference 112 n.1

zero-population movement 272
Zinn, H. 244
Žižek, S. 317–18